UNIX AND C PROGRAMMING

UNIX and C PROGRAMMING

ASHOK ARORA

Visiting Lecturer, Examiner & Software Engineer
(15 years of experience in Teaching & Software Engineering)

On Panel
Institute of Management Technology (IMT)
FORE School of Management (FSM)
All India Management Association (AIMA)

Formerly Senior Faculty
APTECH Computer Education
Sachdeva New PT College

Formerly Software Consultant
Punjab National Bank
Reebak India Company

SHEFALI BANSAL

Visiting Lecturer, Examiner & Software Developer
(7 years of experience in Teaching & Software Development)

On Panel
Institute of Management Technology (IMT)

Formerly Senior Faculty
APTECH Computer Education
First Computers

FIREWALL MEDIA

(An Imprint of Laxmi Publications Pvt Ltd.)

BANGALORE • CHENNAI • COCHIN • GUWAHATI • HYDERABAD
JALANDHAR • KOLKATA • LUCKNOW • MUMBAI • RANCHI
NEW DELHI • BOSTON, USA

Published by :

FIREWALL MEDIA

(*An Imprint of Laxmi Publications Pvt. Ltd.*)

113, Golden House, Daryaganj,

New Delhi-110002

Phone : 011-43 53 25 00

Fax : 011-43 53 25 28

www.laxmipublications.com

info@laxmipublications.com

Price : **Rs. 350.00** *Only.*

First Edition : 2005

Reprint : 2006, 2009

OFFICES

© **Bangalore**	080-26 61 15 61	© **Chennai**	044-24 34 47 26
© **Cochin**	0484-239 70 04	© **Guwahati**	0361-254 36 69, 251 38 81
© **Hyderabad**	040-24 65 23 33	© **Jalandhar**	0181-222 12 72
© **Kolkata**	033-22 27 43 84	© **Lucknow**	0522-220 95 78
© **Mumbai**	022-24 91 54 15, 24 92 78 69	© **Ranchi**	0651-221 47 64

FUN-2817-350-UNIX AND C PROGRAMMING **C—17116/09/02**

Typeset at : ABRO Enterprises, Delhi. *Printed at* : Sanjeev Offset Press, Delhi.

PREFACE

It is a matter of great pleasure for us to write the preface for the first edition of this book. It is organized into 4 units and 20 chapters as per topics outlined in the syllabus. A brief overview of all the units and chapters is given below.

In the first unit, we are discussing the basic concepts of hardware and software along with the popular operating systems—MS DOS and Windows 98. The unit has five chapters, titled 'Concepts of Hardware', 'Concepts of Software', 'Operating System Concepts and File Organisation', 'Getting to know MS DOS' and 'Familiarising with Windows Environment'. The salient feature of the unit is the coverage of all concepts in a simple language with plenty of illustrations.

The second unit describes the popular multi-user operating system. UNIX and the most exciting field of IT, Internet. The unit has six chapters, titled 'Getting Started with UNIX', 'Advanced UNIX', 'Introduction to Internet', 'Browsers', 'Electronic Mail' and 'Introduction to PINE and ELM'. The salient feature of the unit is the detailed discussion on UNIX commands and Internet concepts and services such as E-mail, Telnet, Usenet, Newsgroup, Downloading, etc. The popular mail programs on UNIX systems, PINE and ELM are also discussed in great detail.

The third unit introduces the concepts of programming and computer languages with special emphasis on C Programming Language. The unit has five chapters, titled 'Programming Languages', 'Programming Concepts', 'Introduction to C Programming Language', 'Basic C Features' and 'Conditional Statements and Loops'. The salient feature of the unit is the extensive coverage of programs on simple problems for better understanding of concepts.

In the last unit, we are discussing the advanced features of C programming language. The unit is organized in four chapters, titled 'Functions', 'Arrays', 'Introduction to Pointers' and 'Introduction to Structures'. The salient feature of the unit is the detailed discussion on solving real life problems using C.

The common and unique features of each chapter are :

- Coverage of both theoretical and practical concepts as per the syllabus in a very systematic manner.
- Includes extensive illustrations and examples for better understanding of concepts.
- Includes theoretical/practical exercises at the end of each chapter especially based on latest examination pattern.

To conclude the preface, we express our gratitude to the editorial and production staff of the publisher for editing and good designing of the book. We are indebted to Mr. Saurabh Gupta, Managing Director, Laxmi Publications Pvt. Ltd. for his encouragement and support as he waited patiently for the completion of the book. Finally, we express our best wishes and support to the marketing staff of the publisher for the promotion of this book.

The authors invite feedback from readers. Please do send your comment and suggestions to the publisher or directly mail to us. Thanks.

—Ashok Arora
—Shefali Bansal
E-mail: authorashok@rediffmail.com
E-mail: shefaliindia@rediffmail.com

CONTENTS AT A GLANCE

CONTENTS

Dedicated to
The man behind my success
My Loving Brother,
Shri Baldev Raj Arora

I pay homage to him
Today, 1st Feb, 2003
on his
5th Death Anniversary

Ashok Arora

Dedicated to

The man behind my success

My Loving Brother

Shri Baldev Raj Arora

I pay homage to him,

Today, 17 Feb. 2003

on his

1st Death Anniversary

Ashok Arora

1

CONCEPTS OF HARDWARE

1.1 INTRODUCTION

Information is required at every stage of your life. When you get up in the morning, you read the newspaper to know about last day's happenings and current news about politics, movies, sports, education, etc. When you go to your office, you switch on your computer to read your mails on Internet. When you come back to your home, you switch on your television to listen the news on your favourite channel. So, you need information at every step of your daily life. Comupter is one of your favourite media of information. Computers are being used in almost every field now. There is hardly any area in our society, where computers are not being used. For instance, computers are used in homes, offices, schools, colleges, universities, nursing homes, hospitals, export houses, shops, business establishments, industries, banks, railway stations, airports, research centres and many other organisations. As, computers are performing most of the routine activities in today's society, it has become essential for everybody to learn computers. Computer components are broadly classified into Hardware (physical components) and Software (instructions). In this chapter, we will focus our discussion on hardware concepts. Before starting our discussion on hardware, let us understand computers alongwith their importance, classifications and various uses.

1.2 OVERVIEW OF COMPUTERS

In a layman language, a computer is a fast calculating device that can perform arithmetic operations. Although the computer was originally invented mainly for doing high speed and accurate calculations, it is not just a calculating device. The computer can perform any kind of work involving arithmetic and logical operations on data. It gets the data through an input device, process it as per the instructions given and gives the information as output.

1.2.1 Definition of Computer

We can define a computer as follows :

A computer is a fast electronic device that processes the input data according to the instructions given by the programmer/user and provides the desired information as output.

Various terms used in the above definition are—

- Data–A set of basic facts and entities which itself has no meaning
- Information–Data which has some meaning or value

- Instruction–A statement given to computer to perform a task
- Input–Data and instructions given to computer
- Process–Manipulation of data
- Output–Information obtained after processing of data

1.2.2 Importance of Computers

Computers play a vital role for processing of data in an organisation. Computers help in processing volumes of data efficiently and accurately within a short time. A computer has the following characteristics, which make it so important for an organisation:

- **High Memory.** A computer has much more memory or storage capacity than human beings. It can store millions of data and instructions, which can be retrieved and recalled even after a number of years. This is not possible in case of human brain.
- **Fast.** A computer is so fast that it can perform the given task (arithmetical or logical) in few seconds as compared to man who can spend many months for doing the same task. A computer can process millions of instructions per second.
- **Accurate.** While doing calculations, a computer is more accurate than a man. Man can make mistakes in calculations but a computer does not, if it is provided with accurate instructions.
- **Diligence.** A computer does not suffer from the human traits of tiredness and boredom. Man can feel tired and bored while doing millions of calculations but computer, being a machine, does this job very efficiently and without any tiredness and boredom.
- **No Intelligence.** A computer is a machine and obviously has no intelligence of its own. Each and every instruction must be given to the computer for doing a task. Man has intelligence and it is man who invented computer and gives it all the instructions and logic to work. The main drawback of computer is that it cannot take decisions on its own.

1.2.3 Uses of Computers

During the last four decades, computers have revolutionized almost all disciplines of our life. Computers have made possible many scientific, industrial and commercial advances that would have been impossible otherwise. Computers are being used in many areas of application viz. business, industry, scientific research, defense, space, communications, medicine, education, etc. The utilisation of computers in different fields is summarised in Table 1.1.

Application Area	Use of Computers
Business	Used in banks, airports, share markets, hotels, export houses, Govt offices and others for computerising business applications like MIS, Payroll, Inventory, Finanacial Accounting etc.
Industry	Used in electricity, steel, paper, printing, engineering & other industries forproduction, inventory control & related applications.

Scientific Research	Used to resolve complex scientific problems accurately in a short time
Defense	Used to computeris war planes, ships, radars and many advnaced weapons.
Space	Used to design computerised space satellites, rockets and related technology.
Data Communication	Used to computerise geo-graphically sparated offices through networking.
Telecommunication	Used in ISDN, E-mail, Internet, Intranet, VSAT, Videoconferencing, Paging, Cellular phones etc.
Education	Used in development of CBT (Computer Based Teaching)/ CAT (Computer Aided Teaching) programmes for education.
Libraries	Used to develop Library Management Systems.
Publishers	Used for Desk Top Publishing (DTP) for designing & printing of books.
Law & Order	Used to records data of vehicles, criminals, finger prints etc.
Medicine	Used in hospitals and nursing homes/ clinics for maintaing medical records, prescription writing, diagnostic applications and computerised scanning (CAT Scanning).
Engineering	Used for CAD (Computer Aided Designing)/ CAM (Computer Aided Manufacturing) by enineering companies.
Emerging Technologies	Used in Artificial Intelligence (Expert Systems, Robotics etc.) and Virtual Reality.

Table 1.1 *Role of computers in various fields.*

1.3 CLASSIFICATION OF COMPUTER SYSTEMS

The classification of computers is based on the following four criteria:

(*A*) According to Purpose

(*B*) According to Technology Used

(*C*) According to Size and Storage Capacity

(*D*) According to Historical Advancement

Based on these criteria, the classification of computers is illustrated in Figure 1.1. Let us discuss the classification of computers in detail.

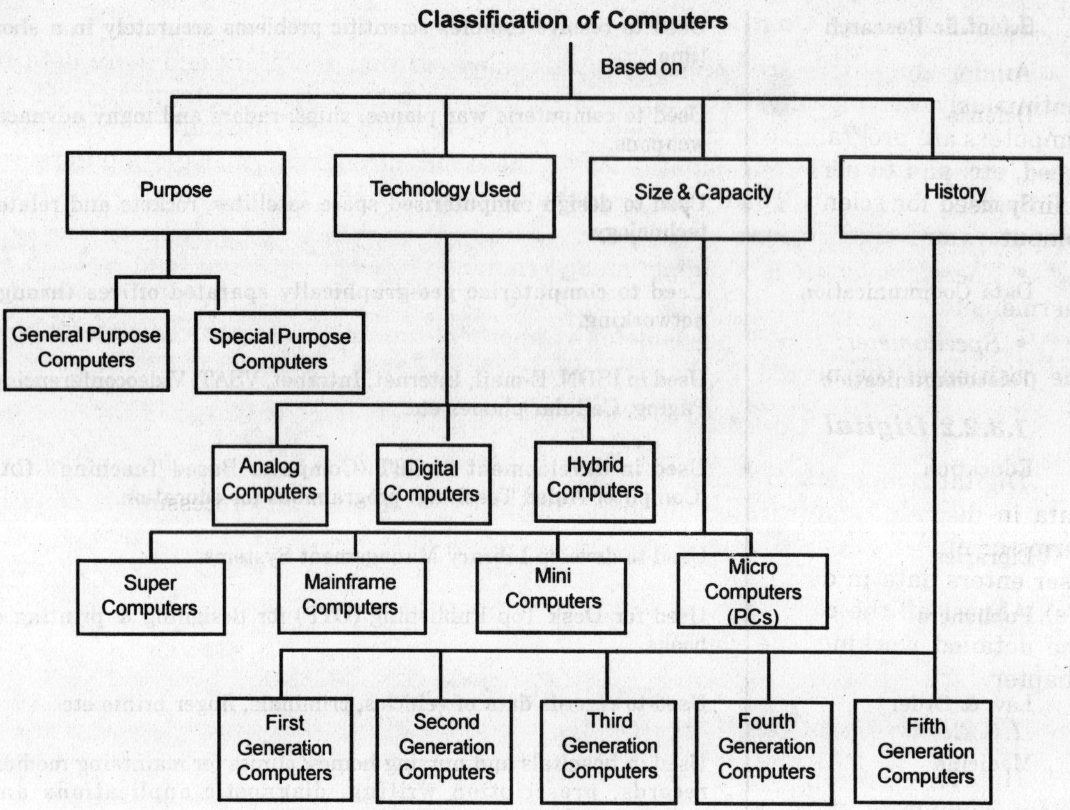

Figure 1.1 *Classification of computers*

1.3.1 According to Purpose

According to the utilisation of computer for different uses, computers are of two types– General purpose and Special purpose. Let us discuss these briefly.

1.3.1.1 General Purpose Computers

Computers that follow instructions for general requirements such as sales analysis, financial accounting, invoicing, inventory, management information, etc. are called General Purpose Computers. Almost all computers used in offices for commercial, educational and other applications are general purpose computers.

1.3.1.2 Special Purpose Computers

Computers that are designed from scratch to perform special tasks like scientific applications and research, weather forecasting, space applications, medical diagnostics, etc. are called Special Purpose Computers.

1.3.2 According to Technology Used

According to the technology used, computers are of three types– Analog, Digital and Hybrid. Let us discuss these briefly.

1.3.2.1 Analog Computers

Analog computers are special purpose computers that represent and store data in continuously varying physical quantities such as current, voltage or frequency. These computers are programmed for measuring physical quantities like pressure, temperature, speed, etc. and to perform computations on these measurements. Analog computers are mainly used for scientific and engineering applications. Some of the examples of analog computers are given below:

- *Thermometer:* It is a simple analog computer used to measure temperature. In thermometer, the mercury moves up or down as the temperature varies.
- *Speedometer:* Car's speedometer is another example of analog computer where the position of the needle on dial represents the speed of the car.

1.3.2.2 Digital Computers

Digital computers are mainly general-purpose computers that represent and store data in discrete quantities or numbers. In these computers, all processing is done in terms of numeric representation (Binary Digits) of data and information. Although the user enters data in decimal or character form, it is converted into binary digits (0's and 1's). Almost all the computers used now days are digital computers and we will discuss the detailed working and components of these computers in subsequent part of this chapter.

1.3.2.3 Hybrid Computers

Hybrid computers incorporate the technology of both analog and digital computers. These computers store and process analog signals, which have been converted into discrete numbers using analog-to-digital converters. They can also convert the digital numbers into analog signals or physical properties using digital-to-analog converters. Hybrid computers are mainly used in artificial intelligence (robotics) and computer aided manufacturing (e.g. process control).

1.3.3 According to Size and Storage Capacity

According to the size and memory/storage capacity, computers are of four types– Supercomputer, Mainframe, Minicomputer and Microcomputer. We are discussing these in detail.

1.3.3.1 Supercomputer

Supercomputer is the biggest, most expensive, sophisticated computer that executes complex calculation at the fastest speed. It is mainly designed for complex scientific applications. It can process huge amounts of scientific data. For instance, an IBM supercomputer built for U.S. Department of Energy is equipped with 2.5 terabytes of memory and can execute 3 trillion program instructions per second. It has many CPUs (Central Processing Units–Main part of a computer) that operate in parallel to make it a fastest computer. It is typically used for following applications:

- Weather Information
- Petroleum exploration and production

- Energy management
- Defense
- Nuclear Energy Research
- Structural Analysis
- Electronic Design
- Rea-time animation
- Medicine

Features of supercomputer. In general, a supercomputer has following capabilities:

- It contains many CPUs operating parallel with processing speed in the range of 400–10.000 MIPS (Millions of Instructions per second)
- It maximizes the number of floating point instruction per second (FLOPS) which is usually above 1 gigaflop per second.
- It has a very high memory and hard disk capacity. Entire memory of a supercomputer consists of high speed.
- Its cycle time is as low as 4 nano second (ns). Thus, it can add two 64-bit data in a single machine cycle.

Examples. Some of the examples of supercomputers are listed in Table 1.2.

Name of Supercomputer	Developer
CRAY X-MP/14,24 & 48	Control Data Corporation
CRAY Y-MP	Control Data Corporation
CRAY 1, 2 & 3	Control Data Corporation
SX-2, SX-3R	Nippon Electric corrporation
HITAC S-300	Hitachi, Japan
VPP 300	Fujitsu
Param,8000,9000 & 10000	C-DAC, India

Table 1.2 *Examples of supercomputers*

1.3.3.2 Mainframe Computer

Mainframe computers are very large and fast computers but smaller and slower than supercomputers. They are multi-user systems, which are designed to be used by thousands of people. They are used in a centralised location where many terminals (input/output devices) are connected with one CPU and thus, allow different users to share the single CPU. They have a very high memory (several hundred Megabytes) and can support thousands of users. They are mainly used for following applications:

- Railway and Airline Reservations
- Banking Applications
- Commercial applications of large industries, companies, Govt. Organisations.

Features of Mainframe computer. A mainframe computer has following capabilities:

- It has very large disks that can store several gigabytes of data.

- It has a very high memory for storing several hundred megabytes.
- It needs a control climate to use. Therefore a mainframe computer is stored in special secure room.
- It can have thousands of terminals (monitors and keyboards).
- It costs several million rupees.
- The processing speed of a mainframe computer is very high i.e. up to several hundred Millions of Instructions Per Seconds (MIPS).

Examples. Some of the examples of mainframe computers are IBM 3090, IBM 4300, IBM 4381, IBM ES 2000, IBM ES 9000 and DEC 10000.

1.3.3.3 Minicomputers

Minicomputers are multi-user, medium scale, smaller and generally slower than mainframe computers. They are mainly used by smaller organisations such as branch of a bank, hotel, hospital, etc. Like mainframes, they have many terminals, which are connected with one CPU and can support many users. The cost of a minicomputer is less as compared to mainframe. Therefore, it is mainly used in applications where processing can be distributed among several minicomputers rather than using a mainframe computer.

Features of a Minicomputer. A minicomputer has the following capabilities:

- It has smaller disks and lesser memory than a mainframe computer.
- Its processing speed is generally slower than a mainframe computer.
- Like mainframes, it can support thousand of users with separate terminals.
- It costs several lacks of rupees.

Examples. Some of the examples of minicomputers are PDP-1, DEC Micro VAX and IBM AS/400. IBM AS/400, which is actually a *midicomputer* (computer with performance between a mainframe and minicomputer) is becoming very popular among minicomputers.

1.3.3.4 Microcomputers

A microcomputer is the least expensive and smallest digital computer, which uses a microprocessor as its CPU. Microprocessor is a single chip (integrated circuit) CPU. Microcomputer is popularly called as Personal Computer (PC). It can be used both as a stand-alone machine and a terminal in a multi-user environment. They are typically single user system but can be used in multi-user environment either by using multi-user Network Operating Systems (such as UNIX, Window NT, etc.) or LAN (Local Area Network.). Microcomputers are becoming very popular now days due to very high processing power and memory. Today, a powerful microcomputer may be used as a substitute for mini or mainframe computer.

Microcomputers are either of desktop or portable models. Portable computers can be carried from one place to another. Some of the models are called as *laptops* while others as *notebook computers*. Notebook computers are smaller, lighter and costlier than laptops. They are small enough to fit in a briefcase, however a laptop cannot be put in a briefcase. *Personal Digital Assistants (PDA)* are also notebook computers with built in software for appointments, electronic mail and scheduling. They are also called *handheld computers*. Desktop computers fit on a desktop and are used widely in offices and homes. The pictures of some of the desktop and laptop computers are shown in Figure 1.2.

Figure 1.2 *Some desktop and laptop computers*

There are many types and models of personal computers, which are summarised in Table 1.3.

CPU Model (MHz)	Clock Bus	Data (BIT)	Register Memory	Max. (RAM)	Comments
8088	8	8	16	1 MB	First 8 bit microprocessor (Original PC)
8086	8	16	16	1 MB	First 16 bit CPU on a chip (PC/XT)*
80286	20	16	16	16 MB	5 times faster than PC/XT (PC/AT)*
80386 SX	33	16	32	16 MB	80386 with an 80286 bus
80386 DX	40	32	32	4 GB	True 32 bit CPU on a chip
80486 SX	40	32	32	4 GB	Math co-processor disabled
80486 DX2	66	32	32	4 GB	More speed with Math co-processor enabled
80486 DX4	100	32	32	4 GB	More speed than 486 DX2
Pentium Pro (P5)	200	64	32	4 GB	Superscope architecture Able to execute 2 instructions simultaneously
Pentium II (P6)	266	64	32	64 GB	Faster than Pentium Pro
Pentium III (PIII)	550	-	-	-	Faster than Pentium II
Pentium 4 (P4)	1000	-	-	-	Fastest PC

* XT stands for Extended Technology and AT for Advanced Technology

Table 1.3 *Different types of microcomputers*

1.3.4 According to Historical Advancement

History of computers begins with the invention of the abacus in 3000 BC, followed by the invention of mechanical calculators in 1500. The years beyond 1642 till 1980 were marked by invention of zeroth, first, second and third generation computers. The years beyond 1980 till today are marked by fourth generation computers. Fifth generation computers are still under research and development. Abacus is a sedimentary first computing device developed in 3000 BC. It consists of a row of series held in a wooden frame having heads stung on them as shown in Figure 1.3. It is used for calculation by the sliding the heads along with the wires. John Napier, a Scottish mathematician invented a mechanical calculator called the *Napier's bones*. He devised a set of eleven rods each having four faces. As these rods were carved from bones, therefore they were called Napier's bones. The rods were used to find products and quotients of large numbers. John Napier also introduced logarithms.

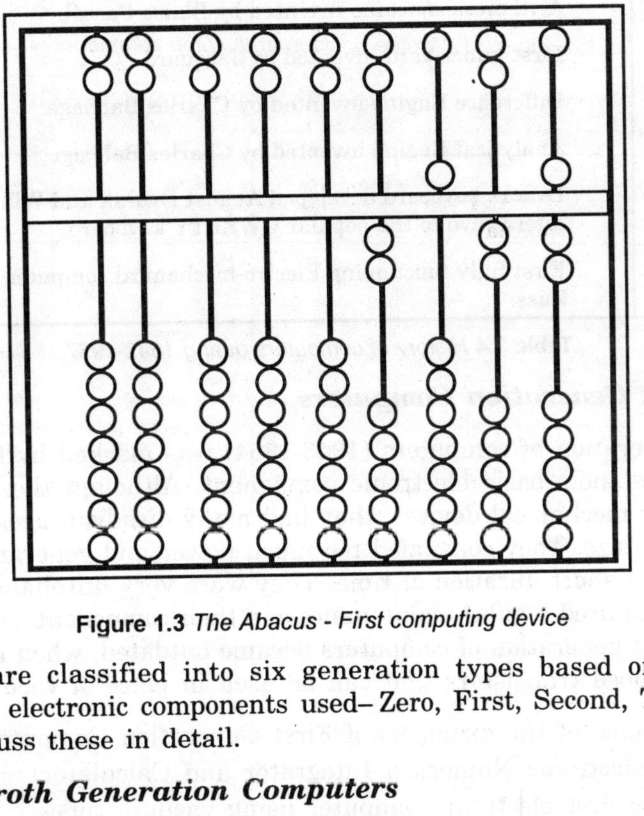

Figure 1.3 *The Abacus - First computing device*

Computers are classified into six generation types based on their historical advancement and electronic components used– Zero, First, Second, Third, Fourth and Fifth. Let us discuss these in detail.

1.3.4.1 Zeroth Generation Computers

The zeroth generation of computers (1642-1946) was marked by the invention of mainly mechanical computers. *Pascaline* was the first mechanical device, invented by Blaise Pascal, a French mathematician in 1642. In this machine, numbers were entered by dialing a series of number wheels. A series of toothed wheels transferred the movements to a disk and hence showed the results. In 1822, Charles Babbage, an English mathematician, designed a machine called *Difference Engine* to compute tables of numbers for naval navigation. Later on, in the year 1834, Babbage attempted to build a digital computer, called *Analytical Engine*. The analytical engine had all the parts of a modern computer i.e. it had four components – the store (memory unit), the mill (computation unit), the punched card reader (input unit) and the punched/ printed output (output unit). As Charles Babbage thought out all basic parts of modern computers, he is known as Father of Computers. In later years, Herman Hollerith invented a machine for counting 1880 US census, which was called the *Tabulating Machine*. In 1944, Howard A. Eiken invented first American general purpose Electro-mechanical computer, called *Mark I* and later on its successor, *Mark II*. The zeroth generation of computers or the era of mechanical computers ended in 1946, when vacuum tubes were invented. Various inventions during era of mechanical computers are summarised in Table 1.4.

Years	Invention
1642	Arithmetic machine invented by Blaise Pascal.
1800	First punch card invented by Jacquard.
1822	Difference Engine invented by Charles Babbage.
1834	Analytical Engine invented by Charles Babbage.
1836	Dvorak keyboard developed August Dvorak and William L. Dealey as an alternative to the popular QWERTY keyboard.
1937	First fully functioning Electro-mechanical computer invented by Konrad Zuse.

Table 1.4 *History of computers during 1642-1937*

1.3.4.2 First Generation Computers

The first generation of computers (1946-1954) was marked by the use of vacuum tubes or valves as their basic electronic component. Although these computers were faster than earlier mechanical devices, they had many disadvantages. First of all, they were very large in size. They consumed too much power and generated too much heat, when used for even short duration of time. They were very unreliable and broke down frequently. They required regular maintenance and their components had to be assembled manually. The first generation of computers became outdated, when in 1954, the Philco Corporation developed transistors that can be used in place of vacuum tubes.

Examples. Some of the examples of First Generation Computers are—

- ENIAC (Electronic Numerical Integrator and Calculator)
  It was the first electronic computer using vacuum tubes.
- EDSAC (Electronic Delay Storage Automatic Calculator)
  It was the first stored-program computer,
- EDVAC (Electronic Discrete Variable Automatic Computer)
  It was successor of EDSAC.
- IAS machine (Princeton's Institute of Advanced Studies)
  It was a new version of the EDVAC, built by von Neumann.

- UNIVAC (Universal Automatic Calculator)
  First commercial computer designed by J. Presper Eckert & John Mauchly

The basic design of IAS machine is now known as *von Neumann machine*, which had five basic parts–the memory, the arithmetic logic unit, the program control unit, the input and output unit as shown in Figure 1.4. Various historical events during 1946-1954 are summarised in Table 1.5.

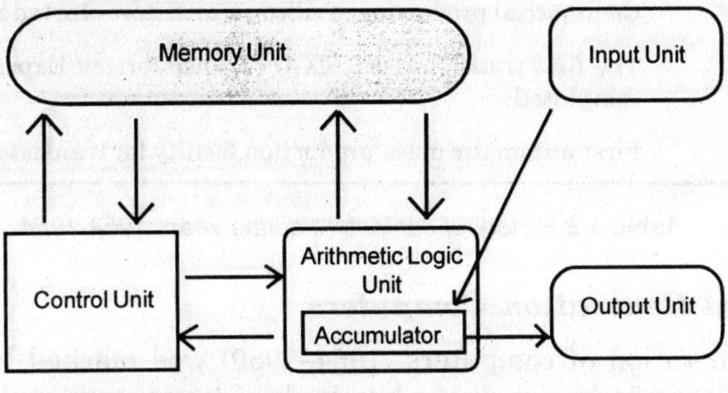

Figure 1.4 *The original von Neumann machine*

Years	Invention
1946	First electronic general purpose computer: ENIAC was invented.
1949	First stored program computer - EDSAC was invented
1951	EDVAC was invented
1952	IAS machine was invented
1953	UNIVAC was invented.

Table 1.5 *History of computers during years 1946-1954*

1.3.4.3 Second Generation Computers

The second generation of computers (1954-64) was marked by the use of transistors in place of vacuum tubes. Transistors had a number of advantages over the vacuum tubes. As transistors were made from pieces of silicon, so they were more compact than vacuum tubes. The second generation computers, therefore, were smaller in size and generated less heat as compared to first generation computers. Although they were slightly faster and more reliable than earlier computers, they also had many disadvantages. They had limited storage capacity, consumed more power and were relatively slow in performance. Like first generation computers, they also required regular maintenance and their components had also to be assembled manually. Manual assembly of components was very expensive and later many attempts were made to reduce such manual assembly. It was in 1964, when it was discovered that a number of transistors could be sealed up into a tiny package, called an *Integrated Circuit* (IC) or a *Chip*. Second generation computers became out-dated after the invention of ICs.

Examples. Some of the examples of Second Generation Computers are:

- **PDP-1**, developed by DEC was the first minicomputer.
- **NCR 304** (National Cash Register) was first all-transistorised computer.

Various historical events occurred during 1954–1964 are summarised in Table 1.6.

Year	Invention
1954	Commercial production of silicon transistors started by Texas Instruments.
1956	The first transistorised, TX-O (Transistorized Experimental computer) is completed.
1960	First automatic mass-production facility for transistors, developed by IBM.

Table 1.6 *History of computers during years 1954-1964*

1.3.4.4 Third Generation Computers

The third generation of computers (1964–1980) was marked by use of Integrated Circuits (ICs) in place of transistors. As hundreds of transistors could be put on a single small circuit, so ICs were more compact than transistors. The third generation computers, therefore, removed many drawbacks of second generation computers. The third generation computers were smaller in size, very less heat generated and required very less power as compared to earlier two generations of computers. These computers required less human labour at the assembly stage. Although, third generation computers were still faster and even more reliable, they also had few disadvantages. They still had less storage capacity, relatively slower performance and thus could not fulfill the requirements of the users and programmers. The third generation computers became outdated, when it was found in around 1978, that thousands of ICs could be integrated onto a single chip, called *LSI (Large Scale Integration).*

Examples. Some of the examples of Third Generation Computers are :

- **IBM 360,** developed by IBM in 1964 was the first product line designed as a family.
- **PDP-8**, developed by DEC in 1965 was the first mass-market minicomputer.
- **PDP-11**, developed by DEC in 1970 was the first highly successful minicomputer.
- **CRAY-1**, developed by Cray in 1974 was the first supercomputer.
- **VAX**, developed by DEC in 1978 was the first supermini computer.

Various historical events during 1964–1980 are summarised in Table 1.7.

Year	Invention
1970	First 4004 microprocessor created by Intel.
1972	The first 8-bit microprocessor (8008) by Intel.
1976	Intel introduces the 5-MHZ microprocessors (8085).
1978	Intel introduces the 4.77-MHZ microprocessors (8086).

Table 1.7 *History of computers during years 1964-1980*

1.3.4.5 Fourth Generation Computers

The fourth generation of computers (1980–till date) was marked by use of Large-Scale Integrated (LSI) circuits in place of ICs. As thousands of ICs could be put onto a single circuit, so LSI circuits are still more compact than ICs. In 1978, it was found that millions of components could be packed onto a single circuit, known as *Very Large Scale Integration (VLSI)*. VLSI is the latest technology of computers that led to the development of the popular Personal Computers (PCs), also called as *Microcomputers*. All present day computers are fourth generation of computers. These computers are very powerful having a high memory and a fast processing speed. Today's PCs are even more powerful than mainframe computers. Although fourth generation computers offer too many advantages to users, still they have one main disadvantage. The major drawback of these computers is that they have no intelligence on their own. Scientists are now trying to remove this drawback by making computers, which would have artificial intelligence.

Examples. Various examples of Fourth Generation Computers are—

- **IBM PC,** developed in 1981 was the first industry standard personal computer, having Intel 8088 memory chip.
- **IBM PC/AT,** developed in 1982 was the first advanced technology PC, having Intel 80286 memory chip.
- **386,** developed in 1985, had Intel 80386 memory chip.
- **CRAY-2,** developed in 1985, was the fourth generation supercomputer.
- **486,** developed in 1989, had Intel 80486 memory chip.
- **Pentium,** developed during 1993 till date, has pentium (80586) memory chip.

Various historical events occurred during 1980–till date are summarised in Table 1.8.

Year	Invention
1980	The 8087 math microprocessors introduced by Intel.
1982	The 6-MHZ 80286 microprocessor introduced by Intel.
1983	IBM announces the IBM PC-XT Model 370.
1984	Intel introduces the 16-MGZ 80286 DX microprocessor
1987	The 80387 math co-processor introduced by Intel.
1988	Intel introduces then 33-MHz 80386 DX microprocessor.
1990	The 33-MMHZ 80486 microprocessor introduced by Intel.
1993	Microsoft introduces 32-bit Pentium-I microprocessor
1997	Microsoft introduces Pentium-II microprocessor
1999	Pentium-III with 450-MHz introduced by Microsoft.
2001	Pentium-IV introduces by Microsoft

Table 1.8 *History of computer during 1980-till date*

1.3.4.6 Fifth Generation Computers

The fifth generation computers (Tomorrow's computers) are still under research and development stage. These computers would have artificial intelligence. They will use USLI (Ultra Large-Scale Integration) chips in place of VLSI chips. One USLI chip contains millions of components on a single IC. The most important feature of fifth generation computers is that they will use intelligent software. This software will enable the user to tell computer 'What to do' and not 'How to do' by using intelligent programming and knowledge-based problem solving techniques. So, the programmers or users would not be required to give each and every instruction to the computer for solving a problem. These computers will also have user interface in form of speech in natural languages.

Example. Fifth generation computers are yet to develop, but **ROBOTS** have few features of fifth generation computers.

The comparative features of various generations of computers are shown in Table 1.9.

Criteria	First Gen. Computers	Second Gen. Computers	Third Gen. Computers	Fourth Gen. Computers	Fifth Gen. Computers
Basic Electronic Component	Vacuum Tubes or Valves	Transistors	Integerated Circuits (ICs)	Very Large Scale Integration (VLSI)	Ultra Large Scale Integeration (ULSI)
Speed	Slowest	Slow	Medium	Faster	Fastest
Size	Largest	Large	Medium	Smallest	Medium
Reliability	Unreliable	Less Reliable	More Reliable	Most Reliable	Yet to judge
Availibility	Out-dated	Out-dated	Out-dated	Current	Yet to build

Table 1.9 *Comparative features of various generation of computers*

1.4 COMPUTER BASED SYSTEMS

Computer based systems are special purpose computers that use either analog technology only or both analog and digital technologies. So both analog and hybrid computers are also called computer based systems. They are mainly used for special purposes like scientific/engineering applications, artificial intelligence (robotics), traffic control, weather forecasting, space applications, medical diagnostics (CAT– Computerised Axial Tomography scan), etc.

Examples. Various examples of computer based systems are–

- *Thermometer.* An analog computer used to measure temperature.
- *Speedometer.* An analog computer used to ensure the speed of car.
- *CAT Scanner.* Computerised Axial Tomography (CAT) machine used to scan various parts of the human body.

- *Smart cars.* Computer-based cars that help the driver to control and maintain the vehicle and its environment and warn the driver about traffic problems.
- *Fly–by-Wire System.* Computerised flight control systems, that control the generations of aircraft and the flight surfaces. They can prevent a pilot from pushing a plane beyond its design limits.
- *ATC (Air Traffic Control) system.* A computer based air traffic control system that increases the spacing between flights to ensure the airplane safety.
- *MRI (Magnetic Response Imaging) Devices.* A computer based imaging device (such as ultrasound) used for diagnosis by doctors.
- *CAM (Computer-aided Manufacturing) devices.* Computer controlled equipment (also called Industrial Robots) used to manufacture/process various products of an industry.

1.5 POPULARITY OF PERSONAL COMPUTERS

IBM PC is the first personal computer, introduced in 1981 by the world's largest computer company - IBM (International Business Machines Corp., New York). This computer was based on Intel's 8088 microprocessor or chip. It became a success almost overnight. In later years, IBM manufactured 80286, 80386, 80486 and recently the Pentium PCs. Although IBM is still the largest supplier of PCs, the majority of PCs are manufactured by other companies as per the standards set by IBM. This whole family of PCs is known as IBM-compatible PCs. So, whenever we talk about a PC, it usually means one of the IBM-compatible PCs. PS/2 and PS/1 (PS stands for Personal System) are IBM computer series introduced in 1987 and 1990 respectively.

Apple Macintosh PC (popularly called as Mac) is another series of 32-bit personal computers, introduced in 1984 by one of the first microcomputer manufacturing company - Apple (Apple Computer, Inc.). Apple is the largest independent manufacturer of non-IBM-compatible PCs. Apple Mac PC uses the Motorola (a leading manufacturer of semiconductor devices) 68000 processor family and a proprietary operating system. As this PC comes with its own operating system, there is no need of DOS (Disk Operating System) or other operating system for operating it. The method of operating a Mac PC is known as *Macintosh user interface.* All Mac PCs have graphic displays, as their operating systems provide graphical user interface (GUI). The Mac PC always displays a row of menu titles at the top of the screen, from which options are selected.

Although the first Mac PC was praised by many users due to its ease of use and low-cost system, it was not exciting for most corporate buyers due to its slow speed, small screen and closed architecture (a system whose technical specifications are not made public). In 1987, Apple manufactured Mac II, which offers full-size screens, high-speed and open architecture (a system whose technical specifications are made public). In 1991, IBM formed an alliance with Apple to fully integrate Macs into IBM enterprise networks for developing PowerPC with Motorola.

IBM-compatible PCs are used as stand-alone machines or as workstations/ file servers in a local area network (we will discuss about local area network in subsequent chapters). These PCs are very popular as stand-alone systems, which run under DOS.

IBM-compatible PCs (80486 & above) are also popular for using as client/server systems (we will also discuss about client/server systems in subsequent chapters). On the other hand, Apple Macintosh PCs are rarely used as the primary client computers in client/ server systems. Macintosh PCs are useful mainly for desktop publishing systems, due to graphical user interface. IBM-compatible PCs, on the other hand, are useful for any kind of business application. They have become very popular among all users in India and abroad.

1.6 STRUCTURE OF COMPUTER

Computer components are broadly divided into two categories– Hardware and Software. Hardware refers to any physical component of computer while software refers to the programs required to run the computer. For example, CPU (Central Processing Unit), Monitor, Keyboard, Hard disk etc. are hardware while DOS (Disk Operating System), BASIC, COBOL, Windows, etc. are software. An analogy of hardware can be book, which you are reading, and software would be the text written on this book. Both hardware and software are dependent on each other. CPU, Memory Unit, Hard Disk etc. are useless unless they are provided with instructions and data for storage and processing. Similarly, DOS or BASIC has no importance unless they are used along with hardware components of the computer.

The internal architectural design of computers differ from one model to another, however the basic components of a computer remain the same for all models. In this section, we will discuss the basic structure of a computer system. The diagram of a generalised architecture of a computer system is shown in Figure 1.5. Before discussing the details of computer architecture, we would define the computer system as follows:

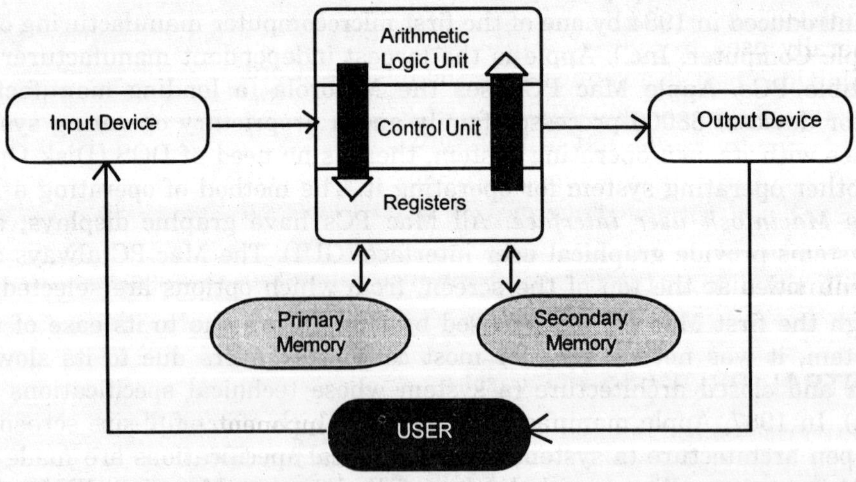

Figure 1.5 *Functional diagram of a generalised architecture of a computer system*

A complete computer installation including the central processing unit, the peripherals such as hard disk drives, floppy disk drives, monitor, printer, mouse and operating system which are designed to work and interact with each other and with the user is called a computer system. A computer system has the following hardware components:

(*a*) **Motherboard.** The system board where all other boards (printed circuit boards having chips or other electronic components) are connected. A motherboard contains the CPU chip, Memory chip (ROM and RAM chips), I/O interface, expansion slots and many other logic circuits. It may also contain a math's co-processor chip.

(*b*) **Input Devices.** Input devices are used to input data, information and instructions into RAM. For example, Keyboard, Mouse, touch screen, Light pen, etc. are the input devices.

(*c*) **Output Device.** Output devices are used to display or print the processed information For example: Monitor and Printer are main output Devices of a PC. Monitor is also called Visual Display Unit (VDU).

(*d*) **Storage Devices.** Storage devices are used to store data, information and software permanently on the computer, so that they can be retrieved whenever required. For example, Hard Disk and Floppy Disk are common storage devices of a PC.

(*e*) **Cards.** Cards are printed circuit boards used to hold the chips (integrated circuits). There are many types of cards used in a PC, the important ones are Video card, Sound Card, I/O card, Controller Card and Memory Card. Video card (Display Card) generates the text and graphic images for the monitor while the sound card generates the sound. I/O card provides a place for connecting input and output devices. Cables of hard disk and floppy disk are connected to controller card. Memory card provides a place for memory chips.

(*f*) **Ports and Cords.** Ports or connectors are the external sockets on a PC used to connect I/O and communication devices. There are many types of ports in a PC, the most important ones are Serial port, Parallel port, Game port and Video port. Serial port is used to connect a mouse, modem or scanner. Parallel part is generally used to connect a printer. Game port is used to connect the joystick while video port is a connector to the monitor. Cords are the cables used to plug into the ports. The important cords used in a PC are keyboard cords, power cords, monitor cords and printer cords.

(g) **Power supply.** Power supply provides the steady power supply to a computer. It provides a voltage range of 4.95 to 5.95 volts for the highest performance of the system.

We will now discuss the details of the most important component of computer *i.e.* CPU.

1.7 CENTRAL PROCESSING UNIT

Central Processing Unit (CPU) is the main component or "brain" of a computer, which performs all the processing of input data. Its function is to fetch, examine and then execute the instructions stored in the main memory of a computer. In microcomputers, the CPU is built on a single chip or Integrated Circuit (IC) and is called as a Microprocessor. The CPU consists of the following distinct parts:

(*a*) Arithmetic Logic Unit (ALU)

(*b*) Control Unit (CU)

(*c*) Registers

(*d*) Buses
(*e*) Clock

Let us discuss them briefly.

1.7.1 Arithmetic Logic Unit

The arithmetic and logic unit of CPU is responsible for all arithmetic operations like addition, subtraction, multiplication and division as well as logical operations such as less than, equal to and greater than. Actually, all calculations and comparisons are performed in the arithmetic logic unit. The data and instructions, which are stored in main memory of computer are transferred to ALU for processing. After processing, many times data move from ALU to memory and vice-versa.

The ALU can be as little as a part of a large scale integration (LSI) chip in a small computer. However, in a large computer, the ALU can consist of a considerable array of high speed logic circuits. Whatever is the size of ALU, the ALU performs the arithmetic and logical operations using the same principles, structure and function.

1.7.2 Control Unit

The control unit is responsible for controlling the transfer of data and instructions among other units of a computer. It is considered as the "Central Nervous System" of computer, as it manages and coordinates all the units of the computer. It obtains the instructions from the memory, interprets them and directs the operation of the computer. It also performs the physical data transfer between memory and peripheral devices.

The control unit performs following important functions.

- Control unit selects, interprets and monitors the execution of the program instructions by generating the timing and control signals.
- It transfers data between memory and input/output devices.
- It synchronises all the ALU operations with its clock.

1.7.3 Registers

Registers are small high speed circuits (memory locations) which are used to store data, instructions and memory addresses (memory location numbers), when ALU performs arithmetic and logical operations. Registers can store one word of data (1 word = 2 bytes & 1 byte = 8 bits) until it is overwritten by another word. Depending on the processor's capability, the number and type of registers vary from one CPU to another. Registers can be divided into six categories viz. General Purpose Registers, Pointer Registers, Segment Registers, Index Registers, Flags Register and Instruction Pointer Register, depending upon their functions.

1.7.4 Buses

Data is stored as a unit of eight bits (BIT stands for Binary Digit i.e. 0 or 1) in a register. Each bit is transferred from one register to another by means of a separate wire. This group of eight wires, which is used as a common way to transfer data between registers is known as a *bus*. In general terms, bus is a connection between two components to transmit signal between them. Bus can be of three major types viz. Data Bus, Control Bus and Address Bus. The differences among these three buses are listed in Table 1.10.

Address Bus	Data Bus	Control Bus
1. Used to send address of the memory on I/O Part.	1. Used to send data among various devices	1. Used to control the various devices of a microcomputer.
2. This bus is unidirectional as most of times CPU generates addresses.	2. This bus is bi-directional as data travels in both directions.	2. This bus is also bi-directional

Table 1.10 *Differences among address bus, data bus and control bus*

1.7.5 Clock

Clock is another important component of CPU, which measures and allocates a fixed time slot for processing each and every micro operation (smallest functional operation). In simple terms, CPU is allocated one or more clock cycles to complete a micro-operation. CPU executes the instructions in synchronization with the clock pulse.

The clock speed of CPU is measured in terms of *Mega Hertz* (MHz) or Millions of Cycles per second. The clock speed of CPU varies from one model to another in the range 4.77 MHz (in 8088 processor) to 266 MHz (in Pentium II). CPU speed is also specified in terms of *Millions of Instructions Per Second* (MIPS) or *Millions of Floating Point Operations Per Second* (MFLOPS).

1.8 MEMORY

Memory Unit is that component of a computer system, which is used to store the data, instructions and information before, during and after the processing by ALU. It is actually a work area (physically a collection of integrated circuits) within the computer, where the CPU stores the data and instructions. It is also known as a Main/Primary/ Internal Memory. It is of the following three types:

(*a*) Read Only Memory (ROM pronounced as "Ra-om")

(*b*) Random Access Memory (RAM pronounced as "R-aem")

(*c*) Complementary Metal Oxide Semiconductor Memory (CMOS)

Let us discuss them in detail.

1.8.1 Random Access Memory

Random Access Memory (RAM) is an important component of Memory Unit. It is used to store data and instructions during the execution of programs. Contrary to ROM, RAM is temporary and is erased when the computer is switched off. RAM is a read/ write type of memory, and thus can be read and written by the user/ programmer. As it is possible to randomly use any location of this memory, therefore, this memory is known as random access memory. The memory capacity of RAM varies from 640 KB to several megabytes (1 Megabyte = 1024 KB) with different models of PC.

1.8.1.1 Types of RAM

There are two types of RAM used in PCs–Dynamic and Static RAM. The differences between these two types of RAM are discussed in Table 1.11.

Dynamic RAM	Static RAM
1. The information stared in Dynamic RAM has to be refreshed after every few milliseconds otherwise it is erased.	1. The information stored In Static RAM need not to be refreshed, but it remains stable as long as powersupply is provided.
2. DRAM has higher storage capacity	2. SRAM has lesser storage capacity
3. It provides lesser speed tocomputer	3. It provides more speed to computer
4. It is cheaper	4. It is costlier

Table 1.11 *Differences between Dynamic and Static RAM*

1.8.2 Read Only Memory

Read Only Memory (ROM) is an essential component of the memory unit. We know that the computer, being a machine, has no intelligence or memory and requires instructions which are given by man. Whenever the computer is switched on, it searches for the required instructions. The memory, which has these essential instructions, is known as Read Only Memory (ROM). This memory is permanent and is not erased when the system is switched off. As appears with its name, it is read type of memory *i.e.* it can be read only and it cannot be written by the user or the programmer. The memory capacity of ROM varies from 64 KB to 256 KB (1 Kilobyte = 1024 bytes) depending on the model of computer.

ROM contains a number of programs (set of instructions). The most important program of ROM is the *Basic Input Output System* (BIOS, pronounced as "bye-os") that activates the hardware (physical components of computer) such as keyboard, monitor, floppy disk, etc. in communicating with the system and application software (set of instructions or programs).

1.8.2.1 Types of ROM

There are many types of ROM available for microcomputers like Mask ROM, PROM, EPROM, EEPROM and EAPROM.

(*a*) **Mask ROM.** Mask ROM is the basic ROM chip. In this type of ROM, the information is stored at the time of its manufacturing. So, it cannot be altered or erased later on.

(*b*) **PROM.** PROM stands for *Programmable Read Only Memory*. In this type of ROM, the information is stored by programmers after its manufacturing. It also cannot be altered or erased later on.

(*c*) **EPROM.** EPROM stands for *Erasable Programmable Read Only Memory*. It is similar to PROM, but its information can be erased later on by ultra violet light and it can be reprogrammed.

(*d*) **EEPROM.** EEPROM stands for *Electrically Erasable Programmable Read Only Memory*. It is similar to EPROM, but its information can be erased by using high voltage current.

(*e*) **EAPROM.** EAPROM stands for *Electrically Alterable Read Only Memory*. As compared to EPROM and EEPROM, the information stored in EAPROM can be altered later.

1.8.3 Complementary Metal Oxide Semiconductor Memory

Complementary Metal Oxide Semiconductor (CMOS) memory is used to store the system configuration, date, time and other important data. When the computer is switched on, BIOS matches the information of CMOS with the peripheral devices and displays error in case of mismatching.

1.9 INPUT DEVICES

You know that the computer is a machine that processes the input data according to a given set of instructions and gives the output. A computer must be given data for processing . After processing, the output must be displayed or printed by the computer. The device used for putting the data and instructions into the computer and displaying or printing output is known as an *Input/Output Unit* (I/O Unit).

The Input Unit is used to enter data and instructions into a computer. There are many peripheral devices that are used as input/output devices for the computer. Keyboard is the main input device. There are some other common input devices like mouse, punched card, tape, joystick, scanner, modem, etc. Input devices are classified into the following two broad categories :

(*i*) Basic Input Devices:

(*ii*) Special Input Devices

Let us discuss them in detail.

1.9.1 Basic Input Devices

The input devices which have now-a-days become essential to operate a PC, may be called as Basic Input Devices. These devices are always required for basic input operations. These devices include Keyboard and Mouse. Today, every PC has a keyboard and mouse as the basic input device as shown in Figure 1.6. Let us discuss these briefly.

Figure 1.6 *A Personal Computer having basic input devices.*

1.9.1.1 *Keyboard*

Keyboard (similar to a typewriter) is the main input device of a computer. It contains 3 types of keys– alphanumeric keys, special keys and function keys. Alphanumeric keys are used to type all alphabets, numbers and special symbols like $, %, @, ^, etc. Special keys such as <Shift>, <Ctrl>, <Alt>, <Home>, <Scroll Lock>, etc. are used for special functions. Function keys such as <F1>, <F2>, <F3>, etc. are used to give special commands depending upon the software used. We can understand the function of each and every key actually by working on a PC. When any key is pressed, an electronic signal is produced. This signal is detected by a keyboard encoder that sends a binary code corresponding to the key pressed to the CPU. There are many types of keyboards but 101 Keys Keyboard, as shown in Figure 1.7, is the most popular one.

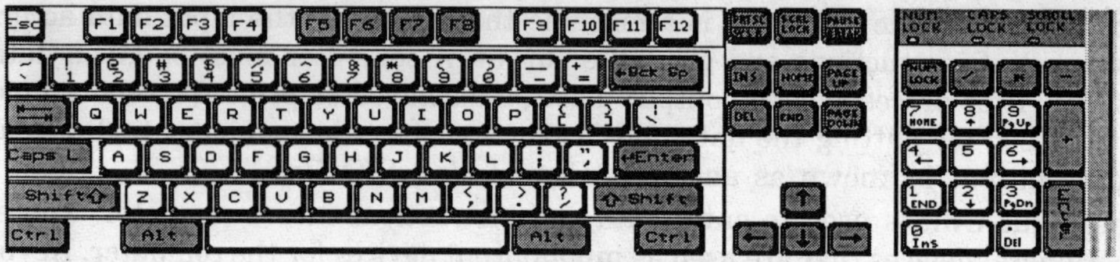

Figure 1.7 *A 101 keys keyboard*

1.9.1.2 *Mouse*

Mouse (similar to a mouse) is another important input device. It is a pointing device used to move cursor, draw sketches/ diagrams, select text/object/menu item, etc. on monitor screen while working on windows (graphics based operating environment of a computer). Mouse is a small, palm size box containing 3 buttons and a ball underneath as shown in Figure 1.8, which senses the movement of the mouse and sends the corresponding signals to CPU on pressing the buttons.

Figure 1.8 *A mouse*

1.9.2 Special Input Devices

The input devices, which are not essential to operate a PC, are called Special Input Devices. These devices are used for various special purposes and are generally not required for basic input operations. These devices include Trackball, Light Pen, Touch Screen, Joystick, Digitizer, Scanner, OMR, OCR, Bar Code Reader, MICR and Voice Input Devices. Let us discuss these special input devices briefly.

1.9.2.1 *Trackball*

A trackball looks like a mouse, as the roller is on the top with selection buttons on the side as shown in Figure 1.9. It is also a pointing device used to move the cursor and works like a mouse. For moving the cursor in a particular direction, the user spins the ball in that direction. It is sometimes considered better than mouse, because it requires little arm movement and less desktop space. It is generally used with portable computers.

Figure 1.9 *A trackball*

1.9.2.2 Light Pen

Light pen (similar to a pen) is a pointing device that is used to select a displayed menu item or draw pictures on the monitor screen as shown in Figure 1.10. It consists of a photocell and an optical system placed in a small tube. When its tip is moved over the monitor screen and pen button is pressed, its photocell sensing element detects the screen location and sends the corresponding signal to the CPU.

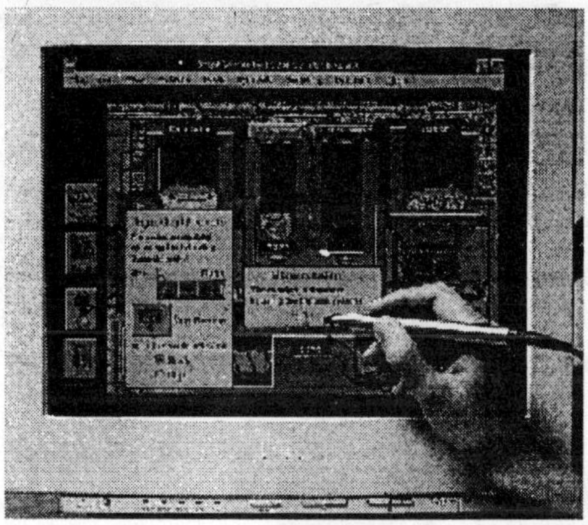

Figure 1.10 *Demonstration of a light pen*

1.9.2.3 Joystick

Joystick is also a pointing device that is used to move cursor position on a monitor screen. Joystick is a stick having a spherical ball at its lower and upper ends as shown in Figure 1.11. The lower spherical ball moves in a socket. The joystick can be moved in all the four directions. The function of joystick is similar to that of a mouse. It is mainly used in Computer Aided Designing (CAD) and for playing computer games.

Figure 1.11 *A joystick*

1.9.2.4 Touch Screen

Some special VDU devices have touch sensitive screens. These screens are sensitive to human fingers and act as tactile input devices. Using touch screen, the user can point to a selection on the screen instead of pressing keys as shown in Figure 1.12. Touch screen helps the user in getting the information quickly. It is mainly used in hotels or airports to convey information to visitors.

Figure 1.12 *Demonstration of touch screen*

1.9.2.5 Scanner

Scanner is widely used in Desktop Publishing (DTP) applications. It is used for digitizing images such as photographs, forms, documents, etc. into computer memory. There are many types of scanners as illustrated in Figure 1.13. Some scanners can also read text by converting them to digital code. The scanners are very useful for converting the typed pages into word processing files. Graphic scanners convert a printed image into video image without converting it to digital code.

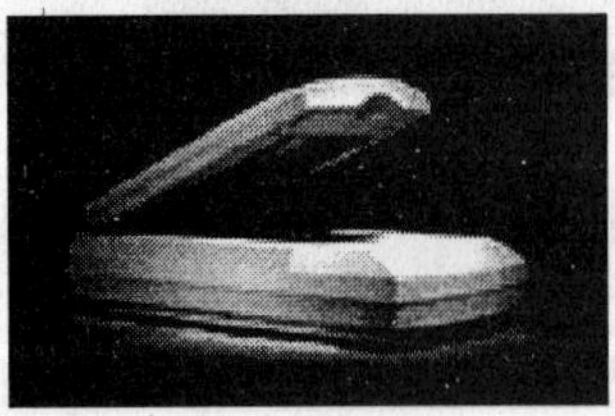

Flatbed Scanner

Optical Scanner

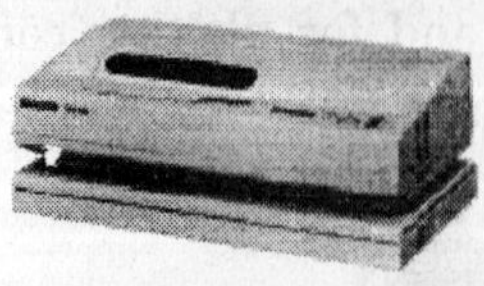

Drum Scanner

Film Scanner

Figure 1.13 *Various types of scanners*

1.9.2.6 Optical Mark Reader (OMR)

Optical Mark Reader is a special type of optical scanner used to recognise the type of mark made by pen or pencil. It is used where one out of a few alternatives is to be selected and marked. It is especially used for checking the answer sheets of examinations having multiple-choice questions. The answer sheet contains special marks such as squares or bubbles. The student fills in these squares with soft pencil or ink to indicate the correct choice as illustrated in Figure 1.14. The OMR detects these marks and sends corresponding signals to the processor. If a mark is present, the amount of reflected light is reduced and thus, OMR detects the presence of mark for each and every answer. Optical Mark Readers are widely used for almost all competitive examinations having objective type questions.

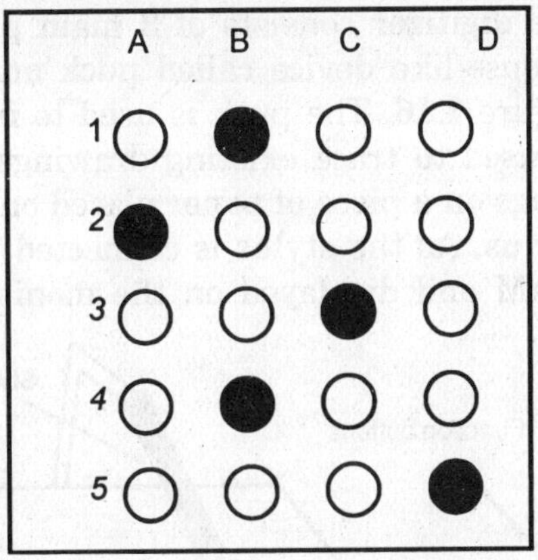

Figure 1.14 *A sample of answer sheet that is checked by Optical Mark Reader*

1.9.2.7 Bar Code Reader

Bar Code Reader is an optical scanner used for reading bar-coded data (data in form of light and dark lines) as illustrated in Figure 1.15. The bar-coded data consists of a number of bars of varying thickness and spacing between them. The bar code reader reads the bar coded data and converts it into electrical pulses, which are then processed by the computer. Bar-coded data is generally used in labeling goods, numbering the books or encoding ID or A/c numbers.

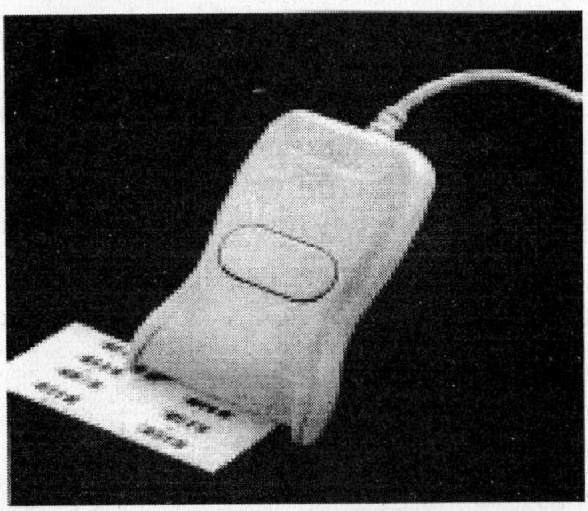

Figure 1.15 *A barcode reader reading bar-coded data*

1.9.2.8 Optical Character Reader (OCR)

Optical Character Reader (OCR) is an optical scanner, which is capable of detecting alphanumeric characters typed or printed on paper using an OCR font. The text, which is to be scanned, is illuminated by a low-frequency light source. The dark areas on the text absorb the light while light areas reflect it. The photocells of OCR device receive this reflected light and provide binary data corresponding to dark and light areas. OCR devices are used for large volume applications like reading of passenger tickets, computer printed bills of credit card companies and reading of ZIP codes in postal services.

1.9.2.9 Digitizer

Digitizer is used to create drawings and pictures using a digitizer tablet by a process called digitizing. The digitizer consists of 3 main parts – a flat surface called tablet, a small hand held mouse-like device called puck and a special pen like device called stylus as shown in Figure 1.16. The puck is used to input existing drawings into the computer. The stylus is used to trace existing drawings placed on the tablet. It is also used to draw new drawings on a piece of paper placed on the tablet. The user makes contact to the tablet with stylus. As the stylus is connected to the tablet by a wire, the traced image is stored in RAM and displayed on the monitor.

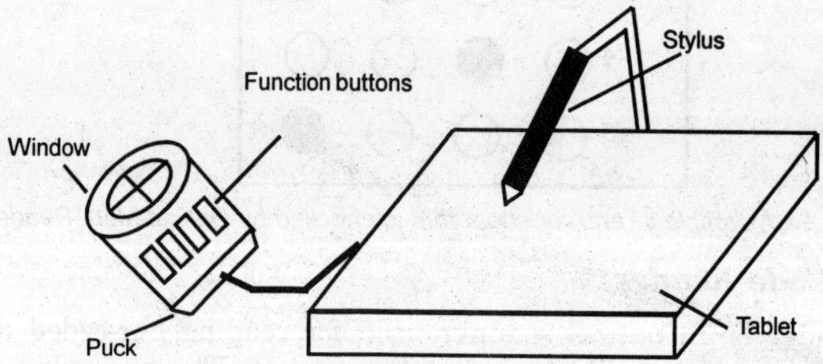

Figure 1.16 *A digitizer*

1.9.2.10 Magnetic Ink Character Recognition (MICR)

Magnetic Ink Character Recognition (MICR) is used to recognise the magnetically-charged characters, mainly found on bank cheques. The magnetically-charged characters are written by a special ink called magnetic ink. MICR device as shown in Figure 1.17 reads the patterns of these characters and compares them with special patterns stored in memory. Using MICR device, a large volume of cheques can be processed in a day. MICR is widely used by the banking industry for the processing of cheques.

Figure 1.17 *An MICR device*

1.9.2.11 *Voice Input Devices*

Voice Input devices are the latest input devices that can recognise the human voice. They seem to be very useful but are not popular due to storage of limited vocabularies and variations in the way of pronouncing words by different persons.

1.10 OUTPUT DEVICES

Output devices are hardware components that are used to display or print the processed information. We are discussing below the structure, working and uses of the common output devices.

1.10.1 Monitor

Visual Display Unit (VDU) commonly called Monitor is the main output device of a computer. It consists of a Cathode Ray Tube (CRT), which displays characters as an output. It forms images from tiny dots, called pixels that are arranged in a rectangular form. The sharpness of the image (screen resolution) depends upon the number of pixels.

1.10.1.1 *Types of Monitors*

There are different kinds of monitors depending upon the number of pixels. Depending upon the resolution, monitors can be classified as follows:

(*a*) CGA (Colour Graphics Adapter)
(*b*) MDA (Monochrome Display Adapter)
(*c*) HGA (Hercules Graphics Adapter)
(*d*) EGA (Enhanced Graphics Adapter)
(*e*) VGA (Video Graphics Adapter)
(*f*) SVGA (Super VGA)

The differences between these monitors are summarised in Table 1.12. Depending upon the colour of display, monitors can be classified as Monochrome (with single colour black/white display) and Colour (with all colours display) Monitors. The pictures of two different models of color monitors are shown in Figure 1.18.

Type of Monitor	Display Type	Text Resolution	Graphics Rsolution (Pixels)
CGA	Text & Graphics	Fair quality	320 × 200
MDA	Text only	Good quality	-
HGA	Text & Mono Graphics	Fair quality	320 × 200
EGA	Text & Enhanced Graphics	Good quality	640 × 350
VGA	Text & Video Graphics	Much better than all the above	640 × 480
SVGA	Text & Video Graphics	Best quality	1600 × 1280

Table 1.12 *Comparison among different types of monitors*

14" Multimedia Colour Monitor 15" Colour Monitor

Figure 1.18 *Two models of colour monitors*

1.10.2 Printer

Printer is the most important output device, which is used to print information on paper. Printers are essential for getting output of any computer-based application. There are many types of printers which are classified on various criteria as illustrated in Figure 1.19. Printers can be broadly categorised into two types–Impact and Non-Impact. Let us discuss these in detail.

1.10.2.1 Impact Printers

The printers that print the characters by striking against the ribbon and onto the paper are called Impact Printers. These printers are of two types: (*a*) Character; and (*b*) Line printers.

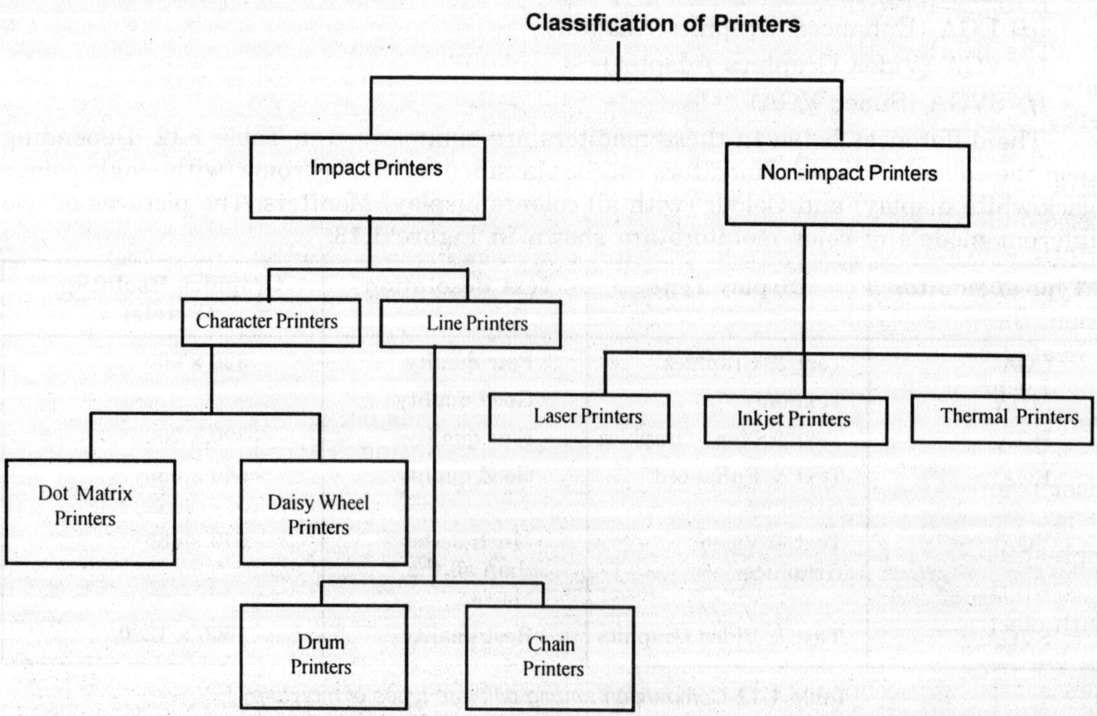

Figure 1.19 *Classification of printers*

(*a*) **Character Printers.** These printers print one character at a time. These printers are again of two types: Daisy Wheel and Dot Matrix Printers.

(*i*) *Daisy Wheel Printers.* These printers print the characters by a mechanism that uses a plastic or metal hub with spokes, called daisy wheel. The characters are embossed on the radiating spokes and printed by striking these spokes against the ribbon and paper. Daisy Wheel printers give a good quality but they are more expensive than Dot Matrix printers are.

(*ii*) *Dot Matrix Printers.* These printers print the characters by putting dots onto the paper. They do not give better printing quality than daisy wheel printers, but are faster in speed. The printing speed of a dot matrix printer can be upto 360 cps (characters per second). They are widely used with microcomputers in most of the offices.

(*b*) **Line Printers.** These printers print one line at a time. Their printing speed is much more than character printers. They are again of two types: Drum Printers and Chain Printers.

(*i*) *Drum Printers.* These printers print the line by a rotating drum having a ring of characters for each print position. The hammers strike each character of the drum simultaneously, so that entire line is printed for one full rotation of the drum. These printers are also called Barrel Printers. The printouts obtained from these printers, have even character spacing but uneven line height.

(*ii*) *Chain Printers*. These printers print the line by a rotating chain having ring characters for each print position. Their printing mechanism is similar to drum printers. The printouts obtained from these printers, have uneven character spacing but even line height.

1.10.2.2 Non-Impact Printers

The printers that print the characters without striking against the ribbon and onto the paper are called Non-Impact Printers. Non-Impact printers are of three types: (*a*) Laser Printers, (*b*) Inkjet Printers, and (*c*) Thermal Printers.

(*a*) **Laser Printers.** These printers look and work like photocopiers. These printers print a complete page at a time, therefore, also called Page Printers. Laser Printers are based on laser technology, which is the latest development in high speed & high quality printing. In these printers, a laser beam is used to write the image on a paper. First, the image is formed by electrically charging thousands of dots on a paper by laser beam. Then, the paper is sprayed with a toner having the opposite charge and is passed over a heated roller to make the image permanent.

Laser printers are very popular and have become an essential part of Desk Top Publishing (DTP). Although laser printers are costlier than dot matrix, they are generally preferred in all offices due to their high quality of printing. There are many models of laser printers depending upon the speed and number of dots printed. The latest model of laser printer is 1200 DPI (Dots Per Inch), which can print 10 pages/minute. Some high-speed laser printers give a speed of upto 100 pages/minute.

(*b*) **Inkjet Printers.** These printers print the characters by spraying the paper with electrically charged ink. These printers give better quality than character printers do but they are not better than laser printers. They are cheaper than laser printers, hence used widely in many offices. They also offer an option of using colour cartridges for multicolour printing.

(*c*) **Thermal Printers.** These printers print the characters by melting a wax-based ink off a ribbon onto a special heat sensitive paper. They give letter quality printing but are relatively expensive in maintenance than other printers.

The pictures of some of the printers are shown in Figure 1.20.

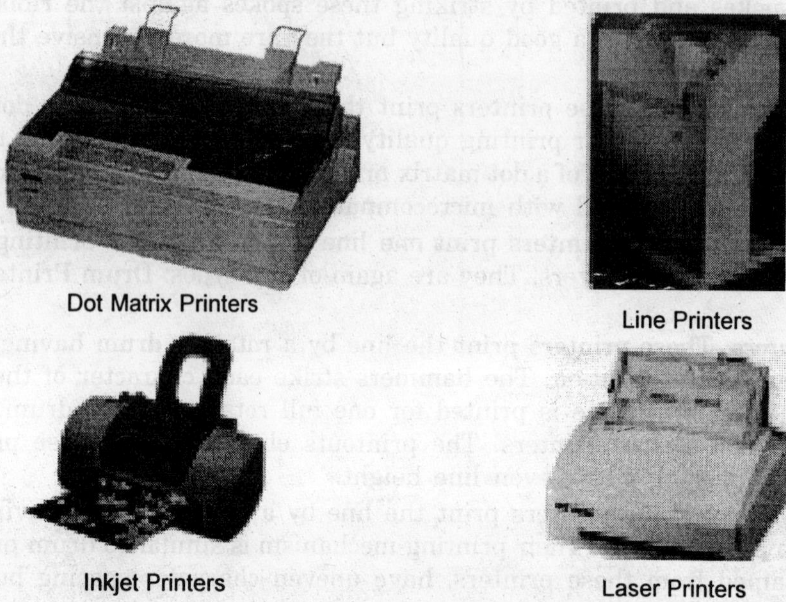

Figure 1.20 *Various types of printers*

1.10.3 PLOTTER

Plotter is an important output device, used to print high quality graphics and drawings. Although the graphics can be printed on printers, the resolution of such printing is limited on printers. Plotters are generally used for printing/ drawing graphical images such as charts, drawings, maps, etc. of engineering and scientific applications. Some important types of plotters are shown in Figure 1.21 and are discussed on next page.

1.10.3.1 Flat Bed Plotters

These plotters print the graphical images by moving the pen on stationary flat surface material. They produce very accurate drawings.

1.10.3.2 Drum Plotters

These plotters print graphical images by moving both the pen and the drum having paper. They do not produce as accurate drawings as printed by flat bed plotters.

1.10.3.3 **Inkjet Plotters**

These plotters use inkjets in place of pens. They are faster than flat bed plotters and can print multicolored large drawings.

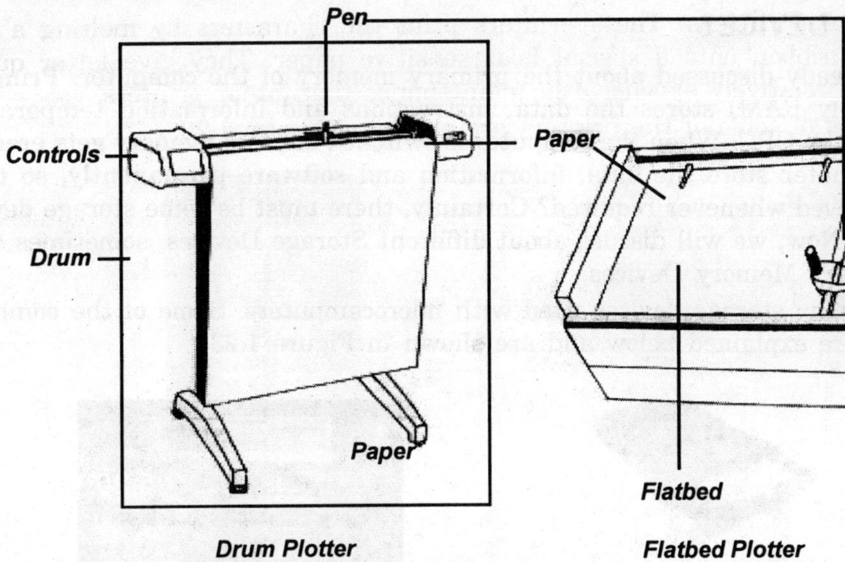

Figure 1.21 *Various types of plotters*

1.10.4 Computer Output Microfilm

Computer Output Microfilm (COM) is a technique to produce output on a microfilm media (microfilm reel or microfiche card) as illustrated in Figure 1.22. A microfilm is a continuous filmstrip that can store several thousands miniaturized document pages. A microfiche card is a 4 X 6 inch film sheet, which can store several hundred pages. The process of producing microfilm or microfiche takes place on a special COM unit. The information recorded on the microfilm is read with the help of a microfilm viewing system. It is generally easier to read a microfiche than microfilm. Computer Output Microfilm is particularly useful for organisations that need to store and manipulate large amount of data. It helps them in tremendous savings in paper and document handling costs.

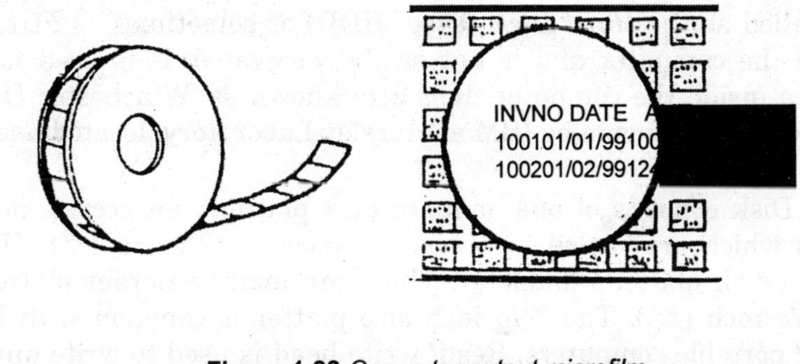

Figure 1.22 *Computer output microfilm*

1.11 STORAGE DEVICES

We have already discussed about the primary memory of the computer. Primary memory (especially RAM) stores the data, instructions and information temporarily during processing by CPU. When the computer is switched off, this memory gets erased. How does a computer store the data, information and software permanently, so that they can be retrieved whenever required? Certainly, there must be some storage device in the computer. Now, we will discuss about different Storage Devices, sometimes also called as Secondary Memory Devices.

There are many storage devices used with microcomputers. Some of the common storage devices are explained below and are shown in Figure 1.23.

Zip Drive

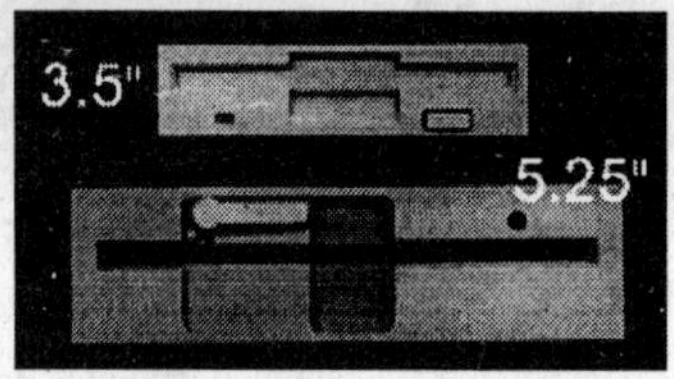

Floppy Disk Drives (3.5" & 5.25")

Hard Disk Drive

CD ROM Drive

Figure 1.23 *Common storage devices*

1.11.1 Winchester Disk (Hard Disk)

Winchester Disk is the most common storage device of present day microcomputers. It is popularly called as the *Hard Disk Drive* (HDD) or sometimes as *Fixed Disk Drive*. It is fixed inside the computer and is not easily removable. It is used for storing the software and data inside the computer. It is also known as 'Winchester Disk', probably because this drive was first made by IBM at Hursley Laboratory, located near Winchester in England.

Winchester Disk consists of one or more disk platters, an access mechanism and read/write heads which are sealed in a case as shown in Figure 1.24. Hard disk size depends upon the disk platter's diameter. There are many different platter sizes (such as $5\frac{1}{2}$, $3\frac{1}{2}$, $2\frac{1}{2}$ inch etc.). The $3\frac{1}{2}$ inch size platter is common with PCs and $2\frac{1}{2}$ inch with laptop/ portable computers. Read/ write head is used to write any information on the disk surface or to read it back.

There are different types of hard disks depending upon their storage capacities. Storage capacities of hard disks range from 10 MB to several GBs, but 1.2 GB to 4.1 GB are now-a-days a common part of Pentium computers.

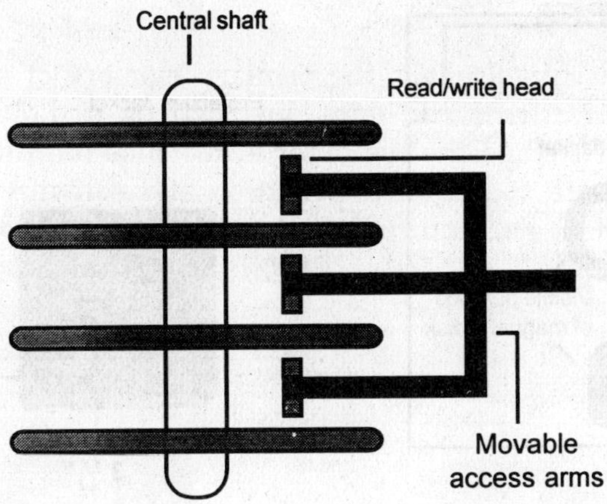

Figure 1.24 Internal structure of a Winchester disk

1.11.2 Floppy Disk

Floppy Disk (FD) is another common storage device that is small, flexible and easily removable. It is made of a plastic disk coated with magnetic material, which is sealed inside a square plastic jacket. It is called as 'Floppy' because it is soft having flexible physical property. Data can be written on or read from this floppy by a drive, called Floppy Disk Drive (FDD), which is fixed inside the computer.

There are many types of floppies depending upon their sizes and storage capacities as summarised in Table 1.13. The original floppy, developed by IBM, is an 8" floppy, but the most popular sizes available for present day PCs are $5^1/_4$" and $3^1/_2$" as shown in Figure 1.25. The storage capacity of floppies varies from 360 KB to 1.44 MB. The floppies can store data on both sides (Double-sided Floppies) or on single side (Single-sided Floppies) depending upon the floppy drive. Double-sided floppy drives are most frequently used in present day PCs. The latest floppy drive, that packs two high density floppy drives (5.25 & 3.5 inch) into a single package, is known as *Combo Drive*.

Type of Floppy	Size	Density	Sectors*	Tracks*	Storage Capacity
DSDD**	5.25 inch	Double	9	40	360 K
DSLD**	3.5 inch	Low	9	80	720 K
DSHD** Big	5.25 inch	High	15	80	1.2 MB
DSHD Small	3.5 inch	High	18	80	1.44 MB

* For definition of these terms, refer to *glossary*

** DS stands for Double Sided, LD for Low Density and HD for High Density

Table 1.13 *Comparison among different types of floppies*

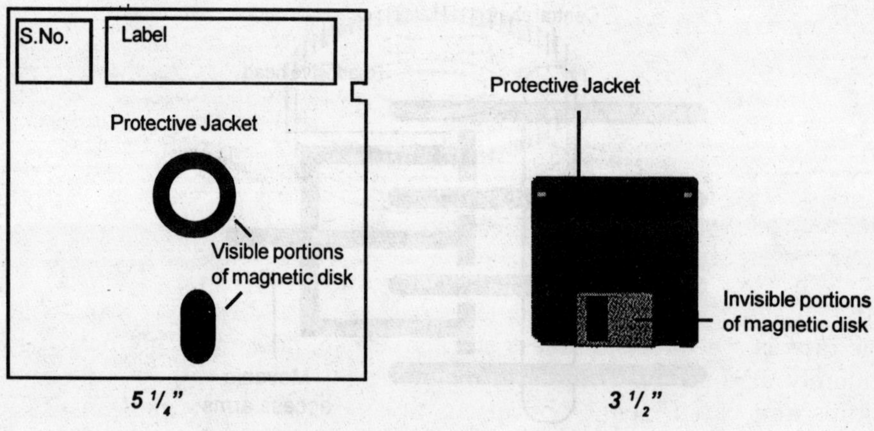

Figure 1.25 The popular sizes of floppy disks

1.11.3 Compact Disk

Compact Disk (CD) is the latest storage device, used to store data, information and software, which can be read only and not be changed or erased. It is an optical read only memory, made up of resin as shown in Figure 1.26. Therefore, it is actually called *Compact Disk Read Only Memory* (CD-ROM). However, the information is stored on CDs by using an expensive drive, called CD-ROM drive.

Figure 1.26 *A CD-ROM Disk*

Now-a-days compact disks are very popular storage devices for microcomputers because a large number of software including multimedia, audio and graphics software is available only on these disks. Compact Disks can store a large volume of data (up to 680 MB), which is almost the same as a storage capacity of a 640 MB Hard Disk.

WORM (Write Once Read Many) is a type of compact disk that can be recorded only once and not erased. It can store more data than a CD-ROM, generally measured in gigabytes.

1.11.4 Magnetic Tape

Magnetic tape is the oldest storage device available for microcomputers. It is generally used to store a large volume of data that is required to be sequentially accessed and processed. The tape is made up of a plastic ribbon coated with an iron-oxide material, which can be magnetised as shown in Figure 1.27. The data stored on tape can be read as well as erased and written again.

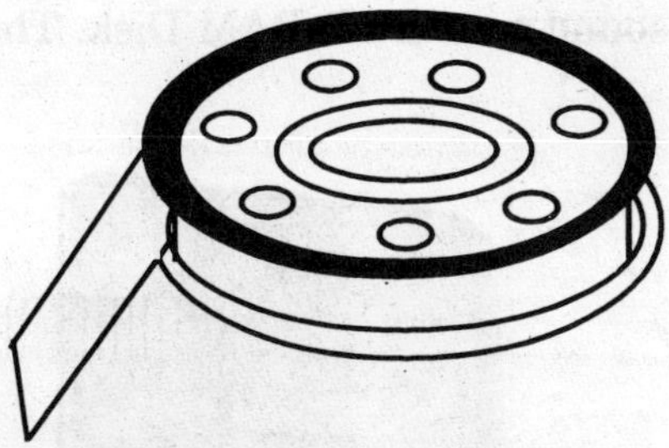

Figure 1.27 *A magnetic tape*

Magnetic tape is a sequential access storage device, hence it is not possible to read the data randomly or directly. Therefore, magnetic tapes are suitable only for storing data for backups and batch mode applications and not for on-line applications. On the other hand, magnetic disks (floppy and hard disks), which are discussed above, are considered best storage devices for on-line applications.

1.11.5 Video Disk

Video disk is used to store text, video and audio data. It is widely used for training applications as it can be played like a phonograph record.

1.11.6 Magneto Optical Drive

Magneto Optical (MO) drive, as shown in Figure 1.28, is the latest of all storage devices. This drive uses both a laser and an electromagnet to record data on a removable cartridge. The surface of the cartridge contains tiny embedded magnets. The unique feature of MO drive is that it has a very high storage capacity. Although MO drive is costlier and slower than HDD, it has a long life and is more reliable.

Figure 1.28 *A magneto optical (MO) disk*

1.11.7 DVD ROM/RAM Disk

DVD ROM and DVD RAM disks are optical disks having a storage capacity of 4.7 GB and 5.2 GB respectively. These disks are becoming the next generation's new standard for higher capacity removable media. They are ideal for storage of huge amount of information required for multimedia applications. One can put 133 minutes of high quality of video with digital sound on a DVD RAM Disk. The picture of DVD RAM disk is shown in Figure 1.29.

Figure 1.29 *A DVD RAM disk*

THEORY QUESTIONS

1. Define computer and briefly explain its main characteristics. Do you think computer is more intelligent than human beings? Discuss.
2. Which major category of computers is used in almost all offices and homes?
3. Explain the salient features of Analog, Digital and Hybrid Computers.
4. What is a Supercomputer? List various uses of supercomputers.
5. Write the differences between mainframe computer and minicomputer.
6. Discuss the development of computers with the reference to various generations.
7. Write a short note on Zeroth Generation of Computers.
8. Why did the First Generation Computers fail? Did the Second Generation Computers become successful? Discuss with examples.
9. Write the differences between Third and Fourth generation of computers.
10. What are the Fifth Generation Computers? Do you think these computers would replace Fourth Generation Computers? Discuss.
11. Do we need computers? Explain various uses of computers.
12. Draw a block diagram of a digital computer and explain the functions of each block in brief.
13. What is a computer system? Describe in brief the architecture of a computer system.
14. Which component of a computer is generally called 'brain' of computer and why? Describe the functions of the distinct parts of this component.
15. Compare and contrast Mainframe computer, Mini computer and Micro computer.
16. What are the main functional units of a Central Processing Unit? Explain in brief.
17. What is a microprocessor? How can a microprocessor be differentiated with CPU? Write the names of any two microprocessors.
18. What is ROM? How does it differ from RAM?
19. Name various types of ROM and describe their main characteristics.
20. How does a Static ROM differ from a Dynamic ROM. Which RAM would you prefer in your computer and why?
21. Define the following terms:
    (*a*) Bus (*b*) Register (*c*) Hardware (*d*) Software
22. Define the term hardware. Discuss in brief the classification of hardware components of a microcomputer.

23. What are Input/Output devices? Explain in brief with example.
24. Name the basic input devices of a PC and explain their functions in brief.
25. What is a trackball? How does it differ from a mouse?
26. Name the input device used -
    (*a*) to create drawings and pictures
    (*b*) for digitizing photographs and documents
27. How does an OMR differ from an OCR? Which of these devices is used for checking the answer sheets of examinations having multiple-choice questions?
28. What are the various output devices? Explain briefly:
29. What is a printer? Name the various types of printers available.
30. Explain the difference between Character, Line and Page Printers. Give examples.
31. What is the difference between impact and non impact printer?
32. What is the difference between main memory and secondary memory?
33. Name the main storage devices of a computer. Elaborate.
34. What is the difference between cards and cords? Explain with examples.
35. What are ports? Explain briefly.

2

CONCEPTS OF SOFTWARE

2.1 INTRODUCTION

In the last chapter, we discussed the basic hardware concepts. We already know that the computer is a piece of hardware and it is useless unless it is provided with the necessary software. Therefore, all computer users must be aware of the basic software concepts. A software is a program or set of instructions, which is required to use the computer. Many types of software are available for various applications. The software development field is so advanced that day-by-day existing software are becoming outdated and new software are coming in the market. So, we must get ourselves aware of the latest developments in the software industry.

In this chapter, we are discussing the important software concepts. We will also try to acquire the latest knowledge of the software available in the market. Though we are also providing you the current information about the latest version of software, we are sure that it will be outdated soon.

2.2 CLASSIFICATION OF SOFTWARE

Software are broadly classified into following two types:

(*a*) System Software

(*b*) Application Software

Let us discuss them briefly.

2.2.1 System Software

Software that is required to control the working of hardware and aid in effective execution of a general user's applications is called System Software. This software performs a variety of functions like file editing, storage management, resource accounting, I/O management, database management, etc. Some of the examples of system software are DOS (Disk Operating System), Windows, BASIC, COBOL and PC TOOLS. This software is developed by System Programmers.

System software is essential to operate a computer. Without an operating system, you cannot even start a computer. Without a language translator (compiler or interpreter), you cannot translate your high-level language program into machine language and hence cannot run it. Without a software utility (such as Norton Disk Doctor - NDD), you cannot detect the problems of the disks. Various system software and their main features are discussed below in brief.

(*i*) **Operating System.** Operating system is the most essential system software that makes your computer ready to use. Without an operating system, it is not possible to use the computer. The computer is useless unless it is provided with essential software that makes it ready to use. Windows provides graphical environment to your PC because of which this operating system has gained widespread popularity these days. We are discussing operating system concepts in the next chapter.

(*ii*) **Language Translator.** The system software that converts the assembly/high level language code into machine language code is called language translator.

(*iii*) **Application Generator.** The system software that helps the programmer to quickly generate a complete or part program according to the specification given.

(*iv*) **Software utilities.** The system software that supports the operation of computer is called a software utility.

2.2.1.1 Types of System Software

System software can be further categorised into following three types :

(*a*) System Management Software
(Operating Systems, DBMSs, Operating Environments)

(*b*) System Development Software
(Language Translators, Application Generators, CASE Tools)

(*c*) System Software Utilities

2.2.2 Application Software

Software that is required for general and special purpose applications like database management, word processing, accounting, etc. are called Application Software. Some of the examples of application software are dBASE, Word Star, Tally, etc. Application software is developed using system software by Application Programmers.

2.2.2.1 Types of Application Software

Application software can be further classified into following two types:

(*a*) General Purpose Application Software
(Database Management Packages, Word Processors, Spreadsheets etc.)

(*b*) Special Purpose Application Software
(Accounting, Inventory, Production Management, etc.)

Let us now discuss these system and application software in detail.

2.3 LANGUAGE TRANSLATORS

Regardless of the programming language used (except machine language), the symbolic instructions have to be translated into a form that can be executed by computer. The software, which converts the codes of other languages into machine code, is collectively called Language Translator. Language Translators are categorised into following three types:

(*a*) Assemblers
(*b*) Interpreters
(*c*) Compilers
Let us discuss them briefly.

2.3.1 Assemblers

Assemblers translate the assembly language code (source program) into machine language code (object program). After assembling, a linker program is used to convert the object program into an executable program. The Microsoft assembler program (MASM) and Borland Turbo assembler program (TASM) are two popular assemblers. Assemblers are used mainly in development of system software.

2.3.2 Interpreters

Instructions of a high-level language are coded in many statements. At the time of their execution, they are converted statement by statement into machine code, by using system software, called Interpreters. For example, programs written in BASIC language are executed by using BASICA or GWBASIC interpreters. Programs written in some fourth generation languages, like dBASE III plus are also executed using dBASE interpreter.

There are certain disadvantages of interpreters. As instructions are translated and executed simultaneously using interpreters, they are very slow for executing large programs. Hence, interpreters are not suitable for most of applications development.

2.3.3 Compilers

As contrast to interpreters, compilers provide faster execution speed. Compilers do not translate and execute the instructions at the same time. They translate the entire program (source code) into machine code (object code). Using linker, the object code is converted into executable code. Compilers are widely used in translating codes of high-level languages (*e.g.* COBOL, FORTRAN, PASCAL, Turbo/ Quick BASIC, Turbo/ Microsoft C etc.) and fourth generation languages (dBASE IV, Foxpro etc.). As compared to interpreters or assemblers, compilers are preferred in development of application software.

2.4 SOFTWARE TOOLS

To develop a large application, lots of effort, money and time are required for designing the systems and writing the program code. The overall goal of computerising an application is to make it more efficient than manual system with optimum utilisation of time, money and effort spent on its development. In order to save the valuable time spent by systems designers and programmers in designing the complete system and writing codes, certain programs are required, which are called software tools.

The selection of software tools has become an important aspect of software development. Software tools assist the programmers/ analyst in the design, coding, editing, compiling, linking and debugging programs. They allow them to focus on the challenging aspects of a system. We are discussing below the important categories of software tools that are normally used.

2.4.1 Application Generators

Application generators are software tools that help the programmer to quickly generate a complete or part program according to the specifications given. The programmer does not write the code but using an application generator, defines the menus, screen, report formats, data elements and processing logics. The application generator generates the program code quickly. Now, the programmer can easily edit and execute the program.

Many application generators are available for different third and fourth generation languages like COBOL, dBASE, Foxpro etc. For example, Pacbase is an application generator for programs written in COBOL language. dBASE and Foxpro have built-in code generation capabilities for designing screen, menu and report formats. Genifer is a full-scale code generator that provides a pattern called a template, from which the code is generated. After defining screens, menus and reports, Genifer creates the data files, index files and programs.

2.4.1.1 Advantages of Application Generators

The major advantages of using application generators are—

- Saving a lot of development time
- Useful as a learning tool for writing programs
- Programs are easy to modify and maintain

2.4.1.2 Disadvantages of Application Generators

Application generators also have certain disadvantages—

- Cannot handle systems having complex processing logic
- Add complexity, if template language differs from native language

2.4.2 CASE Tools

Development of application software is very complex to plan, design, develop and manage. Software engineering is the systematic approach in design, development, operation and maintenance of such software. Its basic aim is to produce high quality software at low cost. Computer Aided Software Engineering (CASE) tool is a group of different software tools that are integrated and used in software engineering. For example, Designer/2000 is Oracle's suite of CASE tools that address the different stages of the application development.

CASE tools simplify all stages of project planning, analysis and design of an application. CASE tools include many important features like graphics library, data dictionary, design methodology, screen/ report designing and systems documentation. CASE tools incorporate modeling techniques for representing the data and processes.

2.5 SYSTEM UTILITY SOFTWARE

System software utilities support the operation of the computer. They provide many features including file management capabilities, data compression, diagnostic routines, virus detection and removal, text editing, performance monitoring and spooling.

There are many types of utilities for carrying different tasks. Utilities are not operating systems, but certain utilities are inbuilt in operating systems. Let us briefly discuss the utilities that are commonly used in computers.

2.5.1 Data Compression Utilities

These utilities compress or decompress files that are stored on floppy and hard disks. As compressed files take up very less space in disks, data compression utilities are widely used during copying of data from hard disk to floppy disks. PKZIP/ PKUNZIP programs are commonly used examples of data compression utilities.

2.5.2 File Management Utilities

These utilities provide file management capabilities like copying, comparing, searching, listing and sorting the files. Although these features are offered by many operating systems, utility programs provide better user-friendly environment along with some additional features. Norton Utilities (NU) and PC TOOLS are the most commonly used file management utilities.

2.5.3 Diagnostic Utilities

These utilities can detect bugs (errors in hardware/ software) in computers. For instance, the problems of floppy and hard disks can easily be detected by a popular utility program called Norton Disk Doctor (NDD). QAPlus and Disk Manager (DM) are other examples of utilities that can detect and remove many bugs in storage devices, software and other components of computers.

2.5.4 Text Editing Utilities

These utilities are used to create, edit and print the non-document texts such as programs, data etc. Norton Editor (NE) is the most common example of text editor. Most operating systems, including DOS, also has inbuilt text editor program.

2.5.5 Virus Detection and Removal Utilities

These utilities are used to detect and eradicate the different types of viruses. Before discussing their importance, let us first discuss, what is a Virus? Virus is an unauthorised software that is used to invade and disrupt the normal working of computer. Like biological viruses, computer virus spreads from one computer to another generally through floppy disks. There are many problems caused by viruses like damage of data, loss of user interface, unexpected screen messages, system crashes etc. The potential problems caused by viruses in today's organisational computer systems are the worst. There are many types of viruses and their number is increasing day by day. The users and managers must take precautionary measures to control the spread of these viruses.

There are many utilities, such as Nashscan, SmartDog, Dr. Soloman's Anti-Virus Toolkit, McAfee VirusScan, etc. that can detect and remove most of the viruses and are popularly called Virus Scanners. These virus scanners must be upgraded from time to time for detection and removal of new viruses. The opening window of a virus scanner, McAfee VirusScan is shown in Figure 2.1.

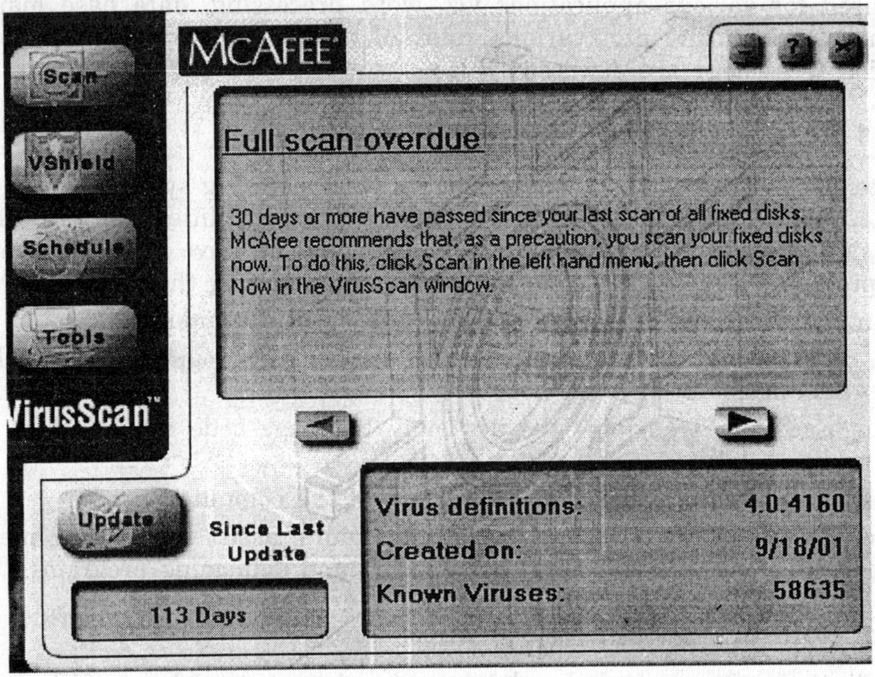

Figure 2.1 *The opening window of a virus scanner*

2.5.6 Spooling Utilities

In multi-user/ networking environments, the input and output devices are generally slow. In such environment, the processing of computer is also slowed down. To control the computer from being slowed down, the spooling programs are used.

SPOOLing (Simultaneous Peripheral Operations OnLine) program is used to buffer data for the printer and remote batch terminals. This program sends the output to the disk and printer does not interact with CPU during printing. Spooling utilities are used mainly in computer systems with multi-user/ networking environment.

2.5.7 Performance Monitoring Utilities

These utilities provide information about the efficiency of computer working. For instance, QAPlus, PC Tools and Norton Utilities provide performance-monitoring capabilities by providing information about speed, storage capacity and other features of the system.

2.6 ROLE OF SOFTWARE IN INFORMATION TECHNOLOGY

Software is essential to use the computer. It is the central element in Information Technology (IT). We have already discussed that software are of two types System and Application software. System software (such as operating systems, compliers etc.) aid in effective execution of general user's application. Application software on the other hand are required for various applications viz. word processing, data base management, spreadsheet, accounting etc, various roles of system and application software in information technology are discussed below.

2.6.1 Role of System Software

System software includes many programs viz. Operating systems (DOS, Windows, UNIX, etc.), compilers, interpreters, assemblers, software utilities (Norton utilities, disk manager, smartdog etc.) and software tools. Although we have already discussed their roles in preceding part of this chapter, we are summarising them below:

- An operating system manages the operation of a computer.
- A compiler/interpreter translates the application program code (in high level language) into machine language code.
- An assembler translates the assembly language code into machine language code.
- Software utilities support the operation of the computer.
- Software tools (such as application generators) assist the programmers/analyst in the design, coding, editing, compiling, linking and debugging programs.

2.6.2 Role of Application Software

Application software includes database management packages (dBase, Fox pro, Oracle, Sybase etc.), word processors (Word, Word perfect etc.), spreadsheets (Excel, Lotus 1-2-3, Quattro Pro etc.), office automation packages (MS office, Lotus SmartSuite, Corel office etc.), desktop publishing (DTP) software (Page Maker, Corel Draw etc.), graphics software (Adobe PhotoShop, Corel Draw etc.), and multimedia software (Macromedia Director, 3D Studio Max etc.). Let us discuss the different application software used today in the next section.

2.7 GENERAL PURPOSE APPLICATION SOFTWARE

Whenever an organisation purchases computers, besides an operating system certain application software are also purchased. These software are required for general purposes like word processing, database management, spreadsheets etc. and are known as General Purpose Application Software. We are now discussing the importance of different general purpose application software along with their major products.

2.7.1 Word Processor Packages

Word processors are application software which are used for word processing. Word processing is the most widely used technique for typing, editing, storing, formatting, manipulating and printing documents with the assistance of computer and printer. It is the most efficient means of generating documents electronically. Let us discuss the advantages of word processing alongwith common word processors.

2.7.1.1 Advantages of Word Processing

Word processing offers several advantages over typewriting. Using the word processing technique, the user can–

- Edit the text as and when required
- Move or copy any part of the text from one location/ file to another location/ file
- Insert or delete the spaces/ text
- Wrap words to the next line (Word Wrapping) and justify text to the right margin (Justification)
- Select different types of fonts and size of characters
- Adjust the margins and page lengths for the desired output
- Find the required word/ group of words and replace with another word/ group of words
- Check the spelling of any word of the document
- Store (save) the document on disk and print single or multiple copies
- Print letters with same text and different names and addresses (mail-merging)

2.7.1.2 Examples of Common Word Processors

There is a wide range of word processors available for both DOS and Windows environment. Word Star, Softword, Akshar, MS Word, Word Perfect and Amipro are some of the common examples of word processors.

Word Star, the most common and popular DOS-based word processor is developed by the MicroPro International Corporation, Inc. U.S.A. There are different versions of Word Star like 1.x, 2.x, 3.x, 4.0, 5.0, 6.0 and 7.0 but the releases 4.0 (also known as Word Star Professional) was the most popular among users during few years back. But now-a-days, after popularity of windows based software, Word Star has become obsolate. Softword is a DOS-based English word processor. Akshar is a DOS-based Hindi word processor. Both of them were developed by an Indian Company, Softech.

Among the Windows-based word processors, MS Word, Word Perfect and AmiPro are the leaders in the markets (DOS based versions of these packages are also available). MS Word, developed by Microsoft Inc. is a part of MS Office professional package. Word 97 and Word 2000 are the most popular versions of Word. Word Perfect (latest version 6.0), developed by Word Perfect Corporation, which provides almost same features as MS Word is also very popular among users. Ami Pro (latest version 3.0)/ Word Pro, developed by Lotus Corporation, is another full-fledged, multi-featured word processor for windows. The important word processors are listed in Table 2.1.

Word Processor	Description
Word Star	Simplest DOS-based word processor
Softword	Similar to Word Star developed by an Indian company
Akshar	Popular Hindi/English word processor developed by an Indian company
Word	Most Popular Windows-based word processor
Word Perfect	Popular Windows-based word processor with DTP features
Amipro	Full-fledged, multi-featured Windows-based word processor with DTP features

Table 2.1 *Common word processors*

2.7.2 Database Management Packages

Business processes are always associated with a huge amount of data. To store, manipulate and process such data, some software packages are needed, which are collectively known as Database Management Packages/ Software/ Systems (DBMS). Data Base Management System is defined as a software that organises and maintains the data in a database for providing information. Before discussing about these packages, let us see what is meant by the terms - data, information, file and database.

2.7.2.1 Data and Information

Data and information are the two basic components of any information system. Data is defined as a set of basic facts and entities which itself have no meaning or value. For example, 5000, 4000, 4500, 4800, 8900.... is a data of employees salaries which itself has no meaning. On the other hand, information is defined as that data which has some meaning or value. For example, the personal data of employee names and their basic salaries represented as "Komal – 5000", "Rajesh – 4000", "Sarika – 4500", "Suchitra – 4800", "Pawan – 8900", etc. is an information because it has some meaning.

2.7.2.2 File and Database

File is a group of related records in a database. For example, a group of personal records of all the employees of a company is a file. However, database is a collection of related files that is created and managed by a database management system. The most important point to remember about database is that it contains data and not necessarily information. Some examples of database are as follows:

(*i*) The vouchers, bills receipt and other financial data of an organisation.

(*ii*) The details of students and their marks obtained for preparing their result in a school.

In the above examples, the data can have some meaning or no meaning in itself until it is processed to get useful information.

2.7.2.3 Examples of Database Management Packages

Many database management packages are available in the market. Managers must be aware of the benefits and limitations of these packages before purchasing and using them. dBASE, Foxbase, Foxpro, MS Access, Paradox, Oracle, Ingres, Sybase, Informix, etc. are the major products of database management systems.

dBASE is the most popular and simplest to learn database management system which is developed by Ashton-Tate, U.S.A. dBASE II was the first product developed for database applications and later on Ashton-Tale developed new versions viz. dBASE III plus, dBASE IV and dBASE V. dBASE III plus and dBASE IV are exclusively DOS based versions while dBASE V is windows-based. FoxBASE+ is a dBASE III plus compatible DBMS, which is originally developed by Fox Software and later on by Microsoft. It is faster and multi-user as compared with dBASE III plus which is slow and single-user. Microsoft developed another dBASE IV compatible DBMS, called FoxPro which has now become very popular among users. FoxPro 1.0, 2.0, 2.5, 2.6 and Visual FoxPro 3.0/5.0 are the different versions of FoxPro. FoxPro offers several advantages over both dBASE and FoxBASE. The differences among dBASE, FoxBASE and FoxPro are given in Table 2.2.

Criteria	dBase	Foxbase	Foxpro
Operating Environment	DOS/Windows	DOS	DOS/Windows
Users	Single-user	Multi-user	Multi-user
Execution Speed	Slow	Medium	Fast
Disk Storage	Less	Average	More
Features	Less	Average	Many
Program Generators	Less	Less	Many
Compiler	Not available	Available	Available

Table 2.2 *Comparison among three popular DBMSs*

MS Access, developed by Microsoft Inc., is also a part of MS Office professional package. It is a relational database management system (RDBMS), which is windows based and is quite similar to Visual FoxPro. Paradox, a part of Corel Office Pro software, is a network RDBMS and is known for its Query By Example (QBE) method of asking questions. Oracle, Sybase, Ingres and Informix are the leaders among RDBMSs. The list of major DBMSs products is illustrated in Table 2.3.

DBMS pacckage	Description
dBase	Most popular DOS/Windows based database management system
Foxbase	Faster, multi-user dBase-compatible DBMS
Foxpro/ Visual Foxpro	DOS/Windows-based DBMS with advanced features
Access	Windows-based DBMS similar to Visual Foxpro
Oracle	Most popular RDBMS for microcomputers
Sybase	Distributed RDBMS that runs on most servers
Informix	Popular RDBMS server mainly for UNIX operating system.
Ingres	Popular RDBMS that runs on many operating systems
Paradox	Netword RDBMS with QBE (Query By Example) features

Table 2.3 *Common DBMS packages*

2.7.3 Spreadsheet Packages

Business applications require a lot of calculation work. In manual system, it is done on a sheet of paper with rows and columns, which is called a 'spreadsheet'. Spreadsheet packages use the concept of an electronic spreadsheet. An electronic spreadsheet (or worksheet) is a very big sheet consisting of thousands of rows and columns, which is used to store information in the memory of a computer. Like databases, electronic spreadsheets have now become an essential tool in developing a computerised management information system. Income statements, annual reports, balance sheet, cost analysis and budgets are some of the applications where worksheets are typically used.

2.7.3.1 *Advantages of Electronic Spreadsheets*

The electronic worksheet offers several advantages over manual and other computer application software. These are described as follows:

- The user can perform any type of calculation involving mathematical, financial, statistical and other functions.
- All recalculations are performed automatically, if any figure is changed.
- As worksheet is very big in size, a large volume of data can be stored on a single worksheet. For example, it is possible to store entire data of accounts of a big organisation on a single worksheet.
- The user can view/ print the data in any desired format.
- Most of the word-processing features like spell checking, find/ replace words can also be performed on a worksheet.
- The data of worksheet can be viewed in many types of graphs/ charts.
- The worksheet can be saved, retrieved, combined to another worksheet and transferred to files of different database and word processing packages.

2.7.3.2 *Examples of Common Spreadsheet Packages*

There are many spreadsheet packages available today. Some of these are exclusively windows based like MS Excel while others are both DOS and Windows based like Lotus 1-2-3. Lotus 1-2-3, developed by Lotus Development Corporation, is the most popular spreadsheet package among DOS users. The different versions of Lotus 1-2-3 are release 1.x, 2.x & 3.x (DOS based) and 4 & 5 (both DOS & Windows based). Lotus 1-2-3 is also available as a part of Lotus Smartsuite office automation package in the market. MS Excel, a part of MS Office, is the most popular Windows based spreadsheet package. The popular versions of Excel are Excel 97 and Excel 2000 but the latest version is Excel 2002. Quattro Pro (latest version 5.0), developed by Borland International is another spreadsheet package that provides advanced graphics and presentation features. Javelin Plus (from Information Resources, Inc.), Multiplan (Microsoft Corp.), Supercalc (Computer Associates International, Inc.) and PlanPerfect (Word Perfect Corp.) are some other examples of spreadsheet packages. The list of major spreadsheet packages is given in Table 2.4.

Spreadsheet Package	Description
Lotus 1-2-3	Most popular DOS/Windows based spreadsheet package
Excel	Most popular Windows based spreadsheet package
Quattro Pro	Spreadsheet package with advanced presentation features
Supercalc	Spreadsheet package from Computer Associates
Multiplan	Spreadsheet package from Microsoft Corp.
PlanPerfect	Spreadsheet package from Word Perfect Corp.
Javeline Plus	Spreadsheet package that uses names to identify calls

Table 2.4 *Common spreadsheet packages*

2.7.4 Office Automation Packages

Word processors, Spreadsheets and Database Management packages are also available as integrated packages generally called Office Automation Packages/.Software Tools or Office Suites. MS Office and Lotus Smartsuite are two most popular examples of office automation packages.

Microsoft Office (MS Office) Professional is a package that contains five powerful general-purpose application packages. It includes Word, Excel, Powerpoint, Access and Mail. We have already discussed about Word, Excel and Access in previous sub-section. Powerpoint is used to create professional presentations in the form of slides. The user can write text, draw figures and organisation charts on these slides. Powerpoint is the most popular and commonly used desktop presentation program for Macintosh and PCs. Powerpoint 97 and Powerpoint 2000 are the currently used versions for Windows 2000. MS Office 2000 is the currently used version for Windows 2000.

Lotus Smartsuite is another popular office automation package that contains five powerful general-purpose application packages. It includes Word Pro, 1-2-3, Freelance Graphics, Approach and Organizer. We have already discussed about Word Pro, and 1-2-3 in previous sub-section. Lotus SmartSuite 7.0 and Lotus SmartSuite 97 are Windows and Web Enabled versions of SmartSuite respectively.

Corel Office, an office suite, contains Word Perfect, Quattro Pro, Paradox, Corel Draw, Netscape Navigator, Presentations, Corel Flow, Sidekick and other general purpose application packages. SideKick is the first popup program (TSR - 'Terminate and Stay Resident' in memory) used for editing programs and non-document files.

2.8 SPECIAL PURPOSE APPLICATION SOFTWARE

Although general-purpose application software are exclusively used by all users for general applications, but there are certain software which are meant for some special applications and organisations. Besides general purpose application software, some organisations also need software for desktop publishing, graphics, multimedia, animations, financial accounting, sales and marketing, inventory, export documentation, etc. These software are collectively known as Special Purpose Application Software. Let us briefly discuss the different types of special purpose application software.

2.8.1 Desktop Publishing Software

Desktop Publishing (DTP) software is used to produce a high-quality document for commercial printing. Using DTP software, text and graphics are combined into a single document that is printed generally on a laser printer. Although this software is mainly useful for publishers but they are also used in general offices and educational institutes for the best presentation of management documents, project reports and thesis works. DTP software can be used in combination with word processors, graphics and CAD (Computer Aided Design) software. First, the document is written using a word processor and the graphics/ diagrams are made using graphics/ CAD software. Then, all documents and graphics are merged into the DTP files for advanced page formatting.

DTP software is widely used by publishers and other organisations. This software requires a special kind of hardware system comprising of high speed PC (preferably 486 or higher), laser printer and scanner/ digitizer.

2.8.1.1 Examples of DTP software

Many desktop publishing software are available in the market with a wide variety of features. PageMaker, Ventura and CorelDRAW are the most common examples of DTP software. PageMaker (latest version 6.5), originally developed from Aldus Corp. and now from Adobe, is extremely famous among Indian users. Although PageMaker was originally introduced for Macnitosh but currently it is available for both Mac and PC (mainly for Windows). Ventura Publisher, developed by Ventura Software, Inc. (a Xerox company), provides full-scale pagination features for very large documents. It is available both for Mac and PCs (under DOS, Windows & OS/2).

CorelDRAW (latest version 10), developed by Corel Systems Corp., is the popular windows-based DTP and Graphics Software for PCs. It is designed to work with high quality graphic images and provides advanced auto tracing features for building a vector-based image. As it does not provide word processing/ DTP page layout features, it is used in combination with word processors and other DTP software like PageMaker.

2.8.2 Graphics, Multimedia and Animation Software

For last few years, Graphics, Multimedia and Animation Software are becoming very popular for high quality presentation of business and other applications. CorelDRAW, Adobe Photoshop, AutoCAD Map and Harvard Graphics are some of the commonly used graphics software. We have already discussed about CorelDRAW in the previous sub-section. Adobe Photoshop is an image editing software with multiple layers, interactive GUI and powerful object-based editing tools. Harvard Graphics, developed by Software Publishing Corp., is a business presentation software. It allows the user to create professional looking presentations in just few minutes.

Multimedia, a latest computer technology, displays information using a combination of full-motion video, text, graphics, animations and sound. A wide range of multimedia and animation software is available in the market. Macromedia Director, 3D Studio Max, AnimatorPro and Animator Studio are some of the commonly used multimedia/ animation software. Macromedia Director is a multimedia authoring software for creating tutorials and CBT (Computer Based Training) software. 3D Studio Max software allows the user to create 3D modelling and animations on a PC. AnimatorPro is an 8-bit, 256 colour, 2D Paint and animation software with in-built C based programming, 3D Studio and customised GUI. Animator Studio is a digital sound studio designer for animation with true colour features.

2.8.3 Business Application Software

Every business consists of many functions that are organised into different departments like Finance, Marketing, Inventory, Production, Research and Development (R&D) and Human Resource Development (HRD). For computerising these departments, special kind of application software are required, which are collectively called as Business

Application Software. These software are available for either general requirements of the users (Standard Software) or can be developed as per the requirement of a specific organisation/ user (Customised Software).

Accord, EX and Tally are some of the examples of popular standard financial accounting software packages among Indian users. Accord, developed by EDP Corporation, is the comprehensive accounting software for preparing MIS and other reports. EX, developed by Tata Consultancy Services, provides business accounting capabilities along with inventory and invoicing features. Tally, developed by Peuronics Pvt. Ltd., is the accounting and book keeping software having the added capabilities of invoicing/ inventory accounting as well.

2.9 EMERGING INFORMATION TECHNOLOGIES

The IT industry is growing very rapidly and many new technologies are coming day by day. There are certain technologies that are still under research and development process. Artificial Intelligence and Virtual Reality are major emerging technologies.

2.9.1 Artificial Intelligence

A computer has no intelligence in itself. It performs tasks by getting instructions from human beings. Scientists are trying to impart certain abilities to the computer, which can enable them to perform tasks intelligently, just like human beings. Artificial Intelligence (AI) is a capability in computer to carry out the tasks that require intelligence if carried out by human beings. The term 'Artificial Intelligence', which was coined in 1956 by John McCarthy at Dartmouth Collge, connotes a futuristic world. Artificial Intelligence is still under research & development program all over the world. Though we are not discussing this vast field of emerging technology in detail, we are presenting a brief outline of main areas of AI briefly.

2.9.1.1 Applications of Artificial Intelligence

There are following five main application areas of AI research:

(*a*) **Expert System.** Expert systems are programs that are like human experts, which possess extensive background knowledge in their specialised field. They are needed because human expert manpower is scarce and expensive. Today, expert systems are available for most of the business applications like finance, marketing, manufacturing etc. besides technical & medical fields. For example, PlanMan, Financial Advisor and Plan Power are some expert systems for financial planning areas. MYCIN was the first expert system project for medical applications. After MYCIN project, new systems like EMYCIN (empty MYCIN) were developed, which were without knowledge base. The expert systems without knowledge base are called expert system shell. Guru and VP Expert are other examples of expert system shell.

(*b*) **Robotics.** Robotics is the major field of artificial intelligence. It is concerned with design, manufacturing and implementation of computer-controlled devices, called Robots. Robots are widely used in many industries like car manufacturing, coal mining, chemical industries etc.

(*c*) **Natural Language Processing (NLP).** NLP is that field of artificial intelligence that allows computers to communicate with users in natural languages like English, French etc. HAL is the popular natural language interface for Lotus 1-2-3. Guru is another example of NLP software with capabilities of database management, word processing, spreadsheets and graphics.

(*d*) **Computer Vision.** This field of artificial intelligence enables computers to recognise shapes and patterns through a technique called Pattern Recognition.

(*e*) **Neural Networks.** Neural networks are knowledge based computer systems that are designed to learn by observations and repetition just like human beings.

2.9.2 Virtual Reality

Virtual reality is a concept that projects users into a three dimensional space generated by computer. Users wear a helmet-like device that completely covers both eyes and ears to create an artificial computer-simulated reality. Users can move and manipulate illusory objects in their view. They can select and organise information with hand and body movements. Several companies are developing business applications for this emerging technology. For instance, a major electronics firm in Japan is developing an application for a 'Virtual Showroom'.

THEORY QUESTIONS

1. Differentiate between system software and application software. Substantiate through an example.
2. What is the difference between an interpreter and compiler? Give two examples of each.
3. What is an assembler? Give examples of two assemblers.
4. What are software tools? Discuss the major categories of software tools with examples.
5. What are application generators? What are their advantages and disadvantages?
6. What are CASE tools? Discuss their importance in the development of a software.
7. What are system software utilities? Discuss the role of commonly used utilities with suitable examples.
8. Discuss the importance of word processors in generating documents. Give some examples of DOS-based and Windows-based word processing packages.
9. Discuss the major features of commonly used Database Management packages.
10. What is an electronic spreadsheet? Describe its major advantages. Name some commonly used spreadsheet packages.
11. What is DTP? Discuss the importance of the DTP software currently available in the market.
12. What is multimedia? Name any four multimedia software which are popular among users.
13. What do you mean by the term 'Artificial Intelligence'? Discuss the major application areas of AI research.
14. What is virtual reality?
15. 'Although computer provides numerous benefits to man, still it can't replace human beings at all'. Discuss.

3

OPERATING SYSTEM CONCEPTS AND FILE ORGANISATION

3.1 INTRODUCTION

You know that the computer is a piece of hardware and it is useless unless it is provided with the necessary software. System software controls the working of hardware and aids in effective execution of a general user's applications. An operating system is the most essential system software that manages the operation of a computer. Without an operating system, it is not possible to use the computer. You can't even make the computer ready to use, unless you provide an operating system to it by a process called booting. In this chapter, we are discussing basic operating system concepts alongwith file organisation.

3.2 FUNCTIONS OF AN OPERATING SYSTEM

An operating system concerns itself with every single and minute detail of your computer working. It manages everything that runs on your computer straight from running an application software, entering data, displaying information on monitor, printing a report, storing data on external storage device (disk), etc. Wherever you are working on your computer, an operating system is always in computer memory. It does many jobs on your behalf without showing you each and every step of processing. For example, if you give a command to open a document file in a word processor, the document is immediately displayed on the screen. But, how this file is opened from the disk (storage device) and how information is displayed on the monitor (output device). All these types of functions are performed by the operating system. In order to enable computer to effectively and efficiently utilise its resources to monitor the system performance and to provide services to the users, an operating system is needed. So, an operating system performs basically three types of functions, which are discussed below in brief.

3.2.1 Essential Functions

The essential functions of an operating system are concerned with effective utilisation of computer resources. Storage management and processor management are two important essential functions of an operating system. Storage management is concerned with allocation and reclamation of storage when a program is initiated and terminated. Processor management is concerned with scheduling of programs in a time sharing system.

3.2.2 Monitoring Functions

These functions are concerned with collection of resource utilisation and system performance information. CPU and I/O devices form the resources whose utilisations are collected and monitored by device management functions of operating system.

3.2.3 Service Functions

These functions of operating system enhance facilities provided to the users. They mainly include automatic procedures for recovery due to hardware errors, file editing facilities and file organisation and access methods.

3.3 OPERATING SYSTEM TECHNIQUES

There are several techniques used in multi-user operating systems for enabling many users to concurrently share the single or multiple CPU (e.g. multiprogramming and multiprocessing). Some techniques are used in single user operating system to handle multiple tasks (multitasking). We will now discuss these common techniques used in different operating systems.

3.3.1 Multiprogramming

It is a process by which single CPU works on two or more programs simultaneously. Using this technique, the operating system keeps the CPU busy. Multiprogramming allows the processor to handle either multiple batch jobs at a time *(Batch Multiprogramming)* or multiple interactive jobs shared among multiple users *(Time Sharing Multiprogramming)*. Time-sharing is a technique that allows a CPU to simultaneously support the activities of several users by allocating fixed time slots (in milliseconds). Examples of operating systems that support multiprogramming are OS/2, UNIX and Macintosh System 7.

3.3.2 Multiprocessing

It refers to the use of two or more CPUs to perform a coordinated task simultaneously. For example, MVS, VMS and Windows NT support multi processing.

3.3.3 Multitasking

It refers to the ability of an operating system to execute two or more tasks concurrently. In multitasking environment, the user opens new applications without closing the previous ones and the information can be easily moved among a number of applications. For example, Windows NT and OS/2 operating systems use this technique.

3.4 HISTORY AND EVOLUTION OF OPERATING SYSTEM

The evolution of operating systems has been driven by technological advances and by the demands and expectations of the users. In the earliest computers, switches and lights were the 'input' and 'output' devices. Each word of the program was to go through a lengthy procedure before it was finally entered into the memory location because this whole process was carried out by using a number of sets of switches. This process was repeated for every word of the program. The program used to get started by setting the program counter to the first word of instruction and then pressing a 'Start' button. This process of programming was very time consuming and it also involved a high risk of error involvement. But the computer users still used to feel satisfied with the results they got. To simplify this process, the basic need was to solve the problem of program loading. The basic idea was to make computer self-efficient in a respect that it automatically read a primitive loader program written on it on start up. This resulted in execution of more extensive loader programs with the help of the basic loader. Thus, this system could then load any user program. This arrangement got the name *'bootstrapping.'* This technique is used these days also. The new name given to bootstrapping is *'booting'*. The evolution of an operating system is described as follows:

(*a*) **Advancement of operating system.** The introduction of program loaders was the very first step to modern operating systems. Another advancement that took place was to improve the output. To display the textual results, output was improved by using a simple character terminal. Finding such terminals was no problem as they were mostly used in the field of communication at that time. These terminals later took the place of input devices using keyboards for low speed input. The keyboard could also be used as a control console helping the operator to communicate with the system. Thereafter, the keyboard was used as the main user interface device for future operating systems.

(*b*) **Used of punched card as input medium.** The punched card was in use long before the arrival of computers or operating systems. The punched cards were used as an input medium in electro-mechanical calculating equipment. The punched cards also offered off time storage as they were also used as output media. The combined card-punch peripheral units could be commonly found out. They could read stacks of cards and produced a considerable amount of noise. These cards were very effectively used to keep track of stock kept in a warehouse for each item.

Due to the improvement of the hardware, the execution time of programs also came down. But this resulted in slowing down of input output devices compared to processor speed because the processor spent most of its time waiting for a card to be read or punched. Moreover, the setup time i.e. the time spent between jobs in order to load the next program and data became disproportionate to the run time of the job.

(*c*) **Introduction of Input Output Control System.** The early programmers felt that a good part of each new program was the same as the previous one. This gave them the idea of writing a standard set of subroutines. It could be loaded into the memory at the time of start-up and kept there for use by the other jobs. This gave rise to the idea of Input Output Control System (IOCS).

Later, magnetic recording was done to digital signals to give magnetic tape drives. They were used as data storage medium instead of using a card punch machine. Magnetic tapes were also used as an input medium. Ultimately, magnetic drums and disks arrived which lead to fast direct access to stored data. These developments complicated the IOCS routines.

(*d*) **Shift from binary language to higher-level languages.** As you already know, binary machine code was used to write earlier programs. This method of writing programs was considered to be a very complicated and time-consuming affair. Thus, the programmers started using the assembly language. Writing larger and more complex programs became practically feasible for them. The assembly language was then followed by higher-level languages like FORTRAN and ALGOL. This was again a step ahead development.

In the year 1960, a new computer called Atlas was developed. This computer was first of its kind that incorporated the design of an operating system. Atlas supported many new features such as interrupts and a virtual memory system. This new idea of virtual memory took some time to make a broad impact. However, the idea of interrupts made quick impact. The reason behind was that it could easily handle many programs and peripheral devices simultaneously. It helped the operating system to look after several programs and I/O activities simultaneously. Around the year 1964, IBM produced the system 370 and then the 303X machines, which are used even today. These range of computers provided a wide range of computing facilities. Thereafter, much advancement was brought out in these machines.

The simple program loader concept helped in reducing the set up time between jobs. It allowed a series of jobs to be loaded automatically from an input device. This was an early form of operating system and was known by several names such as 'supervisor', 'executive' or monitor'. The term 'Operating System ' was used later on. These systems performed the work of an operating system and hence, they have been granted this title. The term batch processing was given where the jobs were given to the computer in batches. Special control cards communicated with the operating system. They used to delimit the various jobs given to the computer and also specified what each job was supposed to do. These cards worked as an interface between the user and the operating system. As the complexity and sophistication with the computers grew, the complexity of these cards also grew. This resulted in the development of JCL's or *Job Control Language.*

As the improvements were brought out in the hardware, it could cope with larger quantities of work. Now, the computer could run several programs at the same time. This is called multi programming. The concept of multi programming is being discussed in greater detail in the subsequent part of the chapter.

3.5 TYPES OF OPERATING SYSTEMS

The variations and differences in the nature of different operating systems may give the impression that all operating systems are absolutely different from each other.

But this is not true. All operating systems contain the same components whose functionalities are almost the same. For instance, all the operating systems perform the functions of storage management, process management, protection of users from one another, etc. The procedures and methods that are used to perform these functions might be different but the fundamental concepts behind these techniques are just the same. The operating systems are categorised according to number of terminals and nature of work performed by them. Now let us quickly look at the different types of operating systems.

3.5.1 According to Number of Terminals Used

Based on number of terminals used in a computer, many types of operating systems are available, which are discussed below.

3.5.1.1 Single-user Operating Systems

These operating systems are mainly used for computers having only one terminal (stand-alone PCs). MS DOS (Microsoft Disk Operating System) and PC DOS (Personal Computer Disk Operating System) are the two important single-user operating systems. Both systems are almost identical and are simply called DOS.

(*i*) **MS DOS.** MS DOS, developed by 'Microsoft Inc.' in 1981, is the most widely used operating system of IBM-compatible microcomputers. The latest version (identification number of a release of software) of MS DOS is 7.

(*ii*) **PC DOS.** PC DOS is essentially the same operating system as MS DOS, but developed and supplied by IBM for its personal computers.

3.5.1.2 Multi-user Operating Systems

These operating systems are used for those computers (micro to mainframe) which have many terminals (multi-user systems). The popular operating systems used for multi-user systems are OS/2, Windows NT, UNIX, NetWare, MVS, OS/400, VMS and Linux.

(*i*) **OS/2.** OS/2 is a multi-user, multi-tasking operating system, developed jointly by IBM and Microsoft. This provides a unique feature of multitasking, where several programs can be run simultaneously. OS/2 was the first operating system that provided users with a Graphical User Interface (GUI).

(*ii*) **Windows NT.** Windows NT (New Technology) is the multi-user 32-bit multi-tasking operating system for 386s and above, developed by Microsoft Inc. Windows NT was driven by a need to exploit the tremendous power of 32-bit microprocessors and runs applications, which are developed for DOS and Windows.

(*iii*) **UNIX.** UNIX was initially developed by AT&T at Bell Laboratories in 1969. UNIX is a highly successful operating system for multi-user systems. Actually, it is more popular among scientific and engineering users rather than business users. In 1980, Microsoft developed its own version of UNIX for 286s and higher PCs which is called XENIX. UNIX System V Release 4 is the latest version of UNIX.

(*iv*) **NetWare.** NetWare is a group of network operating system developed by Novell, Inc., that provides multi-user capabilities.

(*v*) **MVS** (*Multiple Virtual Storage*). MVS is one of the most complex multi-user operating systems ever developed for IBM mainframes. In MVS, each job (time-sharing user or batch program) is assigned its own virtual storage space.

(*vi*) **OS/400.** OS/400 is the IBM's operating system for its AS/400 computer.

(*vii*) **VMS** (*Virtual Memory Storage*). VMS operating system is used on DEC's VAX series of minicomputers.

(*viii*) **Linux.** Linux is a 32-bit UNIX like operating system that has been developed recently for microcomputers. It is the world's first free operating system developed and maintained by thousands of people worldwide.

The applications of different single-user and multi-user operating systems are summarised in Table 3.1.

Operating System	Type	Applications
MS DOS	Single-user	Mostly used for running/developing stand-alone applications/ programs on microcomputers..
PC DOS	Single-user	Mostly used for running/ developing stand-alone applications/ programs on microcomputers.
OS/2	Multi-user	Used for GUI applications and running several applications simulateously on microcomputer.
Windows NT	Multi-user	Used for GUI applications and running several applications simulateously on microcomputer.
UNIX	Multi-user	Most widely used for multi-user applications on all computers.
Netware	Multi-user	Most widely used for LAN (Local Area Network) applications on microcomputer.
MVS	Multi-user	Used widely for large applications needing virtual storage space.
OS/400	Multi-user	Used for large multi-user applications on AS/400 computer.
VMS	Multi-user	Used for large multi-user applications on VAX computer.

Table 3.1 *Applications of some common operating systems*

3.5.2 According to Work Performed

Many types of operating systems are available for computers which are categorized according to the work performed by them. Let us briefly discuss these types of operating systems.

3.5.2.1 Batch Processing Operating System

The main function of a batch processing system is to automatically keep executing one job to the next job in the batch. The main idea behind a batch processing system is to reduce the interference of the operator during the processing or execution of jobs by the computer. All functions of a batch processing system are carried out by the *batch monitor*. The batch monitor permanently resides in the low end of the main store. The current jobs out of the whole batch are executed in the remaining storage area. In other words, a batch monitor is responsible for controlling all the environment of the system operation. The batch monitor accepts batch initiation commands from the operator, processes a job, performs the job of job termination and batch termination. In a batch processing system, we generally make use of the term *turn around time.* It is defined as the time from which a user job is given to the time when its output is given back to the user. This time includes the batch formation time, time taken to execute a batch, time taken to print results and the time required to physically sort the printed outputs that belong to different jobs. As the printing and sorting of the results is done for all the jobs of batch together, the turn around time for a job becomes the function of the execution time requirement of all jobs in the batch. You can reduce the turn around time for different jobs by recording the jobs or faster input output media like magnetic tape or disk surfaces. It takes very less time to read a record from these media. For instance, it takes round about five milli seconds for a magnetic 'tape' and about one milli second for a fast fixed head disk in comparison to a card reader or printer that takes around 50–100 milliseconds. Thus, if you use a disk or tape, it reduces the amount of time the central processor has to wait for an input output operation to finish before resuming processing. This would reduce the time taken to process a job which indirectly would bring down the turn around times for all the jobs in the batch.

Another term that is commonly used in a batch processing system is *Job Scheduling.* Job Scheduling is the process of sequencing jobs so that they can be executed on the processor. It recognises different jobs on the basis of First Come First Served (FCFS) basis. It is because of the sequential nature of the batch. The batch monitor always starts the next job in the batch. However, in exceptional cases, you could also arrange the different jobs in the batch depending upon the priority of each batch. Sequencing of jobs according to some criteria require scheduling the jobs at the time of creating or executing a batch. On the basis of relative importance of jobs, certain 'priorities' could be set for each batch of jobs. Several batches could be formed on the same criteria of priorities. So, the batch having the highest priority could be made to run earlier than other batches. This would give a better turn around service to the selected jobs.

Now, we discuss the concept of *storage management.* At any point of time, the main store of the computer is shared by the batch monitor program and the current user job of a batch. The big question that comes in our mind is how much storage has to be kept for the monitor program and how much has to be provided for the user jobs of a batch. However, if too much main storage is provided to the monitor, then the user programs will not get enough storage. Therefore, an overlay structure has to be devised so that the unwanted sections of monitor code don't occupy storage simultaneously.

Next we will discuss the concept of *sharing* and *protection.* The efficiency of utilisation of a computer system is recognised by its ability of sharing the system's hardware and software resources amongst its users. Whenever, the idea of sharing the system resources comes in your mind certain doubts also arise about the fairness and security of the system. Every user wants that all his reasonable requests should be taken care of and no intentional and unintentional acts of other users should fiddle with his data. A batch processing system guarantees the fulfillment of these user requirements.

All the user jobs are performed one after the other. There is no simultaneous execution of more than one job at a time. So, all the system resources like storage IO devices, central processing unit, etc. are shared sequentially or serially. This is how sharing of resources is enforced on a batch processing system. Now, arises the question of protection. Though all the jobs are processed simultaneously, this too can lead to loss of security or protection. Let us suppose that there are two users A and B. User A creates a file of his own. User B deletes the file created by User A. There are so many other similar instances that can occur in our day-to-day life. So, the files and other data of all the users should be protected against unauthorised usage. In order to avoid such loss of protection, each user is bound around certain rules and regulations. This takes the form of a set of control statements which every user is required to follow.

3.5.2.2 Multiprogramming Operating System

The objective of a multi programming operating system is to increase the system utilisation efficiency. The batch processing system tries to reduce the CPU idle time through operator interaction. However, it cannot reduce the idle time due to IO operations. So, when some IO is being performed by the currently executing job of a batch, the CPU sits idle without any work to do. Thus, the multi programming operating system tries to eliminate such idle times by providing multiple computational tasks for the CPU to perform. This is achieved by keeping multiple jobs in the main store. So, when the job that is being currently executed on the CPU needs some IO, the CPU passes its requirement over to the IO processor. Till the time the IO operation is being carried out, the CPU is free to carry out some other job. The presence of independent jobs guarantees that the CPU and IO activities are totally independent of each other. However, if it was not so, then some times, it could lead to some erroneous situations leading to dependent errors.

A multiprogramming supervisor has a very difficult job of managing all the activities that take place simultaneously in the system. He has to monitor many different activities and react to a large number of different situations in the course of working. The multiprogramming supervisor has to look through the following control functions:

(*a*) **Processor Management.** The supervisor has to decide as to which program should be made to run at the central processor at any given point of time. An important measure to determine the system performance in multi programming is *throughput.* Throughput can be defined as follows:

$$\text{Throughput} = \frac{\text{The number of jobs completed}}{\text{The total time required to complete the jobs}}$$

Hence, when two heavily computational jobs are being multiprogrammed, the throughput becomes low because of the idling of IO channels. So, when the degree of multiprogramming is two, then one job be made as computationally oriented and the other one could be made as IO oriented. The computational job is also known as a CPU bound job. It keeps the processor busy. However, the IO bound job keeps the IO channels busy. Both the jobs work independent of each other. Therefore, the throughput becomes high. When one or more jobs are ready to use the processor, then the supervisor allots the processor to the highest priority job amongst them.

(*b*) **Storage Management.** The supervisor is vested with the important decision of finding out how different storage areas are to be allocated to different jobs present in the system. The storage management function of the supervisor concerns with the allocating of storage to a program when it's processing has been started. The supervisor should avoid the, situation of storage idling. The storage can idle in a situation where the total storage requirement of all jobs in the system is less than the storage capacity of the system. Hence, it becomes the duty of the supervisor to start a new job in the unused area of storage. There is one more possibility to storage idling. It arises in a case when there is enough free storage available, the supervisor also does not have any restrictions on starting a new job but is unable to do so because the free storage is not in a state that can start a program. For instance, small areas of full storage may arise between programs that exist on the system. This situation is known as *storage fragmentation.*

(*c*) **I/O Management.** The supervisor again has to decide as to how and when to start the I/O operations at various IO devices in the system. An operating system can carry out a variety of IO facilities. The supervisor has to manage IO operation because a user program has to be protected from interference by other programs. Any program that wants some IO operation to be done has to first pass on its IO requirement to the supervisor through a trap. This trap is known as the supervisor call trap. The supervisor needs to look into the IO requirements sent by any program because certain IO devices such as disks are sharable among different programs. Thus, the supervisor creates a queue to send all these requests one by one and process them. This can depend on program priority or in an order that optimises the performance of the device. These strategies are called the IO strategy and device strategy respectively.

Sometimes, errors in different devices also occur which are again managed by the supervisor. In order to rectify the error, a transient routine is loaded. It tries to recover from the error by retrying an IO operation. When it has recovered from the error, then it hands over the control to the resident supervisor which performs the standard IO completion actions and then returns to the user program. The supervisor initiates automatic error recovery, therefore, the program in which the problem has occurred will not be aware of IO failure.

3.5.2.3 Time Sharing Operating System

The time sharing systems were developed with a main aim to provide fast response to the requests made by the user. The computing environment which best illustrates the advantages of time-sharing systems over multiprogramming or batch processing systems is one in which a number of interactive terminals are simultaneously used for program development and computational purposes. The response given by the system is shown visually on the screen. The user expects a very fast response from the system if the request made by him requires very less processing by the CPU. For instance, on giving a program statement by the user, the compiler should display the error message quickly. If this interaction takes little time, then the compilation of the user program will proceed rapidly. Both the interactive as well as non-interactive programs can participate in time-sharing. The time sharing systems provide a good rate of program activity for all programs in the system. In order to provide good program activities, certain basic changes are required in the structure of the operation system. These changes mainly involve the processor management and storage management components of the operating system. Let us discuss them in detail.

(*a*) **Processor management.** A time-sharing system provides a good program activity for all programs. In order to provide good service to all the programs, all of them should achieve the highest processing priority. This means that the required CPU attention should be given to each program. Thus, the highest priority would shift from one program to another. It can be achieved practically by using the *round-robin scheduling policy*. The round-robin scheduling policy is shown in Figure 3.1.

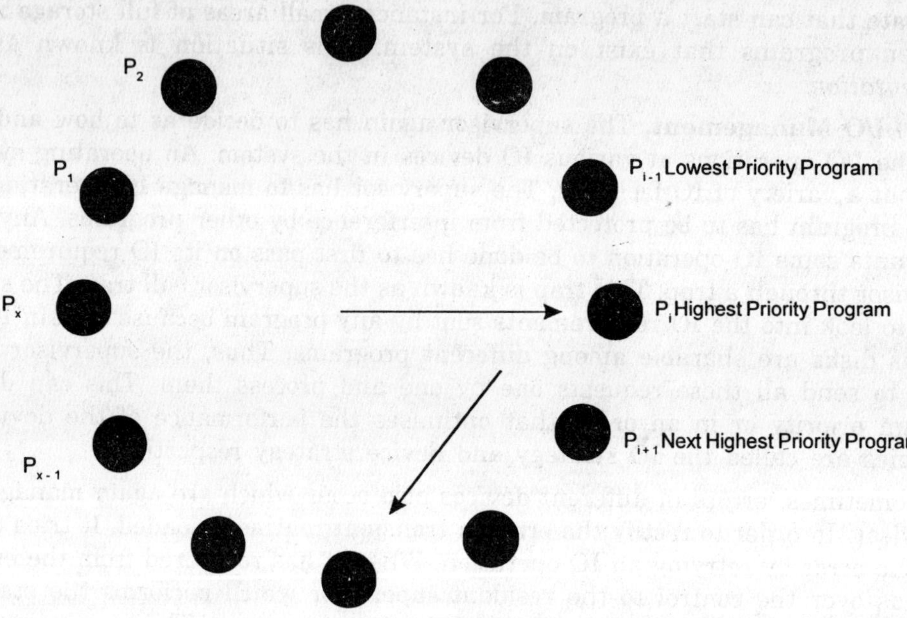

Figure 3.1 *The round-robin scheduling policy*

Under this policy, all 'm' programs in the system form a circular queue. The processor scheduler scans through this queue again and again. It tries to look for the program which is in the 'ready to execute' state. When such a program is found out, then it is scheduled to be executed on the processor. Once the current processing requirements of this program (here Pi) are met with, the scheduler tries to find out the status of the other programs Pi+1, Pi+2 ...Px, P2...Pi in a round fashion. The processor then schedules the first 'ready to execute' program it finds. Now Pi will become the lowest priority program and Pi+1 becomes the highest priority program. This gives the program Pi+1 an opportunity to receive full CPU attention. This is how all programs receive equal CPU attention. If a program is not in a ready to execute state when it is assigned the highest priority, then it will have to wait till its turn comes again.

The advantages of round-robin scheduling are huge over fixed priority scheduling but still it cannot provide good service to all the programs of the system. For instance, think of a situation in which a program Pj were to be a CPU bound program. So, as and when Pj becomes the program of highest priority, the processor would start executing it. Thus, it will not spare CPU for a considerable amount of time. Thus, the service to all programs will be denied till the time the program Pj finishes its task with the CPU. Therefore, the concept of time slicing comes up. It tries to safeguard the system when one or more programs try to eat up a considerable amount of CPU time. The time slice 'd' is the largest amount of CPU time that a program can take up in one turn. Thus, a program can make use of the CPU time till the time it comes across an I/O operation or till the time slice 'd' has finished up, whichever is earlier. Under the time slicing concept, the program cannot monopolise CPU indefinitely.

The concept of time slicing can be carried out through the use of a hardware interval timer. So, when a program is allocated the CPU time, the supervisor has to load the time slice into the interval timer. However, if the program frees the CPU before its time slice expires, then some other program is scheduled by the supervisor and the time slice is loaded once again in the interval timer. At times, the program is not able to release the CPU in the scheduled time, then the interval timer gives rise to a timer interrupt. The supervisor again gets control of the program in order to process the interrupt. He suspends the program that was being executed by the CPU. He performs CPU scheduling once again and executes some other program on the CPU. However, if no other program is ready, then the suspended program is selected and made to run again.

Now, how much time slice should be chosen is a very critical design decision. In order to get a good response, time slice should be as small as possible. However, if 'd' is made very very small, then it can increase the system overheads to a greater extent. Any program that consumes n seconds of CPU should be scheduled to a minimum of (n/d) times. The supervisor also takes away some time of the CPU for scheduling.

(*b*) **Storage Management.** In any time sharing system, the problem of program fragmentation exists because more than one program remains in the main store. The value of the number of programs being executed in the time-shared system is found out irrespective of the program or storage size. It is generally determined by system specification. The time-sharing system should be able to support 32 interactive terminals. All the programs that are being carried out should reside in the main storage. This would help the CPU to change from one program to the other easily. Sometimes all the programs don't reside simultaneously in the memory. In such a situation, the programs reside on secondary storage and are loaded into the computer's main memory before execution. After a program is processed, it is copied onto the secondary storage and new program is put in the main storage. This process is called *program swapping.*

3.5.2.4 Real time Systems

Since the earliest days of computing, the range and complexity of applications into which computers were drawn has risen to a greater extent. A specific class among these is the real time systems. A real time system is said to be one that responds back fastly so that it is able to make an impact on the environment in which it is working. A real time system is actually very fragile because any system interacts with its working environment. The real time system is mostly applied in those systems where the response or the feedback is immediately required. For instance, process control systems in factories or missile tracking system for defence. Another important area of real time system application is in the airline seat reservation system in whose case the availability of a seat is checked, reserved and booked while the operator is interacting with the customer.

Thus, the interaction between the computer and the application environment has to be very quick in case of a real time system. Therefore, the operating system has to be designed in such a manner so that it is able to meet the need of quick response. However, the response requirements of an application are found out by the nature and type of the application. Since the response time requirements of a real time system are critical, a general time-sharing system may not be able to satisfy them. When a real time application is to be supported by a computer system along with general time-sharing series, then the real time application is given the higher processing priority. This helps in giving out a quick response for the application.

3.6 OPERATING SYSTEM AS RESOURCE MANAGER

As we have already seen, a computer cannot be seen without an operating system. All operating systems perform certain basic functions. The operating system manages programs, memory, input and output devices, interprets commands, etc. The operating system acts as a resource manager and performs the following functions:

- The single tasking operating systems are able to run only one application program at one time. Any user who is required to work with many applications at one time faces a great difficulty. Thus in order to switch programs in a single tasking operating system, the user has to quit one program and start working on the second program. The multitasking operating system offers a major advantage over the single tasking operating systems. With the help of a multitasking operating system, a user has the option of working with two or more programs at one time. In such a case, the CPU switches between different application programs as and when required.

- An operating system manages the computer's memory. It allocates the main memory and other storage areas to the system and user programs. The operating system's memory manager provides sufficient memory space so that several processes can be executed at the same time. It provides a satisfactory level of performance (i.e. process execution speed) for the system users. The operating system helps in the sharing of memory space among different processes.

- The operating system makes sure that each process running in a system does not interfere with the code or data of any other process either accidentally or deliberately. The operating system also takes care of data security and integrity. It prevents a process from deliberately invading the privacy of another process.

- An operating system has the ability to interpret commands and the instructions given to it.

- An operating system makes the men-machine interaction easier and more effective.

- Whenever an error is encountered by the computer, an error message is flashed on the screen by the operating system.

- It has the ability to manage and manipulate files present on various storage devices. It can transfer these files from one storage device to another.

- The text editors of an operating system allow us to modify files easily.

3.7 OPERATING SYSTEM AS PROCESSOR MANAGER

The processor management component of operating system organises the execution of user jobs on CPU of the computer. An Operating System processes a user job at three levels—Job Scheduling, Program Initiation and Process Scheduling. Let us discuss these briefly.

3.7.1 Job Scheduling

Job Scheduling determines the time of processing of various jobs. The operating system uses special languages such as Job Control Language (JCL) for executing these jobs sequentially i.e. one after the other. The typical scheduling criteria are–

- Job scheduling on the basis of First-Come-First-Served (FCFS) service
- Job scheduling on the basis of Shortest-Job-Next (SJN) criterion
- Job scheduling according to user specified priority
- Job scheduling according to the user specified deadline for finishing a job.

3.7.1.1 Types of Job Scheduling

There are following two types of job scheduling in processor management.

(*a*) **Non-preemptive Scheduling.** In this type of scheduling, a scheduled job always completes before another scheduling decision is made. FCFS and SJN scheduling are non-preemptive scheduling.

(*b*) **Preemptive Scheduling.** In this type of scheduling, a scheduling decision is made even while the job is under execution.

3.7.2 Program Initiation

Program initiation determines the time and method to initiate processing of next job step.

3.7.3 Process Scheduling

Process scheduling organises the execution of all processes of each job step. The typical process scheduling criteria are—

- Selecting the process to be scheduled next and allocating the processes to the selected process.
- Deleting an existing process and creating a new one.
- Monitor the state of each process.
- Deallocating the processor from a process.
- Supporting a method for communicating between processes.

3.8 OPERATING SYSTEM AS INFORMATION MANAGER

An operating system ensures the efficiency of input/output operations by the information management. The information management component of operating system provides procedures for storing and accessing the information from external storage devices.

3.8.1 Sub-components of Information Management Component

The information management component of operating system comprises of three sub-components, which are discussed below.

3.8.1.1 Physical Input/Output Control Systems

The physical IOCS provides the following functions:

(*i*) Capability of programs to perform their own Input/ Output operations.

(*ii*) Handling of device error conditions.

(*iii*) Ensuring of Input/Output efficiency.

(*iv*) Providing basic device independence.

3.8.1.2 Logical Input/ Output Control System

The logical IOCS provides the following functions:

(*i*) Efficient organisation and access of data on storage devices.

(*ii*) Basic capabilities for file definition.

(*iii*) Selection of data organisation for a file.

3.8.1.3 File System

File system provides the following functions:

(*i*) Protection of existing files.

(*ii*) Controlled sharing of existing files.

(*iii*) Viewing files as objects for manipulation, modification and access.

3.9 FILE ORGANISATION

The Physical concept of data describes how data are actually organized and stored on physical storage media (disk, tape, etc.) Each attribute of an entity is represented in storage by a data item. For example, you can define a data item 'SNAME' for the attribute 'Student Name'. A data item is assigned a name in order to refer to it for storage, retrieval and processing operations. A data item is the elementary unit in data storage. The set of storage locations assigned to a data item is called a field). In physical concept, each instance of an entity is called a record and a collection of related records is called a file. Although a user normally is not required to know how data items are organized and stored in physical storage, the knowledge of physical concept of data helps user to respond to constraints in logical representation arising due to physical storage.

Data Storage and Retrieval are two important driving forces behind data management. Data is not stored in a random fashion but is organised for efficient retrieval. There are many methods of organising data. Before deciding about the method of storage organization, it is important for us to know how the data is likely to be accessed by users. There are four common methods of organising files, which are discussed below in detail:

(*a*) Serial Organisation

(*b*) Sequential Organisation

(*c*) Random file Organisation

(*d*) Indexed Sequential Organisation

Let us briefly discuss about these.

3.9.1 Serial Organisation

In Serial Organisation, the records are stored one after another without any logical order. For example, in Order File with serial organisation, the order no. 198 can be stored after supplier no. S04 as shown in Table 3.2. So, the records need not be stored in ascending or descending order of any field. The records can be added only at the end of a file. The retrieval of a particular record can be done only by reading its preceding records from the beginning of file.

Order No.	Sup. No.	Item Name	Qty Ordered	Price
202	S01	Computer	50	25000
199	S01	Printer	40	5400
198	S04	UPS	100	3500
200	S03	UPS	200	3500
201	S02	Scanner	42	1300

Table 3.2 *An example of file with serial organisation*

3.9.1.1 Advantages of Serial Organisation

The Serial Organisation is the simplest method of file organisation. Serial Organisation is commonly used for storing the transaction data of those applications where records are accessed in the order of their storage.

3.9.1.2 Disadvantages of Serial Organisation

The main disadvantages of serially organised files are :

- The retrieval of records is very slow in these files.
- The deletion and modification of a particular record is difficult and time consuming.

3.9.2 Sequential Organisation

In sequential file organisation, the records are arranged sequentially in a predetermined order. For example, in order file, the record with Order No. 199 will follow the record with Order No. 198 as shown in Table 3.3. In sequential file organisation the records are stored and sorted in continuous blocks on tape or disk. Within each block, the records are sorted in ascending or descending order to simplify the logic for accessing the data.

Order No.	Sup. No.	Item Name	Qty Ordered	Price
198	S04	UPS	100	3500
199	S01	Printer	40	5400
200	S03	UPS	200	3500
201	S02	Scanner	42	4300
202	S01	Computer	50	25000

Table 3.3 *An example of file with serial organisation*

3.9.2.1 Advantages of Sequential Organisation

The sequential file organisation is the traditional and very common way of data storage method due to following two main reasons:

- It is best suited for applications using batch processing; and
- The sequential files can be stored on magnetic tapes which are the least expensive storage devices.

3.9.2.2 Disadvantages of Sequential Organisation

The sequential files have following main disadvantages:

- The sequential files are very inefficient when the number of records is high because for searching a particular record, on average, one-half of the records must be processed.
- When a less number of records are required to be modified or deleted, then the processing becomes time consuming. This is due to the fact that the magnetic tapes do not permit a record to be updated at same location. The entire file must be read first and then rewritten on another tape.

3.9.3 Random File Organisation

As we have discussed, the sequential files have many disadvantages. Their major disadvantage is that it is necessary to read records sequentially. However, it is desired that records can be accessed directly or randomly. The file organisation in which records are organised randomly and need not be in sequence is known as Random or *Direct File Organisation.* In random files, the records are stored at the storage location numbers (address) that can be determined by the record key values.

The record address can be either absolute or relative. To understand the difference between absolute and relative, let us consider an example. In a train, seat no.32 of coach S2 is an absolute address while saying 3rd seat of second coach represents a relative address. Likewise, in case of a file, the record no.3 in sector 1 and track 1 is an absolute address while 3rd record from the beginning of file is a relative address. Therefore, an absolute address represents actual physical location number while relative address represents location number with reference to the beginning of file.

Now, we would discuss the procedure that is generally used to determine the address of a record.

Hashing. The address of a record can be determined by transforming the record key value into an arithmetic formula. The procedure is called hashing or randomising. Using this procedure, each record of the database is stored at a location whose *Storage Record Address* (SRA) is computed as some mathematical function, called *hash function.*

Many hashing techniques are used to compute SRA. The most common technique is to divide the record key value by some prime number and the remainder obtained is considered as a value of SRA as shown in following hash function:

SRA = Remainder of Numeric record key value/prime no.

For example, if the Supplier No. is 101 and it is divided by prime no. 17, then the value of SRA is–

SRA = Remainder of 101/17
= 16

Therefore, the relative address of this record comes to be 16. It means that if a cylinder can store 17 records, then the position of supplier storage no. 101 would be 16th from the 6th cylinder.

3.9.3.1 Advantages of Random File Organisation

The random file organisation has following advantages:

- It provides the fastest direct access to the records.
- It is best suited for applications requiring online inquiry and updating such as Railway Ticket Bookings and Bank Account Statements Program.

3.9.3.2 Disadvantages of Random File Organisation

Although random file organisation is considered best for online applications, it has certain drawbacks. A major problem with hashing technique in random file organisation is the occurrence of synonymous SRA. Hashing can produce identical storage location (SRAs) for two different records. These record keys are called synonyms.

3.9.4 Indexed Sequential Organisation

Index sequentially files are based on the concept of an index. For instance, this book contains different topics which are organised in certain sequence, and it also contains an index in the end. The page number of any topic can be searched by just looking through this index. Similarly, in Indexed Sequential Organisation, the records are stored sequentially on a data file, but a second file *(Index File)* also exists which makes it possible to access any record directly. So, the records of indexed sequential files can be accessed sequentially as well as directly. The files for indexed sequential organization must be stored on a *Direct Access Storage Device* (DASD). The floppy and hard disks are commonly used direct access storage devices.

To understand the indexed sequential organization, let us first discuss the different areas of disk storage. The data is stored in following three areas of storage:

(*a*) **Prime Area.** When an indexed sequential file is originally created, the records are written on an area, called prime area. This area contains records stored in logical sequence of key field. The prime area is similar to a sequential file.

(*b*) **Overflow Area.** This area contains those records that can be added later on and cannot be stored in prime area.

(*c*) **Index Area.** This area contains the values of key fields of records and their storage locations (address) on the disk.

To understand the index sequential organisation, now let us discuss it with an example. Consider a database file having the fields – Employee No. and Name. The records of this file are stored in different area of storage as shown in Table 3.4. In prime area, the employee no. 01, 04 & 10 are stored in block 1 and employee no. 11, 15 & 20 in block 2. Each record is pointing to a main location address (record pointer) and an overflow location address (overflow pointer). Index area contains the employee number (key field) and its main location address for every record. The overflow area contains employee number, employee name and its overflow address for every record which is added later on. For instance, employee no. 01 points to record pointer 1002 and overflow pointer 2000 in prime area. In index area, the index value 1002 corresponds to the employee no. 01. Therefore, this record can be read from prime area by searching its index value. The new record with employee no. 02, when added later on, is stored in overflow area and its overflow pointer value will be 2000. Hence, this new record is also logically in ascending sequence of employee no. but physically stored on another storage area. Likewise, employee no. 5 and 12 will be pointing to overflow pointer values 2010 and 3000 respectively.

Prime Area

Emp. No.	Employee Name	Record Pointer	Overflow Pointer
01	Preeti Arora	1002	2000
04	Sonia	1006	2010
10	Gaurav	1010	2020
11	Dr. Surendra Kumar	1202	3000
15	Sweety	1206	3090
20	Dr. Suhir Khetrapal	1210	3020

Index Area

Emp. No.	Record Pointer
01	1002
04	1006
10	1010
11	1202
15	1206
20	1210

Overflow Area

Emp.No.	Employee Name	Overflow Pointer
02	Mrs. Lajwanti	2000
12	Baldev Arora	3000
05	Anita Arora	2010

Table 3.4 *An example of indexed sequential file showing area of storage*

3.9.4.1 Advantages of Index Sequential File Organisation

The indexed sequential files have following advantages:

• The indexed sequential files provide the user the very powerful tool. The files cannot only be processed sequentially but also randomly.

• The searching is very fast in these files because the file management system accesses the data records in the order of index value. This technique is called the Indexed Sequential Access Method (ISAM). Therefore, these files are also referred as ISAM files.

• When records are updated or inserted, unlike sequential files, there is no need to rewrite the entire file.

3.9.4.2 Disadvantages of Index Sequential File Organisation

The indexed sequential files have following disadvantages:

• These files must be stored on a direct access storage device such as floppy disk, hard disk, etc. and cannot be stored on magnetic tapes.

• These files require regular maintenance otherwise the records added in end overflow area are not incorporated into the main file.

THEORY QUESTIONS

1. What is an operating system ? What are the functions of an operating system?
2. What are the significant features of multitasking and multiprogramming?
3. Discuss the various components of an operating system.

4. How can multiple processors improve the performance of the computer system?
5. Discuss the functions of:
   (*a*) Memory manager in an operating system
   (*b*) Processor scheduler
6. Explain the following terms:
   (*a*) I/O-bound job
   (*b*) CPU-bound job
   (*c*) Turn-around time
   (*d*) Throughput
   (*e*) Job Control Language
7. Differentiate:
   (*a*) Preemptive and non-preemptive scheduling
   (*b*) FCFS and SJN scheduling techniques
   (*c*) Batch processing and Real Time Processing
   (*d*) Single-user and multi-user operating systems
   (*e*) Multiprogramming and time sharing operating systems
8. Explain the following terms:
   (*a*) Batch Processing
   (*b*) Multi Programming
   (*c*) Time Sharing
9. Describe the advantages and disadvantages of time-sharing operating system.
10. Is multiprogramming and multitasking mutually exclusive? Explain your answer briefly.
11. What are the functions of an information manager?
12. How does an operating system :
    (*a*) run several programs concurrently on a single CPU?
    (*b*) allow several programs to use a single printer simultaneously?
13. What is the sequential, direct and indexed sequential file organization?
14. What do you mean by Multitasking system? How is it different from multiprocessing system?
15. What do you mean by file organisation? Explain the main differences between Sequential file and Indexed file.
16. What do you mean by an indexed file? Explain in brief.
17. What do you mean by accessing files? What are the various accessing techniques? Explain.

4

GETTING TO KNOW MS DOS

4.1 INTRODUCTION

MS DOS (Microsoft Disk Operating System) is a product of Microsoft Corporation of USA. It is one of the popular operating systems for PCs. Another operating system available in the market is the PC DOS (Personal Computer Disk Operating System). It is a product of IBM and is very much similar to MS DOS. However, the basic commands of both these operating systems remain the same. In this chapter, we will discuss the basic commands of DOS in detail.

4.2 OVERVIEW OF DOS

DOS is the most commonly used operating system. The full form of DOS is Disk Operating System. It is a single user operating system, which means that only one application can be made to run at one time. DOS provides a 'Platform' or an 'Environment' which lets the application program to interact with CPU and I/O devices. Many application software require DOS for running. The common among these are word processors like WordStar, Professional Write; spreadsheet programs like Lotus 1-2-3, VP Planner Plus; accounting software like Tally, EX, etc. Each software package has a specific command to get itself running on DOS. For example, in order to run the spreadsheet program, Lotus 1-2-3, just type 123 at the DOS prompt. DOS will run Lotus 1-2-3 for you. Once any application software shuts down, the control comes back to DOS and the DOS prompt is seen on the screen. Now, DOS is ready to accept more commands from you.

4.2.1 Hardware Requirements for DOS

In order to run DOS, you simply require the following hardware:

Processor	–	PC/XT, PC/AT 286 or above (Currently PC/XT, PC/AT 286/386/486 computers are outdated and only Pentium III/IV are being manufactured)
RAM	–	8 MB or above
Hard disk	–	Around 10 MB of free space for complete installation

4.2.2 Different Versions of DOS

From the first day, when DOS was written, it has evolved from a simple program loader into a very complex, stable and successful operating system. Let us briefly look at the different faces of DOS from the time it took birth in the year 1981 as shown in Table 4.1.

Year	DOS Version	Feature
1981	MS DOS 1.0	Marked the first operating system on IBM PC. It supported single sided diskette drive which could hold data up to 160 KB only.
1982	MS DOS 1.1	It included double sided disk support.
1983	MS DOS 2.0	It had hard disk and the commands available with it were almost the double of its earlier version. It was introduced with IBM PC-XT and had a hierarchical file strúcture.
1984	MS DOS 3.0	It was introduced with PC/AT. The PC/AT's performed at a speed of 6 MHz. Soon they were able to perform at 8 and 10 MHz. The spped of PC/AT was 67% faster than PC/XT's. The PC/AT had a 1.2 MB floppy disk. A hard disk of larger capacity was also added to it.
1984	MS DOS 3.1	It included a support for Microsoft Networks. Now, PC's could be connected to one another and were able to share data and other resources. This marked the beginning of networking.
1986	MS DOS 3.2	The smaller 3.5 inch diskettes could store twice as much data as a standard 5'¼" diskettes.
1987	DOS 3.3	IBM introduced PS/2 series. It could support higher capacity (1.44 MB) 3'½" drives of PS/2 compatibility. It supported generalized code-page font).
1988	DOS 4.0	Tt was designed to look and function very similarly to OS/2. The shell allows you to use DOS without entering commands at the DOS prompt. By this time, you could also use mouse with the shell.
1991	DOS 5.0	The memory management was improved. The shell and other extended commands were also improved. Now the 2.88 MB floppy diskettes were used.
1993	DOS 6.0	It had advanced features like disk space compression, memory space organiser and disk re-organiser.
1993	DOS 6.2	A few other small changes were brought in.

Table 4.1 *Different versions of DOS*

4.2.3 The Structure of MS DOS

MS DOS is partitioned into many layers. These layers segregate the kernel logic of the operating system, the user's idea of the system, from the hardware on which it is being run. These layers are:

(*a*) The BIOS (Basic Input/Output System)

(*b*) The DOS Kernel

(*c*) The Command Processor (Shell)

Now, let us quickly look at the functions of these layers.

4.2.3.1 The BIOS

Every computer system comes with its own copy of BIOS. The manufacturer of the computer system provides it. It holds the default resident hardware dependent drivers for the following devices:

- Console display and keyboard (CON)
- Date and time (CLOCK $)
- Line Printer (PRN)
- Boot disk device (Block device)
- Auxiliary device (Aux)

The interaction between the MS DOS kernel and the device drives happens through I/O request packets. The device drivers translate all these requests into appropriate commands that are given for the different hardware controllers. In many MS DOS systems, most of the parts of hardware drivers are found in read-only memory (ROM). The main idea is that they can be used by many stand-alone applications, diagnostics and the system startup program. When the system is switched on, at that point of time, BIOS is read into Random Access Memory (RAM). BIOS is a part of a file named IO.SYS. This file has special file attributes like it is marked as hidden and system.

4.2.3.2 The DOS Kernel

The DOS kernel is mostly used by application programs. It is provided by Microsoft Corporation itself and contains a large number of hardware-independent services. These services are called *system functions.* The DOS kernel performs the following functions:

- File management
- Record management
- Memory management
- Character-device input/output
- Access to the real-time clock.

The DOS kernel is read into the memory at the time of system initialization. The DOS kernel forms a part of the file named MSDOS.SYS. This file again has special attributes like hidden and system.

4.2.3.3 The Command Processor (Shell)

The command processor is also called the Shell. It is the shell that provides an interface between the user and the hardware. It helps in carrying out all the commands given at the DOS prompt. It also helps is loading and executing the programs from the storage device. The default shell that carries out all these functions is present in a file called COMMAND.COM. COMMAND.COM is a special file that runs under the complete supervision of DOS. A programmer can replace the COMMAND.COM file by simply adding a SHELL directive to the system configuration file (CONFIG.SYS) on the system startup disk.

4.2.4 The Command.com

The file COMMAND.COM is partitioned into three sections.

(*a*) The resident portion

(*b*) An initialization section

(*c*) A transient module

Let us briefly look at these three sections.

4.2.4.1 Resident Portion

It is loaded above the DOS kernel, its buffers and tables. It contains the routines that process the critical errors, Ctrl-C, Ctrl-Break and termination of other programs. This part of the COMMAND.COM is also responsible for giving error messages.

4.2.4.2 Initialization Section

When the system is geared up, at that point of time the initialization section is loaded exactly above the resident portion. It runs the AUTOEXEC.BAT file created by the user.

4.2.4.3 Transient Module

The transient portion of the COMMAND.COM file is loaded in the high end of memory. Many application programs can very safely use this memory. The transient module helps in displaying the user prompt. It can also read commands from the keyboard. The transient module again executes all these commands.

4.2.5 Types of DOS Commands

DOS offers a variety of commands to perform various functions. With the help of DOS commands, you can display the list of files and directories that are present on the disk, create new files and directories, remove unwanted files and directories and much more. DOS commands can be entered either in uppercase or lowercase letters. The format of a DOS command is called *syntax*. All DOS commands begin with command name. When DOS carries out the instructions given by you, it is called the execution of DOS command.

When any command given by the user is accepted by COMMAND.COM, it belongs to one of the two categories mentioned below:

(*a*) Internal commands

(*b*) External commands

Let us briefly explore these categories of commands as given by the user.

4.2.5.1 Internal Commands

The commands, which are a part of the main files of DOS (i.e. COMMAND.COM and two hidden files), are known as Internal commands. They are loaded in RAM as soon as the computer is switched on. They are executed by the embedded code present in COMMAND.COM. Some of the internal commands are DIR, COPY, DEL, REN, MD, CD, RD, etc. These internal commands are also called *Intrinsic Commands.*

4.2.5.2 External Commands

External commands are separate programs present on the disk. These files have the same primary name as the command name. The extension of these files is either COM or EXE. These commands have to be loaded into the computer's memory before they are executed. All external commands need special program files for their execution. As soon as these commands are executed, they are freed from the memory. So, if you need to execute it again, it has to be reloaded into the computer's memory. Some of the typical examples of external commands are CHKDSK, FORMAT, LABEL, DISKCOPY, BACKUP, RESTORE, etc. External commands are also called *Extrinsic Commands.*

4.2.6 Booting of Computer

In order to use a computer system, the operating system (DOS) must always be present in its memory. So, as and when the computer is switched on, the very first thing that is placed in your computer system's RAM is DOS. Thus, the whole process of loading DOS in computer's memory is referred to as Booting. The process of booting is shown on Figure 4.1.

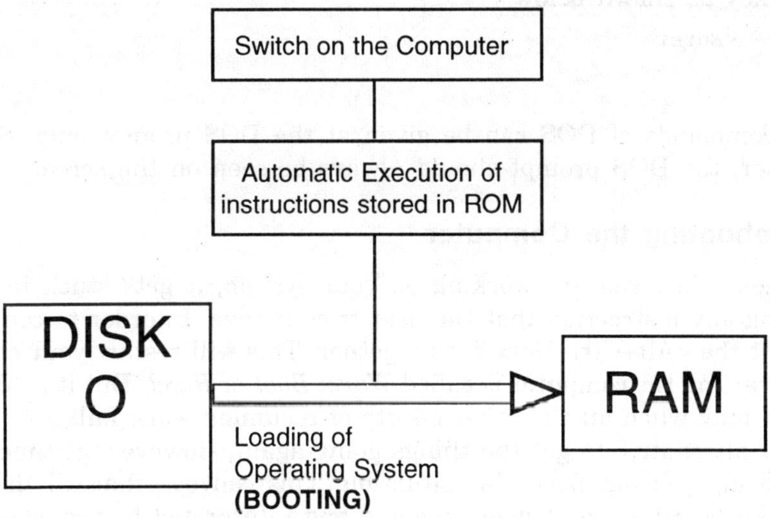

Figure 4.1 *Process of booting*

The booting happens automatically as soon as the computer is switched on, provided DOS is available to it. DOS can be present either on the hard disk or the floppy disk. So, as and when the computer is switched on, DOS is first searched for on the floppy drive. If the computer is able to find DOS on any of the floppy drives, then booting happens from there. However, if DOS is not available on the floppy drive, then it is searched for on the hard disk and then the booting happens from the hard disk. If DOS is not present on hard disk either, then don't forget to insert the floppy carrying the DOS software in the A drive before switching on the system. When the following prompt appears on the screen, you can assure yourself that DOS has been loaded in the computer's memory.

Here underscore character '_' refers to the cursor (blinking mark) on the screen. This prompt will appear only if the booting has been carried out from the floppy drive.

In a case if the booting happens from the hard disk, then the following prompt will be seen on the screen.

C:\>_

Looking at the DOS prompt you can easily make out the currently active drive. In DOS, it is very easy to switch between different drives. Now, if you want to go to the floppy drive then simply type in the drive letter followed by a colon and then hit the <Enter> key as shown below:

```
C:\>A:  <Enter>

A:\>_
```

Note : The commands which have to be typed are written as bold letters throughout this chapter.

Now again if you want to go back to the hard disk drive, then type in C: and press the <Enter> key as shown below:

```
A:\>C:  <Enter>

C:\>_
```

All the commands of DOS can be given at the DOS prompt only. So in order to proceed further, the DOS prompt should always be seen on the screen.

4.2.7 Rebooting the Computer

Sometimes, when you are working on your system, it gets stuck in between and stops accepting any instruction that the user tries to give. In order to come out of such a situation, hit the <Alt+Ctrl+Del> keys together. This will restart your computer. This process of restarting the computer is called *Warm Boot* or *Reset.* But it is always advised to Warm boot only when all the other efforts of resuming work fail. So, this should be used as a last alternative to get the things going again. However, at times Warm Boot also doesn't bring you out from this situation. This conveys that all the instructions given by the keyboard are no longer accepted and interpreted by the computer. In this case, switch off the power supply and wait for a few minutes. Then turn on the power supply and start working again. This is also called *Hard Boot* or *Cold Boot.*

4.3 FILES AND DIRECTORIES IN DOS

File is a collection of related information. Any kind of text, data or program that is entered is stored in a file. It is very essential to organize your files in an ordered manner. This makes the file search easier otherwise, it can really be a difficult and time consuming job to search for a particular file out of the whole lot of files stored on the disk. An example of library can make the explanation of the concept clearer. As you must have already observed, the books in a library are put in big cabinets. Each cabinet is divided into many shelves and sub-shelves. Each shelve or sub-shelve contains books on a particular subject. So, the required book on a particular subject can be found out very easily without wasting much time and effort.

On similar grounds, all the files that are related to each other are clubbed at one place. This is known as a *Directory structure* or simply a *Directory*. A directory structure resembles an inverted tree. The main directory becomes the *Root directory*. The directories and files become the branches of this directory tree. Any number of files and directories can be added to it thus, making the tree grow big downwards. Let us take an example.

Suppose we wish to store two kinds of directories on our disk: MARKET and FINANCE. Further, we wish to keep two more kinds of files (say MUMBAI and DELHI) under MARKET sub-directory. DOS can help you in organizing your files through directory structure which is shown in Figure 4.2.

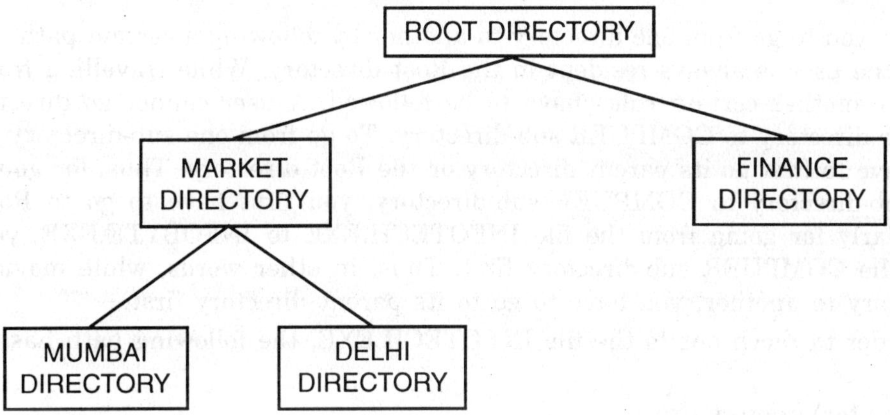

Figure 4.2 *Example of directory structure*

It is clear from the figure that:

1. On the top of the directory structure, there is a Root directory. This directory is always present and is shown by \(backslash) for referencing. Any file or directory that is created is always under the Root directory.
2. MARKET is the sub-directory of the Root Directory.
3. MARKET is the parent directory of the directories MUMBAI and DELHI. It can also be said that the MUMBAI and DELHI are the sub-directories of the MARKET directory. Thus, a directory under a directory is called a *sub-directory.*

It can be clearly seen that the files relating to a particular subject can be put under a directory. For example, all the files relating to marketing in Mumbai zone can be put under MUMBAI sub-directory whereas all the files relating to marketing in Delhi zone can be stored under the sub-directory DELHI.

4.3.1 Referencing Files

It's time to learn as to how to locate a file. The directory structure shown in Figure 4.3 has two sub-directories MATHS and COMPUTER under the Root directory. The sub-directory COMPUTER has two files under it.

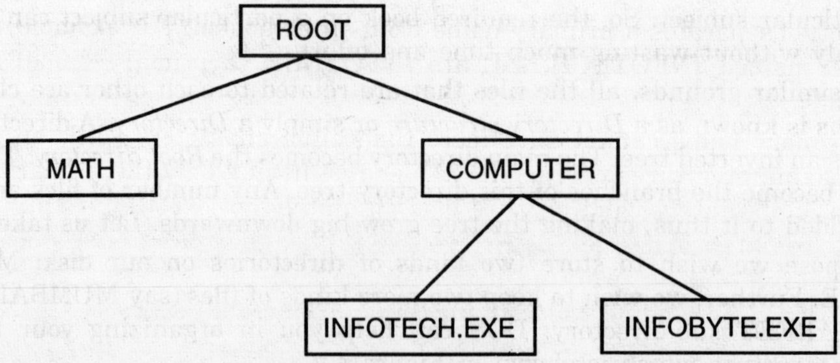

Figure 4.3 *Referencing files*

DOS allows you to go from one directory to another by following a certain path. In the beginning, the user is always resident in the Root directory. While travelling from one directory to another certain rules have to be followed. A user cannot go directly from MATH sub-directory to COMPUER sub-directory. To go from one sub-directory to another, you have to first go its parent directory or the Root directory. Thus, for going from MATH sub-directory to COMPUER sub-directory, you first have to go to Root directory. Similarly for going from the file INFOTECH.EXE to INFOBYTE.EXE, you have to go to the COMPUER sub-directory first. Thus, in other words, while moving from one directory to another, you have to go to its parent directory first.

Now, in order to reach out to the file INFOTECH.EXE, the following path has to be followed:

```
C:\>Computer\Infotech.exe
1          3    4      5
|__________|
     2
```

Here, 1 is the drive name where the file is resident in;
2 is the path which DOS takes to reach to a particular file;
3 is the directory under the Root;
4 is the primary name of the file that is to be accessed; and
5 is the extension name of the same file.

The \ (backslash) has to be used for tracing out the path. The first backslash takes you to the Root directory. The subsequent backslashes separate the directories, sub-directories and the filename that are given in the whole path.

4.3.2 File Naming Conventions

There are certain rules that have to be followed while giving names to your files. A filename has two parts:

(*a*) Primary Name
(*b*) Extension (Secondary Name)

A dot (.) separates a primary name from an extension. For example, the two parts of the file named INFOTECH.EXE are INFOTECH (a primary name) and EXE (an extension).

A primary name cannot have more than eight characters while an extension can have a maximum of three characters. A filename having only the primary name and no extension is absolutely valid because it is absolutely optional to give an extension to a filename. An extension is generally given by the language or software used by the file. For example, if you are working in MS-Word, then the extension given to the file is entering DOC. A filename can contain the following characters:

(*a*) An Alphabet (A-Z) or (a-z)

(*b*) A number (0-9)

(*c*) Special characters such as $, #, &, @, !, %, (,), ~, { , }, ', ^ etc. except *, ?, fullstop (.) and space ( ).

It is a good practice to give meaningful names to your files. However, no two files can have exactly the same name on the disk. Thus, a name given to a file on a disk has to be unique.

A look at a few valid and invalid filenames:

VALID	**INVALID**
GALAXY	S.P.SINGH
456.DOC	SALES*.*
TRIAL	MILKY WAY
INFINITY.DOC	RAJAN.JAIN
EMPLOYEE.EMP	NCLLIBRARY

The rules for naming a directory are the same as that of naming files.

4.4 DIRECTORY MANIPULATION COMMANDS OF DOS

The directory commands help you to create new directories and remove existing ones. They also allow you to travel from one directory to another. You can also view the listing of files and directories that are present on the disk. Let us learn the commonly used directory commands of DOS.

4.4.1 The DIR command

This particular DOS command helps you in displaying a list of files or directories present on a disk. Thus, to see the contents of your hard disk, issue the following command:

```
C:\>DIR <Enter>
```

A sample output as shown in Figure 4.4 can be seen on the VDU. In this figure, each line has five columns that are summarised in Table 4.2.

```
C:\>DIR
     Volume in drive C has no label
     Volume Serial Number is 1421-15AB
     Directory of C:\
     COMMAND    COM              23641     02-01-98     12:12A
     DISKCOPY   COM              4165      05-01-98     4:29A
     CHKDSK     COM              9725      05-03-98     11:30A
     TREE       COM              2473      07-03-98     12:30P
     MATH              <DIR>               10-02-98     12:10A
     COMPUTER          <DIR>               05-05-98     4:30A
     4 file(2)  40,004 bytes
     2dir(s)  231000 bytes free
```

1 2 3 4 5

Figure 4.4 *Displaying the contents of hard disk*

Columns	Contents
1	Primary name (*e.g.* COMMAND)
2	Extension (*e.g.* COM)
3	Size of each file in bytes
4	Date when the file was either created or modified last
5	Time when the file was either created or modified last

Table 4.2 *Contents of the column shown in the directory*

You can view the contents of the floppy drive by following any of the two methods given below:

Method 1: First switch yourself to the floppy drive and then issue the DIR command. The currently active drive becomes A.

```
C:\>A: <Enter>

A:\>DIR <Enter>
```

Method 2: Alternatively, you may issue the following command:

```
C:\>DIR A: <Enter>
```

But in this case, the currently active drive remains C only but the contents of the floppy disk are shown on the monitor.

Figure 4.4 shows two sub-directories MATH and COMPUTER. <DIR> signifies a directory. Now, if you wish to view the contents of the sub-directory COMPUTER, issue the following command:

```
C:\>DIR\COMPUTER <Enter>
```

This command shows you the contents of the sub-directory COMPUTER, which is resident under the Root directory.

Let us assume that there is one more sub-directory by the name INFOCHIP existing under COMPUTER. To view the contents of this sub-directory, issue the following command:

```
C:\>DIR\COMPUTER\INFOCHIP <Enter>
```

This command shows the contents of the sub-directory INFOCHIP, which is under COMPUTER. If you have a large number of files on the disk, then on issuing DIR command, the screen scrolls up and only a few filenames are shown. In such a case, issue the following command:

```
C:\>DIR/P <Enter>
```

This command will show the contents of the disk page-wise. Once the screen is full of file-names, the message 'Press any key to continue' appears at the bottom of the screen and the scrolling will stop. Hit any key on the keyboard. The next screen showing the remaining filenames is displayed. The output of this command is exactly the same as that of DIR command. But if you are interested in seeing the filenames only, issue the following command:

```
C:\>DIR/W <Enter>
```

This command shows the names of files and directories width-wise. So, in one line five names of files and directories are shown. The other details like the size of file, the date and time of each file creation are not shown. The directories are shown in square ([ ]) brackets.

4.4.2 The MD command

In the earlier part of this chapter, we discussed that all the related files should be clubbed at one place, called a directory or sub-directory. So, to club all the related files under one head, new directories and sub-directories have to be created. Let us create a new sub-directory by the name PHYSICS under the Root directory. The following command can achieve this:

```
C:\>MD PHYSICS <Enter>
```

where MD stands for Make Directory

Further, let us create another sub-directory by the name OPTICS under the sub-directory PHYSICS.

```
C:\>MD PHYSICS\OPTICS <Enter>
```

4.4.3 The RD command

With times, certain directories grow old and are no more needed. It is better to delete such directories because they can save you many precious bytes on the disk. So, let us delete the sub-directory OPTICS with the following command:

```
C:\>RD PHYSICS\OPTICS <Enter>
```

where RD stands for Remove Directory

A directory or a sub-directory has to be essentially empty before removing it. For example, in order to remove the sub-directory OPTICS, there should not be any directories and files under it. So, you must first delete all the files and remove all the sub-directories present under the sub-directory OPTICS before removing it. The method for deleting files is being discussed in the later part of this session.

4.4.4 The CD command

Let us again refer to the Figure 4.2. Suppose you are under the MARKET sub-directory and you want to access the files or directories in the FINANCE sub-directory. This would involve the changing of directory from MARKET to FINANCE. This will make the FINANCE directory active. This can be done through the CD command. Look at the following example:

```
C:\>CD FINANCE <Enter>
```

where CD stands for Change Directory

The above command will take you to the sub-directory FINANCE as shown by following prompt:

```
C:\FINANCE>_
```

If you want to go to the sub-directory MUMBAI straight from the sub-directory FINANCE, issue the following command:

```
C:\>CD MARKET\MUMBAI <Enter>
```

After the above command, the following prompt will come:

```
C:\MARKET\MUMBAI>_
```

The command for going to the root directory from the above prompt is:

```
C:\MARKET\MUMBAI>CD\ <Enter>
```

But, the command for going to the parent or previous directory (whether it is root or sub-directory) is:

```
C:\MARKET\MUMBAI>CD.. <Enter>
```

If you are in the sub-directory MUMBAI, the above command will take you to MARKET sub-directory as shown below:

```
C:\MARKET>_
```

The command for displaying the name of the currently active directory is:

```
C:\>CD <Enter>
```

4.5 FILE MANIPULATION COMMANDS OF DOS

DOS offers a number of commands for performing various operations on your files. The commonly used commands for copying, deleting and renaming the files are explained below.

4.5.1 The COPY Command

At times, you may have to work on some other machine. So, this involves copying files from one disk to another. Copying of files can happen from hard disk to floppy or vice-versa. Files can also be copied onto the same disk with a different name. The COPY command helps us to accomplish all these tasks.

The syntax of the copy command is:

```
COPY <Source drive>: (File spec 1) <Target drive>: (File spec 2)
```

where,

Source drive refers to the drive from where the file has to be copied. It can be A, B or C.

'File Spec 1' refers to the path from where the file has to be copied.

'Target drive' refers to the drive where the file is going to be copied.

'File Spec 2' refers to the destination where the file is going to be copied.

(*i*) **Copying a file to another drive under the same name.** A file can have the same name if it is stored on different disks. Thus, to copy a file by the name MYFILE from hard disk to floppy disk, issue the following command:

```
C:\>COPY C:MYFILE A:MYFILE <Enter>
```

After the execution of the above command, the file MYFILE stored on hard disk will be copied to the floppy disk. When the above command is executed, DOS displays the message '*1 File(s) copied*' on the screen. However, if the file has to be copied from the active drive, then specifying the source drive can be avoided. On similar grounds, if the filename remains unchanged then there is no need to specify it after the target drive. Thus, the above command can also be given in the following way:

```
C:\>COPY MYFILE A: <Enter>
```

(*ii*) **Copying a file to another disk under a different name.** The name of the file can be changed very easily while copying. It can be extremely useful when you want to make changes to a particular file without losing the original file. In such a case, you can make a copy of the file with a different name. This makes distinguishing between the two files easier. The following command copies the file MYFILE from the hard disk onto floppy disk by the name NEWFILE.

```
C:\>COPY MYFILE A:NEWFILE <Enter>
```

Thus, we now have two copies of this particular file. The contents of both the files are exactly same. They differ only in terms of name.

(*iii*) **Copying a file with a new name on the same disk.** The file can be copied with a different name on the same disk. Proceeding with the above example, let us save the file MYFILE with a new name, NEWFILE and copy it onto the same disk.

```
C:\>COPY MYFILE NEWFILE <Enter>
```

Once this command is executed, we have the same file under two different names, stored on the same disk.

(*iv*) **Copying files from one directory to another.** Suppose you have placed all your files under the root directory. Now, at a later point of time, you wish to club all the related files at one place. This can be done very easily. Create a directory and copy the required files from the root directory to this newly created directory. DOS allows you to copy files from one directory to another.

Let us assume that you have a file by the name NORTH.TXT in the root directory and you wish to copy this file in the newly created AREA sub-directory. The following command will do this:

C:\>**COPY NORTH.TXT\AREA** <Enter>

Similarly, you can copy files from any directory to any other directory. DOS only needs the specification of full path from you. Let us copy a file OLD.TXT that exists under the sub-directory DATA to the sub-directory INFO which is resident in the floppy disk.

C:\>**COPY DATA\OLD.TXTA:\INFO** <Enter>

4.5.2 The DEL Command

With time, certain files grow old that are no longer required. So, it is desirable to delete such files because unwanted files occupy precious space on the disk. Suppose there is a file on the hard disk by the name SALES.DOC which needs to be deleted. The following command deletes this file:

C:\>**DEL SALES.DOC** <Enter>

Once the above command is executed, DOS does not display any message on the screen. However, if the file SALES.DOC exists on the floppy disk then, you may issue the following command to delete it:

C:\>**DEL A:SALES.DOC** <Enter>

However, it is advised that first you go to the A: prompt and then delete the file as shown below:

C:\>**A:**<Enter>

A:\>**DEL SALES.DOC** <Enter>

The above method will help you to avoid accidental deletion of file SALES.DOC from the hard disk. While deleting any file from a sub-directory, its full path can also be given. Let us assume that the SALES.DOC file exists under a sub-directory MONITOR on the hard disk. Issue one of the following commands:

C:\>**DEL C:\MONITOR\SALES.DOC** <Enter>

OR

C:\>**DEL MONITOR\SALES.DOC** <Enter>

You can also delete the SALES.DOC file by first changing to that sub-directory and then issuing the DEL command as shown below:

C:\>**CD\MONITOR** <Enter>

C:\MONITOR>**DEL SALES.DOC** <Enter>

4.5.3 The REN Command

DOS allows you to give new names to your files. Sometimes, you may find that the old names given to the files are no more appropriate. In such a case, you can rename your files with the help of REN command. Assume that there is a file by the name OLD.TXT and now you wish to give a new name NEW.TXT to it. Carry out the following command to get your work done.

```
C:\>REN OLD.TXT NEW.TXT <Enter>
```

Here, only the name of the file has changed. The contents of the file are same. Again, you can specify the full path to rename your files.

```
C:\>REN DATA\OLD.TXT NEW.TXT <Enter>
```

The file OLD.TXT that resides under the sub-directory Data now has a new name NEW.TXT.

4.6 COMMONLY USED DOS COMMANDS

You have already been introduced with the directory and file commands of DOS. Now, let us make ourselves familiar with other commonly used commands.

4.6.1 The DATE command

Using this command, you can display the system date. You can also enter new date with the help of DATE command as shown below:

```
C:\>DATE <Enter>
```

After issuing the above command the following screen appears:

```
C:\>DATE
```

Current date is SUN 10-25-01

Enter new date (mm-dd-yy):_

So, key in the new date in 'month-date-year' format. However if you do not want to change this date simply hit the <Enter> key. The current date will be taken as new date. A new date can also be given by the following command:

```
C:\>DATE 10-25-01
```

The above command will not show the prompt 'Enter new date' on the screen.

4.6.2 The Time command

The TIME command is used to display and change the current time.

```
C:\>TIME <Enter>
```

On issuing this command, the following screen appears:

```
C:\>TIME
```

Current time is 08:30:15

Enter new time:_

Enter the new time in hours: minutes: seconds format. Hit the <Enter> key if you do not want to change the time. The new time can also be specified along with TIME command.

```
C:\>TIME 11:40 <Enter>
```

So, the prompt 'Enter New Time' will not appear on the screen with above command.

4.6.3 The CLS command

In order to clear a cluttered screen issue the CLS command. This will remove the contents shown on your screen thus making it look neater and cleaner. The CLS command is given in the following manner.

```
C:\>CLS <Enter>
```

4.6.4 The COPY CON command

Text Files can be created with the help of COPY CON command. Look at the following example:

```
C:\>COPY CON MYFIRST.TXT <Enter>
```

This command tells DOS to copy the information from the keyboard or console and put it in the file MYFIRST.TXT. On issuing this command the following screen appears:

```
C:\>COPY CON MYFIRST.TXT

_
```

You will find a blinking cursor in the second line. Enter the text and terminate each line by pressing <Enter> key as illustrated below:

My first DOS file. The name given to this file is MYFIRST.TXT. <Enter>

This is a very interesting session on DOS. <Enter>

Once all the required text is entered, hit the <Ctrl+Z> keys together to mark the end of text. <Ctrl+Z> keys tell DOS that no more text is going to be entered now. Again hit the <Enter> key. Now, the following screen will be displayed:

```
^Z
1 files(s) copied
C:\>_
```

4.6.5 The TYPE command

The contents of any file can be viewed very easily by giving the TYPE command followed by the filename. Let us see the contents of file MYFIRST.TXT that has just been created by issuing the following command.

```
C:\>TYPE MYFIRST.TXT <Enter>
```

It will display the following message on screen:

My first DOS file. The name given to this file is Hello.Txt.

This is a very interesting session on DOS.

However, if the file is very big, then it scrolls upward and only the last page of the file is seen on the screen. The DOS prompt is shown again. You can see the contents of the file page-wise by pressing <Ctrl+S> keys together. Hit any key to see the next page.

You can also send the output of a file to the printer. The following command starts the printing job, provided the printer is on.

```
C:\>TYPE MYFIRST.TXT>PRN <Enter>
```

In case the printer is not ready, the following message will come:

Write fault error, writing device PRN

Abort, Retry, Ignore, Fail?

Set the printer ready and press 'R' to retry otherwise press 'A' to cancel the command.

4.6.6 The ECHO Command

At times you may be required to display a message on the screen while executing a set of commands. The ECHO command helps you to display a meaningful message on the screen. This command is issued as illustrated below:

```
C:\>ECHO Good Morning. The system is booting up. <Enter>
```

The ECHO command is a special DOS command used exclusively in batch files (files containing a set of DOS commands). The concept of batch files is being discussed in the later part of the chapter. There is one more form of ECHO command i.e. ECHO OFF as shown below:

```
C:\>ECHO OFF <Enter>
```

The above command tells DOS not to display other commands in the batch file. It is also used in batch files.

4.6.7 The PROMPT Command

Users always prefer to see the prompt for currently logged sub-directory. The PROMPT command tells DOS to include the sub-directory, greater than (>) sign, date, time or any text as a part of the prompt. The various forms of PROMPT command are discussed below:

(*i*) To display the path designation (*e.g.* \MARKET\MUMBAI) and the greater than sign as a DOS prompt, issue the following command:

```
C:\>PROMPT $p$g <Enter>
```

After giving the above command, if you are logged to MUMBAI sub-directory of MARKET directory in the root, then the following prompt will come on the screen:

```
C:\MARKET\MUMBAI>_
```

(*ii*) To display a text 'Hello' along with path designation and greater than prompt, issue the following command:

```
C:\>PROMPT Hello $p$g <Enter>
```

The above command will display the following prompt:

```
Hello  C:\>_
```

(*iii*) To display date and time along with the C:\>, issue the following command:

```
C:\>PROMPT $d $t $p$g <Enter>
```

The above command will display the following prompt:

```
WED  08-16-1999  15:32:46  C:\>_
```

(*iv*) To display just greater than sign without path designation, you can give the following command:

```
C:\>PROMPT <Enter>
```

The command will display the following prompt:

```
C>_
```

4.6.8 The PATH Command

By this time, you must be familiar with the directory structure of DOS. Suppose your program (say PRINCE.COM file) lies in the GAME sub-directory of the root directory and you want to execute it from any other sub-directory (say WINDOWS). To execute PRINCE.COM file, first you will have to make GAME as the currently active sub-directory and then issue the following command:

```
C:\GAME>PRINCE <Enter>
```

DOS provides a shortcut way to locate and run the above program from any other sub–directory by specifying the path as illustrated below:

```
C:\WINDOWS>PATH C:\GAME <Enter>
```

The above command tells DOS that GAME sub-directory is in the current search path of DOS. DOS will first search the required program file in the currently logged drive and then GAME sub-directory. Thus, the PRINCE.COM file can be executed directly from WINDOWS or any sub-directory as shown below:

```
C:\WINDOWS>PRINCE <Enter>
```

The PATH command is generally used in batch files as discussed in later part of this chapter.

4.7 WILDCARDS

Often you may need to do a similar kind of job on a number of files. If these files have something in common, then we can save the effort of performing repetitive job. So, these files can be referred collectively by using the wildcard facility provided by DOS. The use of wildcards in a DOS command gives greater flexibility when using similar type of filenames. DOS offers two wildcards: ? and *. Each ? can be replaced by exactly one character or none, if it is given at the end of the filename. As and when the ? wildcard is specified in the middle of a filename, it has to necessarily match one character.

The * wildcard can match eight or less characters in the primary name and three or less characters in the extension part. Let us take an example to make the concept of wildcards clear. Suppose the following files are present on your disk:

OLD.TXT	INCOME.PRO
OVER.PRG	ANNUAL.DOC
NEW.DOC	ZEE.COM
OLD.DOC	PAPER.COM
SWEETY	PAGE.IN
GO.EXE	OLD1
DRAGON.EXE	KOMAL
EXPENSE.PRG.	OLD20.BAS

The following commands illustrate the concept of wildcards:

(*a*) If you wish to see all the files that start with the letter O and any extension, then give the following command:

```
C:\>DIR O *.* <Enter>
```

The above command will list the following files:

```
OLD.TXT         OLD1
OVER.PRG        OLD20.BAS
OLD.DOC
```

(*b*) Now, let us copy all the files with any number of characters in the primary name and the extension EXE with the following command.

```
C:\>COPY *.EXE A: <Enter>
```

The above command will copy the files GO.EXE and DRAGON.EXE onto the floppy disk.

(*c*) To delete all the files beginning with OL, having two more characters in the primary name and any extension, issue the following command.

```
C:\>DEL OL??.* <Enter>
```

With this command, the files OLD.TXT, OLD.DOC and OLD1 are going to be deleted because these are the only files present on the disk which match the given wildcard pattern. However, the above command will not delete the files OVER.PRG and OLD20 because the former does not start with OL and the latter has a primary name of 5 characters.

(*d*) Similarly, to copy all files starting with P and an extension comprising of two characters ending with N, issue the following command:

```
C:\>DEL P*.?N <Enter>
```

This will delete the file PAGE.IN because this is the only file matching the given wildcard pattern.

(*e*) For copying all the files having primary name OLD and any extension from floppy to EXPENSE sub-directory of hard disk, issue the following command:

```
A:\>COPY OLD.*C:\EXPENSE <Enter>
```

The above command will copy only two files– OLD.DOC and OLD.TXT.

(*f*) To copy all the files with any primary name and no extension from EXPENSE sub-directory of hard disk to floppy, issue the following command:

```
C:\>COPY\EXPENSE\*.A: <Enter>
```

The above command will copy the files SWEETY, OLD1 and KOMAL.

(*g*) To delete all the files of floppy, issue the following command:

```
A:\>DEL *.* <Enter>
```

After giving the above command, the following message will come on the screen:
Are you Sure (Y/N)?_

Press 'Y' if you really want to delete all files otherwise press any key. Never try the above command on root directory of hard disk, otherwise your most important DOS file COMMAND.COM will also be deleted and thereafter you will not be able to boot the system from the hard disk. Therefore, the use of wildcards with DEL command has to be made with great caution.

4.8 DISK MANIPULATION COMMANDS

In this section, we will learn some of the external commands of DOS such as FORMAT, CHKDSK, LABEL and DISKCOPY.

4.8.1 The FORMAT Command

Before discussing the FORMAT command in detail, let us first see what the term 'Formatting' means. Generally when you purchase a diskette from the market, it is unformatted. It can be compared with a notebook, which has blank pages without any ruler lines. You would prefer to put lines, write page numbers and categorise the pages into equal parts so that an index can be made and the required topic can be searched very easily. Similarly, DOS organises the disk into concentric circles that are called tracks. Tracks are further divided into triangular regions. Each such region is called a sector. The organisation of disk into tracks and sectors is called Formatting. The Figure 4.5 makes the formatting concept clearer.

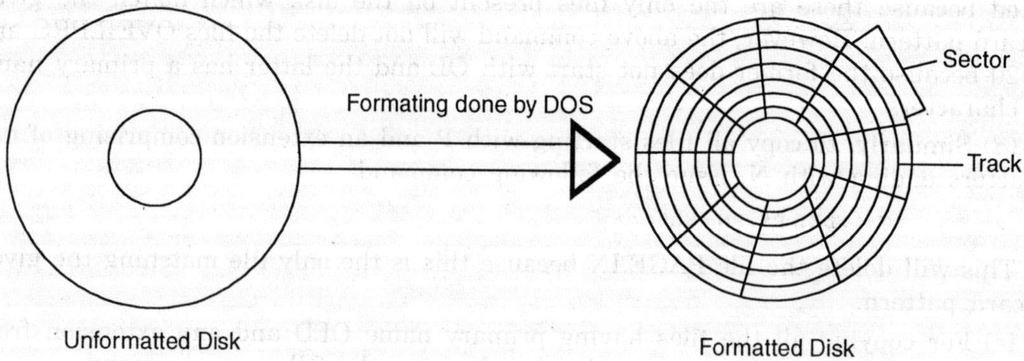

Figure 4.5 *Process of formatting*

FORMAT command is used for formatting a hard disk or floppy disk. As FORMAT is an external command, a file by the name FORMAT.COM should be present on your disk. In order to format the floppy disk, issue the following command:

```
C:\>FORMAT  A: <Enter>
```

Once the above command is executed, the following screen appears:

Insert new diskette in drive A:

and strike ENTER when ready

At this point of time DOS wants you to insert a floppy disk in drive A and hit the <Enter> key. When the formatting of the disk is done, the following message appears on the screen.

Enter Volume Label (upto 11 characters):_

Here, you can give a name to the disk for its easy identification. A label up to 11 characters can be given to the disk after it is formatted. If you don't want that your disk should carry any label, simply press <Enter> key without typing anything. Now, the following message will come:

Format Another (Y/N)?_

Now, if you want to format another disk, then hit 'Y' (for Yes) and insert that disk in the drive. However, if you do not want to format another disk, type in 'N' (for No) or press any key to end the format program.

New disks should always be formatted for using them. But old disks can also be formatted. Formatting will make the disk blank by erasing all its data. You may be required to format an old disk if it has bad sectors and is needed again for usage. However, the FORMAT command should be used with extreme caution. Any disk whether hard disk or floppy disk will lose all data stored on it once the formatting operation is done. Therefore, you should not try the FORMAT command on the hard disk. If you format the hard disk, all the contents stored on it are going to be removed permanently and new tracks and sectors will be created. FORMAT command also provides a method for making your disk bootable. The following command is used for this purpose:

```
C:\>FORMAT A:/S <Enter>
```

With the help of the above command, all the operating system files (COMMAND.COM and two hidden files) are copied from the hard disk to the floppy disk. This floppy can now be used to load DOS in the computer's memory if you are unable to boot the system from the hard disk. The COPY command cannot serve the above purpose because it cannot copy the two hidden files of DOS in the boot sector.

4.8.2 The CHKDSK Command

If a disk is not used properly, then certain sectors of the disk can get corrupted or damaged. The command CHKDSK helps to check the status of the disk. After checking the disk, CHKDSK displays several items of information. However to get executed, this command needs the program file CHKDSK.COM. Let's check the status of the disk in drive A through the following command:

C:\>**CHKDSK A:** <Enter>

On successfully checking the disk, the screen as shown in Figure 4.6 appears.

Figure 4.6 *A screen appearing after the execution of CHKDSK command*

If no drive letter is specified with CHKDSK command, then the currently active drive is checked for.

4.8.3 The LABEL Command

Although you have seen that a volume label to the disk is given at the time of formatting the disk. DOS also provides LABEL command to change, delete or give new label to the disk. This command needs a program file LABEL.COM. Let us give a label to the floppy disk by the following command:

C:\>**LABEL A:** <Enter>

Once the above command is executed the following screen appears:

Volume in drive A has no label

Volume label (11 characters, ENTER for none) _

So hit the <Enter> key if you want to delete the volume label without typing in anything. You can also provide volume label directly with the following command.

C:\>**LABEL A:ABC Ltd.** <Enter>

A new label ABC Ltd. is given to the floppy disk.

4.8.4 The DISKCOPY Command

The DISKCOPY command helps you to copy all the contents of one disk onto the other in such a way that both disks become identical. It copies the contents of the floppy disk present in source drive onto the disk present in the destination drive. If you have a single drive on your computer, then the same drive can act as source as well as the destination drive. The command to copy the contents of one floppy onto the other is given below:

```
C:\>DISKCOPY A:A: <Enter>
```

When you issue the above command a screen like the one shown below appears:

Insert SOURCE diskette in Drive A

Press any key to continue

At this point, insert the diskette whose contents are to be copied and then hit any key. Another message appears on the screen as shown below:

Insert TARGET diskette in drive A

Press any key to continue

So, after this message appears, insert the diskette into which the files are to be copied. Thereafter, press any key to continue the process. Once the process of copying is completed, the following screen appears:

Copy Complete

Copy Another (Y/N)?_

Press the 'Y' (for Yes) key if you want to copy the contents of some other diskette. DOS will again prompt you to enter the source diskette. However, if you want to stop the DISKCOPY process, press 'N' (for No).

DISKCOPY command first formats the target diskette if it is unformatted and then copies files onto it. So, if any contents exist on the target diskette, they are all going to be removed. The DISKCOPY command only works with floppy disk and not with hard disks and both floppies should also be of same capacity (ie. 1.44 MB or 1.2 MB). The DISKCOPY command needs the program file DISKCOPY.COM for execution.

4.8.5 THE XCOPY Command

The XCOPY command is used to copy the files present in sub-directories. The command 'COPY *.*' copies the files of the currently working directory and DISKCOPY command copies the entire contents from one floppy to another. So, they are not helpful in copying files selectively.

The XCOPY command offers three special advantages:

- It prompts you to specify the files that you want to copy.
- It can also copy directories and other lower level directories.
- It can be used to copy files from the hard disk to the floppy disk.

Now, let us explore the XCOPY command. If you wish that DOS should ask for your confirmation for copying a file, then use the /P option along with the XCOPY command. Consider the following example:

```
C:\>XCOPY C:ACCOUNT A:ACCOUNT/P <Enter>
```

If you want to copy the directories and lower level directories, then use the /S option along with the XCOPY command. Look at the following example:

```
C:\>XCOPY C:ACCOUNT A:ACCOUNT/S<Enter>
```

This command will copy the directory and all the sub-directories onto the A disk. However, if the /S option is not specified, then the XCOPY command works within the single directory. You can also use /P and /S option simultaneously with the XCOPY command as shown below:

```
C:\>XCOPY C:ACCOUNT A:ACCOUNT/P/S <Enter>
```

The whole path can be specified with the XCOPY command. This command again needs the program file XCOPY.EXE in order to get executed.

4.9 BATCH FILES

Very often, you keep keying in the same sequence of commands to do a repetitive job. For example, everyday, when you start your work on the computer, you first see the listing of files present on the hard disk. Then, you copy all the files with extension DOC and DBF from the floppy disk to hard disk. For doing this, you have to issue the following commands everyday.

```
C:\>DIR/P <Enter>
C:\>COPY A:*.DOC C: <Enter>
C:\>COPY A:*.DBF C: <Enter>
```

DOS can really simplify your task. All the sequence of commands can be put in a file, which is called a batch file. This file offers a great advantage. Batch files contain lines of text in them. The interpreter reads one line at a time and carries out the instructions contained there in. All the instructions written in the batch file are carried out one by one in the order specified. Any number of commands given in a batch file can be executed by just giving a single command at the DOS prompt. It appears as if all these commands were written individually and executed from the DOS prompt. All the batch files can have any primary name but the extension given to these kinds of files is BAT. The user can create his own batch file.

In order to interpret the user's command, COMMAND.COM first tries to see if the user has given any internal command so that it can be executed directly. Then, it tries to look for an external command or the batch file by the same name. This entire search is carried out first in the current directory of the current disk drive and then in all the directories specified in the PATH command. In each directory, COMMAND.COM first looks for a file that has the extension .COM, then .EXE and finally the .BAT. If COMMAND.COM is not able to locate any of these three file types, then it displays the message 'Bad command or file name' on the screen. However, if the COMMAND.COM is able to locate a .COM file or a .EXE file, then it makes use of the EXEC function of MS-DOS to load that particular file and execute it.

The method of creating a batch file is exactly similar to that of creating any other file on DOS. Let us see it through an example.

```
C:\>COPY CON DAILY.BAT <Enter>
DIR/P <Enter>
COPY A:*.DOC C: <Enter>
COPY A:*.DBF C: <Enter>
<CTRL+Z> <Enter>
```

In the above example, a batch file by the name DAILY.BAT has been created. The contents of the file can be seen using the TYPE command. However, if you want to execute this file, simply type in the name of the file at the DOS prompt as shown below:

```
C:\>DAILY.BAT <Enter>
     or
C:\>DAILY <Enter>
```

The commands given in this batch file are going to be executed one by one in the sequence specified.

4.9.1 The AUTOEXEC.BAT file

The AUTOEXEC.BAT is an auto executable batch file. It is a special kind of a batch file. This file is executed as soon as the operating system is loaded in the computer's memory. The AUTOEXEC.BAT file is needed when you want it to be executed automatically each time the system is switched on. Now, as soon as the computer is switched on, DOS searches for the AUTOEXEC.BAT file in the root directory of the bootable disk. If the system finds this file, then all the commands given in it are executed one by one instantly without even asking for date and time. The AUTOEXEC.BAT file is created like any other batch file. Look at the following example:

```
A:\>COPY CON AUTOEXEC.BAT <Enter>
ECHO OFF <Enter>
CLS <Enter>
ECHO My first Autoexec.bat file successfully
executed <Enter>
PROMPT $P$G <Enter>
PATH C:\DOS;C:\WINDOWS <Enter>
<CTRL+Z> <Enter>
```

Enter the above commands on the root directory of bootable floppy disk. Reset your system. You will notice the above created batch file being executed automatically.

4.10 SECURITY AND RECOVERY OF DATA

The computer and information systems represent valuable assets of the organisation. They are required to be protected against unauthorised access, fraud, embezzlement, fires and natural disasters. Without providing proper safeguards to computer-based resources, an organisation cannot survive. Security of data is mandatory for every organisation. The following commands of DOS are used to recover and secure data:

4.10.1 The Undelete Command

You should be extremely careful while deleting your files. Sometimes, even a good user with disciplined file management habits can accidentally delete and loose important files. The file that you have deleted (using the DEL command) is removed from the directory listing but its contents still remain on the disk. The space occupied by the deleted file is made available for DOS to store new file.

DOS provides a very useful and a very powerful command to restore a file. This is the UNDELETE command. This command works best if you use it immediately after deleting a file. For example, if you delete a file by the name 'Sales' and save another file named 'Purchase' before using the UNDELETE command, then DOS might use the space vacated by the deleted file to save the new file. In such a case, the 'Sales' file cannot be recovered. So, use the UNDELETE command immediately to restore the accidentally deleted file before performing any other DOS actions.

The syntax of the Undelete Command is given below:

```
UNDELETE <File spec>
```

where,

<File spec> is optional. Enter it to undelete a specific file.

If <File spec> is not specified, then all the recently deleted files are restored in your work directory.

For example:

(*i*) Suppose there is a file by the name 'Contract' on your hard disk. Delete this file by issuing the following command:

```
C:\>DEL Contract <Enter>
```

(*ii*) To undelete this file, give the following command:

```
C:\>UNDELETE Contract <Enter>
```

(*iii*) The UNDELETE command displays the name

?ontract and prompts
Undelete (y/n)?

(*iv*) Type 'Y' to undelete this file without pressing the Enter key. UNDELETE prompts

Please type the first character for ?ontract

(*v*) Type 'C' to specify the filename as Contract. UNDELETE displays the following message and you are returned to the DOS prompt:

File successfully undeleted.

4.10.2 The Attrib Command

The attrib command is used to view or set file attributes which helps in indicating a file's status within the DOS filing system. In DOS, four file attributes can be provided:

(*i*) **Read only.** If a read only attribute is set for a file, then that file can be read by DOS and other programs. You cannot modify or delete such a file.

(*ii*) **Archive.** An archive file is a newly created or modified file for which no backup has been taken.

(*iii*) **Hidden.** If the hidden attribute is set for a file, then that file cannot be viewed when you issue the DIR command to see the file listing. You cannot modify or delete this file.

(*iv*) **System.** A system file is used by the DOS operating system and, like a hidden file, cannot be viewed, modified or deleted.

The syntax of the ATTRIB command is given below:

```
ATTRIB (+R or -R)(+A or -A) (+S or -S) {+H or -H} {Filespec} {/s}
```

where,

+	Set an attribute (+R, +A, +S and +H)
-	Clears an attribute (-R, -A, -S and -H)
R	Read only attribute
A	Archive attribute
S	System attribute
H	Hidden attribute.
filespec	File name (with its path) that has to be processed.
/S	Processes files in the specified directory and all its subdirectories

For example:

(*i*) Issue the following command to set the read only attribute on the file East.txt.

```
C:\> attrib+r East.txt <Enter>
```

(*ii*) To view the attributes of the file East.txt, issue the following command:

```
C:\> attrib East.txt <Enter>
```

The read only status is indicated by the R present on the left side of the file name.

(*iii*) To remove the read only attribute on the file East.txt, give the command given below:

```
C:\> attrib-r East.txt <Enter>
```

Using DIR to list files by attribute

You can use the /a switch with the DIR command to list only those files with a specific attribute as illustrated below:

(*i*) /ar	Lists read only files
(*ii*) /aa	Lists archive files
(*iii*) /ah	Lists hidden files
(*iv*) /as	Lists system files
(*v*) -	prefix for 'non' (for example, dir/a-a lists all non-archive files).

4.10.3 The Backup Command

Disk backup is a very crucial and yet a very ignored aspect of our lives. We, as a responsible PC user should adopt a disk file backup routine in our day-to-day life. Single hard disk failure or accidental file/directory deletion can lead to a very miserable time.

So, you should make sure to back up all important data files on a daily basis. You can use the COPY and XCOPY commands to back up selected hard disk files. These commands are very valuable and can give you a good start. The heavy task of backing up the whole hard disk with hundreds of directories and thousands of files under it can be performed by the MSBACKUP command.

MSBACKUP helps you to backup and restore files later on. The number of files can vary from a single file to the entire contents of your hard disk. Using this command, you can easily select files and directories for your backup. The actual backup procedure runs much faster than the COPY or XCOPY commands. Another advantage offered by this command is that it takes less floppy disk space.

To use MSBACKUP command, follow the following steps:

(*i*) Key in the command given below:

```
C:\>MSBACKUP <Enter>
```

(*ii*) If you are running this command for the first time, then follow prompts to configure MSBACKUP for your computer. You are required to run a compatibility test to ensure that this command works properly with your system hardware. Save the configuration settings in a startup screen that appears before you.

(*iii*) Choose the 'Backup' option.

(*iv*) Subsequently, select the files and the directories and/or drives that are to be copied. Thereafter, select the drive (in the 'Backup To' box) on which you want to backup your selected files. Make sure that you have the required maximum number and capacity of floppy disks (as reported by MSBACKUP).

(*v*) Finally, choose the 'Start Backup' option and follow the on screen prompts to perform the procedure.

4.10.4 The Restore Command

You are required to retrieve the files that are backed up using MSBACKUP command. To restore your files, follow the steps given below:

(*i*) Issue the following command to run MSBACKUP.

```
C:\ >MSBACKUP <Enter>
```

(*ii*) In the startup screen, choose the 'Restore' option.

(*iii*) Load the backup catalog that corresponds to the files that are to be restored.

(*iv*) In the Restore dialog box, select the desired backup drive (in the 'Restore To' box).

(*v*) Select 'All Files' for the desired drive (in the Restore Files box). Make sure that you have all of the backup floppy disks.

(*vi*) Choose the 'Start Backup' option and follow the on screen prompts to perform the procedure.

THEORY QUESTIONS

1. What is an operating system? Why is DOS important for a computer system?
2. What is meant by the term Booting? Explain the whole booting process.
3. Explain the directory structure of DOS with examples.
4. What is the difference between a file and a directory?
5. Explain the file naming conventions used by DOS.
6. What are wildcards? Explain by giving appropriate examples.
7. Differentiate between the internal and external commands of DOS by giving suitable examples. Explain and list the internal and external commands of MS-DOS.
8. What is a batch file? What is the difference between a simple batch file and an AUTOEXEC.BAT file?
9. Differentiate between the COPY, XCOPY and DISKCOPY commands with suitable examples.
10. What is the significance of CONFIG.SYS and AUTOEXEC.BAT in DOS?
11. Which of the following are valid file names:
    (*a*) % # $. ABC
    (*b*) Letters.doc
    (*c*) COMPREHEND.A
    (*d*) LYRICS.PATH
    (*e*) 999.53
12. Give the complete syntax of the following commands:
    (*a*) COPY command
    (*b*) RENAME command
    (*c*) FORMAT command
    (*d*) REMOVE DIRECTORY command
    (*e*) CHANGE DIRECTORY command
13. Explain the XCOPY command and the various options (switches) that can be used with it.
14. Write the sequence of commands that will create the following structure of directory:

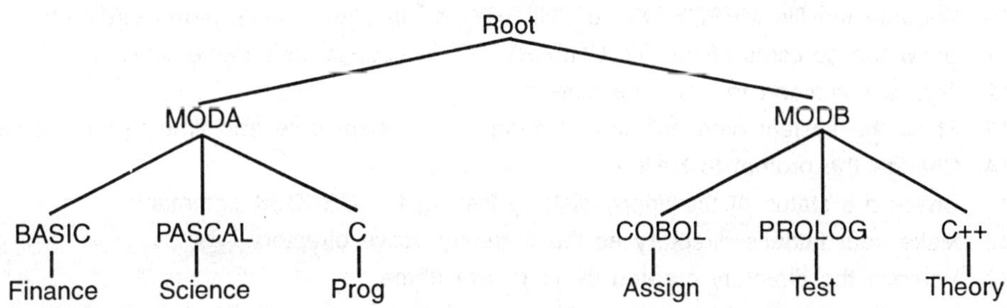

15. Give the syntax of the following commands:
    (*a*) DATE command
    (*b*) RESTORE command
    (*c*) COPY CON command
    (*d*) TYPE command
    (*e*) ATTRIB command
16. Explain the importance of following commands with suitable examples:
    (*a*) CHKDSK
    (*b*) DISKCOPY

(*c*) LABEL
(*d*) FORMAT
(*e*) XCOPY

17. What do you mean by MS-DOS? Why is a file COMMAND.COM considered important as an important file? Write DOS commands to do the following:
    (*a*) To change present working directory to another directory
    (*b*) To check the space available on your hard disk.
18. Write DOS commands to do the following:
    (*a*) Create directory "XYZ" at root.
    (*b*) Copy file "Read me.Txt" from root to "XYZ" directory.
    (*c*) Delete directory "XYZ" with all of its subdirectories and files.

WORKSHOP

Switch on your system. If Windows is installed on your PC, you will see Windows start-up screen. Click at the Start button and choose the 'Shutdown' option. A 'Shut Down Windows' dialog box appears on the screen. Select the 'Restart in MS-DOS mode' option. On the DOS prompt, try the following exercises:

1. Display the listing of files pagewise.
2. Show all the files that are present on your floppy disk widthwise.
3. Give the label by your own name to the disk present in the floppy drive.
4. Insert a new diskette in the floppy drive and format it.
5. Create a sub-directory by your own name in the root directory on the hard disk.
6. Create another sub-directory by your father's name in the root directory on the hard disk.
7. Create a file by the name MERRY.TXT in the directory created by your own name and key in a few lines of text.
8. Copy the file MERRY.TXT into the directory created by your father's name.
9. Delete the file MERRY.TXT from your directory.
10. Rename the file MERRY.TXT to CHERRY.TXT in your father's name directory.
11. Show the contents of the file CHERRY.TXT in your father's name directory.
12. Give a command to clear the screen.
13. Show the system date and time. Change the system date and time to current date and time.
14. Change the prompt to Hello>.
15. Check the status of the floppy disk by issuing the CHKDSK command.
16. Make your father's directory as the currently active directory.
17. Remove the directory created by your own name.
18. Issue the command for going to the root directory.
19. Issue the command for showing the currently active directory.
20. Copy the file CHERRY.TXT to the floppy disk from the hard disk and give it the same name.
21. Copy the file CHERRY.TXT available on the hard disk by a new name Rosy.Txt in the same directory.
22. Delete the file CHERRY.TXT from the hard disk.
23. Copy all the files with an extension EXE onto the floppy disk.
24. Display the message '*It's fun learning DOS*' on the screen.

25. Perform the steps to create a batch file. Create a batch file with name MYFIRST.BAT to do the following steps:
    (*a*) To copy all the files from the floppy disk to hard disk.
    (*b*) To give a listing of all the files present on hard disk.
    (*c*) To delete all the files present on the floppy disk.
26. Create a batch file by the name FUN.BAT that first copies all the files from the floppy disk to the hard disk and then, deletes all the files from the floppy disk.
27. Run the batch file named FUN.BAT.
28. Remove all the directories created by you.
29. Issue the commands–
    (*a*) To create a directory LETTERS on the hard disk.
    (*b*) To create another directory by the name ZONE on the floppy disk.
    (*c*) To go to the root directory.
    (*d*) To display the name of the currently active directory.
    (*e*) To show the listing of files under the root directory (both pagewise as well as widthwise).
    (*f*) To remove all the files with any primary name and extension CAT.
    (*g*) To create a directory PLANNER and copy all the files from the root directory to this directory.
    (*h*) To show all the files having an extension EXE
    (*i*) To create a text file by the name MYFILE.
    (*j*) To rename the file MYFILE as WONDER.
    (*k*) To copy the file Wonder from the root directory to the directory PLANNER.
30. Issue the commands to do the following tasks:
    (*a*) You are currently working in the directory /USR/TEST/PAPER. Change to the directory /SHYAM/PROG/COBOL.
    (*b*) Copy the file from /USR/STUDENT/PROG to /USER/STU/PROG.
    (*c*) Copy a disk floppy in working directory /USER/STU of a hard disk from floppy disk drive A.
    (*d*) Format a floppy disk with boot command file from /USER/STUDENT/TEST in hard disk default drive.

5
FAMILIARISING WITH WINDOWS ENVIRONMENT

5.1 INTRODUCTION

In the last chapter, we discussed about various types of operating systems. We also learnt the concepts of single-user operating system *i.e.* Disk Operating System. In this chapter, we will learn about Windows in quite length. This is most popularly used operating system of today.

5.2 INTERFACE

In order to get all the work done from the computer, interaction with the computer is very essential. However the way you interact with the computer is more important. So, an interface is something that comes to your help. It is a program or a device that bridges the gap between the computer and the user. It can be said that it is the user's gateway into the computer.

UNIX is more popularly known as an interactive system because it responds immediately to your commands. All the systems are not interactive in nature. For instance, the telephone company has got a large number of computers that generate the bill automatically depending upon the number of calls made by the user. These systems are non-interactive. They work on their own according to pre-stored instructions. However, the interactive systems don't do anything by themselves. They allow the different users to work with programs that have been designed and made by programmers. There are a variety of user interfaces available which are discussed below:

5.2.1 Types of interface

Depending on the varied needs of the users, the interface has to comply with all the user requirements. Therefore, there are various types of interfaces available for different types of users. The common types of interface are–

(*a*) System Calls

(*b*) Command Line Interface

(*c*) Graphical User Interface

Let us discuss about these in detail.

5.2.1.1 System Calls

Any user interface requires a software link to the hardware. Therefore, most operating systems provide a set of system calls which are executed by special machine code instructions. However, the use of system calls is absolutely hidden from the user. These system calls can be invoked directly through high-level languages like C, Pascal, etc. by the use of special procedures that are provided in the software package. Invoking a system call is more or less similar to calling any other procedure or function. The main difference is that in a procedure, the object code is part of the calling program whereas in a system call the object code is written in the operating system itself.

5.2.2.2 Command Line Interface

Command line interface allows the user to interact with the operating system through commands given at the command prompt. Such kinds of interfaces are a bit difficult to use. The exact command and its syntax has to be remembered properly for the proper execution of the command. Now, we will see the UNIX and DOS command lines briefly.

(*a*) **Unix Command Interface.** Every command has got syntax or a general format which has to be followed by every user for its execution. For instance, in Unix command system, every command is bound around the following syntax:

```
Command Name [options]    [arguments]
```

In every command, the command name has to be necessarily given. The 'options' and arguments are absolutely optional. The options part comprises of one or more switches. Each switch contains a minus sign followed by one or more characters. For instance, -t, -opt1, etc. The arguments are nothing but values which provide an input to the command. In Unix, the basic interface is the shell. These shells are character-based. So, whenever you use the shell, you have to enter certain commands which are carried out by the shell. For instance, if you want to display the current date, just give in the following command:

```
$date
```

The shell would process your command and would show you the output similar to the one given below:

```
Mon Mar 7 11:40:30 CST 2002
```

Each output line consists of characters which are written at the bottom of the screen. Whenever new output has to be displayed, all the other lines are moved up and the line at the top of the screen disappears. This is called *scrolling*.

Unix provides a command language called *shell*. Commands can be entered directly on the command line. A series of commands can also be gathered and put in a text file to form a shell script. The shell is a very rich system. We will discuss UNIX commands in the next chapter in detail.

(*b*) **DOS Command Interface.** We have already discussed DOS in the previous chapter in great detail. Here, we are just summarising the concept of DOS command interface to distinguish it from the UNIX command interface. As we already know, DOS is a single-user system. Therefore, the MS DOS interface is much simpler than that of UNIX. There are a number of similarities between MS DOS and UNIX like hierarchical directory system and command program files. However, MS DOS does not offer user facilities like login, password, home directory, file ownership and access. The number of commands offered by MS DOS is much less than those offered by UNIX. The general format or syntax of MS DOS commands is similar to UNIX.

```
Command-name [options]    [arguments]
```

In any command, the command name has to be necessarily given. The options switch contains an initial/character. For example,

```
DIR/P
```

where the switch /P shows the output page wise on the screen.

MS DOS uses a program called COMMAND.COM to interpret the commands given by the user. The COMMAND.COM recognises and executes some commands internally. However if COMMAND.COM is not able to recognise any command as internal command, then it needs separate program files for its execution. Some of the commonly used internal commands are DIR, COPY, DEL, CLS, TIME, DATE, etc. Some external commands are FORMAT, XCOPY, CHKDSK, BACKUP, etc. MS DOS also supports batch files that are similar to shell scripts of UNIX. The batch files of MS DOS don't offer very many facilities.

5.2.2.3 Graphical User Interface

The latest advancement in the field of interfaces is the Graphical User Interface (GUI). The GUI is being discussed in detail in the subsequent section.

5.3 OVERVIEW OF GUI

In past, most microcomputers used only DOS as an operating system. Although DOS is essential to operate a computer, but the user interface with DOS is not user friendly. In order to operate the computer, one must learn DOS commands. The user is expected to memorise all DOS commands and understand their correct syntax (rules for writing statements of a language). Therefore, only DOS environment is not considered sufficient for running present day applications on PCs.

5.3.1 What is GUI?

Most of the present day applications related to management and other fields need a graphics-based user interface that is easy to operate. Such a graphics based user interface, that incorporates pull down menus and icons (small pictorial representations of files, programs, storage devices etc.) is known as *Graphical User Interface* (GUI). It provides a very easy and convenient mode of interaction with the user. You are not required to remember the long sequences of command syntax in order to get your work done. GUI's provide everything in the form of pictures and icons. They provide on screen overlapping windows. You can open more than one application at a time. They make use of a pointing device like mouse which enables the user to move the pointer or the cursor on the screen. GUI's provide higher-level devices such as menus, dialog boxes, list boxes, buttons, etc. to ease your work. For example, the operating system of Mac PCs provide graphical user interface (GUI). In IBM-compatible PCs, GUI is provided by an operating environment/ system– 'Windows'.

5.3.2 Features of GUI

GUI's have received widespread acceptance because of the following features:

- Files, directories and other applications can be represented by way of icons which are easy to act upon.
- A number of icons are arranged on the desktop. The desktop can be visualized as a working desk with files organised on it. You can pick any file from the desk, work on it and then close it.
- It extensively makes use of a pointing device called *mouse* which controls the cursor.

- Switching (shooting) facility is provided by GUI's which causes menus to appear and disappear.
- GUI offers facilities such as color dimension, light and video for dynamic interaction.

5.4 WINDOW

A window is rectangular frame in which a file/folder or an application is opened. All the actions such as copying text, deleting text etc. are performed in this window. All windows resemble one another in greater way. The main central area of the window is used to display and interact with the user data which can be either textual or graphical in nature. This window shows only a part of the data that is being processed like a page of a word processed document, etc. You can easily move around the window with the help of a mouse. Figure 5.1 shows the anatomy of a typical window.

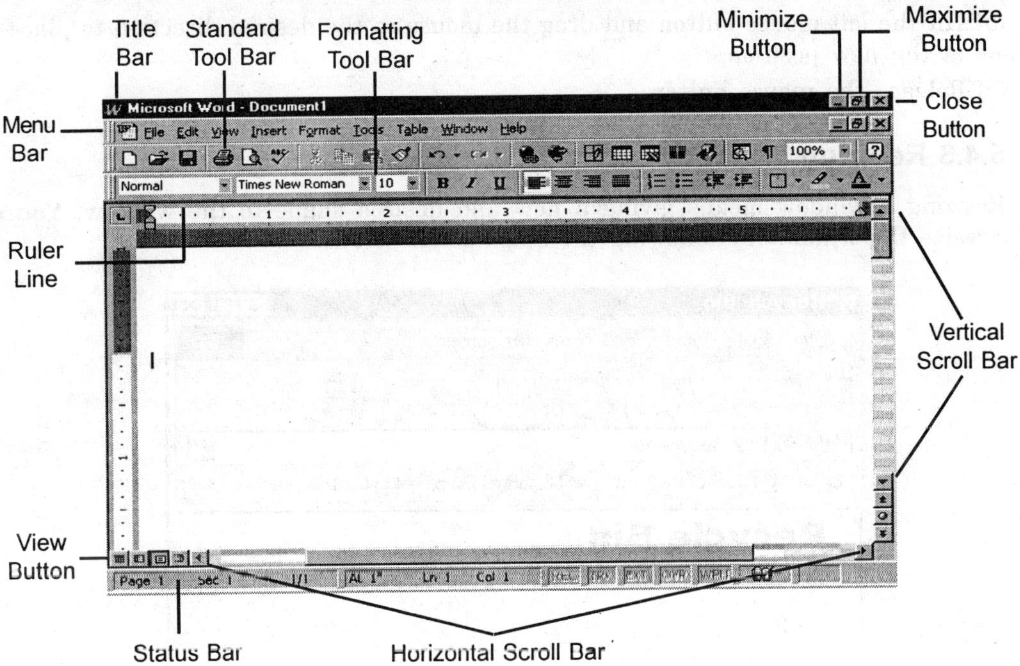

Figure 5.1 *Anatomy of a typical window*

5.4.1 Components of a Window

Let us quickly look at the components of the window shown in Figure 5.1.

(*a*) **Title Bar.** The title bar is always located at the top of the window. It shows the name of the program that is being executed. It also shows the name of the currently open file.

(*b*) **Menu Bar.** Menu bar is located under the title bar and it shows the available menus.

(*c*) **Scroll Bars.** They are used to move through a document or a list when the entire document or list does not fit in the window.

(*d*) **Maximise Button.** It is located in the upper right corner of the screen and it controls the size of the window.

(*e*) **Minimize Button.** It is located in the upper right corner of the screen; towards left of maximize button. It helps to minimize the whole application and show it in the reduced form on the task bar.

(*f*) **Close Button.** This button is present in the upper right corner of the screen. It allows the user to shut down the opened application.

(*g*) **Restore Button.** The maximise button is replaced by the Restore button after the window is enlarged. Clicking at this button returns the window to its previous size.

5.4.2 Moving Windows

A window can be repositioned and resized. Move the window by following the steps given below:

(*a*) Take the mouse pointer at the title bar of the window.

(*b*) Hit the left mouse button and drag the mouse in the desired direction to place the window at the new position.

(*c*) Release the mouse button.

5.4.3 Resizing Windows

Resizing a window means giving a new and desired shape to the window. You can easily resize the window by following the steps given below:

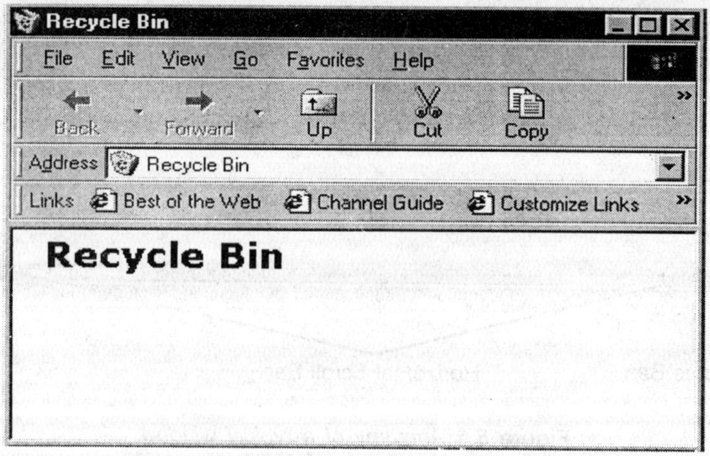

Figure 5.2 *Resizing a window*

(*a*) Take the mouse pointer at the boundary of the window.

(*b*) The pointer will take the shape of a double-headed arrow as shown in Figure 5.2.

(*c*) Hit the left mouse button and drag it in the desired direction.

(*d*) Release the mouse button.

5.5 USING THE MOUSE

A mouse is a pointing device that is extensively used in a graphical environment. The mouse cursor is called the mouse pointer. The main advantage of using a mouse is that it makes navigation very fast and easy in a window. When you move the mouse, the roller present at its back moves which in turn moves the pointer on the screen. You can manage the mouse pointer just by moving the body of the mouse in the direction you want. The tip of the mouse pointer is the action part of the mouse. The mouse pointer takes the shape of a double-headed arrow when taken at the borders of the window. The mouse can perform the following actions:

1. Pointing

Pointing of a mouse refers to the positioning of the mouse pointer at the desired location on the screen. To point at a particular icon or place on the screen, just move the mouse pointer in the direction of the icon or desired location. Stop moving the mouse when the mouse pointer reaches the desired location.

2. Clicking

Clicking of the mouse button is done to activate an icon, menu, menu item, etc. Clicking is the process of pressing and releasing the left mouse button once. To click at an object, first move the mouse pointer and place it on the object. Then press the left mouse button and release it. To right click means to press the right mouse button. A shortcut menu appears when you select an object and right click on it. This shortcut menu offers quick commands that can be performed on the selected object. The shortcut menu shows commands according to the object that has been selected.

3. Double-clicking

Double-clicking refers to the pressing and releasing of the mouse button twice in quick succession. Double-clicking helps in selecting and executing an object. For example, opening a file folder or an application. The keyboard shortcut of double-clicking is the pressing of <Enter> key after selecting it.

4. Dragging and Dropping

Dragging means pressing the left mouse button and moving it while the button is pressed. Dragging is used to move an object on the screen and placing it at a new location. Dragging is also used to select or highlight blocks of text for copying or deleting it. Dropping means placing the object at the desired location by releasing the mouse button.

In short,

- Clicking the left mouse button selects on object without activating it.
- Double-clicking the left mouse button selects an object and activates it.
- Dragging and dropping moves the icons and places them at a new location on the window.

5.6 MENUS AND DIALOG BOXES

You must have observed that many menu options are followed by an ellipsis (...). When such a command is chosen, a box appears in response to that selection which is called a *dialog box*. The dialog box is shown in Figure 5.3. The information is supplied either by typing or by choosing options from the dialog. Let us briefly look at these options.

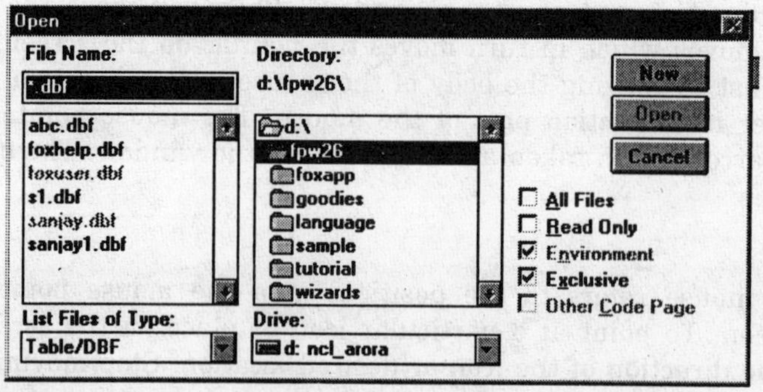

Figure 5.3 *A dialog box*

1. Push button

It is a control that performs an action when chosen. A push button as shown in Figure 5.4(*a*) can be chosen to perform a task immediately. You may be required to provide more information if a push button contains an ellipsis (...)

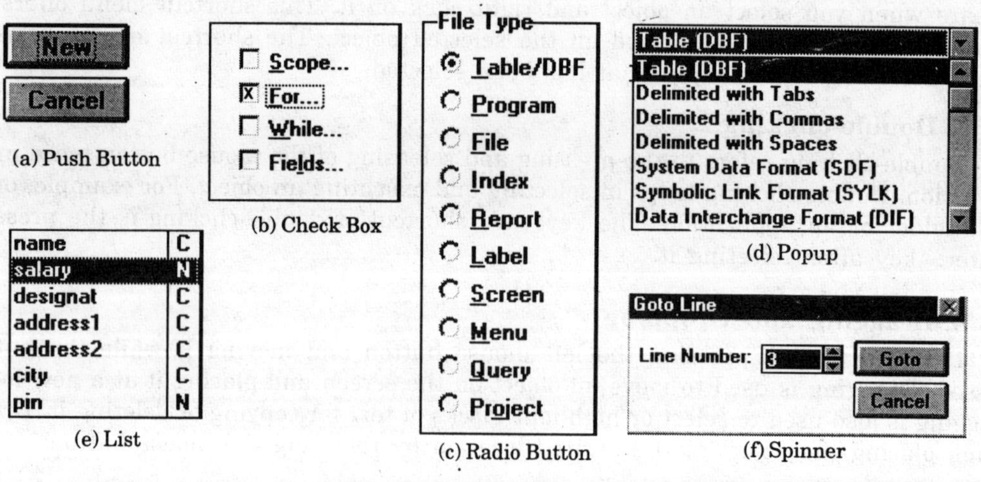

Figure 5.4 *Various buttons of a dialog box*

2. Check Box

It is menu control item that is a small square box followed by a text, label or picture as shown in Figure 5.4(*b*). You can toggle on and off a check box by clicking on it. When a check box is turned on, it displays an {X} in it. Click in the box to turn the check box on or off. You can check multiple boxes simultaneously. Some check boxes are followed by an ellipsis (...). It means that when you choose the check box, another dialog box appears for getting more information.

3. Radio Button

A radio button is a small circular control that resembles a round push button as shown in Figure 5.4 (*c*). It is followed by text. Unlike check boxes, only one radio button in a group can be chosen at once. When a radio button is selected, a bullet appears in the circle and any previously chosen radio button in the group is deselected.

4. Popup

A popup is a rectangle with a down arrow on the right side as shown in Figure 5.4(*d*). Click on the down arrow of the popup to display the list. You can move up and down in the list by using the scroll arrows. Click on the required item to select it.

5. List

A list as shown in Figure in 5.4(*e*) contains choices that can be picked by you. You can scroll through the list that is displayed by using the scroll arrows. Click on the desired item to select it and then choose the appropriate button.

6. Spinner Control

The spinner control is used to spin through the numeric values as shown in Figure 5.4(*f*). A text box is present in the spinner control which is used to enter a number. It contains an up and down arrow. The up arrow increases the value in the associated box on clicking. Likewise, the down arrow decreases the value in the associated text box.

5.7 DIFFERENT VERSIONS OF WINDOWS

Windows is the most popular system software that provides graphical user interface. Windows provides an interface, which is similar to the Macintosh user interface. In such interface, each active application is displayed in a window on the screen as shown in Figure 5.5. The application window can be closed, opened, hidden, displayed, moved, resized, minimised or maximised. The user can run several applications simultaneously, each in its own window. Windows allow the user to share data among different applications. Windows provides an interactive environment, where the user is engaged in continuous dialog with the computer. In windows, although both keyboard and mouse are used as input device, the mouse is the primary tool for selecting and running window applications.

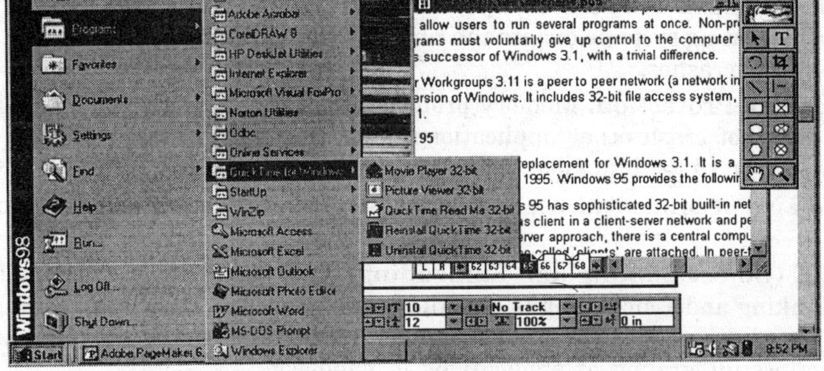

Figure 5.5 *A window screen showing many active applications*

The different versions of windows are Windows 1.x, Windows 2.x, Windows 3.0, Windows 3.1, Windows 3.11, Windows for Workgroups 3.11, Windows 95, Windows 98, Windows 2000 and Windows NT. Windows 1.x, 2.x and 3.0 were the earlier attempts from Microsoft, Inc. for creating graphical user interface but were not very successful. Windows 3.1 and higher versions provide powerful and multi featured GUI capabilities. Windows NT may appear similar to Windows 3.1, but it is based on entirely a different concept.

5.7.1 Windows 3.1/3.11 & Windows for Workgroups 3.11

Windows 3.1 is generally misunderstood as an operating system, but actually it is not an operating system. Windows 3.1 is a graphics-based operating environment that replaces the DOS interface. In order to run Windows 3.1, DOS must be installed on the computer. Windows 3.1 has all the basic features of other GUIs. It also provides non-preemptive multitasking features, which allow users to run several programs at once. Non-preemptive multitasking means the programs must voluntarily give up control to the computer for getting their turn. Windows 3.11 is the successor of Windows 3.1, with a trivial difference.

Windows for Workgroups 3.11 is a peer-to-peer network (a network in which any computer can be server) version of Windows. It includes 32-bit file access system, which is not provided by Windows 3.11.

5.7.2 Windows 95

Windows 95 is a much-awaited replacement for Windows 3.1. It is a 32-bit operating system from Microsoft, released in 1995. Windows 95 provides the following important features:

(*i*) **Built in Networking.** Windows 95 has sophisticated 32-bit built in network components, that allows it to operate both as client in a client-server network and peer-to-peer network operating system. In client-server approach, there is a central computer acting as a file server, with which workstations called '*clients*' are attached. In peer-to-peer networking, every computer connected with network can work as a file server and therefore can share files and printers with other computers.

(*ii*) **Multimedia functions.** Windows 95 provides all multimedia controls and functions. Multimedia is the way of disseminating information in form of text, audio, graphics/animated graphics and full-motion video.

(*iii*) **Preemptive Multitasking.** Windows 95 provides preemptive multitasking features, which are found in operating systems like OS/2 and Windows NT. In preemptive multitasking, operating systems dictate the time slice for each program, resulting in smoother control and fewer crashes.

(*iv*) **Memory Protection.** Memory protection feature of Windows 95 ensures that one application does not crash other applications in memory.

(*v*) **Plug and Play.** Windows 95 automates the hardware configuration process, by knowing the kind of printer, mouse and other peripherals. This feature is known as Plug and Play.

(*vi*) **OLE (Object Linking and Embedding).** OLE is the key technology for Windows 95. Object Linking and Embedding is the Microsoft's standard for creating compound documents (compound document is a document made from different programs) in windows. OLE permits seamless integration of applications in windows.

5.7.3 Windows 98

Windows 98 is the latest upgrade of Microsoft Windows operating system. It makes our computer easier to use by providing new and enhanced features. The major features of Windows 98 are–

(*i*) **Faster than Windows 95.** Windows 98 is a faster operating system. Without adding new hardware, the computer runs faster in Windows 98 as compared to Windows 95. The maintenance wizard of Windows 98 checks the hard disk for problems and frees its space so that the programs run faster.

(*ii*) **Web Integration.** It provides improved web features by combining the power of the computer with the interactive content of the Internet.

(*iii*) **Improved Reliability.** It improves computer reliability by introducing new utilities, wizards and resources which help in running the computer smocthly and efficiently. The new web-based resource site automates driver and system file updates, and provides up-to-date technical support. The system file checker of Windows 98 restores the critical files if they are changed. In Windows 98, scandisk runs automatically if the computer is shut down improperly.

(*iv*) **Multiple Display.** In Windows 98, we can use several monitors simultaneously to run different programs on separate monitors.

(*v*) **Power Management.** Windows 98 improves the startup time of the computer. In Windows 98, we can start the computer in just a few seconds. Windows 98 can restore all the programs in their last saved positions.

(*vi*) **More Entertaining.** Windows 98 provides new features such as enhanced television, video playback and Web TV for Windows that makes our computer more entertaining. Using Web TV for Windows, we can receive and view searchable television program listings provided we have an Internet connection and a TV tuner card installed on our PC.

5.7.4 Windows 2000

Windows 2000 is a line of desktop and NetWare operating systems, which was designed to replace Windows NT. It is built upon the NT Kernel and provides an interface that closely resembles Windows NT and Windows 98. Windows 2000 includes the following parts.

(*i*) **Windows 2000 Professional.** It was designed to replace Windows NT workstation 4.0. It provides improved security, special features for mobile users and better performance.

(*ii*) **Windows 2000 Server.** It was designed to replace Windows NT server 4.0. It provides improved functional and up to two-way Symmetric Multiprocessing (SMP).

(*iii*) **Windows 2000 Advanced Server.** It was designed to replace Windows NT 4.0 Enterprise Edition. It provides large physical memories and up to four-way Symmetric Multiprocessing (SMP).

(*iv*) **Windows 2000 Data Center Server.** It is most powerful server operating system ever offered by Microsoft. It provides up to 64GB of physical memory and up to 16-way SMP.

5.7.5 Windows NT

Windows NT is a secure and an entirely new operating system. It s not a revision of any of the other windows operating systems such as Windows 3.x or Windows for Workgroup

3.x. Unlike earlier versions of Windows, Windows NT is a complete operating system in itself. It does require DOS for low-level functions. When a computer with Windows NT starts up, it starts immediately in Windows NT. Windows NT has successfully overcome the 16-bit limitations (as with the case of MS-DOS). It maintains support for MS-DOS applications as well as Win 16, Win 32, OS/2 and POSIX environments. It comes in two forms:

(*i*) **Windows NT Workstation.** It is designed to work as a client of a Windows NT server domain or as a standalone workstation. It is especially designed for those users who need a reliable operating system with a high level of security.

(*ii*) **Windows NT server.** It is more or less the same as Window NT Workstation. However, it supports some added features that enable it to work as a network operating system.

5.7.5.1 Features of Windows NT

The major features of Windows NT are as follows:

(*i*) **Portability.** Windows NT offers a great flexibility because it can run on a variety of platforms. It frees you from the headache of being tied to a narrow selection of hardware platform. For example, DOS was written for the Intel 8086/8088 family of microprocessors. However, Windows NT was designed to run on Intel 80486 and Pentium based computer as well as Reduced Instruction Set Computers (RISC).

(*ii*) **Multitasking.** Multitasking is the process of running different types of applications simultaneously. In the multitasking environment, one application runs in the foreground and the rest in the background. This is achieved by rapidly switching tasks by scheduling the microprocessor on more than one task at the same time. There are two types of multitasking:

- Co-operative Multitasking
- Preemptive Multitasking

In case of Co-operative Multitasking environment, the control is passed over to a particular application for its execution by the operating system. When that application is over, the control is returned back to the operating system. The control is passed over to the next application so that it can be executed. In this type of environment, the applications perform their work and the control is returned back to the operating system. However, a poorly written application can hang the system because in this case, the control is never returned to the operating system.

In preemptive multitasking environment, the control of the systems always lies with the micro-kernel (as in UNIX). The micro Kernel does the time slicing for the CPU for each process. As and when the allotted time is over, the running process is preempted and the control is transferred to the next process.

(*iii*) **Multithreading.** Windows NT can successfully execute multiple pieces of code or threads from a single application simultaneously. This process is called multithreading. This speeds up the working of the application thereby allowing them to be executed more smoothly.

(*iv*) **Long File Names.** Windows NT offers the "Long File Name" feature of Windows 95/98. The filenames can be 256 characters long.

(*v*) **Security.** Windows NT has been designed keeping security in mind. Windows NT offers the following security features:

- Mandatory logon procedure
- Memory protection, auditing and limited network access.

(*vi*) **Support for many clients.** Windows NT accepts the following clients to serve as its workstation:

- Windows 3.x
- Windows for workgroups
- MS-DOS
- Windows 95/98
- Macintosh
- OS/2
- Windows NT workstation

(*vii*) **Multiprocessor Support.** Windows NT can easily run a computer with multiple microprocessors. This enables multiprocessing applications to run on more than one processor. This capability to support multiple processors is called *scalability*. When running on multiple processors, the Windows NT operating system manages the microprocessors as well as the memory shared by them.

(*viii*) **Compatibility with Applications.** Windows NT can run the following types of applications:

- DOS 16-bit applications
- Windows 3.x 16-bit applications
- POSIX compliant applications
- Win 32 applications

5.8 OVERVIEW OF WINDOWS 98

Window 98, a product of Microsoft is the latest upgrade of its earlier versions (Windows 3.0, 3.1, 3.11 and 95). It is a graphical user interface (GUI) that has been designed to make your work more intuitive and easy. There is no more need of remembering the exact syntax of commands to get your work done. Window 98 is a full fledged operating system. The program files and other resources are generally accessed with the help of mouse. The Windows 98 desktop acts as the primary media for organising your programs, files and resources.

5.8.1 Hardware Requirements

The minimum hardware configuration required for running Windows 98 is given below:

- 486 or Pentium CPU
- At least 8 MB of RAM
- 10 MB to 40 MB of free disk space
- SVGA monitor
- Mouse
- Keyboard

5.8.2 Windows 98 Desktop

So, as and when you switch on your computer, Windows 98 is loaded in the RAM and a desktop appears on the screen as shown in Figure 5.6. This desktop contains folders, files, applications, taskbar and shortcuts. The objects labeled 'My Computer', 'My Briefcase' and 'Network Neighbourhood' are examples of folders. A folder is similar to a directory in DOS. A folder can contain other folders and individual files under it. Thus, to open a folder just double-click it. All the files and folders are shown graphically. Looking at the filename icon, you can easily make out the name of the application to which it is associated. In order to open a file within a folder, simply double-click it. It will open the file with the correct application. Clicking at the object and then holding down the <Ctrl> key on the keyboard and clicking on another object can select multiple objects. You can select as many files and folders as you want.

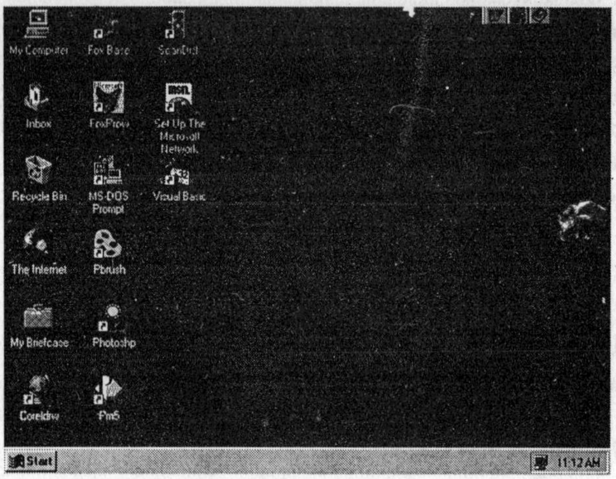

Figure 5.6 *The windows desktop*

Now, to open the folder 'My Computer' just double-click it. All the resources on your computer are shown in it as can be seen in Figure 5.7. Now, if you want to see the files and folders present on your floppy disk, click the object '3 1/2 Floppy (A:)' icon.

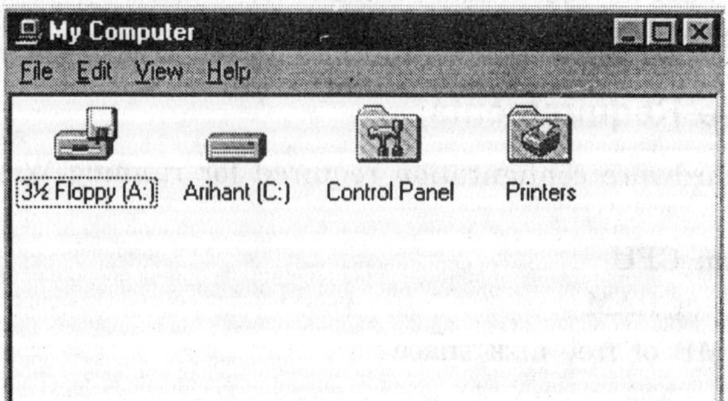

Figure 5.7 *The 'my computer' window*

5.8.3 The Taskbar

Taskbar is located at the bottom of the Windows 98 desktop. It contains a Start button on the left side. On the extreme right side, the taskbar shows the current time. The taskbar also shows all the applications that are currently opened. You can switch between applications using the taskbar. The Figure 5.8 shows that Paint and Aldus Pagemaker 5.0 are the applications that are currently running. The button of the application that is running in the foreground appears depressed. The button that appears raised tells us that the application is running in the background. However, if you want to run any particular application in the foreground, then simply click at that button appearing on the taskbar.

Figure 5.8 *The Taskbar*

5.8.4 The Start Button

The Start Button is a new and much useful feature of Windows 98. Click on it once to display the Start menu. From the Start menu many other menus can be seen. You can activate any of the menu option by selecting it with the help of your mouse pointer. The Start menu is shown in Figure 5.9.

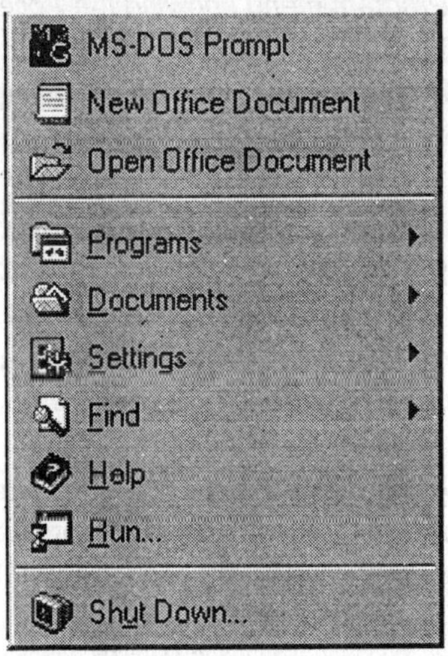

Figure 5.9 *The start button*

(*a*) **The Program Menu.** The Program menu of Windows 98 as shown in Figure 5.10 is exactly similar to the program group found in Windows 3.1. It contains program groups and individual programs. Thus, to launch any program, simply take your mouse pointer at that particular program and click it. In order to open 'Accessories' program group, move the mouse pointer to that group and a cascading menu will appear on the screen. It contains Windows 98 accessory programs such as WordPad, Paint, Notepad, etc.

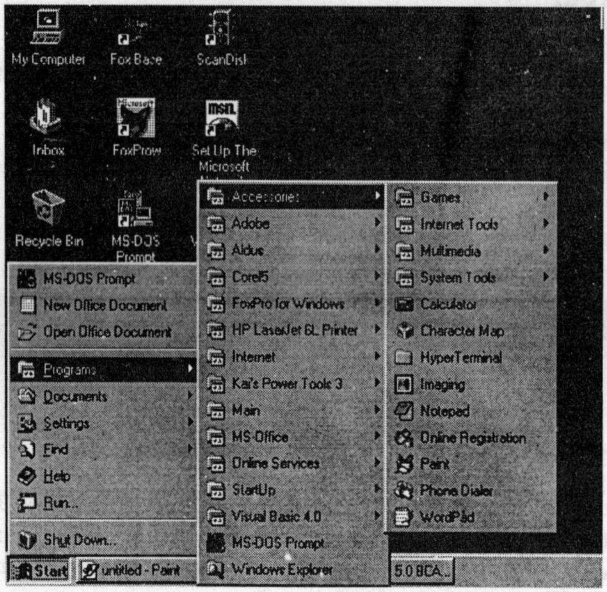

Figure 5.10 The Program menu showing the Accessories group

(*b*) **The Document Menu.** This menu shows you the document that you have recently opened or worked upon. This offers a short way of opening a document. It launches the application in which the document was created. The document menu keeps tracks of the latest fifteen documents that you have used and it puts them in an alphabetical order.

(*c*) **The Settings Menu.** This menu is used for changing the default system setting. You can fiddle with the control panel, printer folder and taskbar setting from here.

(*d*) **The Find Command.** The Find option of the Start menu helps in locating a particular file or a folder. It offers a quick way of finding a file. In the 'Named' box type in the file name you want to search. Accordingly, Windows 98 will return you the full details about the file.

(*e*) **The Help Command.** Windows 98 has got very smart help to offer. In case you find yourself stuck on any issue simply select the Help option from the Start Menu. Above all, you can type in your query in your own words. Windows 98 will display you the related information.

(*f*) **The Run Command.** The Run option of the Start menu helps you to run your file or application straightway. Simply type in the full path and the filename in the 'Open' box and click at 'OK' button. You can also make use of the 'Browse' button in order to locate the required files.

(*g*) **The Shutdown Command.** This command is used for shutting down the system. It offers three options. You can shut down your system, restart your system in windows mode itself or you can switch yourself to DOS mode temporarily. Select appropriate option depending upon your requirement.

5.9 WINDOWS EXPLORER

The File Manager of Windows 3.x is replaced with Windows 98 explorer. It helps you to manage and organise your files and folders. In order to start Windows Explorer, click at the Start menu. Select 'Programs' and then the 'Windows Explorer' option. The 'Windows Explorer' window comes up on the screen as shown in Figure 5.11. This screen lets you explore anything on your desktop. The left part of the explorer screen shows the desktop at the highest level. All the components of the desktop like `My Computer', `Network Neighbourhood', `Recycle Bin', etc. are shown under it. You must have observed that some components of the desktop have a plus sign (+) before them. It shows that there are deeper levels of components under it. On clicking at the plus sign, the next level of the hierarchy is shown. This layering of components continues as long as there are deeper levels of folders or components underneath. The right side of the Explorer screen shows the contents of the folder or the components that are selected in the left part of the Explorer window. The major actions are performed in the right part of the window. Now, we will learn some of the important functions that are performed frequently.

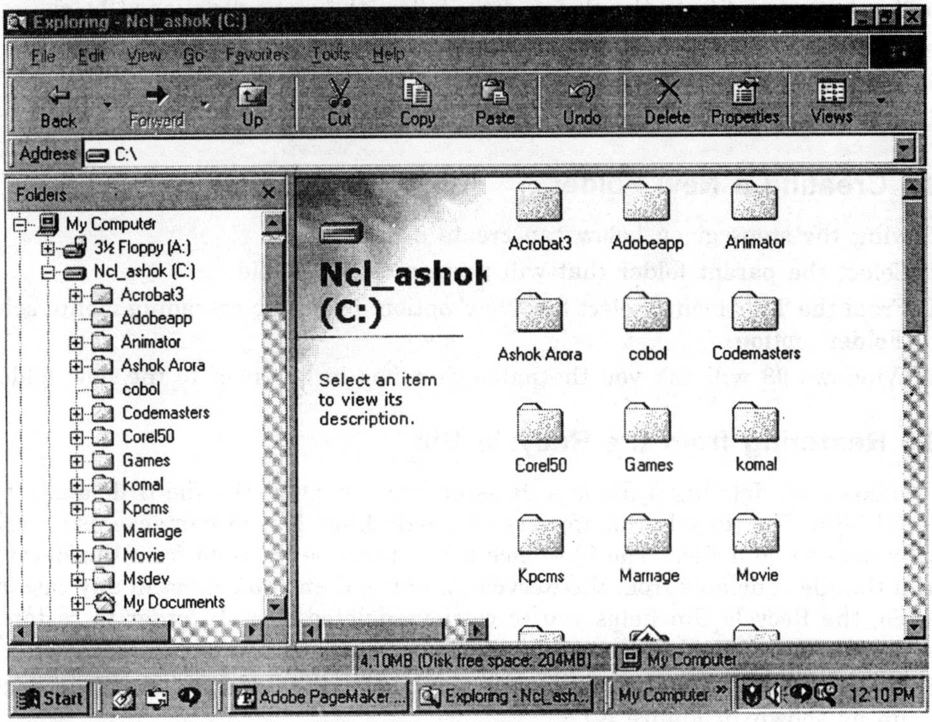

Figure 5.11 *The Windows Explorer*

5.9.1 Renaming a File or a Folder

In order to rename a file or a folder, follow the steps give below:

(*i*) Select the file or the folder that has to be renamed.

(*ii*) Right click the mouse button and select the 'Rename' option.

(*iii*) Type in the new name that you wish to give to the file.

5.9.2 Deleting a File or Folder

A file or a folder can be safely deleted by following the steps given below:

(*i*) Select the file or folder that has to be deleted.

(*ii*) Hit the <Del> key or from the 'File' menu, select the 'Delete' option. Windows 98 will confirm before deleting the file.

5.9.3 Moving a File

Windows 98 allows you to move files from one place to another. A file can be moved from one folder to another by simply performing the following drag and drop procedure:

(*i*) Select the file that you want to move from the right pane of Windows Explorer.

(*ii*) Drag it with the help of mouse and drop it in the new destination.

5.9.4 Copying a File to the Floppy disk

In order to copy a file to the floppy disk, follow the steps mentioned below:

(*i*) Select the file that has to be copied to the floppy disk.

(*ii*) Right click the mouse button and select the 'Send to' option.

(*iii*) From the cascading menu that appears, select the '3 ½ Floppy (A)' option.

5.9.5 Creating a New Folder

Following the steps given below can create a new folder:

(*i*) Select the parent folder that will contain the new folder.

(*ii*) From the 'File' menu, select the 'New' option. From the cascading menu, select the 'Folder' option.

(*iii*) Windows 98 will ask you the name that has to be given to the new folder.

5.9.6 Restoring from the Recycle Bin

In Windows 98, deleting a file is a two-step process. Once the file is deleted, it is put in the Recycle Bin. The Recycle Bin appears on the desktop. It is of immense use if you have accidentally deleted your files. The files once deleted can be restored from the Recycle Bin. However, if the file is deleted from the Recycle Bin also, then you cannot in any case recover your file. So, the Recycle Bin helps you to retrieve deleted files. In order to restore a file from the Recycle Bin, follow the step given below:

(*i*) Double Click the 'Recycle Bin' icon available on the desktop. A dialog box opens up as shown in Figure 5.12.

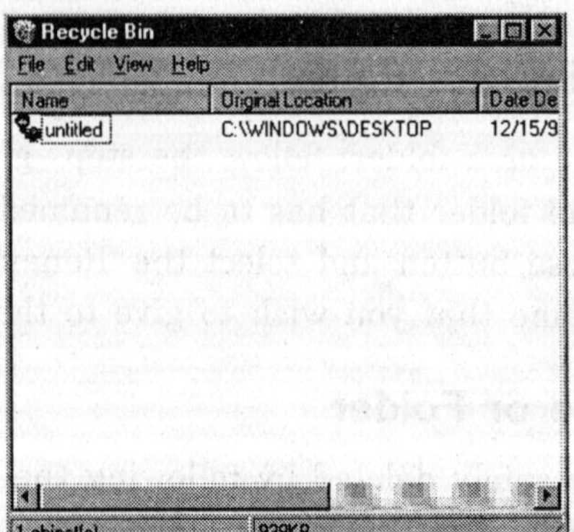

Figure 5.12 *The Recycle Bin*

(*ii*) This window shows all the files that have been deleted. Select the file that you wish to restore.

(*iii*) From the 'File' menu, select 'Restore' option.

5.9.7 Emptying the Recycle Bin

If you wish to delete all the files from the Recycle Bin also, then follow the steps given below:

(*i*) Double-click the 'Recycle Bin' icon present on the desktop.

(*ii*) From the 'File' menu, select the 'Empty Recycle Bin' option.

(*iii*) Windows 98 will ask you to confirm before deleting all the files.

5.10 WINDOWS 98 ACCESSORIES

Windows 98, like its predecessors, contains several built-in accessories that make your computer easier and more convenient to use. In order to access Windows 98 accessories, click on the Start button, move the mouse cursor to 'Programs' and then click at the 'Accessories' option of the cascading menu. We will learn a few of the commonly used built-in accessories of Windows 98.

5.10.1 WordPad

Microsoft WordPad for Windows 98 is a very simple word processing program tnat allows you to create, read and modify simple documents. It is more or less similar to Windows 3.x Notepad program but contains more features and is capable of opening a wider variety of documents. It contains basic file manipulation, editing, viewing and formatting tools that are essential for creating simple documents. It contains standard menu items. The opening screen of WordPad can be seen in Figure 5.13.

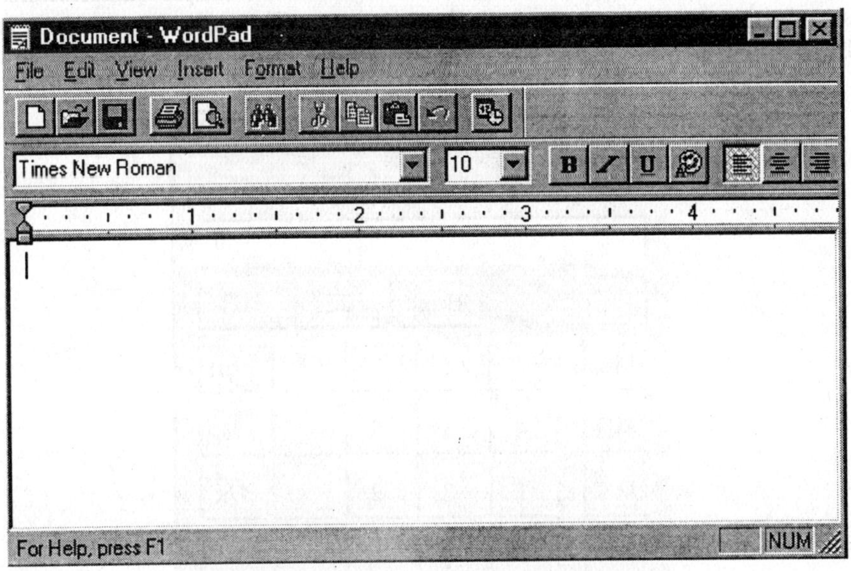

Figure 5.13 *The WordPad application window*

5.10.2 Microsoft Fax

The Microsoft Fax program of Windows 98 helps you to send and receive faxes. It can help you to send the documents that have been created on your computer. You can also send documents directly from compatible applications without even leaving the application e.g. using Word for Windows, you can use the File menu's Send command to direct the output of that application directly to a fax telephone number rather than a printer.

5.10.3 System Tools

Windows 98 contains a number of useful system tools that help you to see and configure your system. Let us briefly discuss a few system tools.

(*i*) **Backup.** This program helps you to perform backups of your computer system.

(*ii*) **Disk Defragmenter.** This system tool reconfigures files on your hard disk so as to speed up disk access times.

(*iii*) **Scan disk.** This utility is more or less similar to the old DOS check disk utility. It scans your disk and gives you the disk status by finding out the used, unused and bad sectors.

(*iv*) **Drive Space.** This utility is a disk compression program that can double up the space on a disk drive. If you need some extra space on your disk you can use this facility.

5.10.4 Entertainment

Windows 98 contains utilities that can control your CD ROM player and multimedia abilities. You can use it to control various aspects of your multimedia system.

5.10.5 Calculator

Windows 98 has a desktop calculator that can perform simple calculations. It contains both the standard as well as the scientific calculator. The calculator has been shown in Figure 5.14.

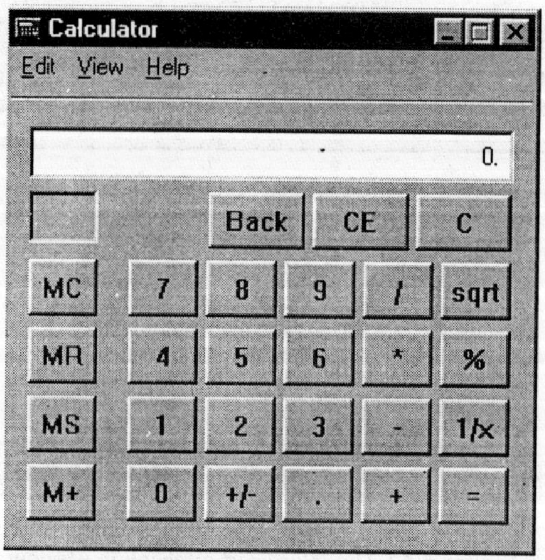

Figure 5.14 *The standard calculator*

5.10.6 Paint

If you are a graphics lover, Window 98 can fulfill your desire. It contains 'Paint' utility that can create simple graphics. You can create, open, view and edit graphic files such as bitmaps, PC Paintbrush files, etc. A typical Paint can be seen in Figure 5.15.

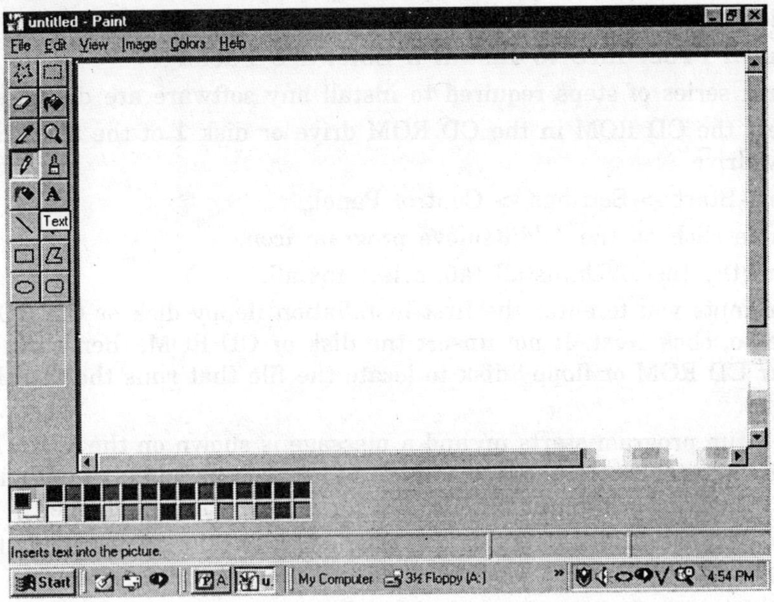

Figure 5.15 *The Paint application window*

5.11 BASIC CONCEPT OF INSTALLING WINDOWS BASED PACKAGES

The very first thing to be done to a new software package is to install it. Earlier, the installation procedure was considered to be very tough and frightening. But, these days, installing software is a very easy work to do because it carries onscreen help instructions. Before installing a software, you have to keep a few things in mind which include checking the hardware and software requirements of the computer system on which the new package has to be installed. Let us discuss them briefly:

1. Hardware Requirements

You should check for the following hardware components before installing a new software package:

- Processor (Whether it is 486 or higher computer)
- RAM (16 MB RAM or higher)
- Sufficient Hard disk space
- CD-ROM drive
- Floppy drive
- Cache Memory
- VGA monitor

The type of processor, RAM and hard disk space requirements vary from one software package to another.

2. Software Requirements

There are many types of operating systems like Windows 98, Windows 2000, Windows NT, UNIX etc. You should select that operating system which fulfills the requirements of the application software package to be installed.

3. General Procedure to Install a Software Package

A general series of steps required to install any software are discussed below:

(*a*) Insert the CD ROM in the CD ROM drive or disk 1 of the $3^1/_2$" installation disk in the floppy drive.

(*b*) Select Start -> Settings -> Control Panel.

(*c*) Double click on the Add/Remove program icon.

(*d*) From the Install/Uninstall tab, select Install.

(*e*) It prompts you to enter the first installation floppy disk or CD ROM. If you have already done so, click Next. If not, insert the disk or CD ROM, then click Next. Windows searches your CD ROM or floppy disk to locate the file that runs the installation. Click at Finish button.

(*f*) The setup program starts up and a message is shown on the VDU. At this stage of the installation, the software package asks you to type your name and other details. In the next step, it asks you to type in the CD Key or a floppy serial number.

(*g*) Now, you are required to give the location where the software has to be saved. So, you can specify the drive along with the folder to install the software.

(*h*) In the next step, you are asked to choose between the typical and the Custom installations. In case of typical installation, the commonly used features are added. The idea behind is to save the disk space. You can add the left out part as and when required. On the contrary the custom installation package adds the whole package. Click at OK button.

(*i*) The installation process begins to copy files to your hard drive. When the software has been installed successfully, a message appears on the screen.

THEORY QUESTIONS

1. What is user interface? How many types of user interface are there?
2. What is Windows 98? Explain the features of Windows 98.
3. What is Windows desktop? Give the names of a few objects present on the desktop.
4. What is Taskbar?
5. Name some of the program groups present in The Program Menu of Windows 98.
6. Write short notes on:
   (*a*) WordPad
   (*b*) Microsoft Fax
   (*c*) System Tools
   (*d*) Multimedia
   (*e*) Calculator
   (*f*) Paint

7. What are GUI's and what are their special features?
8. (*a*) Explain the features of WINDOWS;
   (*b*) How is it different from DOS?
   (*c*) How is the mouse used in WINDOWS?
9. Explain briefly two ways to run an application in Windows 98.
10. What is a compound document and how can it be created?
11. List the different tools provided in the Accessories group.
12. What is a clipboard? How is it useful in Windows based applications?
13. Explain the role of file manager with respect to Windows 98.
14. What are the advantages of using Windows 98 over DOS? Explain the role of the following objects of Windows 98:
    (*a*) The Desktop
    (*b*) My Computer
    (*c*) Recycle Bin
15. Explain the following terms with respect to Windows 98:
    (*a*) My Document
    (*b*) Recycle Bin

WORKSHOP

1. Perform the steps to do the following in Windows 98:
   (*a*) To copy a folder from hard disk to floppy disk.
   (*b*) To create a shortcut for an application.
2. Perform the steps to do the following in Windows 98:
   (*a*) Create a folder in My Document
   (*b*) Copy a file from one folder "A" to another "B"
   (*c*) Send a file from folder "A" to Recycle Bin
3. Perform the steps to rename a folder.
4. Perform the steps to perform the following:
   (*a*) Moving windows
   (*b*) Resizing windows
5. Perform the steps to do the following:
   (*a*) Copying a file to the floppy disk
   (*b*) Restoring files from Recycle Bin
   (*c*) Emptying Recycle Bin

6

GETTING STARTED WITH UNIX

6.1 INTRODUCTION

UNIX is the most popular operating system. UNIX is a multi-user system, which means that more than one person can work at different terminals of the same computer system at the same time. UNIX also supports multitasking. Multitasking means that more than one program can be made to run at the same time. For example, you can initiate a program and leave it by itself to go on and in the meantime you can work on some other program. In this chapter, we will discuss the basic concepts of UNIX operating system alongwith its commands in detail.

6.2 OVERVIEW OF UNIX

Multitasking and multi-user are the two most important characteristics of UNIX that have helped it gain widespread acceptance among a large variety of users. Let us briefly see the hardware requirements, versions and history of UNIX.

6.2.1 Hardware Requirements for UNIX

For any software to run, a certain minimum hardware configuration is required. In order to employ the best ability of UNIX you need:

- 16-bit microprocessor (80286, 386/486, however now only Pentium processor is available).
- An 80 MB of hard disk
- At least 4 MB of RAM
- SVGA monitor
- Keyboard

The UNIX OS files consume 40 MB of the 80 MB disk space. Another 10-20 MB of disk space is eaten up as swap space. This swap space is used at that point of time when UNIX falls short of memory. So, the contents that are not immediately required are stored in the swap space. Any time when the program needs these contents, then they are read from the swap space.

6.2.2 Versions of UNIX

The original version of UNIX actually came from AT&T. Because of the great deal of flexibility offered by UNIX, many new companies emerged and brought out their own variations. Some of the popular versions of UNIX are given in Table 6.1.

Version	Developed by
UNIX	AT & T
AIX	IBM
XENIX	SCO (Santa Cruz Operation)
ULTRIX	DEC (Digital Equipment Corporation)
UNICOS	Cray Research
Sun OS	Sun Microsystems
BSD	University of California at Berkeley
Dynix	Sequent
HP/UX	Hewlett -Packard

Table 6.1 *Popular versions of UNIX*

6.2.3 Brief History of UNIX

The original version of UNIX came in the late 1960's. It was designed by Ken Thompson at AT&T Bell Laboratories. At that point of time, Bell Labs were busy in designing a very big operating system called *Multics*. Their objective was to provide a very sophisticated and complex multi user system which had a support for many advanced features. However, Multics failed because the state of art provided by it at that time was too complex. Therefore, Bell Labs had to withdraw themselves from the Multics project. Ken Thompson then started working on a simpler project and he named it UNIX. This version of UNIX was rewritten in the year 1973. The source code of UNIX operating system was rewritten in C language by Dennis Ritchie, the inventer of C. In order to make UNIX popular among users, AT&T came up with a unique marketing strategy. They started distributing source copies of UNIX to different universities at a very nominal price. This resulted in the widespread popularity of UNIX. In 1974, Thompson and Ritchie described the UNIX System and got it published in a newspaper. This helped in increasing the acceptance level of the UNIX system.

By the year 1977, the UNIX system was installed at around 500 different sites. UNIX system found its major contribution in the operating telephone companies, providing a good environment for program development, network transaction operations services and real time services. A large number of institutions and universities were provided licenses of UNIX system.

So, as the popularity of UNIX grew, many other companies came out with their own versions of UNIX and ported it onto other new machines. From the year 1977 to 1982, Bell Laboratories combined many AT&T variants into a single system and gave it a name UNIX System III. Many new features and advancements were brought out by Bell Laboratories in this version. It was given the name UNIX System V. The people at University of California at Berkeley developed a variant to the UNIX System. Its recent version is called 4.3 BSD for VAX machines. It provided many new and interesting features.

By the beginning of 1984, UNIX system was installed at about 1,00,000 different computer sites. It ran on a wide range of computers ranging from a mini computer to a mainframe. No other operating system can make such a claim. Many of the programs of the UNIX Operating System are written in C. However, the UNIX system can support many other languages also like Fortran, BASIC, Pascal, Ada, COBOL, Lisp and Prolog.

6.2.4 Features of UNIX

UNIX is such an operating system that can be run on a wide range of machines, from micro computers to mainframes. There are a variety of reasons that have made UNIX an extremely popular operating system. Let us discuss these in brief.

(*a*) **Portability.** As of today, there are innumerable computer manufacturers through out the world. Therefore, the hardware configurations also keep varying from one vendor to another. The positive and strong thing about UNIX is that it is running successfully on all these computers. The reason behind UNIX's portability is that it is written in a high-level language that has made it easier to read, understand and change. Its code can be changed and compiled on a new machine. PCs, Workstations, Minicomputers, Super Computers and Mainframes run the UNIX operating system.

(*b*) **Machine Independent.** The UNIX system does not make the machine architecture transparent to the user. Thus, it becomes very easy to write applications that can run on micros, minis or mainframes.

(*c*) **Multi-user Capability.** As discussed earlier, UNIX is a multi-user system. A multi-user system is a system in which the same computer resources like hard disk, memory etc. can be used or accessed by many users simultaneously. Each user is given a terminal (a keyboard and a monitor). Each terminal is an input and an output device for the user. All the terminals are connected to the main computer. So, users sitting at any terminal can not only use the data or the software of the main computer but also the peripherals like printers attached to it. In UNIX terminology, the main computer is called the *server* or the *console*.

(*d*) **Multitasking Capability.** UNIX has the facility to carry out more than one job at the same time. This feature of UNIX is called multitasking. You can keep typing in a program in its editor while at the same time execute some other command given earlier like copying a file, displaying the directory structure, etc. The latter job is performed in the background and the earlier job in the foreground.

(*e*) **Software Development Tools.** UNIX offers an excellent environment for developing new software. It provides a variety of tools ranging from editing a program to maintenance of software.

(*f*) **Built in Networking.** UNIX has got built in networking with a large number of programs and utilities. It also offers an excellent media for communication with other users. The users have the liberty of exchanging mail, data, programs, etc. You can send your data at any place irrespective of the distance.

(*g*) **Security.** UNIX supports a very strong security system. It enforces security at three levels. Firstly, each user is assigned a login name and a password. So, only the valid users can have access to the files and directories. Secondly, each file is bound around permissions (read, write, execute). The file permissions decide who can read or modify or execute a particular file. The permissions once decided for a file can also be changed from time to time. Lastly, file encryption comes into picture. It encodes your file in a format that cannot be very easily read. So, if anybody happens to open your file, even then he will not be able to read the text of the file. However, you can decode the file for reading its contents. This is called *decryption*.

6.2.4.1 What Makes Unix Unique

The following features make UNIX a unique operating system:

- UNIX is the only operating system that is written in a high-level language. This gives it the benefit of machine independence and portability. It becomes very easy to understand, change and move it to other machines.

- It was the first operating system to bring in the concept of hierarchical file structure. It becomes very easy to organise and search for different files.
- It uses a uniform format for files. This makes the application programs to be written easily. This file format is called the *byte stream*. UNIX treats every file as a stream of bytes. Therefore, the user can manipulate his file in the manner he wants.
- It provides primitives that allow the more complex and complicated programs to be built from simpler ones.
- It has a very simple user interface that has the power to provide all the services the users want.
- It hides the machine architecture from the user. This helps the programmer to write different programs that can be made to run on different hardware configurations.
- It provides a simple, uniform interface to peripheral devices.
- It is a multi-user, multiprocess operating system.

6.3 SYSTEM STRUCTURE OF UNIX

The interaction between the user and the hardware happens through the operating system. The operating system interacts directly with the hardware. It provides common services to programs and hides the hardware intricacies from them. The high level architecture of the UNIX system has been shown in Figure 6.1.

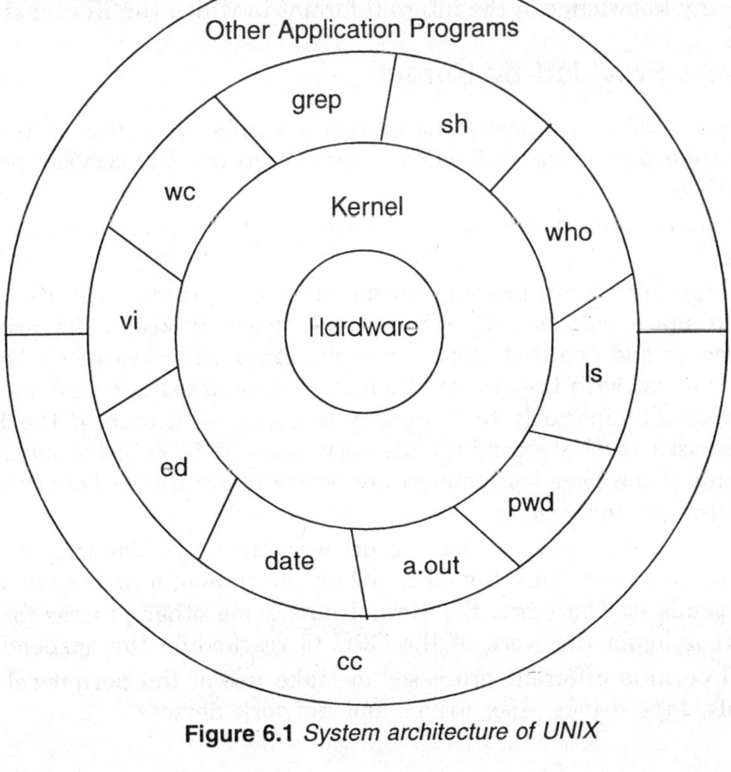

Figure 6.1 *System architecture of UNIX*

The UNIX system seems to be organised as a set of layers. The hardware of a UNIX system is present in the centre of the diagram. It provides the basic services such as memory management, processor execution level, etc. to the operating system. The system Kernel is present in the next layer, which is also called the operating system. The user programs are independent of the hardware on which they are running. Therefore, it becomes very easy to run programs on UNIX system running on different hardware if the programs do make special assumptions. The programs such as the shell and editors like (ed and vi) interact with the Kernel by invoking a well-defined set of system calls. The system calls get various actions done from the Kernel for the calling program. They interchange data between the Kernel and the program. There are many other programs in this layer which form a part of the standard system configurations. These programs are known as *commands*. But there are several other user created programs present in the same layer. It is shown by the program whose name is a.out. 'a. out ' is the standard name for all the executable files produced by the C compiler. The outer most layer contains other application programs which can be build on top of lower level programs. For instance, the C compiler, cc, appears in the outermost layer of the figure. It invokes a C preprocessor, compiler, assembler and link loader. These are all separate lower level programs. The programming style offered by the UNIX system helps us to fulfill a task by combining the existing programs.

The UNIX System V offers somewhere around 64 system calls. However, only 32 system calls are frequently used. These system calls carry very simple options with them. So, it becomes easy to make use of these system calls. The body of the Kernel is formed by the set of system calls and the internal algorithms that implement them. Thus, the Kernel provides all the services to the application programs in the UNIX system. In the UNIX system, the programs do not have any knowledge of the internal format in which the Kernel stores file data.

6.3.1 Services Provided by Kernel

The services provided by the operating system are infact provided by the Kernel. The Kernel performs various operations and acts as a user interface. The services provided by the Kernel are given below:

1. It controls the running of various processes such as their creation, termination and suspension.
2. The Kernel allocates main memory for an executing process. The Kernel allows the processes to share portions of their address space. It keeps the private space of processes secure and does not allow tampering from other processes. However, if the free memory is low with the system, then the Kernel frees out some memory. It then writes a process temporarily to secondary memory. In a case, if the Kernel writes all the processes to the secondary memory, then it is called a *swapping system*. However, only if the pages of memory are written onto the secondary memory, then it is called the *paging system*.
3. The Kernel schedules processes for execution on the CPU. The time-sharing concept allows the processes to share the CPU. When the time of a process has finished, the Kernel suspends it. Therefore, the Kernel puts some other process for execution in the CPU. It is again the work of the CPU to reschedule the suspended process.
4. The Kernel permits different processes to make use of the peripheral devices such as terminals, tape drives, disk drives and network devices.

5. The Kernel allocates the secondary memory for efficient storage and retrieval of user data. The Kernel allocates secondary storage for user files, organises the file system in a well planned manner and provides security to user files from illegal access.

The services provided by the Kernel are absolutely transparent to the user. For instance, the Kernel formats the data present in a file for internal storage. However, it hides the internal format from user processes. Similarly, it makes a distinction between the regular file and a device but hides the distinction from user processes. Finally, the Kernel provides the services so that the user level processes can support the services they must provide. For instance, the Kernel provides the services that the shell requires to act as a command interpreter. Therefore, the Kernel allows the shell to read terminal input, to create pipes (type of files) and to redirect I/O. The computer users can also create private versions of the shell so that they can create an environment according to their own requirements without disturbing the other users.

6.3.2 User Mode and Kernel Mode

Whenever the user on the UNIX system executes a process, then it is divided into two levels: User and Kernel. So, as and when a system call is executed by a process, then the execution mode of the process changes from the user mode to Kernel mode. The Kernel tries to process the requests made by the user. It returns an error message if the process fails. However, if no requests are given to the operating system to service, then also the operating system keeps itself busy with other operations such as handling interrupts, scheduling, processes, managing memory and so on. The main differences between the user mode and the Kernel mode are given below:

1. A process in a user mode can access their own instructions and data but it cannot access the instructions and data of the Kernel. But all the processes present in the Kernel can have the access to both the Kernel and the user addresses.

2. Some machine instructions give an error message when executed in user mode. For instance, a machine may contain an instruction that manipulates the processor status register; processes executing in user mode should not have this capability.

It is very true that the system runs in either the user mode or the Kernel mode. However, the Kernel runs on behalf of the user process. The Kernel is not a separate process running parallel to user processes. The Kernel forms a part of each user process.

6.3.3 Interrupts and Exceptions

The UNIX system allows devices such as I/O peripherals or the system clock to interrupt the CPU abruptly. Whenever the Kernel receives the interrupt, it saves the current work it is doing and services the interrupt. After the interrupt is processed, the Kernel resumes the interrupted work and proceeds as if nothing had happened. The hardware gives a priority number according to the order in which the interrupts should be handled. Thus, when the Kernel looks into an interrupt, it keeps the lower priority interrupt waiting and services the higher priority interrupt.

The term exception is different from the term interrupt. An exception is a condition in which a process causes an unexpected event. For instance, dividing a number by zero, address illegal memory, etc. Exceptions occur in the middle of the execution of an instruction. The system tries to start the instruction again after handling the exception. However, interrupts are considered to happen between the execution of two instructions. The system continues working on the next instruction after servicing the interrupt.

6.3.4 Processor Execution Levels

Sometimes, the Kernel must stop the interrupt from occurring during critical activity. This could corrupt the data being handled. For instance, the Kernel might not want to handle an interrupt when it is working with linked lists (data structures) because handling the interrupt at this point of time might lead to corruption of pointers (memory addresses). Therefore, a better technique has been worked out. The processor execution levels can be set with the help of certain instructions. If you set the processor execution level to certain value, then it can keep away the interrupt from that level and lower levels. It will only allow the high level interrupts to disturb the process.

6.4 PERSONALISED UNIX: PASSWORDS AND LOGIN

In order to communicate with the UNIX command shell, you first need to learn as to how to log in to your account. As you already know, UNIX is a multi-user system, you can start by finding a terminal, a computer or any other way to access the system. You first have to go through the login process no matter how you access UNIX. When you actually login, you will use a name and password initially assigned by the system administrator.

6.4.1 Steps to Login

1. Logging in is a procedure that tells the UNIX System who you are. The system responds by asking you the password. So, in order to log in, first, connect your PC to the UNIX system. After a successful connection is established, you would find the following prompt coming on the screen.

```
Login:
```

Each user on the UNIX system is assigned an account name which identifies him as a unique user. The account name has eight characters or less and is usually based on the first name or the last name. It can have any combination of letters and numbers.

2. Thus, if you want to access the UNIX resources, you should know your account name first. If you don't as yet have an account name, ask the system administrator to assign you one. Now, at the login prompt, enter your account name. Type your account name in lowercase letters. UNIX treats uppercase letters differently from lowercase letters.

```
Login : ritik
Password:
```

3. Once the login name is entered, UNIX prompts you to enter a password. While you are entering your password, it will not be shown on the screen. This is just a security measure adopted by UNIX. The idea behind is that people standing around you are not able to look through the secret password by looking at the screen. Be careful while you are typing your password because you will not be able to see what you have typed. However, if you give either the login name or the password wrong, then UNIX denies you the permission to access its resources. The system then shows an error message on the screen as given below:

```
Login : ritik
Password:
```

```
Login incorrect
Login:
```

Many UNIX systems give you three or four chances to enter your login and password correct. So, key in your correct login name and the password again.

4. Once you have successfully logged on by giving a correct login and password, you are given some information about the system, some news for users and a message whether you have an electronic mail or not.

```
Login: ritik
Password:
Last login: Sun May 14 19:00:29 on ttyAe
You have mail
$
```

The dollar sign is the UNIX's method of telling that it's ready to accept commands from the user. You can have a different prompt also in a case where your system is configured for showing a different prompt. By default a $ is shown for the Korn or Bourne Shells about which we will learn in the next chapter.

5. At this point, you are ready to enter your first UNIX command.

6.4.2 Logging Out

Now, when you are done working on your UNIX system and decide to leave your terminal - then it is always a good idea to log off the system. It is very dangerous to leave your system without logging out because some mischievous minds could tamper with your files and directories. They can delete your files. They can also read through your private files. Thus, logging off the system is always a better idea than turning off your terminal. In order to log off the system, type the following command:

```
$ exit
login:
```

The above command will work if you are using a Bourne or a Korn shell. However, if you are working on C shell, exit will work or you can give another command to log off.

```
$ logout
login:
```

6.4.3 What Can Go Wrong When Logging In?

In order to maintain security, UNIX system is very particular not to allow the unauthorized users to access the system. So, when a message like 'Login denied' comes on the screen, it does not tell you what was wrong with your login. You can say that the UNIX system is a little vague when it denies you access to the system. There could be a few things you could keep in mind while logging in.

1. UNIX is very much case sensitive. Entering SAFARI is different from Safari in UNIX. So, keep in mind the case of characters while entering otherwise it can really frustrate you.

2. While entering a username or password, you could have accidentally mistyped a character. This can change the meaning of the information you have typed in. Thus, in order to remove the mistyped character, make use of the Backspace key. It will help you to erase off the misspelled character.

3. You can also have a slow system. If you have entered the login information and nothing happens, then the system might have slowed down especially when many people are trying to log on simultaneously. However, if your system does not respond after several minutes, then you need to check up with your system administrator to make sure that the system is functioning properly.

Sometimes, it might happen that you have keyed in the correct information and still you are told that the information given by you is incorrect. Under such circumstances, you are required to check up with your system administrator. Possibly, he could have changed your login name or the password.

6.4.4 Choosing a New Login Name and Password

It is a good practice to choose good secret passwords or combinations and keep them secure. Here are a few tips for selecting the right login name and password.

1. Your login name should not be less than two characters and normally should not exceed eight characters. Moreover, it should begin with a lowercase.

2. Choose a password that is greater than at least six characters. The smaller the password, the more vulnerable it is to be leaked out.

3. Don't at all use easily guessable words like sun, moon, stars, etc.

4. Don't choose a password based on personal information like your spouse name, your middle name, your surname, your job title, etc.

5. The password cannot include spaces in it.

6. Never choose a password that is very complicated and not easily memorizable. In such a case, the chances of leaving a copy of the password on a piece of paper near the computer increase. Therefore, keep a password that is neither too short, nor too difficult to remember.

7. You should avoid picking up a password from the computer dictionary.

6.5 DIRECTORIES AND FILES IN UNIX

The operating system is responsible for things like where the parts of a file are physically stored on a disk. The concept of 'directories' originates from the need to know where the operating system stored the file.

6.5.1 What is a Directory?

A directory is a special file that can contain other files under it. The basic idea of a directory structure is to ease the job of finding a file. Thus, a directory can be thought of as a file folder containing files. It is always a good idea to keep all the related files under one directory. You can also keep directories within directories which are in term called *sub-directories*. There is exactly no limit to the number of directories and sub-directories that can be kept under a UNIX system. In a way, you can say that every directory in UNIX is really a sub-directory. You can compare your hard disk to a file cabinet wherein your top-level directories can be thought of as drawers, the sub-directories as file folders and actual files as pieces of paper. Any directory in which you are working is considered to be the current directory. All the directories under the current directory form the sub-directory. You should always avoid keeping all the files under one directory because-this will mess-up your directory structure. In order to keep your directory structure handy and easily manageable, organize your files by creating several directories. A typical directory is shown in Figure 6.2.

The directory structure can be thought of as an inverted tree. It has Root directory at the top. The sub-directories under it form the branches. Thus, the directory structure always keeps growing towards the bottom side. The files form the leaves of the directory structure. You can add any number of files and directories under the Root directory. Let us now see the example given in Figure 6.2. At the top, there is a Root directory. The Root directory contains three sub-directories named 'Purchase', 'Accounts' and 'Sales' under it. Each sub-directory further contains sub-directories under it. For instance, there are two sub-directories 'Computer' and 'Printer' present under the sub-directory 'Purchase'. Each sub-directory such as 'Computer' can contain several files under it. Technically, the file system of UNIX is called a hierarchical file system.

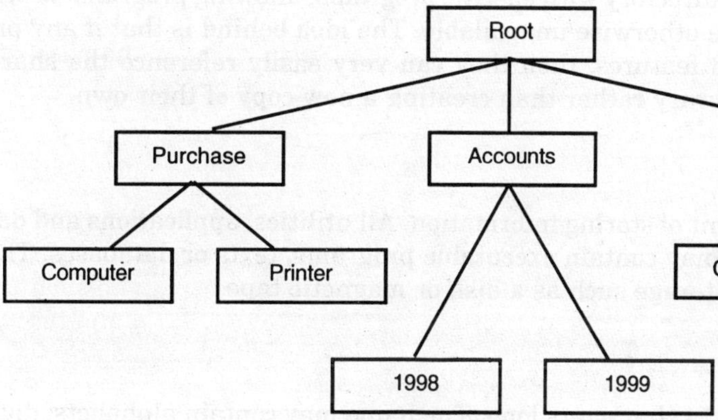

Figure 6.2 *An example of a directory structure*

6.5.2 The Directory Organisation

There are many directories which UNIX keeps and maintains by itself. Some of these directories are discussed below.

6.5.2.1 The bin Directory

The bin directory contains most of the standard UNIX programs and utilities. In UNIX, programs are considered executables because the users can execute such programs. All the programs are compiled in UNIX and then translated into a binary format. The bin directory is place where all the executable binary files are kept.

6.5.2.2 The dev Directory

The dev directory contains device files of UNIX. Without device drivers, you cannot perform major activities on the computer system. For instance, in order to get information on the screen, you need the display device driver. Similarly, to enter information in the computer, the keyboard device driver is used. The floppy disk can be used with the help of floppy device driver. All device drivers that range in hundreds of files are all stored in the standard UNIX dev directory.

6.5.2.3 The etc Directory

The etc directory contains all files except device files and program files. System administrators use this directory to store system configurations as well as user profiles. These files are modified very rarely. Most of these files can be accessed by the system administrator only.

6.5.2.4 The tmp Directory

The tmp Directory is used for storing temporary working files. For instance, if you are a editing file, the program makes a copy of the file and saves it in tmp and you can directly work with that file. This allows you to save the new file back to your original file only when you have completed your work.

6.5.2.5 The lib Directory

UNIX has a central storage place for function and procedural libraries. These specific executables are included in the lib directory with specific programs, allowing programs to offer features and capabilities which are otherwise unavailable. The idea behind is that if any program needs to include some extra features, then they can very easily reference the shared copy of that utility in the UNIX library rather than creating a new copy of their own.

6.5.3 What is a File?

File, in a UNIX system is a unit of storing information. All utilities, applications and data are represented as files. The files may contain executable programs, texts or databases. They are stored on secondary memory storage such as a disk or magnetic tape.

6.5.4 Naming Files

You can give filenames up to 14 characters long. The name may contain alphabets, digits and a few special characters. Files in UNIX do not have the concept of primary or secondary name as in DOS, and therefore file names may contain more than one period (.).

Therefore, the following file names are all valid filenames:

```
mkt.c        name2.c      .star      a.out
```

However, UNIX file names are case sensitive. Therefore, the following names represent two different files in UNIX.

```
mkt.c        Mkt.c
```

6.5.5 File Types

The files under UNIX can be categorized as follows:

1. Ordinary files.
2. Directory files.
3. Special files.
4. FIFO files.

We are discussing about these files below.

6.5.5.1 Ordinary Files

Ordinary files are the one, with which we all are already familiar. They may contain executable programs, text or databases. You can add, modify or delete them.

6.5.5.2 Directory Files

Directory files, as discussed earlier also represent a group of files. They contain list of file names and other information related to these files. Some of the commands, which manipulate these directory files, differ from those of ordinary files.

6.5.5.3 Special Files

Special files are also referred to as device files. These files represent physical devices such as terminals, disks, printers and tape-drives etc. These files are read from or written into just like ordinary files, except that operation on these files activates some physical devices. These files can be of two types – Character device files and block device files. In character device files, data is handled character by character, as in case of terminals and printers. In block device files, data is handled in large chunks of blocks, as in the case of disks and tapes.

6.5.5.4 FIFO Files

FIFO (First-In-First-Out) are files that allow unrelated processes to communicate with each other. They are generally used in applications where the communication path is in only one direction, and several processes need to communicate with a single process. Pipe is an example of a FIFO file in UNIX. This allows transfer of data between processes in a first-in-first-out manner. A pipe takes the output of the first process as the input to the next process, and so on.

6.5.6 UNIX File System Organisation

A key concept, which makes the UNIX hierarchical file system to be so effective, is that anything that is not a directory is a file. In a UNIX system, all programs are considered as files. Device drivers are files, documents and spreadsheets are files, even your keyboard, display and mouse are represented as files.

The top level of the UNIX file structure contains a Root directory. By default, this directory is always present at the top of the directory tree. You as a user cannot create or delete it. The Root directory is represented by / (backslash). The Root directory always contains subdirectories under it such as bin, dev, etc, lib, mnt, tmp and usr. A typical UNIX hierarchical file structure is being shown in Figure 6.3.

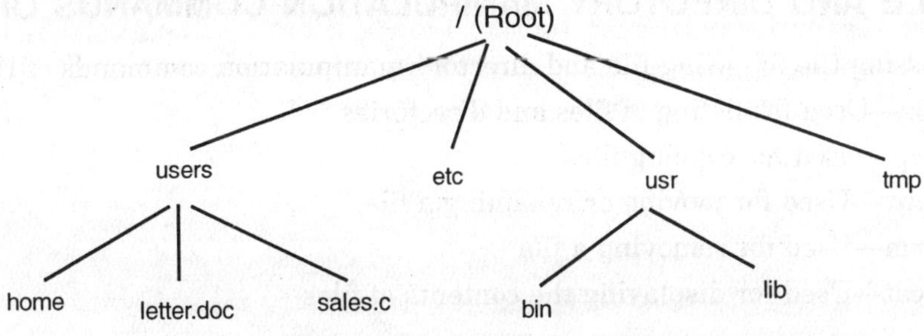

Figure 6.3 *A typical UNIX hierarchical file structure*

However, there is no limit to the number of directories and sub-directories that can be put within the UNIX structure. So, when you login, you are immediately put into the 'home' directory. From the `home' directory only, you can navigate here and there in the file structure.

6.5.7 Relative and Absolute Filenames

Specifying the location of a file in a hierarchy to ensure that the filename is unique is known as the absolute filename. This is regardless of where you are in the whole file system. The absolute filenames always refer to a particular filename. However, the relative filenames help to describe the files that are referenced relative to an assumed position in the file system.

6.6 FILE SECURITY AND OWNERSHIP

The data is centralized on a system working with UNIX. However, if you do not take care of your data, then all other users who login can access it. The first step towards data security is the usage of passwords. The next step should be to guard the data among these users. If the number of users is small, it is not much of a problem. But it can be problematic on a large system supporting many users. UNIX can thus differentiate a file belonging to an individual, the owner of a file or group of users or the others with different limited accesses, as the case may be. The different ways to access a file are:

- Read (r) – You can just look through the file
- Write (w) – You can also modify it
- Execute (x) – You can just execute it

Therefore, if you have a file called vendor.c and that you are the owner of it, you may provide yourself with all the rights rwx [read, write and execute]. You can provide rx (read and execute) rights to the members of your group and only the x (execute) right to all others.

Normally, when you create a file, you are the owner of the file and your group becomes the group id for the file. The system assigns a default set of permissions for the file, as set by the system administrator. The user can also change these permissions at his will. But only a superuser can change these permissions (rwx), ownership and group id's of any file in the system. Giving the execute permission to the data file is absolutely meaningless. Similarly, giving the write (w) permission to an executable file does not carry any sense. The execute (x) permission on directories mean that you can search through the directory and the write (w) permission means that you can create or remove files in the directory. The read (r) permission means that you can list the files in the directory.

6.7 BASIC FILE AND DIRECTORY MANIPULATION COMMANDS OF UNIX

We are discussing the following file and directory manipulation commands of UNIX:

1. ls—Used for listing of files and directories
2. cp—Used for copying files
3. mv—Used for moving or renaming a file
4. rm—Used for removing a file
5. cat—Used for displaying the contents of files

6. pwd—Used for printing current working directory
7. mkdir—Used for making a new directory
8. cd—Used for changing a directory
9. rmdir—Used for removing a directory
10. chmod —Used for changing access permission for files
11. chown—Used for changing owner
12. chgrp—Used for changing group

UNIX Command Structure: Some UNIX commands can be typed as stand alone. For example, is date, pwd, logout and so on. But UNIX commands generally require some additional options and/or arguments to be supplied in order to extract more information. Let us find out basic UNIX command structure.

The UNIX commands follow the following format :

Command[options] [arguments]

The options/arguments are specified within square brackets if they are optional. The options are normally specified by a '-' (hyphen) followed by letter, one letter per option.

6.7.1 The ls Command

The ls command is used for listing information about files and directories.

Syntax: ls [-options] [filename]

Here, filename can be the name of the directory or file. If it is a directory, it lists information about all the files in the directory and if it is a file, it lists information about the file specified.

Options:

-a	–	List all directory entries including . (dot) entries.
-d	–	Give the name of directories only.
g	–	Print group id only in the long listing.
i	–	Print inode number of each file in the first column.
l	–	Lists in the long or detailed format owner's id only in the long listing.
r	–	Reverse the order in which file names are sorted.
s	–	This lists the disk blocks (of 512 bytes each), occupied by a file.
u	–	Sort file names by time since last access.
t	–	Sort file names by time since last modified.
C	–	Display files in columns.
R	–	Recrusively lists all subdirectories.
F	–	Marks type of each file.

You can make use of more than one option at a given time, just group them together and precede them with "-".

Examples:

(*i*) *$ ls -l /usr/mkt*

The above command gives a long listing of the mkt directory, which is inside the usr directory as illustrated below:

drwxr-x—x 3 bobby engineer 79 may 15 15:22 bin

-rwxr-x—x 2 bobby engineers 422 jan 12 10:38 sale.c

(*ii*) `$ ls-1/dev`

The above command gives a typical listing of the dev directory in the root as illustrated below:

crw- -w- -w- 1 root 0,0 Feb 19 12:05 console

brw- - - - - - - 1 root 0,1 Feb 19 11:08 hpob

brw-rw- - - - 1 root 6,2 Jun 06 11:18 ntl

crw-rw- - - - 1 gemale 1,5 Feb 10 12:30 ttyo4

Let us now analyze the different parts of the output shown above:

-	rwxr-x—x	15	bobby	engineer	422	Jan1210:38	purchase.c
1	2	3	4	5	6	7	8

From the leftmost column:

1st column denotes file type. It can be:

-	for ordinary file
d	for directory file
c	for character device file. Here, it is an ordinary file.

2nd column denotes file permissions for the owner, group and others respectively from left. The permissions can be:

r	read permission
w	write permission
x	execute permission
-	no permission

Therefore, here rwxr-x—x means the owner has read, write and execute (rwx) permissions, the group has read and execute (r-x) permissions and all others have only execute (x) permission.

3rd column shows, that there are two links to this file.

4th column shows, that bobby is the owner of this file.

5th column shows, that engineer is the group name to which the owner belongs to.

6th column shows that the file size in bytes is 422.

7th column here shows that Jan 12 10:38 is the date and time when the file was last modified.

8th column here shows that the filename is sale.c

6.7.2 The cp Command

The cp command creates a duplicate copy of a file.

Syntax: `cp file1 file2`

Options: `None`

The cp command of UNIX copies one file to another. It can also copy one or more files to a directory. Here, the file1 is copied as file2. If file2 already exists, the new file overwrites it. The file names specified may be full path names or just the file name (current working directory will be assumed).

Examples:

(*i*) `$ cp mkt.c new_mkt.c`

Here the file 'mkt.c' which is present in the current directory will be copied as 'new_mkt.c' in the same current directory.

(*ii*) `$ cp *.c /usr/mkt`

The above command will copy all the files ending with the letter '.c' to the directory called mkt present under usr directory.

6.7.3 The mv Command

This command moves or renames files.

Syntax : `mv file1 file2`

Options: None

The mv command moves a file from one directory to another. Here 'file1' refers to the source filename and 'file2' refers to the destination filename. Moving a file to another within the same directory is equivalent to renaming the file. Otherwise also, mv does not really move the file, it just renames it and changes directory entries.

Examples:

(*i*) `$ mv *.c /usr/mkt`

This command will move all the files ending with the letter '.c' to the directory called 'mkt'.

(*ii*) `$ mv mkt.c new_mkt.c`

Here, mv will rename the file 'mkt.c' present in the current working directory as 'new_mkt.c' in the same working directory.

6.7.4 The rm Command

The 'rm' command removes files or directories.

Syntax: rm [options] file(s)

This command is used for removing either a single file or a group of files.

Options:

i – confirms on each file before deleting it.

f – removes only those files which do not have write permission.

r – deletes the directory and its contents along with all the sub-directories and their contents.

Examples:

(*i*) `$ rm -ir /usr/mkt/new_mkt.c`

The above command will remove all the files and sub-directories (and their contents) of the mkt directory and the mkt directory itself.

(*ii*) `$ rm /usr/mkt/*.c`

This will remove all the c program files (.c) from the mkt directory.

6.7.5 The cat Command

It displays the contents of a file onto the screen.

Syntax : `cat file....`

The cat writes the contents of one or more files onto the screen in the sequence specified. If you do not specify an input file, cat reads its data from the standard input file, generally the keyboard.

Examples:

(*i*) `$ cat /usr/mkt/new_mkt.c`

This command will display the contents of c program file 'new_mkt.c' onto the screen.

(*ii*) `$ cat`

The above command will get the input from the keyboard as illustrated below:

My first UNIX session.

I am enjoying learning UNIX.

6.7.6 The pwd Command

The pwd command is used for printing the complete pathname of your current working directory, *i.e.* the directory you are presently in.

Syntax: `pwd`

Options: None

Example: `$ pwd`

Output: /usr/project1/mkt

6.7.7 The mkdir Command

This command helps you to create new directories.

Syntax: `mkdir dir1 [dir2.....]`

The mkdir command allows you to create new directories. You can specify more than one directory name in a single command but they should carry different names. The directory names that you specify can be an absolute or relative pathname. The new directories created will be empty except for containing the dot entries, which are used by the UNIX system.

Options: None

Examples:

(*i*) `$ mkdir lesson`

This will create a directory called 'lesson' in you current working directory.

(*ii*) `$ mkdir /usr/plan`

This will create a directory called 'plan' inside the 'usr' directory.

6.7.8 The cd Command

The cd command helps you to change from one directory to another.

Syntax: `cd [directory name]`

The cd command changes from your current directory to the newly specified directory. This command without an argument takes you to HOME directory. You can use pwd to check whether you have arrived at the current directory or not.

Options: None

Examples:

(*i*) `$ cd lesson`

The above command will take you to the 'lesson' directory.

(*ii*) `$cd /usr/plan`

This command takes you to the plan directory under the usr directory.

(*iii*) `$cd`

This takes you to your Home directory.

On issuing the pwd command, you can see your HOME directory.

```
$ pwd
/usr/mkt
```

6.7.9 The rmdir Command

The rmdir removes directories from the disk.

Syntax : `rmdir dir1 [dir2..]`

This command removes one or more directories from the directory system. You can specify more than one directory name but separated by commas. In order to remove a directory, you should have the write permission with you. The directory that you are trying to remove should not contain any files and directories under it. The directory to be removed should not be the current directory.

Examples:

(*i*) `$ rmdir lesson`

This will remove the 'lesson' directory, present in your current working directory.

(*ii*) `$ rmdir/usr/plan`

This will remove the plan directory, present inside the usr directory.

6.7.10 The chmod Command

The command chmod will change access permission to a file.

Syntax: `chmod [for whom] operation permission file name.`

A file is assigned default permissions when it is created so that it is accessed by the owner, group and others. The owner can change these permissions at his discretion using these commands. But only a superuser can change these permissions for any file on the system. In the syntax, 'For whom' denotes the user type, and can be:

u	user or the file owner
g	the group to which the file owner belongs
o	other users, not part of the group
a	all users

'Operation' denotes the options to be done, and can be:

+	add permission
-	remove permission
=	assign permission

'Permission' can be:

r	read permission
w	write permission
x	execute permission

The filename(s) can be:

the files on which you want to carry out this command.

Example:

(*i*) First see the file permissions using the ls –l command for mkt.c as shown below:

```
$ ls -l mkt.c
```

Output:

```
-rwx- -x- -x 2 root other 1428 May 15 07:34 mkt.c
```

i.e. user has rwx, group has x and all others also have x permission.

(*ii*) Now use the chmod command as illustrated below:

```
$ chmod u-x g+w  o+r mkt.c
```

The above command remove execute (x) permission for user, give write (w) permission to group and give read (r) permission to all others.

(*iii*) Then again use the ls -l command to verify, if the permissions have been set or not.

```
$ ls -l mkt.c
```

Output:

```
-rw- -wxr-x 2 root other 1428 May 15 07:34 mkt.c
```

Alternatively, you could have also used the following commands to do the same work:

```
$chmod u=rw g=wx o=rx mkt.c
```

If we use

```
$ chmod a=rwx mkt.c
$ ls -l mkt.c
```

Output:

-rwxrwxrwx 2 root other 1428 May 15 07:34 file.c

In the above command, a=rwx assigns read, write and execute permission to all users.

6.7.11 The chown Command

The chown command changes the owner of the specified file(s).

Syntax : `chown new-owner filename`

The chown command changes the owner of the specified file(s). This command requires you to be in the superuser mode. The new owner can be the user ID of the new owner or the new owner's user number. You can also specify the owner by his name. But the new owner should have an entry in the /etc/passwd file. The filename is the name(s) of the file(s), whose owner is to be changed.

Options: None

Example:

(*i*) `$ chown bobby sales.c`

The above command now makes bobby the owner of sales.c file

(*ii*) `$ ls -l sales.c`

Output:

```
-rwxr-x- - x 1 bobby engineer 1826 May 15 17:56 sales.c
```

6.7.12 The chgrp Command

The purpose of chgrp command is to change the group of a file.

Syntax: `chgrp group filename`

Only the superuser can use this command. This command changes the group ownership of a file. Here group denotes the new group-ID and filename denotes the file who's group-ID is desired to be changed.

Example:

```
$ chgrp shefali sales.c
```

This changes the group-ID of the file 'sales.c' to the group called 'shefali'.

6.8 COMMONLY USED UNIX COMMANDS

There are many commands that are used regularly. Please, make a note that the options that are specified for the commands may not necessarily work on all look-alike UNIX. We are discussing the following commonly used commands of UNIX:

1. banner—Used to display information in bigger size.
2. cal—Used to display calendar on the screen.
3. date—Used to display and set the current system date and time.
4. passwd—Used to install or change the password on the system.
5. who—Used to determine the currently logged users on the system.
6. finger—Used to give specific information about a user.
7. lock—Used to lock the system.

6.8.1 The banner Command

This command displays information. It displays its argument exploded to a bigger size, onto the standard output. The banner command splits up the long arguments on individual word boundaries. It displays the argument up to 10 characters in large letters.

Options: None

Example: `$ banner VICKY`

Output:

6.8.2 The cal Command

The cal command creates a calendar of the specified month for the specified year. If you do not specify the month, it creates a calendar for the entire year. By default this command shows the calendar for the current month based on the system date. The cal writes its output to the standard output.

```
Syntax  :    cal [ [mm]yy]
```

where mm is the month, an integer between 1 and 12 and yy is the year, an integer between 1 and 9999. For current years, a 4-digit number must be used, '98' will not produce a calendar of 1998.

Options: None

Examples:

(*i*) `$ cal`

Output:

May 1999

S	M	T	W	TH	F	S
						1
2	3	4	5	6	7	8
9	10	11	12	13	14	15
16	17	18	19	20	21	22
23	24	25	26	27	28	29
30	31					

(*ii*) `$ cal 2002`

The above command displays the calendar for entire year, 2002. The entire year will whip month by month.

(*iii*) `$ cal 2002/lpr`

The above command prints the calendar for the entire year onto the printer.

6.8.3 The date Command

It shows or sets the system date and time. If no argument is specified, it displays the current date and the current time.

```
Syntax:  date[+options]
```

Options:

%D	–	displays date as mm/dd/yy
%a	–	displays abbreviated weekday (Sun to Sat)
%T	–	displays time as HH:MM:SS
%r	–	displays time as HH:MM:SS(A.M/P.M.)
%d	–	displays only dd
%m	–	displays only mm

Examples:

(*i*) `$ date`

It will display date as – Wed July 9 04: 50:24 EDT 2002.

(*ii*) `$ date +%D`

It will display date as – 11/12/02

(*iii*) `$ date +%r`

It will display time as – 07: 20:50 PM

(*iv*) If you are working in the superuser mode, you can set the date as shown below:

`$ date MMddhhmm[yy]`

where	MM	=	Month (1-12)
	dd	=	day (1-31)
	hh	=	hour (1-23)
	mm	=	minutes (1-59)
	yy	=	Year

It sets the system date and time to the value specified by the argument.

6.8.4 The passwd Command

You can change your password with the 'passwd' command. It is advisable to keep changing your password every few days. This helps in maintaining security. UNIX is very careful about the whole procedure of changing passwords. First UNIX wants you to enter your old password to make sure that a valid user is changing the password. The procedure of changing passwords is very simple. In order to change your password, you first have to log on to the UNIX system. Then issue the 'passwd' command at the UNIX prompt.

```
Syntax:          passwd[user-name]
Options:
```

-d	Deletes your password
-x days	This sets the maximum number of days for the password to be active. After the specified number of days, you will be required to give a new password.

-n days — This sets the minimum number of days the password has to be active, before it can be changed.

-s — This gives you the status of the user's password.

The above options can be used only by the superuser.

Example:

```
$ passwd -x 40 bobby.
```

The above command will set the password of the user as 'bobby' for a maximum of 40 days.

Also note, that passwd program will prompt you to enter your new password twice. If you don't type the same thing both the times, it will give you one more chance to set your password. Thus, UNIX wants you to type in your old password. Then it asks for the new password. Finally, UNIX confirms your new password by asking you to type in the new password again. If by any means, any mismatch happens, then the UNIX system warns you that the information provided by you is inconsistent as shown below:

```
$ passwd: shefali
Changing password for shefali
Enter old password:
Enter new password:
Re-type new password:
Mismatch-password unchanged
$
```

As stated earlier also, UNIX doesn't show the passwords typed by you on the screen because of security reasons.

6.8.5 The who Command

The who command lists the users that are currently logged into the system.

Syntax: `who [options]`

Options:

-u – lists the currently logged-in users.

-T – gives the status of all logged-in users.

am I – this lists login-id and terminal of the user invoking this command.

Examples:

(*i*) `$ who -T`

Output:

Shefali	+	ttyo1	Jan	12	9:50
Bobby	-	ttyo2	Jan	12	10:10

The second column here shows whether the user has write permission or not.

(*ii*) `$ who -u`

Output:

Shefali	ttyo	1	Jan	12	9:50	1235
	Bobby	ttyo2	Jan	12	10:10	2401

The last column here denotes the process-id.

(*iii*) `$ who am i`

Output:

Shefali ttyp 6 Jan 12 14:34

This command shows the account name, where and when I logged in. It also shows the computer terminal being used.

6.8.6 The finger Command

In larger systems, you may get a big list of users shown on the screen. The finger command with an argument gives you more information about the user. The finger command followed by an argument can give complete information for a user who is not logged onto the system.

Syntax: `finger [user-name]`

Options: none

Examples:

(*i*) `$ finger rajiv`

This command will give more information about rajiv's identity as shown below:

```
Login name: rajiv
(512) 222-4444
Directory: /home/rajiv
Last login Fri May 16 12: 14: 40 on ttyol
Project: X window programming
rajiv ttyol May 18 20:05
```

(*ii*) If you want to know about everyone currently logged onto the system, give the following command:

```
$ finger
```

6.8.7 The lock Command

UNIX offers a variety of tools to maintain security. One such tool is the usage of the 'lock' command. This command is found on many systems. The lock command locks your keyboard till the time you enter a valid password, as shown below:

Syntax: lock

Options: none

Example:

```
$lock
Password:
Sorry
Password:
```

If the correct password is not entered, then the lock command does not give control of the keyboard. If the correct password is not entered in a certain number of chances, then the lock command logs you off the system automatically. It is a very powerful tool to use if you are leaving your system just for a few minutes and want to make sure that no mischievous hands fiddle with your files and directories.

6.9 METACHARACTERS

In UNIX, we can refer to a group of files with the help of METACHARACTERS. These are similar to wild card characters in DOS. The valid Metacharacters are *, ? and [ ].

* replaces any number of characters including a null character.

? used in place of one and only one character.

[ ] brackets are used to specify a set of a range of characters.

Examples:

(*i*) `$ ls *.c`

It will list all files starting with any character or characters and ending with the character c.

(*ii*) `$ ls robin*`

It will list all the files starting with robin and ending with any character.

(*iii*) `$ ls x?yz*`

It will list all those files, in which the first character is x, the second character can be anything, the third and fourth characters should be y and z respectively . The rest of the name can be anything.

(*iv*) `$ ls l[abc]mn`

It will list all those files, in which the first character is l, the second character can be either a, b or c the last two characters i.e., 3rd and 4th should be m and n respectively.

Alternatively the above command can also be given in the following manner.

```
$ ls l[a-c]mn
```

6.10 COMPARISON OF DOS AND UNIX

As you already know DOS is a singe user operating system whereas UNIX is a multi-user operating system. Both the operating systems resemble each other in terms of hardware components. DOS as well as UNIX can be installed on a single PC. You can start any one of them. Some programs allow your PC to act as a terminal at some times and a PC at the other times. So, while running DOS programs, you can connect to a UNIX host at the same time. In the comparative study between DOS and UNIX, it also becomes essential to highlight the differences between both the operating systems. So let us now find out how and in what ways does DOS differ from UNIX.

(*a*) All UNIX systems whether large or small require system administration to greater extent. However the larger time-sharing systems need the full time attention of a system administrator to look after the needs of the users as well as the computer. While in case of DOS, the user himself can act as an administrator. Thus, UNIX systems are much more demanding than DOS based systems.

(*b*) UNIX is very much case sensitive. It clearly distinguishes between capital letters and small letters. All the names of commands and programs are given in small letters in UNIX. In UNIX ABC, abc, ABc mean different combinations, each different from the other. However, DOS accepts any mixture of small and capital letters.

(*c*) The UNIX ASCII code does not contain special symbols as found in DOS. The reason behind is that each ASCII character is represented by 8 bits (1 byte) in DOS. Each bit can be either be a 0 or 1. Since there can be two possibilities in which a bit can be represented, the number of different 8 bit patterns is 2^8 which is 256. Out of 256 different codes, UNIX uses 128 codes because the original ASCII code used by it is only 7 bits. So you can form 2^7 or 128 possible combinations of 0's and 1's. At the time when UNIX was invented, only 7 bits were used.

(*d*) The <ESC> key is often used in DOS to cancel the current operation or to go back to the previous position. However, in a UNIX system the <ESC> key is rarely used. The only time wherein the <ESC> key is used is from within the vi editor. It is used to switch over from the insert mode to command mode.

(*e*)In DOS, the <Delete> key is used to erase characters. But in UNIX, the <Delete> key is used to generate the intr (interrupt) code which helps in stopping a program.

(*f*) The command options of UNIX are given by using a minus sign (-). While in DOS, the command options are given after a slash (/). The command options supported by UNIX are much more than DOS. The command options in UNIX can be given either in single or in double and in any sequence.

(*g*) The command used in DOS to erase off the contents of the screen is CLS. The same job is carried by the CLEAR command in UNIX.

(*h*) On a standalone system, the passwords are not very essential and important. The need of password arises more in case of multi-user system. Thus, while using a UNIX system, protect your files and data from damage or accidental usage through passwords.

(*i*) Unlike DOS, all UNIX files have an owner, a user id that controls the file. The idea behind is to protect the file from unauthorised access. The file owner can control the access of his files by setting permissions. The permissions allowed in UNIX are read, write and execute. Contrarily DOS does not support the concept of permissions.

(*j*) Unlike DOS, UNIX maintains a number of directories for its own purposes. In a UNIX directory structure, there is a root directory at the very top. Under the root directory are present seven subdirectories. All the users of the UNIX system can create their files and directories under the usr subdirectory. While in case of DOS, the user can create his files directly under the root directory.

(*k*) The file naming conventions used is UNIX and DOS are also different. In UNIX, the filenames can be up to 14 characters long. The filenames do not carry any extension. The UNIX filenames can contain a period also and should be given in lower case. However, the DOS file naming methodology follows the concept of primary name and an extension. A DOS filename can have a maximum of 8 characters in the primary name and 3 characters in the extension. The extension is optional. The primary name is separated from an extension by a period.

(*l*) UNIX uses forward slashes (/) to separate the names of files and directories while specifying the whole path. However the pathnames are separated by backslashes (\) in case of DOS.

(*m*) UNIX allows you to create empty files while DOS does not.

(*n*) The regular expressions of UNIX can be used to specify filenames, as in the case of DOS wildcards. However, the regular expressions of UNIX are much more powerful than DOS wildcards. The regular expressions of UNIX are ?, *, [ ], - and !. There are only two wildcards found is DOS which are * and ?. Within a regular expression, the ? works the same way as within a DOS wildcard, however the * works differently.

(*o*) The editor used in UNIX is vi whereas the editor used in DOS is EDLIN. The vi editor is much more powerful than EDLIN.

The Table 6.2 summarises a few of the DOS and UNIX commands.

Description	UNIX command	DOS command
1. Change working directory	cd	CD
2. Display working directory	pwd	CD
3. Make directory	mkdir	MD
4. Remove directory	rmdir	RD
5. Rename directory	mv	-
6. Move directory	mvdir	-
7. Copy directory	copy	XCOPY
8. Creating a file	cat > filename	COPY CON:FILENAME.TXT
9. Display filenames in alphabetical order	ls	DIR
10. Display contents of a file	cat	TYPE
11. Display a file page-wised	more or pg	TYPE | MORE

Table 6.2 *Summary of few UNIX commands with their equivalent DOS commands*

THEORY QUESTIONS

1. What is UNIX? What hardware do you require in order to install UNIX?
2. Briefly explain the history of UNIX development.
3. Discuss briefly the different features of UNIX.
4. What makes UNIX unique from other operating systems?
5. Explain the system structure of UNIX in detail.
6. What services are offered by Kernel?
7. Explain the following terms briefly:
   (*a*) Interrupts
   (*b*) Exceptions
   (*c*) Processor Execution levels
8. What is a directory? What is the procedure adopted by UNIX to represent a directory?
9. Discuss briefly the steps to login in a UNIX system.
10. State the reasons why you are sometimes unsuccessful while logging in.
11. How can you change your password in UNIX?
12. Gives a few tips for choosing a new login name and password.
13. Write the syntax of the following commands:
    (*a*) banner (*b*) cal (*c*) date
    (*d*) passwd (*e*) who (*f*) finger

14. What is a directory? Explain in detail giving an example.
15. How does UNIX organise files?
16. Which are the directories that UNIX maintains and keeps by itself?
17. What do you mean by the absolute and relative filenames?
18. What is the convention used to name files in UNIX?
19. Discuss the different types of files present in a UNIX system.
20. What are Metacharacters? Discuss with examples.
21. How is UNIX able to implement file security?
22. What are the different access permissions given to a file?
23. Discuss the options given in the ls command.
24. Give the syntax of the following commands:
    (*a*) chmod (*b*) chown (*c*) chgrp
25. How is the 'chown' command of UNIX different from the 'chgrp' command?
26. Explain the access control mechanism of file and directory attributes in UNIX.
27. List any two major features of UNIX operating system. What is the difference between absolute and relative path names of a UNIX file?
28. Discuss the salient features of UNIX architecture in brief.
29. What is UNIX Kernel? Explain, in brief the role of UNIX Kernel.
30. Give the overall structure of the UNIX operating system and the function of each component.
31. What does the 'exit' command do in UNIX?
32. Why is UNIX more portable than other operating systems?
33. How long can a UNIX filename be?
34. Who can change the attribute of a file or a directory?
35. Which file attribute changes when you copy a file from some other user account?

WORKSHOP

1. Copy a directory mydir1 to mydir2.
2. Remove a directory tree.
3. Create a file and then assign all permissions to the owner and remove all permissions from others.
4. You want to remove files. Some of these files are write-protected, but you donot know which ones are these. Give the commands to remove the desired files.
5. Give a command to list the currently logged users.
6. Give a command to change your password.
7. Assign read and execute rights to the file 'myfile'.
8. Give a command to lock your system.
9. Give a command to change the group from 'first' to 'second'.
10. Give a command to print the currently working directory.

7

ADVANCED UNIX

7.1 INTRODUCTION

We have discussed about various types of UNIX files in the previous chapter. Text files are ordinary files that contain ASCII characters, thus are also called ASCII files. An ASCII (American Standard Code for Information and Interchange) is a standard format to represent all alphabets, numbers and other special symbols and is used to communicate data between different types of computers. In this chapter, we will discuss the programs for creating ASCII files. We will also discuss the advanced features of UNIX which include processes, filters, pipes and shell programming.

7.2 EDITORS

How do we create an ASCII or a text file? In UNIX, a text file is created and modified by a program, called Text Editor or simply Editor. You may have used the common DOS editors, EDLIN and EDIT. Similarly, UNIX operating system also comes with several editors. Let us discuss the features of the common editors along with their important commands.

7.2.1 Types of Editors

In general, we can classify editors into two types—Line Editors and Screen Editors.

(*a*) **Line Editors.** The early UNIX editors that edit processes one line at a time are called Line Editors. So with a line editor, you are required to give many commands to display or edit a set of lines. The common examples of UNIX line editors are ed and ex.

(*i*) *Ed.* Ed was the first line editor of UNIX that is still used sometimes, though it is not popular. Ed was popular on those days when most UNIX commands consisted of only two or three letters. It has become outdated now due to the use of screen editors which provide many more features.

(*ii*) *Ex.* Ex is more powerful and comprehensive than Ed line editor. Some Ex line-oriented commands are also used in few screen editors (such as vi).

(*b*) **Screen Editors:** Editors that make use of the whole screen for editing or processing more than one line at a time, are called screen editors. With screen editors, you can display and edit many lines by giving a single command. The common examples of screen editors are vi and emacs.

(*i*) Vi - Vi stands for 'Visual editor' Vi is the standard full-screen UNIX tool and is the only editor available on SCO UNIX. As most of ed's and ex's features are also available in vi, you can straight away learn vi without learning ed or ex.

(*ii*) Emacs - Emacs is another popular screen editor of UNIX. It is distributed free of cost from Free Software Foundation, Cambridge. Although most vendors distribute emacs with UNIX system, emacs is not a part of UNIX.

In the next section, we are discussing the commands of vi editor in detail. In the later section, we will summarise the important commands of emacs editor.

7.3 VI EDITOR

After comparative study of various types of editors, let us learn the commands of vi editor. As vi editor is difficult to learn due too many commands, we advice you to keep on trying these commands while learning at your terminal.

7.3.1 Starting vi

There are many ways to load editor in the computer memory but the general syntax to start vi is –

```
$ vi [-option (s)] [Filename(s)]
```

where $ is the UNIX prompt

vi is the name of editor

option(s) is/are the letter(s) representing one or more options

File(s) is/are the name of text file(s) you want to open or create

[ ] means these entries are optional and may be skipped

Let us see a few ways to load vi.

(*a*) **Loading vi without a text file.** If you want to load vi without specifying the name of text file to be opened or created, give the following command:

```
$ vi <Enter>
```

You will see a blank screen as shown in Figure 7.1.

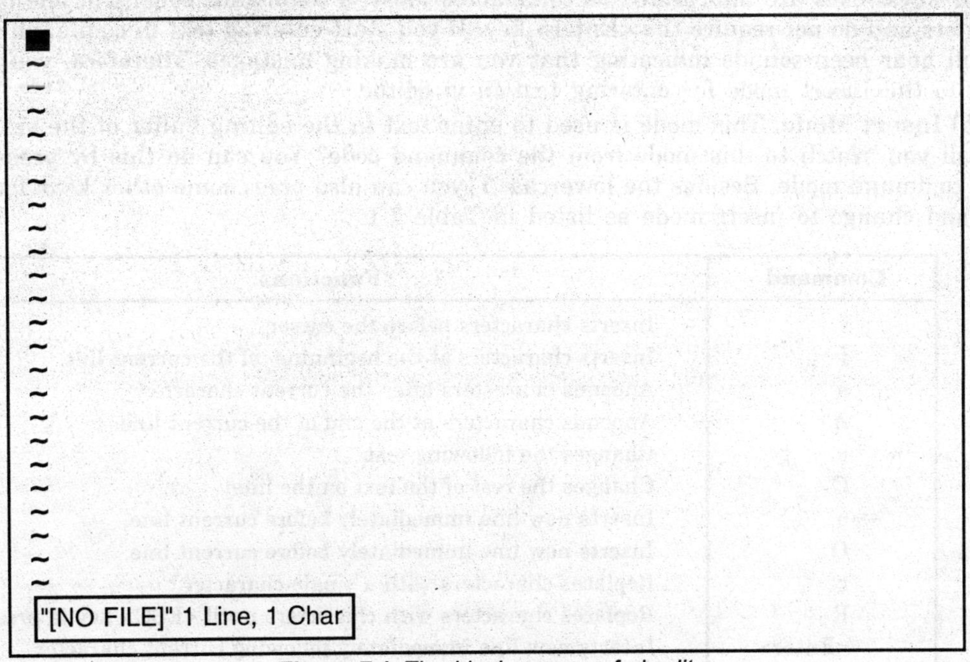

Figure 7.1 *The blank screen of vi editor*

The blank screen is actually not completely blank but is filled with a series of tilde(~) symbols running from upper left corner till the bottom of the screen. These tilde symbols show that the page is blank. At the bottom of screen is the status line showing that no file is opened. The cursor is on 1st line and 1st character position.

(*b*) **Loading vi with text files.** You can also specify the name of one or more text files which you want to create or open at the time of loading vi, by giving the following command:

```
$ vi mohit <Enter>
```

The above command opens the working copy of file 'mohit' in a memory area, called the editing buffer. If there would be no file with name 'mohit' in the current directory, a blank file with name 'mohit' will be stored in the editing buffer. Now, if you enter a new text or modify the existing text, it will be done in the editing buffer. So, your original file will remain unchanged unless you save it.

(*c*) **Loading vi with text file and options.** You can also specify three options while opening the text file as explained below:

(*i*) Sometimes the file might get crashed either due to power failure or other interruption during editing of the file. You can recover the crashed file (say 'mohit') with option -r as shown below:

```
$ vi -r mohit <Enter>
```

(*ii*) To open a file for reading only and not for editing, give the option -R as shown below:

```
$ vi -R mohit <Enter>
```

7.3.2 Modes of Working in vi

You can work in vi in following two modes:

(*a*) **Command Mode.** When vi is started, it is in command mode which means that all your keystrokes are interpreted as commands. Most vi commands consist of one or two characters and do not require the <Enter> key. If you start entering text in command mode you will hear beep sounds indicating that you are making mistakes. Therefore, you must switch to the Insert mode for entering text in vi editor.

(*b*) **Insert Mode.** This mode is used to enter text in the editing buffer of the vi. Now, how will you switch to this mode from the command code? You can do this by pressing i in the command mode. Besides the lowercase i, you can also press some other keys for text entry and change to insert mode as listed in Table 7.1.

Command	Functions
i	Inserts characters before the cursor.
I	Inserts characters at the beginning of the current line
a	Appends characters after the current character.
A	Appends characters at the end of the current line.
c	Changes the following text
C	Changes the rest of the text on the line.
o	Inserts new line immediately before current line.
O	Inserts new line immediately before current line.
r	Replaces characters with a single character.
R	Replaces characters with characters until <ESC> key is pressed.
<Enter>	Inserts new line immediately following current character.

Table 7.1 *Various keystroke commands for switching to insert mode and entry of text*

7.3.3 Editing Text in vi

After coming to the insert mode, you can type your text. Type 4-5 lines of any text in the vi text editor screen by pressing <Enter> key after end of each line. When you want to end the text entry, press <ESC> key for returning to command mode.

7.3.4 Saving Text in vi

While entering text, always remember to save your file. If the power goes off, you will lose all the currently edited text. For saving the file for the first time, give the following keystroke commands at the command mode:

```
:w  sweety
```

The text file will be saved with name 'sweety 'and you can still continue editing the text. If you don't want to save the file and want to quit vi give the following command:

```
:q!
```

There are many options for saving or abandoning a file in vi, which are listed in Table 7.2.

Command	Function
:W(Filename)	Saves the text file with the new name, (Filename) and resumes editing.
:w	Saves the file with existing name and resumes editing.
:q!	Quits vi editor without saving the file.
:Q	Quits vi editor only when file is saved.
:x	Saves the file and quits vi editor.
:wq	Same as :x
zz	Same as :x

Table 7.2 *Various options for saving/abandoning a file in vi editor*

7.3.5 Moving the Cursor while Editing

The cursor, you know is a blinking underscore character that marks a position on the screen, where the user can enter or modify the text. In vi, the line on which cursor is positioned is called the *current line*. In vi, you can move cursor in both command and inser modes. Some useful cursor commands of vi editor are summarised in Table 7.3.

Command	Function
(left arrow)	Moves the cursor to the beginning of current line.
(Right arrow)	Moves the cursor to the end of current line.
(Up arrow)	Move the cursor to left character on same line.
(Down arrow)	Move the cursor to right character on same line.
O	Same as left arrow key
$	Same as right arrow key.
–	Moves cursor to the beginning of the previous line.
<Ctrl>M	Moves cursor to the beginning of the next line.
b	Moves cursor to the beginning of the previous word.
e	Moves cursor to the end of the next word
w	Moves cursor to the beginning of the next word.
G	Moves cursor to the last line of the file.
nG	Moves cursor to the beginning of line n (e.g. 5G moves to 5th line)
n!	Moves cursor to the beginning of column n (e.g. 5moves to 5th column on same line)
H	Moves cursor to top line of the screen.
M	Moves cursor to middle of the screen.
L	Moves cursor to bottom of the screen
B	Same as b, but ignores punctuation in text.
E	Same as e, but ignores punctuation in text.
w	Same as w, but ignores punctuation in text

Table 7.3 *Some useful cursor commands of vi*

7.3.6 Moving the Screen

Beside the cursor, you can also move the screen in vi. You can scroll the screen upward or downward by the commands listed in Table 7.4.

Command	Function
<Ctrl> U	Scrolls half of the screen upwards.
<Ctrl> D	Scrolls half of the screen downwards
<Ctrl> B	Scrolls the full screen backward (Up)
<Ctrl> F	Scrolls the full screen forward (down)

Table 7.4 *Screen movement command of vi*

7.3.7 Modifying the Text

Modifying the text in vi is a difficult process because you cannot overwrite the characters. If you want to change a character of the word, then either you first delete that character and write new one or use a command to replace that character. For example, if your text contains a word 'unix' and you want to write u in capital letter, then you cannot straight away position the cursor to 'u' and type 'U'. This is not allowed in vi editor. For changing 'unix' word with 'Unix', you must follow one of the methods given below:

Method I – Deleting and changing the character

Step 1: Move the cursor to character 'u' of the word 'unix'.

Step 2: Press x in the command mode. This will delete the character 'U'

Step 3: Press i for switching to the insert mode.

Step 4: Enter U at the cursor position to i.e. before the word 'nix'.

Method II – Replacing the character

Step 1: Same as step 1 of method I

Step 2: Press r in the command mode for replacing the character.

Step 3: Enter U immediately after pressing r.

Method III – Changing the case of letter

Step 1: Same as step 1 of method I

Step 2: Press tilde (~) character in the command mode. This will change lowercase 'u' to uppercase `U'. The tilde (~) can also be used to change an uppercase letter to lowercase.

Any one of the above methods will change 'unix' word to 'Unix'. So, you must have realised that editing is not so easy in vi as in a word processor. Various useful commands for deleting and undeleting the text are listed in Table 7.5.

Command	Function
x	Deletes a character at the cursor position
d	Deletes the next character
D	Deletes characters to the end of the line
dd	Deletes the current line
: D	Same as dd
: x	Same as x
:X	deletes the previous character
: D$	Same as D
: U	Undoes the last deletion
p	Puts the last deleted text after the cursor
P	Puts the last deleted text before the cursor
u	Undoes the last change made to the text
U	Restores the line to its pervious condition

Table 7.5 *Important commands for deleting and undeleting the text*

7.3.8 Cutting the Text

While editing a text file, we often require to move a block of text from one position to another within a file. In order to move the text, first we cut the text, then place the cursor at the position where the text has to be placed and finally we paste it. There are many commands to cut (or yank) the text in vi editor, which are called *Yanking commands* and some of them are listed in Table 7.6.

Command	Function
y	Cuts the characters at cursor position
yy	Cuts the current line
Y	Same as yy
yn	Cuts the n number of characters from cursor position
nyy	Cuts the n number of lines from current line
y$	Cuts from cursor position to end of line
yw	Cuts the word at cursor position

Table 7.6 *Important commands for yanking (cutting) the text*

7.3.9 Searching a Text Pattern

At times, you are required to search a particular word or group of words in the text file. For example, in order to search a word 'hello' in the text file, issue the following command at the command prompt:

```
/hello
```

The above command will position the cursor at the first occurrence of the word 'hello' from the current line. Suppose, you want to find the next occurrence of the word 'hello', then simply press / at the command prompt. If there is no more same pattern, you will see the following message:

pattern not found

You can also search backward by giving the following command.

```
?hello
```

Similarly, to continue searching, you can press only ?. Some of the important options for searching a text pattern are listed in Table 7.7.

Command	Function
/pattern	Search forward a string 'pattern' in the text file
/	Search forward for the previous pattern
?pattern	Search backward a string 'pattern' in the text file
?	Search backward for the previous pattern
n	Repeat last / or ? Command and search forward
N	Repeat last / or ? command and search backward

Table 7.7 *Options for searching a text-pattern*

7.3.10 Repeating vi Commands

You can execute vi commands repeatedly by adding a number to the command. This number indicates the number of times a command is to be repeated. You can use this method to repeat commands with any of the text-manipulation commands (such as deletion, cursor movements, cutting the text, etc.) discussed in this chapter.

Examples:

(*i*) To delete five characters from the cursor position, give the following command:

```
:X5
```

(*ii*) To delete three lines from the current line, give the following command:

```
:D5
```

(*iii*) To move the cursor to the beginning of next three words, give the following command:

```
W3
```

7.4 EMACS EDITOR

Besides vi editor, emacs is also a popular text editor. Although the earlier versions of emacs were difficult to learn, the latest one is easier due to a user-friendly interface. This version of emacs supports a mouse and provides pull-down menus. You can also issue commands from the keyboard by using <Ctrl> and <Alt> keys.

7.4.1 Starting emacs

To start emacs, enter the following command:

```
$ emacs
```

You will see a startup screen followed by almost a blank screen with a status line at the top/bottom. As emacs work in only single mode, you can straight away enter the text. You are also required to press <Enter> key after each line as you do in vi editor. Type 3-4 lines of text and save the file.

7.4.2 Saving the File

In emacs, you can save the file with one of the following ways:

(*a*) If you want to resume editing after saving the file, press <Ctrl> X followed by <Ctrl> S key.

(*b*) If you want to quit emacs after saving the file, press <Ctrl> X followed by <Ctrl> C key.

In either of the above commands, emacs will ask you to enter the name of the file, if you are saving the file for the first time.

7.4.3 Important Commands

Though we are not discussing emacs in detail, we are summarising the frequently used commands of emacs in Table 7.8.

Command	Function
Alt <	Moves the cursor to the beginning of file.
Alt >	Moves the cursor to the end of file.
Ctrl V	Moves the cursor to the next screen
Alt V	Moves the cursor to the previous screen
Ctrl D	Deletes a character at the cursor position
Del	Deletes all characters from beginning of line to the cursor position
Ctrl K	Deletes all characters from the cursors position to the end of line.
Ctrl @	To mark the beginning/end of a block for copying and moving the text
Ctrl w	To delete the marked block of text
Ctrl Y	To paste the marked block of text

Table 7.8 *Some frequently used commands of emacs*

7.5 PROCESS

Program, you know, is a set of instructions and is useless until it is loaded into computer's memory. When a program is loaded into the memory, it starts and we call it a process. So a process is an executable program in memory. When we run a UNIX command (say ls), we are actually running a process. Similarly when an operating system is loaded into memory (*i.e.* your computer is booting), a series of processes (can be in thousands in number for multi-user operating systems) are running. Now, let's define the process in relation to the operating system.

A process is defined as an entity that represents the basic unit of work to be implemented in the system.

The basic unit of work in an operating system could be a single program or a concurrently executable section of a program. So, if a program consists of three executable sections, there would be three processes running in memory.

How does UNIX identify a process? UNIX provides a unique identification number to each process during the time of its execution. The identification number of a process is called Process id. In this section, we will discuss about processes along with multi-processing features of UNIX operating system.

7.5.1 Process Table

As there are many processes running or waiting to run, their details must be stored in some area of computer memory. The process table is the name given to a data structure that stores the details about all processes. In UNIX, when the Kernel is loaded in RAM, the process table is initialised. The process table contains details of every process that is initialised. When the process is completed such details are deleted from the process table.

7.5.1.1 The ps Command

You can display the contents of the process table in UNIX by the ps command. The ps command displays the status of all active processes. The various forms of ps command are explained on the next page:

(*i*) The simplest form of ps command is without any options as shown below:

```
$ps
```

The above command displays the process id (PID), name of the terminal (TTY), time used by the process (TIME) and the name of the command (COMMAND) that is executing as illustrated below:

PID	TTY	TIME	COMMAND
39	console	0.12	sh
410	tty01	0.02	ps
432	tty02	0.09	vi

(where sh stands for shell)

(*ii*) If you want to view the information about each process, give ps command with -f (full listing) option as shown below:

```
$ ps -f
```

You will get information in more columns as illustrated below:

UID	PID	PPID	STAT	STIME	TTY	TIME	COMMAND
Rosy	39	1	S	11:35:15	console	0.12	sh
Rosy	410	1	R	12:05:02	tty01	0.09	ps
Rosy	432	540	W	14:12:31	tty02	0.09	vi

(where UID stands for User id
PPID stands for Parent Process id
STAT stands for Process status
STIME stands for Starting time of process)

The process status can have either of following main states:

Run State (R) – The process currently running
Sleeping state (S) – The process not currently required to run
Wait state (W) – The process waiting to run.

(*iii*) If you want to view little information about all the processes running on the entire system, give the following command:

```
$ ps -e
```

You will see the listing of process in four columns as illustrated above in ps command without any options. The ps command without any options provide information for your system only while the ps with –e option for the entire system.

(*iv*) If you want to view all the information about all the processes running on the entire system, give the following command:

```
$ ps -ef
```

(*v*) The –e option with ps command displays all the processes on entire network whether they are actively doing something or not. For instance, -e option also displays those processes that are running other processes. These processes are generally called *process group leaders* and are of little interest for the user. So, if you want some new information about processes other than process group leaders, give the following command:

```
$ ps -d
```

The above command will show the listing of only currently active process group.

(*vi*) If you want to view all important information about processes that are associated with a terminal, give the following command:

```
$ ps -a
```

(*vii*) You can also use –f option with above command in order to display complete information as shown in following command:

```
$ ps -af
```

7.5.2 Process Priorities

The process scheduler allocates fixed time slots for each and every process waiting for its turn to avail the processor. However, certain important processes are required to be processed earlier before their turns to come. In UNIX, you can assign higher priorities to these processes by using the nice command.

7.5.2.1 The nice Command

The nice command executes a command with a different priority. Normally, all commands run at priority 20, but if you want to run a command (say ps –af) at priority 10, give the following command under C shell:

```
$ nice 10 ps -af
```

The lower the number means higher the priority to run the process and the higher the number means, lower the priority. As a priority can have values ranging 0 to 120, 0 is the highest and 120 is the lowest priority.

Under the Bourne Shell, the priority number must be proceeded by a '-' as illustrated below:

```
$ nice -5 ps -af
```

The above command will lower the priority by 5 and thus set it to 25 (As by default priority is 20). Under the C shell, you can use both 't' and '-' before the priority number as illustrated in following commands:

```
$ nice +5 sort shalu > shalu1
$ nice -5 sort shalu > shalu1
```

The above first command will raise the priority by 5 and thus set it to 15 and the second command will lower it by 5 and set it to 25.

7.5.3 Foreground and Background Processes

The processes use the terminal for input and output while executing commands. These processes are called *Foreground Processes*. When the processes execute on their own, without reading from the terminal, they are called *Background Processes*. For example, you can run the sort command in background by ending the command with an $ (ampersand) character as shown below:

```
$ sort shalu > shalu1 &
```

The above command sorts a file named shalu and creates the sorted file with name shalu1. As the command runs in background, your terminal is freed for reading more commands.

7.5.4 Terminating a Process

If a process has been launched by another user at another terminal, you can stop that process. You can also terminate a process running in the background. In order to terminate a process, use the kill command with the syntax shown below:

```
$ kill [-signal] PID
```

where signal specifies the particular event occurred in a process and PID indicates the process id.

Examples:

(*i*) To terminate a process with process id 125 and signal number 9 give the following command:

```
$ kill -9 125
```

The signal 9 indicates that the terminating process cannot be ignored and process must be stopped in any case.

(*ii*) You can also use signal 15, but under certain circumstances a process can ignore this terminating signal. If you do not use any signal number, then the signal number 15 is taken as default signal. So, the following two commands do the same function:

```
$ kill -15 125

$ kill 125
```

(*iii*) If many processes are running in background, you can stop all of them by specifying the process id 0 and no signal number as shown below:

```
$ kill 0
```

7.6 BOOTING PROCESS IN MULTITASKING SYSTEM

Multitasking refers to the ability of an operating system to execute two or more tasks concurrently. In multitasking environment, the user opens new applications without closing the previous ones and the information can be easily moved among a number of applications. In simple words, multitasking means that the operating system can perform more than one task at a time. UNIX is a multitasking operating system. When you boot your computer with UNIX operating system, many processes run at a time, so the operating system is performing a series of tasks. These processes compete with each other for computer resources. In order to allocate resources efficiently, many processes are run in the background. Background processes are the major components of a multitasking system.

When you boot a multitasking system particularly UNIX, the following processes are run:

(*i*) Process 0. First process launched by UNIX.

(*ii*) Init. Process 0 launches another process called init. Init is the mother of all processes.

(*iii*) Parent. Init launches other process called *Parent Process* which launches additional processes. Init is also considered as parent to other processes.

(*iv*) Child. The parent processes launch other processes called *Child Processes*. Child processes are actually ancestor of all the processes running on the system.

7.7 CONTROLLING INPUT/ OUTPUT

UNIX is known for having many powerful features which includes controlling the input and output. In UNIX system, every program and UNIX commands are connected to three files – the standard input, the standard output and the standard error. Let us discuss about these files briefly:

1. Standard Input

The basic source from which UNIX programs read their input is called the standard input. By default, the standard input is assigned to the special file representing the key-board that is the actual source of the input data.

2. Standard Output

The basic target to which UNIX programs write their output is called the standard output. By default, the standard output is assigned to the special file representing the screen of your terminal that is the usual target of the output.

3. Standard Error

The output target to which UNIX programs write their error messages is called the standard error. By default, the standard error is also assigned to special file representing the screen of your terminal.

7.7.1 Redirection

Although most of the time, standard input, standard output and standard error are acceptable to the user, you can also change them. You can change the input source or the output target. For instance, sometimes you may require getting input from the file instead of the keyboard or you may want output on printer instead of the monitor. In such circum-stances, you need to redirect the standard input, standard output or standard error. Redi-rection is a technique in UNIX to reassign the standard input, standard output or standard error to a specified file.

7.7.1.1 Redirecting the Standard Input

You can redirect the standard input for a command by writing the command in follow-ing way:

(*i*) First type the command;

(*ii*) Put < (less than) symbol; and

(*iii*) Then write the name of the input file.

Example:

You can take the input from the file 'account', instead of the standard input (keyboard) by the following command:

```
$ cat < account
```

7.7.1.2 Redirecting the Standard Output

You can also redirect the standard output for a command by writing the command in following way.

(*i*) First type the command.

(*ii*) Put > (greater than) symbol and

(*iii*) Then write the name of the output file.

Examples:

(*i*) To redirect the contents of the file 'preeti.c' to the file 'vandana.c' instead of the showing the contents on the screen, give the following command:

```
$ cat preeti.c > vandana.c
```

(*ii*) To redirect the listing of ls –l command to a file, 'sachin' instead of screen, give the following command:

```
$ ls -l > sachin
```

(*iii*) You can redirect the listing of ls –l command on other terminal (say tty 02), give the following command:

```
$ ls -l > /dev/tty02
```

7.7.1.3 Redirecting the Output in Append Mode

If you redirect the output to a file and if the file already exists, it is over written by new data. So, in that case, you can redirect the output to already existing file in append mode by using >> instead of >.

Example:

To redirect the output of the ls –l command to the already existing file 'sachin', give the following command:

```
$ ls -1 >> sachin
```

If the file 'sachin' does not exist, the shell will create this file otherwise new output will be appended at the end of this file.

7.7.1.4 Redirecting the Standard Error

Error messages are normally displayed on the screen, but you can also redirect them to a file or printer by using 2> as explained in following examples:

(*i*) To execute a program 'invoice' by sending the output to file 'invlist' and the error messages to another file 'errors', give the following command:

```
$ invoice > invlist 2> errors
```

(*ii*) If you want to redirect both the standard output and the standard error to a file 'invrepo', use 2>&1 symbol as shown in following command:

```
$ invoice > invrepo 2>&1
```

7.7.1.5 Redirecting the Standard Error in Append Mode

As you do in standard output, you can use >> symbol for appending the standard error to a file as illustrated in following commands:

```
$ invoice >> invlist 2>> errors
$ invoice << invrepo 2>>&1
```

7.7.1.6 Redirecting both Input and Output

You can redirect the input and output at the same time. For example, to obtain input to cat command from the file 'infile' and to redirect its output to another file 'outfile', give the following command:

```
$ cat <infile> outfile
```

7.8 FILTERS

Filters are the programs (or commands) that read from standard input file process (or filter) it and write the output to the standard output file. Most UNIX commands are filters as they use standard input and output. For example, cat is a filter command that joins the contents of the two files into one long stream of data as illustrated below:

```
$ cat student1 student2 > class
```

The above command creates a temporary file 'class' by combining two files 'student1 and 'student2'.

The importance of filter commands is that these commands can be combined. The data from one filter can be passed to another filter. For instance, by using cat filter, you can create a temporary file and by using the n1 filter, you can add the line numbers and store the output in another temporary file.

7.8.1 Filter Commands

We are discussing below the important filter commands.

7.8.1.1 The tee Command

The tee is a useful filter command. It not only reads the standard input and sends the output onto the standard output, but also redirects a copy of what it has read, into the file of your choice. It thus forms the concept of T used by the plumbers. Therefore, you can extract some of the data from the middle using the tee command.

Examples:

(*i*) You can send the contents of file 'sonia.c' to both printer and another file 'gandhi.c' by the following command:

```
$ cat sonia.c | tee gandhi.c | lpr
```

The above command is equivalent to following two commands:

```
$ cat soina.c > gandhi
$ lpr gandhi
```

(*ii*) If you wish to append a file using tee, just use –a option as shown below:

```
$ ls -l | tee -a gandhi c | lpr
```

7.8.1.2 The pg Command

This command displays the contents of a file(s) one page at a time. The format of the command is as follows:

```
pg  [filename....]
```

where, the filename is the name of the file(s), you wish to view. You can specify either the absolute pathname or the relative pathname. If you do not specify any filename, it takes its inputs from the standard input file. This command is generally used at the end of the pipeline, because its output is not useful in midway.

After displaying one screen, it displays ':' at the bottom of your screen, and waits for your response. If you press <RETURN> key it shows the next screen and so on. The various options used with pg command are listed in Table 7.9.

Option	Function
: n <Enter>	Skips the n number of pages before displaying the next page *e.g.* : 4 <Enter> Skip 4 pages before displaying another page. :-3 <Enter> Skip back 3 pages before displaying another page
: p Program <Enter>	Cause pg to search forward for the first occurrence of the string Program or program
: n [gG]oa <Enter>	Causes pg to search forward for occurrence of the string Goa or goa.
: . Enter>	Causes the current line to be redisplayed.
: $ <Enter>	Causes the last screen of the file to be displayed
: q <Enter>	Quits the pg program, out to the shell.
: h <Enter>	Displays the list of pg commands
: p <Enter>	Takes you to the beginning of the previous file.

Table 7.9 *Options used with pg command*

7.8.1.3 The more Command

This command displays the contents of a file(s) one screen (or page) at a time. The format of this command is as follows:

```
more  [filename......]
```

This command is similar to the pg command, but with very limited options. At the end of one screen display, it displays the following message:

```
—more— (20%) at the bottom of the file.
```

Here 20% means that 20% of the file contents are yet to be listed. It waits for your response. Pressing spacebar will display the next screen. Pressing <Enter> will cause one line at a time to be displayed. Typing 'q' will quit the more program. 'More' command displays the contents of one file after the other if you specify more than one filename.

7.8.1.4 The head Command

This command displays the first n lines of a file. The format of the command is as follows:

```
head [-n] [filename.....]
```

where n is the number of lines. If you don't specify a value for n, the default value is 10 lines. head is a filter program and can be used anywhere in the pipeline.

Examples:

(*i*) `$ head manoj.c`

This command will display the first 10 (default) lines of 'manoj. c'

(*ii*) `$ head -4 manoj.c`

This command will display the first 4 lines of 'manoj. c'

(*iii*) `$ head -4 <bill> billrepo 2>> &1`

This will take input from the file 'bill' and output the first 4 lines in the file 'billrepo'. The error messages if any will also be stored in the output file 'billrepo'.

7.8.1.5 The tail Command

This command displays the last n lines of a file. The format of the command is as follows:

```
tail [+/-n] [filename]
```

Where n, denotes the number of lines. If you do not specify any value for n, by default it displays the last 10 lines. The filename is the name of the file you wish to view. But unlike head command, you can specify only one filename here. If you do not specify any filename, it takes its input from the standard input file.

Examples:

(*i*) `$ tail manoj.c`

This will display the last 10 lines of the file 'manoj.c'

(*ii*) `$ tail -3 manoj.c`

This will display the last 3 lines of the file 'manoj.c'

(*iii*) `$ tail +30 bill.c`

This will display all lines starting from the 30th line to the end of the file.

7.8.1.6 The wc Command

This command counts characters, words, and lines in the input file. The format of the command is as follows:

```
wc [options] [filename.....]
```

If you don't specify a file name, we take its input from the standard input file and write it to the standard output. You can specify more than one filename at a given time. It will then list the count statistics for each of the file specified, one after the another. If you don't specify an option, it reports all the three counts: Characters, words, and lines.

Example:

(*i*) `$ wc sarika`

This command counts characters, words and lines in the file 'sarika'

(*ii*) `$ wc -cw sarika`

This command counts characters and words in the file 'sarika'

7.8.1.7 The cut Command

The cut is a filter program and can be used anywhere in a pipeline. This command is a bit different from the earlier commands. It allows some field(s) or columns(s) of the file to be manipulated. It cuts the fields specified from a file(s) separated or delimited by a character. The default delimiter is the tab character. If you do not specify a filename, cut will take its input from the standard input file. You can also specify more than one file name. It will first cut from the first file, then the second file and so on. This command cuts specified characters or field(s) from a given file(s). The format of this command is as follows:

```
cut option [file name....]
```

The various options used with this command are listed in Table 7.10:

Option	Function
-d	delimiter, separating the fields
-c	character to cut
-f	fields to cut

Table 7.10 *Options used with cut command*

It is compulsory to specify either the c or the f option with the cut command, without which it will give an error.

Example:

Consider the file 'laxmi' with following data:

Roll no	Name	Class
101	Ravinder	BCA
102	Mohit	BCA
105	Vandana	PGDCA
104	Pawan	PGDCA
103	Puja	BCA

(*i*) `$ cut -d" " -f1 laxmi`

The above command will display –

101

102

105

104

103

Here the first field (-f1) was cut, and that the delimiter is a space (" ").

(*ii*) `$ cut -f2,3 -d" " laxmi`

The above command will cut the 2nd and the 3rd field from file 'laxmi'. The output will be as follows:

Ravinder	BCA
Mohit	BCA
Vandana	PGDCA

(*iii*) `$ cut c4, 5 stud_mas`

This will cut the 4th and 5th (character) of the file stud_mas.

7.8.1.8 The paste Command

This command concatenates data from files line by line. The format of the command is as follows:

```
paste [-d <character>] filename....
```

where "d" defines the delimiter character, when joining files. Tab is the default delimiter.

Example:

```
$ cut -f1 -d" " < laxmi > file1
$ cut -f2 -d" " < laxmi > file2
$ paste -d" " filel1 file2
```

Output:

01	Ravinder	BCA
02	Mohit	BCA
03	Vandana	PGDCA

7.8.1.9 The cmp Command

This command compares two files and reports the occurrence of the first difference between the two files. The format of the command is as follows:

```
cmp filel1 file2
```

The cmp, command compares the two file on a line wise line basis. The moment it encounters a difference, it comes out of the program, back to the shell prompt, with a message as illustrated below:

```
File2 file1 differ : char 31 line 5
```

i.e. the first difference occurs on 31st character from starting of file1 and it is on 5th line (of filel). If there is no difference between the two files, then cmp just takes you back to the shell prompt.

7.8.1.10 The diff Command

This command compares two files and reports of their differences. The format of the command is as follows:

```
diff [-e] file1 file2
```

The diff command compares the two files on line wise line basis and even if the two lines differ by one character, the whole line is reported.

7.8.1.11 The sort Command

This command sorts the file on the key field(s) and options specified. Sorting is based on the ASCII collating sequence. The sort is a filter program and it sorts lines form an input file based on the key field(s) and option(s), you specify. The various options used with sort command are listed in Table 7.11.

Option	Function
-t	Specifies the field separator or the filed delimiter. Default is the tab character.
-n	Indicates numeric sort.
-i	Reverses the sort.
-f	Ignore case while sorting
-u	Unique sort-i.e. only one copy of lines with duplicate keys goes to the output.
+(n)	skips first n fields and sort on (n+1)th field.
-n	stop considering after nth field
-m	It merges the specified files. Input files must be already sorted according to the same specification
-o	Use the file named in the following arguments as the output file.

Table 7.11 *Options of sort command*

Example:

(*i*) The command used to sort on first field in the ascending order is given below:

```
$ sort laxmi
```

The above command will sort on the first field and the following result is given:

```
01    Ravinder    BCA
02    Mohit       BCA
03    Puja        BCA
04    Pawan       PGDCA
05    Vandana     PGDCA
```

(*ii*)

```
$ sort -t" " +1 laxmi
```

This will sort the file excel on the student name, with space as the delimiter for fields. The output would be as follows:

```
02    Mohit       BCA
04    Pawan       PGDCA
03    Puja        BCA
01    Ravinder    BCA
05    Vandana     PGDCA
```

(*iii*) `$ cat laxmi | sort -t" " +1 | pg`

This will show the sorted output listing page by page. If you specify more than one filename, the sort will sort all the lines of all the input files together. So, sort command can merge the files also.

7.8.1.12 The grep Command

This command searches the input file(s) for a matching pattern. The grep is an acronym for "globally find regular expression and print". It is very efficient command for searching a pattern of character strings in one or more files. You can use both regular expressions containing ordinary character and metacharacters, in the search pattern. If you do not specify an input file, it takes its input from the standard input file. grep can be used any where in the pipeline.

The format of the command is as follows:

grep [options] search-pattern [filename....]

The options of the grep command are listed in Table 7.12.

Option	Function
-c	Reports only the count of matching lines.
-i	Reports only the names of files containing lines, with the search pattern.
v	Displays those line, not having the search pattern.
n	Precede each line by the line number in the input file.

Table 7.12 *Options of grep command*

Examples:

(*i*) `$ grep std *.c`

The above command will display all lines containing words such as stdin, stdout, stderr, etc.

(*ii*) If you want to search the exact match of the "std" string then enclose it within quotes, as shown below:

```
$ grep "std" *.c
```

(*iii*) The following command will display all lines beginning with an uppercase letter.

```
$ grep " ^ [ A-Z]. *
```

(*iv*) The following command will display all lines that begin with a blank.

```
$ grep "^.*" manoj.c
```

7.8.1.13 The find Command

This command is one of the most powerful commands of UNIX, with a very complex line structure. Sometimes, you know the name of a file, but you do not know where it is in the directory system. Manually, it could take a lot of time to search every directory. The find command can be used to find a file in the directory system. The format of the find command is as follows:

Find pathname ...... option......

The find command searches through the directory hierarchy and looks for all those files that match the options specified. It searches every directory path starting with the directory specified in "pathname". This command will report the filenames, with full path names, for each file that meets all the conditions specified by the options. The various options used with find command are listed in Table 7.13.

Option	Function
-atime n	The file must have been accessed in the last n days where 'n' is an integer.
-time n	The file must have been changed in the last n days where 'n' is an integer.
-exec command	This executes a UNIX command for each file which meet all the conditions specified in the findcommand options.
-group name	This selects all files belonging to the group specified.

Table 7.13 *Options used with find command*

Note: Each option, as usual is preceded by "-". Some options will be followed by an argument. A "+" sign before a number ("n") in an option means "more than". A "-" sign means "less than" For example: the option -atime +10 means "all files that have not been accessed for 10 days". If you specify a "-" as the pathname, the search starts with your current working directory.

Examples:

(*i*) `$ find | -name 'shalu.c' -print`

This finds a file called shalu.c, starting the search at the root directory.

(*ii*) `$ find | -name 'a*' - print`

This finds all those files which begin with the letter 'a'.

(*iii*) `$ find | usr | project1 - newer '|etc| manoj -print.`

This finds all those files which are newer than |etc| manoj. The search will start with |usr|project1 directory.

(*iv*) `$ find | -name 'dev' - type d -print`

This prints all directories named 'dev' in the system.

7.9 PIPES

In UNIX, you can combine certain commands into one command by a technique called pipe or piping. Pipe is the mechanism that combines two adjacent programs or commands by connecting the standard output of one program (or command) to the standard input of the next program (or command). So, the output of one command becomes the input of the next command. Piping is done by using the symbol '|' called a *pipe symbol*. The syntax of piping command is as follows:

```
$ command1 | command2 | command 3......
```

Examples:

(*i*) You can pipe the output of who command to the command wc for counting the number of users logged onto your system by giving the following command:

```
$ who | wc -l
```

As wc –l counts the number of lines from the listing of who command, you will get the output in a number (such as 4 or 5) indicating the number of users.

(*ii*) To list the programs (e.g. 'prog1' and 'prog2') give the following command:

```
$ cat prog1 prog2 | n1 | more
```

The cat command combines the two data files 'prog1' and 'prog2' , and n1 command reads from these files and adds line numbers. The more command displays the data screen by screen.

7.9.1 Importance of Pipes

Piping is one of the powerful features of UNIX. Using pipes, you can perform a complex task by combining several simple commands. Pipes save your time and disk space. If you use pipes, there is no need to create temporary files that may occupy much of your disk space. For instance, if you do not use pipes to display listing of more than one program (as illustrated in previous command), you will need to create temporary files as shown by the following commands:

(*i*) First, you will combine the two files ('prog1' and 'prog2') and temporary file 'temp' by giving following command:

```
cat prog1 prog2 > temp
```

(*ii*) Then, you will read the file 'temp', add the line numbers and store the output in second temporary file 'temp2' by giving the following command:

```
n1 < temp > temp2
```

(*iii*) Now, you will read the file 'temp2' for displaying the data by the following command:

```
more < temp2
```

Thus, two temporary files 'temp' and 'temp2' will use your disk space unnecessarily and you will require to delete these files by giving the following command:

```
$ rm temp temp2
```

So, piping not only makes your task easier but also saves the disk space.

7.10 SHELL SCRIPT

The shell script is similar to the batch files of DOS, where a sequence of frequently used UNIX commands is stored in a file and shell is made to read the file and execute the command. Such a file is called a shell script. For example, let us create and execute a shell script.

1. Open a file say Test1 using vi editor.
2. Enter the following commands and save the file.

```
who
ls -l
```

3. To execute the script, enter the following commands.

```
sh Test1
```

Or

```
chmod u +x Test1
```
(Change the mode of the file)

```
$ Test1
```

sh is a command which creates a sub-shell generally called a *child shell process*. This child shell reads the Test1 file, executes the commands contained in the file and thereafter returns control to the original shell.

7.10.1 Shell Types

The following types of shell are available in the UNIX system:

1. **Bourne Shell.** Bourne shell is the original command processor developed by At&T and named after its developer Stephen R. Bourne. It is the fastest and the widely used UNIX command processor and can be used on all UNIX systems. The executable filename is sh.

2. **C Shell.** C shell is another command processor developed by William Joy and others at the University of California at Berkeley. Its name has originated from the programming language 'C', as it resembles its syntax. The executable filename is csh.

3. **Korn Shell.** Korn shell is developed by David Korn which combines the best features of both the above shells. Its executable filename is ksh.

7.10.2 The Echo command

The echo command is used to display the messages on screen. In other words, it simply echoes back its argument on to the terminal (screen). For example, the output of the following command is 'Welcome to World of Computers'

```
$ echo Welcome to World of Computers
```

It is preferred to enclose the message that has to be echoed in double-quotes. Some of the options used with the echo command are shown in Table 7.14:

Character	Function
\c	Keeps the cursor on the same line of the screen after displaying the argument.
\n	Displays an additional blank line after the argument.
\007	Displays the argument and then sounds the system bell on the next line.

Table 7.14 *Options used with echo command*

7.10.3 File Expansion : Shell Metacharacters

As discussed earlier, the shell offers certain unique features like filename expansion variables, etc. which make it a powerful command language. The shell uses a set of symbols called *metacharacters*, to form a pattern to match various classes of filenames that can replace full filenames. These metacharacters are "*", "?" and "[ ]" symbols.

In certain circumstances metacharaters are to be used literally, for example:

```
$ echo Display filenames of all * in current directory
```

On execution of the above statement when executed, the * is replaced by a list of all the filenames in the current directory. UNIX also provides certain neutralise metacharacters such as backslash (\), Single quotes (') and double quotes (") as listed in Table 7.15.

Character	Function
\ (black slash)	Negate special properties of the single character following it.
' (pair of single quotes)	Negates special meaning of all characters enclosed within the quotes.
"" (pair of double quotes)	Negates special meaning of all enclosed characters except $',

Table 7.15 *Neutralise metacharacters of the shell*

The other shell metacharacters are discussed below:

1. Word separators (space, tab, newline) – These are special set of three characters used to separate one word from the next.

2. Command terminators (newline, semicolon and ampersand) - Newline is the simplest way of telling the shell that a command has ended. This is inserted on hitting the <Enter> key. For example:

```
$ pwd <Enter>
/user/templ
```

Semicolon (;) can be used to terminate commands. It helps to put several commands on the same line. For example:

```
$ cal ;date
```

Ampresand (&) is another command terminator that causes the command preceding it to run in the background.

7.11 VARIABLES

Like other programming language, shell provides the user the ability to define variables and assign values to them. A shell variable name must always begin with an upper-case or lower-case letter and may contain numbers and underscore character. There are certain system variables that have special significance.

7.11.1 System Variables

System (environmental) variables are those that are available to each process as it begins execution as shell maintains its own set of variables. Some of the standard environmental variables found in many systems are mentioned below:

(*a*) **Path.** It contains the search path string. The commands given by the user are searched in the directories specified in the path string. An error message is displayed on failure.

Example : `/bin/usr/bin`

(*b*) **Home.** It specifies the full path name for the user's login directory. The cd command without any argument will look for the contents of this variable and change the directory accordingly.

Example: `/usr/user1`

(*c*) **Term.** It holds the terminal specification. Being a UNIX system it can have different types of terminals. Typical entries found are vt100, vt200, ansi, etc.

(*d*) **Logname.** It holds the user login name.

Example: `user1`

(*e*) **PS1.** It stores the primary prompt string, which is the dollar sign ($). To change the prompt, simply assign the new value to this variable.

Example: `$ PS1="Trial" will change the prompt to 'Trial'`

(*f*) **PS2.** It specifies the secondary prompt string, which is displayed for the continuation of commands into the next line. Usually a greater than symbol (>) is assigned to it.

(*g*) **Shell.** It stores the name of the shell (Bourne, Korn or C). In Bourne shell, the entry sh is found in this variable.

7.11.2 Creating a Variable

The format for creating a variable is:

```
<variable_name>=
```

There should be no spaces on either side of the assignment operator.

```
$ name ="Vivek"
```

To refer the contents of a variable the $ symbol is used.

```
$ echo $name
Vivek
```

7.11.3 Reading a Value into a Variable

Along with assigning a value to a variable, the shell also allows a user to enter a value into a variable during execution of a shell script by using the read command.

Example: Let us write a shell script which will accept the Roll No, Name and Course Name from the user and display the same on the terminal screen.

1. Open a file called Test2 using vi editor.
2. Enter the following lines and save it.

```
echo "Enter your Roll_No : \c"
read r_no
echo "Enter you Name :\c"
read name
echo "Enter your Course_Name :\c"
read c_name
echo "Roll_No: $r_no, Name: $name, Course: $c_name"
```

3. `sh Test2 <Enter>`

7.11.4 Simple Arithmetic on Shell Variables

The command expr can be used to evaluate arithmetical computations on the shell variables having integer values.

```
$ expr 4+10
14
$ expr 8 - 2
6
$ expr 3 \* 4
12
$ expr 45 /5
9
```

The arguments of the expr command must be separated by a blank space from one another. The special symbols must be preceded by a back slash (\) so that the shell does not expand them. The division of expr is an integer division, i.e. it displays only the integer portion of the result. The output of the expr command can be stored in a variable. Arithmetic computation of variables is also possible through the expr command.

Examples:

```
$ sum='expr 25 + 5'
$ echo $sum                  will display 30
$ x=12
$ y=80
$ echo sum is $x + $y
                             sum is 12 + 80
                             will display the arguments.
$ echo sum is `expr $x + $y'
                             sum is 92
$ sum='expr $x + $y'         will store 92 in the variable sum
```

7.11.5 Local and Global Variables

By default the shell variables are 'local' to the shell that create them. The values of these shell variables are not available to the newly created child process.

The export command is provided by UNIX, which can be used to declare a variable as global so that these variables are available to the child process.

The following example explains the concept of local and global variables.

```
$ City = Jaipur
$ echo "${City}"
Jaipur
$ sh                     Creates a new shell
$ echo "${City}"         No response
```

`$ City =Agra`	Assigning a new value 'Agra' to city
`$ echo "${City}`	
Agra	
`$ ctrl d`	Returns to parent shell
`$ echo "$" {City}`	Returns 'Jaipur'. Parent is unaware of 'Agra'
`$ sh`	Creates a child shell
`$ echo "${City}`	value 'Agra' destroyed
`$ ctrl d`	Return to parent

At this stage users can use export command with variable used in the shell so that t' other programs can use it.

`$ City = Jaipur`	
`$ export City`	
`echo "${City}"`	
Jaipur	
`$ sh`	Creates a new child shell
`$ echo "${City}"`	Child shell has the variable 'City'
Jaipur	
`$`	
`$ City = Agra`	Assign a new value to City
`$ echo "${City}"`	
Agra	
`$ ctrl d`	Return to parent
`$ echo "${City}"`	Parent shell retains its original value 'Jaipur'

The last two commands display that the variables can be exported or passed on to sub shells, but the reverse is not true. Export command causes a copy of the variables and values to be passed onto a child shell.

7.12 OPERATORS

UNIX employs different types of operators. Let us discuss them briefly.

7.12.1 Operators on Numeric Variables

In shell, the following operators on numeric variables are used:

-eq : equals to
-ne : not equal to
-gt : greater than

-lt : less than
-ge : greater than or equal to
-le : less than or equal to

Examples:

```
$x=10;  y=25
$test  $x  -eq  $y
$echo  $?
1
$
```

`$test $x -eq $y` — testing for equality of the variables 'x' and 'y'

`$echo $?` — Checking the exit status

`1` — false, as value of 'x' is not equal to the value of 'y'

7.12.2 Operators on String Variables

In shell, the following operators on string variables are used:

= : equality of strings
!= : not equal
-z : zero length (string contains zero characters: null string)
-n : string length is non zero

Examples:

```
$  emp_name="Vinay"
```

`$ test -z $emp_name`	will return the exit status 1 as the string name is not null
`$ test -n $emp_name`	will return 0 as the string is not null
`$ test -z "$emp_address"`	will return 0 as the variable has not been defined
`$ test $name ="Vinay"`	will return 1 as the value of name is not equal to "Vinay"

7.12.3 Operators on Files

In shell, the following operators on files are used:

-f : the file exists and is an ordinary file
-s : the file exists and the file size is non zero
-d : directory exists
-r : file exists and has read permission
-w : file exists and has write permission
-x : file exists and has execute permission

Examples:

`$ if test -f "test.doc"`	will check the existence of the file test.doc, if it exists and it is an ordinary file.

```
then echo "It's a Ordinary file"
else echo "Its not a Ordinary file"
fi
```
returns 0 else 1

`$ test -r "test.doc"` will check for the read permission for the file test.doc

`$ test -d "$HOME"` will check for the existence of the user's home directory

7.12.4 Logical Operators

The logical AND, logical OR and logical NOT operators are used for combining more than one condition.

-a : logical AND

-o : logical OR

! : logical NOT

Examples:

`$ test -r "test.doc" -a -w "test.doc"`

will check both the read and write permission for the file 'test.doc' and returns either 0 or 1 depending upon the result.

`$ echo $?<Enter>` will show the status of the above command.

7.13 CONSTRUCTS USED IN SHELL SCRIPTS

Like other programming languages, the UNIX shell also offers certain constructs for looping and decision making which can be used in shell scripts. Let us discuss these.

7.13.1 The if...then...else construct

The if construct is usually used in conjunction with the 'test' construct. The test command is used to test for the position of files and values of variables. The result of the test command is always 'true' or 'false'.

```
If <condition>
then command(s)
else commands(s)
fi
```
<indicates the end of the if construct>

7.13.2 The Case...Esac construct

The shell script uses this construct to perform a specific set of instructions depending on the value of a variable and can be used in place of the if construct.

The syntax is as follows:

```
case variablename in
        pattern) command;;
        pattern) command;;
        *) default;;
esac
```

The case statement allows a shell script to choose from a list of alternatives. This statement compares the value of the variable with the patterns from top to bottom and performs the commands associated with the first pattern that matches. The patterns are written using the shell's pattern matching rules. Each action is terminated by the double semicolon ';;'. The word 'esac' marks the end of case construct.

In case, nothing matches the pattern then the command following the "*)" label is executed, it is used as the last choice. If it were provided as the first choice then the commands following it will be executed always and the case statement will ignore all the following patterns.

The case...esac construct is commonly used for setting up menus, where the course of action is to be decided from a set of alternatives.

Example:

```
case ${opt} in
        1) ls
        2) who
        3) date
        4) cal
esac
```

7.13.3 The for ... do ... done Construct

The for construct is the only shell control flow statement that is commonly typed at the prompt rather than putting it in a script file. The commands to be executed are specified between the words do .. done.

The syntax for the for statement is as follows:

```
for <variable> in <list>
do
        <commands>
done
```

Examples:

(*i*) A for loop construct to display names one file per line is given below:

```
$ for i in Jaya Aruna Rahul
>do
>       echo $i
>       done
$
```

(*ii*) **Shell script using for loop is given below:**

```
For i in 1 2 3 4 5 6 7 8 9 0
do
        echo $i
done
```

The above loop executes for 10 times and displays the numbers 1 2 3 4 5 6 7 8 9 0.

7.13.4 The while loop

This loop uses the exit status from a command to control the execution of the command(s) in the body of the loop. The loop is executed repeatedly until the set of commands condition returns a non-zero status.

The syntax of the while loop is as follows:

```
while <command>
do
        <commands>
        # loop body executed as long as command returns true (a zero)
done
```

Example:

The shell program for printing the first 10 positive numbers using the while loop is given below:

```
# using while loop
ctr=1                          #assign a value 1 to a variable ctr
while [$ctr -le 10]
do
echo $ctr
num='expr $ctr+ 1'             # increment num by 1
done
#end of script
```

7.13.5 The until loop

This loop checks the exit status of the command, and executes the command(s) enclosed within the do and done statement, until the condition command returns true (a zero status). The syntax for the until loop is:

```
until <command>
do
        <command(s)>
        # loop body executed as long as command returns false.
done
```

Example:

Printing the first 10 positive numbers using until loop.

```
val =1
until [ $val -gt 10]
do
        echo $val
        num='expr $val + 1'
done
```

7.13.6 The Break ... continue construct

At times, you may require to skip the remaining commands of a loop and return to the beginning of the loop. Sometimes, a need may arise to terminate and exit the loop. The shell provides the commands break and continue for these purposes.

The continue command will skip the remaining statements or commands in a loop and return to the beginning of the loop. Whereas the break command will terminate the loop and exit the loop.

Example:

Let's consider the previous example.

```
while true
do
      echo "Enter your option"
      echo "Press 5 to exit"
      read opt
      case ${opt} in
            1) ls;;
            2) who;;
            3) date;;
            4) cal;;
            5) break;;
            *) echo "Invalid Option"
      esac
done
$
```

Whenever user presses 5, the break command is executed and while is terminated.

7.14 PARAMETER HANDLING IN SHELL SCRIPTS

The shell interprets commands in UNIX. Whenever a command is entered and the <enter> key is pressed, the shell puts word on the command line into special variables as follows:

$0 is the variable used to put command name.

$1 is the variable used to put the first argument.

$2 is the variable used to put the second argument.

And so on.

The UNIX shell creates variables up to $9. The variables $1 through $9 are also called *positional parameters of the command line*. Depending upon the number of arguments specified in the command, the shell will assign values to some or all of these variables.

Example:

```
cat  test.doc
```

$0 contains the command name *i.e* cat

$1 contains the first argument *i.e* test.doc

$2 does not contain anything (since there are no more arguments)

Apart from the variables $0 to $9, the shell also assigns values to the following variables when a command is entered:

$* contains the entire string of arguments.

$# contains the number of arguments specified in the command.

Example:

```
cat  testfil1  testfil2
```

$* it will contain the string of arguments "testfil1 testfil2"

$# it will contain the value 2 since the number of arguments are 2.

THEORY QUESTIONS

1. What are editors? Describe various types of editors.
2. Describe various ways to start vi editors.
3. Discuss different modes of working in vi.
4. How can you modify the text in vi editor? Write the important commands for deleting and undeleting the text.
5. How can you search a text pattern in vi?
6. What is Emacs? Write the important commands used in Emacs editor.
7. Define a process. Name the data structure that stores the details about all processes.
8. How can you display the contents of a process Table in UNIX? Write the various forms of ps command.
9. How can you assign higher priorities to various processes in UNIX? Write the commands.
10. What are background processes? Write the commands to terminate a background process.
11. What is multitasking? Explain the booting process in a multitasking system.
12. Define the following terms:

    (*a*) Standard input

    (*b*) Standard output

    (*c*) Standard error

13. What is redirection? How can you redirect the standard input, standard output and standard error. Explain with commands.
14. What are filters? Explain their importance.
15. Write a short note on following filter commands:

(*a*) tee	(*b*) pg	(*c*) cut
(*d*) paste	(*e*) head	(*f*) tail
(*g*) grep	(*h*) sort	

16. How do you search a text pattern? Explain with commands.
17. How do you find a text pattern? Explain with commands.
18. What are pipes? What is the importance of pipes.
19. What is UNIX shell? What are the different types of shell available in the UNIX system?
20. What are shell metacharacters? Explain by giving appropriate examples.
21. State and explain the system environmental variables of UNIX.
22. What are the different numeric, file and logical operators offered by UNIX.
23. What do you understand by environment variables? What environment will it create after the execution of the following sequence of commands?

    HOME = /home/preeti

    LOGNAME = preeti

    MAIL = /ver/mail/preeti

    PATH = /use/bin

    PS1 = '$'

    PS2 = '>'

    SHELL = /bin/sh

    TERM = ansi
24. How can you run a process in the background?
25. How is a process created in UNIX. Explain in brief.

WORKSHOP

1. Write and run a shell script which will take a filename as input and copy it.
2. Write and run a shell script which will accept the employee name and his basic as input and print his name, basic and HRA. HRA is based on the following information:

    If basic >2000 HRA = 550 else HRA = 350
3. Write and run a shell script that will take two filenames as input and remove one, if both are equal.
4. Write and run a shell script which will display the following menu:

    (*a*) Display who all are logged in.

    (*b*) Display long listing of files including hidden files page by page.

    (*c*) Display today's date and time.

    (*d*) Exit

    Depending upon the choice of the user, the appropriate actions should be performed. For choice 'a' to 'c' appropriate messages should be displayed before the desired output.

5. Perform following operations in vi editor:
   (*a*) To search a string 'Shyam' and change it to 'Ram'.
   (*b*) Delete a word
   (*c*) Insert text into a file
6. Give a command in UNIX to find out all the users from the /usr and also sort them.
7. Perform the following operations in vi editor.
   (*a*) Copy 7 lines of text to another file.
   (*b*) Delete contents of a file.
   (*c*) Set the line numbers.
   (*d*) Display the lines that are common in both the files.
8. Write and run a single command line statement (using redirection, pipes and tees) that will accept lines typed through the keyboard and copy them in sorted order in a file 'newsort' and also count the number of lines and store the count in another file named 'count_lines'.
9. Give the command to terminate a process.
10. Write and run a shell script that accepts the Roll No., Name and Course Name from the user and display the same on the terminal screen.

8

INTRODUCTION TO INTERNET

8.1 INTRODUCTION

Internet, the largest computer network, is very popular among millions of users world-wide. It helps people to communicate with each other sitting at any corner of the world. It is a major media for creating and viewing any kind of information. It has now become a vast virtual market place for advertising and selling products. In fact, there is no area left where Internet is not helping us. Therefore, you must learn Internet in order to get its full benefits.

In this chapter, we will discuss basic concepts of Internet along with its tools. We will also discuss various modes of connecting to Internet.

8.2 OVERVIEW TO INTERNET

Internet is a technology for linking Local Area Networks (LANs) into a huge global computer network. Before discussing its importance and applications, let us first define Internet.

8.2.1 Definition of Internet

Internet is defined as a network of networks. Internet is the world's largest computer network, which connects several computers of different types belonging to various networks all over the globe.

8.2.2 Difference between Internet and Online Services

Online services are commercial networks that are owned by different agencies, while there is no owner of Internet. Online services charge users for access while no one pays for using Internet. Online services are profit making firms that offer current news, chat rooms and other information to their subscribers over standard telephone lines. They also provide Internet Access. Internet, on the other hand, is a large network of networks that facilitates data communication services. The commercial networks that charge user for access are:

- America On Line (AOL)
- Compu Serve
- MCI Mail

8.2.3 Authorities Governing Internet

Internet is not governed by a single authority. There are many authorities that control the Internet today. They are:

(*a*) **Internet SOCiety (ISOC).** It is a voluntary membership organisation, which promotes global interchange of information on Internet.

(*b*) **Internet Service Provider (ISP).** It sells Internet subscriptions to the public.

(*c*) **Internet Architecture Board (IAB).** It provides addresses for computers on the Internet and sets rules for naming addresses.

(*d*) **Internet Engineering Task Force (IETF).** The technical and operational problems on Internet are solved by Internet Engineering Task Force.

Various authorities governing Internet are shown in Figure 8.1.

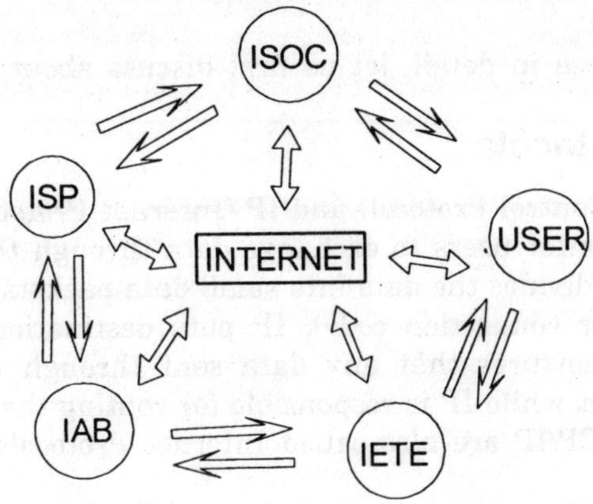

Figure 8.1 *Various authorities governing Internet*

8.2.4 Applications of Internet

Internet is the world's largest computer network, which connects several computers of different types belonging to various networks all over the globe. Various applications of Internet are–

- It helps people to communicate with each other sitting at any corner of the world.
- It is the major media for creating and viewing any kind of information related with Science, Art, Music, History, Computers, Engineering, Medicine, Management, Religion, Movies, Games, Sex, etc.
- We can do audio and video conferencing on Internet.
- Internet helps students to learn and find suitable jobs for them.
- It helps people to chat with each other so that they can make friends across the world.
- Internet provides all types of entertainment to people by games, movies, etc.
- Internet helps organisations to link their widely spread offices and employees.
- Using E-mail services, people can send messages to any part of the world within few minutes.
- Internet is the vast virtual market place for advertising and selling products through the latest concept of E-commerce.
- We can see our horoscope on Internet.
- We can also watch news, sports, movies on Internet.

- Web publishing (Electronic Publishing) is the new approach of publishing, which is replacing paper books with electronic books.

8.3 CONNECTING TO INTERNET

Connecting to the Internet through host machine by providing user name and password is called logging In. There are four modes of connecting to the Internet, which are–

(*a*) Host/Terminal connection

(*b*) Individual Computer TCP/IP Link

(*c*) Dial-up Access through LAN

(*d*) Dedicated Access

Before discussing these in detail, let us first discuss about Internet Protocols.

8.3.1 Internet Protocols

TCP (Transmission Control Protocol) and IP (Internet Protocol) are the standards (set of rules) that enable computer users to exchange data through the Internet while sending a large block of data. TCP divides the data into small data packets and adds some additional information (such as error connection code). IP puts destination address information on such data packets. TCP ensures that any data sent through the Internet reaches the destination computer intact while IP is responsible for routing the data packets to a desired destination IP address. TCP/IP are also called Internet Protocols.

8.3.2 Host/Terminal Connection

Host/Terminal connection is the least expensive type of Internet access. In this method, our computer is not really connected to the Internet but we are using it as a terminal, which is remote to an Internet host or server. This method requires a modem and a phone line. Using host/terminal connection, only text based applications can be accessed on the Internet and we cannot access graphical applications. Using this method, we get access to the shell of a UNIX computer, therefore it is also called *Shell Access Connection*. Host/Terminal Connection offers following advantages:

- Ideal for University and College students as it is more economical.
- Provides good speed for accessing text only documents.

8.3.3 Individual Computer TCP/IP Link

TCP/IP is an abbreviation of two Internet protocols, Transmission Control Protocol (TCP) and Internet Protocol (IP). TCP permits two Internet-connected computers to get a reliable connection. IP is responsible for routing the data packets to a desired destination IP address. TCP/IP link requires a modem or an ISDN adapter and an analog phone line or an ISDN line. With this link, the user computer is assigned a temporary IP address and is directly connected to the Internet.

TCP/IP links can either be SLIP or PPP links. The differences between SLIP and PPP links are listed in Table 8.1.

SLIP Link	PPP Link
1. SLIP stands for Serial Line Internet Protocol.	1. PPP stands for Point to Point Protocol.
2. SLIP is an older protocol.	2. PPP is a new protocol.
3. It is slower in speed.	3. It is faster in speed.

Table 8.1 *Difference between SLIP link and PPP link*

Individual Computer TCP/IP Link offers following advantages:

- Most suitable for Internet cafes because using a phone line and a hub, many computers can be simultaneously connected to Internet with cheaper cost.
- Most suitable for homes as a single PC can be easily connected to Internet using a modem and a telephone line. Moreover, the Internet and phone line charges per hour are also not very high.
- Using ISDN line, the Internet access becomes cheaper and faster.

8.3.4 Dial-up through LAN

Dial-up through LAN is an intermediate type of connection between TCP/IP link and Dedicated link as it provides some features of both these connections. It is set between LAN and Internet servers. It is generally used to exchange a large volume of E-mail messages on a little Internet traffic. Dial-up Access through LAN is ideal for those organisations which need to send large volumes of E-mails to their branch offices and customers on daily basis because this mode provides a high speed.

8.3.5 Dedicated Access

Dedicated link connection is a permanent Internet connection. It allows the user's computer to remain connected to the Internet round the clock. It can be set up over a telephone line using a router or a modem. A router is an electronic device that examines each data packet on receiving and provides the way to send it towards its destination. So, the router transmits data from one network to another. We can also use a modem in place of a router. A router provides higher transmission speed (more than 56.6 kbps) while a modem provides low speed (*i.e.* 28.8 kbps). Dedicated link offers following advantages:

- Dedicated link connections are generally used by big organisations for providing on line Internet services to their customers. It is ideal for big organisations needing Internet with permanent connection.
- Ideal for institutes providing on-line education through Internet.
- Ideal for E-commerce and web publishing due to highest speed and round the clock access.

The differences among various ways of connecting to Internet are shown in Table 8.2.

Host/ Terminal Connection	Individual Computer TCP/IP Link	Dial-up Access through LAN	Dedicated Access
1. No direct connection with Internet.	1. Direct Temporary connection.	1. Direct Temporary connection.	1. Direct Permanent connection.
2. Requires a modem and phone line.	2. Requires a modem/ ISDN adapter and phone line/ISDN line.	2. Requires LAN modem and phone line.	2. Requires modem/ router and phone line.
3. Limited Access with slow speed.	3. Average access with average speed.	3. Average access with high speed.	3. High access with high speed.
4. Does not provide GUI interface.	4. Provides GUI interface.	4. Provides GUI interface.	4. Provides GUI interface.
5. Used by students on UNIX machines.	5. Used by individuals & Internet cafes at homes or small offices.	5. Used by organisations to exchange large volume of E-mails.	5. Used by big organisations for all internet applications.

Table 8.2 *Various ways of connecting to Internet*

8.4 INTERNET TOOLS

Internet provides the following important tools and services:

(1) Browsers
(2) Search Engines
(3) Electronic Mail
(4) File Transfer Protocol
(5) Usenet
(6) Telnet
(7) Internet Relay Chat
(8) Other Tools

Let us discuss about these tools in detail.

8.4.1 Browsers

Surfing refers to the searching of information on Internet without knowing what we are searching for. Surfing on Internet is done by programs, which are called browsers. Browsers help non-technical people to work on Internet because they are very user friendly. You need not remember the commands. Browsers always help you while surfing the Internet. The differences between a text only browser and a graphical browser are shown in Table 8.3.

The popular browsers are:

(*a*) World Wide Web (WWW)
(*b*) Gopher
(*c*) Netscape Navigator
(*d*) Microsoft Internet Explorer

Text Only Browser	Graphical Browser
1. It shows web pages with text only without graphic and animation. 2. It is very fast. 3. Example: Lynx	1. It shows complete web pages with text, graphics, animations and sound. 2. It is comparatively very slow. 3. Examples: Netscape Navigator, Internet Explorer and NCSA Mosaic.

Table 8.3 *Difference between a text only browser and a graphical browser*

We will discuss about these browsers in the next chapter.

8.4.2 Search Engines

Search engine is an Internet accessible search service that enables us to search for information on the Internet using a browser. The commonly used Search Engines are–

- Yahoo
- Rediff
- Infoseek
- Lycos
- Webcrawler

We will discuss about these search engines in the next chapter.

8.4.3 Electronic Mail

E-mail is the most common service available on Internet. E-mail stands for Electronic Mail. Using E-mail, we can send mail to any part of the world in the form electronic documents, which can include both text and graphics. Users of Internet create their own E-mail accounts which can be accessed by giving passwords so that no unauthorised person can access their mails. E-mail is becoming so popular that people prefer it in place of postage mail. We will discuss E-mail in detail in Chapter 10.

8.4.4 Downloading

Downloading refers to copying software from a remote computer to your computer through Internet. Using FTP (File Transfer Protocol), Internet users can copy any file from remote computer to their computer.

We will discuss the process of downloading in the next chapter.

8.4.5 File Transfer Protocol

File Transfer Protocol (FTP) is a tool of Internet used for copying any file from one Internet host to another. Copying a file from any remote server to our host computer is called *downloading*. FTP downloads files to our server from any remote server on Internet. There are two types of FTP– Regular FTP and Anonymous FTP. In Regular FTP, Internet users can transfer files from those remote computers where they have their own account and identification using passwords. In Anonymous FTP, files are available to all Internet users for downloading. In this method of FTP, Internet users log on by entering the words 'anonymous', 'guest' or 'ftp' instead of a user name and provide their E-mail addresses as their passwords. Anonymous FTP is the easiest way to upload and download files, however users are restricted by the security system of the remote computer. Anonymous sites permit us to access their files without establishing an account with them. By using anonymous FTP, we can access public archives on the Internet. There are two modes for transferring flies in FTP—ASCII mode and Binary mode. In ASCII mode, we can download mainly plain text and postscript files. However, most files in Internet are transferred in binary mode. For example, zip, jpg, mpeg, com, exe and gif files are transferred in binary mode. Program files such as .c and .h files are transferred in ASCII mode.

Using FTP Internet users can also transfer files to servers and save them to a directory on remote computer. This is called *upload*.

8.4.5.1 Connecting to FTP

We can connect to an FTP site in one of the following two ways:

(*a*) **Using FTP via VSNL.** We can connect to FTP using UNIX command interface via an Internet Service Provider such as VSNL. In this way, we have to provide commands by typing them on a keyboard. To use FTP via VSNL, we follow the procedure explained below:

- While connecting with Internet, instead of typing 'PPP', enter 'telnet' followed by host-name e.g. 'del2'.
- A menu will be displayed. We now select the option 2, which is 'FTP'.

  The FTP prompt 'ftp>' will be displayed on screen. Now we open the FTP site by entering the following command:

  ```
  ftp>open  <site-name>
  ```

  where <site-name' is the name of FTP site.
- For downloading a file, enter the following commands:

  ```
  ftp>ascii
  ftp>get  <file-name>
  ```

  where ascii command specifies that the file is a text file and <file-name> is the name of file. Now if we want to download a binary file, specify 'bin' instead of 'ascii' as shown below:

  ```
  ftp>bin
  ```

  If we want to see the contents of a text file while downloading, give the following command:

  ```
  ftp>get  <file-name>  |more
  ```

  For uploading a file, give the following command:

  ```
  ftp>put  <file-name>
  ```

Frequently used FTP commands are given in Table 8.4

Command	Purpose
ascii	Specify that the file to be downloaded is a text file.
bin	Specify that the file to be downloaded is a binary file such as exe, com etc.
dir	To see the list of files in a current directory.
ls -l	Same as dir.
cd <dir-name>	To change to a sub-directory.
dir <dir-name>	To see the list of files in directory specified.
del <file-name>	To delete a file on remote computer.
get <file-name>	To download a file.
mget <file-name1> <file-name2> ...	To download many files.
put <file-name>	To upload a file.
mput <file-name1> <file-name2>	To upload many files.
bye	To quit FTP.
quit	same as bye.

Table 8.4 *Frequently used FTP commands*

(*b*) **Using a Web Browser.** We can also connect to FTP using a Web browser such as Internet Explorer or Netscape Navigator. This is the Graphical User Interface (GUI) way of connecting to an FTP site. This is the simplest way as we need not remember the UNIX commands and can select options using both mouse and keyboard.

8.4.6 Usenet

It is a world-wide computer based discussion system on Internet. It consists of special groups set up by Internet user on a range of topics from entertainment activity to scientific research. These groups of topics in Usenet are called *Newsgroups*. Usenet consists of thousands of newsgroups, each of which consists of articles sent by Internet Users.

8.4.6.1 Accessing the Usenet

A special type of program called a *newsreader* accesses Usenet. This program helps us to handle the volume of news available on Usenet. With newsreader, we can select the news, which we want to read or discard the news, which we do not.

8.4.6.2 Newsgroups

Various groups of topics in Usenet are called *Newsgroups.* Usenet is a forum in which people share news on a defined topic through large electronic bulletin-boards on Internet. Newsgroups are open and hence discussion become scattered on Usenet newsgroups. Usenet newsgroups are organised into various categories called *Hierarchies*. These hierarchies include following 3 sub-categories:

(*a*) **Standard newsgroups.** These include high quality discussions, which can not be established without a formal voting procedure. The top-level standard newsgroup hierarchies are described in Table 8.5.

Hierarchy Name	Description
Comp	Every thing related to computers
Sci	Discussions on science and Engineering
Soc	Social groups
News	News about usenet
Rec	Recreational subjects such as sports, aviation, music, arts, etc.
Talk	Random discussions on controversial subjects, including sex, politics, religion, etc.
Misc	Other topics viz health, law, books, etc.

Table 8.5 *The top level newsgroups hierarchies*

(*b*) **Alt newsgroups.** These include discussions, which can be established by anyone with the requisite technical knowledge.

(*c*) **Biz newsgroups.** These include discussions for commercial uses.

The Newsgroup Client

Google Group is one of the popular newsgroup clients. You can connect it by entering the URL as `http://groups.google.com` as shown in Figure 8.2. In order to participate in a newsgroup, either enter the name of topic in the search box and click on 'Google Search' button or browse through the groups and select a category as shown in Figure 8.3.

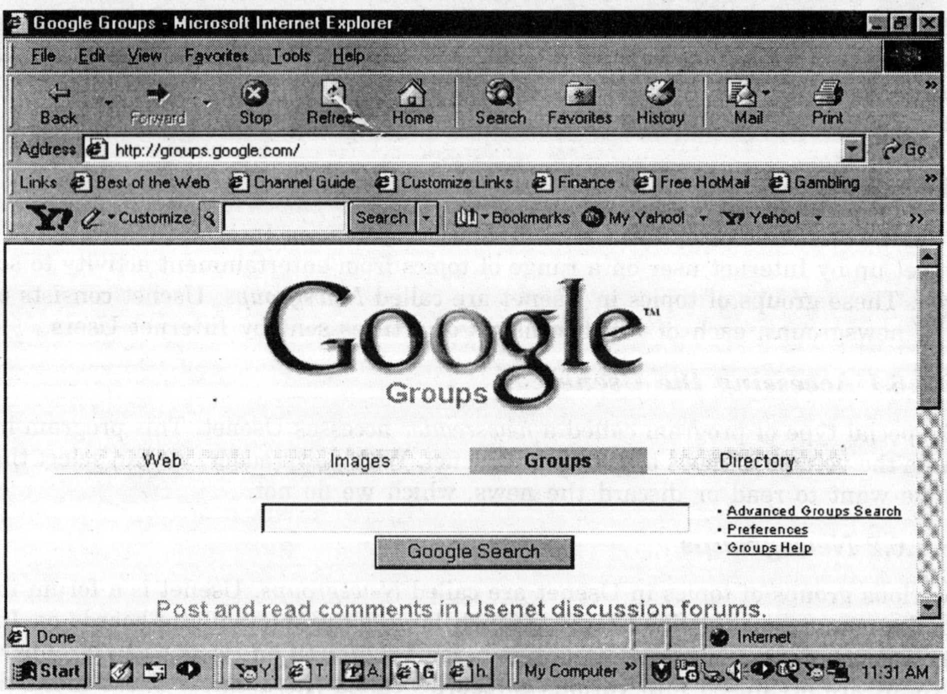

Fig. 8.2 *The google group*

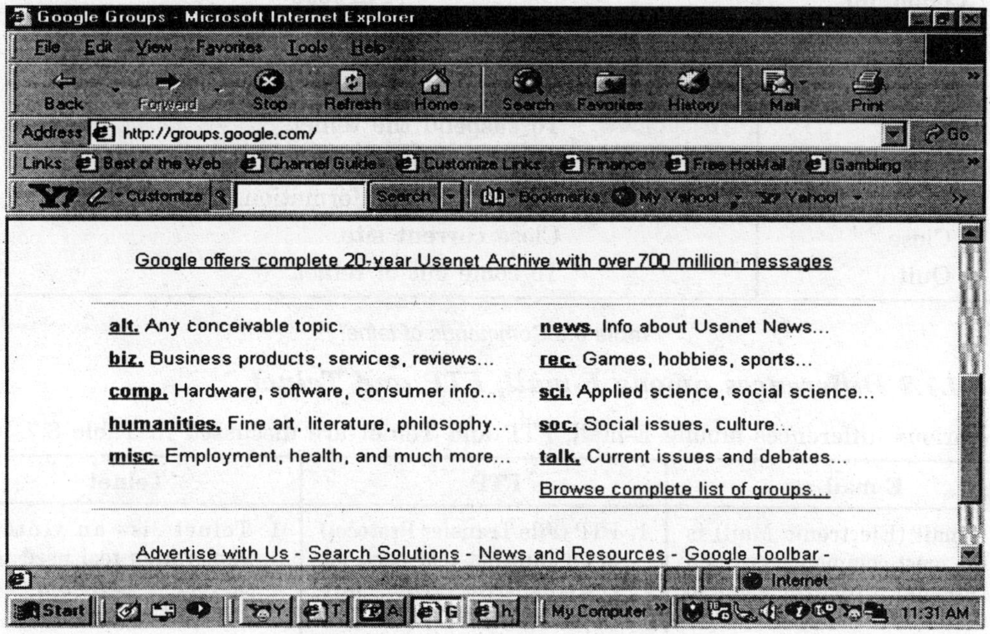

Fig. 8.3 *Categories in the google group*

8.4.7 Telnet

Telnet is an Internet exploration tool that is used for logging on remote computers on the Internet. Using Telnet, we can communicate with a wide range of remote systems with which we have an account. Telnet is mainly used to access databases on other systems. It is frequently used by libraries. Using telnet, we can use our computer from anywhere in the world. Telnet is actually an Internet standard protocol for remote terminal connection service. Telnet is one of the simplest tool on Internet. With telnet, employees of branch office can access data on the computer in the head office. Using telnet, we can also log on to and use third party computers that have been made assessable to the public. For example, using telnet we can read the catalog of the United States library of Congress. We can also use telnet to obtain other services such as Gopher and Web servers.

8.4.7.1 Using Telnet via VSNL

To use Telnet via VSNL, we follow the procedure explained below:

(*a*) While connecting with Internet, instead of typing 'PPP', enter 'telnet' followed by host-name e.g. 'del2'.

(*b*) A menu will be displayed. We now select the option 3, which is 'Telnet'.

(*c*) Use telnet commands as given in Table 8.6.

Command	Purpose
Open	To connect to a site.
Send	To send special characters.
z	To suspend the telnet.
Status	To print status information.
?	To print help information.
Close	Close current site.
Quit	To come out of telnet.

Table 8.6 *Commands of telnet*

8.4.7.2 Differences among E-mail, FTP and Telnet

Various differences among E-mail, FTP and Telnet are discussed in Table 8.7

E-mail	FTP	Telnet
1. E-mail (Electronic Mail) is the most common service on Internet which is used to send mail to any part of the world in the form of electronic documents.	1. FTP (File Transfer Protocol) is an Internet tool used for copying file from one Internet host to another.	1. Telnet is an Internet exploration tool used to log on remote computers on the Internet.
2. E-mail is similar to postage mail.	2. FTP is entirely different from postage mail.	2. Telnet is also not related to postage mail.
3. Each Internet user requires an E-mail address and password to use an E-mail service.	3. FTP works in two modes one mode requires user ID and password on remote machine while in another user can be anonymous or guest.	3. Telnet also works in two modes - one requiring the user identification and another does not require user ID and user can be anonymous or guest.
4. E-mail service offers an address book containing addresses of E-mail users.	4. FTP does not provide any address book or other database.	4. Telnet helps users to access database on remote machines.

Table 8.7 *Differences among E-mail, FTP and telnet*

8.4.8 Internet Relay Chat

Internet Relay Chat (IRC) is the most popular tool and Internet used by people to talk to each other using the computer. It is the only place where we can go and talk to people from anywhere in the world in the form of exchanging text and audio. It is used by people sitting at their homes anywhere in the world to talk to each other electronically using computer. It is generally called as *chatting*. In chatting, discussions of each participant are displayed on the screen of all the other participants taking part in a conversation. We can either join an existing conversation or start our own conversation on any topic. There are no constraints on the topics that may be discussed. We can discuss on sports, religion, health, sex education, etc. Now-a-days, chatting has become a great fun. People spend hours in Cyber-Café for chatting. They make new friends, some fall in love and few even marry. Chatting has become a most interesting tool on Internet.

8.4.9 Other Tools

Let us conclude this chapter with a brief discussion on some other tools of Internet.

8.4.9.1 Veronica

VERONICA stands for Very Easy Rodent Oriented Net-wide Index to Computer Archives. It is an index of Internet Gopher items and titles which provide keyword searches of Gopher items and titles. It is menu-driven and hence is very easy to operate.

8.4.9.2 Wais

WAIS stands for Wide Area Information System. It searches text documents containing the specified keywords. It identifies documents, which are most closely related to the topic specified.

8.4.9.3 Archie

Archie is an Internet search program used to locate files and directories on anonymous FTP servers on the Internet.

THEORY QUESTIONS

1. Define Internet and discuss why is it so popular? Describe various applications of Internet.
2. Differentiate Internet from Online services. Name three Online Services.
3. What are TCP/IP? Discuss their role in Internet.
4. What is logging in? Explain various modes of connecting to Internet.
5. What are various tools and services available on Internet? Explain them briefly.
6. Explain the following terms:
   (*a*) WWW (*b*) Usenet (*c*) Newsgroups (*d*) IRC
7. Differentiate among the following terms:
   (*a*) FTP and Telnet
   (*b*) Download and Upload
   (*c*) Alt and Biz Newsgroups
   (*d*) SLIP and PPP Links
   (*e*) TCP/IP link and Dedicated link connections
8. Give full form of the following abbreviated terms:
   (*a*) FTP (*b*) TCP (*c*) IP (*d*) WWW
   (*e*) WAIS (*f*) ISP (*g*) ISOC
9. Explain the use of following tools of Internet:
   (*a*) WAIS (*b*) VERONICA (*c*) Archie (*d*) Browser
10. Name the authorities that control the Internet today.
11. What is the use of FTP? Explain two ways by which you can connect to an FTP site.

12. Write the commands of FTP connected via VSNL –
    (*a*) To specify that the file to be downloaded is a text file.
    (*b*) To see the list of files in a current directory.
    (*c*) To see the list of files in directory specified.
    (*d*) To download a file.
    (*e*) To upload many files.
13. Write the function of following commands of Telnet connected via VSNL:
    (*a*) Open (*b*) Close (*c*) z (*d*) ?
14. What is chatting? Why it is so popular among Internet users?
15. Are a browser and a search engine same? Explain with examples.

WORKSHOP

1. Connect to the Internet using the type of connection available in your institute.
2. After connecting to Internet, load the graphical browser available in your system.
3. Use various search engines for reading today news. Name the search engine, which you find convenient to use.
4. Chat with your friend using IRC services provided by various search engines. Name the search engine, which you find convenient for chatting.
5. Find out various newsgroups on Internet through a search engine. Name the newsgroup for discussion on engineering education.
6. Log on to your remote computer using Telnet via VSNL (if VSNL connection is available in your computer lab).

9
BROWSERS

9.1 INTRODUCTION

In the last chapter, we discussed various applications of Internet. Surfing is the common activity of all Internet users. Surfing refers searching information on Internet without knowing what we are searching. As all Internet users are not computer professionals, surfing on Internet is done by programs, which help non-technical people to work on Internet. In this chapter, we will discuss about these programs. We will also discuss about other programs, which help us searching the required information on Internet. We will also discuss the procedure for copying information and programs on our computer from the Internet servers.

While working on Internet, you will find use of term cyberspace. Cyberspace describes the place where you are when you are traversing the virtual geographical space of Internet. To know where you are, you must know the addresses of Internet servers and services. Let us begin our discussion with various address systems of Internet.

9.2 UNIFORM RESOURCE LOCATOR (URL)

The addressing system on Internet is called Uniform Resource Locator (URL). It has following two forms:

(*a*) Letter Addressing System or Domain Name System (DNS)

(*b*) Number Addressing System or Internet Protocol (IP) Addressing System

Let us discuss these.

9.2.1 Letter Addressing System or Domain Name System (DNS)

Domain name is a readable computer address that identifies the location of a computer on the Internet. Domain Name System is the conceptual system of naming domains that form the hierarchical organisation of the Internet. This system is also called Letter Addressing System. The general format of this system is:

`Name-of-user@Name-of-host.subdomain.domain`

where,

`Name-of-user` is the name of Internet account for logging into the host computer

`Name-of-host` is the name of each computer on the Internet.

`Subdomain` is generally the name of organisation.

`Domain` is a group of computers that are administered as a unit in Internet letter addressing system, which is easily understood by a person.

There are two types of domains—Geographic and Non-geographic domains.

9.2.1.1 Geographic Domain

The last part of domain name indicates the name of the country where the computer is located. This is called Geographic Domain. The examples of few geographic domains are listed in Table 9.1.

Domain Name	Country
.au	Australia
.ca	Canada
.cu	China
.in	India
.jp	Japan
.uk	Great Britain
.us	USA

Table 9.1 *Examples of geographic domains*

9.2.1.2 Non-geographic Domain

The part of domain that indicates the type of organisation where computer is located is called Non-geographic Domain. The examples of non-geographic domains are listed in Table 9.2.

Domain Name	Type of organisation
.gov	Government Agencies
.edu	Educational Institutions
.com	Commercial
.mil	Military
.net	Network
.org	Organisations other than Educational & Commercial

Table 9.2 *Examples of non-geographic domains*

9.2.2 Number Addressing System or Internet Protocol (IP) Addressing System

In this system, a unique 32-bit address is assigned to each computer that is connected to the Internet. It is given in four-part decimal number (*e.g.* 132.116.42.51). Each part represents 8 bits of the 32-bits address, which cannot exceed 255. The 32-bit address is called a *doted quad* while each 8 bit part is called an *octet*. The 32-bit address is also called *IP address* or *Internet Address*. For example, 5.232.59.82 is an IP address where 5,232,52, and 82 are octets. IP address identifies the location of a particular computer on the Internet. IP addresses are organised from left to right and consist of sequence of domain and sub-domain codes. This system of addressing on Internet is also called Number Addressing System. It is directly understood by the machine.

9.3 OVERVIEW OF BROWSERS

Browsers are the programs for surfing on the Internet. As these programs are very user-friendly, you need not remember the commands. Browsers help you always while surfing on the Internet. Browsers can be broadly classified into two types—Text Only Browsers and Graphical Browsers. The difference between a text only browser and a graphical browser is described in Table 9.3. All Internet users mostly use graphical browsers. The popular graphical browsers are–

(*a*) World Wide Web (WWW)

(*b*) Gopher

(*c*) Netscape Navigator

(*d*) Microsoft Internet Explorer

Let us discuss about these in detail.

Text Only Browser	Graphical Browser
1. It shows web pages with text only without graphics and animation 2. It is very fast. 3. *Example:* Lynx	1. It shows complete web pages with text, graphics, animations and sound. 2. It is comparatively very slow. 3. *Examples:* Netscape Navigator, Internet Explorer and NCSA Mosaic.

Table 9.3 *Difference between a text only browser and a graphical browser*

9.3.1 World Wide Web (WWW)

World Wide Web is the most popular browser of Internet. It is a series of servers that are inter-connected through hypertext and hyperlinks. It is the most favorite means of browsing the Internet. It is simply known as the *Web*. It is very popular because -

- It is very easy to use.
- It is attractive in screen layouts
- It provides information to any one interested
- It provides user a simplified way to access text, graphics, animation, sound and other forms of information.

9.3.1.1 Hypertext, Hypermedia and Hyperlinks

Hypertext is the text that contains connections within the text to other documents besides the regular text. It is actually a way of presenting information on the web. Using hypertext, the user can jump from one page to another by clicking on the underlined or highlighted words called hyperlinks as shown in Figure 9.1. Hypermedia is higher version of hypertext that contains links not only to text but also to other forms of information such as sound movies, pictures etc. It enables user to retrieve multimedia resources on Internet.

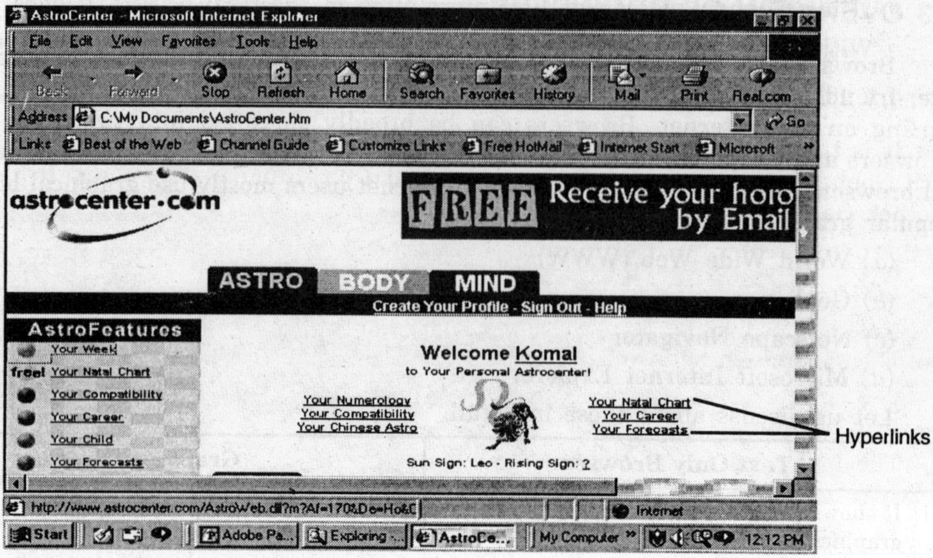

Figure 9.1 *A web page showing hyperlinks*

9.3.1.2 HTML

HTML stands for HyperText Markup Language. It is the encoding scheme used to create and format a Web page. It is an improved version of Sandard Generalised Markup Language (SGML). HTML is a versatile language and can be used on any platform. It can be used to display any type of document on the host computer, which can be geographically at a different location. HTML provides tags to make the Web page look attractive. We can use graphics, colors, fonts, etc. to enhance the presentation of Web page using HTML. HTML allows the creation of hyperlinks to any limit.

9.3.2 Gopher

Gopher is a browser for locating information on the Internet. It enables the user to locate all textual information stored on Internet servers through a series of easy to use, hierarchical menus. Internet has thousands of gopher servers around the world. Each gopher site has thousands of listing orgainised in form of menus and submenus. We surf the Internet by selecting various items from these menus. Gopher is based on the concept of clients and servers. Clients are the software that requests information for a user. Servers are the software that provide information to clients. When the user initiates the gopher software for surfing and selects an item from the menu, the server transfers the user to the appropriate file on the selected server. Now, the user jumps to another server and in this way the process continues and user move from one site to another while surfing on Internet. The salient features of Gopher are—

- It is an Internet-based document retrieval system.
- It displays a set of resources on Internet in the form of menus.
- It is very simple to operate as we need not know the address of sites and UNIX commands.

- Using Gopher, we can gather information in the form of text, images and sound.
- With Gopher we can also access services in the form of Telnet connections.

9.3.2.1 Gopherspace

It is the universe of Gopher servers connected to the Internet throughout the world. Each Gopher server has an Internet address and port number of its own. It also has links to other Gopher servers.

9.3.3 Netscape Navigator

Netscape Navigator is a popular graphical browser for Internet. We can download it free of cost from the site `http://home.netscape.com`.

9.3.3.1 Menu Options of Netscape Navigator

The menu options of Netscape Navigator are–

(*i*) FILE Menu Options:

1. *New Web Browser.* Used to open a new window of browser.
2. *New Mail Message.* Used for creating a new mail message.
3. *New Document.* Used to open a blank document, a document from template or a document from a wizard.
4. *Edit Document.* Used to open a saved document.
5. *Save As.* Used for saving the current document as a file.
6. *Open Location.* Used to open a web site.
7. *Open File in Browser.* Used to open a file in browser.
8. *Open File in Editor.* Used to open a document in Editor.
9. *Upload File.* Used to transfer file to a FTP location.
10. *Print.* Used to print a document.
11. *Page Setup.* Used to set the page layout.

(*ii*) EDIT Menu Options:

1. *Undo/Redo.* Used to reverse the last action performed in Netscape window.
2. *Cut.* Used to cut the selected text and place in clipboard.
3. *Paste.* Used to paste the selected text from clipboard at the current cursor position.
4. *Delete Document.* Used for deleting the document.
5. *Find.* Used to find the selected text in current document.
6. *Find Again.* Used to find the previous selected text in the current document.

(*iii*) VIEW Menu Options:

1. *Reload.* Used to reload the document from server.
2. *Refresh.* Used to redraw the present document.
3. *Load Images.* Used to load the images embedded in the document.
4. *Reload Frame.* Used to reload the active frame in the current document.
5. *Document Source.* Used to display message in HTML format.

6. *Document Information.* Used to display structure of the current document along with the associated HTML files.
7. *Frame Source.* Used to display the source code of current frame of the document.

(*iv*) GO Menu Options:

1. *Back.* Used to load previous page.
2. *Forward.* Used to load next page that was loaded earlier.
3. *Stop Loading.* Used to stop the loading of page.
4. *Home.* Used to load home page of site.

(*v*) BOOKMARKS Menu Options:

1. *Add Bookmark.* Used to add the current page name to bookmark list.
2. *Go to Bookmark.* Used to select a page name from bookmark list.

(*vi*) OPTIONS Menu Options:

1. *General Preferences.* Used to change font, colours, images etc. of pages.
2. *Editor Preferences.* Used to change general appearance and editing options of pages.
3. *Mail and News Preferences.* Used to change mail and news configuration.
4. *Networking Preferences.* Used to change memory cache, disk cache etc.
5. *Connections.* Used to open more than one connection to server so that simultaneously many sites can be connected.
6. *Proxies.* Used to access Internet through a firewall.
7. *Protocols.* Used to set rules that govern transmission of data.
8. *Languages.* Used to enable a language JAVA or JAVASCRIPT that will be understood by browser.
9. *Auto Load Images.* Used to load inline images automatically.
10. *Show Toolbar.* Used to display toolbar in browser window.
11. *Show Location.* Used to display location bar in browser window.
12. *Show Directory Button.* Used to display directory buttons in browser window.
13. *Security Preferences.* Used to set passwords, site certificates etc.

(*vii*) DIRECTORY Menu Options:

1. *Netscape's Home.* Used to open Netscape's home page. This can also be opened by entering URL `http://home.netscape.com`.
2. *What's new.* Used to display new items on Internet.
3. *What's cool.* Used to view cool sites such as movies, music, sports, food etc.
4. *People.* Used to search E.mail addresses of people.
5. *Internet Search.* Used to search web using a search engine (Yahoo, Rediff etc.)
6. *Customer Showcase.* Used to display name of organisations using Netscape servers.
7. *About Internet.* Used to open sites which helps us in learning Internet.

(viii) WINDOW Menu Options:

1. *Netscape Mail.* Used to read or send E.mail messages.
2. *Netscape News.* Used to read news.
3. *Bookmark.* Used to open bookmark list window.
4. *History.* Used to delete history list.
5. *Address Book.* Used to create/open address book of E.mail addresses.

(ix) HELP Menu Options:

1. *About Netscape.* Used to display information such as version no., copyright etc. of Netscape program.
2. *Software.* Used to display information about upgrades in Netscape software.
3. *Registration Information.* Used to provide product registration information.
4. *About Plug.ins.* Used to provide information about plug.ins for Netscape.
5. *Web Page Starter.* Used to provide information about new web publishers.
6. *Handbook.* Used to see online manual of Netscape.
7. *Release Notes.* Used to provide information about Netscape version.
8. *How to Give Feedback.* Used for giving feedback.
9. *How to Get Support.* Used to get support from Netscape.
10. *How to Create Web Services.* Used to create web services.
11. *FAQs.* Used to get answers for frequently asked questions about Netscape.

9.3.4 Microsoft Internet Explorer

Microsoft Internet Explorer is the most popular browser for Internet. It is based on MCSA Mosaic. It is distributed under a licensing agreement with Spyglass Inc. It is shareware software that can be downloaded from Internet. It enables us to connect to the Internet for gaining access to the huge volume of information on millions of computers connected with Internet. The opening screen of Microsoft Internet Explorer is shown in Figure 9.2.

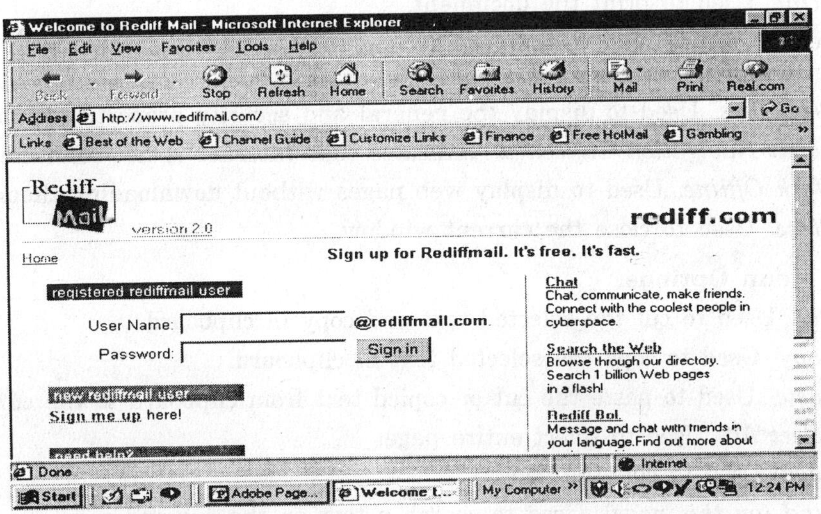

Figure 9.2 *The opening screen of microsoft internet explorer*

9.3.4.1 Features of the Microsoft Internet Explorer

Microsoft Internet Explorer offers following features:

- It offers channels by which the latest web contents are automatically delivered to us from the world's best content providers. We can view these channels on right side of our computer monitor screen (desktop).
- We can subscribe to our favourite sites so that the contents are automatically updated. Updated web sites can be downloaded in the background while we are doing other things on our PC.
- We can add a web page to our list of favourites for easy access.
- We can search the web sites using explorer bar that appears in the left side of the browser window when we click the 'Search' button on the toolbar.
- We can view web pages in many languages.
- Microsoft Internet Explorer offers a feature AutoComplete by which we can type first few characters of URL and Internet Explorer writes the complete address.
- We can browse the web safely in Microsoft Internet Explorer as there are different levels of security for different areas of the web to protect our PC.

9.3.4.2 Menu Options of Microsoft Internet Explorer

Various menu options available in Microsoft Internet Explorer are—

(i) FILE Menu Options:

1. *New.* Used to open a new file in a new window so that user can view many web pages at the same time.
2. *Open.* Used to open a site by entering the address or selecting it from the browser list.
3. *Save.* Used to save the current document as a file.
4. *Save as.* Used to save the already saved current document with a new name.
5. *Page Setup.* Used to change page layout.
6. *Print.* Used to print the document.
7. *Send.* Used to send the current document as a mail to another user or to send it on floppy.
8. *Properties.* Used to display the general and security properties of document.
9. *About Navigation Cancelled.* Indicates that Internet is not connected.
10. *Work Offline.* Used to display web pages without downloading them.
11. *Close.* Used to close the current window.

(ii) EDIT Menu Options:

1. *Cut.* Used to cut the selected text and copy in clipboard.
2. *Copy.* Used to copy the selected text in clipboard.
3. *Paste.* Used to paste the cut or copied text from clipboard to the cursor position.
4. *Select All.* Used to select entire page.
5. *Page.* Used to edit the page.
6. *Find (on this page).* Used to search a text on the current page.

(iii) VIEW Menu Options:

1. *Toolbars.* Used to show or hide toolbars.
2. *Status Bar.* Used to show/hide status bar.
3. *Explorer Bar.* Used to show/hide explorer bar.
4. *Fonts.* Used to select the size of fonts.
5. *Stop.* Used to stop the current operation such as loading of web site etc.
6. *Refresh.* Used to display the current page again.
7. *Source.* Used to display the HTML code of the current page.
8. *Full Screen.* Used to display Explorer window on the entire screen without showing menu options.
9. *Internet Options.* Used to change various setting such as colur of the test, the format of showing URL, Security, Connection, Programs etc.

(iv) GO Menu Options:

1. *Back.* Used to go to the previous web page.
2. *Forward.* Used to go to the next web page.
3. *Up one level.* Used to go one level up.
4. *Home Page.* Used to show way that was loaded in the beginning of current session.
5. *Channel Guide.* Used to open the channel guide web page.
6. *Search the web.* Used to search the web.
7. *Mail.* Used to open the mail program.
8. *News.* Used to open the newsreader program.
9. *My Computer.* Used to open my computer window for file operations.
10. *Address Book.* Used to open the address book.
11. *Internet Call.* Used to open the Internet call and meeting program.

(v) FAVORITES Menu Options:

1. *Add to Favourites.* Used to add the current page to a list of favorite pages.
2. *Organise Favorites.* Used to display the list of favorite pages and to select one from the list.
3. *Manage Subscriptions.* Used to view the status for all subscriptions.
4. *Update All Subscriptions.* Used to update all subscriptions.
5. *Channels.* Used to view various channels viz. ABCL Online, CNN Interactive etc.
6. *Links.* Used to link with best of the web, channel guide etc.
7. *Software Updates.* Used to update Microsoft Internet Explorer.
8. *My documents.* Used to display my documents for file operations.

(vi) HELP Menu Options:

1. *Contents and Index.* Used to display contents and index on topics.
2. *Products Update.* Used to provide help updating the product.
3. *Web Tutorial.* Used to learn Internet Explorer through web.

4. *Online Support.* Used to get online support.
5. *Microsoft on the web.* Used to get information on various products of Microsoft.
6. *About Internet Explorer.* Used to display program information, version no and copyright notice.

9.4 SEARCH ENGINES

Search engine is an Internet accessible search service that enables us to search for information on the Internet using a browser. Yahoo and Rediff are commonly used Search Engines. Let us discuss the procedure for using a popular search engine Rediff.

9.4.1 Using a Search Engine

We can search any information using a search engine. Let us consider an example. Various steps to search information about Intel P-III processor using REDIFF search engine are as follows:

1. Load REDIFF web site by entering its URL `http://www.rediff.com`. Now type 'Pentium III Processor' and click on 'Go' button as shown in Figure 9.3.

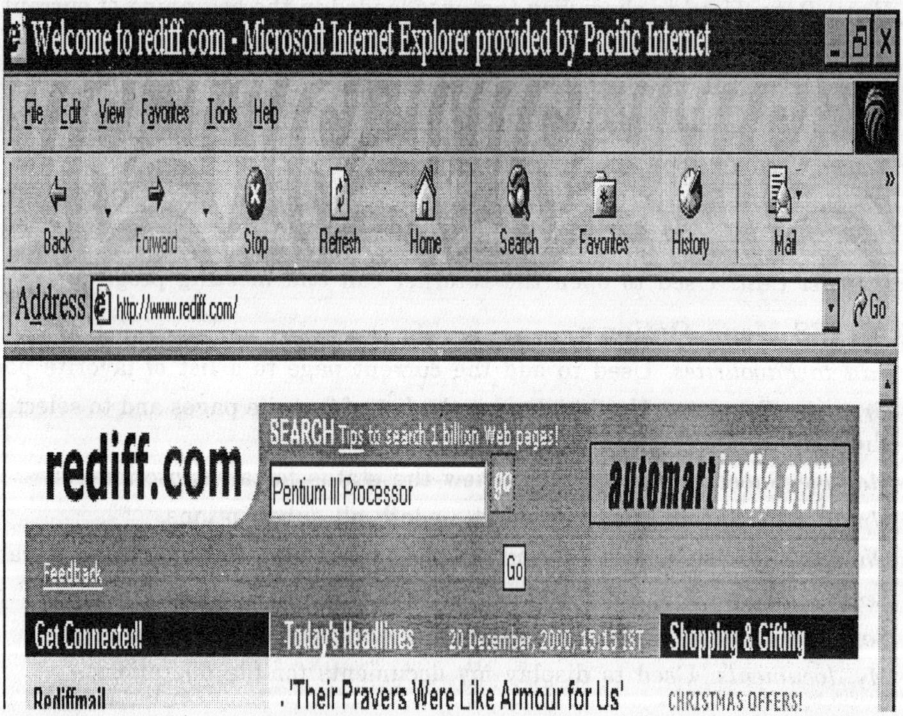

Figure 9.3 *Screen 1 of searching about P-III processor using rediff search engine*

2. The REDIFF will search the web for those sites which contain information relating to Pentium III Processor. Now, the web page as shown in Figure 9.4 is displayed.

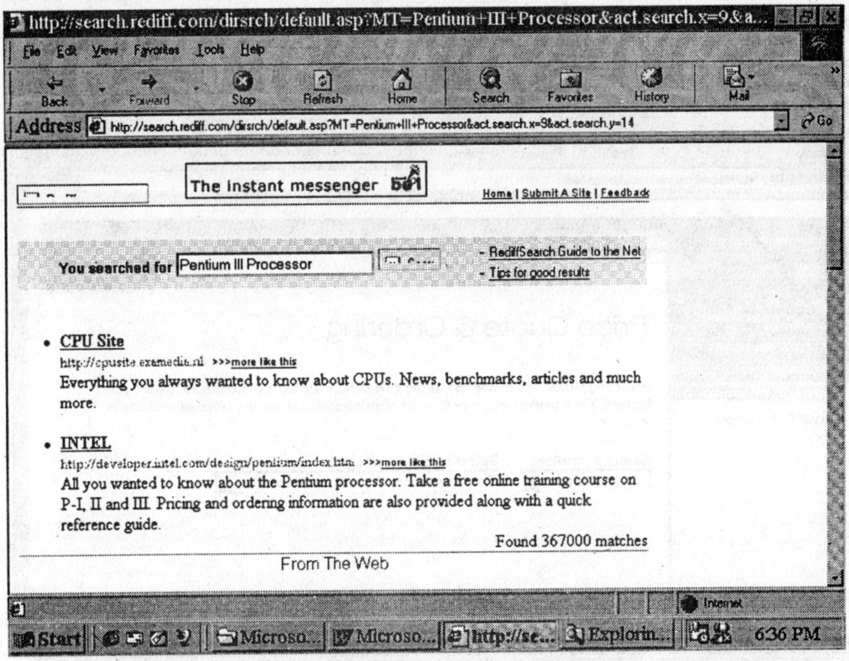

Figure 9.4 *Screen 2 of searching about P-III processor using rediff search engine*

3. Now, click on 'INTEL' site to know about Intel Processors. The screen as shown in Figure 9.5 is displayed.

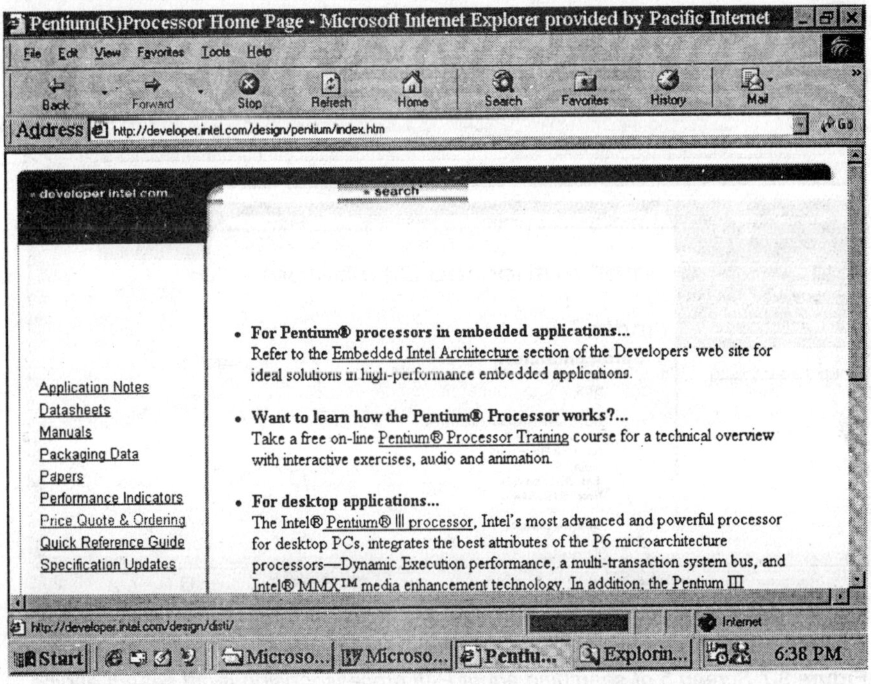

Figure 9.5 *Screen 3 of searching about P-III processor using rediff search engine*

4. Now, click on 'Price Quote & Ordering' option shown in left part of screen. This displays the screen as shown in Figure 9.6.

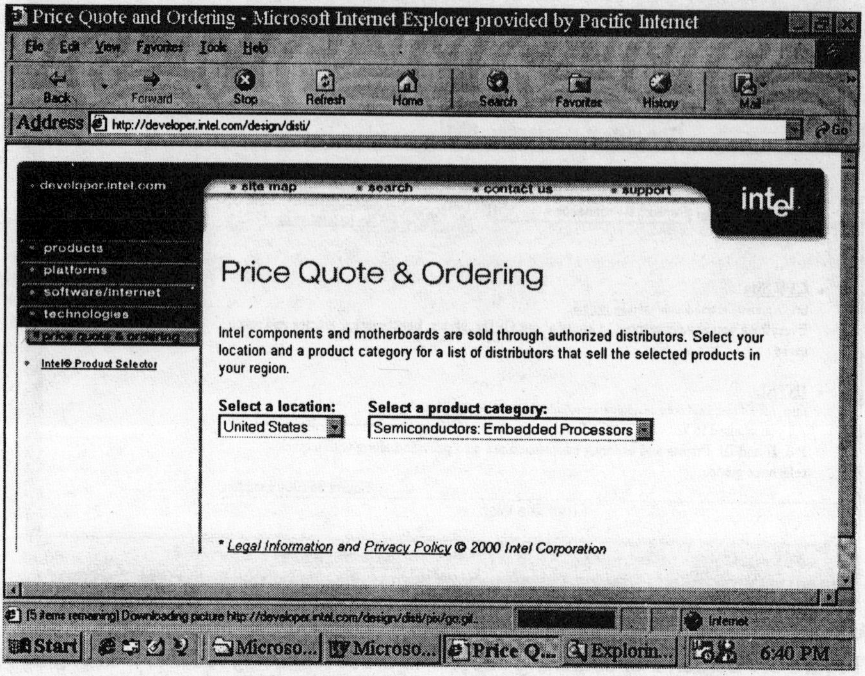

Figure 9.6 *Screen 4 of searching about P-III processor using rediff search engine*

5. Now, select a location (country name) and product category to display the Intel authorised dealers as shown in Figure 9.7.

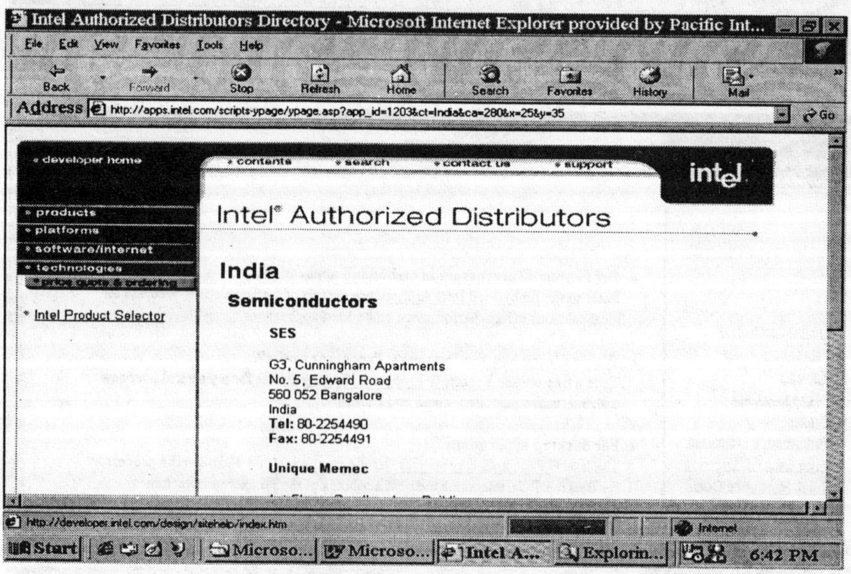

Figure 9.7 *Screen 5 of searching about P-III processor using rediff search engine*

9.5 DOWNLOADING

Downloading refers to copying software from a remote computer to your computer through Internet. Let us discuss the process of downloading using the search engine - Yahoo.

9.5.1 Process of Downloading

We can download a software *e.g.* JAVA Development Kit from a site of 'Sun Microsystems' by the following way:

1. Open YAHOO site by entering its URL `http://yahoo.com` and type 'download jdk' where jdk stands for java development kit at search box followed by clicking on 'search' button as shown in Figure 9.8.

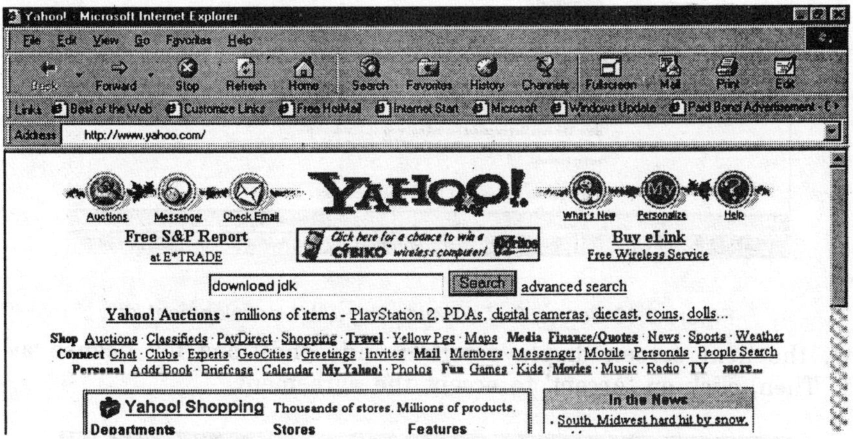

Figure 9.8 *Screen 1 of downloading JAVA development kit*

2. Now the screen as shown in Figure 9.9 is displayed. Then, click at 'Java ™ Development Kit 1.1x'.

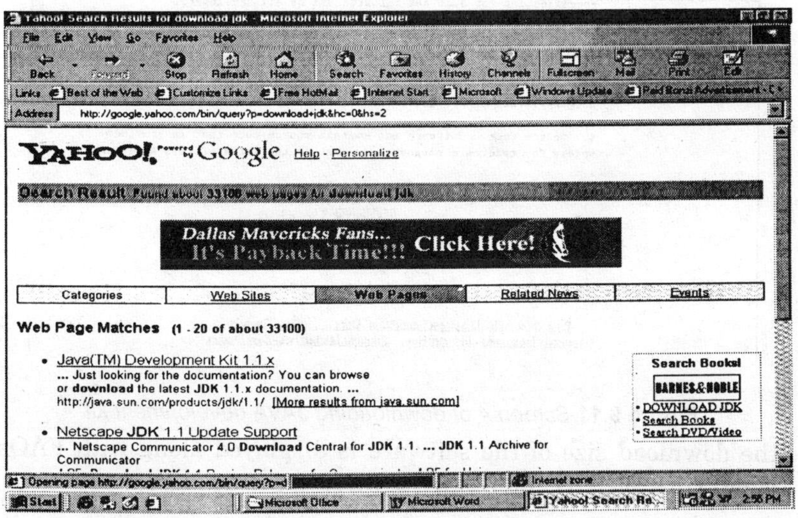

Figure 9.9 *Screen 2 of downloading JAVA development kit*

3. The web page of java.sun.com is displayed as shown in Figure 9.10. Click on 'Continue' button.

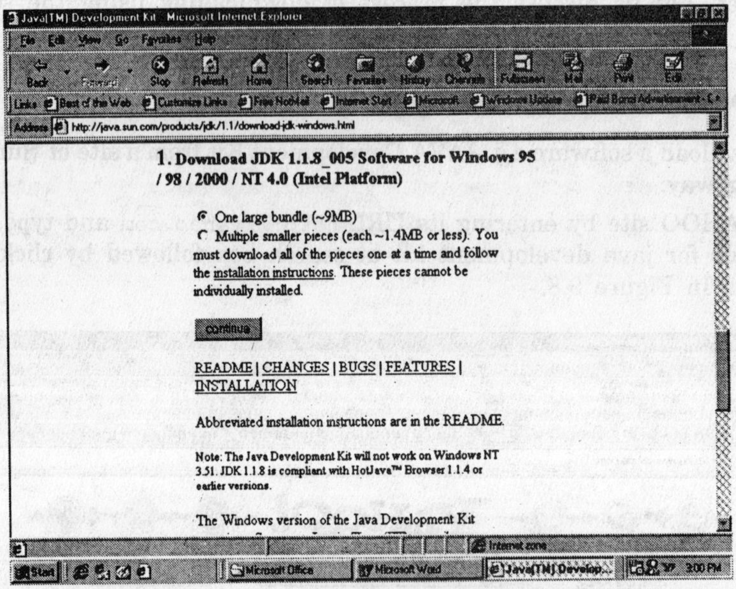

Figure 9.10 *Screen 3 of downloading JAVA development kit*

4. Now, the next screen displays terms and conditions for license as shown in Figure 9.11. Then, click on 'Accept' to accept the agreement.

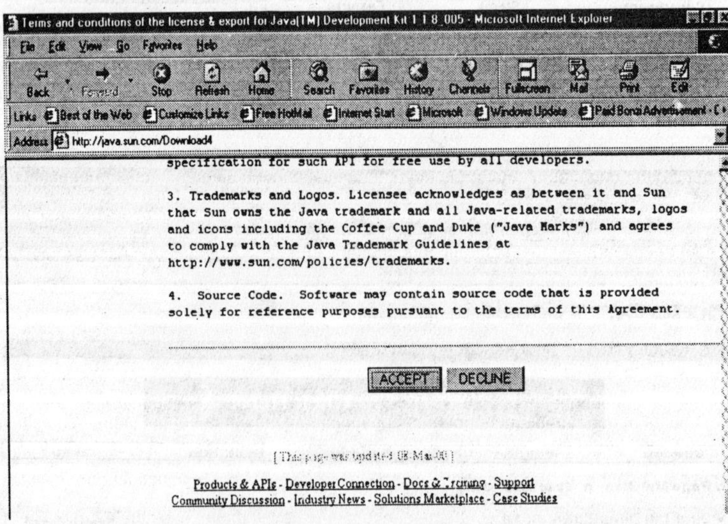

Figure 9.11 *Screen 4 of downloading JAVA development kit*

5. Now, the download size of the software is displayed along with FAQs as shown in Figure 9.12. Then, click at 'FTP download' button.

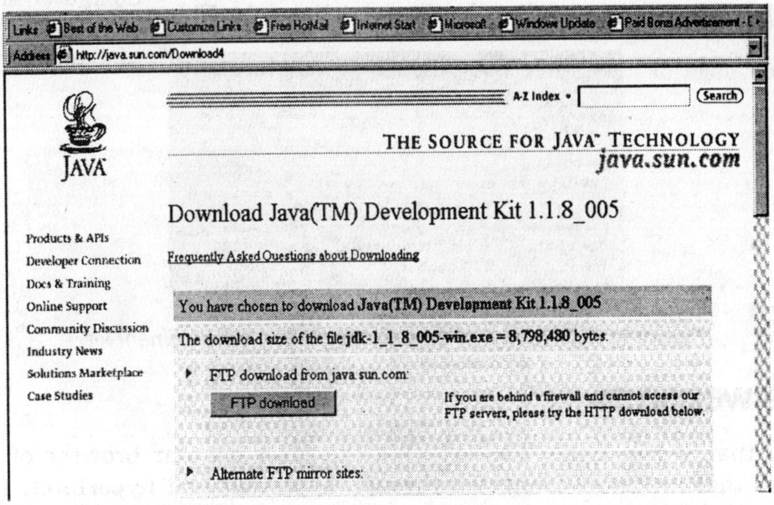

Figure 9.12 *Screen 5 of downloading JAVA development kit*

6. Now, the file download dialog box is displayed which asks whether you want to save the file on disk or not as shown in Figure 9.13.

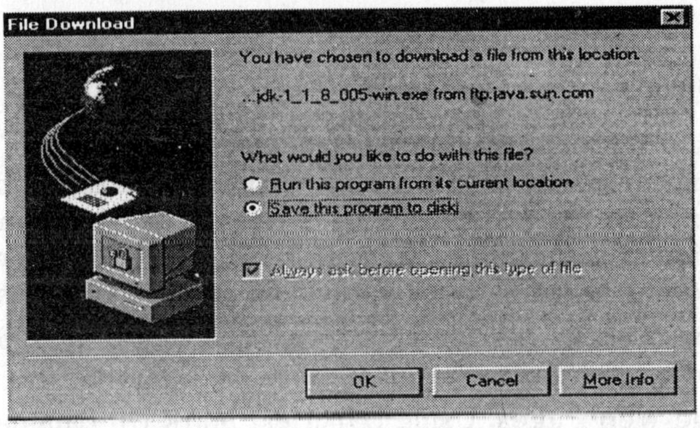

Figure 9.13 *Screen 6 of downloading JAVA development kit*

7. Now, first click on radio button of 'Save download on disk' and finally click on 'OK' button. The 'Save as' dialog box is displayed as shown in Figure 9.14. Select the folder and write the file name and click on 'Save' button.

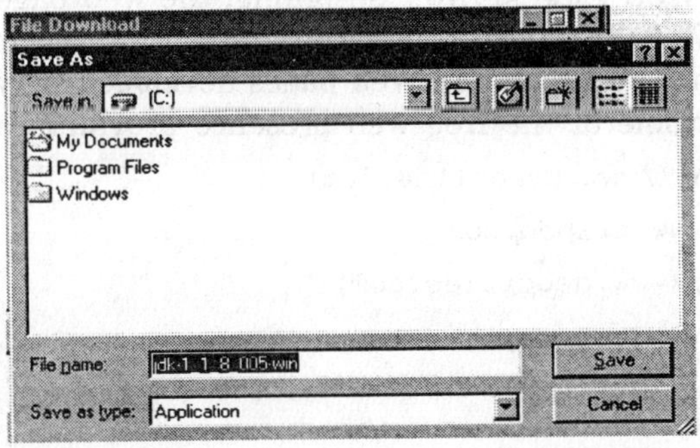

Figure 9.14 *Screen 7 of downloading JAVA development kit*

8. Now, the software starts downloading as shown in Figure 9.15.

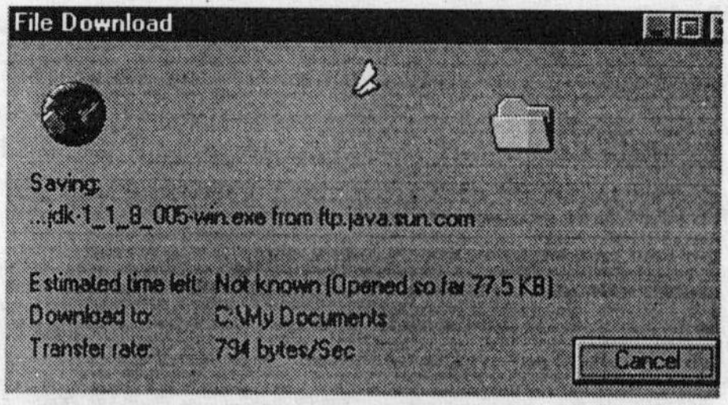

Figure 9.15 *Screen 8 of downloading JAVA development kit*

9.6 VISITING WEBSITES

You know that World Wide Web (WWW), the most popular browser of Internet is a series of servers that are inter-connected through hypertext and hyperlinks. It is the most favourite means of visiting a web site. There are billion of websites on Internet. With WWW, browsing the Internet becomes easier. The WWW is a powerful tool that helps you to find and retrieve the information using links to other Web pages. Before discussing the procedure for visiting these Web pages, let us first understand the popular terms 'Web Page' and 'Portal'.

9.6.1 Web Page

A Web page is a document containing single unit of information that is available via World Wide Web. It may contain text, graphics, images, pictures, sound, video, animation, hypertext, hypermedia and hyperlinks. Using hypertext and hypermedia, you can move from one page to another by clicking on hyperlinks (the underlined or highlighted words). You can perform following three basic operations on these Web pages:

1. Accessing the Web Pages. Using a browser such as Microsoft Internet Explorer and Netscape Navigator, you can visit to a website for accessing the Web pages.

2. Designing the Web Pages. Using Hypertext Mark Up Language (HTML), you can design web pages. HTML is a subset of Standard Generalised Markup Language (SGML), which is an international standard for defining and managing the HTML contents. Web pages can be made more interactive and user-friendly using the new language called DHTML (Dynamic Hypertext Mark Up Language).

3. Uploading the Web Pages. After designing, the web pages are uploaded onto the Internet using various Web Presence Providers. The web presence providers host the web sites by allocating memory space for the Web pages developed by you either free of cost or by paying the charges. Some of the free web presence providers are.

- USAonline (`http://www.usaonline.com`)
- Tripod (`http://www.tripod.com`)
- Geocities (`http://www.geocities.com`)

9.6.2 Portal

Portal is a website that contains hyperlinks to many other websites based on the required information. For example, Yahoo, Rediff, MSN India, Indya, JobsDB, Top-education, etc. are some of the popular portals.

9.6.2.1 Types of Portals

There are two types of portals—Horizontal Portals and Vertical Portals.

1. Horizontal Portals (Hortals). These are websites, which contain links to information on a broad range of subjects such as education, sports, music, health, jobs, sex, romance, religion, etc.

Examples:

- Yahoo (http://www.yahoo.com)
- Rediff (http://www.rediff.com)
- MSN India (http://msn.co.in)
- Indya (http://indya.com)
- India.com (http://www.india.com)

2. Vertical Portals (Vortals): These are websites, which contain links to information on a particular subject.

Examples:

- Jobs (http://jobs.com)
- Tourism (http://tourism.com)
- Sports (http://sports.com)
- Science (http://science.com)
- Travel (http://travel.com)

9.6.3 Procedure for Visiting Websites

A website is a collection of Web pages that usually consists of a home page and many related pages and links. Web pages reside on an HTTP (HyperText Transfer Protocol) server. HTTP is a method of exchanging information between servers and their clients on Internet. If you want to visit a website to access Web pages, there are following four main ways:

1. Using Address of Website
2. Using Address of Portal
3. Using 'Favourite' button as menu option
4. Using Search Engine

Let us discuss these with illustrations.

9.6.3.1 Using Address of Website

To visit a website, you can enter its URL (Uniform Resource Locator) in the address bar of the browser as illustrated below:

(*a*) Start the Internet browser by double clicking on the browser shortcut icon *e.g.* Microsoft Internet Explorer.

(b) Enter the URL of the website e.g. `http://www.top-education.com` **to be visited in the address bar of Internet Explorer opening screen. You will see the top part of the home page of this website as shown in Figure 9.16. Using the vertical scroll bar, you can see the next part of the home page as shown in Figure 9.17.**

Figure 9.16 *Screen 1 of visiting a web site using its address*

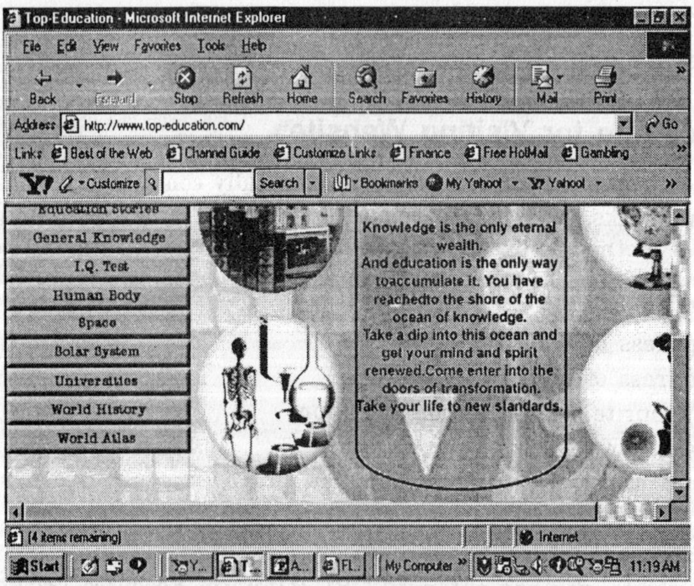

Figure 9.17 *Screen 2 of visiting a web site using its address*

(*c*) Click on the 'Universities' hyperlink button to go to websites containing information about universities of India. You will go the main index page of linked site `http://top-education.com/university/index.html` as shown in Figure 9.18.

Figure 9.18 *Screen 3 of visiting a web site using its address*

(*d*) Click on the 'Science' subject. You will go the top part of technical page of linked site `http://top-education.com/university/technical.html` as shown in Figure 9.19. Using the vertical scroll bar, you can see the remaining parts of this page as illustrated in Figure 9.20.

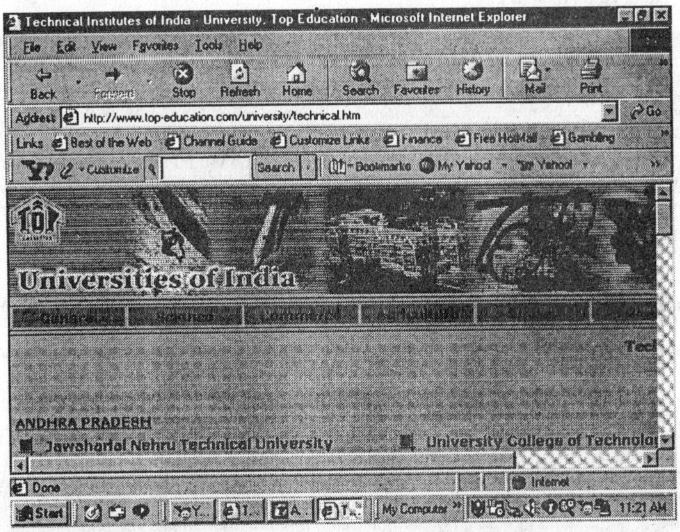

Figure 9.19 *Screen 4 of visiting a web site using its address*

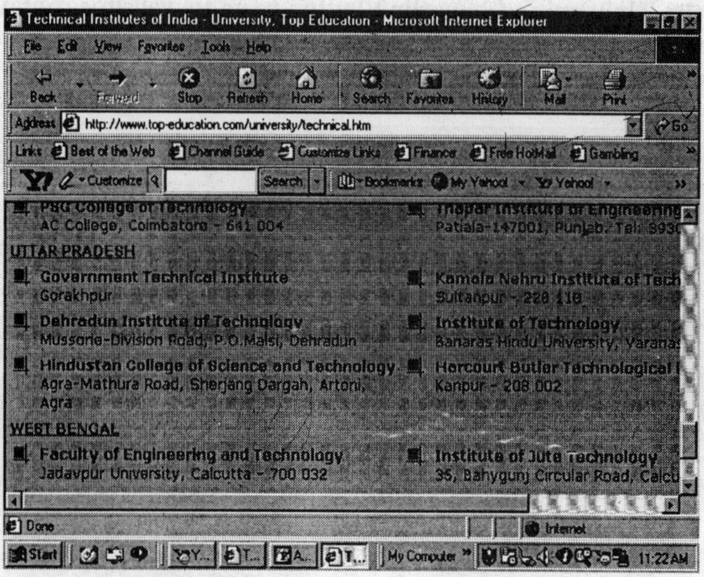

Figure 9.20 *Screen 5 of visiting a web site using its address*

9.6.3.2 Using Address of Portal

You can also visit to a website by entering URL of a Hortal (e.g. Yahoo) or a Vortal (*e.g.* Tourism) in the address bar of the browser as illustrated below:

(*a*) Start the Internet browser by double clicking on the browser shortcut icon e.g. Microsoft Internet Explorer.

(*b*) Enter the URL of the Vortal e.g. `http://www.jobs.com` to be visited in the address bar of Internet Explorer opening screen. You will see the top part of the home page of this Vortal as shown in Figure 9.21.

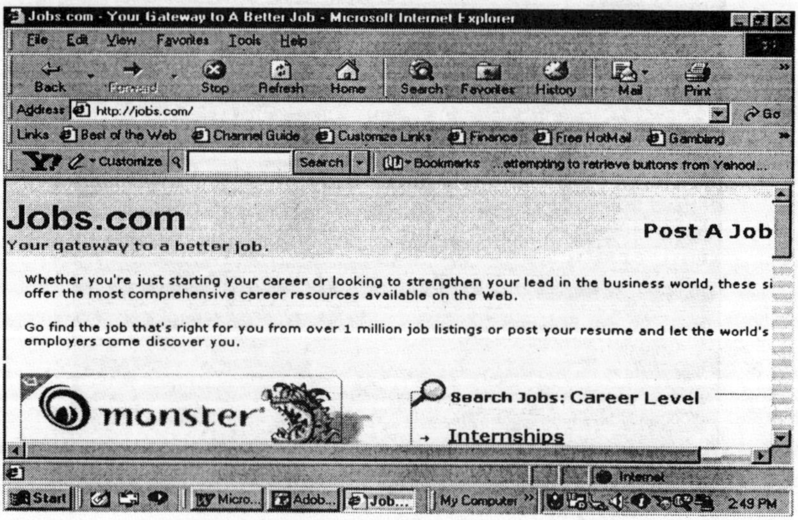

Figure 9.21 *Screen 1 of visiting a web site using address of a vortal*

(*c*) Click on the 'Monster' hyperlink button to go to this website. You will see the home page of this website having URL. `http://www.monster.com` as shown in Figure 9.22.

Figure 9.22 *Screen 2 of visiting a web site using address of a vortal*

9.6.3.3 *Using 'Favorites' Button or Menu Option*

The third way to visit a Website is by using 'Favorites' button or option of the Microsoft Internet Explorer menu as illustrated below:

(*a*) Start the Internet browser by double clicking on the browser shortcut icon *e.g.* Microsoft Internet Explorer.

(*b*) Click on the 'Favorites' button or choose 'Favorites' option from the menu. Place the mouse pointer on 'Links' option of the 'Favorites' menu and click on 'Sports' option of the 'Links' menu as illustrated in Figure 9.23. You will directly jump to the Web page having URL `http://sureseeker.com/newsearch.pl?search=sports`' of the Web site `sureseeker.com` as shown in Figure 9.24. In order to visit one of these sites, you can click on the title of site (e.g. Site titled 'MLB Tickets Available 24/7').

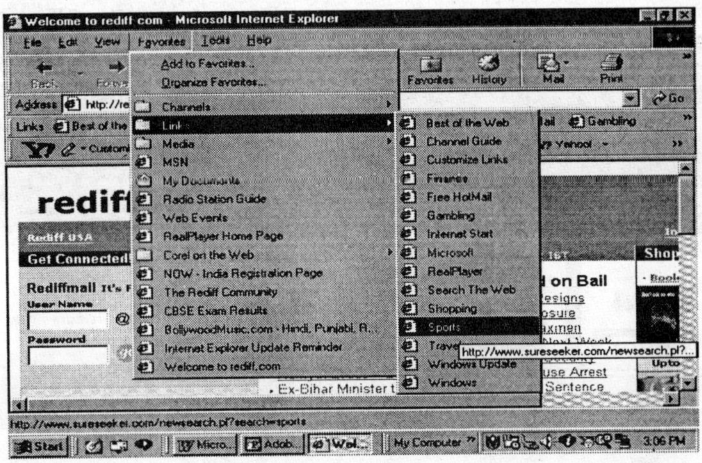

Figure 9.23 *Screen 1 of visiting a web site using 'favorites' menu*

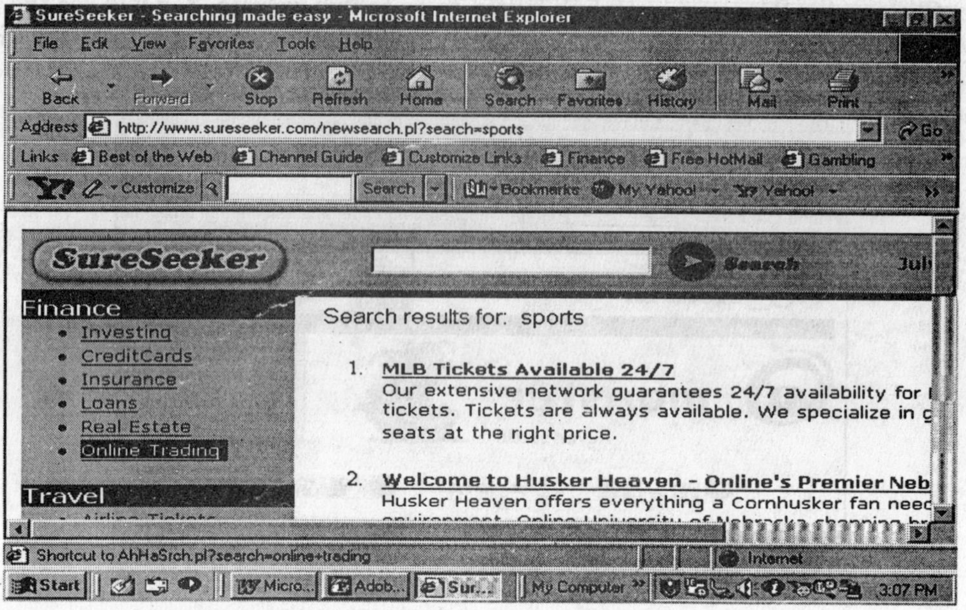

Figure 9.24 *Screen 2 of visiting a Web site using 'Favorites' menu*

Adding a Website to Favorites

You can add your site to one of the options of 'Favorites' menu by following way:

(*a*) Start the Internet browser by double clicking on the browser shortcut icon e.g. Microsoft Internet Explorer.

(*b*) Visit to the site by typing its URL (e.g. `http://www.travel.com`) in the address bar of Internet Explorer as shown in Figure 9.25.

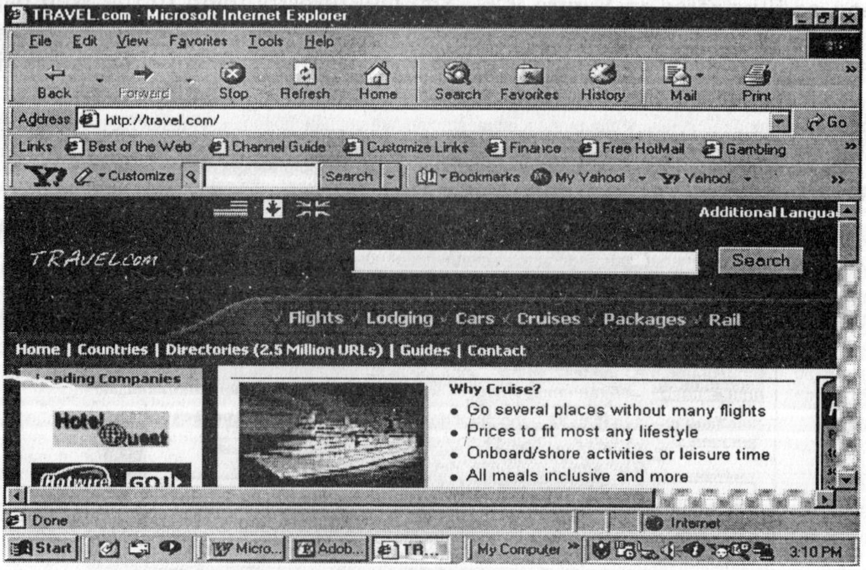

Figure 9.25 *Screen 1 of adding a website to 'favorites' menu*

(*c*) Click on the 'Favorites' menu and select 'Add to Favorites...' option from the this menu as shown in Figure 9.26.

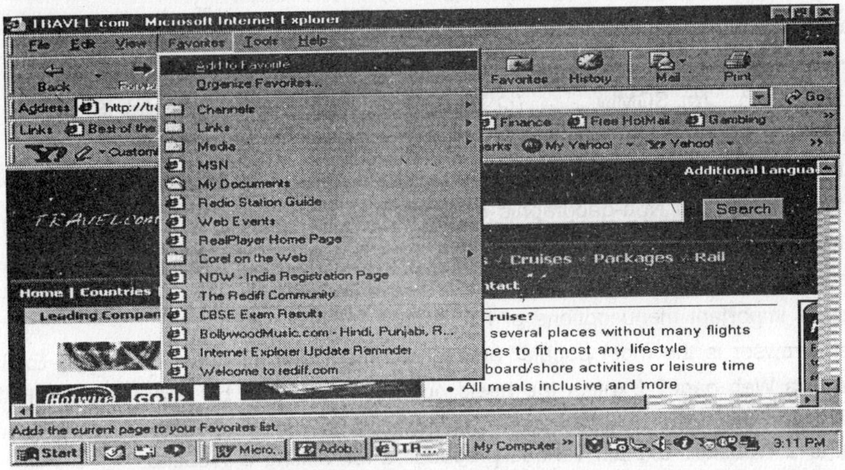

Figure 9.26 *Screen 2 of adding a website to 'favorites' menu*

In this way, the name of site will become an option in 'Favorites' menu. You can also delete this option by choosing 'Organize Favorites...' option from the 'Favorites' menu.

9.6.3.4 Using Search Engine

The fourth way to visit a Website is by using a search engine such as Yahoo, Rediff, etc. by entering the type of information required in its search box as explained earlier in Section 9.4 (Search Engines).

THEORY QUESTIONS

1. Explain the two addressing systems on Internet.
2. What is surfing? Name three popular browsers used for searching on the Internet.
3. Write short notes on the following terms (with examples):
   (*a*) Domain Name System
   (*b*) Search Engine
   (*c*) Hyperlinks
   (*d*) Gopherspace
4. How will you get the information about Intel Pentium 4 processor using a search engine? How will you purchase it through Internet.
5. Differentiate between following browsers:
   (*a*) Gopher and WWW
   (*b*) Internet Explorer and Netscape Navigator
   (*c*) Hortal and Vortal
6. Explain the working principle of Gopher.

7. Explain the procedure of using following search engines:
   (*a*) Rediff
   (*b*) Yahoo
8. What is downloading? Explain the process of downloading with suitable example.
9. Give the full form of following abbreviated terms:
   (*a*) HTML (*b*) SGML (*c*) DNS (*d*) FAQ (*e*) ISP (*f*) URL
10. Differentiate between following terms:
    (*a*) Domain and Subdomain
    (*b*) Geographic and Non-geographic domains
    (*c*) Hypertext and Hypermedia
11. Describe important menu options of Netscape Navigator.
12. Describe important menu options of Microsoft Netscape Navigator.
13. Which browser is the most popular among common Internet users and why? Explain.
14. What is a Web page? Explain the basic operations that can be performed on the Web pages.
15. What is a Website? Explain various procedures for visiting a Website.

WORKSHOP

1. Connect to Internet and open the Web Browser available in your system. See the functions of various menu options of this browser.
2. Find the sites that contain information on 'Job Opportunities for Engineering Students in India' using YAHOO and Rediff search engines. Analyse their performances with respect to their efficiency in exact matching of information.
3. Search the Web site of your university. Note down the name of its web site. Visit its various web pages and note down their domain names and IP addresses. Analyse and compare various components of these domain names and IP addresses.
4. Download Java Development Kit from the web site. `'http://sun.com'` using the Web browser.
5. Visit to the following Website(s) by the most efficient procedure:
   (*a*) `http://intel.com`
   (*b*) Websites for Shopping
   (*c*) Websites on computer books
   (*d*) Websites providing information about Hotels.

10

ELECTRONIC MAIL

10.1 INTRODUCTION

Electronic mail (E-mail) is the most common service available on Internet. E-mail is becoming so popular that people prefer it to postage mail. Many search engines such as Rediff, Yahoo, etc. provide this service free of cost to users. In this chapter, we will discuss about various procedures for sending and receiving mails over Internet. We will also discuss the method for storing E-mail addresses for getting maximum benefit from E-mail service of Internet. Let us begin our discussion with an overview of electronic mail.

10.2 OVERVIEW OF ELECTRONIC MAIL

Electronic mail is defined as electronically transfer of mails from one computer to another over Internet. Using E-mail, we can send mail to any part of world in the form electronic documents, which can include both text and graphics. Users of Internet create their own e-mail accounts along with giving the passwords so that no unauthorised person can access their mails. E-mail is very popular among Internet users as users can send unlimited number of free E-mail messages to any of millions of E-mail users around the world. E-mail is an easiest way to contact with friends and relatives staying in any part of the world. After learning Internet, you would like to prefer E-mail to postal mail. Why? Let us discuss the similarities and dissimilarities between E-mail and postal mail.

10.2.1 Comparison between E-mail and Postal Mail

Email is similar to Postal Mail in the following ways:

- Both E-mail and Postal mail are forwarding to a mailing address.
- Sender does not know when E-mail and Postal mail will be read by receiver.
- Both mails come back when they are not received.
- Both mails can be read by unauthoised pesons.
- Mailing list subscription can be provided to both E-mail and Postal Mail.

However, E-mail differs from Postal mail in following ways:

- E-mail is delivered within few minutes while Postal Mail may take days, weeks or even months in reaching its destination.
- E-mail service is free of cost while Postal Mail requires postage.
- E-mail can be received by the receiver from any computer in the world having Internet connection while Postal Mail can be received only from the delivered address.

Now, you can easily understand why you would prefer E-mail to postal mail.

10.2.2 Differences between E-mail Server and E-mail Client

The differences between E-mail server and an E-mail client are shown in Table 10.1.

E-mail Server	E-mail Client
1. It runs on the computer of Internet Service Provider (ISP) viz. VSNL, MTNL, NOW, etc. 2. It receives the mail sent by user and send it to its destination over the internet	1. It run on the computer of Internet user. 2. It enables the user to read the mails received, to compose new mails and to send to E-mail server.

Table 10.1 *Difference between E-mail Server and E-mail Client*

10.2.3 E-mail Protocol

E-mail protocols are communication standards of E-mail. Various E-mail Protocols are:

(1) **SMTP.** SMTP stands for Simple Mail Transfer Protocol. It specifies the procedure for sending and receiving text messages over Internet by the E-mail servers. It also specifies the format of E-mail message.

(2) **POP or POP3.** POP stands for Post Office Protocol. In this protocol, the E-mail server stores the incoming messages only temporarily. When messages are downloaded by E-mail client, they are deleted from the server.

(3) **IMAP or IMAP4.** IMAP stands for Internet Message Access Protocol. It stores messages on the mail server rather than facilitating downloading to the user's computer. It is more convenient that POP3 as all of user's mail is kept in one central location where it can be organised and achieved.

10.2.4 E-mail Addressing

E-mail address consists of following three parts:

(*i*) **Mailbox Name.** It is the first part of E-mail address which indicates the user name. For example, in E-mail address 'authorashok@rediffmail.com' authorashok is the Mailbox name that indicates the name of the user.

(*ii*) **The @ sign.** It separates the first and third part of E-mail address.

(*iii*) **Server Name.** It is the name of user's Internet mail server. For example, in E-mail address 'authorashok@rediffmail.com' rediffmail.com is the name of Server.

Examples of E-mail Addresses:

- shefaliindia@rediffmail.com
- authorashok@rediffmail.com
- pnigam@hotmail.com
- guptas@global.t-bird.edu
- kccsw@nda.vsnl.net.in
- colaxmi@hotmail.com

10.2.5 Getting E-mail Account

You can get your E-mail account on Internet in the following two ways:

1. Through ISP. When you get an Internet connection, Internet Service Provider provides you an E-mail account with your user name, Internet address of your mail server and your password. The password can also be changed by the user.

2. Through Free E-mail Service. Some Web-based companies such as Hotmail, Yahoo, Rediff, etc. offer free E-mail services to Internet users. Free E-mail services are very popular among all users because we can access our E-mail from anywhere in the world. Moreover, our E-mail address is never changed. To get your free E-mail account, follow the procedure discussed below:

(*a*) Start the Internet browser (*e.g.* Microsoft Internet Explorer) by double clicking on the browser's shortcut icon.

(*b*) Open the Website of Rediff by entering its URL `http://www.rediff.com` in the address bar of the Microsoft Internet Explorer. The home page of Rediff Website will be displayed on the screen as shown in Figure 10.1. Now, click on 'New User? Sign up' hyperlink in Rediffmail box.

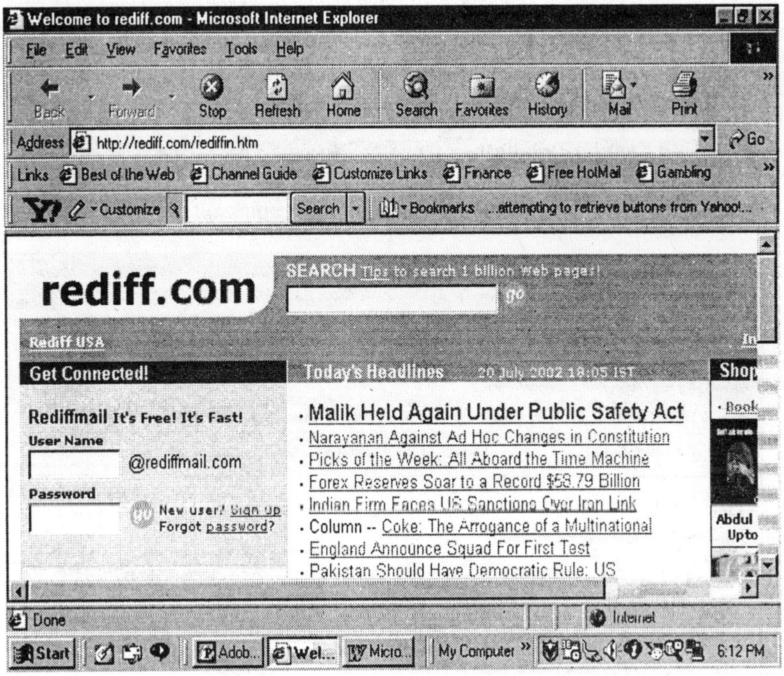

Figure 10.1 *The home page of rediff website*

(*c*) The top part of opening page of Rediffmail Registration Form will be displayed on the screen as shown in Figure 10.2. Using the vertical scroll bar, go the next part of this page, which is shown in Figure 10.3. The Rediffmail offers two types of accounts to users – Free Personal Account and Paid Business Account. Click on the 'SIGN UP NOW!' hyperlink. Now the top or first part of Rediff Registration Form *i.e.* Rediffmail Account Details will be displayed on the screen as shown in Figure 10.4. Enter your login name and password twice as illustrated in Figure 10.5.

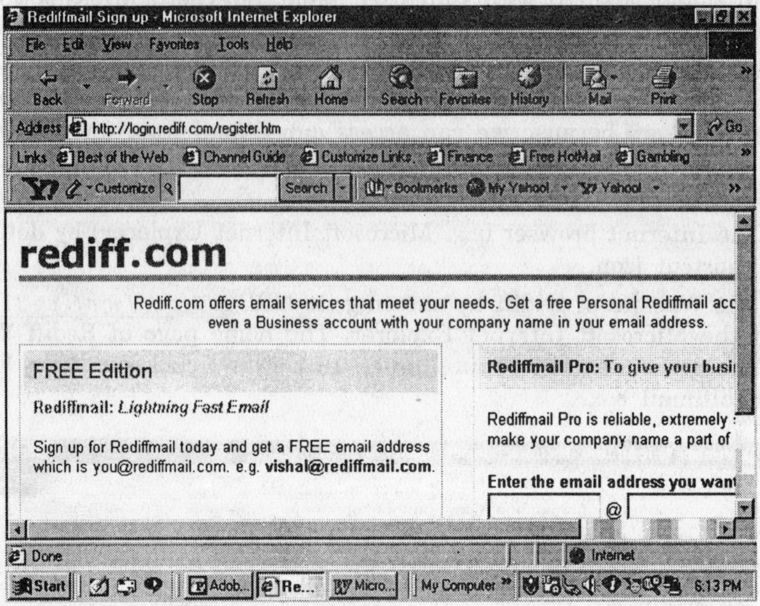

Figure 10.2 *The top part of opening page of rediffmail registration form*

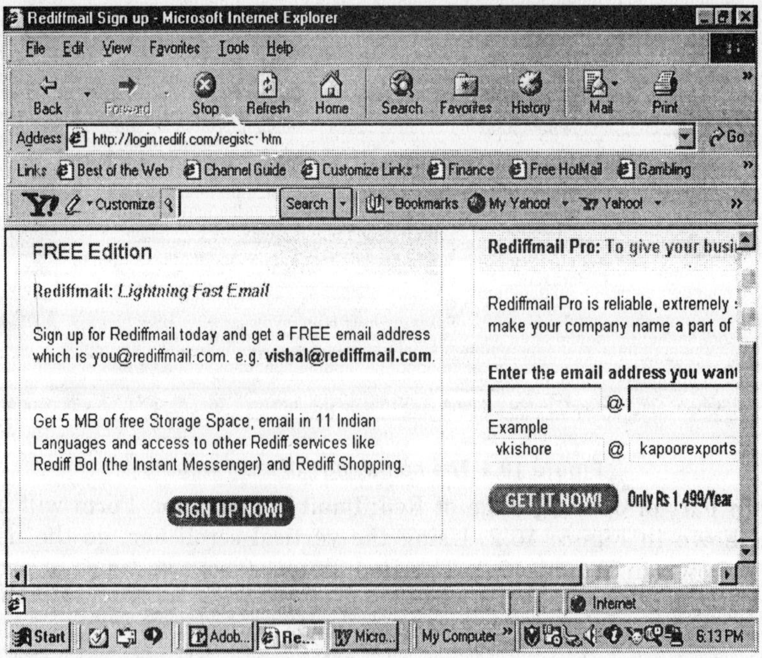

Figure 10.3 *The bottom part of opening page of rediffmail registration form*

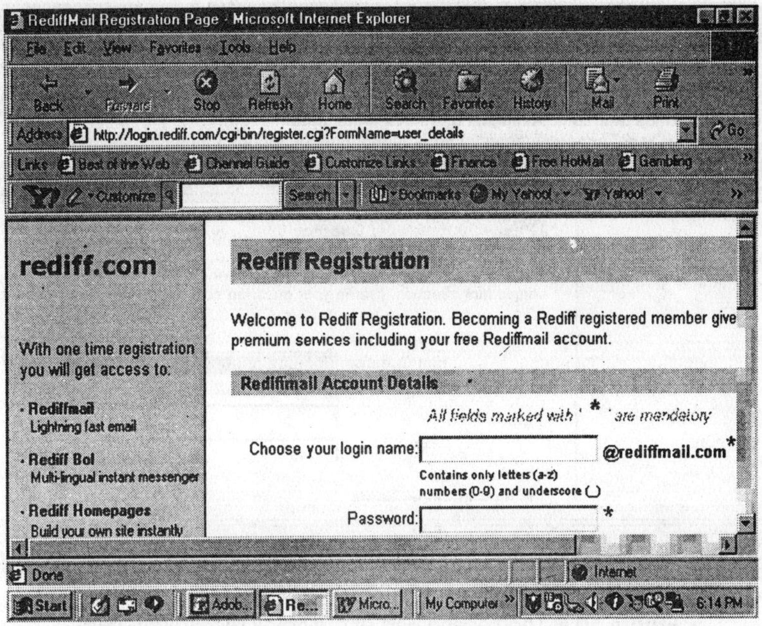

Figure 10.4 *The first part of rediffmail registration form*

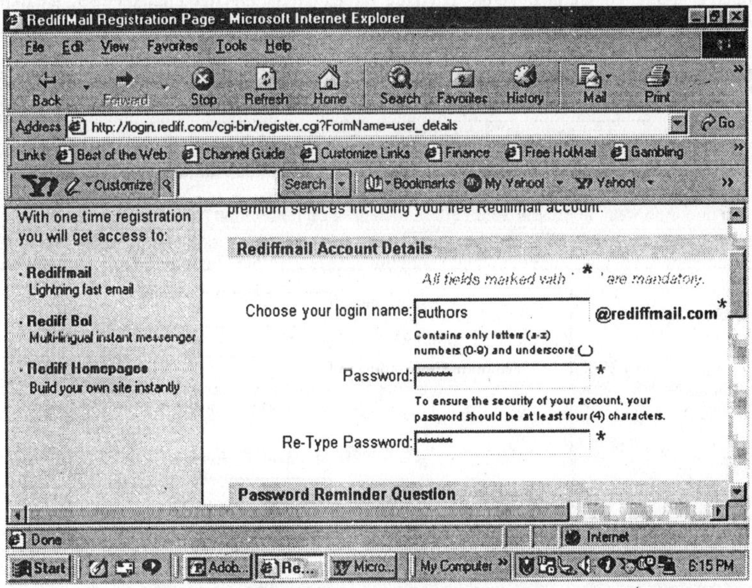

Figure 10.5 *Entering details in the first part of rediffmail registration form*

(*d*) Using the vertical scroll, move to the second part of Rediff Registration Form as shown in Figure 10.6 to enter Password Reminder question and answer. This will help you to remember the password in case you forget it in future.

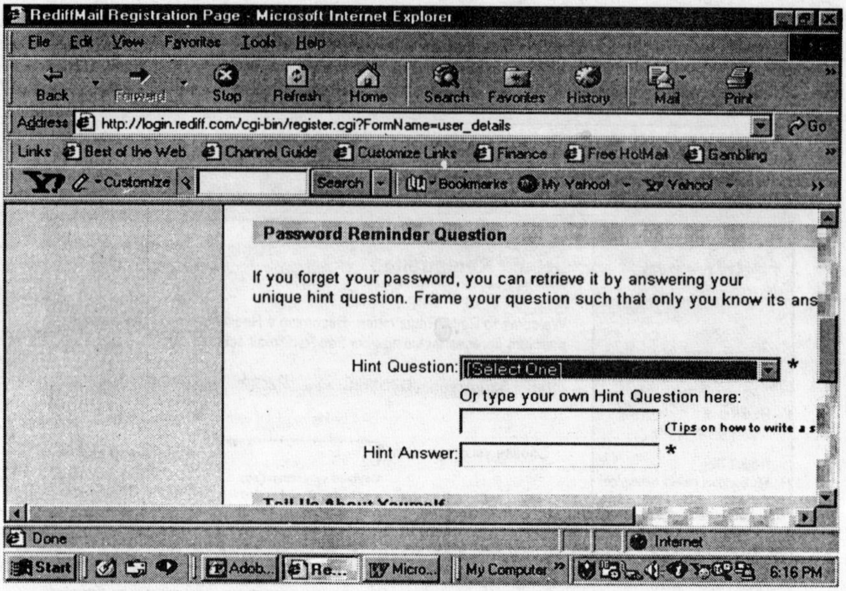

Figure 10.6 *The second part of rediffmail registration form*

(*e*) Again using the vertical scroll, move to the third part of Rediff Registration Form as shown in Figure 10.7 to enter your name, alternate E-mail address, gender and country. Now click on 'Continue' button.

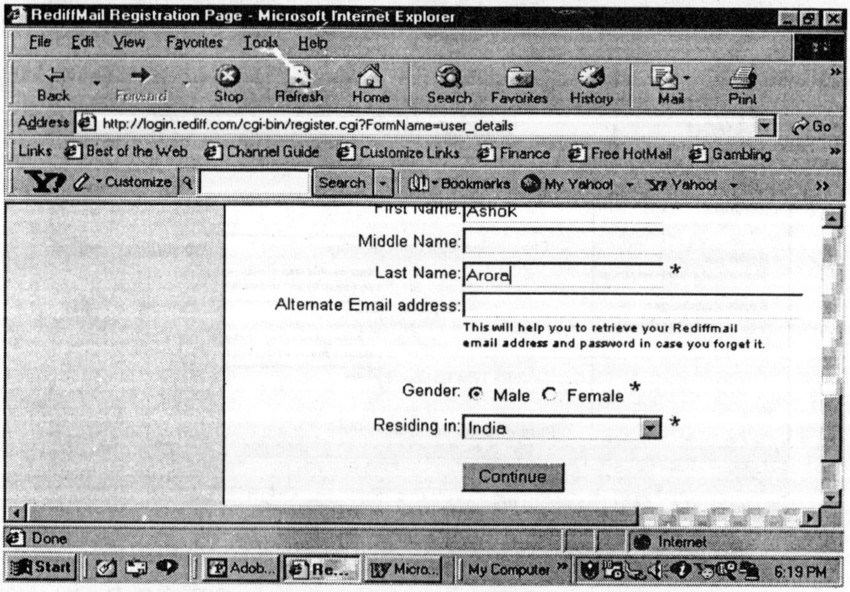

Figure 10.7 *The third part of rediffmail registration form*

(*f*) Rediffmail will now verify the details entered by you and check whether your Login Name already exists on Internet server. If it already exists, the message saying 'Sorry! The User Name already exists' will be displayed in the top of Rediffmail Registration Form as shown in Figure 10.8. Rediffmail will also give you suggestions of few user names, which do not exists and you can select one of them. Now, enter the Login Name, Password (twice) and Password Reminder question with answer again. Then again click on 'Continue' button. This message will keep on coming until you enter the Login name that does not exist.

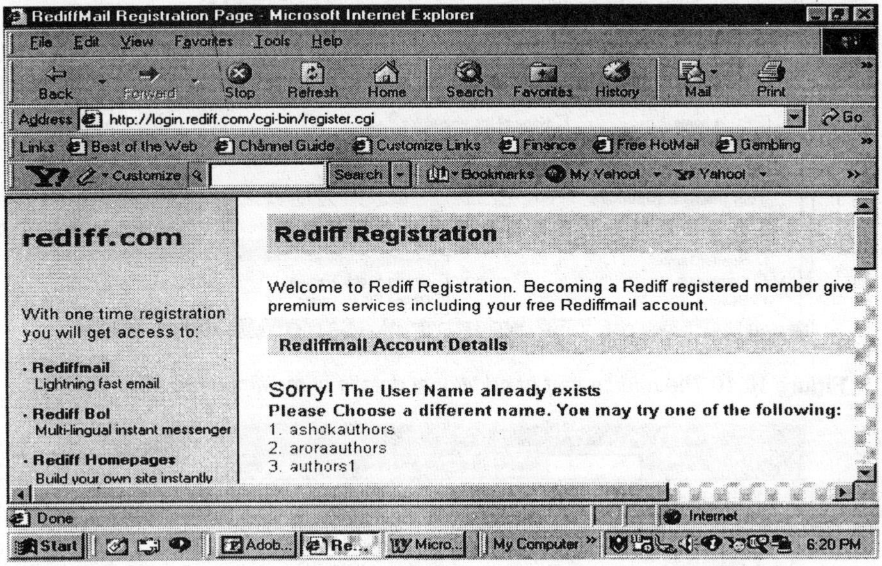

Figure 10.8 *Rediffmail registration form showing a message in case user name already exists*

(*g*) If server accepts the Login name, you will need to enter additional details in rest of the Rediffmail Registration Form as shown in Figures 10.9. 10.10 and 10.11. Finally click on 'Register Me' to finish the registration procedure of Free E-mail account.

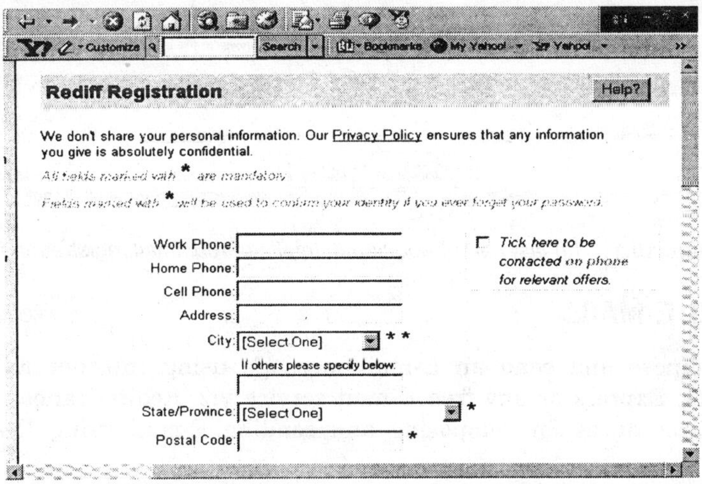

Figure 10.9 *The top part of additional details of rediffmail registration form*

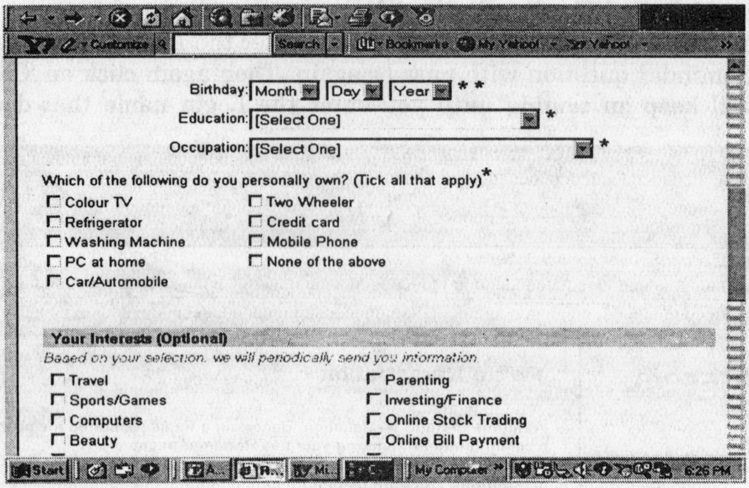

Figure 10.10 *The middle part of additional details of rediffmail registration form*

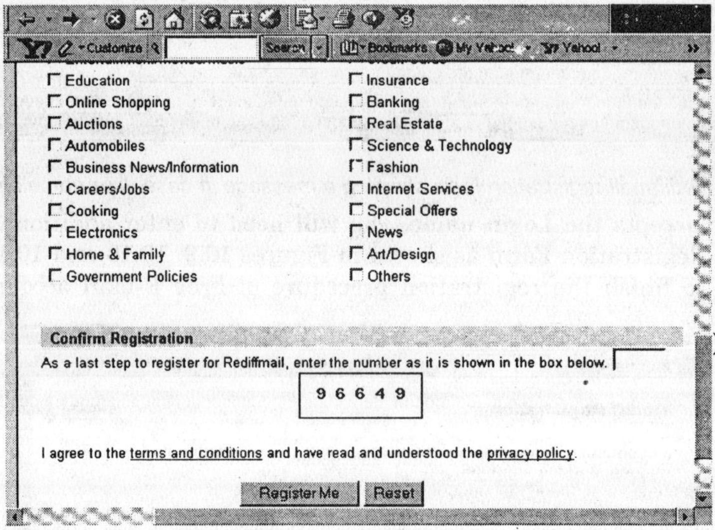

Figure 10.11 *The last part of additional details of rediffmail registration form*

10.3 SENDING E-MAIL

We can compose and send an E-mail message using Internet Explorer, Netscape Navigaor, Outlook Express or any free E-mail service viz. Rediff, Yahoo, Hotmail, etc. Let us discuss the procedures for composing and sending E-mail using Rediff and Outlook Express.

10.3.1 Composing and Sending E-mail using Rediff

The procedure to compose and send an E-mail message using Rediff is described below:

(*a*) Open the Website of Rediff by entering its URL `http://www.rediff.com` in the address bar of the Microsoft Internet Explorer. The home page of Rediff Website will be displayed on the screen (Refer Figure 10.11) (*b*) To open your mailbox, enter the user name and password and click on 'Sign in' as shown in Figure 10.12.

Figure 10.12 *Opening mailbox by entering user name and password in rediffmail*

(*c*) The incoming message list of your mailbox will be displayed as shown in Figure 10.13. In order to compose a message, click on the 'Compose' button.

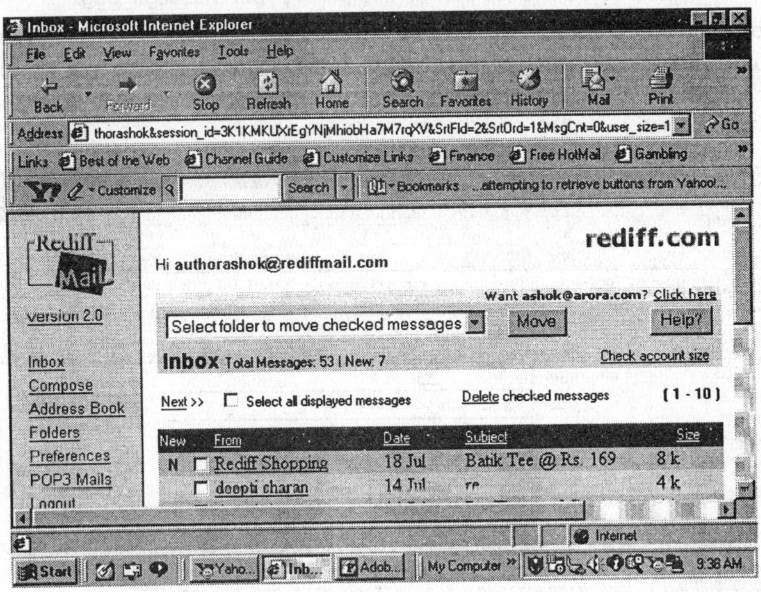

Figure 10.13 *Incoming message list of the mailbox (Inbox)*

(*d*) Now, you will see the top part of 'Compose your message' page as shown in Figure 10.14. Enter the E-mail address of recipient's mailbox in 'To' box. Enter the subject of your message in 'Subject' box. Write the E-mail addresses where you want to send the copies of your message in 'Cc' box (cc stands for carbon copy). You can also send the extra copy of your mail by specifying address of its recipient in 'Bcc' box (bcc stands for blind carbon copy).

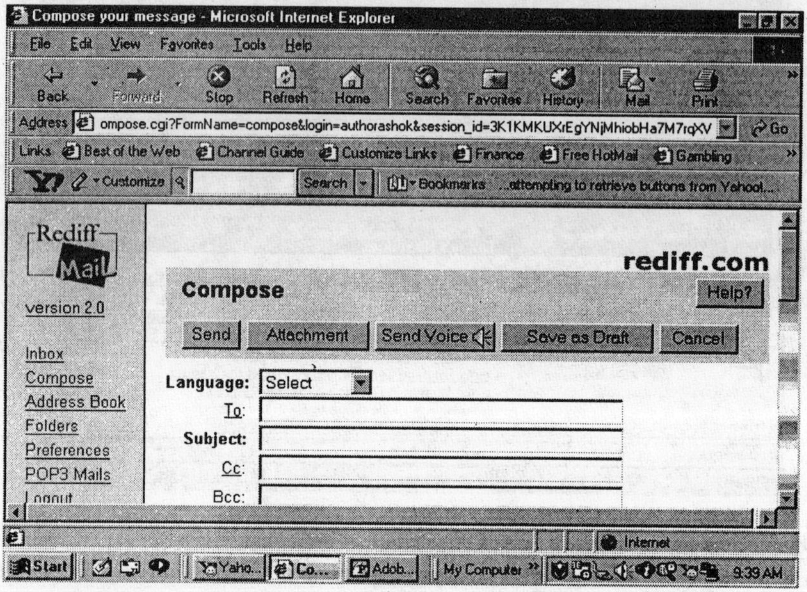

Figure 10.14 *The top part of 'composing your message' page*

(*e*) After entering details in top part of the 'Compose you message' page, use vertical scrollbar to move to message part of this page. Now, type the message in message box as illustrated in Figure 10.15. You can also save this message in your mailbox by clicking on the 'Save in Sent folder'.

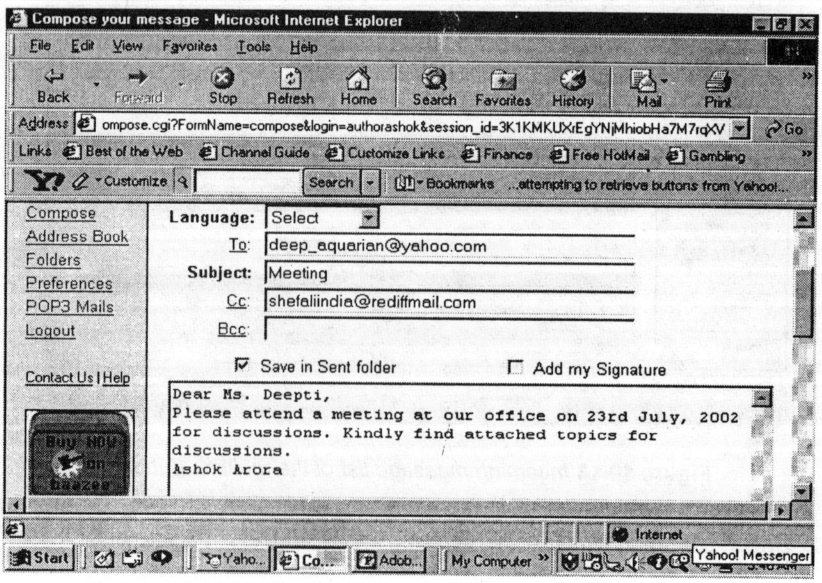

Figure 10.15 *The message part of 'composing your message' page*

(*f*) Using the vertical scrollbar, now you move to the bottom part of 'Compose your message' page. Click on 'Attachments' button as shown in Figure 10.16 to attach a file with your message.

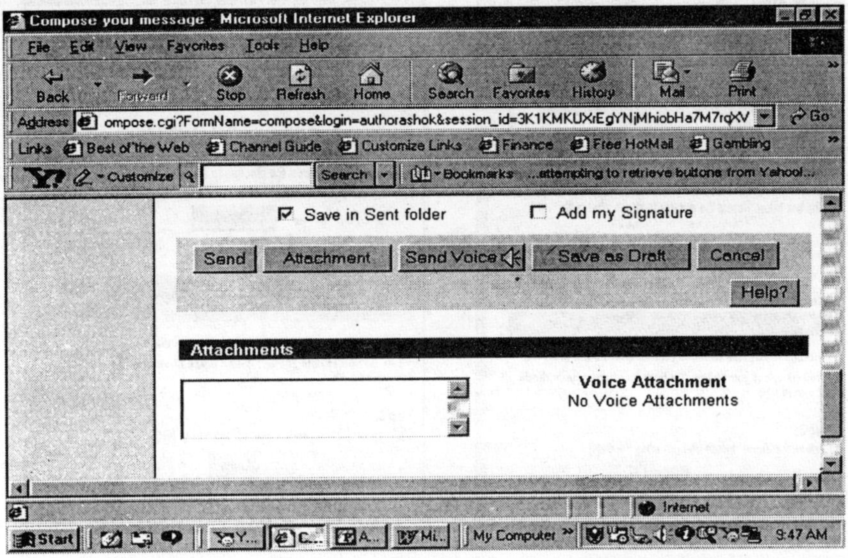

Figure 10.16 *The bottom part of 'composing your message' page*

(*g*) Now, the 'Attachments' page will be displayed in a separate window as shown in Figure 10.17.

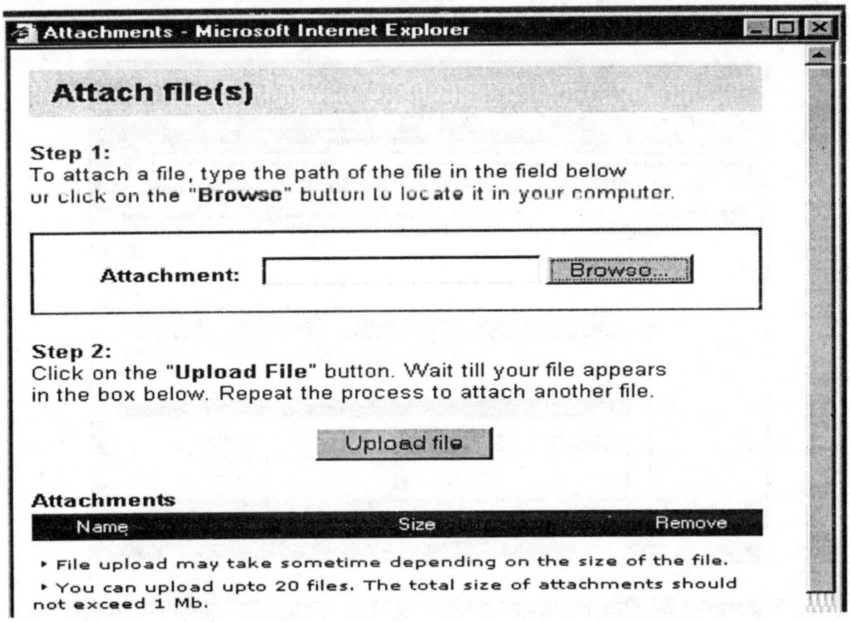

Figure 10.17 *The 'attachments' page of rediffmail*

(*h*) You can attach one or more files with your mail by a three-step process illustrated in Figures 10.18 and 10.19.

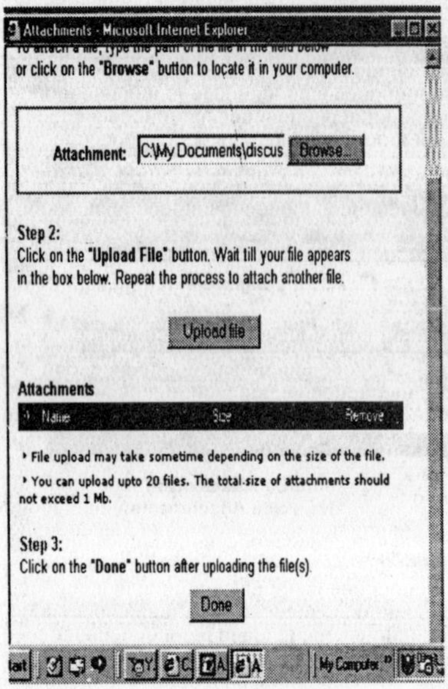

Figure 10.18 *Steps 1 and 2 of three-step process for attaching files*

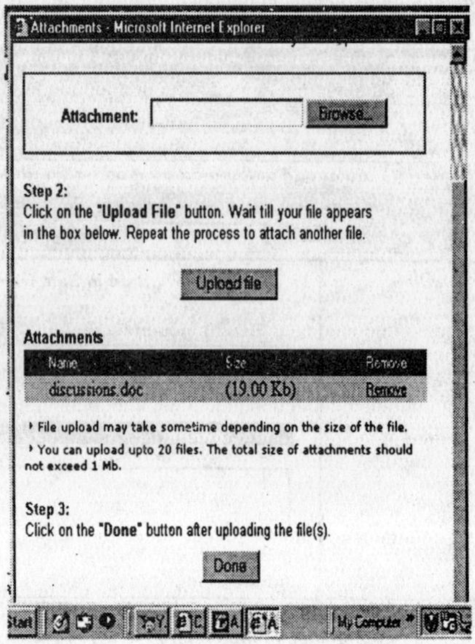

Figure 10.19 *Step 3 of three-step process for attaching files*

(*i*) After attaching file(s) you will come back to the 'Compose your message' page as shown in Figure 10.20. Finally click on 'Send' button to send the message along with attachments to the specified recipients.

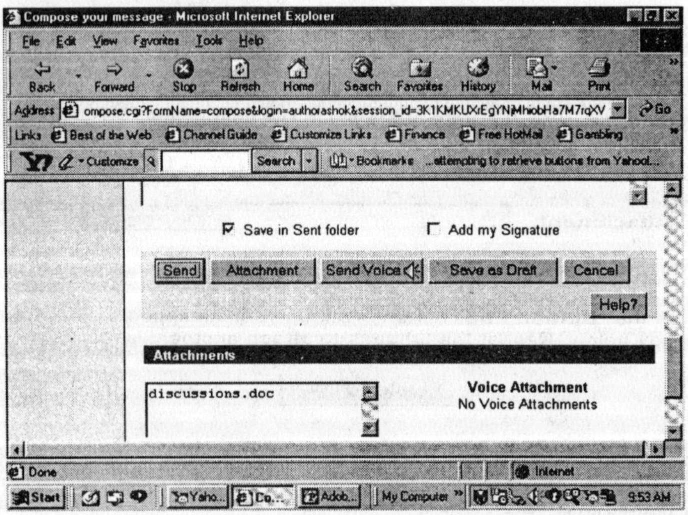

Figure 10.20 *The 'compose your message' page after attaching a file*

(*j*) In the end, you will see the 'Sent Message Confirmation' page as shown in Figure 10.21. This page will inform you that the message has been sent to one or more recipients.

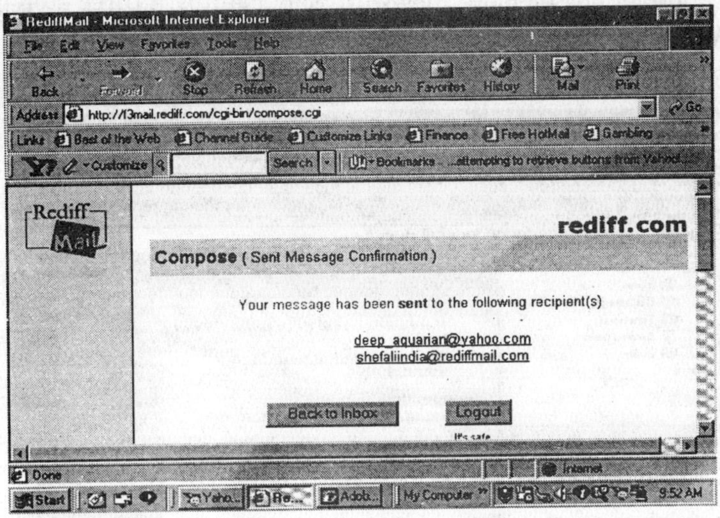

Figure 10.21 *The 'sent message Confirmation' page displayed after sending e-mail*

In this way, you can compose your message and send it to one or more E-mail users.

10.3.2 Composing and Sending E-mail using Outlook Express

The procedure to compose and send an E-mail message using Outlook Express is described below:

1. After connecting to Internet, click on 'Start' button of Windows and choose 'Outlook Express' option from 'Programs' menu as shown in Figure 10.22.

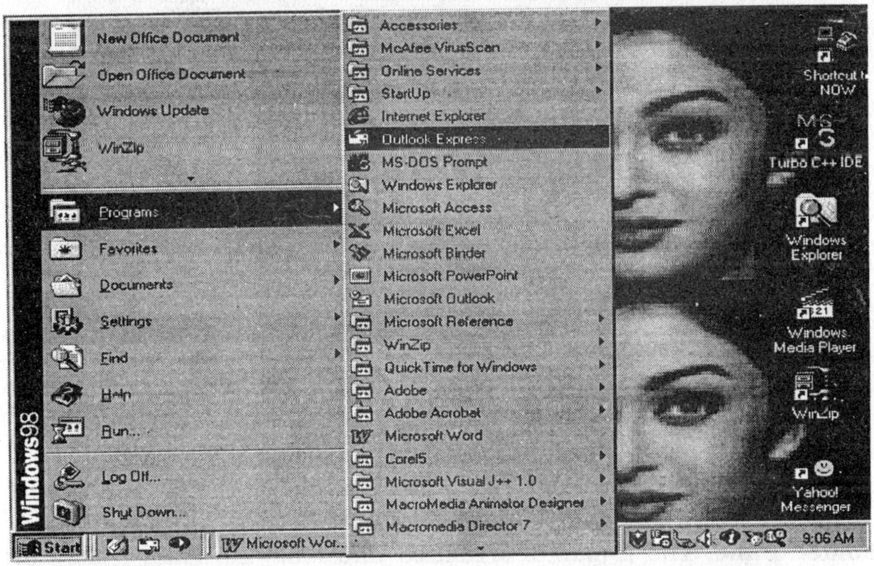

Figure 10.22 *Starting outlook express from 'start' button of Windows 98*

2. You will see the opening screen of Outlook Express as shown in Figure 10.23. This screen is called Message Component Window or E-mail Client's Window. To see all parts of this window, click on 'Read Mail' button.

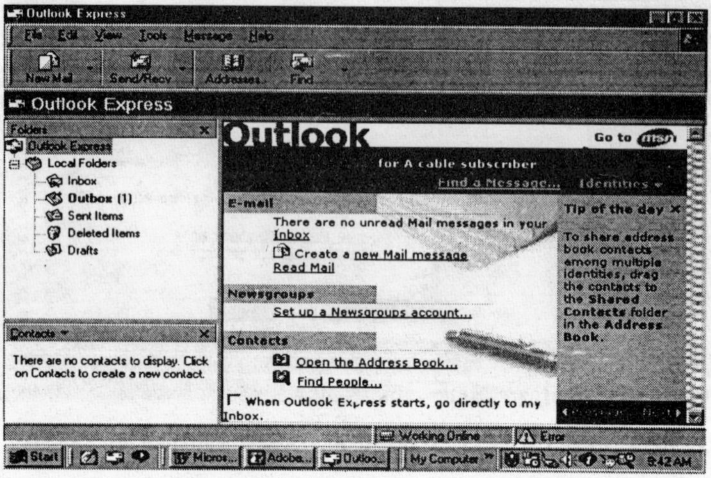

Figure 10.23 *Opening screen of outlook express*

Parts of a Message Component Window

The Message Component Window or the E-mail Client Window as shown in Figure 10.24 has following four parts:

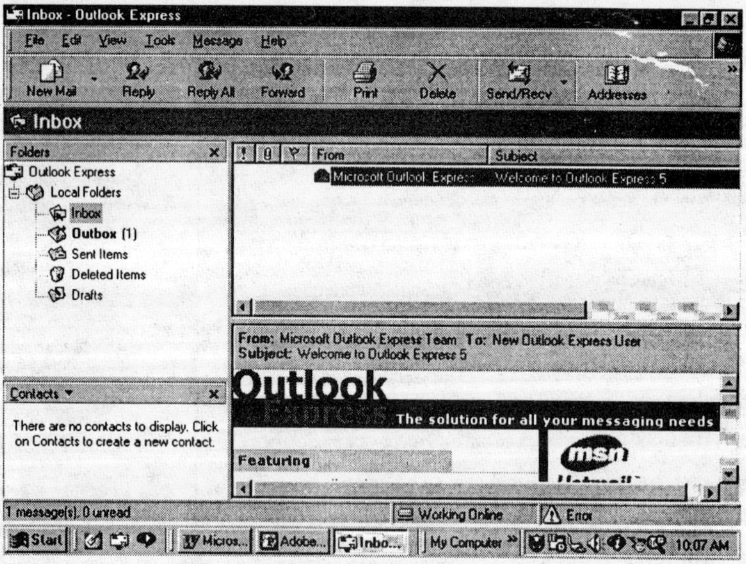

Figure 10.24 *Message component window*

(*a*) **Folder Pane.** The E-mail is organised into following main folders by Netscape Navigator.

(*i*) *Inbox.* It stores incoming mails.

(*ii*) Outbox: It stores outgoing mails composed by us.

(*iii*) Sent Items: It contains copies of mails sent by us.

(*iv*) Deleted Items: It contains messages that are deleted.

(*v*) Drafts: It contains messages drafted by us.

(*b*) **Message Header Pane.** It contains the list of messages contained in the selected folder. It displays the following columns:

(*i*) Name of Sender or Recipient

(*ii*) Subject line of the message

(*iii*) Received or Sent Date of Message

(*iv*) Read Icon indicating the message is read or not

(*c*) **Message Window.** The contents of the message selected from Message Header Pane are displayed in this window.

(*d*) **Contacts Window.** It displays the page name or file name (if any) attached with the mail.

3. First choose 'File – New – Mail Message' options from the menu or click on the 'New Mail' tool as shown in Figure 10.25.

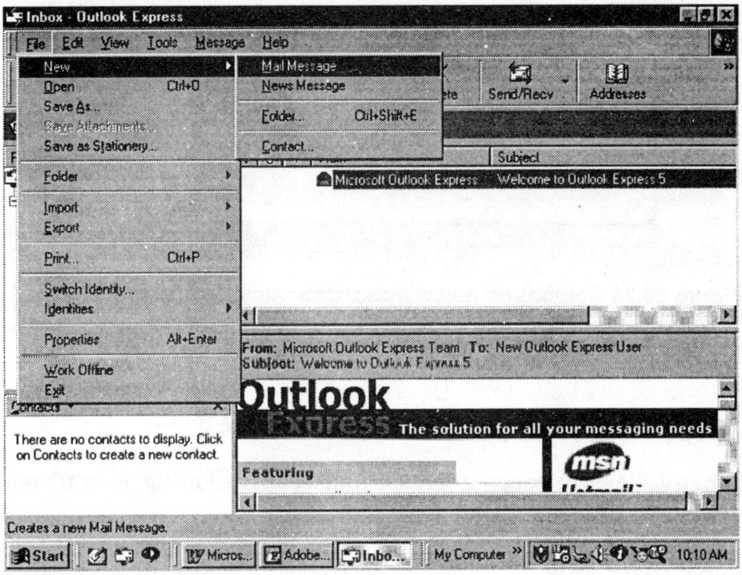

Figure 10.25 *Opening new message window in outlook express*

4. Now compose a new message as shown in Figure 10.26. This message component window has following fields:

(*a*) To. Write the E-mail address of the receiver in this field.

(*b*) Cc. Write the E-mail addresses where we want to send the copies of our message. Cc stands for carbon copy.

(*c*) Subject. Specify here the subject of our message.

We can also display the following additional fields in the message component window by choosing required 'View' options from the menu:

(*a*) From: It displays the sender E-mail address.

(*b*) Reply To: It contains E-mail addresses when we send replies to E-mails received.

(*c*) Blind cc: It contains E-mail address where extra copy of mail is sent.

(*d*) File cc: It contains the folder name where copies of sent messages are stored.

(*e*) Newsgroup: It contains name of Usenet Newsgroup where we want to sent message.

(*f*) Followup To: It contains name of Usenet Newsgroup where we want to post a reply.

(*g*) Attachment: It displays the name of file or page name enclosed with message.

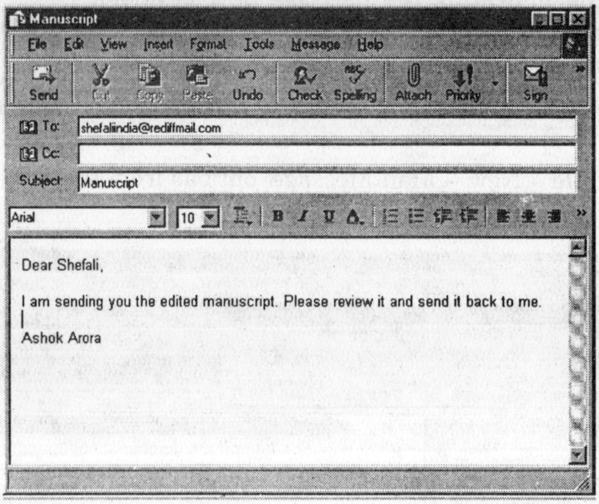

Figure 10.26 *Composing a new message in message component window*

5. Finally to send the composed message to E-mail addresses specified, click on 'Send' button of message component window.

10.4 RECEIVING, CHECKING & READING E-MAIL

There are many ways to receive, check and read incoming E-mail messages, however the following two ways are generally used by users:

(*a*) Using Outlook Express.

(*b*) Using Address of Internet Server.

Let us discuss these methods with illustrations.

10.4.1 Reading E-Mail using Outlook Express

You can read your E-mail using Outlook Express by following way:

1. After connecting to Internet, click on 'Start' button of Windows and choose 'Outlook Express' option from 'Programs' menu (Refer Figure 10.22).

2. You will see the Message Component Window of Outlook Express (Refer Figure 10.23). Click on 'Read Mail' button. Alternatively, you can also click on the 'Send and Receive' button on the toolbar in 'Outlook Express'.

3. Then we click the Inbox icon on either the Outlook bar or the Folders list. To view the message in the preview pane, we click the message in the message list and to view the message in a separate window, we double-click the message in the message list. The message screen (Refer Figure 10.24) shows following icons with message list:

(*i*) **Question Mark (?).** It indicates that the status of mail server can not be checked automatically.

(*ii*) **Envelope.** It indicates that there is no more message for us.

(*iii*) **Explanation Mark (!).** It indicates that there are new messages for us.

4. If we want to view all the information about a message, such as when it was sent, first we click on the 'File' menu, and then click on 'Properties'.

5. To save the message in our file system, we click on 'Save as' and then select the required format and folder where we want to save.

10.4.2 Reading E-mail using Address of Internet Server

You can read your E-mail using address of Internet server (such as Rediff) by following way:

1. Enter the address of Internet Server (*e.g.* `http://www.rediff.com`) in 'Address' box of Internet Explorer or Netscape Navigator window (Refer Figure 10.1).

2. Now enter the user name and password and click on 'Sign in' (Refer Figure 10.12). The incoming message list is displayed (Refer Figure 10.13). Click on the required message to read the mail.

10.4.3 Managing Folders in E-mail

The mails received in the mailbox of your server are stored in Folders. There are following four types of folders in Rediffmail as shown in Figure 10.27:

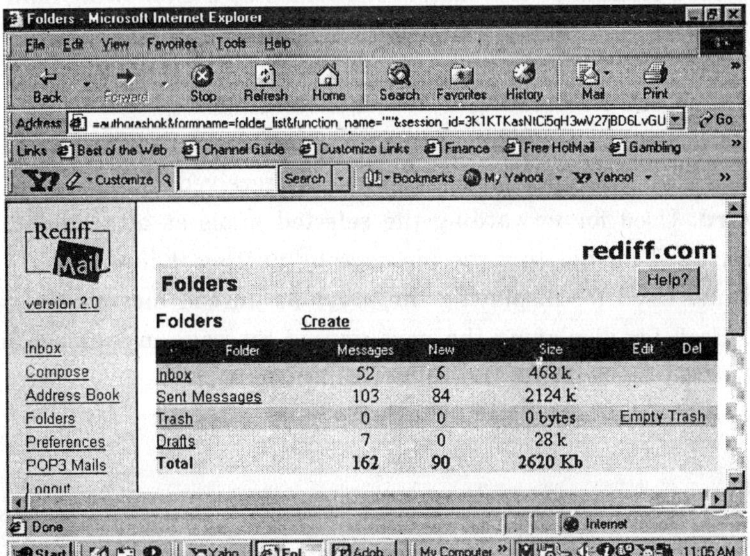

Figure 10.27 *Types of folders in rediffmail*

(*a*) Inbox. The messages coming on the mailbox are stored in Inbox folder.

(*b*) Sent Messages: If you save your E-mail message while sending it, the message will be stored in 'Sent Messages' folder.

(*c*) Trash. The mails deleted by you are transferred to Trash folder from Inbox folder.

(*d*) Draft. After composing the mail, you can store it in 'Draft' folder by choosing 'Save as Draft' button in 'Composing your message' page (Refer Figure 10.16).

You can manage these folders either by deleting or moving message(s) in following ways

I. Moving Messages:

(*a*) Select the message(s) by marking on the message title box (Refer Figure 10.13).

(*b*) Move the selected messages by selecting the folder from 'Select folder to move checked messages' box and clicking on 'Move' button (Refer Figure 10.13).

II. Deleting Messages:

(*a*) Double-click on the folder to see its messages (Refer Figure 10.27).

(*b*) Select the message(s) by marking on the message title box (Refer Figure 10.13).

(*c*) Click on the 'Delete' button (Refer Figure 10.13).

(*d*) If you want to delete all messages from 'Trash' folder, click on the 'Empty Trash' button (Refer Figure 10.27).

10.5 E-MAIL COMMANDS OF NETSCAPE NAVIGATOR

We are discussing now various commands of E-mail, which are provided by mail toolbar buttons and menu options of Netscape Navigator.

10.5.1 Function of Mail Toolbar Buttons available in Netscape Navigator

Commonly used commands of E-mail are provided by the following mail toolbar buttons of Netscape Navigator:

(*a*) **Get Mail.** Used for connecting to mail server and receiving the mail.

(*b*) **To: Mail.** Used for creating a new mail message.

(*c*) **Re: Mail.** Used for replying to the received mail message.

(*d*) **Re: All.** Used for replying to the all mails received.

(*e*) **Forward.** Used for forwarding the selected mails as attachment.

(*f*) **Delete.** Used for deleting the message by putting it into Trash folder.

(*g*) **Previous.** Used for displaying the previous unread message in message list.

(*h*) **Next.** Used for displaying the next unread message in message list.

(*i*) **Print.** Used for printing the selected message(s).

(*j*) **Stop.** Used for stopping the transmission of message.

10.5.2 Functions of Mail menu options in Netscape Navigator

Various mail menu options available in Netscape Navigator are described below:

1. FILE Menu Options:

(*a*) *New Mail Message.* Used for creating a new mail message.

(*b*) *New Folder.* Used for creating a new mail folder.

(*c*) *Save As.* Used for saving the message as a file.

(*d*) *Get New Mail.* Used for connecting to mail server and receiving the mail.

(*e*) *Send Mail in Outbox.* Used to send outgoing message in outbox folder.

(*f*) *Empty Trash Folder.* Used to permanently delete the messages stored in Trash folder.

(*g*) *Print Messages.* Used for printing the selected message(s).

(*h*) *Close.* Used for closing the mail window.

2. EDIT Menu Options:

(*a*) *Undo/Redo.* Used to reverse the last action performed in mail window.

(*b*) *Cut.* Used to cut the selected text and place in clipboard.

(*c*) *Paste.* Used to paste the selected text from clipboard at the current cursor position.

(*d*) *Delete Message.* Used for deleting the message by putting it into Trash folder.

(*e*) *Delete Folder.* Used for deleting the selected folder and its contents.

(*f*) *Select Thread.* Used to select all messages in the current thread (group).

(*g*) *Select Flagged Messages.* Used to select flagged messages in the current thread.

(*h*) *Select All Messages.* Used to select all messages in all threads.

(*i*) *Find.* Used to find the selected text in current message.

(*j*) *Find Again.* Used to find the previous selected text in the current message.

3. VIEW Menu Options:

(*a*) *Reload.* Used to reload the message from server.

(*b*) *Refresh.* Used to redraw the present message.

(*c*) *Sort.* Used for arranging the messages date-wise, name-wise, subject-wise etc. in ascending or descending order.

(*d*) *Unscramble.* Used for decoding of received message using shifting of character mechanism.

(*e*) *Wrap Long Lines.* Used for word wrapping of text exceeding right margin to next line.

(*f*) *Load Images.* Used for displaying those images of present message which are not loaded with message.

(*g*) *Document Source.* Used to display message in HTML format.

(*h*) *Attachments Inline.* Used to display page attachment as part of message.

(*i*) *Attachments as Links.* Used to display page attachment as a hyperlink. The attached page is displayed on clicking on these links.

4. MESSAGE Menu Options.

(*a*) *Reply.* Used to reply the sender by writing new message.

(*b*) *Reply to All.* Used to reply the sender and all recipients to whom sender has send the incoming message.

(*c*) *Mark as Read.* Used to mark the message that has been read.

(*d*) *Mark as Unread.* Used to mark the message that has not been read.

(*e*) *Flag Message.* Used to put icon in current message's flag column.

(*f*) *Unflag Message.* Used to remove icon in current message's flag column.

(*g*) *Forward.* Used for forwarding the selected mails as attachment.

(*h*) *Forward Quoted.* Used for sending the current message as quoted text.

(*i*) *Move.* Used for sending the current message to selected folder.

(*j*) *Copy.* Used for sending a copy of current message to selected folder.

(*k*) *Add to Address Book.* Used to add the sender's E-mail address in address book.

5. GO Menu Options.

(*a*) *Previous Message.* Used to display the previous message.

(*b*) *Next Message.* Used to display the next message.

(*c*) *First Unread.* Used to display the first unread message.

(*d*) *Previous Unread.* Used to display the previous unread message.

(*e*) *Next Unread.* Used to display the next unread message.

(*f*) *First Flagged.* Used to display the first marked message.

(*g*) *Previous Flagged.* Used to display the previous marked message.

(*h*) *Next Flagged.* Used to display the next marked message.

(*i*) *Stop Loading.* Used for stopping the transmission of message.

6. OPTIONS Menu Options.

(*a*) *Show all Messages.* Used to display all messages.

(*b*) *Show only Unread Messages.* Used to display only unread messages.

(*c*) *Document Coding.* Used to select a character set encoding scheme.

(*d*) *Show Headers:*

(*i*) All. It displays all headers.

(*ii*) Normal. It displays primary address columns.

(*iii*) Brief. It displays only subject and recipient columns.

10.6 ADDRESS BOOK

Address book provides a simplified method to store E-mail addresses for easy retrieval by Microsoft Outlook Express. In the Address Book, we can store multiple E-mail addresses, residential and official addresses and phone/fax numbers of our contacts. We can also store personal and official Internet addresses and link directly to them from the Address Book. The extra information about our contacts can be provided in a section for notes in address book. In addition to storing addresses, the address book provides following important features:

(*a*) **To find people and organisations by using LDAP directory services.** LDAP stands for Lightweight Directory Service Address Protocol. The address book supports LDAP for using directory services provided through Internet. While addressing E-mail messages, these directory services can be used very easily.

(*b*) **To create a Business Card.** We can create a business card in address book. This card in stored in Visiting Card format that can be exchanged with different programs such as personal planners, E-mail etc. Business card is the latest way to send contact information on Internet.

(*c*) **To create a group of contacts.** We can create a group of contacts such as Business Associates, Friends, Relatives, Film Stars etc. in address book. In this way, we can send E-mails to all people in a group very quickly and easily.

(*d*) **To import names from other address books.** We can import addresses from address books created in other programs such as Microsoft Exchange, Netscape Communicator etc. to Microsoft outlook express address book.

(*e*) **To give a nick name to an address.** We can give a nick name to an E-mail address in address book by simply specifying nickname in 'Mail to:' field instead of writing E-mail address.

10.6.1 Creating an Address Book

To create an address book in Microsoft Outlook Express, we follow the procedure described below:

1. First we click on the 'Address Book' icon in Outlook Express toolbar. The 'Address Book' window as shown in Figure 10.28.

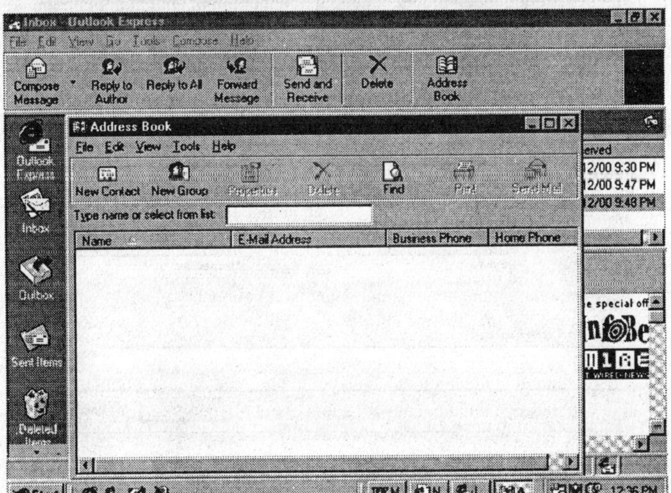

Figure 10.28 *The 'address book' window*

2. Now click on 'New Contact' icon and Enter personal information in the 'Properties' window as illustrated in Figure 10.29.

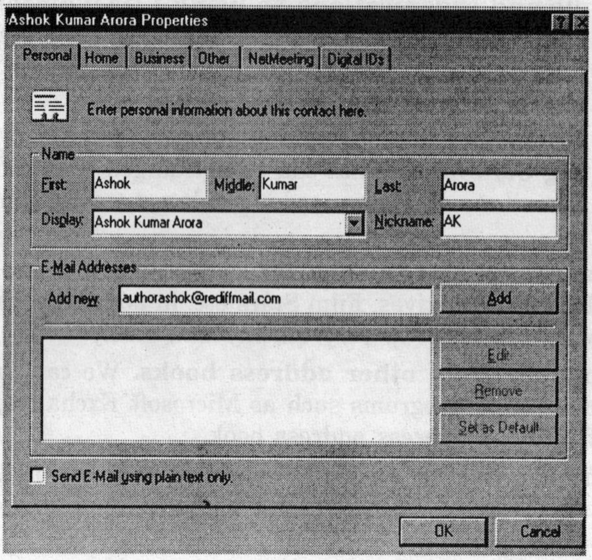

Figure 10.29 *Entering personal information in address book*

3. Now we click on 'Home' tab and enter home address as illustrated in Figure 4.47. Similarly we can enter business and other details by selecting respective tabs and finally we click on 'Add' button. All the information is added to the address book and the screen as shown in Figure 10.30.

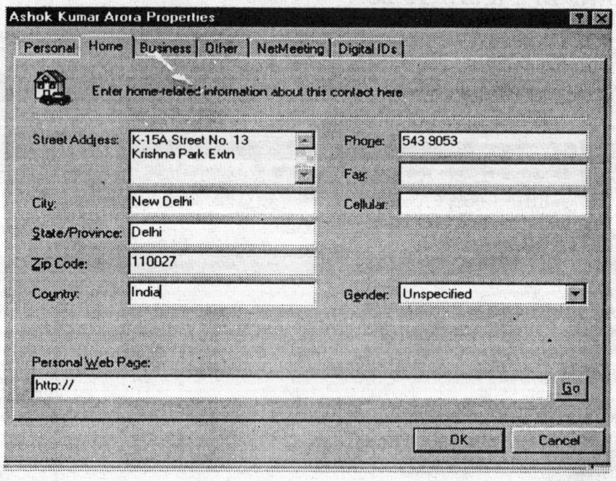

Figure 10.30 *Entering home-related information in address book*

4. Now, we create a group by clicking on 'New Group' icon in the Outlook Express toolbar. The window of a group properties as shown in Figure 10.31 is displayed where we type a name for the group and select members of the group by clicking on 'Select members' button. After selecting all the members of a group, we click on 'OK' button.

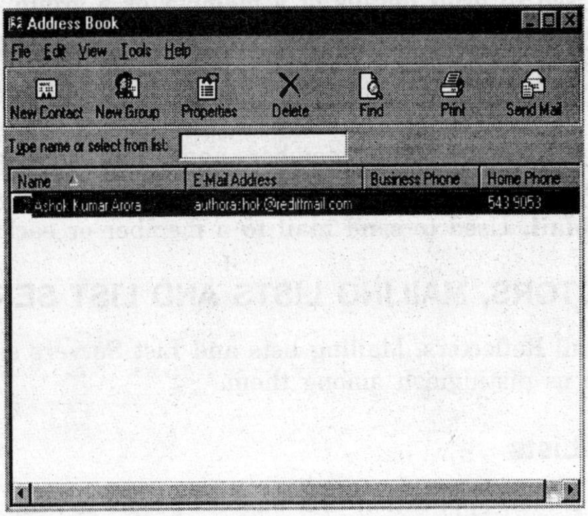

Figure 10.31 *Screen displayed after entering all information in address book*

5. Now, the screen as shown in Figure 10.32 is displayed where we select or type name of other groups and select members of that group.

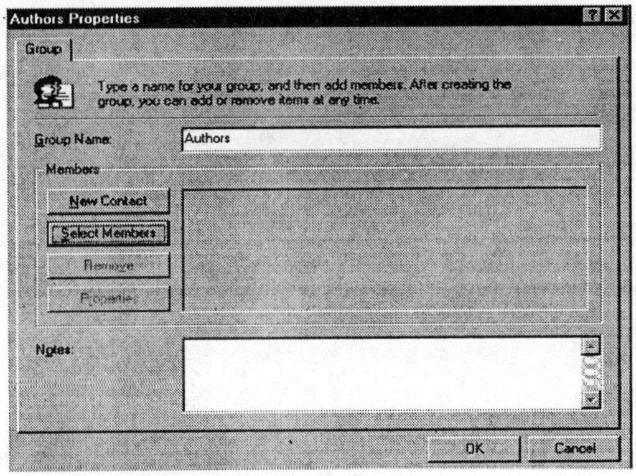

Figure 10.32 *Properties window of address book*

6. We can now send the mails to all members of a group or a particular member from the address book by clicking on 'Send Mail' icon in the address book.

10.6.2 Menu Options of the Address Book

Important menu options available in the address book are described below:

1. **File–New Contact.** Used to enter addresses of new contact.
2. **File–New Group.** Used to enter addresses of new group.
3. **File–Properties.** Used to display or edit data of a particular member or group.
4. **File–Delete.** Used to delete a member or a group.
5. **File–Import.** Used to import address book or card from other programs.
6. **File–Export.** Used to export address book or card to other programs.

7. **File–Print.** Used to print details of a member or a group.

8. **File–Close.** Used to close the address book.

9. **Edit–Find.** Used to find the member by specifying its name, address, E-mail address etc.

10. **View–Sort By.** Used to arrange members name wise, address wise, phone no. wise etc. either in ascending or descending order.

11. **Tools–Send Mail.** Used to send mail to a member or each member of a group.

10.7 MAIL REFLECTORS, MAILING LISTS AND LIST SERVERS

The terms like Mail Reflectors, Mailing lists and List Servers seem to be similar, but they are different. Let us distinguish among them.

10.7.1 Mailing Lists

Mailing list is an E-mail application that enables people to send messages to everyone who has subscribed to the list. It consists of a special group of persons having common interests. To join a mailing list, user must subscribe. Generally, a user subscribes by following method:

- Send an E-mail message to the list's server address.
- Type word 'subscribe' in the message's body.
- Enter name of mailing list.
- Enter his/her name.
- Give confirmation to subscribing.

10.7.2 Mail Reflectors

Mailboxes that receives the mail and sends it to all the members of the mailing list are called Mail Reflectors.

10.7.3 List Server

The programs that manage the mailing list are called list server. For examples, LISTSERV is a list server developed by a program named Eric.

10.8 BOUNCED MAIL

An E-mail that is not received by the receiver and hence comes back to the sender is called **bounced mail**. A mail is bounced due to following reasons:

- The E-mail address of sender may be wrong.
- The E-mail address may be typed in different case (upper or lower) as the address is case sensitive.
- The names of user or host may be unknown or not existing.
- There may be no free space in the receiver's mail box.

10.8.1 Handling Bounced Mail

The bounced mail is handled by special programs called *daemons* (pronounced as DEE-MON). A daemon is a program that does repetitive tasks for them and listens for requests coming into an Internet server. It is started automatically at the time of booting. The daemon tells the problem of bounced mail and thus user can handled the bounced mail.

THEORY QUESTIONS

1. What is E-mail? How will you compose and send a message using E-mail to your friend using Outlook Express? Explain.
2. What are E-mail Protocols? Explain them briefly.
3. (*a*) What is an E-mail address book? Explain its various menu options.
   (*b*) Explain the procedure of creating an address book with suitable example.
4. Explain the components of e-mail in (*a*) Outlook Express, and (*b*) Rediff.
5. Explain with example the procedure of creating and sending mail using address of the Internet server.
6. Explain the procedure of reading your mail using (*a*) Outlook Express, and (*b*) address of the Internet server.
7. How do you attach one or more files with your mail while sending the E-mail? Explain with suiable example.
8. Write short notes on following terms:
   (*a*) Netiquette
   (*b*) List Server
   (*c*) Daemons
9. Differentiate between the following terms:
   (*a*) E-mail and Postal Mail
   (*b*) E-mail Client and E-mail Server
   (*c*) SMTP and IMAP
   (*d*) Mail Reflectors and Mailing list
10. (*a*) Name three E-mail service providers who provide E-mail facility to personal users free of cost.
    (*b*) How will you create your E-mail account on any of these service providers? Explain the composition of your E-mail address.
11. Give the full form of following abbreviated terms:
    (*a*) POP3 (*b*) SMTP (*c*) DNS
12. What are folders in E-mail? Explain their functions in brief.

WORKSHOP

1. Create your free E-mail accounts on a) Rediff, and b) Yahoo servers.
2. Open your E-mail account and compose a mail by writing feedback of this book. Send it to authors of this book at address 'authorashok@rediffmail.com' with cc to 'shefaliindia@rediffmail.com'.
3. Open your mailbox using (a) Outlook Express, and (b) Address of Internet server.
4. Create an address box with E-mail addresses of your friends and relatives.
5. Send the mails read by you to the respective folder of your mailbox.

11
INTRODUCTION TO PINE AND ELM

11.1 INTRODUCTION

In the last chapter, we discussed the procedures of sending and receiving electronic mails over Internet using Outlook Express and address of various Internet servers (such as Rediff, Yahoo, etc.) in Windows operating environment. In this chapter, we will discuss the procedures of sending and receiving electronic mails in UNIX environment. On UNIX platforms, you need special programs for sending and receiving mails. PINE and ELM are two such E-mail programs, which run on UNIX systems over Internet. Let us discuss these in detail.

11.2 OVERVIEW OF PINE

PINE is a popular character-based E-mail client program. It is a UNIX mail system that was developed by the company 'Computing and Communications' at University of Washington in 1989. It was written as an alternative to ELM which is another UNIX mail system. Although PINE was developed for students and teachers of University of Washington, it has become a popular E-mail program for UNIX on Internet and online services around the world. Let us first see, what is PINE and why it has become so popular?

11.2.1 What is PINE

PINE is an acronym for "Program for Internet News and E-mail". It is an easy-to-use program for reading, sending and managing Internet electronic mails and news (Usenet) messages. PINE is a Mail User Agent (MUI), which is a program for composing and reading messages using Internet mail standards. It also allows you to read and post news messages on Usenet provided your site operates a suitable news server.

PINE supports the following Internet protocols:

(*a*) **Simple Mail Transport Protocol (SMTP).** It is the standard protocol used for sending mail.

(*b*) **Internet Message Access Protocol (IMAP).** It permits the client E-mail program (such as PINE) to access remote messages that are kept on the mail server.

(*c*) **Network News Transport Protocol (NNTP).** It allows distribution, inquiry, retrieval and posting of news articles on Usenet.

(*d*) **Multipurpose Internet Mail Extensions (MIME).** It allows you to attach any type of file (binary files) to your message provided the recipient client also has MIME-capable mail program.

11.2.2 Features of PINE

PINE program provides the following features:

- PINE is so well designed that you can easily use it while working. You are not even required to read its manual for using it.
- The message composition editor of PINE (PICO) is a simple-to-use text editor with text justification and spell-checking features. PICO is an acronym for PINE's message composition editor.
- PINE provides a mail index, which displays the summary of messages.
- It contains an address book for saving addresses and their nick names, which can be remembered easily.
- It provides folders for storing received and sent messages. These folders can be easily accessed and managed.
- In PINE, you can view and process mails with single character commands such as I to view the Index, R to reply the message and C for composing the message.
- On-line help, specific to each screen is available in PINE.
- As PINE supports MIME protocol, the graphics and sound files can be attached to the mail messages.

11.2.3 Requirements for Using PINE

In order to use PINE, you require the following software:

(*a*) UNIX operating system.

(*b*) Telnet client software such as NCSA Telnet or Host Explorer Telnet. Host Explorer Telnet comes with Windows Internet Access Kit.

(*c*) Besides these software, you need an Internet connection which can be dial-up or by way of Ethernet.

11.2.4 Starting PINE

Follow the steps given below for starting PINE:

1. Dial in an Internet connection, in case you are using Dial-up connection. If you use Ethernet, your connection will be automatically available.
2. Connect to the Login services using the Telnet software at login. `ith.umich.edu.`
3. At the UNIX prompt, type the following command:

```
$ pine<Enter>
```

You will see the opening screen of PINE showing the Main Menu as shown in Figure 11.1. Various commands of main menu are described in Table 11.1.

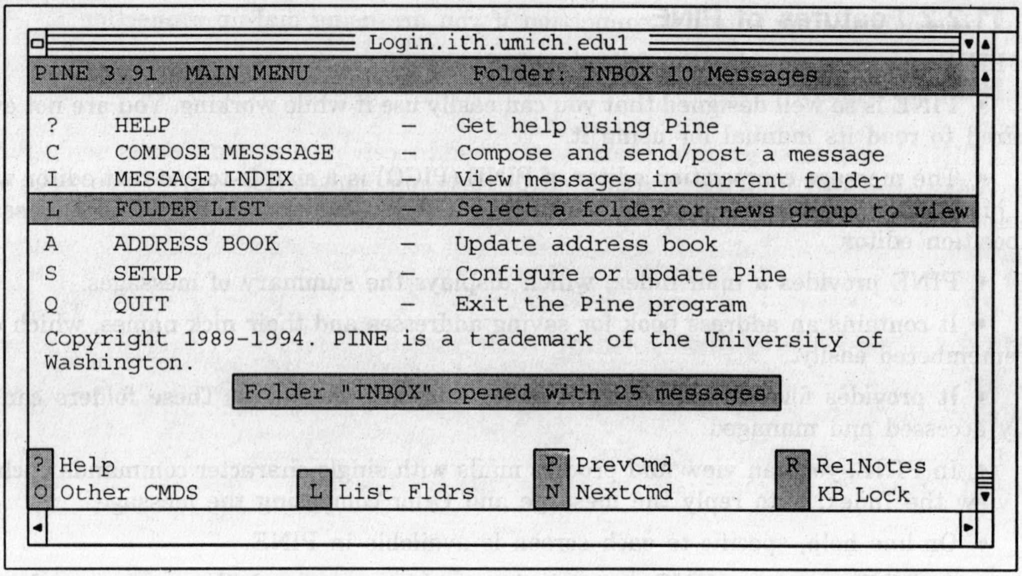

Figure 11.1 *Opening screen of PINE*

Command	Function
? (Help)	To access on-line help from PINE.
C (Compose Message)	To compose and send/post a mail/news message to recipient(s)/News group(s).
I (Message Index)	To display a one-line summary of each message in the current folder.
L (Folder List)	To select and maintain a folder or news group from the displayed list of folders.
A (Address Book)	To maintain a personal address book for storing individual/group of E-mail addresses.
S (Setup)	To change password and configure the Printer Command.
Q (Quit)	To come out of PINE program
O (Other Cmds)	To display other commands.
P (PrevCmd)	To run previous comamnd.
N (NextCmd)	To run next comamnd.
R (Rel Notes)	To display notes on the latest version of PINE program.
K (KB Lock)	To lock the keyboard.

Table 11.1 *Commands of main menu in PINE*

11.2.5 Quitting PINE and Logging Out

Follow the steps given below to quit PINE and log out of the login services:

1. Type Q in the main menu.
2. Type the following command at UNIX prompt for logging out of the login services:
```
$ exit
```
3. To close Telnet software, choose 'Quit' (or 'Exit') from the File menu.

4. Disconnect from Internet connection if you are using dial-up connection.

11.3 E-MAIL WITH PINE

As PINE is a menu-driven program, sending and receiving electronic mails using PINE is very easy. You will find the function of all the commands on screen, so you need not remember them. Besides this each screen has a help option, which you can use in case of any problem. Let us first discuss the procedure of composing and sending a message in PINE.

11.3.1 Composing and Sending a Message

Follow the steps given below to compose and send a message in PINE:

1. Type C in the main menu. You will see the Compose Message Screen as shown in Figure 11.2. This screen comprises three parts: (*i*) Header Part (*ii*) Message Part and (*iii*) Menu Part. Various elements of the Compose Message Screen are shown in Table 11.2

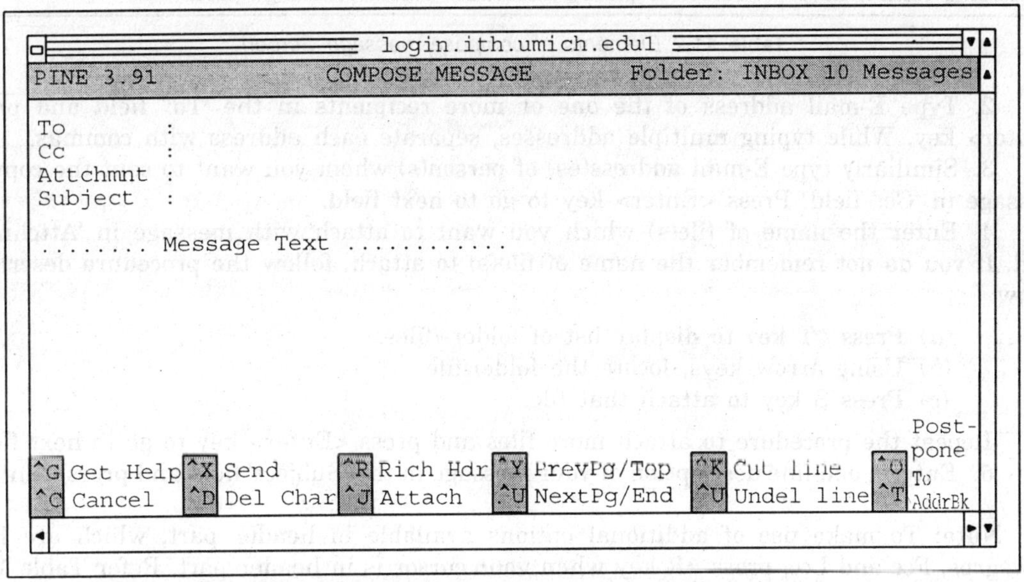

Figure 11.2 *Compose message screen of PINE*

Screen Element	Description
Header Part of Screen:	
To	Used to specify the E-mail address(s) of recipient(s).
Cc	Cc stands for Carbon Copy. Used to specify E-mail address(es) of person(s), whom you want to send copy of the message.
Attchmnt	Used to specify the name of file, which you want to send as attachment to the message.
Subject	Used to specify one line description of the message.

BCC	BCC stands for Blind Carbon copy. Used to send a copy of message to person(s) whose address(es) you want to keep confidential and not to disclose the recipient(s).
Newsgrps	To specify Usenet Newsgroup(s) to which you want to post the message.
FCC	FCC stands for File Carbon copy. Used to display the default folder where you want to store outgoing message.
LCC	LCC stands for List Carbon copy. Used to send a message to a list of people generally created in address book without sharing their addresses to other people in the list.
Message Part of Screen:	
Message Text	Area of screen where message of any number of lines is entered and edited using PICO or other text editor.
Menu Part of Screen:	
Various commands such as ^G, ^X keys etc. (^ means pressing & holding control key)	Bottom part of screen that displays various commands of Compose Message Screen and PICO editor based on the position of cursor. The functions of some commands vary depending upon whether the cursor is placed in Header part or Message part.

Table 11.2 *Elements of compose message Screen*

2. Type E-mail address of the one or more recipients in the 'To:' field and press <Enter> key. While typing multiple addresses, separate each address with commas.

3. Similiarly type E-mail address(es) of person(s) whom you want to sent the copy of message in 'Cc:' field. Press <Enter> key to go to next field.

4. Enter the name of file(s) which you want to attach with message in 'Attchmnt' field. If you do not remember the name of file(s) to attach, follow the procedure described below:

(*a*) Press ^T key to display list of folders/files.
(*b*) Using arrow keys, locate the folder/file.
(*c*) Press S key to attach that file.

Repeat the procedure to attach more files and press <Enter> key to go to next field.

5. Enter a one-line description of your message in the 'Subject' field and press <Enter> key.

Note: To make use of additional options available in header part, which are Bcc, Newsgrps, Fcc and Lcc, press ^R key when your cursor is in header part. Refer Table 11.2 to know the functions of these options.

6. Now, type your message in the 'Message Text' area of Compose Message Screen. If you have already typed the message and stored in a text file, you can place that text in this area of screen by pressing ^R key provided your cursor is placed in message part of screen. You can add more text with this stored message. You can edit the text of your message by using various commands of PICO editor which are discussed in Table 11.3. Press ^G keys in message area if you need any help from the editor.

Command	Function
Cursor Control Commands:	
^F	To move the cursor forward by a character
^B	To move the cursor backward by a character
^P	To move the cursor to the previous line
^N	To move the cursor to the next line
^A	To move the cursor to the beginning of the current line
^E	To move the cursor to the end of current line
^C	To determine the position of cursor in the document
^Y	To move back an entire page of text
^V	To move forward an entire page of text
Editing Commands:	
^D	To delete a character at the cursor position
^K	To delete the entire line or block
^U	To undelete/paste the last deleted line(s)/block
^I	To insert a tab character at cursor position
^R	To insert a text file at cursor position
^J	To justify the text in a paragraph
^L	To refresh the displayed text on screen
^T	To invoke the spelling checker program iSpell
<Ctr> +^	To mark a block of text
^W	To find a word or phrase
File Commands:	
pico file1.txt	To create or edit a text file (file1.txt) from UNIX prompt
Select 'File' –'DirEd'–'C'	To create a new file from the Menu system
Select 'File' –'DirEd'–'E'	To edit an existing file from the Menu system
^X–Y	To exit and save changes
^X–N	To exit and abandon changes
^O	To save changes

Table 11.3 *Commands of PICO editor*

7. After composing the message, press ^X keys to save message and exit PICO editor. PINE program will prompt you – Whether to send message?

Press 'Y' or <Enter> key to send the message. The message will be sent to the recipient(s) address(es) and copied to your sent-mail folder. If you do not want to send the message, press 'N' key. The message is not sent and you can continue to work on it.

Note: If you want to send the message later on, press ^O keys instead of ^X. The message will be saved in postponed messages folder and sending of message will be postponed. If you want to delete the message or cancel it before sending, press ^C keys instead of ^X.

11.3.2 Reading, Replying and Forwarding a Message

In PINE, you can read, reply and forward your mail from the message/mail index screen.

11.3.2.1 Reading the Message

To read your mail, follow the procedure discussed below:

1. From the main menu, press I to go to the message/mail index or Folder Index Screen, which will look similar to Figure 11.3.

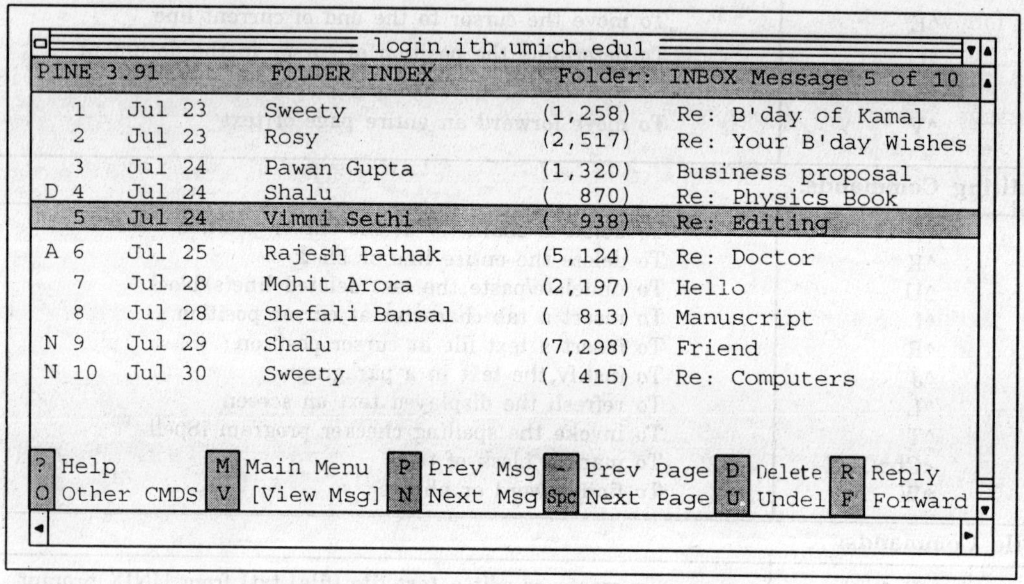

Figure 11.3 *Folder index screen of PINE*

In Folder Index Screen, an index of messages is displayed in five columns– Serial Number, Date, Sender's Name, No. of Bytes and Subject of message besides the beginning column containing symbols N, A or D. N means the message is new (unread), A means the message has been answered (reply) by you and D means the message is marked for deletion.

2. Use the arrow keys to select the message to read. Thereafter press <Enter> key. The complete message will be displayed on separate screen in one or more pages. Press <spacebar> key to go to next page and <–> key to go to previous page. In this way you can read your message.

Viewing Attachments

To view an attached document, type V (View Attch) to open the Attachment Index Screen. You will see numbered lines showing the description type of attached file. Use the arrow keys to select the attached file and type S (Save). The following message will come on screen:

```
Copy attachment to file in home directory: <file name>.
```

Press <Enter> key to save attachment to your home directory. You will see a confirmation message that atachment was sent to home directory. Now Type E to exit attachment.

11.3.2.2 Replying the Message

To reply this message, follow the procedure discussed below:

1. If you want to reply this message, press R while reading the message. You will see the following message on screen:

```
Include original message in Reply?
```

Press 'Y' if you want to send the original message alongwith the reply otherwise just press <Enter> key.

2. Now, PINE will ask you whether you want to send reply to all recipients by displaying the following message:

```
Reply to all recipients?
```

Press 'Y' if you want to send the reply to all those recipients who received the original message. By default the answer is No, so just press <Enter> key if you want to reply only the sender of message.

3. After this, the Compose Message Screen will be displayed on screen. You can compose and send the message as discussed in previous sub-section.

11.3.2.3 Forwarding the Message

While reading your message, you can send the same message to someone else by the procedure discussed below:

1. Press 'F' key while reading the message or while you are in Folder Index Screen. PINE will open the Message Compose Screen containing the original message.
2. Type the recipient's address whom you want to forward the message in "To:" field.
3. Type an introductory message above the original message.
4. Press ^X keys to send/forward the message as explained in previous sub-section.

11.3.3 Printing the Message

There are two ways to print a message in PINE. The simpler method is to save the message to a file and then use an FTP program to retrieve it from your home directory. You can print this file in the same way as you print other files.

Another method of printing is to use the print commands of PINE. This method works if the Telnet client you are using supports printing. For instance, Better Telnet and Host Explorer support printing while Niffy Telnet does not. To use this method, follow the procedure as discussed below:

1. First, you need to set up the printer by pressing S in the PINE Main Menu. PINE will display a menu of setup tasks and will ask you to choose one of them. Press P to configure your printer. Now, 'Select Printer' screen as shown in Figure 11.4 will be displayed.

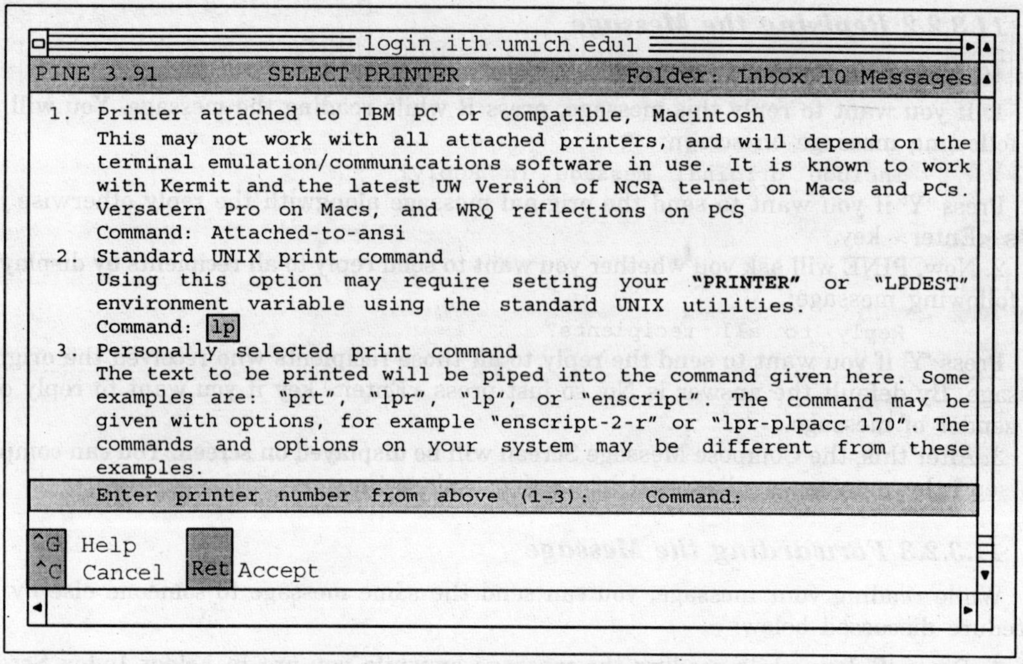

Figure 11.4 *Select Printer Screen of PINE*

2. Choose the printer number (say 1) from the options displayed in 'Select Printer' menu.

3. Now press I to go to Mail Index/Folder Screen and select or open the message to print (say message No. 5).

4. Press '%' or 'Y' key as print command. You will see the following confirmation message on screen:

```
Print Message 5 using "attached-to-ansi"?
Y N ^C
```

Enter Y to confirm the printing of message.

In this way, you will print your message on a locally attached printer to your workstation

11.4 ORGANISING FOLDERS AND MESSAGES IN PINE

No we are in a position to compose, read, reply, forward and print E-mail messages. Let us learn to organise these messages. This is essential for proper management of your E-mail. As you may get many E-mails in a single day, you need to delete already read or unwanted mails. This is possible if your mails are stored or saved in respective folders. Let us discuss the role of Folders in PINE and how they are organised.

You know, electronic mails are stored in mail boxes on the server. A collection of mails sent, received and saved by you are stored in various groups called Folders. By default, PINE provides following three folders:

(*a*) INBOX—This folder stores all incoming messages.
(*b*) Sent-mail—It stores a copy of each message sent by you.
(*c*) Saved-messages—It stores all messages saved by you.

There is one more folder, postponed-msgs, which is created when first time you postpone the sending of a message by pressing ^O keys instead of ^X. Besides this, you can also create your own folder. Let us now discuss the procedure of creating a new folder and operations that can be performed on PINE folders.

11.4.1 Adding a Folder

To add a new folder, follow the procedure discussed below:

1. In the Main Menu, press L to display list of folders, you will get the Folder List screen with default folders, a part of which is shown in Figure 11.5.

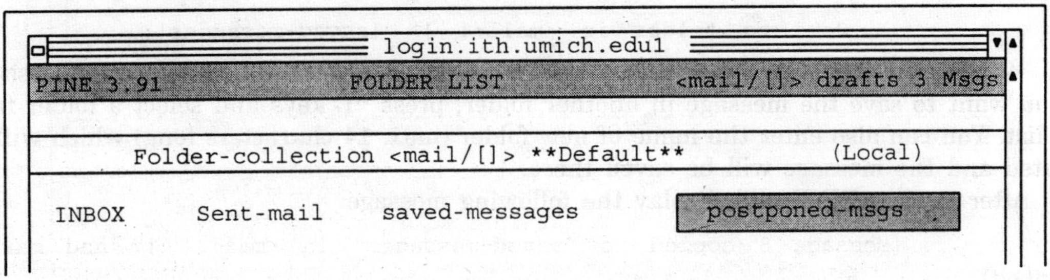

Figure 11.5 *A part of folder list screen showing default folders of PINE*

2. To add a folder to the list, press A. PINE will display the following message on screen:

```
Name of folder to add:
```

3. Enter the name of folder you want to add and press <Enter> key. If you do not want to add new folder, press ^C keys. PINE will display following message:

```
[Addition of new folder cancelled]
```

4. Press M to go to Main Menu.

11.4.2 Deleting a Folder

You can delete any folder in PINE except INBOX folder. However, it is advised that you should never delete other two default folders—sent-mail and saved-messages as they may contain important messages. As there is no way to undelete a folder, you should be very careful while deleting it. The procedure to delete a folder is discussed below:

1. In the Main Menu, press L to go to Folder List Screen.
2. Using the arrow keys (or using P or N key), move to the folder you want to delete. Press <Enter> key or type V (View Fldr) if you want to see the index of messages in that folder and come back again to Folder List.
3. Press D to delete the highlighted or selected folder. PINE will ask you:

```
Really delete "<folder name>"?
```

4. Press Y if you are sure to delete this folder. PINE will display the following message:

```
[Folder "<folder name>" deleted]
```

If you do not want to delete that folder, press N. PINE will now display the following message :

[No folder deleted]

In this way, the folder deleted by you will disappear from the Folder List.

11.4.3 Saving Messages to a Folder

You can save your received messages in saved-messages or any other folder created by you. The procedure to save a message to a folder is discussed below:

1. In the Main Menu, press I to go to the Folder Index Screen.
2. Highlight or select the message (say message no. 8) using arrow keys (or using P or N key).
3. Press S to save the message. PINE will prompt you:

```
Save to folder in <mail/[ ]> [saved-messages]:
```

4. Press <Enter> key if you want to save the message in default folder—saved-messages. If you want to save the message in another folder, press ^L keys and select a folder from the list. You can also enter the name of new folder (max. 14 characters long) which will be created and the message will be saved there.

After saving, PINE will display the following message:

```
[Message 8 copied to "saved-messages" in <mail/[ ]> and marked deleted]
```

In this way, the message in current-folder (INBOX) is marked for deletion and copy of it is saved in saved-messages folder. If you do not want to delete message in current folder, press U to undelete this message.

11.4.4 Deleting Messages in a Folder

Accumulation of unwanted and already read messages occupies useful space of server's memory. Therefore, you should keep on deleting such messages. There are two steps to delete a message— (*a*) Marking a message for deletion, and (*b*) Expunging a message. Let us discuss these steps in detail.

11.4.4.1 Marking a Message for Deletion

Follow the procedure discussed below to mark a message for deletion:

1. In the Main Menu, Press L to go to the Folder List Screen.
2. Using the arrow keys [or using P or N key], select the folder which contains the message that needs to be deleted.
3. Press <Enter> key or type V [ViewFldr] to see the index of messages in selected folder.
4. Using the arrow keys [or using P or N key], select the message you want to delete.
5. You can delete the message either while viewing the message or while it is selected at the Folder Index/Message Index screen. In any of the cases, press D (Delete).

If you press D while viewing the message, PINE displays the following message:

```
[Message <No.> marked for deletion]
```

If you press D while the message is highlighted at Message Index Screen, a 'D' mark is displayed to the left of the message.

6. Repeat the above process until you have marked all unwanted messages for deletion.

11.4.4.2. *Expunging a message*

You can permanently delete the messages marked for deletion by one of the following methods:

Method I

1. When you quit PINE or leave a folder (other than INBOX) and the folder(s) contain some messages that are marked for deletion, you will see the following prompt:

```
Expunge the # deleted message(s) from <folder name>?
```

2. Press Y to expunge or N to not expunge.

Method II

1. In the Main Menu, press I to go to Folder Index Screen.
2. Press X (expunge). PINE prompts you:

```
Expunge "#" message(s) from <folder name>
```

3. Press Y to expunge or N to not expunge.

11.4.5 Undeleting Messages in a Folder

Once a message has been marked for deletion, you can undelete it by following the steps given below :

1. In the Main Menu, press L to go the Folder List Screen.
2. Using the arrow keys (or using P or N key), select the folder which contains that message (marked for deletion) needs to be undeleted.
3. Press <Enter> key or type V [View Fldr] to see the index of messages in selected folder.
4. Using the arrow keys (or using P or N key), select the message you want to undelete. Press <Enter> key to view this message.
5. You can undelete the message either while viewing the message or while it is selected at the Folder Index Screen. In any of the cases, press U (Undelete).

If you press U while viewing the message marked for deletion, PINE displays the following message:

```
[Deletion mark removed, message won't be deleted]
```

If you press U while the message is highlighted at the message index screen, 'D' mark disappears from the left of the message.

6. Repeat the above process until you have undeleted the required messages marked for deletion.

11.5 ADDRESS BOOK IN PINE

It may be difficult for you to remember a number of E-mail addresses of your friends, relatives and associates. In PINE, you can easily build a list of E-mail addresses by creating their nick-names. You can remember these nick-names very easily. While composing and sending mails, you can use these nick-names instead of writing the complete E-mail addresses.

Besides giving nick-names for individuals, you can also give a common nickname to a group of people. The collection of nick-names for individuals/groups along with names and

E-mail addresses of people is called an *Address Book*. Let us first discuss the procedure for adding new addresses to PINE's Address Book.

11.5.1 Adding New Address to Address Book

There are following two ways to add new adresses to the Address Book:

(*a*) Adding Address from Main Menu.
(*b*) Adding Address from Message Index Screen.
Let us discuss these methods in detail.

11.5.1.1 Adding Address from Main Menu

Follow the steps discussed below to add new addresses in Address Book from the Main Menu.

1. In the Main Menu, press A. PINE will display an Address Book screen as shown in Figure 11.6 (Assume only 3 addresses are entered).

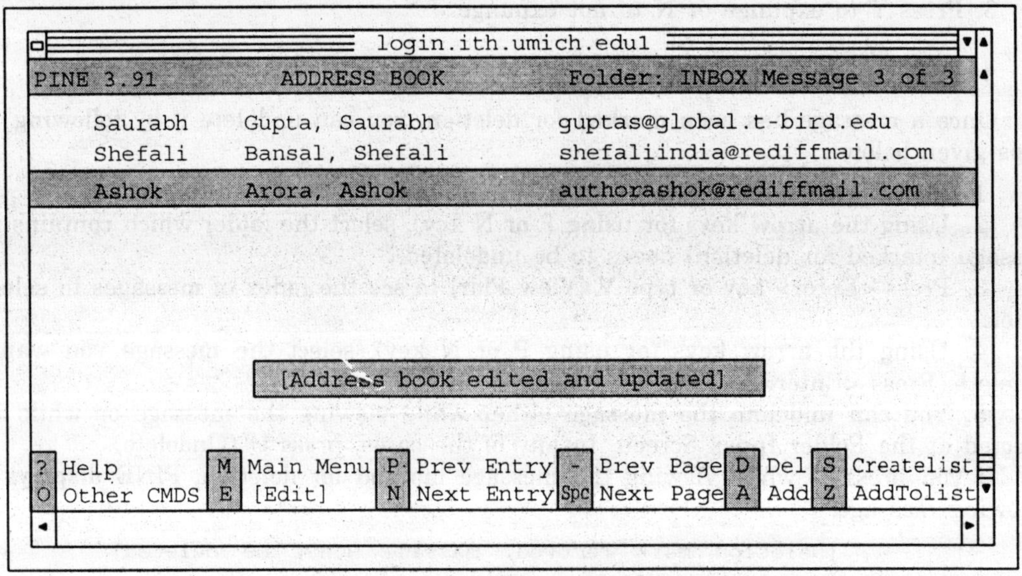

Figure 11.6 *Address book screen in PINE*

As shown in the Figure, each entry in the address book has the following three fields:

(*i*) Nick name: The short name of E-mail address e.g. Saurabh.
(*ii*) Description: The description of E-mail address e.g. Gupta, Saurabh.
(*iii*) Address: The E-mail address e.g. guptas@global.t-bird.edu

2. To add a new address, press A (Add) again. An Address Entry Screen that looks similar to the compose message screen will be displayed. It contains the following fields:

(*i*) Nickname– Enter a nickname which is easier to remember.
(*ii*) Full name– Enter the name of person whose E-mail address you are going to add.
(*iii*) Fcc– Fcc stands for File carbon copy. Leave this field blank. By default PINE saves the message in 'sent-mail' folder.

(*iv*) Comment– Enter description of entry for your own purpose.

(*v*) Addresses– Enter the E-mail address of person.

After entering data in all these fields, press ^X to save and exit. Press ^C keys if you want to cancel adding the new entry.

11.5.1.2 Adding Address from Message Index Screen

You can also add address to the Address Book by taking an individual address from a message you are reading or have selected in the message index by following the steps discussed below:

(1) Press T (Take Addr) in the Message Text or Message Index Screen.

(2) If the message contains more than one address, PINE will prompt you:

```
[Single mode: Use "P" or "N" to select desired address]
```

Now, select the address using arrow keys (or using P or N key).

(3) Now PINE will prompt you:

```
Enter new or existing nickname (one word and easy to remember):
Enter a nickname and press <Enter>
```

(4) Now PINE will display the Address Entry Screen with nickname as entered by you and E-mail address of the message. Enter the rest of the fields as discussed in step 2 of 'Adding Address from Main Menu'.

11.5.2 Adding a Group (List) Address

Sometimes you need to send messages to a group of people. You can create a list address for giving a nickname to such a group. As there are two ways to add individual address to the address book, there are same ways for creating a list address as discussed below:

11.5.2.1 Adding a list Address from Main Menu

Follow the same steps as discussed in sub-section 11.5.1.1 on topic 'Adding Address from Main Menu' except that you will press S (Create List) key instead of A (Add) in step 2.

11.5.2.2 Adding a list Address from Message Index Screen

Follow the same steps as discussed in sub-section 11.5.1.2. on topic 'Adding Address from Message Index Screen' except that you will press L (List Mode) in step 2.

11.5.3 Using the Address Book

While composing a message, you can use the address book very easily by one of the following two ways:

(*a*) Type the nickname of address in To: or Cc: fields.

(*b*) Select a name from the address book by following the steps given below:

(*i*) When the cursor is in To: or Cc: field, press ^T to go to Address Book.

(*ii*) Use the arrow keys to highlight the address.

(*iii*) Type S or <Enter> key to select the address.

11.6 OVERVIEW OF ELM

Elm is another popular mail system for UNIX. It is a screen-oriented, interactive program for sending and receiving electronic mails via telnet or modem. It was developed in 1986 by Dave Taylor, a programmer. Elm is the first screen-oriented E-mail program as the earlier mail programs (such as mail and mailx) were line-oriented. In those line-oriented programs, only single line was visible at the bottom of the screen. Elm was developed to display messages on the full screen. Let us discuss about this program in detail.

11.6.1 What is Elm

Elm is an acronym for "Easy Little Mailer". Using elm, you can compose, send, receive, reply, forward and save your messages. It is easier to use than mailx but difficult than PINE. Elm is a recommended system at many universities all over the world for handling E-mails on UNIX systems. Elm is available on the central UNIX system run by the computing service such as UCS Sun Workstation. Although UNIX operating system provides the mail command for handling E-mails, but elm provides many useful additional features. Let us discuss these features of Elm, which have made it popular on UNIX systems in academic institutions.

11.6.2 Features of Elm

Elm provides the following main features:

- Elm is user-friendly, prompt driven program. As you will perform functions on elm, elm will ask questions. This feature makes it user-friendly.
- It is screen-oriented program as full screen is available for writing and displaying text of messages.
- All commands of Elm are keyboard driven.
- Elm, like PINE provides the facility of creating mailing lists (aliases).
- Like PINE, messages can be saved in folders for later retrieval.
- Mail tool facility provided by Sun workstations provides a graphical interface to elm mail system.

11.6.3 Requirements for Using Elm

For using elm, you require the following software:

(*a*) UNIX operating system.

(*b*) Telnet client software.

Besides these software, you must have connection to a UCS Sun Workstation through an account (such as UCS account or SUNet ID) and an access to a UNIX server.

11.6.4 Starting Elm

Follow the steps given below for starting elm:

1. Dial in an Internet connection, if you want to login remotely. Connect to the login services using the Telnet software at `login.ith.umich.edu`.

If you login directly, log into your UCS or other account and establish a command prompt.

2. Type elm at the UNIX command prompt as shown below:

```
$ elm<Enter>
```

Elm will display its main screen similar to Figure 11.7. The main screen of elm has following 3 parts:

(*a*) Top Line—It shows the name of file that contains your mailbox, the number of messages and the version of elm.

(*b*) Index—It lists the summary of messages with following six columns:

(*i*) Status Codes: The first column indicates the status of the message by following codes—

- N indicates that the message is new and not yet read.
- O indicates that the messages is old and not yet read.
- Blank indicates that the message has been read but neither saved nor deleted.
- D indicates that the message is marked for deletion.
- M indicates that the message contain a MIME (Multipurpose Internet Mail Extensions) attachment having non-textual data.
- U indicates that message was marked "urgent" by the sender.

(*ii*) Serial No: The second column indicates the message number.

(*iii*) Date: The third column displays date when message was sent.

(*iv*) Name: The fourth column displays the name of sender.

(*v*) No. of lines: The fifth column displays the number of total lines in the message.

(*vi*) Subject: The sixth column displays the subject of message as written by the sender.

(*c*) Help and Command lines— The bottom of screen contains help and command lines. Enter all your commands at the command linę. Various commands of this screen are described in Table 11.4.

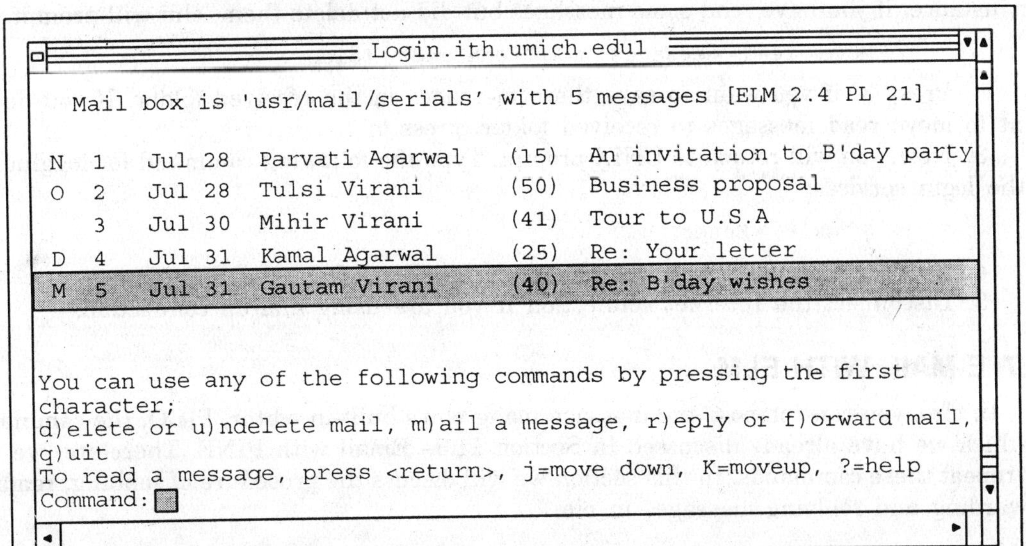

Figure 11.7 *The main screen of Elm*

Command	Function
d	To delete (mark for deletion) the mail message.
u	To undelete the message marked for deletion.
m	To send a mail message.
r	To reply to the highlighted mail message.
f	To forward the highlighted mail message.
q	To quit elm.
<return>	To read the highlighted mail message.
j	To move down on next message.
k	To move up on previous message.
?	To get help from elm.

Table 11.4 *Commands of main screen of Elm*

11.6.4.1 Starting Elm First Time

When you start the elm program first time, you will see this message on the screen:

```
Notice: This version of elm requires the use of a.elm directory in
your home directory to store your elmrc and alias files.

Shall I create the directory.elm for you and set it up (y/n)?
```

Press 'y' to create the directory. After this the main screen as discussed above will be displayed.

11.6.5 Quitting Elm and Logging out

Follow the steps given below to quit elm and logout of the login services.

1. Type q in the main screen of elm.

   Note: Remember to type q in small case as elm program is case-sensitive. So, type all commands as written (capital or small) in the book/manual/help screen.

2. Elm may prompt you to respond some questions depending on your current session. For instance, if you have read some messages but did not delete them, elm will prompt you:

   ```
   Move read messages to "received" folder? (y/n)
   ```

   Press 'y' if you want to save these messages in the received folder. If you do not want to move read messages to received folder, press 'n'.

3. Now, you will return to UNIX prompt. Type the following command for logging out of the login services:

   ```
   $ exit <Enter>
   ```

4. To close Telnet software, choose 'Quit' (or 'Exit') from the File Menu.
5. Disconnect the Internet connection if you are using dial-up connection.

11.7 E-MAIL WITH ELM

In elm, you can compose the message using elm's built-in editor, PICO, the commands of which we have already discussed in Section 11.3– Email with PINE. Therefore, we will not repeat these commands. In this section we will discuss the procedure of sending, reading, forwarding and replying messages in elm.

11.7.1 Sending a Message

Follow the steps given below to send a message to one or more recipients:

1. In the main screen, type m(mail) at command prompt. Elm will ask you the mail ids of recipients as shown below:

```
Send the message to:
```

Type the E-mail address(es) of recipient(s). For multiple addresses, separate each address with a space.

2. Now, elm will prompt you:

```
Subject of message:
```

Enter a one-line description of your message. If you leave it blank and press <Enter> key, Elm will prompt you:

```
No subject-continue with message? (y/n) n
```

Press 'y' to continue.

3. After this, Elm will prompt you to enter address of the recipients to whom you want to send a copy of message as shown below:

```
Copies to:
```

Enter the addresses or leave it blank, and press <Enter> key.

4. Now, Elm opens the PICO text editor. Compose your message and save it by pressing ^X keys. You will come out of PICO editor and elm will display the following message on screen:

```
And now:
e)dit message, h)eaders, i)spell, !)shell, a)attachment, s)end,
or f)orget
```

5. If you want to edit the earlier composed message, press e and do the changes. Save the changes and exit.

6. If you want to edit the header of the mail, press h. Elm will display the Header Edit screen as shown in Figure 11.8.

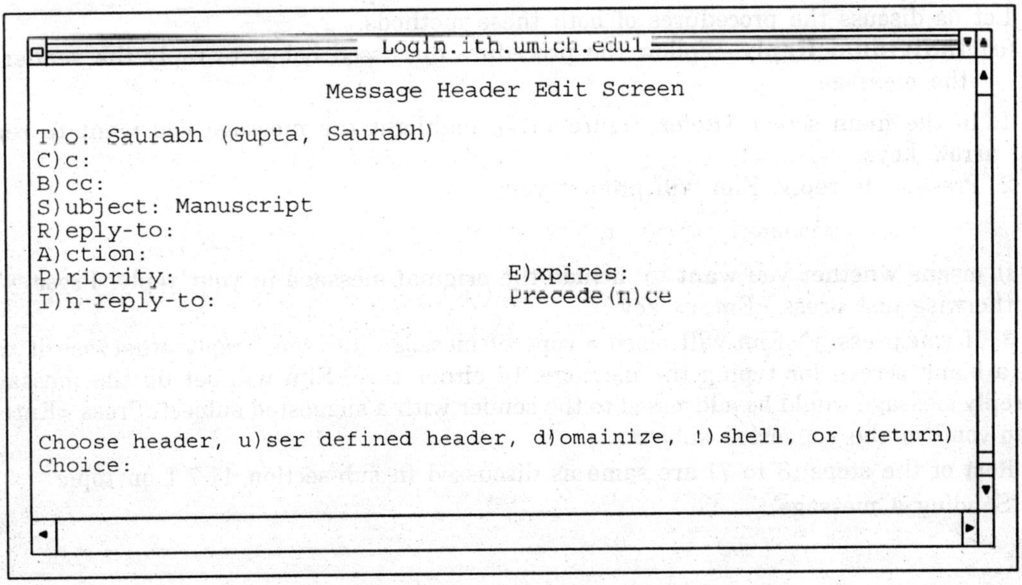

Figure 11.8 *The Header Edit screen of Elm*

The Header Edit screen allows you to modify or expand your original header (To/Cc) choices. To change or add to your original header choices, press the indicated letter such as t, c, b, etc.) from one of the header items. In Message Header Edit Screen, only some items such as To, Cc, Bcc and Subject are generally used, which we have already discussed in the chapter. As other items are advanced options, we are not discussing them.

After you have finished editing the header information, press <Enter> key at command prompt.

7. Now, press s to send the message.

11.7.2 Reading, Replying and Forwarding a Message

In elm, you can read, reply and forward your mail from the main screen. Let us discuss these in detail.

11.7.2.1 Reading the Message

To read your mail message, follow the procedure discussed below:

1. In the main screen (Refer Figure 11.7), highlight the message you want to read by arrow keys or type message number at command prompt.
2. Press <Enter> key to read the highlighted message. The message will be displayed on screen.
3. Follow the instructions on the bottom of the message screen to press the following keys to view more of that message or to return to the main screen:
   (*i*) <Enter> — To display the next line of message.
   (*ii*) <Spacebar> — To display the next screen of message.
   (*iii*) i — Type i at command prompt to return to the main screen.

11.7.2.2 Replying the Message

There are following two ways to reply a message:
(*a*) Individual Reply— Reply to sender.
(*b*) Group Reply— Reply to all receipients of message.
Let us discuss the procedures of both these methods.

(*a*) **Individual Reply**—Follow the procedure discussed below to reply the sender of the message:

1. In the main screen (Refer Figure 11.7), highlight the message you want to reply using arrow keys.
2. Press 'r' to reply. Elm will prompt you:

```
Copy message? (y/n) n
```

It means whether you want to include the original message in your reply. Press 'y' if yes otherwise just press <Enter> key.

3. If you press 'y', Elm will place a copy of message into your reply otherwise it will open a blank screen for typing the message. In either case, Elm will set up the message. The reply message would be addressed to the sender with a suggested subject. Press <Enter> key to confirm the suggested subject.

Rest of the steps (3 to 7) are same as discussed in sub-section 11.7.1 on topic 'Sending a message'.

(*b*) **Group Reply:** The procedure for replying all recepients of original message is same as discussed above in 'Individual Reply' except that you will press 'g' instead of 'r' in the main screen.

11.7.2.3 Forwarding the Message

Follow the procedure discussed below to send a copy of message to someone else:

1. In the main screen (Refer Figure 11.7), highlight the message which you want to forward using arrow keys.
2. Press 'f' to forward. Elm will prompt you whether you want to edit the message before forwarding, as shown below:

```
Edit outgoing message? (y/n) y
```

Press <Enter> to forward or type n for not forwarding the message.

Rest of the procedure is similar to sending a message.

11.7.3 Printing the Message

1. In the main screen (Refer Figure 11.7), highlight the message which you want to print using the arrow keys.
2. Press 'p' to print the message

11.8 ORGANISING FOLDERS AND MESSAGES IN ELM

Folders, you know are the mail boxes where messages are stored. These folders reside in your 'Mail' directory. When you start elm first time, a folder (mailbox) is set up for incoming mail. You can create additional folders for organising your messages. Let us learn to organise these folders and messages.

11.8.1 Creating Folders and Saving Messages

Elm allows you to save a message to an existing or a created folder. The commands used to perform these functions are Save and Copy. Let us discuss them briefly.

11.8.1.1 The Save Command

The Save command not only saves a message into the specified folder but also creates the folder. Let us discuss this with an example. Suppose you want to save a message received from a person named Tulsi Virani in folder 'Actor', you are required to follow the steps discussed below:

1. In the main screen (Refer Figure 11.7), highlight the message, which you want to save using arrow keys.
2. Press 's' to save. Elm will prompt you:

```
Save message to: ~/Mail/Virani
```

'Virani' is the folder name suggested by Elm. ~ stands for the home directory and Mail is the directory name. The complete path of folder is ~/Mail/Virani.

Type the new folder name either by first deleting 'Virani' and typing 'Actor' or by putting the equal sign (=) before the folder name 'Actor' after deleting the entire path '~/Mail/Virani' as shown below:

```
Save message to : = Actor
```

'= Actor' and '~/Mail/Actor' are both same notations for your mail directory or folder. If this folder does not exist, elm will create it automatically.

Note: As Elm is case-sensitive, use folder name as you have typed.

In this way, with save command, the message is saved into specified folder and is removed from the original mail box folder.

11.8.1.2 The Copy Command

The Copy command is similar to Save command. The only difference between the two commands is that the former does not erase the message from original folder but sends the copy of it to specified folder. Type 'C' (Capital C) to give Copy command in the main screen. Rest of the procedure is same as discussed in Save command.

11.8.2 Changing Folders

For accessing messages from different folders, you need to change folders by following the procedure discussed below:

1. In the main menu, type 'c' (small c) to change folder. Elm will prompt you:
   ```
   Change to which folder:
   ```
2. Enter the name of folder at the displayed prompt (e.g. Actor) as shown below:
   ```
   Change to which folder: = Actor <Enter>
   ```

If you have forgotten the name of folder, type '*' and press enter at the above prompt. Elm will give you a listing of folders and files from which you can read the name of your folder and type its name at the same prompt—'Change to which folder:'

11.8.3 Deleting a Message in Folder

You can mark the messages for deletion in a folder by following the steps given below :

1. Change to the folder, which contains message you want to delete by following the procedure discussed in sub-section 11.8.2.
2. Highlight the message you want to delete using the arrow keys.
3. Press 'd' to delete. The letter D will be displayed before the message number, indicating that the message is marked for deletion.
4. When you quit Elm, you will be asked to delete messages which are marked for deletion. Press 'y' for yes otherwise press 'n'.

11.8.4 Undeleting a Message in Folder

You can undelete the messages marked for deletion in a folder by following way:

1. (See Step 1 of sub-section 11.8.3).
2. (See Step 2 of sub-section 11.8.3).
3. Press 'u' to undelete. The letter D will disappear from the message number.

11.9 ALIASES IN ELM

An alias is an easily remembered name for an E-mail address. Elm's Alias feature allows you to create nicknames for your recipients whose addresses are difficult to remember. Alias in Elm is functionally same as Address Book in PINE.

Let us discuss the procedures to create, delete and use aliases.

11.9.1 Creating an Alias

You can create an alias by one of the following ways:

(*a*) Adding a new alias from received message.

(*b*) Creating aliases from Main Screen.

Let us discuss these in detail.

11.9.1.1 Adding a New Alias from Received Message

Follow the steps discussed below to add a new alias from the message you received:

1. In the main screen (Refer Figure 11.7), highlight the message whose alias is to be added using the arrow keys.

2. Type 'a' at command prompt. Elm will prompt you:

```
alias:
```

3. Type 'a' again at alias prompt to make an alias for current message.

4. Elm will now prompt you to enter an alias for the sender address of the current message. Type the nickname (e.g. Tulsi) at this prompt as shown below:

```
Current message address aliased to: Tulsi
```

5. Elm will then prompt you to enter last name of the person you are aliasing as shown below:

```
Enter last name for Tulsi: Virani  'Virani' name is sugested by Elm.
```

Press <Enter> key to accept this name or type new name and press <Enter> key.

6. Now Elm will prompt you to enter the first name of that person as shown below:

```
Enter first name for Tulsi: Tulsi
```

Similarly, either type new name and press <Enter> key or just press <Enter> key.

7. Finally, you will be prompted to enter comment for the person. Type Comment or leave it blank and press <Enter> key.

8. Now, Elm will display all the information entered by you and will wait for your confirmation as shown below:

```
Alias: Add address from current message . . .
Accept new alias? (y/n) y
New alias: Tulsi is "Tulsi Virani"
Messages addressed as: tulsi@global.actor.edu
Press 'y' to accept the new alias or press 'n' to cancel
      this alias.
```

9. Elm will return you to the alias prompt. Enter another alias command or type 'x' to exit the alias function and return to command prompt.

11.9.1.2 Creating Aliases from Main Screen

Follow the procedure discussed below to create new aliases from the main screen of Elm:

1. Type 'a' at command prompt of Main Screen.
2. Elm will prompt you:

```
Alias:
Type 'n' at this prompt
```

3. Now, Elm will prompt you to enter alias name, last name for the alias, first name for the alias, comment and address for the alias as discussed in previous sub-section.

4. Finally Elm will confirm the entries from you.
5. To return to command prompt, press 'x'.

11.9.2 Deleting an Alias

To delete an alias, follow the procedure discussed below:

1. Highlight the message in Main Screen (See Figure 11.7) using arrow keys.
2. Type 'a' at command prompt.
3. Elm will prompt you:

```
alias:
    Type 'd' at this prompt
```

It will display the letter 'D' (capital D) in front of the alias and hence alias will be marked for deletion.

4. When you exit Elm, all aliases marked for deletion will be removed permanently.

11.9.3 Distribution Lists

A group of addresses having a common name is called a *distribution list* or *group alias*. To create a distribution list, follow the procedure discussed below:

1. Type 'a' at command prompt of Main Screen.
2. Elm will prompt you:

```
Alias:
```

Type 'n' at this prompt.

3. Now, Elm will prompt you:

```
Enter alias name:
```

Type name of alias e.g. actors and press <Enter>.

4. Then, Elm will prompt you:

```
Enter last name for actors:
```

Type last name for the alias e.g. actors mails and press <Enter>.

5. Similary, Elm will prompt you to enter last name and comment which can be left blank. Press <Enter>.
6. Now, Elm will prompt you to type addresses. Type the addresses of people each separated by commas and press <Enter> key.
7. Finally, Elm will confirm the entries from you.
8. To return to command prompt, press 'x'.

11.10 DIFFERENT WAYS TO START ELM

Before concluding this chapter on PINE and ELM, let us discuss other ways of starting Elm. Normally, you start Elm by typing 'elm' at UNIX prompt. Other forms of starting Elm are:

(*a*) Starting Elm to send a message.
(*b*) Starting Elm to read a message.

Let us discuss these with examples.

11.10.1 Starting Elm to Send a Message

Various ways of starting Elm for sending a message are:

1. $ elm <recipient alias>

   e.g.

   ```
   $ elm tulsi
   ```

   The above command will send message to recipient with alias 'tulsi' and Elm will prompt you to enter subject and 'copies to'. After that elm will open editor for typing the message.

2. $ elm –S <Subject> <receipient alias>

   e.g. `$ Elm "Birthday Wishes" tulsi`

   The above command will send a message to recipient with alias 'tulsi' along with subject "Birthday Wishes". Elm will again prompt you to confirm subject and enter 'copies to'. After that Elm will open editor for typing the message.

3. $ elm –S <Subject> <recipient address> <<file name>

   e.g.

   ```
   $ elm -S "Birthday Wishes" tulsi@global.actor.edu<notes
   ```

   The above command will send the contents of file 'notes' to specified receipient address along with specified message.

11.10.2 Starting Elm to Read a Message

Various ways of starting elm for reading a message are

1. $ elm –f <folder name>

   e.g.

   ```
   $ elm -f Actor
   ```

   The above command will display message index of folder 'Actor'.

2. $ elm –m –f <folder name>

   e.g.

   ```
   $ elm -m -f Actor
   ```

   The above command will display message index of folder 'Actor' by turning off the menu at bottom of screen.

THEORY QUESTIONS

1. Discuss and compare the features of PINE and elm.
2. Describe the requirements of your system for using (*a*) PINE and (*b*) Elm.
3. Discuss the steps to
   (*a*) Start PINE
   (*b*) Start Elm
   (*c*) Quit PINE
   (*d*) Quit Elm
4. Describe the commands of Main Menu in PINE.
5. How will you compose and send a message in–
   (*a*) PINE
   (*b*) Elm

   Explain with examples.

6. Discuss various parts and elements of Compose Screen in PINE.
7. What is PICO ? Describe its commands in brief.
8. How will you read and reply a message in–
   (*a*) PINE
   (*b*) Elm
   Explain with examples.
9. How will you print a message in–
   (*a*) PINE
   (*b*) Elm
10. What are Folders? Name the default folders of PINE. How will you add a new folder ?
11. How do you
    (*a*) Save a message in PINE
    (*b*) Save a message in Elm
    (*c*) Delete a message in PINE
    (*d*) Delete a message in Elm
12. What are Address Books in PINE ? How do they differ from aliases in Elm ? Explain.
13. How will you create an alias in Elm ? Describe various methods.
14. Write the full form of following abbreviations:

(*a*) PINE		(*e*) Lcc
(*b*) Elm		(*f*) SMTP
(*c*) PICO		(*g*) MIME
(*d*) Fcc		(*h*) IMAP

15. Write the steps to perform the following operations in PINE–
    (*a*) Forward a message
    (*b*) Attach a file
    (*c*) View an attachment
16. Write the steps to perform the following operations in Elm–
    (*a*) Starting elm to send a message
    (*b*) Starting elm to read a message
    (*c*) Forward a message
    (*d*) Create a distribution list
17. How will you
    (*a*) Undelete a message in PINE
    (*b*) Undelete a message in Elm
    (*c*) Delete an alias in Elm
    (*d*) Expunge a message in PINE
18. How will you use an address book in PINE ? Explain with example.
19. Explain the function of following commands in Elm–

(*a*) d	(*e*) c	(*i*) i
(*b*) m	(*f*) p	(*j*) q
(*c*) j	(g) s	(*k*) r
(*d*) c	(*h*) f	(*l*) ?

20. Explain the function of following commands in PINE/PICO–

(*a*) C	(*e*) ^G	(*i*) D
(*b*) A	(*f*) ^T	(*j*) spc
(*c*) S	(g) ^X	(*k*) V
(*d*) I	(*h*) ^O	(*l*) O

WORKSHOP

1. Start PINE and send a mail message to your friend by composing it with PICO editor.
2. Read your mails in PINE and reply to one sender of your mails.
3. Forward a message to your friend in PINE.
4. Add the following folders in PINE:
   (*a*) Mywork (*c*) Univ
   (*b*) Myfriends (*d*) College
5. Transfer all the messages from INBOX folder to Mywork folder in PINE.
6. Delete the following folders in PINE
   (*a*) Univ (*b*) Myfriends
7. Permanently delete unwanted files of each of the following folders in PINE :
   (*a*) Sent-mail (*b*) Mywork
8. Create an address book of your friends in PINE by adding addresses from Message Index Scree
9. Create an address book of your teachers in PINE by adding addresses from main-menu.
10. Start Elm and send a mail message to your teacher after composing it.
11. Read your mails in Elm and forward a message to your friend.
12. Add the following folders in Elm:
    (*a*) Cricket (*c*) Teachers
    (*b*) Models (*d*) Filmstar
13. Transfer all the messages from mailbox to the folder named 'Cricket' in Elm.
14. Delete unwanted messages of mailbox and cricket folders.
15. Create an alias of your friends in Elm from received messages.
16. Create a group alias of your cricketers in Elm.
17. Start elm to read messages of your teachers by opening its folder 'Teachers'.
18. Reply to a message recieved in mailbox of Elm.

12

PROGRAMMING LANGUAGES

12.1 INTRODUCTION

We are already aware of this fact that computer has no intelligence of its own and each and every instruction should be given to it for performing any task. The set of instructions given to computer to process the data or perform a certain task is called *a Program*. Programming is the technique for writing the programs. The programming process is a set of activities that are carried out to develop and implement a program. You must understand this process in order to become a programmer. Programming is required at all levels from manufacturing of the computer to its operation by the user. Programming, which is done at systems level for developing systems software, is known as *Systems Programming* (Systems Development). Systems Programs are written in low-level languages like Machine/Assembly Language and some high level languages like C, C++ etc. Programming, which is done at the user level, for development of application software, is known as *Applications Programming* (Applications Development) or simply *Programming*. Application Software is generally developed using high-level languages, Database Management Systems or Front End Tools.

In this chapter, you will study these approaches of programming, steps in programming and various types of computer languages.

12.2 PROGRAMMING APPROACHES

Before discussing the classification of programming languages, let us first discuss the two approaches used in programming which are–

(*a*) Procedure Oriented Programming.

(*b*) Object Oriented Programming.

12.2.1 Procedure Oriented Programming

Procedure oriented programming is the traditional way of programming, where an application problem is viewed as a sequence of steps (algorithms). As per the algorithm, the problem is broken down into many modules (functions) such as data entry, reporting, querying modules, etc. as shown in Figure 12.1. There are two types of data, which are associated with these modules–one is global and another is local data. Global data items are defined in main program, whereas local data is defined within associated functions. Many of the functions share global data, as this kind of data is available to all functions. Procedure oriented programming is the conventional approach of programming for developing application software. High-level languages like COBOL, Pascal, BASIC, Fortran, C etc. are based on procedure oriented approach, and hence are also called *procedural languages*.

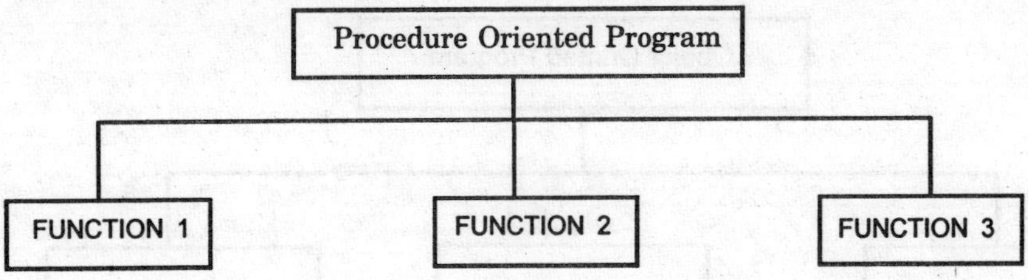

Figure 12.1 *Generalised structure of a procedure oriented program*

12.2.1.1 Advantages of Procedure Oriented Programming

The main advantages of procedure oriented programming are as follows :

(*i*) It is easy to port programs as compilers for procedural languages are easily available.

(*ii*) It is easier to learn procedure oriented programming as compared to the other new ways of programming.

12.2.1.2 Disadvantages of Procedure Oriented programming

Although procedure oriented programming is the conventional approach of programming, it has certain drawbacks. The main disadvantages of this approach are as follows :

(*i*) As most of the functions share global data, this data is freely available to all functions. Although this freely available data is easily accessed by any function, it can create certain problems. When a new function is written for analyzing this data in different way it is possible that data may be changed accidentally or deliberately. Therefore, there is no security of data in procedure oriented programs.

(*ii*) Another problem is that whenever data structure is required to be changed, all the functions using that data must also be changed. So, procedure oriented programs (especially for complex applications) are extremely difficult to modify and maintain.

(*iii*) Procedure oriented programming does not model the real world problem.

12.2.2 Object Oriented Programming

Object oriented programming is the latest approach of programming. It attempts to eliminate most of the drawbacks of procedure oriented programming by incorporating new concepts. It is a new way of organising programs, which is not dependent upon any particular language. In object oriented programming, a problem is not viewed as a sequence of steps to be done, but as a collection of different units (called objects). These objects model the real world things. The structure of an object-oriented program is shown in Figure 12.2. The 'Object oriented' concept can be better understood by discussing about the definitions of an object and its related terms. So, let us discuss the basic terminology used in Object Oriented Programming (OOP).

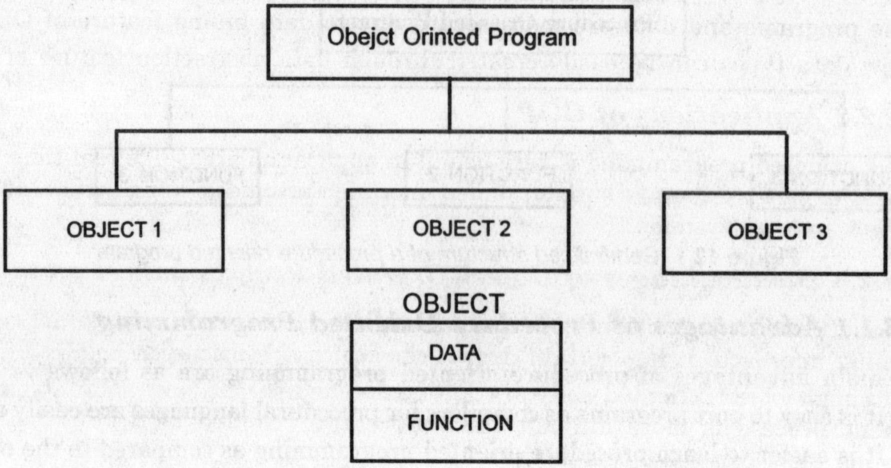

Figure 12.2 *Generalised structure of an object oriented program*

Object. The fundamental idea behind OOP is to store the data and functions operating on that data into a single unit, called an object. An object may represent a person, a student, an employee, an account, an examination or any item that closely resembles the objects of real world.

Class. A class is a collection of similar objects. For example, if 'Car', 'Bus' etc. are different objects than 'Vehicle' is a class.

Encapsulation. The wrapping of data and functions in an object or class is known as encapsulation.

Data Hiding. Data hiding is an extremely important feature of OOP, by which data is not accessible to other functions outside the objects.

Data Abstraction. The act of representing essential features of the objects without giving details is known as data abstraction. Classes use this concept and represent essential properties of the objects.

Inheritance. An object of one class (base class) can inherit the properties of another class (derived class) by a process, called inheritance. For example 'Petrol Vehicle', is one class that inherits the properties of another class 'Vehicle'.

Polymorphism. The ability of objects to exhibit different behaviors in different instances is known as polymorphism. For example, an additional function of an object generates a sum if the data is in numeric form or it concatenates the strings if the data is in character form.

12.2.2.1 Advantages of Object Oriented Programming

Object oriented programming offers several benefits over the procedure oriented approach. The main advantages of using object-oriented approach in software development are given below:

- Reusability of the code is the major benefit of object oriented programming. Redundant code can be eliminated through the inheritance feature of OOP. The generation of windows, menus, dialog boxes, etc. are few examples of programming codes that can be reused. So, a lot of time of programmers is saved during development of application software.

• In object oriented programming, as the emphasis is on data rather than algorithms, a program can easily be broken down into objects, which model truly the real world objects.

• The programs and data are more secure due to data hiding feature of OOP.

• New data types can be easily created through data abstraction feature of OOP.

12.2.2.2 Applications of OOP

Object oriented programming is very useful in application areas like real-time, artificial intelligence, expert systems, computer aided manufacturing/designing, office automation and decision support systems.

12.2.2.3 Disadvantages of Object Oriented Programming

Although the object oriented approach is the latest and most widely accepted programming approach, it has certain drawbacks which are discussed below:

• Although object oriented software are easier to upgrade and maintain, first time development process is more difficult than procedure oriented software. Use of latest programming tools can solve this drawback.

• All languages cannot easily implement object oriented approach. So, object oriented programming is limited to few languages (object oriented languages).

12.3 ROLE OF PROGRAMMERS AND SYSTEMS ANALYST

A single person does not manage software development project. It is teamwork. A person called, project leader, manages software project. The project leader is generally a system analyst, who analyses and designs the complete software. Software professionals, called *Programmers*, develop programs. System programmers develop systems software while application programmers are involved in the development of application software.

Systems analyst and programmers play a vital role in development of an application or systems software. The analyst plays the role of a specialist in computer-based applications. Programmers are responsible for coding, editing, testing and debugging the programs. Systems analyst and programmers work together as a team.

12.3.1 Role of System Analyst

A system analyst is a person who is overall responsible for development of software. He is the computer professional who takes charge of analysing, designing and implementing computer-based information systems. He is the crucial interface among users, programmers and MIS managers. He performs the following roles for an organization:

(*a*) **Investigation of problem.** The analyst studies the problems and needs of an organisation during development of a system. He visits various departments of the organisation and interviews the users. He analyses the problems of the current system and collect their requirements.

(*b*) **Solving the problem.** The analyst solves the problems of the current system faced by the users. He determines how people, method and technology can improve the current system. He presents the system proposal to the management and after acceptance of proposal develop the system along with his team consisting of analysts, programmers and users.

(*c*) **Managing the project.** The analyst monitors the development and implementation of software in relation to quality, cost and time. He works with the project team for managing the project properly.

(*d*) **Motivation.** The analyst motivates users to participate in development and implementation of the proposed system.

12.3.2 Role of Programmers

Programmers are the members of a project team. They perform the following roles during development of a system:

(*a*) **Development of System.** As per the design prepared by analyst, the programmers design the database files and write the programs. During database design, the programmers create, organise and maintain data files depending upon the requirement specifications, hardware configurations and the features of programming language and DBMS used. During programs design, the programmers write programs (called *coding of programs*) as per the logic developed by analyst. Programmers also enter/edit programs using a text editor, compile, execute and debug programs.

(*b*) **Testing of System.** The programmers play a vital role during testing of complete system. They prepare test data with the help of users and test programs using various techniques.

(*c*) **Implementation and Maintenance of System.** The system analyst implements the tested software at the user's place along with his team. The programmers may prepare the manuals, conduct training programs and convert data files from old to new system during implementation. Programmers as per guidance of analyst also undertake maintenance of system.

12.4 TYPES OF COMPUTER LANGUAGES

One man communicates with another in a language, which another man can understand. Similarly, man communicates with computer in a language which machine can understand. This language consists of a set of commands, which is understood by the computer either directly or after translating. This language is known as Computer Programming Language. There are the following four types of programming languages:

(*a*) Low Level Languages

(*b*) High Level Languages

(*c*) User Friendly Languages

(*d*) Object Oriented Languages

Let us discuss these languages briefly.

12.4.1 Machine or Low level Languages

In early days of computers, only those languages were used for programming, which could be directly executed on computer. Languages, which computer can understand directly and are machine dependent, are known as Machine languages or Low Level Languages. For example, Assembly Language is a low level language. Machine language is the oldest and most difficult of all the languages.

12.4.1.1 Reasons for learning Assembly Language

We learn Assembly language due to the following reasons:

- Although programmers prefer high level languages (such as C or Pascal) to Assembly language for developing application software, they use Assembly language combined with a high level language to speed up certain time dependent routines.

• Assembly language helps us to understand the computer architecture. The intimate knowledge of the computer helps us to write very efficient programs both in assembly and high level language.

• Assembly language does not impose many rules and restrictions for writing a program. On the other hand high level language imposes many rules. Therefore, Assembly language is mostly used to write system programs, which are difficult to develop using HLL. For example, we can easily write a program to change hardware settings (such as Monitor Display Mode, Keyboard characters set etc.) in assembly language, which is difficult to write in high level language particularly COBOL, BASIC, Fortran etc.

• In assembly language, the code of programs is much smaller than those of HLL programs. This is due the fact that many lines of instructions written in a high level language can be written using simple one-line instructions of assembly language.

• As assembly language is a low-level language, each line of the source program corresponds to one machine instruction. So, the program code is smaller and hence program runs faster.

12.4.2 High Level Languages

Development of applications using low level languages requires a deep understanding of the hardware. In order to facilitate the programmers to write programs without knowing the internal details of computer components, many languages were developed. These languages use common English words and are translated into low-level languages before processing by the computer. These languages, which computer cannot understand directly and are not machine dependent, are called High Level Languages (HLL). Some of the high level languages are BASIC, LOGO, COBOL, FORTRAN, etc.

12.4.3 User Friendly Languages

Although high level languages are simpler to codify than low-level languages, they still require a lot of time to learn programming syntax. Therefore, a new category of languages have been developed which are user-friendly, very easy to codify and simplest to learn. These languages are called User Friendly Languages. Some of the user friendly languages are dBase, FoxPro, etc.

12.4.4 Object Oriented Languages

The object oriented programming is the latest approach in programming. The languages that are based on object oriented programming (OOP) approach, are called Object Oriented Languages. Some of the popular object oriented languages are Smalltalk, C++ and Object COBOL, Object Pascal, Simula, Eiffel, Java & Visual J++.

12.5 PROGRAMMING LANGUAGES USED FOR SCIENTIFIC AND COMMERCIAL APPLICATIONS

High level languages are mainly used for scientific and commercial applications. The languages such as BASIC, COBOL, C, etc. are especially developed for commercial applications while FORTRAN is exclusively used for developing engineering applications where a lot of mathematical calculations are required. The language PASCAL is used for both commercial and scientific applications. Let us discuss about these languages in detail.

12.5.1 BASIC (Beginners All Purpose Symbolic Instruction Code)

BASIC is the first programming language to be made standard with personal computers. It was first developed by John Kemeny and Thomas Kurtz, two professors from Dartmouth College, U.S.A in 1964. It was primarily developed to teach programming to students of Dartmouth college, but later, it became so popular that today it is being taught in primary classes of most schools for learning programming. This is because that BASIC is very easy to learn and use, as it uses common English words as shown in Figure 12.3.

PROGRAM TO CALCULATE PERCENTAGE OF MARKS OBTAINED

```
10 REM
20 INPUT "Enter your Name", N$
30 INPUT "Enter you Marks obtained:, MO
40 INPUT "Enter your Maximum Marks", MM
50 LET P=(MO * 100)/mm
60 PRINT "YOUR PERCENTAGE IS", P
70 END
```

Figure 12.3 *An example of a BASIC program showing use of common English words*

12.5.1.1 Features of BASIC

The BASIC language offers the following features:

- The programming is in easy language i.e. in everyday English.
- Program if contains any error, can be edited easily.
- This language can be used for both mathematical and commercial problems.
- It can be used on both small (microcomputers-PCs) and large computers.
- The BASIC programs can be run on different computers with little or no modifications.
- Graphics and computer games can be easily made by using BASIC.

12.5.1.2 Versions of BASIC

BASIC is available in interpreter and compiler versions, the former being more popular for beginners. The different versions of BASIC language are–

(*a*) **ANSI BASIC.** It is an interpreter-based version of BASIC standardized in 1978 by the American National Standards Institute (ANSI).

(*b*) **BASICA (Advance BASIC).** This interpreter-based version of BASIC was developed by Microsoft corporation for the IBM PC Compatible computers.

(*c*) **GW-BASIC (Gee Whiz BASIC).** It is the BASIC Interpreter that was accompanied with MS DOS in versions prior to 5.0.

(*d*) **QBasic.** It is the BASIC interpreter that was accompanied with MS DOS and PC DOS version 5.0. It supersedes GW-BASIC and includes a program REMLINE.BAS that can convert GW-BASIC programs to QBASIC code.

(*e*) **Quick BASIC.** It is the popular BASIC compiler from Microsoft that adds advanced features to the BASIC language.

(*f*) **Visual BASIC.** It is the most popular version of QUICK BASIC for developing of window-based applications. It is considered a new programming language and environment (developed in 1990) which is based on BASIC language.

12.5.2 LOGO

LOGO is a high-level programming language, created by Seymour Papert in the mid 1960s for teaching programming to young children for making drawing. LOGO is so simple to learn that children studying in 1st class can use it. Using LOGO, children can create simple to complex patterns on screen very easily. LOGO is also called *Turtle Graphics* as you can create patterns consisting of lines rectangles, squares, circles etc. by moving the turtle (a triangular shaped cursor) with simple commands as shown in Figure 12.4.

```
FD 50
RT 90
FD 25
RT 90
FD 20
RT 90
FD 25
```

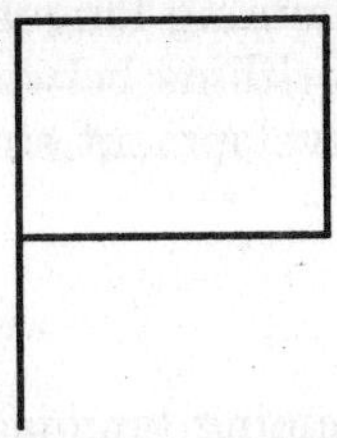

Figure 12.4 *An example of a LOGO program with output*

12.5.3 COBOL (Common Business Oriented Language)

COBOL has been the most popular high-level language for developing business applications mainly on mainframes and minis. It was developed in around 1960 and is still being used for developing business applications that typically run on mainframes. One time, COBOL was also popular on PCs but now it has become obsolete on microcomputer's environment. There are different versions of COBOL- COBOL ANSI'74, COBOL 85 and Microsoft COBOL. The ANSI'74 version of COBOL was standardised in 1974 by American National Standards Institute. COBOL 85 and Microsoft COBOL have been the most popular versions of COBOL.

COBOL is the most structured programming language because its instructions can be read and understood easily by the programmers who have not written them. All COBOL programs are divided into four parts, called divisions. The first division, called IDENTIFICATION DIVISION, documents the program's name, author, date-written, etc. The second division, called ENVIRONMENT DIVISION specifies the hardware and software environment of the program. The third division, called DATA DIVISION, defines the names and formats of the files and variables used in the programs. The last division is the PROCEDURE DIVISION, which describes the step-wise instructions and statements of the program. Although COBOL programs are lengthy in coding, they follow the rules of structured programming techniques. So, if you can learn COBOL, you can learn any programming language very easily.

12.5.4 FORTRAN (Formula Translator)

FORTRAN is the first high level programming language, developed by John Backus of IBM during 1956-57. Although it was originally designed to express mathematical formulas and is used occasionally for business applications, it is still the most popular language for developing scientific and engineering applications to solve mathematical problems.

12.5.4.1 Version of Fortran

The popular versions of FORTRAN are FORTRAN II, FORTRAN IV, FORTRAN 77 and FORTRAN V. FORTRAN II was the first version of FORTRAN used during 1950-60. FORTRAN IV was standardized, by ANSI in 1966. In 1977, an updated version of FORTRAN IV was announced which is called FORTRAN 77 and was standardized in 1978 by ANSI. FORTRAN V is the latest version of FORTRAN.

12.5.5 ALGOL (ALGOrithmic Language)

ALGOL is a high level programming language that was developed as an international language for the expression of algorithms between people and machines in 1960. Algol-60 was a turning point in language development since it was designed to reflect mathematical algorithms.

12.5.6 Pascal

Pascal is a high level programming language developed by a Swiss Professor Niklaus Wirth in the early 1970s. It was named after Blaise Pascal, a French mathematician who built the first desk-calculator type adding machine in the seventeenth century. Pascal is a structured programming language like COBOL, but it is not only used for developing business applications but also for scientific applications. Infact, you can write program for any application in Pascal. Pascal is a compiler-based language, built upon ALGOL by simplifying syntax and adding data types and structures such as files, records and sets.

12.5.6.1 Turbo Pascal

There are many versions of Pascal programming language, but Turbo Pascal, developed by Borland International in 1983 is the most popular one. There are also different versions of Turbo Pascal viz. 1.0, 2.0, 3.0, 4.0, 5.0, 5.5 and 6.0. Turbo Pascal 6.0, developed in 1990, is the latest version of Turbo Pascal.

12.5.7. Ada

Ada is a high level language, based on concepts developed in Pascal language. It was designed for embedded application where a computer forms part of a specialised system such as a cruise missile. It was developed as a result of search for a new programming language organised by the US Department of Defense in the late 1970s. Ada was named after August Ada Byron (1815-1852), counters of Lovelace and daughter of Lord Byron. Lady Ada was a mathematician and colleague of Charles Babbage (Father of Computers), who built a digital computer, called *Analytical Engine*. As the software for the Analytical engine was developed by Lady Ada, therefore she is known as the world's first programmer. The language Ada is named in her honor.

12.5.8 LISP (LIST Processing)

LISP is a high-level language, developed in the early 1960s by John McCarthy. LISP was designed mainly for the manipulation of LIST and tree structures of various kinds.

LISP is used in Artificial Intelligence application and compiler creations. It is available both in interpreter and compiler versions.

12.5.9 PL/I (Programming Language I) and PL/M (Programming Language for Microcomputers)

PL/I is a high level language developed by IBM, during 1964-69. It was designed to bring together the key features of FORTRAN, COBOL and ALGOL. It also introduced new concepts like multitasking. PL/I did not become popular, as it was very complex.

Later on, in the early 1970, Intel Corporation modified PL/I and developed a new language for microcomputers, called PL/M, which was mainly used for developing operating systems.

12.5.10 C

C is the most powerful high-level language, developed by Dennis Ritchie at AT&T's Bell Laboratories of USA in 1972. It was developed to replace the popular language of that time like ALGOL, PL/I, PL/M etc. The statements of C are very similar to those of Pascal.

12.5.10.1 Historical Development of C

The history of developing C started in 1960, when ALGOL language was developed by an international committee in search of a new language that could program all types of applications. ALGOL 60 did not become popular, as it was very abstract and general. Later on, in 1963, a new language called *CPL (Combined Programming Language)* was developed at Cambridge University. CPL was hard to learn and more difficult to implement. Thus, in 1967, Martin Richards at Cambridge University modified CPL and developed a new language called *BCPL (Basic Combined Programming Language)*. But BCPL could deal with only specific problems and was not accepted. In 1970, Ken Thompson at AT&T's Bell Laboratories developed language called *B*. But again B language could deal with only specific problems. Finally, in 1972, Dennis Ritchie developed the C language.

12.5.10.2 Features of C

C language offers features of both low-level (2nd generation) and High-level (3rd Generation) languages as discussed below:

(*a*) **Pointers.** In C, we can refer the memory locations by its internal address, called pointers. Pointers are one of the features of low-level languages.

(*b*) **Dynamic Allocation of memory.** In C, the programs during execution can request operating system to release memory for its use, which is called Dynamic Allocation of Memory. This is again one of the features of low-level language.

(*c*) **Bit Manipulation.** In C, data can be manipulated in its lowest form of storage i.e. BITS, which is again one of the features of low-level language.

(*d*) **Recursion.** In C, one function may call itself again and again, which is called Recursion. Recursion is a feature of high-level language.

12.5.10.3 Uses of C

As C provides features of both low and high level languages, it can be used to develop both system and application software. C can be used to develop operating systems, compilers, interpreters and other system software. You can also use C to develop both commercial and business application software.

12.5.10.4 Versions of C

There are many versions of C viz. ANSI C, Microsoft C and Turbo C. Turbo C is the most popular one.

High level languages were widely used for applications development, but most of them are now outdated due to popularisation of 4GLs. The uses of some of the high level languages are summarised in Table 12.1.

Language	Uses
BASIC (Beginner's All Purpose Symbolic Instruction Code)	Used for all purposes (Commercial, Scientific, Educational, Graphics etc.) by beginners.
LOGO	Used by young children to make drawings on computer.
COBOL(Common Business Oriented Language)	Mainly used for development of commercial applications on all types of computers.
FORTRAN (Formula Translator)	Used for development of scientific (mathematical) applications.
ALGOL (ALGOrithmic Language)	Used to reflect mathematical algo rithms.
PASCAL (Name of a Mathematician)	Used for both commercial and scientific applications.
ADA (Name of a Programmer)	Used to develop embedded applications for defense.
LISP (LiSt Processing)	Used to develop artificial intelligence applications.
PL/I and (Programming PL/M Language I Programming Language for Microcomputers)	Used to develop system software and mainly operating systems.
C (No full form)	Very powerful language for development of both system and application software.

Table 12.1 *Uses of high level languages*

12.6 GENERATION OF LANGUAGES

As we already know that the earlier programs were written in low languages comprising of 0's and 1's. Because it was very difficult to code in binary language, efforts were made to make coding easier and less complicated. This journey of development and sophistication has led to the development of higher level languages. A programming language has passed through the five generations. Let us discuss them in detail.

12.6.1 First Generation Language

Machine language is also known as the first generation language. When the computers were just invented, only those languages were used for programming, which could be directly executed on computer. These languages used machine dependent code comprising of 0's and 1's. A set of 1's and 0's as 11001010 has a specific meaning for the computer. Such a binary code was easily understood by the computers. Machine language is the oldest and most difficult of all the languages.

12.6.2 Second Generation Languages

A number of efforts were made to eliminate the difficulties faced while using the machine language. The very first language that looked English-like was developed in 1950 and it was known as Assembly Language or *Symbolic Programming Language*. The main idea was to bring man and machine closer to each other. Both of these used different languages but could easily understand each other. This language is easier than machine language and is known as Second Generation Language. In Assembly Language, instructions are given using mnemonic operation codes (such as ADD, MUL etc.) instead of binary digits.

12.6.3 Third Generation Languages

Even though the Assembly language was much closer to English, an effort was still made to simplify programming. Development of applications using low level languages requires a deep understanding of the hardware. In order to facilitate the programmers to write programs without knowing the internal details of computer components, many languages were developed. Each high level language was developed to fulfill some basic requirements for particular type of problems. These languages use common English words and are translated into low-level languages before processing by the computer. These languages, which computer cannot understand directly and are not machine dependent, are called Third Generation Languages. These languages are also known as *High Level Languages* (HLL).

12.6.4 Fourth Generation Languages

Although high level languages are simpler to codify than low-level languages, they still require a lot of time to learn programming syntax. Hence, these languages are beyond the reach of many computer users, who do not want expertise in programming. Therefore, a new category of languages have been developed which are user-friendly, very easy to codify and simplest to learn. These languages are called *User Friendly Languages* and popularly known as *4GLs* (Fourth Generation Languages). Fourth generation languages may be classified into two categories-Xbase and structured query language.

12.6.4.1 Xbase

Xbase is generic term denoting any of the programming environment based on the original dBASE programming language. XBase languages include dBASE, Fox Base, Clipper and FoxPro, out of which FoxPro is still being used by programmers while others are outdated.

(*a*) **dBase.** dBase is the first developed popular fourth generation language, on which the other Xbase languages (Foxbase, Clipper and FoxPro) are based. It is a relational Database Management System (DBMS) for PCs, developed by Borland. dBase is an interpreter based language but its programs can be compiled with Clipper. You can write program for any type of application in dBase (*e.g.* Preparation of the results of students).

Versions of dBase: Various versions of dBase are:

- Vulcan. dBase was originally named Vulcan by Wayne Ratliff, who created it to manage a company football pool.
- DBase II. Hal Lashlee and George Tate renamed Vulcan with dBase II in 1981 and formed Ashton-Tate company to market it. In 1991, Ashton-Tate company was acquired by Borland.
- DBase III. In 1984, dBase II was was upgraded to dBase III.
- DBase III plus: In 1986, new features are added to dBase III and dBase III plus was introduced.
- DBase IV. It is a major upgrade of dBase III plus with features like report/screen generation, SQL (Structured Query Language) and QBE (Query By Example) interfaces.

(*b*) **FoxBase.** FoxBase is a Xbase development system from Microsoft which is similar to dBase. Foxbase was originally developed by Fox Software for DOS. FoxBase+ is the most popular version of FoxBase. It gained a reputation for its higher speed and more compatibility than dBase III plus. As programming in FoxBase+ was quite similar to that in dBase III+, programmers preferred the former due to its higher speed.

(*c*) **Clipper.** Clipper (latest version 5.2) is the most popular dBase-compatible application development system. Originally, it was being used as a dBase compiler for programmers, but later on it became a stand-alone development system with many unique features. Although, now nobody uses clipper, earlier, it was very popular among dBase programmers due to following features:

- Clipper is a flexible Xbase language for writing efficient, encapsulated, and reusable program modules.
- It provides a powerful, flexible and replaceable database engine.
- It provides the simplest and efficient way to develop sophisticated and friendly user interfaces.

(*d*) **FoxPro.** FoxPro is the dBase IV compatible Xbase language from Microsoft. FoxPro is an enhanced version of FoxBase, which includes GUI (Graphical User Interface), SQL (Structured Querry language) and QBE (Querry By Example) interfaces. Various versions of FoxPro include FoxPro 1.0, FoxPro 2.0, FoxPro 2.6 for DOS /Window and Visual FoxPro 3.0/5.0/6.0. Visual FoxPro 6.0, the latest version of FoxPro is currently very popular among programmers for application development due to object-oriented features and client/server support.

12.6.4.2 Structured Query Language (SQL)

Structured Query Language (SQL), developed by IBM, is a standard data definition and data manipulation language (DDL/ DML) of relational databases. It is designed to define, access, query, organise and update the data and information in relational databases. It is now provided with most RDBMS and non-relational DBMS. SQL is generally hidden by user friendly interfaces in an end-user environment. It is an English like query language, intended for interactive use by untrained end users and was originally spelled *SEQUEL (Structured English Query Language)*. Although SEQUEL consists of basic vocabulary of English-like words like SELECT, INSERT, DELETE actually it has not much resemblance with English language. Therefore, now, it is generally pronounced as SQL. SQL has now become favorite among programmers who write programs that access relational databases.

The uses of different 4GLs are summarised in Table 12.2.

Language	Uses
dBASE	Used for development of mainly single user DOS based database appliactions.
FoxBase	Used for development of both single and multiuser DOS based database applications.
FoxPro	Used for development of both DOS and Windows based database applications.
Clipper	Used for development of both single and multiuser DOS based database applicaions.
SQL (Structure Query Language)	Used to define, access , querry, organised and update data in relational databases.
PL/SQL (Procedural Language/ Structured Language)	Used as a development tool that extends the facilities of oracle's SQL database language.
PRO * C	Used to generate native C code by embedding SQL commands.

Table 12.2 *Uses of 4GLs*

12.6.5 Fifth Generation Languages

We have discussed that the object oriented programming is the latest approach in programming. The languages that are based on object oriented programming (OOP) approach, are called *Object Oriented Languages*. They may be classified into Fifth Generation Languages. Object oriented languages are especially useful for development of GUI (Graphical User Interface) applications. These languages also offer a unique feature of Reusable Code. Some of the popular object oriented languages are Smalltalk, C++ and Object COBOL, Object Pascal, Simula, Eiffel, Java & Visual J++. C++ and Java, are widely used for development of Windows-based applications.

(*a*) **C++.** C++ is an object oriented version of C. It was developed by Bjarne Stroustrup at Bell Labs in the early 1980s. It has become very popular because it incorporates Object-Oriented Programming (OOP) features in traditional C programming. So, C++ is a superset of C. The structure of a C++ program resembles with those of C with few changes in syntax. The popular version of C++ is Turbo C++ (latest version 6.0).

(*b*) **Java.** Java is an object oriented programming language from the Java Soft division of Sun. Java is mainly used for developing Internet and Intranet applications. Using Java, you can develop client/server applications for the World Wide Web. Although Java is similar to C, C++ and objective C, it is not based on any of these languages.

The uses of different object oriented languages are summarised in Table 12.3.

Language	Uses
Smalltalk	Used for development of mainly graphical applications.
C++	Used for development of all types of objectoriented applications
Object COBOL	Used for development of object oriented applications on mainframe computer.
Object PASCAL	Used for general object oriented applications.
Simula	Mainly used in a research environment.
Eiffel	Used for general object-oriented applications.
Visual J++	Very popular for development of Windows based applications.

Table 12.3 *Uses of object-oriented languages*

12.6.5.1 Object Based Languages

There are certain languages which support most of the features of object oriented programming except inheritance. These languages are not pure object oriented languages and are known as Object Based Languages. For example, Ada, a high level language designed for process control, is an object based language.

12.7 CONCEPTS OF NETWORK PROGRAMMING LANGUAGE

The Java programming language has emerged as a language for Internet programming. The Java Virtual Machine (JVM) is considered to be the standard platform for mobile code in network programming. These days much of the programming of distributed applications is also being done using Java. Java, however, has limitations. Therefore, it is unreliable and subject to run-time errors. Most of the run-time errors are caught by the JVM but they can still lead to application failure. Java finds its major application in network programming. Java provides no specific language support for network programming. Code mobility is provided through class loaders, which only allow code to be dynamically linked across the network. Mobile agent systems provide much wider functionality, allowing running computations to move from machine to machine. Such functionality promises to revolutionize the field of electronic commerce, allowing user agents to roam the Internet negotiating commercial transactions on behalf of the user.

12.7.1 Features of Java

Java language offers following features:

- Java is an interpreter-based language. First, the source code of a Java program is converted into byte code, which is then converted into machine code during execution by the Java interpreter, called *Java Virtual Machine*. With Java Virtual Machine, Java programs can be run on any computer and hence they are hardware independent.
- Java is difficult to learn language. So, it is not meant for the beginners.
- Java provides a special class called *Java Applet*, which can be run by an already running Java application such as a Web browser. Java applets can be downloaded and run on any Web browser (e.g. Internet explorer, Netscape Navigator, etc.) capable of interpreting Java.

• Java provides a reusable object called *Java Bean*. A Java Bean can execute only on computers supporting OLE (Object Linking and Embedding) at the operating system level. Using Java Beans, the developer can quickly create applications.

THEORY QUESTIONS

1. What do you mean by computer languages? Differentiate between High Level, Assembly and Machine Languages.
2. How are the programs written in a high level language executed? Name second and third-generation-languages.
3. List the salient features and typical application areas of the following high level languages:
   (*a*) C
   (*b*) BASIC
4. What is a fourth generation language? How does it differ from a conventional high level language?
5. Mention three factors that make high-level languages more advantageous than machine level languages?
6. (*a*) Give examples of high level languages?
   (*b*) Why do you require so many different languages?
   (*c*) What are their special features?
7. List the special features of third generation languages.
8. What do you understand by the following and give examples to justify your answer:
   (a) Scientific programming languages.
   (*b*) Business oriented programming languages.
9. Explain the characteristics of procedural and non-procedural languages.
10. What are the important characteristics of the following:
    (*a*) System Software
    (*b*) Commercial Software
    (*c*) Scientific Software
    Name the high level languages suitable for writing each of the above categories of software.
11. Mention the characteristics of C language. Why is it known as an intermediate language?
12. List the advantages of Higher level languages over Lower level languages.
13. Why are the Fourth Generation Languages called the User-Friendly Languages?
14. Which programming languages are used for scientific and commercial applications? Substantiate through an example.
15. Discuss the different Programming approaches by giving suitable examples.

13
PROGRAMMING CONCEPTS

13.1 INTRODUCTION

Having understood the importance of programming and programming languages in developing a system, we are now in a position to discuss the steps of a programming process carried out by each programmer. As you already know, a program is a set of instructions to be executed by the computer to accomplish a particular task. The programming process is a set of activities that are carried out to develop and implement a computer program. Writing a program consists of various steps. In this chapter, we will discuss these steps including the programming tools such as flowcharts and pseudocodes in detail.

13.2 PROGRAMMING PROCESS

A program is developed in the following steps:

(*a*) Understanding the problem.
(*b*) Understanding the requirements.
(*c*) Developing the algorithm.
(*d*) Checking the algorithm.
(*e*) Coding the algorithm.
(*f*) Entering the program.
(*g*) Translating the program.
(*h*) Executing and Testing the program.
(*i*) Debugging the program.
(*j*) Documenting the program.

Let us discuss them in detail.

13.2.1 Understanding the Problem

The first prerequisite you need to fulfill before designing the program model is a clear statement of the problem that the program is supposed to solve. A problem definition defines what the problem is without any reference to the possible solutions. It is a simple statement, may be one to two pages and it should sound like a problem. The problem definition should be in user language and the problem should be described from the user's point of view. It usually should not be stated in technical computer terms. As the analyst assigns the programs to different programmers module-wise, the programmers understand the problem to be solved. The programmers define the problem of each program on a document and proceed for the next step.

13.2.2 Understanding the Requirements

After understanding the problem definition, the programmers study the input, output and processing requirements of the program that form the basis for program requirements analysis. The programmers obtain the input, output and processing requirements for the programs to be written. They also study the data flow diagrams, data dictionary and process descriptions (structured English statements, decision tools and decision tables) for obtaining the program requirements. The programmers are also required to review the database design before proceeding for the next step. Specifying requirements adequately is a key to the program's success. Essentially, we must look for three main components which are—

1. What is given as input?
2. What is expected as output?
3. How to arrive at the solution?

Hence, while determining program requirements we have to discern from the problem statement what exactly constitutes input, what is expected as output and how the processing is to be done. It will not be out of place to mention here that a given problem or business solution may be solved in a particular way manually and we may or may not choose to adopt the same processing logic while developing a solution to be computerised.

13.2.3 Developing the Algorithm

After defining the problem and understanding the requirements, the next step of a programming process is to develop algorithm. This is the most time consuming and crucial part of a programming process. An algorithm is a step-by-step procedure for solving a programming problem. The algorithm develops and designs the logic of a program. To be useful as a basis for writing a program the algorithm must:

- arrive at a correct solution within a finite time
- be clear, precise unambiguous and
- be in a format which lends itself to an elegant implementation in a programming language.

The common tools for developing an algorithm are—

(*i*) Flowcharts: Visual and graphical representation of the program.

(*ii*) Pseudocodes: Descriptive representations of the program logic in a simple English like language.

These tools are generally called *Program Tools*. We will discuss about these tools with few examples in subsequent part of this chapter.

13.2.4 Checking the Algorithm

The algorithm must be complete and correct in order to ensure the efficient execution of the program. Therefore, it becomes mandatory to check the algorithm before coding it. There are many methods to check the algorithm. Some of them are–

(*a*) *Dry run.* Manual way of checking algorithm by finding the values of each variable after every step of algorithm.

(*b*) *Review.* Studying the logic and comparing it with specifications.

(*c*) *Structured walk through.* Presentation of algorithm to the team members.

13.2.5 Coding the Program

After checking the algorithm and its final approval, the programmers start coding. *Coding* involves writing of program as per the algorithm using a programming language and database environment specified in the SRS (System Requirements Specification) document. Here we choose a programming language and using the syntax and semantics of that language, convert our algorithm which is in the form of a flowchart/pseudocode.

Syntax means the correct way or "grammar" of writing a command or series of commands, including all the proper options and command-line statements.

Semantics means the logical meaning of a statement, separate from the grammatical structure. The programmers may do the coding manually or by using application generators and CASE tools. Screen generators, menu generators and report generators are widely used CASE tools for generating program codes. Although, code generators may generate many lines of program statements, they cannot generate whole code. The programmers are still required to modify the generated code and write new code manually.

13.2.6 Entering the Code

After writing the program, it is entered into the computer using a text editor. Text editors are used to create, edit and print the programs. The interpreters and compilers of most programming languages (such as Turbo C, C++, Pascal, Foxpro, etc.) have inbuilt text editors.

13.2.7 Translating program

After feeding the program into the computer, it is required to be translated to a machine code using language translators. Compilation means converting the source code i.e. the user's program which is written using a high level language, into machine code which is machine understandable language.

Compilation results in certain kinds of errors which are indicated by the computer after the process is over. These errors have to be corrected and then the program recompiled. The process continues until the program is error free. Next, we must verify that our program does everything that it is supposed to do. Invariably, computer programs do not work properly the first time. The three types of errors that are normally encountered are discussed below.

13.2.7.1 Syntax Errors

Syntax errors occur when a computer language compiler cannot understand a command entered by the programmer. When such an error is encountered the computer rejects the program and prints out an error message. These errors are encountered during compilation and are very easy to correct. In many cases, these errors arise due to spelling mistakes, missing commas, etc. and incorrect syntax. For example, in FoxPro if we type APEND instead of APPEND, this causes a syntax error.

13.2.7.2 Execution Errors

These errors are encountered after error-free compilation, at the time of execution of the program. Execution errors are also called *runtime errors*.

Typical examples are—

- infinite loops

- correct outputs only for selected data
- data incorrect or in wrong order

13.2.7.3 Logical Errors

Logical errors are due to mistakes made by the programmer while coding the program. The computer does not detect logical errors.

For example, for calculating the net salary of an employee the formula is

```
Net_Sal = Basic_Sal + Allowances - Deductions
```

but through oversight, while coding, the formula is written as

```
Net_Sal = Basic_Sal - Allowance + Deductions
```

This will obviously produce a wrong result. Such errors can be detected only by a dry run.

13.2.8 Executing and Testing the Program

After translating, the program is executed and tested with test data. The test data is prepared as per the requirement specifications of the program. The test data is fed into the computer and outputs are compared with the required reports. The program is tested for the following aspects:

- The data entry should be user-friendly with all possible error messages.
- Online help should be provided throughout the time of execution.
- The execution speed should be as per the requirements.
- The output should be as per required formats.
- The modifications and deletions should be easy and correct.
- The database must be maintained as per the requirements.

Besides the above guidelines, there may be many more aspects for testing. However, the basic aim of testing is that the program should run efficiently, correctly and according to the specifications given in SRS document and guidelines of the analyst.

13.2.9 Debugging the Program

While testing, the program may have some bugs (errors) which must be corrected. The bugs of a program are removed by a programming technique called *debugging*. During debugging, the program code and algorithm are reviewed and corrected. The debugged program is fed into the computer again. It is translated, executed and tested unless it is found 100 percent error free.

13.2.10 Document the Program

Once the program is found error-free, the program algorithm and code is properly documented. A program code is documented as per the documentation techniques of programming. A project report is prepared by the programmer and submitted to the analyst or project leader. The documentation of program is a major part of systems documentation. Documentation of a program will consist of flowcharts/pseudocodes, program listings and detailed written statements of algorithms and procedures involved. Documentation is necessary for program maintenance. Without proper documentation, it will be difficult to change a program at a later date.

It is a wrong notion that documentation is the last step in the algorithm development stage. In fact, it should be interwoven with the entire phase of the programming process, especially with the design and implementation, because documentation is supposed to enable individuals to understand the logic of programs.

13.3 DESIRABLE PROGRAMMING STANDARDS

Programming standards are required to provide a degree of predictability in programs of a common type, written in a common language or written for a common computer installation.

A standard contributes to–

- Simplification of program design
- Simplification of program maintenance and
- Efficiency of computer resource utilisation.

Let us briefly discuss the standards to be followed for program design and maintenance.

13.3.1 Standards for Program design

1. **Use standard algorithms.** It is always better if individuals or groups in an organisation adopt standard approaches to common situations. There are standard algorithms for table searching, file updating, sorting etc. which are available by reference to published works. The use of common techniques will free maintenance programmers from having to be familiar with many other methods of tackling the same procedure.

2. **Use standard structure patterns.** Any programmer must as far as possible adhere to the structured and consistently construct programs in the same pattern. He must use a main module or driving module to control the overall execution of a program. Use subroutines to perform the individual tasks constitution to get the program's operations.

3. **Use standard control mechanisms.** Whenever a program module is to be repeated many times depending on the occurrence of a nominated condition, adopt a consistent procedure to handle the status items which control the iteration of the procedure.

13.3.2 Standards for Program maintenance

1. Defining data items

- Use meaningful names where the syntax of the language permits. for example:

```
BASIC_PAY
NET_SAL
CASH_SALE
```

- Never rely on data items having a specific initial content other than that which your program explicitly assigns to them. For example, a counter or a total must start with an initial value of zero, ensure that a program instruction puts that value in the data item. Never presume that such an item automatically starts at zero.

2. Procedural code (Instruction)

- Write one instruction per line.
- Separate program modules or related groups of instructions by a few blank lines to enhance comprehensibility.

• Indent related instructions in loops and conditional statements where the syntax of the language permits, for example:

```
FOR I IN RANGE 1 TO 5
DO
          AREA   = L  *  B          ***  Indented
          SUM    = NUM1  +  NUM2    ***  Indented
ENDDO
ENDFOR
```

• Construct the program from a number of small, independent, functionally oriented modules. Each program module should conform to the following criteria:

a. It should have a meaningful name (*e.g.*, NET_SAL) where the syntax of the language permits, otherwise it should have a comment statement to indicate its function.

b. Unless its purpose is plainly apparent from its instruction, it should contain a few comment lines explaining its purpose within the program.

c. It should carry out a single function.

d. It should consist of relatively few instructions, say a maximum of 50 lines of code.

13.4 STRUCTURED PROGRAMMING

Structured programming techniques imply that the program development and coding must follow a top-down approach and structured programming constructs.

Top-down approach implies planning the program as hierarchy of modules. Programming begins with the top (main) module. When the main module is programmed, second level modules are then programmed.

In order to support the discipline of top-down programming, the following basic structured programming constructs are followed in programming:

- Sequence
- Selection
- Repetition

Sequence indicates that if there is no intervening control structure, the flow of control normally passes from one instruction to the next in sequence.

Selection indicates a decision, from among several options. You may branch out to one of multiple locations within the program depending on the decision.

Repetition, or looping constructs occur when a set of instructions are to be repeated several times. It saves the trouble of writing the same set of statements repeatedly.

13.5 PROGRAMMING TOOLS

The tools that are used by programmers for developing the logic of a program are called *Program Tools*. There are two major types of Program Tools available, which are Program Flowcharts and Pseudocodes. The programmers make use of these tools to design program logic. Let us discuss about these tools in detail.

13.5.1 Program Flowcharts

A *program flowchart* is the graphical representation of the steps followed for solving any programming problem or for accomplishing a task. It is the best tool to develop the program logic. It includes all necessary steps of a program. It is called a flowchart, because it charts the flow of a program. It is a symbolic representation of each input, output and processing step. Besides being a good method of writing down the algorithm, it is also a part of program documentation and helps in understanding, debugging and maintaining programs.

Before coding a program in any programming language, the programmers are always advised to draw the flowcharts first. In the flowcharting technique, operations are represented by drawing appropriate symbols for the actions. The important symbols used in a flowchart are shown in Figure 13.1. These flowchart symbols are connected by arrows to illustrate the sequence of operations. Let us briefly discuss the significance of these symbols:

Symbol	Explanation
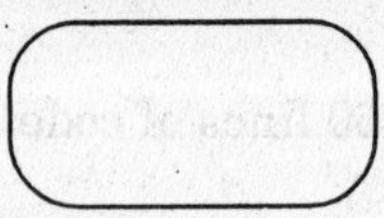	Terminator – Used in start and end of a flowchart.
	Input/output– Used to accept the data or display/print the output.
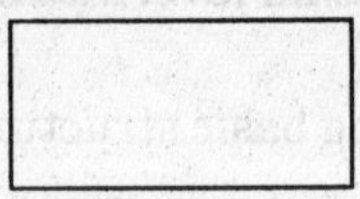	Process– Used to show the activity or processing to be performed an data.
	Flow lines– Used to connect other symbols in a flowchart for showing the sequence of their execution. The default direction of execution is from top to bottom and from left to right for reverse directions the arrow must be used.
	Decision Box – Used to check a condition whether it is true or false. Depending upon the condition, the program branches in two directions.
	Connector– Use to connect two parts of a flowchart.
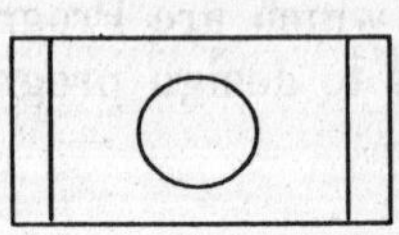	Predefined Process– Used to represent a module of a program.

Figure 13.1 *Symbols used in a Flowchart*

1. The Input/Output Symbol

This symbol is used to represent the input/output operations (I/O operations) such as read and write. This is illustrated in Figure 13.2.

Figure 13.2 *The Input/Output symbol*

2. The Process Symbol

This symbol is used to represent process like assigning a value to a variable or adding a number. It has one arrow going inside to denote the input data to the process and another arrow leaving it to denote that the processed data leaving this process. In other words, it has one entry and one exit as shown in Figure 13.3.

In Figure, 13.3 "SUM = NUM1 + NUM2" is a process which adds the two numbers and stores the result in Sum. For this process, the input is numbers flowing in (represented by in-going arrow from the process).

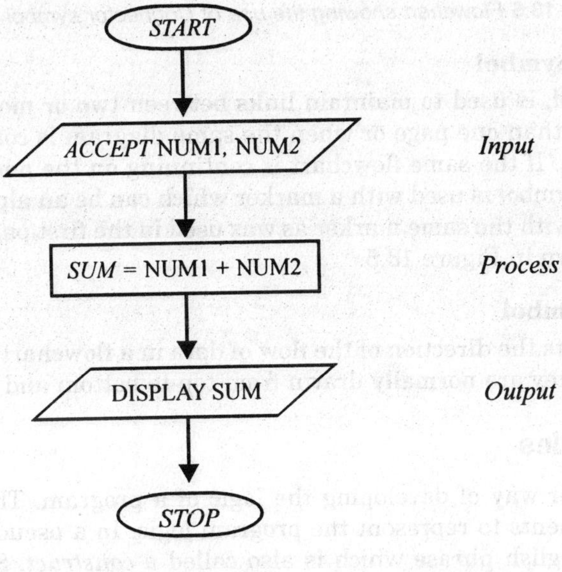

Figure 13.3 *Flowchart to add two numbers*

3. The Terminal Symbol

This symbol indicates the beginning or the end of a flowchart as shown in figure 13.4.

Figure 13.4 *The Terminal symbol*

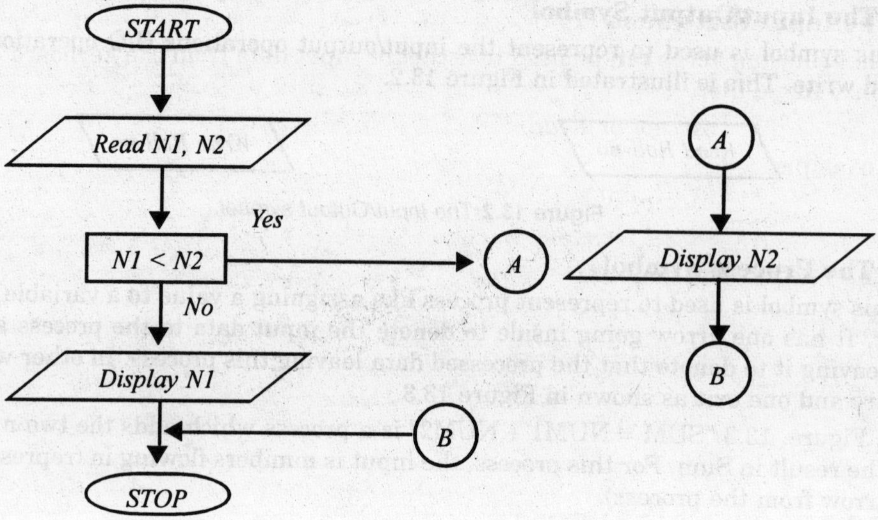

Figure 13.5 *Flowchart showing the use of Connector symbol*

4. The Connector Symbol

The connector symbol, is used to maintain links between two or more flowcharts when the flowchart runs longer than one page or when the same diagram is continued at different locations of the same page. If the same flowchart is continuing on the next page, then at the end of the first page this symbol is used with a marker which can be an alphabet or a number. The same symbol is used, with the same marker as was used in the first page, at the beginning of the second page as shown in Figure 13.5.

5. The Flowline Symbol

This symbol represents the direction of the flow of data in a flowchart. These are straight lines with arrow heads. They are normally drawn from top to bottom and left to right.

13.5.2 Pseudocodes

Pseudocode is another way of developing the logic of a program. The *pseudocode* uses simple English like statements to represent the program logic. In a pseudocode, each step is written using a simple English phrase which is also called a *construct*. Some programmers prefer pseudocode as compared to flowcharts because writing the logic of a program sometimes is easier than drawing the diagrams. Some programmers make use of both the tools by first drawing the flowcharts and then writing pseudocodes. Some of the conventions which are used while writing pseudocodes are as follows:

1. All statements in a loop should be indented.
2. All alphanumeric values should be enclosed in single or double quotes.
3. The beginning and end of a pseudocode is marked with keywords like 'start' and 'end' respectively.
4. All statements must include certain keywords which denote an operation.

Some books follow the convention of ending each statement with a semicolon. Let us briefly discuss some of these conventions:

1. The Input Statement

The following verbs can be used to accept or input data from the keyboard or from an existing form like a file.

Accept or Read

For example,

Accept Name
Read Name

2. The Output Statement

The following verbs can be used to output data.

Write or Display

For example,

Write Name
Display Name

13.6 PROGRAMMING EXAMPLES

Let us see some solved examples on flowcharts.

13.6.1 Examples of flowcharts

Example 1

A student appears for a test in 3 subjects. Each test is out of 100 marks. The percentage of each student has to be calculated and depending on the percentage calculated, grades are given as under:

Percentage	Grade
=>90	E+
80-90	E
70-79	A+
60-69	A
50-59	B+
<50	FAIL

Draw a flowchart for the stated problem.

Solution: Flowchart for the same is given in Figure 13.6.

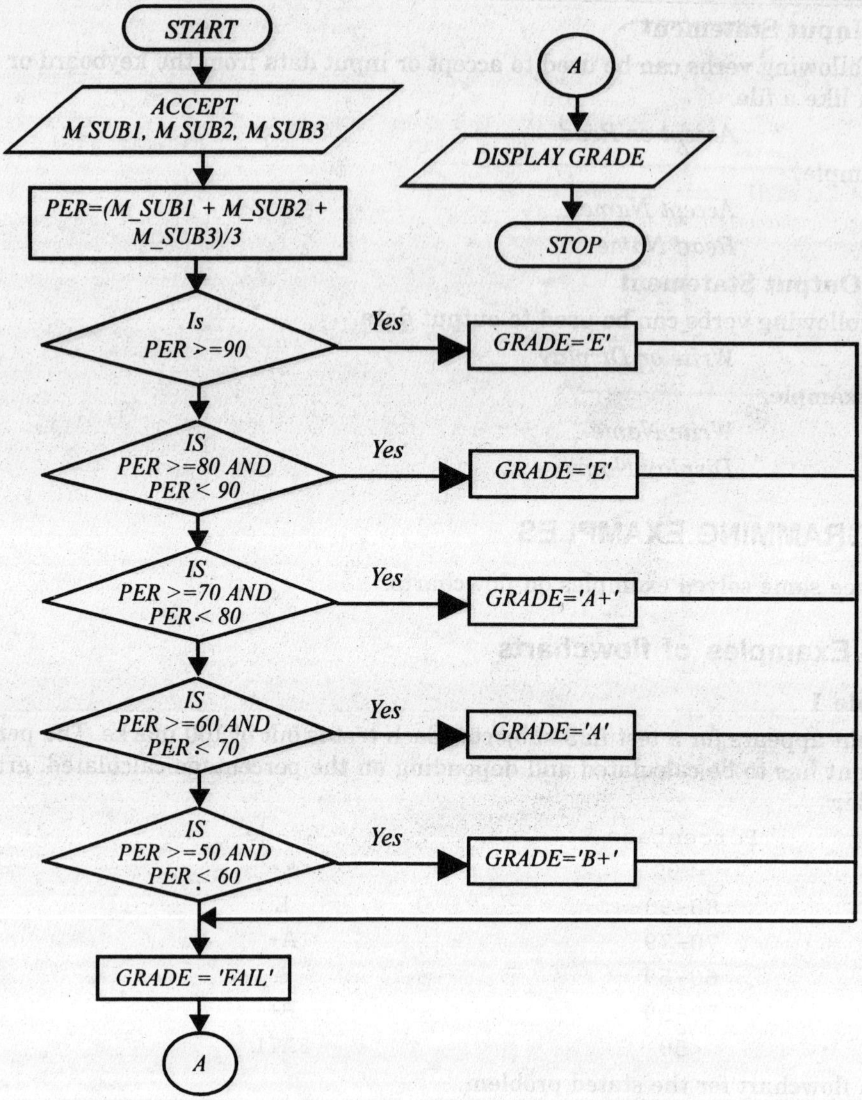

Figure 13.6 *Flowchart showing the calculation of Percentage and Grades*

Example 2

Draw a flowchart to find the factorial for any given number. Factorial means the product of the positive integers 1, 2, 3 up to and including a given integer. Applying the following equation derives factorial:

n! (factorial of n) = n* (n-1)* (n-2)* (n-3)........*3*2*1

Solution: Flowchart for the stated problem is given in Figure 13.7.

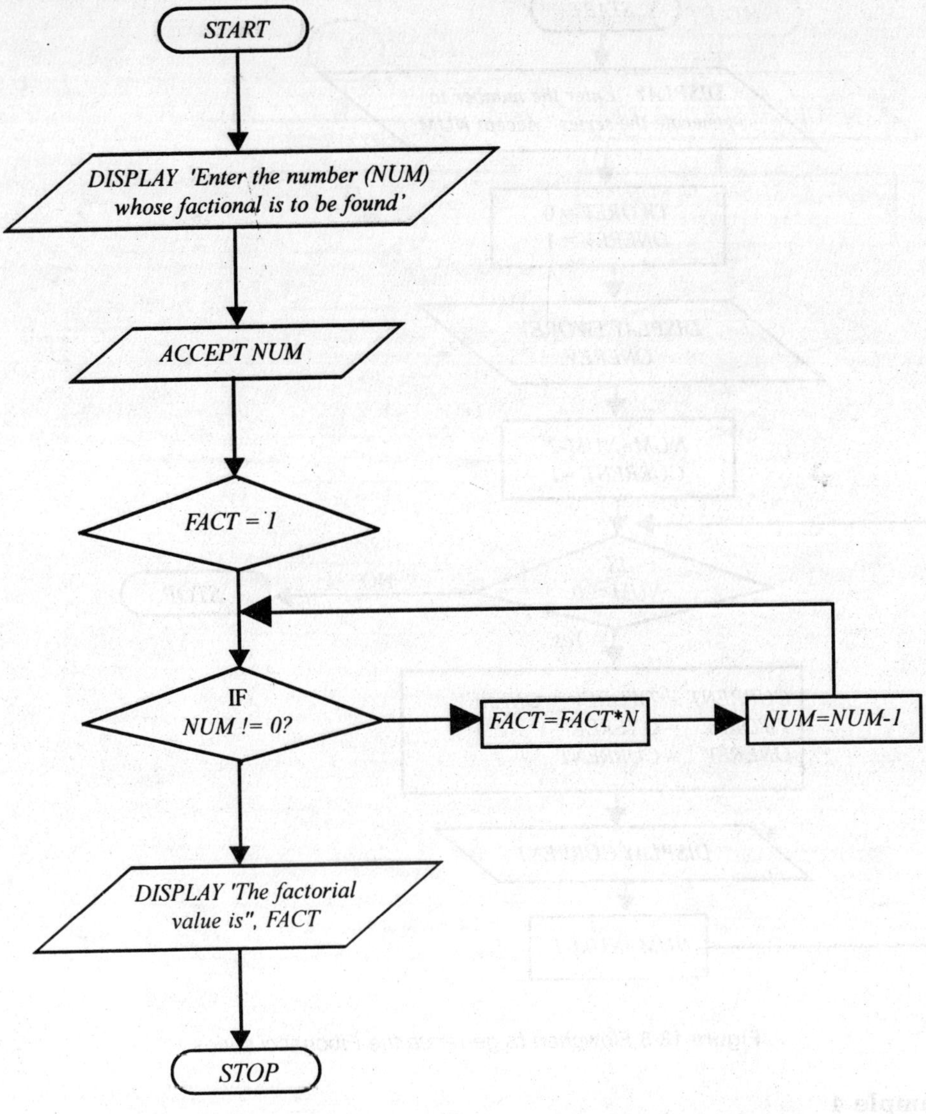

Figure 13.7 *Flowchart to find the factorial for any given number*

Example 3

Generate the first 20 numbers in the fibonacci series. Fibonacci series is a series of integers in which each integer is equal to the sum of the two preceding integers in the series. The series is formulated mathematically by Xi = Xi-1 + Xi-2, where X0 = 0 and X1=1; that is 0,11,2,3,5,8.....

The series looks like:

0+1 = 1, 1+1 = 2, 1+2 =3, 2+3 = 5, 3+5 =8, etc.

If we were required to generate 5 numbers then, the series would look like: 0 1 1 2 3 5...

Solution: The flowchart for this problem is shown in Figure 13.8.

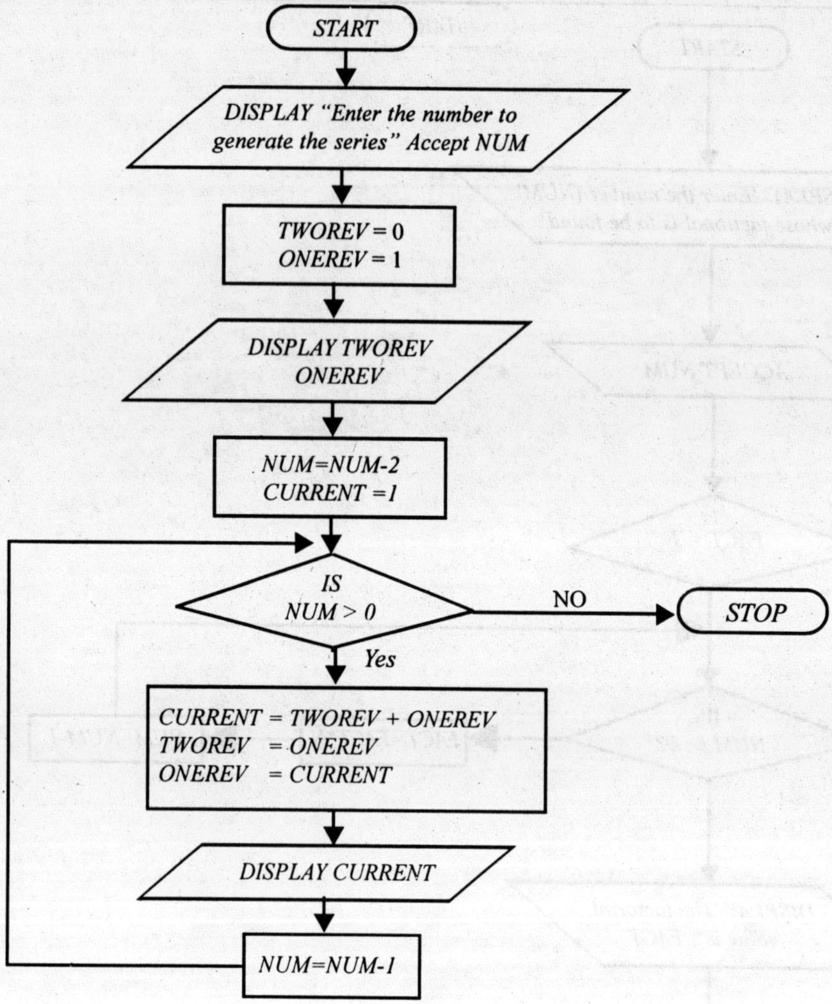

Figure 13.8 *Flowchart to generate the Fibonacci series*

Example 4

Draw a flowchart which finds the sum of all odd numbers in the range 1 to 10 (*i.e.* 1+3+5+7+9=25).

Solution: The flowchart to solve this problem is shown in Figure 13.9.

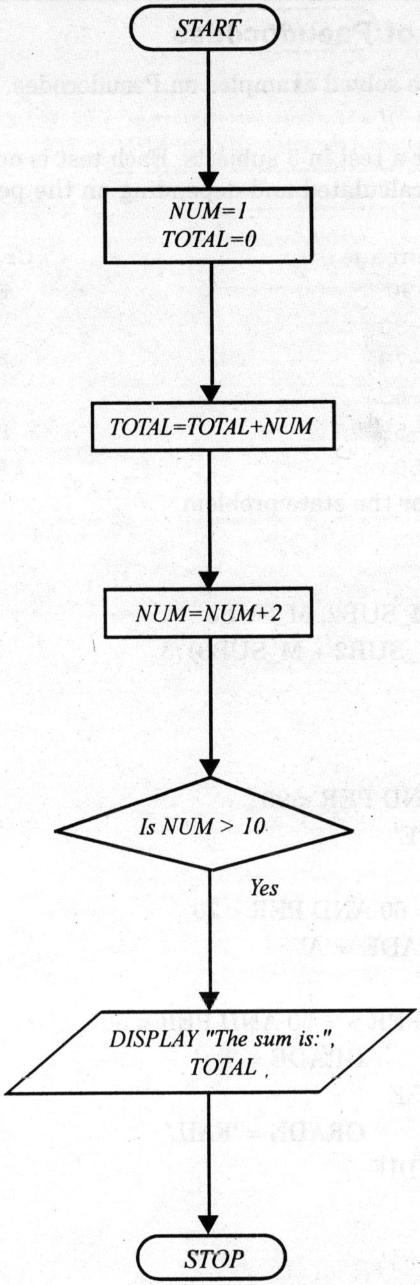

Figure 13.9 *Flowchart to find the sum of all odd numbers in the range 1 to 10*

13.6.2 Examples of Pseudocodes

Let us see some of the solved examples on Pseudocodes.

Example 1

A student appears for a test in 3 subjects. Each test is out of 100 marks. The percentage of each student has to be calculated and depending on the percentage calculated, grades are given as under:

Percentage	Grade
=>90	E+
80-90	E
70-79	A+
60-69	A
50-59	B+
<50	FAIL

Write a pseudocode for the state problem.

Solution:

```
START
ACCEPT M_SUB1, M_SUB2, M_SUB3
PER = (M_SUB1 + M_SUB2 + M_SUB3) /3
IF PER > = 90
   GRAD = 'E+'
ELSE
   IF    PER >= 80 AND PER < 90
         GRADE = 'E'
   ELSE
         IF PER > = 60 AND PER < 70
               GRADE = 'A'
         ELSE
               IF PER > = 50 AND PER < 50
                     GRADE = 'B+'
               ELSE
                     GRADE = 'FAIL'
               ENDIF
         ENDIF
   ENDIF
ENDIF
ENDIF
DISLAY GRADE
END
```

Example 2

Write the pseudocode to find the factorial for any given number. Factorial means the product of the positive integers 1, 2, 3 up to and including a given integer. Factorial is derived by applying the following equation:

n! (factorial of n) = n* (n-1)* (n-2)* (n-3)........*3*2*1

Solution:

```
START
DISPLAY 'Enter the number (NUM) whose factorial is to be found'
ACCEPT NUM
FACT = 1
WHILE n ! = 0                ** ! = is a symbol for not equal to
DO
   FACT = FACT *NUM
   NUM = NUM – 1
ENDDO
DISPLAY 'The factorial value is :', FACT
END
```

Example 3

Write a pseudocode to generate the first 20 numbers in the fibonacci series. Fibonacci series is a series of integers in which each integer is equal to the sum of the two preceding integers in the series. The series is formulated mathematically by Xi = Xi-1 + Xi-2, where X0 = 0 and X1=1; that is 0,1,1,2,3,5,8....

The series looks like:

0+1 = 1, 1+1 = 2, 1+2 =3, 2+3 = 5, 3+5 =8, etc.

If we were required to generate 5 numbers then, the series would look like: 0 1 1 2 3 5..

Solution:

```
START
DISPLAY 'Enter how many numbers to generate:'
ACCEPT NUM
TWOREV = 0
ONEREV = 1
DISPLAY TWOREV, ONEREV
NUM = NUM – 2
CURRENT = 1
WHILE NUM > 0
DO
   CURRENT = TWOREV + ONEREV
   TWOREV = ONEREV
   DISPLAY = CURRENT
   DISPLAY CURRENT
   NUM = NUM -1
ENDDO
END
```

Example 4

Write a pseudocode to find out the sum of all odd numbers in the range 1 to 10 (i.e. 1+3+5+7+9=25).

Solution:

```
START
NUM = 1
TOTAL = 0
REPEAT
   TOTAL = TOTAL + N
   NUM = NUM + 2
UNTIL NUM > 10
DISPLAY 'The sum is: ', TOTAL
END
```

13.6.3 More Examples of Flowcharts and Pseudocodes

Now, let us take few common examples on pseudocodes and flowcharts.

Example 1

Write a pseudocode and then draw a flowchart that accepts there numbers, adds them and displays the result.

Solution:

The flowchart for the stated problem is shown in Figure 13.10.

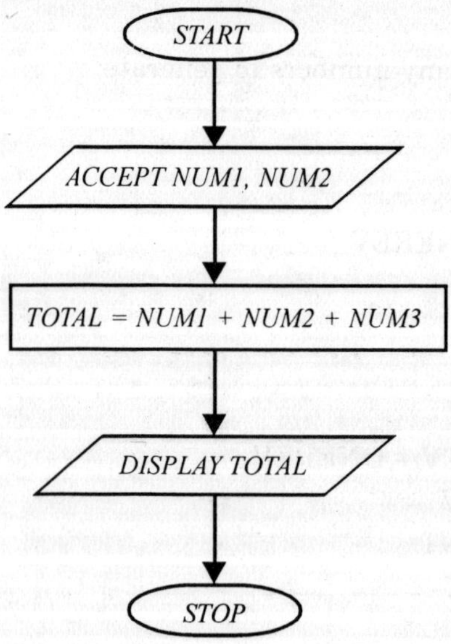

Figure 13.10 *Flowchart to add three numbers*

The pseudocode for the above problem statement is given below:

START
ACCEPT NUM1
ACCEPT NUM2
ACCEPT NUM3
TOTAL = NUM1 + NUM2 + NUM3
DISPLAY TOTAL
END

Example 2

Aman's monthly salary consists of Basic salary, traveling allowances and a 15% commission on sales made. At the end of the month we need to calculate his salary. Draw a flowchart and write the pseudocode statements for the stated problem.

Solution: The flowchart is shown in Figure 13.11.

The pseudocode for the problem statement is given below:

START
ACCEPT B_SALARY, TRA_ALL, SALES
COMMISSION = SALES * 0.15
TOT_SAL = B_SALARY + TRA _ ALL + COMMISSION
DISPLAY TOT_SAL
END

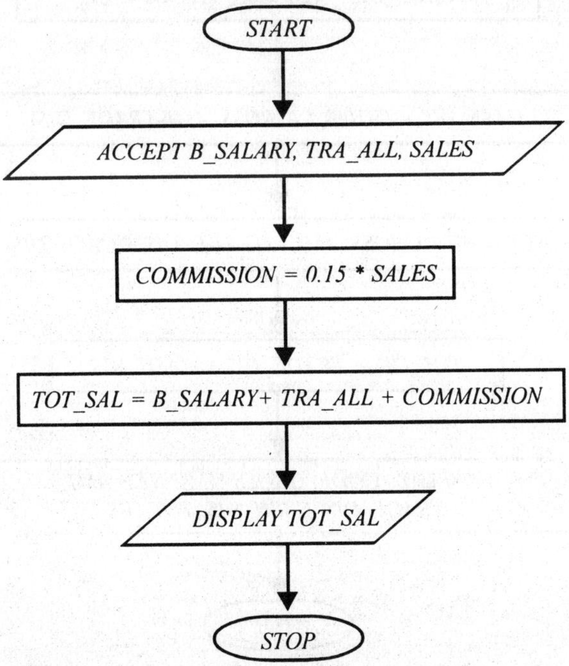

Figure 13.11 *Flowchart to calculate the Monthly Salary*

Example 3

SNOW, a grocery store gives discount to its regular customers. The discounts are given irrespective of the amount of purchase. The store gives two types of discounts. A trade discount of 20% on total value of in purchase and a cash discount of 5% on the value of the purchase less trade discount.

Let us calculate and display the gross amount due, the net amount due, the value of the quantity discount, the value of the cash discount and the total discount along with the product code. You are required to draw a flowchart and write pseudocode statements.

Solution: The flowchart is shown in Figure 13.12.

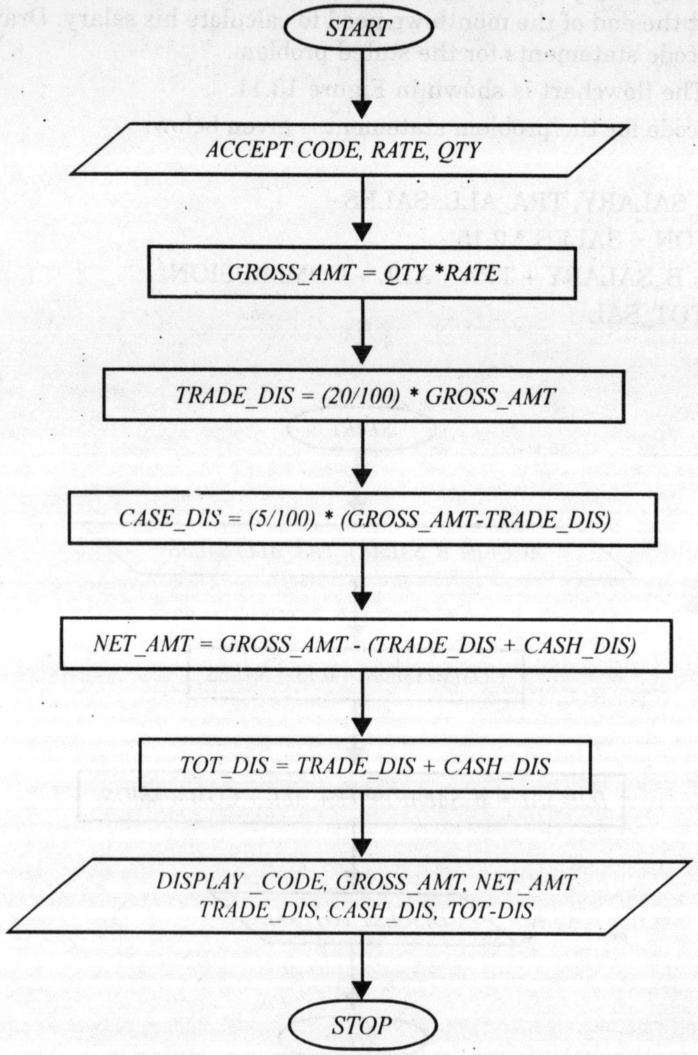

Figure 13.12 *Flowchart to calculate the total discount*

The following statements show the pseudocode of the stated problem.

```
START
ACCEPT CODE, RATE, QTY
GROSS _ AMT = QTY * RATE
TRADE _ DIS = 20 / 100 * GROSS _ AMT
CASH _ DIS = 5 / 100 * (GROSS _ AMT – TRADE _ DIS)
NET _ AMT = GROSS _ AMT = (TRADE _ DIS + CASH _ DIS
TOT _ DIS = TRADE _ DIS + CASH + DIS
DISPLAY CODE, GROSS_AMT, NET_AMT, TRADE_DIS,
CASH_DIS, TOT_DIS
END
```

Here	CODE	=	Product Code
	RATE	=	Product rate
	QTY	=	Product quantity
	GROSS_AMT	=	Gross amount
	TRADE_DIS	=	Trade discount
	CASH_DIS	=	Cash discount
	NET_AMT	=	Net amount
	TOT_DIS	=	Total discount

Example 4

Draw a flowchart to calculate area of Circle and Rectangle. Also write the pseudocode statements for the same.

Solution: The flowchart is shown in Figure 13.13.

The following statements show the pseudocode of the stated problem.

```
Main Routine
Step 1    Start
Step 2    Accept FIG
Step 3    If FIG = "CIRCLE"
          do CIR_ROUTINE
   Else
          If FIG = "RECTAGLE"
                    do RECT_ROUTINE
   Else
                    goto Step 2
Step 4    Display AREA
Step 5    Stop

CIR_ROUTINE
Step 1    Input RADIUS
Step 2    Calculate AREA = 3.14 * RADIUS * RADIUS
Step 3    Return to main routine
```

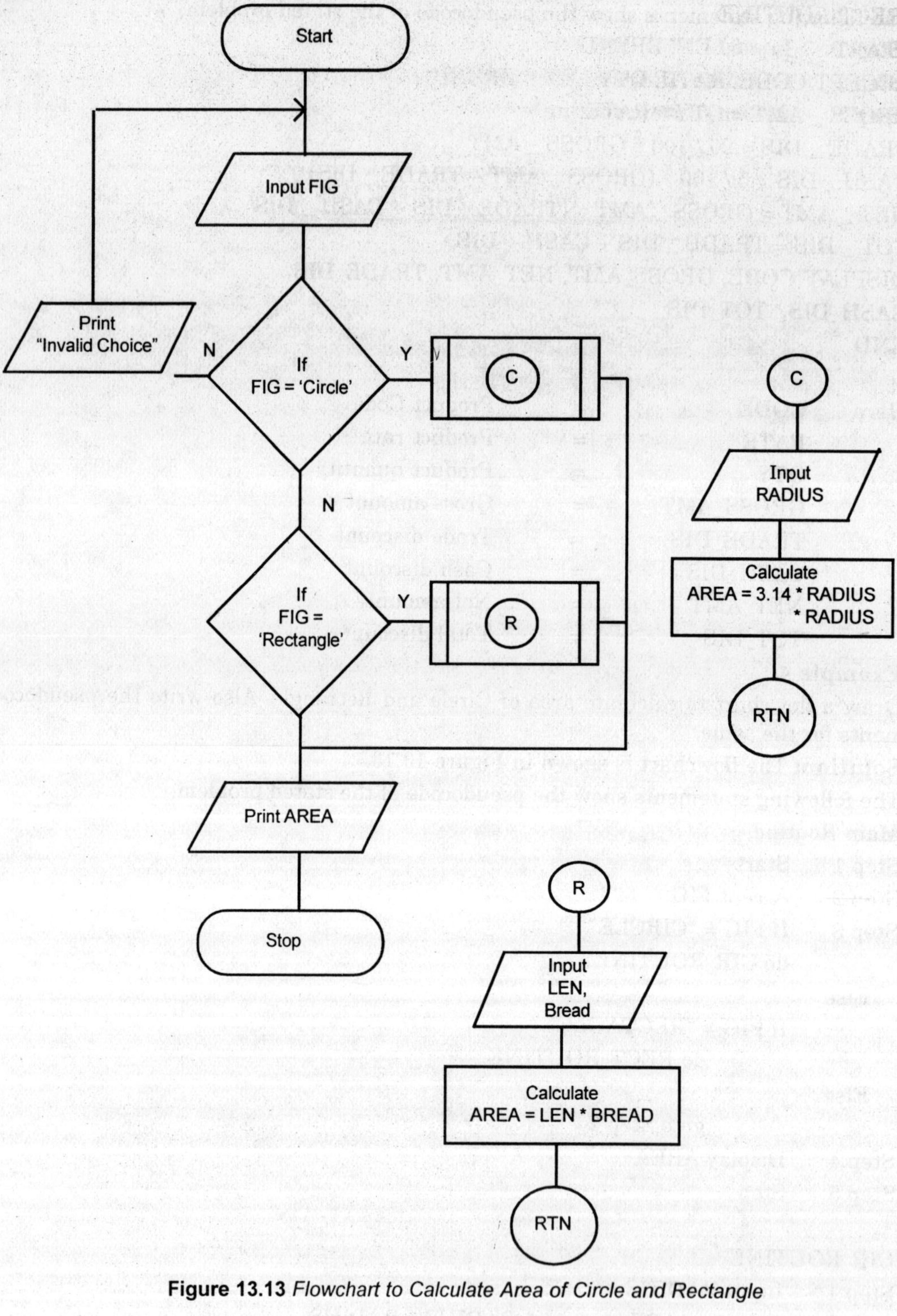

Figure 13.13 *Flowchart to Calculate Area of Circle and Rectangle*

RECT-ROUTINE

Step 1 Input LEN, BREAD

Step 2 Calculate AREA = LEN * BREAD

Step 3 Return to main routine

THEORY QUESTIONS

1. Discuss the programming process in detail.
2. Define the terms: Syntax and Semantics.
3. Why is documentation necessary?
4. Describe the steps you will follow in program development?
5. What is meant by structured programming?
6. What is a flowchart?
7. What is a pseudocode?
8. Draw and explain different symbols used in drawing a flowchart.
9. What are the three types of errors that are normally encountered while compiling a program?
10. What are the standards used for program design and program maintenance?
11. Draw a flowchart that adds N natural numbers.
12. Draw a flowchart that determines the smallest number out of given N numbers.
13. Draw a flowchart for fibonacci series.
14. Draw a flowchart to count non-zero digits in a set of 100 digits.
15. Write the steps for executing a program written in C and draw its flowchart.
16. Draw a flowchart to print the largest number amongst a list of n numbers.
17. Draw a flowchart to calculate the roots of the equation $ax^2 + bx + c = 0$.
18. Write pseudocode statements to add first 10 even numbers.
19. Write pseudocode statements to find out the smallest number out of the given N numbers.
20. Write pseudocode statements to find out the perimeter of a rectangle.
    Perimeter of a rectangle = 2 (l + b)
    where l is the length of the rectangle,
    b is the breadth of the rectange.

14
INTRODUCTION TO C PROGRAMMING LANGUAGE

14.1 INTRODUCTION

The C programming language is unique among languages because it has uncommon power. Power in a language or utility is the ability of a language to do a good job with very little code. C is a general purpose and structured programming language. C resembles high-level programming languages such as Pascal and FORTRAN–77 because it uses keywords like if, else, for, do and while. The 'C' language also possesses the powerful low level features of 2nd generation languages like pointers, memory allocation, bit manipulation, etc. It also makes use of a number of operators and a variety of data structures which are said to be the features found in the 3rd generation languages. Thus, the combined features of 2nd and 3rd generation languages make 'C' a very powerful and widely used language. Therefore, this language is considered good for systems programming like development of compilers, interpreters, operating systems, graphics and general utilities. C language is also used for the development of commercial applications. Thus, C bridges the gap between the machine language and the more conventional high level languages. C has a great ability to write very small source programs. It contains small instruction set. It also makes extensive usage of library functions which enhance the basic instructions. Besides that, C language allows users to write additional library functions which can be added to the existing list of library functions.

Another reason for the wide popularity of C language is that its programs are highly portable. The reason behind this is that every version of C is accompanied by its own set of library functions. These are written for the particular characteristics of host computer. These library functions have been standardized so that each library function is generally accessed in the same manner from all the versions of C. This is the reason why most of the C programs can be run on many different computers with almost no alteration.

Moreover, the functions available in C work as building blocks to develop more functions. As discussed earlier also, C is a structured programming language which means that in programs, we can write logically defined functions, functions that return value, functions that keep private variables, etc. In fact, the C language offers very few functions which form the core of C language. Using these core functions available in the library, you can build rest of the other functions. This feature of C has given it immense power and scope. Thus, you can develop your own functions and store them as independent modules in the C library. Thereafter, these functions can be used as and when required.

You will be immensely surprised to know that out of a total of 13,000 lines of code for Unix operating system all, except 800 lines have been written in C language. Apart from that the C compilers are being written in earlier versions of C language. There are other language compilers also such as databases, spreadsheets, word processors, etc. which are being developed in C language.

In the subsequent pages of this chapter, we will discuss about the historical development of C language, features of C and the structure of a C program.

14.2 HISTORY OF C LANGUAGE

The history of C language traces back to the year 1969 when Ken Thompson and Dennis Ritchie designed a file system that could provide a more convenient environment for programming at Bell Labs Inc. (now known as AT&T Bell Laboratories). This language was far better than the earlier two languages called, BPCL and B. These languages were also developed at Bell Laboratories. These two languages were very specific and less powerful. Thus, Ritchie developed the C language that was compiler based. He inherited some of the features from BPCL and B, added new features and this is how a new language called C language was developed. Till 1978, C was mostly used within Bell laboratories. By mid 1980's, C had gained widespread popularity. Many computer professionals were impressed by C's many desirable features. Therefore, they started promoting this language. Many commercial applications, which were originally written in other languages were rewritten in C.

14.3 FEATURES OF C

Let us discuss some of the features of C because of which C has become a widely accepted language :

1. **Pointers.** Pointer is a reference to a memory location by its internal address or byte number. Like other languages, C allows reference to a memory location by a name assigned to it or by way of pointers.

2. **Bit-Manipulation.** The C language allows the manipulation of data in BITS which is the lowest form of storage. This feature is not supported by most of the other programming languages available today.

3. **Memory Allocation.** In most of the programming languages, the memory to a variable name is assigned at the time of its definition in the program. However, apart from this, C language also allows dynamic allocation of memory. It means that the program can request the operating system to release memory for the use of the program at the time when the program is being executed.

4. **Recursion.** Recursion is an extremely powerful feature of C language. Recursion is the ability of a function to call itself again and again. We will discuss about recursion in detail in the subsequent part of this book.

14.4 STRUCTURE OF A C PROGRAM

Each and every C program consists of atleast one function which is called the *main*() function. This is the very first function to be executed by a program. The other functions are followed by the main() function. Let us briefly discuss the structure of a single level and multiple level functions:

1. **Single Level Functions.** A single level function is the one that contains one and only one function called main() function. It neither carries any other function name nor does it make a call to any other function. Let us see the syntax of a simple C function:

```
main()
{
    printf("Learning  C");
    /* Message printed on the screen */
}
```

Let us discuss the different components of this function:

main( ) — It is the very first function to be executed by a program. It should be present in all the C programs. The main() function is like any other function available in the library or the one written by the user.

Paranthesis ( ) — Round brackets are present at the end of all the function names. They are used to pass parameters to a function.

{ ; } — The curly brackets mark the beginning and end of any function. They are mandatory for all the functions.

/* */ — They are used to write comment lines in a function and are used only for documenting and providing information for later use. The comment line can be given either in a single line or may be comprised of a number of lines. It is absolutely optional to give a comment line. Thus, while executing any C program, the compiler ignores the text written as comment lines.

; — Semicolon is used for marking the end of an executable line. As many executable lines are there, those many semi-colons are required to be given at the end of each executable line.

printf( ) — It is a C function used for displaying constant or variable data on the screen. This function will be discussed in detail in the next chapter.

2. **Multiple level functions.** A multiple level function is the one in which one function makes call to another function. However, there is no precise limit to the number of functions that can be stored in a single program. Let us see an example of a multiple level function:

```
main()
{
    printf("Learning  C.");
    /* printing message on the screen */
    show-msg();
    printf("learning C.");
}
    show-msg()
    {
        printf("I am enjoying  ");
        /* printing another message */
    }
```

The output to this program will be like:
Learning C. I am enjoying learning C.

Here,

main( )	The first function to be executed.
printf( )	A function provided by C.
show-msg( )	It is a function defined by the programmer *(User-defined Function)* and can be independently called by another function.
( )	The round brackets are used at the end of each function name. It is used for passing values to functions. It may or may not contain any values.
;	A semi-colon is used to terminate all executable lines. If you have noticed carefully in the above example, a statement calling or executing a function needs to be terminated by a semi-colon (for example, show-msg( );). However, a statement that marks the beginning of a function definition does not require a semi-colon at the end (for example, show-msg( )).

In nutshell, each function must contain:

1. A function *heading*, which consists of the function name. The function name might contain an optional list of arguments enclosed in paranthesis.
2. A list of argument *declarations*, if arguments are included in the heading.
3. A *statement* which forms the rest of the function.
4. *Parameters* or *arguments* that represent information to be passed between the function and other parts of the program.
5. *Expression statements* which end with a semi-colon (;).
6. *Comments* can be given anywhere in the program to explain the underlying logic of a program. Comment lines are placed within the delimiters /* and */. Comments are optional and may or may not be given in a program.

These program components will become clearer to you by going through various C programs which will be discussed in greater detail in the subsequent chapters of this book. Now, let us discuss the basic elements used to construct simple C statements. These elements include the C character set, constants, identifiers, keywords, data types, declarations, expressions and statements. Let us discuss about them briefly.

14.4.1 The C Character Set

The C character set includes uppercase characters A to Z, lowercase alphabets a to z, digits 0 to 9 and certain special symbols to represent information. They act as building blocks to form basic program elements such as constants, variables, operators, etc. Table 14.1 shows the C character set.

Alphabets	A,B,C,D,........, X,Y,Z a,b,c,d,........, x,y,z
Digits	0,1,2,3,........, 7,8,9
Special symbols	! ~ ‘ ’ # % ^ & * ( ) - _ + = : [ ] { } ; \ : | " . < > / ? , (blank)

Table 14.1 *The C character set*

Certain other characters such as @ and $ are sometimes included within strings and comments.

The C language makes use of certain combination of characters such as \b, \n and \t to represent special conditions such as backspace, newline and horizontal tab, respectively. These special combination of characters are known as escape sequences and are treated as a single character.,

14.4.2 Constants

A constant can be defined as a value that remains fixed and does not change. This value can be stored in a memory location of the computer. The C constants can be broadly categorised into three types. They are numeric constants, character constants and string constants. Let us discuss about these types of constants briefly.

14.4.2.1 Numeric Constants

Numeric constants represent numbers. A numeric constant is again of two types which are integer constants and Floating point constants. Let us outline about these numeric constants briefly:

(*a*) **Integer Constants.** An integer constant is a number that is integer-valued. It comprises a sequence of digits. However, to form an integer constant, it must have atleast one digit. Integer constants do not carry a decimal point. They can be either positive or negative. However, if no sign is present before the integer constant then they are considered as positive. An integer constant cannot include commas or blank spaces. An integer constant can be written in three different number systems which are decimal (base 10), octal (base 8) and hexadecimal (base 16). The integer constants can have a value between –32768 to +32767.

Examples of Valid Integer Constants:

14
749
–8400
32765
–4328

(*b*) **Floating Point Constants.** Floating point constants are also known as real constants. A *real constant* is a base-10 number that can contain either a decimal point or an exponent (or both). A floating point constant comprises a sequence of digits with a decimal point. However, if no decimal point is present in the floating point constant then it is assumed to be present at the right side of the last number. A floating point constant can carry either a positive or a negative value. By default, the sign given to a floating point constant is positive. Like integer constants a floating point constant too cannot carry a comma or a blank space.

Examples of Valid Floating Point Constants

0.2
12.3
+346.48
–43.78
326.0098

Floating point or real constants are represented in exponential form if the value of the constant is either too small or too large. In the exponential form, a real constant comprises two parts i.e. mantissa and exponent. This will become clearer through an example. Suppose, there is a number 1.4×10^{-8} whose exponential form is written as 1.4 e – 8. The mantissa and exponent part of this number are shown below:

1.4 e	–8
mantissa	Exponent

Thus, mantissa appears before 'e' and exponent appears after 'e'. Thus, the mantissa and the exponent part are separated from each other by the letter 'e'. The mantissa may have a positive or a negative sign. If no sign is present in the mantissa part, then it is considered to be positive. However, the exponent part should essentially contain either a positive sign or a negative sign. The default sign of the exponent is positive. The magnitude of a floating point constant ranges between 3.4 E –38 to 3.4E + 38.

Examples of Floating Point Numbers Represented in Exponential Form:

+1.2e–6
–1.2e–6
2.1e+8
3.0e+5
–3.1e–6

14.4.2.2 Character constants

A character constant is a single alphabet, digit or special symbol enclosed in apostrophes or single quotation marks (' '). Both the inverted commas should point to the left side. The maximum length of a character constant is just one character.

Examples of Character Constants:

'A'
'c'
'7'
'$'
'!'

Most personal computers make use of the ASCII (American Standard Code for Information Interchange) character set. In ASCII character set, each single character is numerically encoded with its own unique 7-bit combination. In all, a total of $2^7 = 128$ different characters have been standardized by ASCII. Table 14.2 shows the ASCII character set. If you have observed this table carefully, you will notice that the characters are ordered as well as encoded. The digits are ordered in the numerical sequence like 0, 1, 2, ...7, 8, 9 and the alphabets are arranged in an alphabetical order. The uppercase letters precede the lowercase letters.

ASCII Value	Character	ASCII Value	Character
000	NUL	008	BS
001	SOH	009	HT
002	STX	010	LF
003	ETX	011	VT
004	EOT	012	FF
005	ENQ	013	CR
006	ACK	014	SO
007	BEL	015	SI

ASCII Value	Character	ASCII Value	Character
016	DLE	060	<
017	DC1	061	=
018	DC2	062	>
019	DC3	063	?
020	DC4	064	@
021	NAK	065	A
022	SYN	066	B
023	ETB	067	C
024	CAN	068	D
025	EM	069	E
026	SUB	070	F
027	ESC	071	G
028	FS	072	H
029	GS	073	I
030	RS	074	J
031	US	075	K
032	blank	076	L
033	!	077	M
034	”	078	N
035	#	079	O
036	$	080	P
037	%	081	Q
038	&	082	R
039	’	083	S
040	(	084	T
041	)	085	U
042	*	086	V
043	+	087	W
044	,	088	X
045	–	089	Y
046	.	090	Z
047	/	091	[
048	0	092	\
049	1	093	]
050	2	094	↑
051	3	095	—
052	4	096	
053	5	097	a
054	6	098	b
055	7	099	c
056	8	100	d
057	9	101	e
058	:	102	f
059	;	103	g

ASCII Value	Character	ASCII Value	Character
104	h	116	t
105	i	117	u
106	j	118	v
107	k	119	w
108	l	120	x
109	m	121	y
110	n	122	z
111	o	123	{
112	p	124	|
113	q	125	}
114	r	126	~
115	s	127	DEL

Note: The first 32 characters and the last character are control characters; they cannot be printed.

Table 14.2 *The ASCII character set*

14.4.2.3 String constants

A string constant is a constant that comprises any sequence of characters (including non-alphabetic characters) which are enclosed in double quotation marks (" "). Infact, strings are character arrays. Each string constant has one extra character than the actual characters input to accomodate a string terminator represented by \0. This string terminator is not displayed when the string is printed. The compiler automatically places a null character (\0) or a string terminator at the end of every string constant, as the last character within the string.

Examples of String Constants:

"red"
"Mumbai"
"Red Fort, Delhi"
"East West North South"
"Welcome to C"

It is worthwhile to note here that a character constant (e.g., 'C') and the coresponding single-character string constant (e.g., "C") are not equivalent. Here the character constant has an integer value of 1 whereas the string constant comprises of two characters *i.e.* the specified character followed by the null character (\0).

14.4.3 Identifiers

Identifiers are the names given to various elements of a program. These include variables, functions and arrays. An identifier may consist of numeric and alphabetic characters. The first character of an identifier must essentially start with a character. An identifier can be formed by both uppercase and lowercase characters, though both of them have different ASCII represersation. The C compiler considers A and a as different alphabets as has already been discussed. It is recommeded to use lowercase letters for most of the identifiers. Thus, both the uppercase and lowercase characters are not interchangeable. The underscore is also a recognizable character. An underscore is often used in the middle of an identifier.

An underscore can also be given in the beginning of the identifier but this practice is generally not followed.

An identifier can be arbitrarily given. Some versions of C recognize only the first eight characters. The ANSI standard, however, recognises 31 characters. A programmer must give meaningful names of identifiers and the number of characters in an identifier must be kept as small as possible.

Examples of Identifiers:

add num	magnitude	sum
power	num	acctspay

The following are invalid identifiers:

"Name"	(Illegal quotes)
add-num	(Illegal character)
multiply numbers	(Space included)
56 abc	(The first character is a digit)
break	(keyboard)

14.4.4 Keywords

Keywords are reserved words that have been made standard and have predefined meanings in C. Their meaning has already been explained to the C compiler. These keywords cannot be used as variables, function names or constants. However, some C compilers allow you to construct variable names which exactly resemble the keywords. It is recommended not to mix up the variable names and the keywords. All the keywords are given in lowercase characters. As you are already aware, the C compiler treats the uppercase letters different from the lowercase characters, you can use an uppercase keyword as an identifier. Generally, this is considered as a bad programming practice. As far as possible you should try not to use the uppercase keywords as identifiers. Table 14.3 shows the list of keywords used in C.

auto	double	if	static
break	else	int	struct
case	enum	long	switch
char	extern	near	typedef
const	float	register	union
continue	far	return	unsigned
default	for	short	void
do	goto	signed	while

Table 14.3 *A list of C keywords*

14.4.5 Data Types

In C language, different types of data can be entered. Each of these types of data are represented differently in the computer's memory. The C data types are of two types–Fundamental and Derived data types. Let us discuss these briefly.

14.4.5.1 Fundamental Data Types

The fundamental data types are the data types at the lowest level. These are actually used for representing data in the memory. All the other data types are derived from fundamental data types. The fundamental data types include—

(*a*) **Characters.** This data type is used to represent individual characters or strings. Hence, a char type requires only 1 byte of memory.

(*b*) **Integer.** This data type is used for representing integer quantities.

(*c*) **Float.** This data type represent numeric values having decimals in between.

Table 14.4: shows the storage requirements of the above data types.

Data Type	Description	Typical memory Requirements	Minimum Value	Maximum Value
char	Single Character	1 byte	0	255
int	Integer quantity	4 bytes (or 1 word)	2^32	(2^32)–1
float	Number containing a decimal decimal	4 bytes (or 1 word)	6 digits of precision	6 digits of precision

14.4.5.2 Derived Data Types

Derived data types are the data types that are based on fundamental data types. These data types are represented in memory as fundamental data types. The derived data types include short int, long int, double float, etc. A short int may require less memory than an ordinary int or it may require the same amount of memory as ordinary int but it will never exceed an ordinary int in word length. On similar grounds, a long int may require either equal memory or more memory as compared to ordinary int but it will never be less than ordinary int. Double float is a double-precision floating point number. It may require 2 words or 8 bytes of memory. The derived data types are summarised in Table 14.5.

Data Type	Description	Total memory Requirement	Minimum value	Maximum value
short int	Integer quantity	2 bytes	–2^16	(2^16)–1
long int	Integer quantity	4 bytes	–2^32	(2^32)–1
double float	Double precision floating point number	8 bytes	12 digits of precision	12 digits of precision

Table 14.5 *Derived data types of C*

14.4.6 Variables

A variable is a named entity which may vary during the execution of a program. A variable represents a single data item that can be either numeric or character. A variable name is a name given to the memory locations of the computer where different constants are stored. At any point in the program, the data item must be assigned to the variable. This data item can then be accessed later in the program by referring to the name of the variable. A variable name is a combination of 1 to 8 alphabets, digits or underscores. All the variable names must start with an alphabet and it cannot include commas or blanks within. No special symbol other than the underscore (–) is allowed within a variable name.

Examples:

```
char name;
int num1, num2;
```

A given variable can be assigned different data items at various places within the program. Thus, the values stored in a variable can change during the execution of a program. During program execution, the data types of the variables cannot change.

14.4.7 Arrays

The C language makes extensive usage of arrays. An array can be defined as an identifier or a variable name given to a collection of data items. The data items must be of the same data type. The array elements represent the individual data items. For instance, the first array element represents the first data item, the second array element represents the second data item and so on. We will discuss about arrays in detail in latter part of this book.

14.4.8 Declarations

Declarations generally appear in the beginning of a program. A declaration groups a set of variables with a specific data type. All the variables must be properly declared before they can appear in executable statements. Declarations comprise of a data-type followed by one or more variable names. These variable names are separated from each other by commas. A declaration ends with a semi-colon. In nutshell, a declaration can take the following form.

```
data type (list of variable names)
```

or

```
data type var1, var2, . . .  varn;
```

Each array variable must be followed by a pair of square brackets containing a positive integer which signifies the size of the array. The size of array represents the number of elements present in an array.

Example:

```
int num1, num2;
char name, add;
```

Here, num1 and num2 are the variables of integer type. On similar grounds, name and add are two variables having character data type.

The above-mentioned declarations can also be written as:

```
int num1;
int num2;
char name;
char add;
```

In general practice, the variables having the same data type are clubbed in a single declaration. The memory is allocated to the variables automatically.

Integer type variables can be declared as short integer or long integer. Less storage space is allocated to short integers as compared to long integers. Typically 2 bytes are allocated to short integer variable and 4 bytes or 1 word each to ordinary integer variable. A long integer variable typically gets 8 bytes or 2 words of memory. To declare a short integer variable, simply write short int or short. Similarly, to declare long integer just write long int or long.

Example:

```
short int add, sub;
long int mul, divide;
int num1, num2;
```

The above declarations can also be written as:

```
short add, sub;
long mul, divide;
int num1, num2;
```

Now, you can easily make out the amount of memory allocated to each of these variables. The variables add and sub are allocated 2 bytes each. The variables mul and divide get 8 bytes each and the variables num1, num2 get 4 bytes each.

An integer variable can also be declared as unsigned by specifying either unsigned int or simply unsigned. Unsigned integer variables can be larger than ordinary integer variables by approximately twice the size. The unsigned integer variables can have a positive value only and they cannot be negative.

Example:

```
int temp, ctr;
unsigned int a, b, c;
```

The above declarations can also be written as:

```
int temp, ctr;
unsigned a, b, c;
```

You can assign initial values to the variables within a type declaration. This is called initialization of a variable. To initialize a variable, the declaration must comprise a data type variable name, an equal sign (=) followed by a constant of an appropriate type. The declaration must end with a semicolon.

Example:

```
int ctr = 1;
char ans='y';
```

Here, ctr is an integer variable that has the initial value as 1 and ans as charactertype variable initially assigned the character 'y'.

You can also initialize a character type array within a declaration. This is done by explicitly giving an array name, square brackets, equal to sign followed by a string which is enclosed in quotes. Generally, the size of the array is not explicitly specified i.e. the square brackets are kept empty. As usual, the declaration ends with a semicolon.

Example:

```
char city[ ] = "Mumbai"
```

This will create an array by the name city whose size is 7 elements. The first six characters represent the six characters of the word Mumbai and the seventh element represents the null character (\0). The null character is added automatically at the end of the string. The above-mentioned declaration can also be given as:

```
char city[7] = "Mumbai";
```

Here, the size of the array has been explicitly defined. If the size of the array is specified too small, then the characters at the end of the string are lost. For instance,

```
char city[4] = "Mumbai";
```

Here, the last three words i.e.; ai and \0 of the word Mumbai will be lost.

If the size of the array is too large, then the extra array elements are either filled with zeros or meaningless characters.

14.4.9 Expressions

An expression comprises a single data item. This data item can be a character or a number. An expression can be formed from a single entity such as a constant, a variable, an array element or a reference to a function. An expression can also be made from a combination of these entities which are connected to each other by operators. One or more operators are commonly used in C language to form expressions. Logical conditions can also be specified with the help of expressions. Logical conditions signify either true or false and are represented by the integer values, 1 and 0, respectively. It can be safely said that the logical-type expressions represent numerical quantities.

Examples:

```
x + y
l = m
sum = num1 + num2
a < b
a = = b
```

• Here, the first expression makes use of the addition operator (+). It represents the addition of the values stored in two variables named x and y.

• The second expression uses the assignment operator (=). Here, the value stored in the variable named m is assigned to another variable named *l*.

• The third expression adds the values stored in two variables i.e. num1 and num 2 and the added up value is assigned to the third variable named sum.

• The fourth variable represents the logical condition and this expression will have the value 1 (true) if the value of a is less than the value stored in the variable b. Otherwise, the expression contains the value false (0).

• The last expression uses the comparison operator (==). If the values of both the variables i.e. a and b are equal. Then the expression stores a value of 1 (true). Otherwise, it stores a value of 0 (false).

14.4.10 Statements

Statements are the executable code in C. They cause the computer to carry out some action. C language has three different types of statements which are expression statements, compound statements and control statements. Let us discuss each of these types of statements briefly.

14.4.10.1 Expression Statements

An expression statement comprises an expression followed by a semicolon. When the C compiler executes an expression statement, then this expression is evaluated.

Examples:

```
sum = 3;
add = sum + num1;
++i;
;
```

In the example, the first two expression statements are assignment statements. Both these statements cause the value stored in the variables on the right hand side to be assigned to the variables present on the left hand side of the assignment operator (=).

The third expression statement causes the value of the operator i to be increased by 1. This is also called *increment operator (++)*. The last expression statement is a null statement. It does not do anything because it comprises of a semicolon only.

14.4.10.2 Compound Statements

A compound statement comprises a number of individual statements that are enclosed within a pair of braces. It allows you to embed a number of statements within other statements. A compound statement does not end with a semicolon.

Example:

```
{
    pi = 3.141593;
    surface_area_of_sphere = 4*pi*radius*radius;

    volume_of_sphere = 4*pi*radius*radius*radius;
}
```

This compound statement comprises of three expression statements. It is considered a single entity when it appears in a program.

14.4.10.3 Control Statements

Control statements are used where a program employs special features such as logical tests, loops and branches. Many other statements are included in a single control statement.

Example:

```
while (ctr <= 10)
{
    printf("Sum is:");
    scanf("%f",&sum);
    sum = sum + 10;
    ctr = ctr + 1;
}
```

This statement is a control statement and it further contains one compound statement and four expression statements within a compound statement. The compound statement will be executed till the value of the variable ctr does not exceed the value of 10.

14.5 CREATING PROGRAMS IN C

In C language, creating and executing a program is a four step process. Firstly, you are required to create a disk file that contains your source code. This is done with the help of an editor. Secondly, an object file is created by compiling the source code. Thirdly, the compiled code is linked so that an executable file is created. In the fourth step, you run the program. Let us discuss these four steps briefly:

14.5.1 Creation of Source Code

Source code is a series of statements or commands that form a program. These statements when executed help to achieve the desired tasks. This source code is entered into an editor. Most compilers have a built-in editor that allow you to enter your source code. However, if your compiler does not have one, then you can make use of many other alternative editors. Many computer systems have a program that can be used as an editor.

The UNIX system has many editors such as ed, ex, emacs or vi. If you are using Microsoft Windows, Notepad is available. The Edit editor is available on MS DOS 5.0 or later versions. If you are using a version of DOS before 5.0, then you can make use of the EDLIN editor. The summarised list of various editors that can be used for entering the C source code is given in Table 14.6.

Operating system	Editors
UNIX	ed ex edit emacs vi
Microsoft Windows	Notepad
MS-DOS 5.0 or before	Edlin
MS-DOS 5.0 or later	Edit
PC/DOS 6.0 or later	E
OS/2	E EPM

Table 14.6 *List of available editors*

If you do not want to use any of these editors, then you can buy a different editor from the market. They are available as commercial packages or shareware.

After entering the source code in a file, it must be given a name and saved. It is recommended that you should give meaningful names to your files. The extension given to a C file is .c, for example, myfirst.c is valid filename.

14.5.2 Compiling the Source Code

After entering the source code in a file, you are required to compile it. Compiling the source code would change it into machine language that is easily understood by the computer. The computer cannot directly understand your source code. Hence, the source is changed into binary or digital code with the help of a program known as *compiler*. The compiler takes your source code file as input and produce a file that has corresponding machine language instructions. These machine language instructions are called the *object code* and the file that contains these instructions is called the *object file*. There are a number of compilers available which convert your source file into object file. Each of these compilers has its own set of commands to create the object code. To compile your source code, you are required to give the command to run the compiler followed by the source filename. If you are to compile a file named myfirst.c on a UNIX machine, just issue the following command:

```
cc myfirst.c
```

Table 14.7 shows the commands that are given to compile a source file using various DOS/Windows compilers.

Compiler Name	Command
Microsoft C	cl myfirst.c
Borland's Turbo C	tcc myfirst.c
Zortec C	ztc myfirst.c
Borland C	bcc myfirst.c

Table 14.7 *Commands to compile a file using different compilers.*

Compiling is easy if you are using a graphical environment. In graphical development environment, compiling is done by simply selecting the compile icon from the menu. Now, to run the compiled file, you are required to choose the run or related option from the menu.

Once the compiling is done, an object file is created. This object file has the same primary name as that of your source file but the extension given to this file is .OBJ instead of .c. The .OBJ extension is recognised as an object file and is used by the linker. On UNIX systems, the object files get the extension .O instead of .OBJ.

14.5.3 Linking

In C language, the source code that you write is converted to object code by the compiler. This object code is converted to an executable file by a program called linker. The process of creating an executable file from the object code is called *linking*.

There are some predefined functions which are available from the C function library. These predefined functions contain the C code that has already been written and supplied in the ready-to-use state with your compiler package such as printf( ), scanf( ), etc. These functions perform frequently needed tasks such as displaying information on the screen, reading data from disk files, etc. If your program makes use of these library functions, then the object file produced must be associated with the object code from the function library to create the final executable program. The final executable program means the program that is ready to be run or executed on your computer.

14.5.4 Executing

You can run your program once it has been successfully compiled and linked to create an executable file. To run your file, simply type in the name of the file at the system prompt. If you feel that the program is not producing the desired results then you have to restart the process straight from first step. It would involve making changes to the source code, recompiling the source code, relinking the program to create a new version of the executable file. Finally, you are required to run the file by typing its name at the system prompt. You will have to repeat this process till the time you are not satisfied with the output produced by the program.

14.6 TURBO C COMPILER

The Turbo C compiler is also known as Borland Turbo C compiler. It is a good debugging tool which is very inexpensive. It has a good support of graphics. Table 14.8 summarises the commonly used Turbo C commands:

Hot Key	Menu Function
<F1>	Displays Help Screen (Help)
<F2>	Saves active editor file (File/Save)
<F3>	Opens a file (File/Open)
<F4>	Executes to cursor location (Run/Go to Cursor)
<F5>	Zooms the active window (Window/Zoom)
<F6>	Cycles through open windows (Window/Next)
<F7>	Traces into subroutines (Run/Trace into)
<F8>	Steps over subroutine calls (Run/Step Over)
<F10>	Activates the menu bar
<Alt+F1>	Displays previous Help Screen (Help/Previous topic)
<Alt+F3>	Closes active window (Window/Close)
<Alt+F5>	Displays user screen (Window/User Screen)
<Alt+F9>	Compiles active program (Compile/Compile)
<Alt+Spacebar>	Goes to System menu
<Alt+C>	Goes to Compile menu
<Alt+D>	Goes to Debug menu
<Alt+E>	Goes to Edit menu
<Alt+F>	Goes to File menu
<Alt+H>	Goes to Help menu
<Alt+O>	Goes to Options menu
<Alt+R>	Goes to Run menu
<Alt+S>	Goes to Search menu
<Alt+W>	Goes to Window menu
<Alt+X>	Exits Turbo C to DOS (File/Exit)
<Ctrl+F9>	Executes active program (Run/Run)

Table 14.8 *Commonly used Turbo C commands*

Let us briefly see the Turbo C operation commands. These commands are summarised in Table 14.9.

Function	Keystroke
Character left	<Left arrow> or <Ctrl+S>
Character right	<Right arrow> or <Ctrl+D>
Word left	<Ctrl+left arrow> or <Ctrl+A>
Word right	<Ctrl+right arrow> or <Ctrl+F>
Line up	<Up arrow> or <Ctrl+E>
Line down	<Down arrow> or <Ctrl+X>
Page Up	<PgU> or <Ctrl+R>
Page down	<PgDn> or <Ctrl+C>
Beginning of line	<Home> or <Ctrl+Q/S>
End of line	<End> or <Ctrl+Q/D>
Insert line	<Ctrl+N>
Delete line	<Ctrl+Y>
Delete block	<Ctrl+K/Y>
Delete till end of line	<Ctrl+Q/Y>
Delete a character to the left of cursor	<Backspace> or <Ctrl+H>
Delete character at current cursor	<Delete> or <Ctrl+G>

position	
Copy block of lines to edit a file	<Ctrl+K/C>
Copy block of lines to clipboard	<Ctrl+Ins> or <Edit/Copy>
Delete block	<Ctrl+Del> or <Edit/Clear>
Mark block begin	<Ctrl+K/B>
Mark block end	<Ctrl+K/K>
Move block from clipboard	<Shift+Ins> or <Edit/Paste>
Invoke main menu	<F10>
Language help	<Ctrl+F1>
Open file	<File/open> or <F3>
Save file	File/save> or <F2>

Table 14.9 *Commonly used Turbo C operation commands*

THEORY QUESTIONS

1. What are the characteristics or features of C language?
2. Discuss briefly the history of C.
3. What is the structure of a C program? What is the significance attached to the name mai?
4. Differentiate between single level and multi-level functions.
5. What is a compound statement? How is a compound statement written?
6. What is an expression statement? Can an expression statement be included in a compound statement?
7. What are comments and how are they included within a C program?
8. What punctuation mark is used to end most of the C statements? Do all statements require this punctuation mark?
9. List the merits and demerits of C language.
10. What are data types? Differentiate between fundamental and derived data types.
11. What is meant by identifiers? How is a user-defined identifier different from a keyword?
12. What are structured languages? Is C a structured language?
13. Define the following terms:
    (*a*) Constants
    (*b*) Variables
    (*c*) Arrays
    (*d*) Declarations
    (*e*) Control Statements
14. Write the steps to create a program in C.
15. Differentiate between a compiler and a linker.
16. Name the operating systems and the editors supported by them.
17. Name the different compilers available in the market and the corresponding commands to compile a file temp.c.
18. Write the command to run an executable file.
19. Write the commands in Turbo C to perform the following actions:
    (*a*) To activate the menu bar
    (*b*) Open a file
    (*c*) Save a file
    (*d*) Insert a line
    (*e*) Compile active program
20. How is short int different from long int?

15
BASIC C FEATURES

15.1 INTRODUCTION

In the last chapter, we discussed about the structure of a C program briefly. We also learnt as to how to enter and run a C program. In this lesson, we will discuss about the different operators used in C. Specifically, we will get ourselves acquainted with arithmetic operators, relational operators, logical operators, unary operators, assignment operators, etc. We will also discuss about the different functions provided by the C library. There are other standard C functions as well which are included in almost all the C programs. These standard functions include the getchar( ) function, the putchar( ) function, the scanf( ) function, the printf( ) function etc. In the latter part of the chapter, we will be discussing about these functions along with some programming examples which make use of these functions.

15.2 OPERATORS IN C

The C language includes a number of operators. These operators are used in different combinations to form expressions. An *operator* can be defined as a symbol that specifies an operation to be performed. The data items on which the operators act upon are called *operands.* Some operators require a single operand while others might require two operands to act upon. The order in which the operations are performed by operators is known as the *order of precedence.* As discussed earlier also, C has rich set of operators. It makes extensive use of a variety of operators. Let us now discuss these different categories of operators available in C language.

15.2.1 Arithmetic Operators

Arithmetic operators are used to form arithmetic expressions. The arithmetic operators used in the C language are listed in Table 15.1.

Operator Name	Operator Symbol	Meaning
Addition	+	Addition
Subtraction	–	Subtraction
Multiplication	*	Multiplication
Division	/	Division
Modulus	%	Remainder

Table 15.1 *The Arithmetic Operators*

Example:

Let var1 and var2 be the two integer variables having the value 20 and 6, respectively. Form various arithmetic expressions using operators and find the resulted output.

Expression		Result
var1 + var 2	20 + 6	26
var1 – var 2	20 – 6	14
var1 * var 2	20 * 6	120
var1 / var 2	20 / 6	3
var1 % var 2	20 % 6	2

Thus, the operands can have an integer value, floating point number or characters. The character constants are represented as integer values, as determined by the ASCII character set.

Example:

Suppose v1 and v2 are two character type variables having the characters A and S, respectively. The arithmetic expressions that make use of these variables and the resultant output is shown below :

Expression	Result
v1	65
v2	83
v1 + v2	148
v1 + v2 + 7	155
v1 + v2 + '7'	203

Note that the characters A and S hold the values 65 and 83 respectively in the ASCII character set.

If any of the operands represent negative values, then the usual rules of algebra apply to them for performing any arithmetic operation.

As discussed earlier also, the operations carried out in the arithmetic expression follow an order of precedence. Operations having higher precedence are carried out first. The multiplication, division and remainder operations enjoy higher precedence over addition and subtraction. The natural order of expression evaluation can be modified with the use of parentheses.The associativity of these operators is from left to right.

15.2.2 Relational Operators

The relational operators required for evaluating the conditions are similar to those in other languages. C has four relational operators which are listed in Table 15.2.

Operator Symbol	Meaning
<	Less than
<=	Less than or equal to
>	Greater than
>=	Greater than or equal to
==	Equal to
!=	Not equal to

Table 15.2 *The Relational Operators*

The relational operators mentioned in Table 15.2 are used to form logical expressions. These logical expressions form conditions which either have the value true or false. The conditions true or false are represented as integer values and have the values 1 or 0 respectively. Thus, a true condition is represented by the integer value 1 and the false condition is represented by the integer value 0. All these operators have the left-to-right associativity.

Example:

Suppose there are two integer variables p and q having the values 10 and 20. Several expressions formed using relational operators are :

Expression	Result	Value
p < q	true	1
p > q	false	0
p != q	true	1
p == 10	true	1

Example:

Assume that p is an integer variable having the value 17 and C is a character variable holding the character 'n'. Let us assume that the ASCII character set rules apply to this character variable. Several expressions using these variables and relational operators are shown below :

Expression	Result	Value
p < 20	true	1
p == 17	true	1
c == 110	true	1
c != a	true	1
p > 20 * (c)	false	0

15.2.3 Logical Operators

Logical operators are used to evaluate conditional statements. They are also used to combine conditions. The logical operators act upon operands. C supports three logical operators that are shown in Table 15.3.

Operator Symbol	Operator Name
||	OR
&&	AND
!	NOT

Table 15.3 *The logical operators*

The logical operators help to combine the individual logical expressions which form complex conditions. The result of a logical operation is either true or false. The result of a logical OR operation is true if either or all of the operands in the logical expression are true. Hence, if all the operands are false, then only the result of a logical OR operation is evaluated as false.

The result of the logical AND operator is true if all the operands present in the logical expression are evaluated as true. However, if even a single operand has a false value, then the net result of the logical AND operator is evaluated as false.

The logical NOT operator is used to reverse the meaning of a logical expression. For instance, if the logical expression is evaluated as true, then the NOT operator causes the expression to become false and vice-versa. In simple words, the NOT operator negates the result of the logical expression.

Example:

Let p and q be two integer variables having the values 10 and 15 respectively. The logical expressions formed using logical operators are shown below :

Expression	Result
(p <= 10) && (q ≥ 15)	true
(p <= 10) || (q < 10)	true
! ((p <= 10) || (q < 10))	false

As far as precedence of logical operators is concerned, the logical NOT operator is evaluated before AND which is evaluated before OR. However, this precedence can be changed with the use of parentheses (). The associativity of the logical operators is from left to right.

15.2.4 Unary Operators

The unary operator is so called because it acts upon a single operand only. Unary operators are generally given before the operand but sometimes, they can also be given after the operand. In C language, all numeric constants are positive. The most widely used unary operator is unary minus. A minus sign is given before a numerical constant, variable or an expression. In short, a negative number in C language is nothing but a unary minus operator followed by a positive numeric constant. For instance, –437, –14.2, –(a * b * c), etc. In all these examples, a minus sign is followed by either a numeric constant, a numeric variable or an arithmetic expression. Unary operators are further classified as—

(*a*) Increment Operator

(*b*) Decrement Operator

Let us discuss about these operators briefly.

15.2.4.1 Increment Operators

The increment operator increments the value of the operand by 1. For instance, if there is an integer variable p having the value 15, then using the increment operator (++p) will increase its value by 1 thus making 16. Its equivalent logical expression is p = p+1.

15.4.2.2 Decrement Operators

Unlike increment operators, the decrement operators decrease the value of the operand by 1. For instance, if there is an integer variable q having the value 15, then using the decrement operator (-- q) will tend to reduce its value by 1, thus, giving it the final result as 14. The logical expression formed using decrement operator is q = q–1.

The increment and decrement operators can be given either before or after the operand and likewise, they convey different results. For instance, let there be two numeric variables tot and sub_tot, then using the increment operator before and after the operand has different results.

```
tot = sub_tot++;
```

and

```
tot = ++sub_tot;
```

The first statement is equivalent to:

```
tot = sub_tot;
sub_tot = sub_tot+1;
```

whereas, the result of the second statement is as:

```
sub_tot = sub_tot + 1;
total = sub_total;
```

The ++ increment operator in sub_tot++ is known as the *post increment operator* whereas the ++sub_tot is known as the *pre increment operator*.

The above rules hold true for decrement operators as well.

Unary operators have higher precedence over the arithmetic operators. The associativity of unary operators is from right to left.

15.2.5 Assignment Operators

Assignment Operators are used to form assignment expressions. C supports a rich variety of assignment operators. The assignment operators help in assigning the value of an expression to an identifier. The most widely used assignment operator is =. The syntax of the assignment expression which use this operator is given below:

```
variable = expression;
```

where expression can be a constant, a variable or an expression.

For instance,

```
num = 54;
add = sum 1 + sum 2;
a = b;
```

The first assignment expression assigns the value 54 to the variable named num. The second assignment expression causes the result of the arithmetic expression (sum 1 + sum 2) to be assigned to the the numeric variable add. The third assignment expression causes the value of the variable b to be assigned to the numeric variable a.

The operands in an assignment expression should be of same data types. However, if the operands are of different data types, then the value of the right hand operand will automatically be converted to the type of the variable on the left. This way the complete assignment expression will comprise of variables having the same data types. Sometimes, this type of practice can result in the modification of the data being assigned to the variables. For instance, a floating–point value may be truncated if assigned to an integer variable.

Note : It is important to notify that the assignment operator (=) is different from the equality operator (==). As discussed earlier also, the assignment operator is used to assign a value to a variable. For instance, ctr = 2. However, the equality operator is used to test for equality between the values of two expressions. For instance, ctr1 == ctr2. Thus, both these operators cannot be used in place of each-other.

The C language has other assignment operators as well. These are +=, –=, *=, /= and %=. Let us see how they are used to form assignment expressions.

```
ctr 1 += ctr 2;
```

is equivalent to

```
ctr1 = ctr1 + ctr 2;
```

On similar grounds,

```
ctrl -= ctr2;
```

is equivalent to

```
ctrl = ctrl - ctr2;
```

Rest of the assignment operators are also used in a similar manner.

Example:

Assume that there are three numeric variables a, b and c having the values 6, 9 and 12, respectively. Let us formulate different assignment expressions.

Expression	Interpretation	Result
a += 6	a = a + 6	12
b –= a	b = b – a	3
c *= (b – 1)	c = c * (b – 1)	96
c /= 3	c = c/3	4
c %= (b – a)	c = c % (b – a)	0

The associativity of the assignment operators is from right to left. As far as precedence is concerned, the assignment operators have the lowest precedence over all other operators such as unary operators, arithmetic operators, relational operators, equality operators and logical operators.

15.2.6 Conditional Operators

Conditional operators are used to carry out simple conditional operations. The expressions formed from conditional operators are known as *conditional expressions.* The syntax of the conditional expression is given below:

```
expression1 ? expression2 : expression3
```

The conditional operators are represented by the symbols ? :. While evaluating a conditional expression, the expression1 is evaluated first. If it is true, then the expression2 is evaluated and its value is given as result otherwise the value stored in expression3 is given as result.

In any case, while evaluating if the expression1 turns out to be false, then the expression2 is not evaluated. Instead expression3 is evaluated and this becomes the result of the conditional expression. Thus, the result of the conditional expression comes either from expression2 or expression3. For instance, examine the following conditional expression

```
(p < q ? p : q)
```

Here, the expression1 is evaluated first. If the value of the variable p is less than the value of the variable q, then p is given as output otherwise q is given as output.

Table 15.4 shows the precedence as well as the associativity of different operators discussed so far.

Operator Type	Operator Symbol	Associativity
Unary Operators	– ++ – – !	R ⟶ L
Arithmetic Operators	* / % + –	L ⟶ R
Relational Operators	< <= > >= == !=	L ⟶ R
Logical Operators	! && ||	L ⟶ R
Conditional Operators	? :	R ⟶ L
Assignment Operators	= += –= *= /= %=	R ⟶ L

Table 15.4 *Operator Precedence and Associativity*

15.3 LIBRARY FUNCTIONS IN C

The C language comprises a library of standard functions. Most versions of C provide the libraries in both source code and relocatable code. The relocatable code is already compiled into an intermediate code which is linked with the compiled main program to form the final object code program. These standard functions perform most of the commonly used operations or calculations such as input/output operations (read and write characters), open and close files, functions that perform operations on characters (conversion from lower case to uppercase and vice-versa), functions to carry out mathematical calculations (finding square roots, evaluate trigonometric expressions), functions that perform operations on strings (comparing two strings, concatenating strings), etc.

You can also add new functions to the existing library by typing the source code in any text editor. Then, you are required to recompile the library source code. Now, when the library is linked by the linker, the new functions can be incorporated by the linker into the object code. You should be extremely cautious while attempting to add functions to the standard library.

The functions which are functionally similar can be clubbed together and compiled in separate library files as object programs. You can access the function by simply writing the function name followed by a list of arguments. Some commonly used library functions of C are given in Table 15.5.

Function	Type	Purpose	Include File
abs(i)	int	Returns the absolute value of i.	stdlib.h
atof(s)	double	Converts string s to a double-precision quantity.	stdlib.h
atoi(s)	int	Converts string s into an integer.	stdlib.h
atol(s)	long	Converts string s to a long integer.	stdlib.h
exit(u)	void	Closes all files and buffers and terminates the program.	stdlib.h
fclose(f)	int	Closes file f. Returns 0 if the file is successfully closed.	stdio.h
fgetc(f)	int	Enters a single character from file f.	stdio.h
fgets(s,i,f)	char	Enter string s, containing i characters, from file f.	stdio.h
fopen(s1,s2)	FILE*	Opens a file named s1 of s2 type. Returns a pointer to a file.	stdio.h
fprintf(f,...)	int	Sends data items to file f.	stdio.h
fputc(c,f)	int	Sends a single character to file f.	stdio.h
fputs(s,f)	int	Sends string s to file f.	stdio.h
fread(s,i1,i2,f)	int	Inputs i2 data items each of size i1 bytes, from file f to string s.	stdio.h
free(p)	void	Frees a block of allocated memory whose starting address is indicated by p.	malloc.h or stdlib.h
fscanf(f,...)	int	Inputs data items from file f.	stdio.h
fseek(f,l,i)	int	Moves the pointer for file f at distance 1 bytes from location i (i may represent pointer position or end-of-file).	stdio.h

ftell(f)	longint	Returns the current pointer position within file f.	stdio.h
fwrite(s,i1,i2,f)	int	Sends i2 data items, each of size i1 bytes from string s to file f.	stdio.h
getc(f)	int	Inputs a single character from file f.	stdio.h
getchar()	int	Inputs a single character from the standard input device.	stdio.h
isalnum(c)	int	Determines if argument is alphanumeric.	ctype.h
isalpha(c)	int	Determines if the argument is alphabetic. Returns non-zero value if true; 0 otherwise.	ctype.h
isascii(c)	int	Determines if the argument is an ASCII character. Returns non-zero value if true, 0 otherwise.	ctype.h
isdigit(c)	int	Determines if argument is a decimal digit. Returns non-zero value if true; 0 otherwise.	ctype.h
islower(c)	int	Determines if argument is in lower-case character. Returns non-zero if true, 0 otherwise.	ctype.h
isspace(c)	int	Determines if argument is a whitespace character. Returns non-zero value if true; 0 otherwise.	ctype.h
isupper(c)	int	Determines if argument is in upper case. Returns non-zero value if true; 0 otherwise.	ctype.h
malloc(u)	void	Allocates u bytes of memory. Returns a pointer to the beginning of the allocated space.	malloc.h or stdlib.h
pow(d1,d2)	double	Returns d1 raised to the power d2.	math.h
printf(...)	int	Sends data items to the standard output device.	stdio.h
putchar(c)	int	Sends a single character to the output device.	stdio.h
puts(s)	int	Sends the string s to the standard output device.	stdio.h
scanf(....)	int	Allows input of data items from the standard ouput device.	stdio.h
strcmp(s1,s2)	int	Compares two strings. Returns a –ve value if s1 < s2, 0 if s1 = s2, +ve if s1 > s2.	string.h
strcpy(s1,s2)	char*	Copies string s2 to string s1.	string.h
strlen(s)	int	Returns the number of characters in string s.	string.h
toascii(c)	int	Converts value of argument to ASCII.	ctype.h
tolower(c)	int	Converts value of argument to lower-case.	ctype.h or stdlib.h
toupper(c)	int	Converts letter to upper-case.	ctype.h or stdlib.h
rewind(f)	void	Moves the pointer to the beginning of file f.	stdio.h

Table 15.5 *Library functions of C*

To use the standard library functions, we have to include certain specific information within the main portion of the program. This type of information is stored in special files. These special files are accessed with the preprocessor statement #include and followed by the filename as shown below:

```
#include < filename>
```

These special files are generally supplied with the compiler. The commonly used filenames are stdio.h, stdlib.h etc. The suffix "h" denotes a "header" file. This file has to be included at the beginning of the program.

15.4 STANDARD INPUT OUTPUT FUNCTIONS

In the last section, we discussed about a number of standard library functions. Some of these functions include a number of input/output (I/O) functions such as getchar( ), putchar( ), scanf( ), printf( ), gets( ), puts( ), etc. The C environment considers the keyboard as the standard input, the VDU as the standard output and the VDU as the standard error device. The standard input/output functions allow the transfer of information between the computer and the standard input/output devices. The functions, getchar( ) and putchar( ) are known as character based input/output functions and allow single character to be transferred in and out of the computer. The gets( ) and puts( ) functions are also known as the string based input/output functions because they alllow a stream of characters (strings) to be transferred between the input and the output devices. Any input or output operation takes place as a stream of characters.

The standard input/output functions are buffered *i.e.,* each device has an associated buffer through which any input or output operation takes place. You must make sure that after any input operation from the standard input device, the standard input buffer is cleared otherwise the contents of the previous buffer will interfere in the subsequent input operations. You are required to clear the output buffer only if a newline character is used or an input function is used or the buffer is explicitly cleared.

You can access an input/output function simply by writing the function name followed by a list of arguments enclosed in parentheses. However, some input/output functions do not require any arguments. In that case, a function name followed by empty parentheses is given.

15.4.1 Character based Input Function–The getchar( )

The getchar function is used to enter a single character into the computer. It accepts a single character from the keyboard. The getchar( ) function belongs to the standard Input/ Output library of C language. A pair of parentheses follows the function name. The function does not require any arguments. The syntax of the getchar function is:

```
char_variable name = getchar();
```

where char_variable name is the name of the variable which is of character type. This variable name has to be explicitly declared.

Example:

```
char str[ ];
.......
.......
ctr = getchar();
```

Here, in the first statement the variable of character type is declared which has the name ctr. The second statement accepts input from the standard input device which is generally keyboard and assigns it to the variable ctr.

15.4.2. Character based Output Function–The putchar( ) Function

The putchar( ) function is used to display a single character on the standard output device which is generally a monitor. The putchar( ) function also belongs to the standard Input/Output library of C language. The character to be displayed on the standard output device is expressed as an argument to the putchar function. It is represented as a character type variable and enclosed in parentheses after the putchar( ) function name. The syntax of the putchar function is:

```
putchar(character-variable-name)
```

where

character–variable–name is a character type variable declared earlier in the program.

Example:

```
char ctr;
...........
...........
putchar(ctr);
```

In the first statement, a variable is declared by the name ctr which is of character type.

In the second statement, the value assigned to the character variable ctr is displayed on the screen using the putchar function.

Let us write a small program which accepts a character from the standard input device and displays it on the standard output device using the two standard Input/Output functions discussed earlier.

Program 15.1

```
#include<stdio.h>
main()    /* First function to be executed */
  {
     char temp;          /*A character type variable is declared*/
     temp=getchar();     /*Accept a character*/
     fflush(stdin);      /*Clears the stdin(standard input) buffer*/
     putchar(temp);      /*Displays a character*/
  }
```

In the above program,

(1) The #include<stdio.h> includes the contents of the standard input-output file (stdio.h) at the time of compilation. This file is compiled along with the function to be compiled.

(2) The function main() is the first function to be executed and has to be necessarily included in all the functions.

(3) All the statements after the main() function are included in opening and closing brackets.

(4) A variable of character type is declared which has the name temp.

(5) The function getchar() accepts one character from the standard input device (keyboard) and assigns it to the character variable temp which was declared earlier.

(6) The fflush() clears the associated buffer with a specified input/output device (stdin in this case). It is advisible to clear the buffers.

(7) The putchar( ) function is used to display one character onto the standard output (monitor) device and the character variable which holds the output to be displayed is given as an argument.

15.4.3 String Based Input Function–The gets( )

The getchar() and putchar() are the character based Input/Output functions. Besides these, C provides the gets( ) function for string-based input. The gets( ) function accepts the input in a string variable. The string is input into the computer via the standard input device and terminates with a newline character. The gets( ) function is also a part of the standard Input/Output library of C language. The syntax of the gets function is:

```
char str[];
..........
..........
gets(str);
```

In the first statement, a string is declared and in the second statement the string input is accepted in the string variable named str using the gets( ) function.

15.4.4 String Based Output Function–The puts( )

The puts( ) function is again a part of the standard Input/Output library of C language. The puts( ) function is used to display a stream of characters on the standard output device. The function puts() accepts a string variable to be displayed on the standard output device as an argument. The puts() function causes the cursor to jump to the next line after printing the string. The syntax of the puts function is given below:

```
char str[];
char str[];
.........
........
puts(str);
```

In the first statement, a string is declared which has the name str. In the second statement, the puts( ) function is used to display the stream of characters stored in the string variable named str.

Let us write a small program which makes use of the gets( ) and puts( ) function to accept and display a string of characters.

Program 5.2

```
#include<stdio.h>
main()
{
    char str[15];
    puts("Enter a string upto 15 characters");
         /*Displays the message given in parentheses on the screen*/
    gets(str);       /*Accepts a string*/
    fflush(stdin);   /*Clears the buffer*/
    puts(str);       /*Display the stream of characters stored in the/
                     /*input string*/
}
```

15.4.5 Formatted Input Data Function–The scanf( )

The scanf( ) function forms a part of the standard Input/Output library of the C language. This function is used to enter data which can comprise characters, strings or numbers. The syntax of the scanf() function is given below:

```
scanf(format, data1, data2,....);
```

The scanf() function reads and converts characters from the standard input according to the format specification string and the input is stored in memory locations as given by the arguments. For instance,

```
scanf("%c%d",&n,&d);
```

Here %c and %d are format specification strings. &n and &d are data names provided as arguments in the scanf() function. Please note that the data names (&n and &d) are preceded with the & sign. All data names are preceded with this symbol except string type data names.

The format string in the scanf() function can comprise whitespace characters which are blank spaces, tabs or newline characters. The format string consists of individual groups of characters. One character group signifies one input data item. Each character group has to begin with a percent sign (%). Thus, a single character group consists of the percent sign and the conversion character.

Table 15.6 shows the commonly used conversion characters:

Conversion Character	Interpretation
c	Single character
d	Decimal integer
f	Floating point value
h	Short integer
s	String followed by a whitespace character shown by \0. This is also known as the null character which is added automatically at the end of the string.
u	Unsigned decimal integer
x	Hexadecimal integer

Table 15.6 *Commonly used conversion characters*

15.4.6 Formatted Output Data Function–The printf( )

The printf( ) function allows the output to be written onto the standard output device. This function also forms a part of the standard Intput/Output library functions of C. The printf( ) function is used to output any combination of numerical values, single character or strings. The parameters to the printf() function are the format specification string along with the data to be displayed. The syntax of the printf() function is:

```
printf(format, data1, data2,.......);
```

where format refers to the format specification string. This string contains a specification beginning with the symbol % followed by a character called as *conversion character* for each variable that is to be displayed.

data1, data2, ... are the arguments that represent the individual data items to be displayed. The arguments in the printf() function donot represent any memory addresses. Therefore, they are not preceded with the ampersand(&) symbol.

Table 15.7 shows the commonly used conversion characters.

Character Conversion	Interpretation
c	Data is displayed as single character.
d	Data is displayed as a decimal integer.
e	Data displayed as a floating point value with an exponent.
f	Data displayed as a floating point without an exponent.
s	Data displayed as a string and printed until a NULL character is reached.

Table 15.7 *Commonly used conversion characters for data output*

Other symbols which are permitted in the format specification string are *\n* (for new line) and *\t* (for tab equivalent to 8 spaces). You can give a minus sign, a digit or a period between % and the conversion character.

Let us discuss about these in details:

- a minus sign signifies the adjustment of data to the left side.
- a digit specifies the minimum width in which the data is to be output. If the specified width is less than the data, then the width occupied by the output is larger. However, if the data consists of lesser characters than the specified, width then it is shifted to the right side if minus sign is present. Otherwise, it is shifted to the left side.
- a period separates the width from the next digit.
- a digit following a period specifies the number of decimal places for numeric data or the maximum number of characters to be displayed.

Table 15.8 shows some examples of the formatted output.

Format Specification	Data	Output
[%2d]	6	[6]
[%2d]	456	[456]
[%04d]	6	[0006]
[%-2d]	6	[6]
[%5.3d]	6	[006]
[%5s]	"My name is"	[My name is]
[%15s]	"My name is"	[My name is]
[%15.5s]	"My name is"	[me is]
[%.5s]	"My name is"	[My na]
[%-15.5s]	"My name is"	[My na]
[%f]	98.48	[98.480000]
[%4.1f]	98.48	[98.4]

Table 15.8 *Some examples of formatted output*

The following program reads your age and then writes it on the standard output. This program shows the usage of the scanf() and printf() functions.

Program 15.3

```
#include<stdio.h>
main()
  {
      int age;  /*Declares a variable of Integer type*/
      printf("Enter your age\n");   /*Prints the message on the screen*/
      scanf("%d",&age);   /*Accepts intput*/
      fflush(stdin); /*Clears buffer*/
      printf("Your age is : %d\n",age);  /*Displays the message as well as*/
                                           /*the input age on the screen*/
  }
```

15.5 SIMPLE C PROGRAMS

Let us write some simple programs in C on the following problems to illustrate the concepts discussed in this chapter.

(*a*) To calculate sum and average of two numbers.

(*b*) To accept and display your name and address.

(*c*) To find whether the input character is Y, y, N, n or other.

15.5.1 Finding Sum and Average of two Numbers

Program 15.4

```
/*Program to calculate sum and average of two numbers*/
#include <stdio.h>
main()
  {
      float num1, num2, sum, avg;   /*Declaring variables*/
      num1 = 560.10; /*Assigning a value*/
      num2 = 290.20; /*Assigning a value*/
      sum = num1 + num2;  /*Calculating sum*/
      avg = sum/2;   /*Calculating average*/
      /*Displaying the output in formatted form*/
      printf("\n\n\n\n\n");
      printf("\t\t\t------------------------------");
      printf("\n\t\t\t\t First No.  :%7.2f\n",num1);
      printf("\n\t\t\t\t Second No. :%7.2f\n",num2);
      printf("\n\t\t\t\t Total      :%7.2f\n",sum);
      printf("\n\t\t\t\t Average    :%7.2f\n",avg);
      printf("\t\t\t------------------------------");
      getche(); /*waits until user presses a key");
  }
```

Output

When the above program is executed, the following output is generated on screen.

First No.	:	*560.10*
Second No.	:	*290.20*
Total	:	*850.30*
Average	:	*425.15*

15.5.2 Accepting and Displaying Strings

Program 15.5

```
/*Program to accept and display your name and address*/
#include <stdio.h>
main()
  {
     char name[21], address[31];   /*Declaring two string variables*/
     puts("Enter your name-max 20 characters");  /*Display message*/
     gets(name);     /*Accept name*/
     fflush(stdin); /*Clear buffer*/
     puts("Enter your address-max 30 characters"); /*Display a message*/
     gets(address); /*Accept Address*/
     fflush(stdin); /*Clear buffer*/
     /*Display output*/
     puts("Your name is");
     puts(name);
     puts("Your address is");
     puts(address);
     getche(); /*Wait until user presses a key*/
  }
```

Sample Input/Output

When the above program is executed, the computer asks you to enter your name as shown below:

Enter your name–max 20 characters

Enter your name(say Tulsi Virani). Now the computer asks you to enter your address as shown below:

Enter your address–max 30 characters

Enter your address(say 5, Nariman Point). Now, you will get the following output.

Your name is
Tulsi Virani
Your address is
5, Nariman Point.

15.5.3 Finding the Validity of Input Character

Program 15.6

```
/*Program to find the validity of input character*/
#include <stdio.h>
{
    char inpchr;   /*Declare a variable for character*/
    int result1, result2, result3;    /*Display variables for storing*/
                                      /*logical results*/
    printf("\n Enter 'Y' for Yes or 'N' for No:");
    inpchr = getchar(); /*Accept a character*/
    fflush(stdin); /*Clear buffer*/
    /*If the input character is not Y, y, N or n*/
    result1 = (inpchr != 'Y' && inpchr != 'y' && inpchr !='N' && inpchr != 'n');
    /*Value of result1 would be 1 if the above condition is true*/
    printf("\n Result of First Logical Expression %d",result1);
    /*If the input character is Y or y*/
    result2 = (inpchr == 'Y' || inpchr == 'y');
    /*Value of result 2 would be 1 if the above condition is true*/
    printf("\n Result of Second Logical Expression %d",result2);
    /*If the input character is N or n*/
    result3 = (inpchr == 'N' || inpchr == 'n');
    /*Value of result3 would be 1 if the above condition is true*/
    printf("\n Result of Third Logical Expression %d",result3);
    getche(); /*Wait until user presses a key*/
}
```

Sample Input/Output: When the above program is executed, the following message is displayed :

Enter 'Y' for Yes or 'N' for No :

Based on the input character, the following outputs are generated :

(*a*) If input character is y, the output would be :

Result of First Logical Expression 0
Result of Second Logical Expression 1
Result of Third Logical Expression 0

(*b*) If input character is n, the output would be :

Result of First Logical Expression 0
Result of Second Logical Expression 0
Result of Third Logical Expression 1

(*c*) If input character is d, the output would be :

Result of First Logical Expression 1
Result of Second Logical Expression 0
Result of Third Logical Expression 0

THEORY QUESTIONS

1. What is an operator? How many types of operators are there? Discuss.
2. Distinguish between operators and operands.
3. What are arithmetic operators? How many types of arithmetic operators are there ? What are the rules that apply to these operators?
4. What is operator precedence?
5. What is associativity? What is the associativity of the different types of operators?
6. What is a unary operator?
7. Distinguish between the increment and the decrement operators.
8. What are relational operators? Discuss.
9. Distinguish between the two equality operators available in C.
10. What is the relative precedence of the relational, equality and logical operators with respect to each-other?
11. What is a conditional operator? Discuss.
12. Discuss any five library functions of C.
13. Are the library functions a part of the C language? Discuss.
14. What are the commonly used input/output functions in C?
15. What is the getchar() function? How is it written in C language?
16. What is the name of the standard Input/Output header file? How is it included in a C program?
17. What is the putchar() function? How is it used in a C program?
18. Discuss about the following functions briefly:
    (*a*) The gets() function
    (*b*) The puts() function
    (*c*) The scanf() function
    (*d*) The printf() function

WORKSHOP

1. Suppose num1, num2 and num3 are integer variables having the values 10, 8 and 6, respectively. Find out the value of each of the following arithmetic expressions by writing and executing a program:
    (*a*) `num1 + num2 + num3`
    (*b*) `num1 – num2 + num3`
    (*c*) `num1 * (num2 / num3)`
    (*d*) `num1 % num3`
    (*e*) `(num1 * num2) % num3`
2. Write a program to accept and display the element number and the weight of an Electron. The element must be of integer type and weight must be of float type. After entering the data, display it in a formatted form.
3. Write a program that accepts your name and age and displays this information on the screen in formatted way.
4. Write a program to find whether the input character is M, m, F, f or any other character using logical operators by assigning the result of expressions to integer variables.

16
CONDITIONAL STATEMENTS AND LOOPS

16.1 INTRODUCTION

Till now, you have learnt to write very simple programs in C, where instructions are executed in the same order in which they appear in the program. Such programs cannot solve the real life problems. In most situations, we need to take decisions based on certain conditions and are required to execute statements in any order regardless of their appearance in the program. Such type of program execution is called conditional execution and is unavoidable in real life programs. In this chapter, we will learn various conditional statements used in C programming.

In real life problems, we also need to repeat a job. You can repeat a set of instructions until some condition is satisfied by a process called *looping*. In this chapter, we will also learn different types of looping statements.

16.2 DECISION MAKING

In your daily life, you come across too many situations, where you have to take decisions. Suppose you are making a cup of tea. You will add tea to water only when the water is boiled. You put milk when the colour of boiled mixture changes to yellowish brown. So, you take decisions based on certain conditions. Similarly, while writing a program you need to consider various conditions of the problem on which different results are generated or control of program is transferred to another part of the program. In C, decision making is done by statements, called *Conditional Statements* or *Decision Making Statements.* Let us discuss about these briefly.

16.2.1 Conditional Statements

C language provides the following conditional statements or constructs (*construct* generally refers to a group of statements):

(*a*) The if construct

(*b*) The if-else construct

(*c*) The goto statement

(*d*) The switch-case construct

(*e*) The conditional operator statement.

Out of the above five conditional constructs or statements, the first two *i.e.* the if construct and the if-else construct are widely used in C programming. Let us first understand them with suitable examples. You will learn the other statements/constructs in later part of the chapter.

16.3 THE if AND if-else CONSTRUCTS

Decision making in C becomes easier by using the if and if-else constructs. In chapter 13 (Programming Concepts), we have discussed the two major types of program tools Flowcharts and Pseudocodes, which are used by programmers to develop logic of programs. While drawing a flowchart, we use decision symbol to represent a conditional statement. Based on the condition, the control of the program jumps to one of many statements. In a pseudocode, such construct is represented using if/if-else words. Similarly, we write such conditional statements using if and if-else constructs in a program. Let us learn these.

16.3.1 The if Construct

The if construct is used to execute one or more statements in a program based on certain condition. The general form of the if construct with single statement is as follows:

```
if(expression)
    statement;
```

where expression can be formed by arithmetical, relational and logical operators. The statement is executed only when the expression is true.

The general form of if construct with multiple statements is represented as follows:

```
if(expression)
    {
        statement 1;
        statement 2;
        .
        .
        .
        statement n;
    }
```

Where statement 1, statement 2, ... statement n are various *n* no. of statements. Note that the expression is always written within parentheses and the multiple statements are written within brackets { }.

Let us write a program to understand the if construct.

Program 16.1

```
/*Program to demonstrate the use of if construct with single statement*/
/*Program to check if y is input*/
#include <stdio.h>
main()
    {
        char ans;
        puts("Enter y for yes");
        ans = getchar();
        fflush(stdin);
        if(ans=='y');
          puts("You entered y");
        puts("Thanks");
        getche();
    }
```

In the above program, ans variable is declared as character data type for storing the input character. The messages are displayed using puts() functions. The statement, ans = getchar() accepts the character from the user. The fflush(stdin) statement clears the buffer of standard input device *i.e.,* keyboard. This is required as the user needs to press <Enter> key after typing the character and the <Enter> key has some value (13 in ASCII) which may create problem in correct execution of subsequent statements. (You may try a program without writing fflush(stdin) statement and see the problem). So, you should always write fflush(stdin) statement after gets() and getchar() functions to avoid such problems. In the above program, the if construct is written as follows:

```
if (ans == 'y')
    puts("You entered y");
```

where (ans == 'y') is the expression. If this expression is true *i.e.,* ans is equal to y the subsequent puts() statement is executed and the message "You entered y" is displayed on the screen. The second last statement of program, puts("Thanks") is always executed no matter you enter y or any other character. The last statement getche() asks the computer to wait until the user presses any key. Let us run this program and see the output. When the above program is executed, the computer asks you—

Enter y for yes

Suppose you enter y, you will get the following output:

You entered y
Thanks

If you enter any other character (say n), you will get the following output:

Thanks

The above program illustrates the use of if construct with a single statement. Let us now write another program that illustrates the use of if construct with multiple statements.

Program 16.2

```
/*Program to demonstrate the use of if construct with multiple statements*/
/*Program to display multiple messages based on a condition*/
#include <stdio.h>
main()
  {
      char choice;
      puts("Good Morning");
      puts("Enter C to continue");
      choice = getchar();
      fflush(stdin);
      if(choice == 'C')
        {
            puts("  Welcome");
            puts("    To");
            puts("World of C");
        }
      puts("Thanks");
      getche();
  }
```

The above program is somehow similar to previous one, except the use of multiple statements within if construct. When the program is executed, computer displays the following messages:

Good Morning
Enter C to continue

If you enter C, you will get the following output:

Welcome
To
World of C
Thanks

If you enter any other character, the following output will come on the screen:

Thanks

The if construct has certain limitations. With this construct, only a single set of instructions are executed based on the validity of expression. There is no way by which you can execute another set of instructions if the expression is false. C provides the if-else construct which is used for solving such problems. Let us learn this construct.

16.3.2 The if-else Construct

The if-else construct is used to execute two different sets of instructions based on validity and invalidity of certain condition. The general form of the if-else construct with single statement is as follows:

```
if(expression)
    statement-t;
else
    statement-f;
```

where statement-t is the statement executed when the expression is true and statement-f is the statement executed when the expression is false.

The general form of the if-else construct with multiple statements is as follows:

```
if(expression)
  {
    statement-t-1;
    statement-t-2;
        .
        .
        .
    statement-t-n;
  }
else
  {
    statement-f-1;
    statement-f-2;
        .
        .
        .
    statement-f-n;
  }
```

where statement-t-1, statement-t-2, ... statement-t-n are *n* no. of statements executed when the expression is true and statement-f-1, statement-f-2,........statement-f-n are *n* no. of statements executed when the expression is false.

Let us understand the use of if-else construct by writing some programs.

Program 16.3

```
/*Program to demonstrate the use of if-else construct with single statement*/
/*Program to check whether product of two numbers is >= 100*/
#include <stdio.h>
main()
  {
     float a, b, x; /*Declaration of variables*/
     printf("Enter 1st No."); /*Display a message*/
     scanf("%f",&a);       /*Accept first no. into variable a*/
     printf("Enter 2nd No."); /*Display a message*/
     scanf("%f",&b);       /*Accept second no. into variables b*/
     x = a * b;      /*Store product of a and b into x*/
     if (x>=100)
        printf("Product is greater than or equal to 100");
     else
        printf("Product is less than 100");
  }
```

When the above program is executed, you get the following message:

Enter 1st No.

Enter the first no. (say 15). Now, the computer will display the following message:

Enter 2nd No.

Enter the second no. (say 20). The computer will calculate the product and you will get the following output:

Product is greater than or equal to 100

Let us analyse the output. As the product of entered numbers is 300 and is greater than 100, the statement following the conditional statement, if (x >= 100) gets executed. Hence, you get the above output.

If you will enter the first no. 5 and the second no. 8, the product will be 40 (which is less than 100) and the statement following the else (as the condition becomes false) gets executed. Hence, you will get the following output:

Product is less than 100

As we have stated in the general form of if-else construct, you can also write multiple statements in if-else construct. Let us modify the above program to illustrate this concept. Suppose you also want to display that with how much value the product is less or greater than 100 besides displaying whether the product is greater than or equal to 100 or less than 100. For this, the if-else statements can be written as follows:

```
if(x>=100)
  {
     printf("\n Product is greater than or equal to 100");
     printf("\n It is more than value %d",x-100);
  }
else
```

```
{
    printf("\nProduct is less than 100");
    printf("\nIt is less than value %d",100-x);
}
```

Now, if you will enter the first no. 5 and the second no. 8, you will get the following output :

Product is less than 100
It is less than value 60

You can also write multiple statements after if statement and single statement after else statement and vice-versa. The important point to note is that whenever you write multiple statements, do not forget to put braces as illustrated above. However, while writing a single statement in if construct, the braces are optional and hence are generally not put.

We have just discussed simple if-else constructs where only single if-else expressions are used. You can put one if-else expression within another if-else expression by a procedure called *nesting*. Let us discuss nested if-else constructs.

16.3.3 Nested if-else Construct

The nested if-else construct is used to execute multiple sets of instructions based on validity and invalidity of multiple conditions. Such construct is required to solve complex conditional problems. There are many forms of nested if-else construct. Let us write a few general forms of this construct.

Form 1:

```
if(expression-1)
  if(expression-2)
      statement-1;
  else
      statement-2;
else
  statement-3;
```

Where expression-1 and expressions-2 are two conditional expressions; statement-1, statement-2 and statement-3 are three sets of single or multiple statements.

In the above construct, statement-1 is executed if both expression-1 and expression-2 are true. The statement-2 is executed, if the expression-1 is true and the expression-2 is false. The statement-3 is executed if the expression-1 is false (the expression-2 is not checked here as it is checked only when expression-1 is true). It is important to note that the first 'else' corresponds to the second 'if' and the second 'else' corresponds to the first 'if' statement.

Form 2:

```
if(expression-1)
  statement-1;
else
  if(expression-2)
      statement-2;
  else
      statement-3;
```

In the above construct statement-1 is executed if the expression-1 is true otherwise expression-2 is checked. If expression-2 is true, than statement-2 is executed otherwise statement-3 is executed. So, statement-3 is executed only when both expression-1 and expression-2 are false.

Form 3:

```
if(expression-1)
  if(expression-2)
      statement-1;
  else
      statement-2;
else
  if(expression-3)
      statement-3;
  else
      statement-4;
```

In the above construct, there are four sets of statements and three expressions. The statement-1 is executed, if both expression-1 and expression-2 are true. The statement-2 is executed if expression-1 is true and expression-2 is false. The statement-3 is executed if expression-1 is false and expression-3 is true. The statement-4 is executed if both expression-1 and expression-3 are false.

Similarly, you can write many more forms of nested if-else constructs. The important point to remember is that the else clause is always associated with the closest preceding if statement (Indentation makes this clear). The above discussed nesting is two-layer, you can also do nesting in more than two layers.

Let us understand these forms of nested if-else constructs by writing some programs.

Program 16.4

```
/*Program to demonstrate the use of Nested if-else construct using Form 1*/
/*Program to find grade of marks obtained*/
#include <stdio.h>
main()
  {
     int perc;
     printf("\n Enter percentage of your marks obtained");
     scanf("%d",&perc);
     if(perc<60)
       if(perc>=50)
          printf("\n Grade B");
       else
          printf("\n Grade C");
     else
       printf("\n Grade A");
     getche();
  }
```

When the above program is executed, you get the following message on the screen:

Enter percentage of your marks obtained

Suppose you enter your percentage as 56, you will get the following output:

Grade B

This is because perc is less than 60 and greater than 50, hence the first conditional statement is executed.

Now, if you will enter percentage as 42, the second conditional statement will be executed because second expression is false and first expression is true. Hence, the output would be as follows:

Grade C

If you will enter percentage as 60, you will get the following output:

Grade A

This is because the third conditional statement is executed when the perc is not less than 60 *i.e.,* first expression is false.

The above program illustrates the use of first general form of nested if-else construct as stated earlier. Let us now write one more program that illustrates the use of second general form of nested if-else construct.

Program 16.5

```
/*Program to demonstrate the use of Nested if-else construct using form 2*/
/*Program to check if input character is Y/y, N/n or any other*/
#include <stdio.h>
main()
  {
    char ch1;
    printf("\n Enter 'Y' for Yes or 'N' for No");
    ch1 = getchar();
    fflush(stdin);
    if (ch1 == 'Y' || ch1 == 'y')
      printf("\n Yes");
    else
      if (ch1 == 'N' || ch1 == 'n')
          printf("\n No");
      else
          printf("\n Invalid Input");
    getche();
  }
```

When the above program is executed, you get the following message:

Enter 'Y' for Yes or 'N' for No

If you will press 'y' you will get the following output:

Yes

If you will press 'N' you will get the following output:

No

In case, you will press any character other than Y, y, N, or n, you will get the following message:

Invalid Input

In the above program logical operator for OR, || is also used in if expressions.

Now let us write another program to illustrate the use of third general form of nested if-else construct.

Program 16.6

```
/*Program to demonstrate the use of Nested if-else construct using form3*/
/*Program to find whether the input character is capital, small or any other*/
#include <stdio.h>
main()
  {
     char ch;  /*Declare a character variable*/
     printf("\n Enter a character");     /*Display a message*/
     ch = getchar();       /*Accept a character in ch*/
     fflush(stdin); /*Clear the input buffer*/
     if (ch >= 'A')
       if (ch <= 'Z')
          printf("\n The input character is in Capital letter");
       else
          if (ch >= 'a')
            if (ch <= 'z')
               printf("\n The input character is in Small letter");
            else
               printf("\n The input character is greater than z");
          else
            printf("\n The input character is less than a but greater
               than z");
     else
       printf("\n The input character is less than A");
     getche();
  }
```

The above program seems complicated, however if you read it carefully by analysing indentation, the logic of program would be very clear to you. Let us first execute this program and see its output with different inputs.

The above program finds whether the input character is a capital letter, small letter or any other character. A character is a capital letter if it is greater than or equal to 'A' and is smaller than or equal to 'Z'. Similarly, a character is a small letter if it is greater than or equal to 'a' and is smaller than or equal to 'z'. Using nested if-else statements, such conditions can be easily written as illustrated in the above program. When the above program is executed, you get the following message:

Enter a character

Suppose you enter 'D', you will get the following output:

The input character is in Capital letter

Why? Because the first two expressions written with nested if-else statements, if (ch >= 'A') and if (ch <= 'Z') becomes true. Similarly if you enter 'x', the statements, if (ch >= 'a') and if (ch <= 'z') will become true and you will get the following output:

The input character is in Small letter

Now, if you enter { you will get the following output:

The input character is greater than z

Why? Because the ASCII value of { is 123 while ASCII value of z if 122. Similarly, if you enter =, you will get the following output:

The input character is less than A

This is because the ASCII value of = is 61 while ASCII value of A is 65.

Will you ever get the following output?

The input character is less than a but greater than z.

Never. Why? Because there is no such character as ASCII value of a is 97 while ASCII value of z is 122. No value can be less than 97 and greater than 122.

The logic of the above program must be clear to you. If you still find the above nested if-else construct difficult to understand, there is another way to write the same construct. You can use logical operator AND, && in place of nested if statements as illustrated below:

```
if (ch >= 'A' && ch <= 'Z')
  printf("\n The input character is in Capital letter");
else if (ch >= 'a' && ch <= 'z')
  printf("\n The input character is in small letter");
else
  printf("\n The input character is not an alphabet");
```

However, as you can see with the above construct, you cannot display other messages associated with seperate if-else conditions (as you did in previous program).

Let us discuss another conditional statement, the goto statement which is rarely used and is not recommended for structured programming.

16.4 THE goto STATEMENT

The goto statement is used to transfer control to some other part of program. The general form of the goto statement is as follows:

```
goto label;
```

where label is an identifier of the statement where the control is transferred. The general form of label statement is as follows:

```
label: statement
```

Each label is unique and hence no two statements can have the same label in a program.

The goto statement is generally required to come out of nested loops (loops will be discussed in the later part of the chapter) but it should be avoided. The main drawback of the goto statement is that you can jump to any part of the program by goto statement which makes the program really very difficult to understand and maintain. Instead of using goto statement, you should use structured progamming techniques. There are many other ways to come out of loop and jump to other parts of the program.

We will discuss these ways while discussing looping in later part of this chapter and functions in Chapter-18.

Let us now write a simple program to understand the use of goto statement.

Program 16.7

```
/*Program to demonstrate the use of goto statement*/
/*Program to display an error in input*/
#include <stdio.h>
main()
  {
    char alpha;
    printf("\n Enter only alphabet");
```

```
    alpha = getchar();
    fflush(stdin);
    if (alpha >= 'A' && alpha <= 'Z')
     printf("\n Alphabet is Capital");
    else if (alpha >= 'a' && alpha <= 'z')
     printf("\n Alphabet is small");
    else
     goto errorline;
    errorline:printf("\n Invalid Input");
 }
```

Although in the above program, the label statement, errorline: printf("\nInvalid Input") is written immediately after the if-else construct, it can be put anywhere in the program (but in the same function, functions will be discussed in Chapter-18) if the program is long. When the above goto statement is executed, the control will jump to errorline statement if the input is not an alphabet.

We will not use goto statement again in any of our programs as you will never require to use and we do not recommend you to use it.

Let us now discuss the commonly used conditional statements, the switch-case construct which can be used in place of certain if-else constructs.

16.5 THE switch-case CONSTRUCT

The switch-case construct or switch statement is used to choose a particular group of statements from several available groups based on the value of an integer expression. The general form of the switch-case construct is as follows:

```
switch(expression)
 {
    case value-1:
          statement-1;
    case value-2:
          statement-2;
          .
          .
          .
    case value-n:
          statement-n;
    default:
          statement-d;
 }
```

where expression is the expression that generates an integer value (it can be of char type as char has ASCII value). The value-1, value-2, ... value-n are n number of different values of expressions. The statement-1, statement-2, ... statement-n are the statements executed based on value-1, value-2, ... value-n, respectively. The statement-d is executed when no match is found with any of the case statements. The case and default statement are labels that identify the different alternatives. The case label must be unique within the switch-case construct. It is actually the value of expression followed by word case. These case values are matched one by one with expression values and if there is a match, subsequent statement is executed. After this all subsequent case and default statements are also executed. Consider the construct where there is no statement after case value as illustrated below:

```
case value-1a:
case value-1b:
     statement-1;
case value-2a:
case value-2b:
     statement-2;
          .
          .
          .
```

In the above case statements, statement-1 is executed if value of expression is either value-1a or value-1b. Similarly, if expression gives result as value-2a or value-2b, statement-2 will be executed.

As we have just discussed that in switch-case construct, a statement of that case is executed where a match is found and all subsequent statements of other case and default labels are also executed. How will you come out of switch construct if a match is found? This can be done by using the break statement. After every case statement, the break statement is written as shown below:

```
switch(expression)
    {
     case value-1:
          statement-1;
          break;
     case value-2:
          statement-2;
          break;
          .
          .
          .
     case value-n:
          statement-n;
          break;
     default:
          statement-d;
    }
```

Note that no break statement is written after default statement. Why? Because default is the last label of switch construct, the control will automatically come out of switch-case construct after executing statement-d. Hence, there is no need to write break statement here.

Let us write few programs to understand the switch-case construct. To make the concept clearer, first we will write a program using nested if-else construct and then we will modify it using swith-case construct.

Program 16.8

```
/*Program to display a message depending upon the choice of user*/
/*Using nested if-else construct*/
#include <stdio.h>
main()
  {
    int choice;
    printf("\n Menu");
    printf("\n 1. Breakfast");
    printf("\n 2. Lunch");
    printf("\n 3. Dinner");
    printf("\n Enter your choice");
    choice = getchar();
    fflush(stdin);
    if (choice == 1)
      printf("\n Good Morning Sir, What do you want in Breakfast");
    else if (choice == 2)
      printf("\n Good Afternoon Sir, What do you want in Lunch");
    else if (choice == 3)
      printf("\n Good Evening Sir, What do you want in Dinner");
    else
      printf("\n Invalid Choice Sir, I cannot help you");
  }
```

When the above program is executed, the following messages are displayed:

Menu

1. Breakfast

2. Lunch

3. Dinner

Enter your choice

Different output messages will be displayed based on the choice entered by you. If you enter 1, the following message will come on the screen:

Good Morning Sir, What do you want in Breakfast

Similarly, other messages are displayed based on the choice. If you enter 4, you will get the following message:

Invalid Chioce Sir, I cannot help you

Let us rewrite this program using switch-case construct.

Program 16.9

```
/*Program to display a message depending upon choice of user*/
/*Using switch-case construct*/
#include <stdio.h>
main()
  {
    int choice;
    printf("\n Menu");
    printf("1. Breakfast");
```

```
        printf("2. Lunch");
        printf("3. Dinner");
        printf("\n Enter your choice");
        choice = getchar();
        fflush(stdin);
        switch(choice)
          {
              case 1:
                    printf("\n Good Morning Sir, What do you want in Breakfast");
                    break;
              case 2:
                    printf("\n Good Afternoon Sir, What do you want in Lunch");
                    break;
              case 3:
                    printf("\n Good Evening Sir, What do you want in Dinner");
                    break;
              default:
                    printf("\n Invalid Choice Sir, I cannot help you");
          }
      }
```

The above program performs the same function as the previous one. Which of these programs do you find easier to write and understand? And why? The switch-case construct is easier to write for such problems because the coding is compact and more understandable.

Let us write one more program using switch-case construct to understand more features of this construct.

Program 16.10

```
/*Program to determine whether the input alphabet is a vowel*/
/*Using a switch-case construct*/
#include <stdio.h>
main()
  {
      char alpha;
      puts("Enter an alphabet");
      alpha = getchar();
      fflush(stdin);
      switch (alpha)
        {
            case 'a':
            case 'A': puts("a is vowel");
                  break;
            case 'e':
            case 'E': puts("e is vowel");
                  break;
            case 'i':
            case 'I': puts("i is vowel");
                  break;
```

```
        case 'o':
        case 'O': puts("o is vowel");
              break;
        case 'u':
        case 'U': puts("u is vowel");
              break;
        default: puts("Entered character is not vowel");
    }
}
```

When the above program is executed, you will get the following message:

Enter an alphabet

Suppose, you enter I, you will get the following output:

i is vowel

Similarly, if you will enter i, you will also get the above output.

If you enter f, you will get the following message:

Entered character is not vowel

So, default statement is executed when none of the case value is matched with entered character.

Can you use switch-case construct for all types of problems? No. You cannot write conditional statements using switch-case construct for problems where it is checked whether the entered number is greater or smaller than a particular value. So, you cannot write Program 16.4 and Program 16.6 (discussed earlier in the chapter) using switch-case construct. That is the limitation of switch-case construct. However, the problems discussed in Program 16.9 and Program 16.10 are generally solved using switch-case constructs.

Let us now discuss one more conditional statement, the Conditional Operator Statement which has limited use.

16.6 THE CONDITIONAL OPERATOR STATEMENT

The concept of conditional operators has already been discussed in chapter-15 on Basic C Features (See Section 15.2.6). Here, we will implement this concept in a program.

The simple if-else construct can be easily written using a conditional operator statement. You know that the general form of if-else construct with single statement is as follows:

```
if(expression)
  statement-t;
else
  statement-f;
```

where statement-t is executed if expression is true otherwise statement-f is executed.

Such construct can be converted to a compact form using conditional operator statement as shown below:

```
(expression? statement-t: statement-f)
```

If expression is true, statement-t is executed and if expression is false, statement-f is executed.

Let us rewrite the if-else construct of Program 16.3 using conditional operator statement. The if-else construct was written as follows:

```
if (x >= 100)
        printf("Product is greater than or equal to 100");
else
        printf("Product is less than 100");
```

The above statements can be written using conditional operator as illustrated below:

```
(x >= 100? printf("Product is greater than or equal to 100"):
printf("Product is less than 100"));
```

You can also assign the value of statement-t and statement-f to another variable as shown below:

```
a = (expression? statement-t: statement-f)
```

where a is an integer or char variable.

Let us understand this concept by writing a small program.

Program 16.11

```
/*Program to demonstrate the use of conditional operator statement*/
/*Program to find whether rank is 1 or 2*/
#include <stdio.h>
main()
  {
        int marks,rank;
        printf("\n Enter your marks");
        scanf("%d", &marks);
        if (marks < 99 || marks > 100)
                printf("\n No rank");
        else
                rank = (marks == 100? 1: 2);
        printf("\n Rank = %d", rank);
  }
```

When the above program is executed, you get the following message:

Enter your marks

Suppose, you enter 105, you will get the following message:

No rank

If you enter 100, you will get the following output:

Rank = 1

Similarly, if you enter 99, you will get the following output:

Rank = 2

In the above program, the values 1 and 2 are assigned to variable rank based on the condition. If marks are equal to 100, 1 is assigned to rank and if marks are equal to 99, 2 is assigned to rank.

Conditional operator statements are rarely used due to their limited use, however they make code compact for simple if-else constructs.

This finishes our discussion on conditional statements. Now, we will discuss the most useful concept of programming *i.e.,* looping in the remaining part of this chapter.

16.7 LOOPING

Many times you need to repeat a job again and again. You may need to repeat the job either for fixed number of times or until a certain condition is satisfied. For instance, your teacher may ask you to write your name for 100 times as a punishment. She may ask you to keep on saying "Sorry Madam" until she keeps on checking your homework. So, you perform a task repeatedly until a condition is satisfied. When the condition becomes false, you stop performing the task. Similarly, you can repeat a set of statements of your program based on certain condition. You can repeat the same set of instructions for a fixed number of times. Repetition of instructions in a program is done by a construct, called *looping* or *iteration*. We will now discuss various statements of C used for looping. Such statements are really very useful and most of the times are necessary for writing C programs.

16.7.1 Looping Statements

C language provides the following three types of looping statements:

(*a*) The while statement

(*b*) The do-while statement

(*c*) The for statement

The first two statements are used to repeat a set of instructions until a condition is true. The last statement is used to repeat a task for a fixed number of times. Let us discuss all these statements.

16.8 THE while STATEMENT

The while statement is used to execute a statement (simple or compound) repeatedly until the logical expression is true (*i.e.,* having non-zero value). The general form of while statement is as follows:

```
while(expression)
    statement;
```

where expression is usually a logical expression (*i.e.,* conditional expression) having value either true (non-zero) or false (0). The statement can be simple or compound. If the statement is compound, you can also represent the general form of while statement as follows:

```
while(expression)
   {
      statement-1;
      statement-2;
         .
         .
         .
      statement-n;
   }
```

Let us write a simple program to understand the while statement.

Program 16.12

```
/*Program to demonstrate the use of while statement*/
/*Program to display sum of many sets of two numbers until the user wants to continue*/
#include <stdio.h>
main()
  {
    int a, b, c;  /*Declaration of variables*/
    char choice;  /*Declaring a flag for condition*/
    choice = 'Y'  /*Initialisation of flag*/
    while (choice == 'Y' || choice == 'y')  /*While loop begins*/
      {
        printf("\n Enter First No.?");    /*Displaying a message*/
        scanf("%d", &a);    /*Accepting first no. in a*/
        printf("\n Enter Second No.?");   /*Displaying a message*/
        scanf("%d", &b);    /*Accepting Second no. in b*/
        c = a + b;     /*Storing sum of a and b in c*/
        printf("\n Total = %d", c);   /*Displaying output*/
        printf("\n Do you want to continue? (Y/N):");
                                          /*Displaying a message*/
        choice = getchar(); /*Accepting choice of user in choice*/
        fflush(stdin); /*Clears input buffer*/
      }  /*End of while loop*/
  }
```

Let us understand the logic of this program. In the above program, three variables, a, b and c of integer type are declared to store first number, second number and sum of numbers, respectively. The variable choice is declared as char type as a flag to be used in while expression and is initialised with value 'Y'. Initialisation of flag is required because a loop is executed until a condition is true and in the beginning, we need to make condition true. After initialising, we begin the loop by writing while statement, which has been written as follows:

```
while(choice == 'Y' || choice == 'y')
```

In the above statement, we have written a compound expression (condition) which tells C compiler to execute the subsequent simple or compound statements until choice is equal to 'Y' or 'y' (This is required as the user can type in small or uppercase letter). The compound statement is enclosed within braces, { }. The closing brace } indicates the end of while statement or loop.

Within the loop, the statements are written to accept two numbers from the user and store them in variables a and b. The sum of these two numbers is stored in variable c using an arithmetic expression and is displayed on the screen using printf() statement. After this, the user is asked whether he wants to continue and the choice of the user is stored in flag, choice. If the user enters 'Y' or 'y', the control goes back to the beginning of while loop and all statements of the loop are executed again. If the user enters any other character other than 'Y' or 'y', the condition of while statement becomes false and the statements of the loop are not executed. So, the program comes to an end depending upon the choice of the user.

The above program shows the use of while statement based on the choice of user. The while statement can also be used to execute a set of statements for a fixed number of times. Can you tell how? It is very simple. Just declare a counter (integer variable) instead of flag (char variable) and initialise it with a numeric value (say 1). Perform the loop statements until the value of counter is less than or equal to the desired value (number of times you want to execute the loop) and increment the counter by 1. The following part of the program will make this concept very clear:

```
int n;
n = 1;
while (n <= 5)
  {
     printf("\n I am learning loops");
     n++;
  }
```

What will be the output of this part of the program? It will display the same message in 5 lines as shown below:

I am learning loops
I am learning loops
I am learning loops
I am learning loops
I am learning loops

The logic of the above while loop is quite simple. As *n* is initialised to 1, the expression (*n* <= 5) becomes true. So, the loop statements are executed and the message is displayed on the screen using printf() statement. The next statement, n++ increments *n* to 2 and again the expression (*n* <= 5) becomes true. Hence, the loop is executed again and the message is again displayed on next line (due to \n in printf). The n++ is again incremented to 3 and the loop is executed again. After the message is displayed on fifth line, *n* becomes 6 which makes the expression (*n* <= 5) false. So, the loop is not executed and the program control comes out of the loop.

You can also decrement the counter within a loop as illustrated below:

```
int n = 5;
while (n >= 1)
  {
     printf("\n I am learning loops");
     n--;
  }
```

What will be the output of this sub-program? Same as discussed earlier. Why? This is because here again loop is executed 5 times, no matter what remains the value of *n* in each loop. Initially *n* is 5 which satisfies the condition (*n* >= 1), then *n* is decremented to 4, 3, 2, 1 and 0 during each loop. When *n* becomes 0, the condition (*n* >= 1) becomes false and the control comes out of the loop.

Let us write one more program which illustrates the use of while loop in executing same set of instructions for a fixed number of times.

Program 16.13

```
/*Program to demonstrate the use of while statement*/
/*Program to calculate average of 10 numbers*/
#include <stdio.h>
main()
```

```
{
    int n, s, c;    /*n is number, s is sum & c is counter*/
    float a;        /*a is average*/
    s = 0;          /*Initialise sum to zero*/
    c = 0;          /*Initialise counter to 0*/
    while(c < 10)
      {
         printf("\n Enter a number %d", c);
         scanf("%d", &n);
         s = s + n;       /*Add number to sum*/
         c++; /*Increment counter*/
      }
    a = (float)s/c;      /*Calculating average*/
    printf("\n Average = %f", a);
}
```

The above program accepts 10 numbers from the user and calculates their average. The logic of the program can be explained as follows:

We initialise three variables, *n*, *s* and *c* for storing the number, sum and counter respectively. The average of numbers is stored in variable a which is of float type (average can be in decimals). Outside the loop we initialise *s* and *c* with zero. Why? Because *s* is an accumulator (which stores arithmetic results) which needs to be initialised with 0 otherwise it may contain some garbage value and *c* is a counter which is used to count the numbers entered by the user (outside loop no number is entered, hence it is 0). The loop is executed until *c* is less than 10. Within the loop, the number (*n*) is accepted and added to sum (*s*). The counter *c* is also incremented whenever a number is accepted. When the loop finishes, *s* contains the sum of 10 numbers entered by the user. After the loop, average is calculated by the following expression:

```
a = (float) s/c;
```

As a is of float type, s and c are integers, therefore (float) expression is written before the expression, s/c in order to convert the integer output to float type. This is called *type casting of operands or variables.*

Finally, the average is displayed using printf() statement.

Let us see the output of the program with some sample data.

Sample Input/Output

Enter a number 1 50
Enter a number 2 10
Enter a number 3 40
Enter a number 4 30
Enter a number 5 20
Enter a number 6 50
Enter a number 7 90
Enter a number 8 40
Enter a number 9 10
Enter a number 10 60
Average = 40.000000

In all the examples of while statement, which we have discussed, the compound statements are written where it is necessary to put braces { }. However, if you write a single simple statement in while loop, there is no need to put braces as illustrated below:

```
int i = 1;
while (i <= 100)
      printf("\n Looping is quite interesting");
```

What will be the output of the above sub-program ? It is an endless loop as you are not incrementing the variable, i. So, the message 'Looping is quite interesting' will keep on displaying on your computer monitor and you will have to reboot your system.

Let us now learn another type of looping statement, which is quite similar to while statement *i.e.,* do-while statement.

16.9 THE do-while STATEMENT

The do-while statement is almost similar to while statement functionally, except that the while statement checks condition first and then execute statements of loop. However, the do-while statement execute statements of loop first and then checks condition. Let us first write the general form of do-while statement and then discuss it:

```
do
  {
      statement-1;
      statement-2;
          .
          .
          .
      statement-n;
  }while(expression);
```

As it is clear from the general form of do-while statement, the do statement marks the beginning of loop and while statement marks its end. The statement-1, statement-2, ... statement-n are executed first and then the validity of expression (condition) is checked. If it is true, then the loop is again executed. So, do-while loop is always executed once no matter the condition is true or false as contrary to while loop which is never executed if the condition is false.

In order to compare while and do-while loops, we will discuss the same examples again as we discussed in previous section for the while loop.

Let us first discuss the example of the Program 16.12 for displaying sum of many sets of two numbers until the user wants to continue. The while loop discussed there can be re-written using do-while as illustrated below:

```
char choice;
do
  {
      .
      .
      .
      choice = getchar();
  }while(choice == 'Y' || choice == 'y');
```

Note that in the above example, we have not initialised the variable choice with 'Y' as we did in while loop. This is because here there is no need of initialisation as the condition is checked only when the user enters data to choice variable and the loop is executed once no matter what is the value of choice. You can modify Program 16.12 by writing do statement instead of while as explained above. You will see that it will not affect the execution of the program in any way. So, both while and do-while loops do same job, it is the choice of the programmer to use any of them in different situations. Just like while loop, you can also use do-while loop to execute a set of statements for a fixed number of times. Can you convert the following statements of while loop (already discussed) into do-while statements ?

```
int n;
n = 1;
while (n <= 5)
  {
      printf("\n I am learning loops");
      n++;
  }
```

Yes, you can. The above sub-program can also be written using do-while loop as shown below :

```
int n;
n = 1;
do
  {
      printf("\n I am learning loops");
      n++;
  }while(n <= 5);
```

Have you seen the similarity in while and do-while statements ? Both are almost similar in the writing of expression except that 'do' statement marks beginning of do-while loop and 'while' expression ends the do-while loop. The expression is same in both while and do-while statements.

Both do-while and while statements are generally used for solving those problems where you do not know how many times a loop will be executed and the loop is executed based on the choice accepted from the user as illustrated in Program 16.12. Although you can use both do-while and while statements for solving the problems where you know how many times a loop will be executed as illustrated in Program 16.13. C language provides another looping statement, the for statement exclusively for solving such problems. Let us discuss this widely used for loop statement.

16.10 THE for STATEMENT

The for statement is the most widely used looping statement of C. It is mainly used to execute a simple or compound statement for a fixed number of times. Its syntax is so compact that in a single for statement, you can initialise the variable (generally a counter), increment or decrement it and check the condition. Let us see how? The general form of for statement is as follows:

```
for (initialisation expression; conditional expression; increment/
                                                  decrement expression)
  {
      statement-1;
      statement-2;
```

```
        .
        .
        .
        statement-n;
    }
```

where initialisation expression initialises the counter with an integer or float value, conditional expression specifies the simple or complex condition and increment/decrement expression alters the value of counter.

If we compare the general form of for statement with the while statement, the while statement can also be represented as follows:

```
initialisation expression;
while(conditional expression)
  {
     statement-1;
     statement-2;
        .
        .
        .
     statement-n;
     increment/decrement expression;
  }
```

So, you can observe the difference between the two. In while statement, three expressions are written at three different positions but in for statement, all the three expressions are written at one position only.

Let us rewrite the following instructions (discussed earlier) of while loop using the for statement:

```
int n;
n = 1;
while (n <= 5)
  {
     printf("\n I am learning loops");
     n++;
  }
```

Using the for statement, the above sub-program can be written as follows:

```
int n;
for (n=1; n <= 5; n++)
     printf("\n I am learning loops");
```

In the above for statement, first n is initialised to 1 and the printf() statement is executed. Then, n is incremented by 1 and condition ($n <= 5$) is checked. As it is true, the printf() statement is again executed. The loop continues until $n <= 5$ and when n becomes 6, the control come out of loop.

So, you see it is extremely easy to code such a looping problem as compared to while or do-while statement.

Let us write some programs to illustrate the use of the for statement.

Program 16.14

```
/*Program to demonstrate the use of for statement*/
/*Program to display multiplication table of 2*/
#include <stdio.h>
main()
 {
    int i, n;
    printf("\n Table of 2\n\n");
    for(i=1;i<11;i++)
      {
         n = 2 * i;
         printf("2x%2d = %2d\n", i, n);
      }
    getche();
 }
```

The above program displays the multiplication table of 2 as shown in the following output:

```
Table of 2
2 × 1  =  2
2 × 2  =  4
2 × 3  =  6
2 × 4  =  8
2 × 5  = 10
2 × 6  = 12
2 × 7  = 14
2 × 8  = 16
2 × 9  = 18
2 × 10 = 20
```

Let us analyse various statements of the program. Two variables *i* and *n* are declared to store the counter and product. The heading 'Table of 2' is displayed using printf() statement outside the loop. The for statement is written as follows:

```
for(i=1;i<11;i++)
```

The above for statement, initialises *i* to 1 and executes the loop until $i < 11$. The counter *i* is incremented after each loop. Within the loop, 2 is multiplied with *i* to give product *n*.

So, during the first execution, 2 is multiplied with 1 to give product 2. Now the output is displayed using printf() statement. After this *i* is incremented, condition is checked and as the condition is true, loop is again executed. In this way, the loop is executed for 10 times and multiplication table of 2 is generated.

The for statement can also be written in some other ways by omitting the initialisation expression and/or increment/decrement expression. However, it is essential to write conditional expression in the for loop. Let us understand this concept with few examples:

(1) Initialisation can be done in the separate statement and for statement is written using conditional and increment/decrement expressions only as illustrated below:

```
int j;
j = 1;
for(;j<=5;j++)
  printf("\n%d",j);
```

(2) Increment/decrement expression can be written within the loop and for statement is written using initialisation and conditional expressions only as illustrated below:

```
int k;
for(k=20;k>=1;)
  {
      printf("\n%d",k);
      k--;
  }
```

(3) Both initialisation and increment/decrement expressions can be written as separate statements and for statement is written using conditional expression only as illustrated below:

```
int d = 2;
for(;d<=10;)
  {
      printf("\n%d",d);
      d++;
  }
```

Note that it is essential to put semicolons (;) if we do not write an expression in the for statement as shown above.

We have discussed all these types of looping statements. Like nested if-else statements, looping statements can also be nested. Let us learn how?

16.11 NESTED LOOPS

You can embed one loop within another which may be similar or dissimilar to outer looping statement. For instance, you can embed a for loop within another for loop or a for loop within a while loop or vice-versa. There can be many possibilities of such nested loops. Nesting can be at more than two levels. However, upto three level nesting is common. Let us understand these nested loops with few examples.

16.11.1 Nested for Loops

Consider the following statements to understand the nested for loops:

```
for(i=1;i<=5;i++)
  for(j=10;j<=12;j++)
     printf("\n%d\t%d",i,j);
```

The above statements describe a nested for loop. There are two for statements – one marks the beginning of outer loop and another marks the beginning of inner loop. When the outer loop is executed first time, the value of *i* is initialised to 1. Now, the program control goes to the inner for statement which initialises the value of *j* to 10. The next statement is printf() statement which displays the value of *i* as 1 and *j* as 10. Now, *j* is incremented and it becomes 11. As 11 is less than 12, the expression, $j <= 12$ becomes true and the inner loop is again executed. So, you get the output for *i* and *j* as 1 and 11, respectively. Now *j* is incremented to 12, which again satisfies the expression, j <= 12.

The inner loop is again executed and you get the output for *i* and *j* as 1 and 12, respectively. Now *j* is incremented to 13 which makes the expression $j <= 12$ false. Hence, the inner loop is completed and the program control again goes to outer for statement, where *i* is incremented and it becomes 2. As *i* is less than 5, the expression, $i <= 5$ remains true. Now, the program control goes to inner for statement and *j* is again initialised to 10. So, the value of *i* and *j* are displayed as 2 and 10 respectively. In this way, for each value of *i*, the inner loop is executed for 3 times (as *j* ranges from 10 to 12) and as *i* ranges from 1 to 5, the printf() statement is executed for 15 times (3 × 5). Hence, the following values of *i* and *j* are displayed on the screen:

```
1    10
1    11
1    12
2    10
2    11
2    12
3    10
3    11
3    12
4    10
4    11
4    12
5    10
5    11
5    12
```

Nesting can be done at three levels as illustrated below:

```
for(a=0;a<=1;a++)
  for(b=10;b>=8;b--)
      for(c=100;c>=101;c++)
         printf("\n a=%d  b=%d  c=%d",a,b,c);
```

How many times, the printf() statement will be executed ? As outer loop executes for 2 times, middle for 3 times and the inner for 2 times, the printf() statement will be executed for 2 × 3 × 2 = 12 times as shown in the following output:

```
a=0    b=10    c=100
a=0    b=10    c=101
a=0    b=9     c=100
a=0    b=9     c=101
a=0    b=8     c=100
a=0    b=8     c=101
a=1    b=10    c=100
a=1    b=10    c=101
a=1    b=9     c=100
a=1    b=9     c=101
a=1    b=8     c=100
a=1    b=8     c=101
```

As clear from the output, first the inner loop is completed, then middle and finally the outer loop.

Nested for loops are generally used to manipulate arrays (an array is a collection of similar data elements) which are discussed in detail in chapter-18 on Arrays (See Programs 18.3, 18.15, 18.16, 18.17 and 18.18).

Just as for loops can be nested, while and do-while loops can also be nested. You can also nest a for loop within a do-while or while loop or vice-versa. Let us learn these.

16.11.2 Nested Other Loops

You can place a while loop within another while loop as shown below:

```
ans='Y';
while(ans=='Y')
  {
     chioce='N';
     while(choice=='N')
       {
          .
          .
          .
       }
  }
```

Similarly, you can place a do loop within another do loop as illustrated below:

```
do
  {
     do
       {
          .
          .
          .
       }while(choice=='N');
  }while(ans=='Y');
```

You can also nest these loops in three or more levels. You can also nest dissimilar type of loops within one another. Let us write a program to demonstrate the nesting of dissimilar types of loops.

Program 16.15

```
/*Program to demonstrate nesting of dissimilar types of loops*/
/*Program to display a multiplication table of any number entered by the user*/
#include <stdio.h>
main()
  {
     int num, x, ctr;
     char ans;
     do
       {
          printf("\n Enter a no.");
          scanf("%d", &num);
          printf("\n Table of %d\n\n",num);
          for(ctr=1;ctr<=10;ctr++)
            {
               x=num*ctr;
```

```
                printf("%d × %d = %d\n", num, ctr, x);
            }
            printf("\n Do you want to continue ? Y/N");
            scanf("%\s", &ans);
        }while(ans=='Y'|| ans=='y');
    }
```

The above program is similar to the previous program, which displays the multiplication table of 2. This progam displays the multiplication table of any number entered by the user. So, in this program a value is accepted from the user and is stored in variable num. So, within the for loop 1, the variable, num is multiplied with the counter (ctr) to generate the product (x). This program accepts the value of num within an outer do loop which is executed until the user wants to keep on displaying table of any required number. The user's choice is accepted in the char variable, ans and the loop is executed until ans is equal to 'Y' or 'y'. Let us run the program and see the output. When you execute this program, you will get the following message:

Enter a no.

Suppose, you enter the number as 5, you will get the following output:

Table of 5
5 × 1 = 5
5 × 2 = 10
5 × 3 = 15
5 × 4 = 20
5 × 5 = 25
5 × 6 = 30
5 × 7 = 35
5 × 8 = 40
5 × 9 = 45
5 × 10 = 50

16.12 THE break AND continue STATEMENTS

Nested loops are very useful for solving real life problems. Sometimes, we need to come out of any of the nested loops under certain conditions. Sometimes we need to bypass the statements inside the loop. C language provides two statements, break and continue for handling such situations. Let us conclude the chapter with a brief discussion on these statements. Both these statements can be used with any type of looping statement.

16.12.1 The break Statement

The break statement is used to come out of a loop without executing the subsequent statements and checking the condition. The general form of the break statement is as follows :

```
break;
```

Let us understand the importance of this statement by writing a program.

Program 16.16

```
/*Program to demonstrate the use of break statement*/
/*Program to find whether the entered number is a prime no.*/
#include <stdio.h>
```

```
main()
  {
      char pflag;    /*pflag is a flag to check whether no. is prime*/
      int n, ctr;    /*n is a number & ctr is a counter for loop*/
      printf("\n Enter a no.");
      scanf("%d",&n);       /*Accepting the no.*/
      ctr=2;    /*Initialise ctr so that you can first divide n by 2*/
      while(ctr<n)
        {
            pflag='N';      /*Assume no. is not prime*/
            if(n%ctr==0)    /*if remainder is equal to zero*/
              {
                  pflag = 'N';    /*No. is not prime*/
                  break;          /*come out of loop*/
              }
            else
              pflag='Y';    /* No. is prime*/
            ctr++;
        }
      if(pflag='Y' || n==1 || n==2)
        printf("\n%d is a prime no.",n);
      else
        printf("\n%d is not a prime no.",n);
  }
```

Let us understand the logic of the above program. Which is a prime number? A number which is divisible by itself only. For example, 1, 2, 3, 5, 7, 11, 13 .... are prime numbers. To find whether a number is prime or not, you can keep on dividing the number by all numbers starting from 2 and ending one less than the number. Therefore, we used the following condition in the loop:

```
while(ctr<n)
```

where ctr is a counter and n is a number entered by the user. We initialise the ctr to 2 because we want to divide n from 2 onwards. If the number is divisible by 2 or higher number, the number is not a prime number and we should come out of loop. This is accomplished by following the if construct and using the break statement:

```
if(n%ctr==0)
  {
      pflag='N';
      break;
  }
```

If the remainder obtained after dividing n by ctr is zero, the number is divisible and hence not prime. Therefore in that situation, we assign 'N' to pflag which signifies that the number is not prime. If the remainder is not zero, the pflag is set to 'Y' and ctr is incremented to continue the loop. Outside the loop, the message stating whether the number is prime or not is displayed depending on the value of pflag. Let us run the above program with some sample inputs and see the output:

Sample Inputs/Outputs

1. *Enter a no. 1*
   1 is a prime no.
2. *Enter a no. 3*
   3 is a prime no.
3. *Enter a no. 6*
   6 is not a prime no.

With this program, the importance of break statement must be clear to you. Sometimes, we do not want to come out of loop but just want to skip the subsequent statements. This can be done using another statement, continue. Let us learn this.

16.12.2 The continue Statement

The continue statement is somehow opposite to the break statement. With continue statement, the loop does not terminate and only looping statements after continue are skipped. So, the program control goes directly to conditional looping statement and the loop remains continued based on the condition. The general form of the continue statement is as follows:

```
continue;
```

Let us understand the use of this statement by writing a program.

Program 16.17

```
/*Program to demonstrate the use of continue statement*/
/*Program to accept a valid choice of menu*/
#include <stdio.h>
main()
  {
   int chioce;     /*Declare a variable for chioce*/
   do
     {
        printf("\n Main Menu");
        printf("\n1. Enter Data");
        printf("\n2. Make Querries");
        printf("\n3. Print Reports");
        printf("\n4. Exit");
        printf("\n Enter your choice:");
        scanf("%d",&choice);
        fflush(stdin);
        if(choice<1 || choice>4)
          {
            printf("\n Invalid chioce");
            continue;
          }
        switch(choice)
          {
            case 1:
            case 2:
            case 3:
            case 4:
```

```
                    printf("\n Your choice is %d",choice);
            }
        }while(choice!=4);
    }
```

The above program displays a menu and accepts the choice from the user by making a do-while loop. Based on the chioce, the appropriate message is displayed. The user can enter 1, 2, 3 or 4 as valid choices and any other choice is treated as invalid. If the choice is invalid, the program control skips the subsequent switch construct by checking the following condition:

```
if(choice<1 || choice>4)
{
    printf("\n Invalid Choice");
    continue;
}
```

So, the continue statements bypass the subsequent statements of the current loop (If it is a nested loop, the loop where continue is written).

So, the break and continue statements are quite useful to control the execution of loop by bypassing the remaining statements of loop. The only difference between these two statements is that the break statement stops while the continue statement continues the loop.

With this discussion, the chapter on conditional and looping statements is concluded. Now, we will revise the concepts discussed in the chapter by writing some programs on typical problems.

16.13 TYPICAL APPLICATIONS OF BRANCHING AND LOOPING

Here, we are writing programs to solve the following typical problems:

(*a*) To generate a table of triangular numbers
(*b*) To find result and division of a student
(*c*) To find the validity of a triangle
(*d*) To count number of vowels and non-vowels
(*e*) To calculate sum of digits of a number
(*f*) To generate a Floyd's triangle of numbers

We are explaining the logic of programs only and not the meaning of statements while writing these programs as we have already disussed these concepts in detail.

16.13.1 Generating Table of Triangular Numbers

Triangular numbers are 1, 3, 6, 10, 15, 21, 28............ and so on. If n is 1, 2, 3, 4, ... and so on, the triangular numbers (*tn*) are generated by adding from 1 to *n* as shown below :

n	*tn*
1	1
2	3 (1 + 2)
3	6 (3 + 3)
4	10 (6 + 4)
5	15 (10 + 5)

To solve this problem, you can keep on adding *n* to *tn* by making a loop. Let us write the program.

Program 16.18

```
/*Program to generate a table of triangular nos.*/
#include <stdio.h>
main()
{
   int n, tn;    /*tn is a triangular no. of n*/
   printf("\n\n\t\t\t Table of Triangular Numbers\n\n");
   printf("\t\t\t------------------------------\n");
   printf("\t\t\t     n    Sum from 1 to n\n");
   printf("\t\t\t------------------------------\n");
   tn=0; /*Initialise triangular no as zero*/
   for(n=1;n<=10;++n)
     {
       tn=tn+n;
       printf("\t\t\t    %2d       %2d\n",n,tn);
     }
   printf("\t\t\t------------------------------\n");
}
```

Sample Output

When the above program is executed, we get the following output:

Table of Triangular Numbers

n	*Sum from 1 to n*
1	*1*
2	*3*
3	*6*
4	*10*
5	*15*
6	*21*
7	*28*
8	*36*
9	*45*
10	*55*

16.13.2 Finding Result and Division

Let us write a program to calculate the percentage of marks obtained by a student and to find the result and division of the student on the following conditions:

(*a*) The student is passed if percentage >= 40
(*b*) The student is failed if percentage < 40
(*c*) The division is I if percentage >= 60
(*d*) The division is II if percentage >= 50 but <=60
(*e*) The division is III if percentage >= 40 but < 50

The program accepts the name, marks obtained and maximum marks from the user and displays the result and division in a proper format.

The logic of the program is quite simple and need not require any explanation.

Program 16.19

```
/*Program to find result and division*/
#include <stdio.h>
main()
  {
     char name[20];
     float mobt, mm, perc;
     printf("\n------------------------------");
     printf"\n FINDING THE RESULT & DIVISION");
     printf("\n------------------------------");
     printf("\n\n Name          :");
     gets(name);
     fflush(stdin);
     printf("\n Marks obtained :");
     scanf("%4f", &mobt);
     fflush(stdin);
     printf("\n Maximum Marks :");
     scanf("%4f", &mm);
     fflush(stdin);
     perc = mobt * 100/mm;
     printf("\n Percentage     :");
     printf("%7.2f", perc);
     printf("\n Result         :");
     if(perc>=40)
       printf("Pass");
     else
       printf("Fail");
     printf("\n Division       :");
     if(perc>=40 && perc<50)
       printf("III Division");
     if(perc>=50 && perc<60)
       printf("II Division");
     if(perc>=60)
       printf("I Division");
     printf("\n------------------------------");
     getche();
  }
```

Sample Input/Output

When the program is executed, after entering the data the output is generated as shown below :

```
-----------------------------------------------
FINDING THE RESULT & DIVISION
-----------------------------------------------
Name              : Sonali
Marks Obtained    : 1000
Maximum Marks     : 1600
Percentage        : 62.50
Result            : Pass
Division          : I Division
-----------------------------------------------
```

16.13.3 Finding Validity of Triangle

A triangle has three sides where the sum of any two sides is greater than the third side. So, it is possible to draw a triangle if it satisfies this condition.

Let us write a program to input the size of three sides of a triangle and find out whether it is possible to draw a triangle or not.

Program 16.20

```
/*Program to determine whether a triangle is valid*/
#include <stdio.h>
main()
  {
      int s1, s2, s3;     /*Variables for 3 sides*/
      int t1, t2, t3;/*Variables to store sum of two different sides*/
      printf("\n Enter the size of 3 sides of triangle");
      printf("\n Side 1 :");
      scanf("%d",&s1);
      printf("\n Side 2 :");
      scanf("%d",&s2);
      printf("\n Side 3 :");
      scanf("%d",&s3);
      t1 = s1 + s2;  /*Calculating Sums*/
      t2 = s1 + s3;
      t3 = s2 + s3;
      if(t1>s3 && t2>s2 && t3>s3)
        printf("\n Triangle is valid");
      else
        printf("\n Triangle is not valid");
  }
```

Sample Input/Output

When the above program is executed the following outputs are generated when some data are entered:

1. *Enter the size of 3 sides of triangle*
   Side 1 : 3
   Side 2 : 2
   Side 3 : 5
   Triagle is valid

2. *Enter the size of 3 sides of triangle*
   Side 1 : 8
   Side 2 : 2
   Side 3 : 3
   Triagle is not valid.

16.13.4 Counting Vowels and Non-vowels

Let us write a program to input characters one by one and to count the number of vowels and non-vowels entered by user. The logic of this program is also quite simple. Just accept a character within a while or do-while loop and use switch construct to check whether the entered character is a vowel or non-vowel. Ask user to press '!' to finish the entries. The number of vowels and non-vowels can be stored in separate variables. They can later on be displayed on the screen after coming out of loop.

Program 16.21

```
/*Program to count no. of vowels and non-vowels*/
#include <stdio.h>
main()
  {
     char alpha = ' ';    /*Declare & initialise alpha with space*/
     int vow, nvow; /*Vow for vowel, nvow for non-vowel*/
     vow = 0;         /*Initiative counters*/
     con = 0;
     while(alpha != '!')
       {
          printf("\n Enter a character :");
          alpha = getchar();
          fflush(stdin);
          switch(alpha)
            {
               case 'A' :
               case 'a' :
               case 'E' :
               case 'e' :
               case 'I' :
               case 'i' :
               case 'O' :
               case 'o' :
               case 'U' :
               case 'u' :
                           vow++;    /*Increment vowel counter*/
                           break;
               default:
                           nvow++;   /*Increment non-vowel counter*/
            }
       }
```

```
        printf("\n No. of vowels entered are %d", vow);
        printf("\n No. of non-vowels entered are %d", nvow);
    }
```

Sample Input/Output

When the program is executed, the folllowing output is generated after entering the input:

Enter a character: a
Enter a character : e
Enter a character : W
Enter a character : i
Enter a character : !
No. of vowels entered are 3
No. of non-vowels entered are 1

16.13.5 Calculating Sum of Digits

You can calculate the sum of digits of a number by the following logic :

(*a*) Divide the number by 10 and find the remainder. The remainder would be rightmost digit.
(*b*) Add remainder to a variable sum.
(*c*) Assign value of quotient obtained to the number.
(*d*) Repeat the process until the number becomes zero.

Let us write the program to accept a number from the user and calculate the sum of its digits using the above logic.

Program 16.22

```
/*Program to calculate sum of digits*/
#include <stdio.h>
main()
  {
     int n;     /*n is a number*/
     int rd;    /*rd is the right most digit*/
     int sum = 0;    /*Initialise sum to zero*/
     printf("\n Enter a no.");
     scanf("%d",&n);
     do
        {
           rd = n % 10;    /*Assign remainder to rd*/
           sum += rd;      /*Same as sum = sum + rd*/
           n/=10;     /*Same as n = n/10*/
        }while(n>0);
     printf("\n Sum of digits is %d", sum);
  }
```

Sample Inputs/Outputs

When the above program is run, you get the following output when some sample input number is entered:

(1) Enter a no. 591
Sum of digits is 15
(2) Enter a no. 2874
Sum of digits is 21

16.13.6 Generating Floyd's Triangle

A Floyd's triangle contains the following series of numbers:

1
2 3
4 5 6
7 8 9 10
11 12 13 14 15
.
.
.
79 80 81 82 83 84 85 86 87 88 89 90 91

If you write the whole series, you will find that this series generates a triangle of numbers in 13 rows and 13 columns. If *r* is the row no and *c* is the column no., you can develop the following logic for writing this program:

(1) Declare 3 variables *r, c* and *n* for row no., column no. and number to be displayed. Initialise *n* to 1.
(2) Make an outer loop where *r* changes from 1 to 13 incremented by 1.
(3) Make an inner loop where *c* changes from 1 to *r* incremented by 1.
(4) Display *n* and increment it within inner loop.

With above logic, you can generate the Floyd's triangle very easily. Let us write the program.

Program 16.23

```
/*Program to generate Floyd's triangle of numbers*/
#include <stdio.h>
main()
  {
      int r, c; /*r for row & c for column*/
      int n =1; /*Initialise the number with 1*/
      for(r=1;r<=13;r++)
        {
           printf("\n");
           for(c=1;c<=r;c++)
             {
                printf("%d",n);
                n++;
             }
        }
      getche();
  }
```

Sample Output:

When the above program will be executed, you will get the following output:

```
1
2   3
4   5   6
7   8   9   10
11  12  13  14  15
16  17  18  19  20  21
22  23  24  25  26  27  28
29  30  31  32  33  34  35  36
37  38  39  40  41  42  43  44  45
46  47  48  49  50  51  52  53  54  55
56  57  58  59  60  61  62  63  64  65  66
67  68  69  70  71  72  73  74  75  76  77  78
79  80  81  82  83  84  85  86  87  88  89  90  91
```

THEORY QUESTIONS

1. What are conditional statements is C? Discuss in brief.
2. What is if construct? How does it differ from if-else construct? Explain with example.
3. What is nested if-else construct? Explain various forms of nested if-else constructs with suitable examples.
4. Explain the following statements with suitable programs:
   (*a*) The goto statement.
   (*b*) The switch statement.
5. Write a program to determine whether a given year is a leap year or not. A leap year is that year which is divisible by 4 but not by 100 or is divisible by 400.
6. What are looping statements in C? Explain in brief.
7. Compare the following statements.
   (*a*) If-else and switch-case
   (*b*) do-while and while
   (*c*) continue and break
8. What is a for statement? Discuss the importance of a nested for loop by writing a program.
9. Can you nest do-while and while loops? Explain with examples.
10. Write a program to find factorial of a number. (Factorial of 5 is $5 \times 4 \times 3 \times 2 \times 1 = 120$.)

WORKSHOP

1. Enter the following programs discussed in the chapter on your computer:
   (*a*) Program 16.6
   (*b*) Program 16.10
   (*c*) Program 16.14

(*d*) Program 16.16

(*e*) Program 16.27.

Enter data wherever required and analyse the output.

2. Write a program to find sum of odd and even numbers separately between 1 to 50. Enter the program on your computer and see the output.
3. Write a program to display multiplication tables of 2 to 5. Enter it on your computer and see the output.
4. Write a program to display the fibonacci series *i.e.*, 1, 1, 2, 3, 5, 8, 13, ... upto first *n* numbers. Enter it on your computer and see the output.
5. Write a program to reverse the digits of a number entered by user. Enter it on your computer and see the output by entering different data.
6. Write a program to display the following output.

   1
   2 2
   3 3 3
   4 4 4 4
   5 5 5 5 5

   Enter it on your computer and see the output.

17
FUNCTIONS

17.1 INTRODUCTION

Functions are the building blocks of C programs. We introduced the term 'function' in the very first chapter while discussing our first program in C. You already know that main( ) is a function, which must be present in all C programs as it is the first function executed by the C compiler. Some other C functions which are familiar to you are: printf( ), scanf( ), getchar( ) and putchar( ). All these functions are available in the C library. Besides these library functions, you can build your own functions in C, which are called *user-defined functions*. Any C program is a combination of either library functions only or both library and user-defined functions. Till now, you have written many programs in C. Have you ever realised that a lengthy program in C can be broken down into smaller modules? When so many library functions are already available in C, then why do we need user-defined functions? You will get answers to these questions when you learn functions.

In this chapter, we will discuss the need, importance and use of the user-defined functions in a program. As a user-defined function is simply called function in C programming, we will use the general term 'function' while discussing it. However, we will use the term 'Standard Library Function' for a function that is available in C library. We are providing a brief description of important library functions in Appendix-D. Now, let us discuss functions, which are very easy-to-define and we can use them in our programs for solving any problem in a structured and simpler way.

17.2 OVERVIEW OF FUNCTIONS

If you are familiar with other high level languages, such as BASIC, COBOL, FORTRAN or Pascal, you must be familiar with Subroutines, Procedures or Paragraphs, which are sections of programs created by programmers. C functions are equivalent to these subroutines, procedures or paragraphs. They are actually the subprograms, which perform specific tasks and can be independent to other parts of a program. Let us first define the term 'Function'.

A *function* is a section of program that performs specific task, can be independent to other parts of the program, can return a value to the calling function and has a unique name in the program.

For understanding this definition, let us write a simple function in C and use it in our program. In C programming, writing the statements of a function is called *Defining the Function* and using it in the program is called *Calling the Function.*

17.2.1 Defining and Calling a Simple Function

A simple function is defined in the following form:

```
function-name()
{
     Statement-1;
     Statement-2;
          :
          :
}
```

However, when the function is called it is written in the following form:

```
function-name();
```

Note that a function is defined by writing its name without putting any semicolon after it, followed by a pair of braces within which the statements are written. However, when you call a function, you need to put semicolon after the name of function.

The following program defines and calls a function for displaying some message on the screen.

Program 17.1

```
/*Program that defines and calls a simple function*/
#include <stdio.h>
main()
{
     printf("\n Hello Students!");
     /*Calling the function*/
     message();
     printf("\n Functions");
}
/*Defining the function*/
message()
{
     printf("\n Let us learn");
}
```

In the above program, message( ) is the name of the function, which is called from the main( ) function. On execution of this program, the following output is displayed on the screen:

Hello Students !
Let us learn
Functions

Now, let us see how the above program is executed. You know that main( ) function is always executed first (no matter wherever it is written within the program). When the main( ) function is executed, first of all the string "Hello Students !" is displayed on the screen. The next statement message( ) calls the function message( ) and executes the statement written within the pair of braces. Hence, the string "Let us learn" is displayed. After executing the single statement written within function definition, the control goes back to the main( ) function and the statement next to message( ) statement gets executed. So, finally the string 'Functions' is displayed on the screen.

A calling function can call another function as illustrated in following example:

Program 17.2

```
/*Program where calling function calls another function*/
#include <stdio.h>
main()
{
     printf("\n Hello Students!");
     /*Calling first function*/
     message();
     printf("\n Functions");
}
/*Defining the first function */
message()
{
     printf("\n Let us learn");
     message1();
}
/*Defining the second function */
message1()
{
     printf("and understand");
}
```

What will be the output of the above program? On execution, the above program displays the following output:

Hello students!
Let us learn and understand
Functions

So, you see the first function 'message( )' calls another function 'message1( )'. Therefore, the string 'Let us learn and understand' is displayed before the control returns to the main( ) function.

In this way, any function can call another function and so on. There is no limit on the number of functions present in the C program. The main( ) function can also call more than one function any number of times as illustrated in the following example:

Program 17.3

```
/*Program to demonstrate the calling of multiple functions*/
#include <stdio.h>
main()
{
     func1();
     func2();
     func1();
     func3();
}
func1()
{
     printf("\n Good Morning");
```

```
}
func2()
{
     printf("\n Ladies");
}
func3()
{
     printf("\n Gentlemen");
}
```

On executing the above program, the following output will be displayed:

Good Morning
Ladies
Good Morning
Gentlemen

So, you see how easy it is to define and call a function. But it is not as easy as it seems. Sometimes, you need to pass values of the variables (called arguments or parameters) to the calling functions for doing some calculations or any other processing. How will you pass values to calling functions and return any value back to the called function? Now let us discuss the method of defining and calling functions with arguments or parameters.

17.2.2 Defining and Calling a Function with Parameters

Using parameters, a calling function can convey information to the called function. You have used parameters while writing printf( ) and scanf( ) functions. For example, in the statements scanf("%d", &x); and printf("%d", x); - x is a parameter. Similarly, you can use parameters in the functions defined by you. The general form of defining a function using parameters is as follows:

```
function-name1(parameter1, parameter2, ....)
data-type parameter1, parameter2, ....
{
     Statement-1;
     Statement-2;
          :
          :
     return(return-variable);
}
```

The general form of calling a function with parameters is:

```
return-variable = function-name1(parameter1, parameter2, ...);
```

Note that only one value (*i.e.*, return-variable) can be returned to a calling function and more than one parameters can be passed to the called function. While calling a function with parameters, you also need to put semicolon after the calling function statement.

Let us write a program to understand the method of passing values to a function.

Program 17.4

```
/*Program to calculate area of rectangle*/
#include <stdio.h>
main()
{
     int l, b, area;
     printf("\n Enter length of rectangle");
     scanf("%d", &l);
     printf("\n Enter breadth of rectangle");
     scanf("%d", &b);
     /*Calling the function by passing parameters*/
     area=areafunc(l,b);
     printf("\n The area of rectangle is %d", area);
}
/*Defining the function having parameters*/
areafunc(a,b)
int a, b;
{
     int c;
     c = a * b;
     return(c);
}
```

On executing this program, the following message appears:

Enter length of rectangle

Type the length say 5 and press <Enter key>. Now, the computer prompts you to enter breadth of rectangle. Type 4 and again press <Enter> key. Finally, you get the following output:

The area of rectangle is 20

Let us see how the program gets executed:

1. The beginning statements of main( ) function accept the length and breadth of rectangle from the user.

2. The next statement area = areafunc(l, b) calls the function by passing values of l and b.

Actual Parameters. The parameters (*e.g.*, l and b) defined in calling function statement are called Actual Parameters or Actual Arguments.

3. Now, the control goes to the function definition statement areafunc(a, b). This statement specifies that the values of l and b are stored in parameters a and b, respectively.

Formal Parameters. The parameters (*e.g.*, a and b) defined in the definition of function are called Formal Parameters or Formal Arguments.

4. The next statement int a, b defines the data type of formal arguments. The data type, number and order of formal arguments must match with the actual arguments. Note that the statement declaring data types of formal parameters is always written before the beginning brace of the function definition.

5. The first statement within braces of function definition is int c, which declares the variable c as integer type for storing the return value.

6. The next statement c = a * b calculates the area of rectangle by multiplying a with b and storing the result in variable c.

7. The last statement of function definition return(c) returns the result to the main( ) function and stores it into the variable area. So, the control goes back to the calling function.

8. The last statement of main( ) function, printf( ) displays the output on the screen.

Now, you must have understood the method of passing values to another function and returning the value back to the called function.

17.2.2.1 Call by Value

When values of the variables are passed to functions, such function calls are called *call by value*. These values occupy separate locations in memory and are accessed by formal parameters. Using 'call by value' function calls, you can return only a single value back to the calling function as illustrated in previous program. However, sometimes you need to return more than one value. How will you do that? This concept will be discussed in detail in chapter–19 (pointers) where you will learn to pass memory addresses to the functions.

17.2.2.2 Alternate Methods

Let us now discuss four more ways of writing the above discussed program.

Method 1

The one approach of defining the function is to write expression within return statement instead of first storing the result of expression in another variable and then returning it. For example, the areafunc( ) function could be defined as follows:

```
areafunc(a,b)
int a, b;
{
    return(a*b);
}
```

Method 2

The second approach of calling the function is to call the function within the printf( ) statement instead of calling it by a separate statement as illustrated below:

```
printf("\n The area of rectangle is %d", areafunc(l,b));
```

Method 3

The third approach of defining the function is to use variable names for formal parameters, same as that of actual parameters. For example, you can use same l and b variable names as formal parameters while defining the function. Although the variable names for actual and formal parameters could be the same but the compiler treats them as different variables due to their presence in different functions.

Method 4

The fourth approach of defining function is to define data type of formal parameters within function definition statement as illustrated below:

```
areafunc(int a, int b)
```

You can use any or all of these methods for calling and defining functions with parameters.

17.3 IMPORTANCE OF FUNCTIONS

Why do programmers need functions? What is the importance of functions in a program ? After understanding the ways of defining and calling functions, you may have realised the importance of functions in your programs. Let us discuss two main advantages of functions in a program - structured programming and reusability of code.

17.3.1 Structured Programming

Functions allow you to write a structured program. In a structured program, complex programming problems are broken down into a number of smaller and simpler tasks, where each task is performed by a separate function. Structured programming provides you the following benefits:

- It is easier to write a structured program because writing a structured program follows some rules of writing a good program.
- It is easier to debug a structured program because a structured program is always properly documented and follow rules of structured programming.
- Programming project can be divided into modules which can handled by different programmers simultaneously.

So, there is a division of labour in writing programs for complex and big problems and hence, important time of a programmer is saved. Structured programs are easier to modify and maintain due to proper documentation.

17.3.2 Reusability of Code

Another important benefit of functions is the reusability of code for the same kind of problems. You can use same section of code in different parts of your program for solving similar and repetitive problems. For instance, you can write a function for converting the amount written in figures into words. Whenever you need to display some figure in words, you can call this function. Similarly, you can write functions for many types of arithmetic, statistical or financial calculations, which can be reused by any of your program. So, reusability of code reduces the effort of writing hundred lines of code again and again for solving problems of similar nature.

17.4 FUNCTION PROTOTYPES

You know that a function may return a value. By default, this value is always of int data type. Sometimes, you need to return float, double, char or other type of value. For example, if you are passing parameters of float type to a function, the value returned must be either float or double. If you will not specify the return type, the value returned would be int, so you may get incorrect results. Therefore, it is important to specify the return type of data and also the type of parameters passed before defining the function, specially if the return type is other than int. A function prototype provides a return type, function name and types of parameters passed along with the name of parameters (optional) as shown in following format:

```
return-type function-name (parameter-type parameter-name-1, parameter-type
                                              parameter- name-2, ....)
```

For example, if the return-type of function func1 is float and you are passing two parameters a and b with type int and float respectively, the function prototype would be written as follows:

```
float func1(int a, float b)
```

Or

```
float func1(int float)
```

If you are specifying parameter names in the function prototype, they can be different than those specified in function definition. The only requirement is that they should have same type, number and in the same order.

If a function does not return any value then you specify void as return-type in function prototype as illustrated below:

```
void func-message()
```

Or

```
void func-message(void)
```

It means neither you are passing any parameters to the called function nor the called function is returning any value to the calling function. This is generally used when you call a function just for displaying messages. Normally, you need not write function prototype for functions which do not return any value. Let us now understand the importance of function prototypes.

17.4.1 Importance of Function Prototypes

A function prototype informs the compiler about the number, name and type of parameters which are passed to the called function. It also informs the compiler about the type of value (int, float, char, etc.) which will be returned to the calling function. Such type of information helps compiler in verifying the correctness of the type and number of parameters passed to the called function and the value returned to the calling function. If there is an error, the compiler gives an error message during compilation. It will help you in debugging your program. If you do not use function prototype, you may get incorrect results on execution of program. For instance, if you expect that certain function should return a float value but it may return an int value if you do not specify the return type of function by the use of function prototype. Therefore, it is a good practice to use function prototype whatever value the function may return. Let us write two programs – one using function prototype and another without it and compare their results.

17.4.2 Examples of Programs with/without Function Prototype

The following program calculates the area of a circle using a function without declaration of its prototype:

Program 17.5

```
/*Program to calculate the area of a circle without using
                                        function prototype

#include <stdio.h>
main( )
{
        float r, area;
        printf("\n Enter radius of the circle:");
        scanf("%f", &r);
        area = areafunc(r);
        printf("\n Area of the circle is %f", area);
}
```

```
areafunc(float r)
{
     float a;
     a = 3.14*r*r;
     return(a);
}
```

On execution, the above program prompts you:

Enter radius of the circle:

Type 2 and press <Enter> key, you will see the following output:

Area of the circle is 12.000000.

Is the result correct? No. The correct result is 12.56. Now, again execute the program and enter the radius 3, you will see the result 28.00000, which is again incorrect. The correct result is 28.26. So, you see without using function prototype, the called function returns int value. To correct the program, use function prototype as shown in the following program.

Program 17.6

```
/*Program to calculate the area of a circle using function prototype*/
#include <stdio.h>
/*Function prototype declaration*/
float areafunc(float);
main()
{
     float r, area;
     printf("\n Enter radius of the circle:");
     scanf("%f", &r);
     area = areafunc(r);
     printf("\n Area of the circle is %f", area);
}
float areafunc(float r)
{
     float a;
     a = 3.14*r*r;
     return(a);
}
```

When the above program is executed, you get the correct result because float value is returned as is specified in the function prototype. Enter the program in computer and see the results for different values of radius.

17.5 RECURSIVE FUNCTIONS

The most useful feature of functions is recursion. When a function calls itself, it is called *recursion*. Such a function is called recursive function. For example, the following message( ) function is a recursive function:

```
message()
{
     printf("\n Hi! How are you?");
     message();
}
```

If you call this function from the main( ) function, what will be the output? The program will display the same message 'Hi ! How are you?' again and again and will go in an end-less loop.

What is the need of calling the function itself? You see, a recursive function just repeats a set of statements. You can do this simply by making a loop as illustrated in the following function:

```
message1()
{
        int i;
        for(i=1; i<=100; i++)
              printf("\n Hi! How are you?");
}
```

The above program will display the message for 100 times and will not go in an end-less loop. So, what is the benefit of recursive functions? To understand the importance of recursion, we will first write two programs for calculating factorial of a number-one using non-recursive function and another using recursive function. Later on, we will compare these two programs to find the better one.

17.5.1 Example of Non-recursive Function

Let us write a program to calculate the factorial of a number without using a recursive function, but just using a loop. Before writing the code, you must first develop logic of the program.

To develop the logic of program, let us calculate factorial of 5 *i.e.*, 5!

We know,

5! = 5 × 4 × 3 × 2 × 1 = 120

Let x is a number whose factorial has to be calculated

a is the factorial

i is a counter for loop

then, the steps to calculate factorial of 5 (Assume x = 5) are:

Step 1: Let a = 1 and i = x (*i.e.*, i = 5)
Calculate a = a × i
So, a = 1 × 5 = 5.

Step 2: Decrement i, so i = 5 – 1 = 4
Again calculate, a = a × i
So, a = 5 × 4 = 20.

Step 3: Decrement i, so i = 4 – 1 = 3
Again calculate a = a × i
So, a = 20 × 3 = 60.

Step 4: Decrement i, so i = 3 – 1 = 2
Again calculate a = a × i
So, a = 60 × 2 = 120.

Step 5: Decrement i, so i = 2 – 1 = 1
Again calculate a = a × i
So, a = 120 × 1 = 120.

The calculation stops when i = 1. The above discussed logic is shown in Figure 17.1.

Variables a i a	Condition for loop
Step 1 1 × 5 = 5	i >= 1 where i
Step 2 5 × 4 = 20	is a counter.
Step 3 20 × 3 = 60	Assume in step 1
Step 4 60 × 2 = 120	Factorial, a = 1
Step 5 120 × 1 = 120	i = 5
So, Factorial of 5 = 120	

Figure 17.1 *Logic for Calculation of Factorial of a Number*

Now, we can easily write code for the program.

Program 17.7

```
/*Program to calculate factorial of a number*/
/*Without using recursive function*/
#include <stdio.h>
main()
{
     int n, f;
     printf("\n Enter a number:");
     scanf("%d", &n);
     f=fact(n);
     printf("\n Factorial of %d is %d", n, f);
}
fact(int x)
{
     int a=1, i;
     for(i=x; i>=1; i- -)
          a=a*i;
     return(a)
}
```

On execution, the program prompts you:

Enter a number:

Type 5 and press <Enter key>.

You will see the following output:

Factorial of 5 is 120

You can see the output for some other numbers after executing the program again and again. Now, let us solve the same problem of factorial by writing a recursive function.

17.5.2 Example of Recursive Function

To calculate the factorial of 5 using recursive function, let us recall the logic discussed earlier. As you know,

5! = 5 × 4 × 3 × 2 × 1

This is same as

5! = 5 × 4 !

where, 4! = 4 × 3 !

where, 3! = 3 × 2 !

where, 2! = 2 × 1 !

and 1! = 1

So, in order to calculate 5!, first you have to calculate 4! and to calculate 4!, you have calculate 3! and so on. We also know that the factorial of 1 is 1. This logic is the basis of writing a recursive function. Let us write the steps for developing the logic for calculating 5! using recursion.

Again, assume x is a number whose factorial has to be calculated and a is the factorial.

Step 1: Calculate a = x × Calculate factorial of x – 1
So, a = 5 × Calculate factorial of 4

Step 2: Calculate, Factorial of x – 1 = x – 1 × Calculate factorial of x – 2
So, Factorial of 4 = 4 × Calculate factorial of 3

Step 3: Calculate, Factorial of x – 2 = x – 2 × Calculate factorial of x – 3
So, Factorial of 3 = 3 × Calculate factorial of 2

Step 4: Calculate, Factorial of x – 3 = x – 3 × Calculate factorial of x – 4
So, Factorial of 2 = 2 × Calculate factorial of 1

As 1! = 1, the calculation stops here and the value of a is obtained. In simple words, the logic of program to calculate factorial of 5 (5!) using recursion is described in following steps:

(*a*) First of all 1! is calculated, which is 1.
(*b*) 1 is multiplied with 2 to obtain 2!, which is 2.
(*c*) 2 is multiplied with 3 to obtain 3!, which is 6.
(*d*) 6 is multiplied with 4 to obtain 4!, which is 24.
(*e*) Finally, 24 is multiplied with 5 to obtain 5!, which is 120.

This logic is illustrated in Figure 17.2.

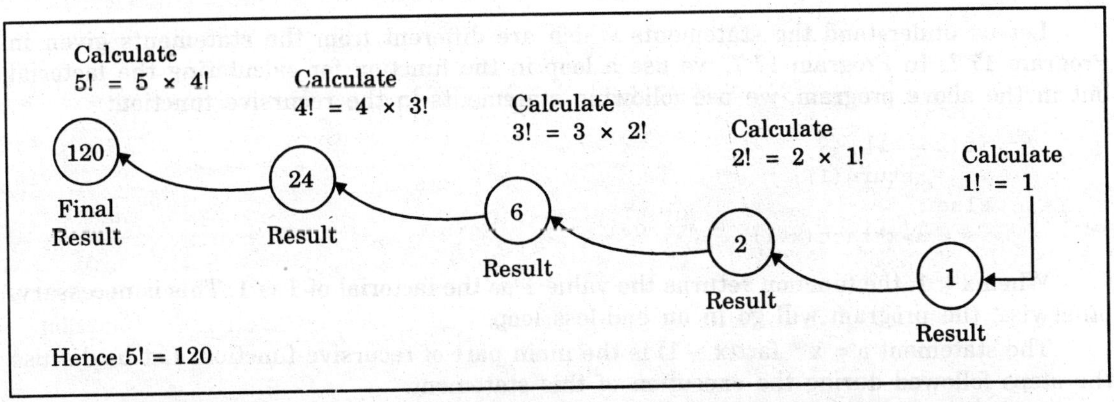

Figure. 17.2 *Diagrammatic Representation of Program Logic for Calculating Factorial of 5 using Recursion*

The program logic discussed above is similar to following steps:

Step 1: 1 × 2 = 2

Step 2: 2 × 3 = 6

Step 3: 6 × 4 = 24

Step 4: 24 × 5 = 120

Although you can develop program using this logic through simple looping (similar to Program 17.7), we will develop program through a recursive function for understanding the importance of recursion. Let us now write the program.

Program 17.8

```
/*Program to calculate factorial of a number using recursion*/
#include <stdio.h>
main()
{
     int n, f;
     printf("\n Enter a number:");
     scanf("%d", &n);
     f=fact(n);
     printf("\n Factorial of %d is %d", n,f);
}
/*Defining the recursive function*/
fact(int x)
{
     int a;
     if(x==1)
          return(1);
     else
          a=x*fact(x-1);
     return(a);
}
```

On execution, the program gives same messages and output as discussed in Program 17.7.

Let us understand the statements which are different from the statements given in Program 17.7. In Program 17.7, we use a loop in the function for calculating the factorial but in the above program, we use following statements in the recursive function:

```
if(x==1)
     return(1);
else
     a=x*fact(x-1);
```

When x = 1, the function returns the value 1 as the factorial of 1 is 1. This is necessary, otherwise, the program will go in an end-less loop.

The statement a = x * fact(x – 1) is the main part of recursive function. Let us discuss the steps followed during the execution of this statement.

Step 1: In the beginning, the value of x is 5, so a = 5 × fact (5 – 1) = 5 × fact (4). Now, the function calls itself with value of x = 4.

Step 2: As x = 4, a = 4 × fact (4 – 1) = 4 × fact (3). Now the function calls itself again with value x = 3.

Step 3: As x = 3, a = 3 × fact (3 – 1) = 3 × fact (2). Similarly, the function calls itself again with value of x = 2.

Step 4: As x = 2, a = 2 × fact (2 – 1) = 2 × fact (1). Finally, the function calls itself again with value of x = 1.

Step 5: As x = 1, so the condition (x = = 1) becomes true and hence the value 1 is returned to the previous calling function of step 4.

Step 6: 1 is multiplied with 2 and 2 is returned to the previous calling function of step 3.

Step 7: 2 is multiplied with 3 and 6 is returned to the previous calling function of step 2.

Step 8: 6 is multiplied with 4 and 24 is returned to the previous calling function of step 1.

Step 9: Finally 24 is multiplied with 5 and 120 is returned to the main( ) function.

In this way, the factorial of 5 is obtained which is 120.

Now, you must have understood the logic of recursion. We will discuss some more programs on recursion in later part of this chapter. Let us now compare the discussed recursive and non-recursive functions. Which one of these do you find easier to write? Which one of these uses simpler and compact code?

17.5.3 Recursive v/s Non-Recursive Functions

Non-recursive function is easier to write than a recursive function, but a recursive function also has its own importance in C programming. Let us first discuss the advantages and disadvantages of a non-recursive function.

17.5.3.1 Advantages and Disadvantages of Non-Recursive Functions

A non-recursive function provides mainly two benefits to the programmers:

- It is very easy to write a non-recursive function because the statements are written within a loop.
- A non-recursive function is easier to debug due to simple programming constructs.

However, a non-recursive function has mainly following two drawbacks:

- A non-recursive function is not the direct way to code an algorithm. Programmers generally code an algorithm to solve the problem in an indirect way so that it becomes easy.
- Programs written using non-recursive functions are lengthy due to indirect logic of program.

17.5.3.2 Advantages and Disadvantages of Recursive Functions

A recursive function is very useful as it provides following advantages to programmers:

- Recursion is the most direct way of converting a program algorithm into code. It is clear from the factorial problem that the statement a = x * fact(x – 1) is similar to the algorithm step written as 5! = 5 × (5 – 1)!
- A recursive function makes the code compact, so programs become smaller.
- Complicated problems where same steps are repeated again and again can be easily solved by writing recursive functions.

Inspite of these advantages, programmers generally avoid using recursive functions in their programs due to the following reasons:

- Writing recursive functions is a complicated task for beginners.
- It requires experience and good understanding in developing program logic.
- Recursive functions are somehow difficult to debug.

17.6 SCOPE OF VARIABLES

The scope of a variable means as to which functions of a program the value of a variable is available. The value of a variable may be available either to all functions of a program or to only that function where the variable is declared. The scope of a variable depends on its location where it is declared in the program. Based on this, the scope of a variable could be either global or local. The scope of a variable also depends on the type of storage class. Let us discuss various types of scopes and storage classes of variables in detail.

17.6.1 Global and Local Scope

If a variable is declared outside the function definition, generally before main( ) function, its value is available to all the functions. If the value of this variable is changed in one function, it is reflected in another function. Such type of scope of variables is called *Global Scope* and such variables are called *Global Variables*. However, if a variable is declared within the function definition, its value is available only to that function where it is declared. If the value of this variable is changed in that function, it is not reflected in other functions. Such type of scope of variables is called *Local Scope* and such variables are called *Local Variables.* Let us understand this concept with an example.

Program 17.9

```
/*Program to demonstrate the difference between local and global*/
/*variables*/
#include <stdio.h>
int a=1;
void func1(void)
main()
{
     printf("\n Value of a in main = %d", a);
     a++;
     printf("\n Value of a in main after increment = %d", a);
     func1();
     printf("\n Value of a in main after calling function = %d", a);
}
void func1()
{
     int b=20;
     printf("\n Value of a in func1 = %d", a);
     printf("\n Value of b in func1 = %d", b);
     a++;
     printf("\n Value of a in func1 after increment %d", a);
}
```

What will be the output of this program? On execution, the following output will be displayed on the screen:

Value of a in main = 1
Value of a in main after increment = 2
Value of a in func1 = 2
Value of b in func1 = 20
Value of a in func1 after increment = 3
Value of a in main after calling function = 3

Let us analyse the execution of this program. In this program, we have declared two variables a and b. The variable a is a global variable as it is declared outside the functions. The variable b is a local variable as it is declared inside the function *i.e.,* func1( ). As a is initialised to 1, the first output of a in main( ) function is 1. After increment in main( ) function, its value is displayed as 2. Now, the function func1( ) is called. In func1( ) function, another variable b is initialised as 20. As the scope of variable a is global, the value of a in func1( ) function is displayed as 2. Note that no value is passed to func1( ) as it is clear from the definition of function prototype (void func1(void)) itself. The value of b is displayed as 20 as the scope of variable b is local. In the next statement of the program, the variable a is incremented again. After incrementation, the value of a is displayed as 3 in func1( ) function. Now, the control goes to the main( ) function. Note again that no value is returned to main( ) function as there is no return statement and it is also clear from the definition of function prototype. What will be the value of variable a now? Will it be 2 or 3? It will be 3 because the scope of variable a is global and hence the change in value is reflected in calling function.

Now let us assume that a is initialized again in func1( ) function with value 10, then what will be its value in func1( ) after increment? Will it be 3 or 11? When same variable is declared again in another function, it becomes a new local variable for that function. As local variable gets preference over global variable (if variable names are same), the value of a after increment will be displayed as 11 and not as 3. Now, what will be the value of a in main( ) function after calling the function? Will it be 3 or 11. It will be 3 as the scope of variable a is global for the main( ) function.

We believe that the concept of local and global scope of variables is clear to you. We will discuss this concept again while discussing storage classes.

17.6.2 Storage Classes

As we already know, all variables in C have a data type. Besides having a data type, a variable also belongs to a particular storage class. The features of a variable depend on that particular storage type. Till now, we have not defined any storage type for variables, but they assume the default storage class if it is not defined. There are four storage classes in C, which are defined as follows:

(*a*) Auto
(*b*) Static
(*c*) Extern
(*d*) Register

Let us discuss these storage classes in detail.

17.6.2.1 Auto

By default, all variables have auto storage class. In C, auto storage class is declared as follows:

```
auto int n;
auto char ans;
```

As the default storage class for a variable is auto, there is no need to write 'auto' word before data type as illustrated below:

```
int n;
char ans;
```

The word 'auto' is generally written just to emphasise that the variable has auto storage type. A variable with auto storage class has following features:

- The variable is stored in memory.
- The scope of variable is local to the function.
- By default, the variable has an unpredictable initial value. It means if you do not initialise the variable, it contains a garbage value, but not zero.
- The variable is created each time the function is invoked.

The following program illustrates the features of a variable having auto storage class

Program 17.10

```
/*Program showing features of auto storage class*/
#include <stdio.h>
void dispmsg(void);
main
{
    auto int x=10;
    printf("\n Value of x in main before call = %d", x);
    x++;
    dispmsg();
    printf("\n Value of x in main after call = %d", x);
}
void dispmsg()
{
    auto int x=100;
    printf("\n value of x in dispmsg = %d", x);
    x++;
}
```

On execution, the program gives the following output:

Value of x in main before call = 10

Value of x in dispmsg = 100

Value of x in main after call = 11

Were you expecting this output? It is obvious that value of x in the main( ) function before calling another function dispmsg is 10. After this, x is incremented in the main( ) function and dispmsg( ) function is called. Now, x is declared again as auto with value 100. Therefore, the value of x in dispmsg( ) function is displayed as 100 and not 11. Why? This is because the scope of auto storage class is local to the function where it is declared. Now, the control goes back to the main( ) function after incrementing x again. Although in dispmsg( ) function, now the value of x is 101, in main( ) function it is displayed as 11. This is again due to local scope of auto storage type variable. From the output of this program, it is also clear that auto variable is created each time the function is invoked. If you call dispmsg( ) function again. The value of x would again become 100.

Let us now discuss another storage class where a variable is created and initialised only once.

17.6.2.2 Static

Static storage class is similar to auto storage class in only two features—one, the static variable is stored in memory and its scope is local to the function. However, static storage class differs from auto storage class by having default zero initial value and initialization of value only once. As variable of static storage class is created only once and its value, persists between different function calls, it is so called 'static'. In C, static storage class for a variable is declared as follows:

```
static int a;
```

Let us understand the features of a variable declared as static with the help of a program.

Program 17.11

```
/*Program to demonstrate features of static storage type*/
/*It also compares static with auto storage class*/
#include <stdio.h>
void static1(void);
void auto1(void);
main()
{
     /*Calling function having static variable*/
     static1();
     static1();
     /*Calling function having auto variable*/
     auto1();
     auto1();
}
void static1()
{
     static int x=100;
     printf("\n Value of x = %d", x);
     x++;
}
void auto1()
{
     auto int y=100;
     printf("\n Value of y = %d", y);
     y++;
}
```

On execution, the program displays the following output:

Value of x = 100
Value of x = 101
Value of y = 100
Value of y = 100

Are you surprised with this output? As we know that static variable is initialised only once, no matter how many times that function is called where it is declared. Therefore, first time you get value of y as 100 and second time you get as 101. The auto type of variable is initialised each time the function is called. Therefore, you get both times the values of x as 100.

17.6.2.3 Extern

Extern refers to External variable. From the name, it is clear that extern type of variable is declared outside all the functions. As the values of extern variables are available to any function, their scope is global. Like static, extern variables are initialised with default value of zero. Their values persist till the program ends. Like both auto and static, extern variables are stored in memory. The extern declaration is required for those variables whose values are defined in other program files (such as header files of C libraries). In C, extern storage class for a variable is declared as follows:

```
process()
{
     extern int x;
     /*x is defined in another program file*/
     :
     :

}
```

You can also use extern declaration for global variables defined in the same program file, but it is not necessary and moreover not required.

17.6.2.4 Register

Till now, we have discussed three storage classes — auto, static and extern. The variables of all of these storage classes are stored in memory. Sometimes you need to store a value of variable in registers as registers provide faster access. Generally you need to store frequently used variables such as counters, flags in registers. In that case, you can declare a variable of storage type register.

Like auto storage class, the default initial value stored in register type of variable is garbage value and the scope of this variable is local to the function. Actually the variables of register storage class offer same features as of auto storage class except that they are stored in registers instead of memory. As registers are limited in CPU, you can declare only few variables as register type to get advantage. In C, a variable with register storage class is declared as follows:

```
register int x;
```

The following program illustrates the use of register storage class:

Program 17.12

```
/*Program using variable of register storage class*/
#include <stdio.h>
```

```
main()
{
      register int n=0;
      do
      {
            printf("%d", n);
            n++;
      } while(n<10);
}
```

On execution, the program gives the following output:

0 1 2 3 4 5 6 7 8 9

As register storage type is almost similar to auto storage type, you do not need any explanation about the execution of this program.

Having understood about various storage types, we can compare their features in a tabular form as described in Table 17.1.

Criteria	Auto	Static	Extern	Register
1. Scope	Local	Local	Global	Local
2. Storage location	Memory	Memory	Memory	Registers
3. Default value on initialisation	Unpredictable	Zero	Zero	Unpredictable
4. Creation	Each time the function is called	Only once	Each time the function is called	Each time the function is called
5. Typical use	Local variables	Recursive function	Global variables	Counters, flags, etc.

Table 17.1 *Comparison of various storage types in C*

17.7 TYPICAL APPLICATIONS OF FUNCTIONS

Let us revise the chapter by writing functions for solving a few problems in C. We are providing the complete programs along with sample inputs/outputs on typical problems. As we have already discussed the concepts used in these programs, we are not explaining you the execution of programs. You are advised to enter and execute these programs on computer and analyse their outputs.

17.7.1 Finding Prime Numbers

Program 17.13

```
/*Program to find out whether the number*/
/*entered by user is a prime number*/
#include <stdio.h>
main()
{
      int num, a;
      printf("\n Enter a number:");
      scanf("%d", &num);
```

```
        /*Calling the function*/
        a = prime(num);
        if ((a==1 || num==1 || num==2)
            printf("\n %d is a prime number", num);
        else
            printf("\n %d is not a prime number", num);
        getche();
    }
    int prime(int n)
    {
        int a, i=2;
        while (i<n)         /*beginning of loop for dividing n with i*/
        {
            a=0;            /*a is a flag to check no. is prime or not*/
            if(n%i==0)      /*If remainder is zero*/
            {
                a=0;        /*No. is not prime*/
                break;      /*come out of loop*/
            }
            else
                a=1;        /*no. is prime*/
            i++;
        }
        return(a);
    }
```

Sample Inputs/Outputs:

1. *Enter a number : 5*
   5 is a prime number
2. *Enter a number : 93*
   93 is not a prime number
3. *Enter a number : 1*
   1 is a prime number
4. *Enter a number : 2*
   2 is a prime number

Program 17.14:

```
/*Program to display first n prime numbers*/
#include <stdio.h>
main()
{
    int num=1, a, x, p=0;
    printf("\n How many first prime numbers you want to display?");
    scanf("%d", &x);
    printf("\n First %d prime numbers are", x);
    while(p<x)
```

```
        {
            a=prime(num);
            if  ((a==1) || num==1 || num==2)
            {
                printf("%d",  num);
                p++;
            }
            num++;
        }
        getche();
    }
    int prime(int n)
    {
        int a, i=2;
        while (i<n)       /*beginning of loop for dividing n with i*/
        {
            a=0;          /*a is a flag to check no. is prime or not*/
            if(n % i == 0)  /*If remainder is zero*/
            {
                a=0;      /*No. is not prime*/
                break;    /*come out of loop*/
            }
            else
                a=1;      /*no. is prime */
            i++;
        }
        return(a);
    }
```

Sample Inputs/Outputs

1. *How many first prime numbers you want to display? 5*
   First 5 prime numbers are 1 2 3 5 7
2. *How many first prime numbers you want to display? 9*
   First 9 prime numbers are 1 2 3 5 7 11 13 17 19

17.7.2 Finding Sum of Cubes of Digits

Program 17.15

```
/*Program to find 3-digit numbers whose sum of*/
/*the cubes of their digits is equal to number itself*/
#include <stdio.h>
main()
{
    int n, x;
    printf("\n Numbers that are equal to sum of the cubes of their digits are");
    for(n=100; n<=999; n++)
    {
        x=findnum(n); /*Calling the function*/
        if(x==1)      /*if no. is found*/
```

```
            printf("\n %d", n);
        }
        getche();
    }
    findnum(int a)
    {
        int sum=0, storen, found, digit; /*found is a flag*/
        storen=a; /*No. is stored in variable which does not change*/
        do
        {
            digit=a%10;     /*Divide no. by 10*/
                              /*to find right most digit*/
            sum=sum + digit * digit * digit
                            /*The remainder or right most is cubed */
                            /*and added to sum*/
        } while(a!=0);      /*loop continue till all digits are obtained*/
        if(sum==storen);    /*compare sum with no.*/
            found=1;        /*No. is found*/
        else
            found=0;        /*No.is not found*/
        return(found);
    }
```

Sample Inputs/Outputs

Numbers that are equal to sum of the cubes of their digits are:

153

370

371

407

17.7.3 Finding Square of a Number

Program 17.16

```
    /*Program to calculate square of a number*/
    include <stdio.h>
    main()
    {
        int x, sqr;
        printf("\n Enter a number:");
        scanf("%d", &x);
        sqr = square(x);
        printf("\n Square of %d is %d", x, sqr);
        getche();
    }
    int square(a)
    int a;
```

```
{
    int s;
    s=a*a;          /*Calculating square*/
    return(s);
}
```

Sample Inputs/Outputs:

1. *Enter a number: 5*
   Square of 5 is 25
2. *Enter a number: 8*
   Square of 8 is 64

17.7.4 Finding Fibonacci Numbers

Program 17.17

```
/*Program to display Fibonacci series*/
#include <stdio.h>
main()
{
    int n, i, f;
    printf("\n How many first fibonacci numbers you want to display?");
    scanf("%d", &n);
    printf("\n The first %d Fibonacci numbers are", n);
    for(i=1; i<=n; i++)
    {
        f=fib(i);       /*Calling the function*/
        printf("%d", f);
    }
    getche();
}
int fib(int a)
{
    if(a<=2)      /*First 2 fibonacci nos. are 1,1*/
        return(1);
    else
        return(fib(a-1)+fib(a-2));
    /*recursive call*/
    /*a-1 is first previous number in series*/
    /*a-2 is second previous number in series*/
    /*Fibonacci no. is calculated by adding 2 previous nos.*/
}
```

Sample Inputs/Outputs

1. *How many first Fibonacci numbers you want to display? 5*
   The first 5 Fibonacci numbers are 1 1 2 3 5.
2. *How many first Fibonacci numbers you want to display? 15*
   The first 15 Fibonacci numbers are 1 1 2 3 5 8 13 21 34 55 89 144 233 377 610.

17.7.5 Reversing the Number and Finding Number of Digits

Program 17.18

```
/*Program to display number in reverse order*/
/*and to calculate number of its digits*/
include <stdio.h>
main()
{
    int x, d;
    printf("\n Enter a number:");
    scanf("%d", &x);
    d=numofdigit(x); /*Calling the function*/
    printf("\n No. of digits in this number are %d", d);
    getche();
}
int numofdigit(int x)
{
    int rm, d1=0; /*rm for right most digit*/
    printf("\n The number in reverse order is");
    while(x!=0)          /*Execute statements till quotient not equal*/
                         /*to zero*/
    {
        rm=x%10;         /*Divide number by 10 and*/
                         /*store remainder in rm*/
        printf("%d", rm);
        x=x/10;          /*Store quotient in x*/
        d1=d1+1;         /*Increment d1 to find no. of digits */
    }
    return(d1);          /*return no. of digits */
}
```

Sample Inputs/Outputs

1. *Enter a number: 6549*
   The number in reverse order is 9456
   No. of digits in this number are 4
2. *Enter a number: 13098*
   The number in reverse order is 89031
   No. of digits in this number are 5

17.7.6 Finding Roots of Quadratic Equation

Hint: Formula to find the roots of the quadratic equation, $ax^2 + bx + c = 0$:

$$x = \frac{-b \pm \sqrt{b^2 - 4ac}}{2a}$$

Assume, a, b and c are floating point numbers x_1 and x_2 are floating point variables for roots $b^2 > 4ac$.

Program 17.19

```
/*Program to find roots of the quadratic equation*/
#include <stdio.h>
#include <math.h>
void quad(float, float, float);
main()
{
     float a, b, c;
     int invalid=0;
     while(invalid==0)    /*loop for valid entry*/
     {
          printf("\n Enter value of a, b and c:");
          scanf("%f %f %f", &a, &b, &c);
          if(b*b <= 4*a*c)        /*To check b² <= 4ac*/
          {
               printf("\n Invalid data, enter again");
               /*data is invalid if real roots are not possible*/
               invalid=0;
          }
          else
               invalid=1;
     }
     quad(a, b, c);    /*Calling the function*/
     getche();
}
void quad(float a, float b, float c)
{
     float d, x1, x2;
     d=b*b-4*a*c;         /*d = b² - 4ac*/
     x1=(-b + sqrt (d))/2*a;
     x2=(-b+sqrt (d))/2*a;
     printf("\n The real roots of quadratic equations are %d and %d", x1, x2);
}
```

Sample Inputs/Outputs

1. *Enter value of a, b and c: 1 3 1*
   The real roots of quadratic equations are 0 and –24576
2. *Enter value of a, b and c: 2 6 3*
   The real roots of quadratic equations are 0 and 8192
3. *Enter value of a, b and c: 1 –4 3*
   The real roots of quadratic equations are 0 and 0
4. *Enter value of a, b and c: 4 1 2*
   Invalid data, enter again
   Enter value of a, b and c: 1 4 2
   The real roots of quadratic equations are 0 and 16834

17.7.7 Computing sin x

Hint: Formula to compute the value for sin x for summing the first n terms

$$\sin x = x - \frac{x^3}{3!} + \frac{x^5}{5!} - \frac{x^7}{7!} + \ldots\ldots$$

Or

$$\sin x = \frac{x^1}{1!} - \frac{x^3}{3!} + \frac{x^5}{5!} - \frac{x^7}{7!} + \ldots\ldots$$

Where x is in radians (3.14 radians = 180°).

Program 17.20

```
/*Program to compute the value of sin x*/
#include <stdio.h>
#include <math.h>
float calsinx(float, int);
float fact(int);
main()
{
     int n;
     float x, sin x;      /*x is in radians */
     printf("\n Enter the value of x and n:");
     scanf("%f %d", &x, &n);
     sinx=calsinx(x, n); /*Calling the function*/
     printf("\n sin x=%f", sin x);
     getche();
}
float calsinx(float x, int n)
{
     float s=0, t;
     int i, p=1;          /*t is one term for p and p+2*/
     for(i=1; i<=n; i++)
     {
          t=pow(x, p)/fact(p)  - pow(x, p+2)/fact(p+2);
          /*Calculate term by*/
          /*subtracting second part from first part of term*/
          p=p+4           /*Adding 4 to p*/
                          /*makes xp to xp+4 e.g., x1 to x5*/
          s=s+t; Add term to s
     }
     return(s);
}
float fact(int p)
/*function to calculate factorial of p*/
{
     if(p==1)
          return(1);
     else
          return(p*fact(p-1));
}
```

Sample Inputs/Outputs

1. *Enter the value of x and n: 1.57 2*

   sin x = 0.999843

   ***(Note:** sin 90 = 1 and 90 degree = π/2 or 1.57 radians)*
2. *Enter the value of x and n: 2 3*

   sin x = 0.909296
3. *Enter the value of x and n: 0 4*

   sin x = 0.000000

17.7.8 Finding Sum of a Series

Program 17.21

```
{
      /*Program to obtain sum of series*/
      /*1+x+x^2+x^3+.....+x^n*/
      int n, x, sum;
      printf("\n Enter value of x and n:");
      scanf("%d %d", &x &n);
      sum=sumofseries(x, n);       /*Calling the function*/
      printf("\n The sum of series is %d", sum);
      getche();
}
int sumofseries(int x1, int n1)
{
      int i, series, sum1=0;
      printf("\n The series is");
      for(i=0; i<=n1; i++)
      {
           series = pow(x1, i)           /*Calculating a term of series*/
           printf("%d", series);
           sum1 = sum1 + series;  /*Adding term to sum1*/
      }
      return(sum1);
}
```

Sample Inputs/Outputs:

1. *Enter value of x and n: 4 2*

   The series is 1 4 16

   The sum of series is 21
2. *Enter value of x and n: 6 4*

   The series is 1 6 36 216 1296

   The sum of series is 1555

THEORY QUESTIONS

1. What are functions? How will you define and call a function without arguments? Explain with example.
2. What are parameters? What is the difference between actual and formal parameters? Explain with a program.
3. Discuss the importance of functions in C programming.
4. What are Function Prototypes? Discuss the importance of function prototypes with examples.
5. (*a*) What do you mean by term 'void'? Explain with example.

   (*b*) How do you return a value to the calling function? Explain with a program.
6. What is 'Call by Value' function call? Explain with an example.
7. (*a*) What is recursion? Write a recursive function.

   (*b*) Compare recursive and non-recursive functions with suitable examples. Which of these functions you find easier to write? Why?
8. Differentiate between the following terms:

   (*a*) Global and Local Variables.

   (*b*) Auto and Static Storage Class.

   (*c*) Extern and Register Storage Class.
9. Write a program to find out the sum of digits of a given number.
10. Write a function to calculate greatest common divisor of two non-negative integers.
11. Write a recursive function to calculate factorial of 5.
12. Write a program to display sum of first n odd numbers.
13. Write a program to calculate perimeter of rectangle using a function.
14. Write a program to display nth prime number in the range 1 to 100.
15. Write a program to find nth fibonacci number in the first 50 numbers in fibonacci series.

WORKSHOP

1. Write a program using a function to reverse the integer entered by user. Enter the program in computer and execute it using following data:

   (*a*) 3129

   (*b*) 19732

   (*c*) 98789

   (*d*) 0

   See and analyse the outputs.
2. Write a program to calculate area of circle by defining a function. Enter and execute the program using following inputs:

   Enter Diameter: 5.37

   Enter Diameter: 18.21.
3. Enter the Program 17.17 (given in chapter) and execute it. See the outputs by enterning some sample data.
4. Write a program to display te following series (Lucas sequence):

   1 3 4 7 11 18 29

   Enter the program and see the output.

5. Enter the Program 17.18 (given in chapter) and execute it. See the outputs by entering the value of x for calculating sin 60, sin 45 and sin 180.

   (**Note:** π radians = 180 degree where π = 3.14)
6. Enter the program written by you in Theory Question 14 and execute it.
7. Enter the program written by you in Theory Question 15 and execute it.
8. Write a program to calculate sum of n even numbers starting from the given number. Enter and execute this program.
9. Enter the following program and see the output on its execution.

```
#include <stdio.h>
main()
{
      int x, i;
      for(i=1; i<=5; i++)
      {
            x=series(i);
            printf("%d", x);
      }
}
int series(int x)
{
      int n;
      n=x*x*x;
      return(n);
}
```

10. Enter the following program and see the output after entering data an execution.

```
#include <stdio.h>
main()
{
      int x, y, z, max;
      printf("\n Enter value of x, y and z");
      scanf("%d %d %d", &x, &y, &z);
      max=large(x, y);
      printf("\n Maximum no is %d", large(z, max));
}
large(int a, int b)
{
      int c;
      if(a>=b)
            c=a;
      else
            c=b;
      return(c);
}
```

18

ARRAYS

18.1 INTRODUCTION

Till now you have learnt to define and use different types of variables in your programs. Most of the times you need to create a collection of variables for data items, which are similar to one another. In this chapter, we are going to discuss the declaration, use and application of these collection of similar variables, called Arrays, in our programs. Using arrays, a large quantity of data can be conveniently stored, referred, accessed and processed in memory. As it is easier to refer an entire collection of data items at one time rather than referring each data item individually, the knowledge of arrays is mandatory for programmers. Let us gain this knowledge and apply it in our programs.

18.2 OVERVIEW OF ARRAYS

An *array* is a collection of related or similar data elements stored in a contiguous area in the memory, which is referred by a common name. To understand the meaning of an array, consider the following problem:

Let us assume that you want to store the roll numbers of 10 students along with their percentage of marks obtained in the computer memory. After entering all the data, you also want to display information of each student on monitor. How will you solve this problem?

You can easily solve this problem by writing a program in C. As you want to input roll number and percentage of marks obtained of each student, you can declare two variables: rollno1 and perc1 for storing data of first student. Similarly for storing data of second student, you can declare variables: rollno2 and perc2. As there are 10 students, you will be required to declare 20 variables to store their roll numbers and percentages. You can use these variables in your program while writing code for entering and displaying data. This program, on execution, will store the roll number and percentage of each student in separate variables. Hence, you can display information of each student by displaying contents of the 20 variables. Can you easily think of different name for each variable? It is difficult, but you can. Now, suppose you want to store the data of 1000 students of a school. Can you, then easily think of 2000 different variable names and use them in your program? It is extremely difficult and seems to be somehow impossible, though you still can. The program would be extremely lengthy and it would be really difficult for you to develop logic and code for the program. Such a program would be very unstructured.

All programming languages (including C) provide us a very easy method to solve such problems. Such problems can be solved conveniently by the use of arrays. Using an array, a group of similar data elements (such as roll numbers) are referred with a common name. For example, for solving the problem discussed above, the roll numbers and percentages of all students can be referred by common names such as rollno[i] and perc[i], respectively, where i is the location number of each student's data in memory. In C, the beginning location of an array element is referred as 0 as distinguished from some other programming languages like BASIC, where it is referred as 1. Hence, rollno[0], rollno[1] and rollno[2] refer to the roll numbers stored on location numbers first, second and third, respectively. Similarly, perc[0], perc[1] and perc[2] refer to the percentages stored on location numbers first, second and third, respectively. What are these location numbers called? Let us discuss below.

18.2.1 Subscripts

Subscripts are defined as numbers that denote the positions or locations of particular data elements in an array. For example, in the above discussed problem, variables rollno[0] and perc[0] are the elements of arrays, rollno[i] and perc[i], respectively, where i is the subscript. So, 0 and 1 are the subscripts of rollno[0] and rollno[1] variables, respectively. The variables having subscripts are called subscripted variables. Therefore, arrays are nothing but subscripted variables. A subscript can be constant or numeric variable. Based on the number of subscripts in an array, arrays are of many types. Let us discuss various types of arrays.

18.2.2 Types of Arrays

Arrays are classified into two categories– One-dimensional and Multi-dimensional arrays. Let us discuss these.

18.2.2.1 One-dimensional Arrays

An array containing a single subscript is called a *one-dimensional array*. For example, in above discussed example, rollno[i] and perc[i] are one-dimensional arrays. In one-dimensional arrays, the data elements are arranged in linear order in memory as illustrated in Figure 18.1.

	07	13	02	09	08	11	12	01	03	04
rollno	[0]	[1]	[2]	[3]	[4]	[5]	[6]	[7]	[8]	[9]
	35	41	72	100	13	92	81	78	62	49
perc	[0]	[1]	[2]	[3]	[4]	[5]	[6]	[7]	[8]	[9]

Figure 18.1 *Linear representation of One-dimensional Arrays*

18.2.2.2 Multi-dimensional arrays

An array containing multiple or more than one subscripts is called a *multi-dimensional array*. A multi-dimensional array is generally either a two-dimensional (2-D) or a three-dimensional (3-D) array. More than three subscripts are also possible in an array but they are rarely used. Let us understand the arrangement of data elements in 2-D and 3-D arrays.

(*a*) Two-dimensional Arrays

To understand a two-dimensional array, consider an example. A company markets its products in 3 regions and each region has 5 sales executives. The company wants to store the sales made by each sales executive of all the regions separately. To solve this problem, study the data which is organised in a tabular form as shown in Table 18.1.

Sales in Rupees					
Region No.	**Sales Executive No.**				
	1	**2**	**3**	**4**	**5**
1	2000	492	3120	251	8972
2	1500	5152	530	1730	1498
3	1375	109	4320	450	540

Table 18.1 *An example of data of sales made by 5 executives each in 3 regions*

In this table, there are three rows and five columns. The data of such a table can be stored by the use of a 2-D array. In a 2-D array, the two subscripts are used-the first one specifies the row number and the second specifies the column number. For example, sales[0][2] denotes the variable for storing the sales data of row 1 and column 3 *i.e.,* sales made by sales executive no. 3 of region no. 1 (which is Rs. 3120). Similarly, the sales of Rs. 5152, made by sales executive no. 2 of region no. 2 will be stored in data element sales[1][1] (Remember that subscripts in C begin from 0 and not from 1).

A two-dimensional array is also called a *matrix*. Although, the data of 2-D array is viewed logically as organised in a table, it is stored in memory in linear order, just like one-dimensional array, as illustrated in Figure 18.2. Each row of a 2-D array can be considered a one-dimensional array. So, a 2-D array is an array of 1-D arrays.

0th 1-D array					1st 1-D array					2nd 1-D array				
2000	492	3120	251	8972	1500	5152	530	1730	1498	1375	109	4320	450	540

Sales [0] [0][0] [1][0] [2] [0] [3] [0] [4] [1] [0] [1] [1] [1] [2] [1] [3] [1] [4] [2] [0] [2] [1] [2] [2] [2] [3] [2] [4]

Figure 18.2 *Linear Representation of Two-dimensional Array*

(*b*) Three-dimensional Arrays

In order to understand a three-dimensional array, let us review the problem discussed above in 'Two-dimensional array'. The company manufactures two categories of items— one Tooth-pastes and another Tooth-powders. Suppose, the company wants to analyse the sales of each category of item in different regions. The data of these items are represented in tabular form as shown in Table 18.2.

Sales in Rupees										
Region No.	**Product: Tooth Paste**					**Product: Tooth Powder**				
	Sales Executive No.					**Sales Executive No.**				
	1	2	3	4	5	1	2	3	4	5
1	1500	292	1620	150	5813	500	200	1500	101	3159
2	1250	1835	20	1500	1100	250	3317	510	230	398
3	375	100	4100	350	270	1000	9	220	200	270

Table 18.2 *An example of sales of 2 types of products made by 5 executives each in 3 regions*

A three-dimensional array can be thought of as an array of 2-D arrays, where a 2-D array is an array of 1-D arrays. In a 3-D array, three subscripts are used, where first subscript denotes the two major parts of a table where both parts represent same number of rows and columns with similar data. For instance, in Table 18.2, the data of two products tooth paste and tooth powder are shown in two parts of table. Each part of table has data organised in 3 rows and 5 columns logically represented as a 2-D array. The data of this table can be represented as a 3-D array, sales [*p*][*r*][*s*] where *p, r* and *s* are subscripts representing product no., region no. and sales executive no., respectively. For example, the data element, sales [0][0][0] represents sales of tooth paste made in region 1 by sales executive no. 1 (*i.e.,* Rs. 1500). Similarly, sales [1][2][2] represents sales of tooth powder made in region 3 by sales executive no. 3 (*i.e.,* Rs. 220).

Like 1-D and 2-D arrays, the data of a 3-D array is also stored in memory in linear order as illustrated in Figure 18.2. By analysing the data shown in this figure, you will come to know that a 3-D array is nothing but an array of arrays.

270	Sales [1] [2] [4]
200	Sales [1] [2] [3]
220	Sales [1] [2] [2]
9	Sales [1] [2] [1]
1000	Sales [1] [2] [0]
298	Sales [1] [1] [4]
230	Sales [1] [1] [3]
510	Sales [1] [1] [2]
3317	Sales [1] [1] [1]
250	Sales [1] [1] [0]
3159	Sales [1] [0] [4]
101	Sales [1] [0] [3]
1500	Sales [1] [0] [2]
200	Sales [1] [0] [1]
500	Sales [1] [0] [0]
270	Sales [0] [2] [4]
350	Sales [0] [2] [3]
4100	Sales [0] [2] [2]
100	Sales [0] [2] [1]
375	Sales [0] [2] [0]
1100	Sales [0] [1] [4]
1500	Sales [0] [1] [3]
20	Sales [0] [1] [2]
1835	Sales [0] [1] [1]
1250	Sales [0] [1] [0]
5813	Sales [0] [0] [4]
150	Sales [0] [0] [3]
1620	Sales [0] [0] [2]
292	Sales [0] [0] [1]
1500	Sales [0] [0] [0]

(Each group of five consecutive elements forms a 1-D array; each group of three 1-D arrays forms a 2-D array.)

Figure 18.3 *Linear Representation of Three-dimensional Array*

18.3 ONE-DIMENSIONAL ARRAYS

After having an overview on arrays, let us discuss the ways to declare, initialise and manipulate one-dimensional arrays.

18.3.1 Declaration of 1-D Arrays

A one-dimensional array is declared in the following format:

```
<data-type> <array-name> [No. of elements];
```

For example, an array to store roll numbers of 10 students is declared as follows:

```
int rollno[10];
```

Similarly, you can store the prices of 100 items in an array, which is declared as follows:

```
float price[100];
```

You can also declare an array for storing a string of characters such as name of students, as illustrated below:

```
char name[21];
```

In the above declaration of array, each character of name is stored in separate data element, such as name[0], name[1], name[2]... name[20] and the last name [21] data element stores the string-terminator character, '\0' (NULL).

In general, you can declare an array of any data type (fundamental or derived) in C. An array can be declared both inside or outside the function.

18.3.2 Initialisation of 1-D Arrays

After declaration, you can initialise array element with values. Initialisation is important as it provides some specific values to array elements. If you do not initialise an array, the array elements may contain some garbage values, which may effect the results or output of your program. Therefore, initialisation is always advisible though it is not mandatory. There are two ways by which you can initialise the data elements of a one-dimensional array.

(*a*) Initialisation using a single instruction, and

(*b*) Initialisation using a set of instructions. Let us discuss these.

18.3.2.1 Initialisation Using a Single Instruction

You can initialise a one-dimensional array using a single instruction as illustrated in following examples:

(*i*) `char name[ ] = {"SHIVANI"};`

(*ii*) `char month[ ] = {'M', 'A', 'R', 'C', 'H', '\0'};`

(*iii*) `int age[ ] = {32, 41, 17, 19, 22, 0};`

(*iv*) `float price[ ] = (352.50, 5059.00, 450.50, 0};`

As shown in first two examples, a string can be initialised in two ways. In first example, the complete string is enclosed in double quotes (") to initialise a string variable. In second example, each data item of the array is initialised with characters enclosed in single quotes (') and separated by commas. Note that NULL character is stored in last data element, which is not required in first example while storing the entire string in the array.

Similarly, a string-terminator is not required in last data element of numeric arrays, however you may store 0 in last data element just to simplify logic of the program (as illustrated in examples (*iii*) and (*iv*) above. The important requirement for initialization using a single instruction is that the array needs to be initialised outside the function.

18.3.2.2 Initialisation Using a Set of Instructions

Using single instruction method, a limited number of data elements of an array can be initialised. Suppose, an array contains 50 data elements and you want to initialise each data element of the array with same value, then the single instruction method of initialisation is not convenient. Such an array is initialised using a set of instructions written inside the function in the form of a loop. For example, to initialise each element of an array, maxmarks[50] with value 100, write the following statements within the function:

```
int i, maxmarks[50];
for (i = 0; i < 50; i++)
    maxmarks[i] = 100;
```

A limited number of data elements can also be initialised separately without a loop construct with same or different values, inside the function. For example, if an array, price[ ] has only 5 data elements and you want to initialise each element separately with some value; you can write the following statements within the function:

```
float price[5];
price[0] = 35.50;
price[1] = 50.00;
price[2] = 71.50;
price[3] = 192.50;
price[4] = 49.00;
```

Besides initialisation, you can also accept data from the user by using standard Input/Output functions such printf( ) and scanf( ) while manipulating arrays. Let us now discuss the manipulation procedure of one-dimensional arrays.

18.3.3 Manipulation of 1-D Arrays

We have just discussed the methods for declaring and initialising one-dimensional arrays. Manipulation of an array includes– entering data into array elements, reading that data and performing calculations during the execution of program.

Let us discuss the way to enter data into a one-dimensional array.

18.3.3.1 Entering Data into 1-D Arrays

The standard Input/Output functions, printf( ) and scanf( ) are used along with a loop construct to accept data from the user during execution of the program. Consider the problem of storing roll numbers and percentages in an array discussed in the beginning of this chapter. Write the following statements within the function to store roll numbers and percentages of 10 students in 1-D arrays, rollno[10] and perc[10];

```
int i, rollno[10], perc[10];
for (i = 0; i < 10; i++)
```

```
{
 printf("\n Enter Roll No. of Student %d:", i+1);
 scanf("%d", &rollno[i]);
 printf("\n Enter Percentage of Student %d:", i+1);
 scanf("%d", &perc[i]);
}
```

Let us analyse these statements. The first statement, int *i* , rollno[10], perc[10]; declares three integer variables- one is the counter *i*, second an array rollno[10] and third an array perc[10]. Input/Output statements are written within the for loop construct.

The first printf( ) function displays the message "Enter Roll No. of Student" followed by the student no. *i.e.*, i + 1 (As initial value of *i* is 0, therefore i + 1 refers Ist student). The first scanf( ) function accepts data from user and stores into the array element, rollno[*i*] where *i* is subscript or loop counter. As initial value of *i* is 0, the roll number of first student will be stored in array element, rollno[0]. Similarly, the second printf( ) function displays the message "Enter Percentage of Student" followed by the student no. *i.e., i* + 1. The second scanf( ) function accepts data from user and stores into the array element, perc[*i*]. After execution of loop for the first time, *i* is incremented and thus data for second student is accepted. In this way, the program will accept data of all 10 students and will store it in two 1-D arrays, rollno[10] and perc[10]. How will you read this data to display output? Let us discuss.

18.3.3.2 Reading Data from 1-D Arrays

After entering data, you can read it from memory using the printf() function within a loop construct as illustrated below:

```
printf ("\n Roll No.\t Perc.");
for (i = 0; i < 10; i++)
    printf ("\n %d\t%d", rollno[i], perc[i]);
```

The above statements will display the output in following form:

Roll No.	Perc.
07	*35*
13	*41*
:	:

In this way, all the data of two arrays, rollno[10] and perc[10] will be displayed. You can also display data of selective data elements. For example, to display roll no. and percentage of 6th student, write the following statements:

```
printf ("\n The roll no. of 6th student is %d" rollno[5]);
printf ("\n The percentage of 6th student is %d" perc[5]);
```

Besides reading the data from an array, you can perform calculations on the values of data elements. All types of calculations can be performed on array elements similar to numeric variables. Let us discuss how?

18.3.3.3 Calculations on 1-D Arrays

To understand, how you will perform calculations on data elements of an array, let us consider the following three array declarations:

```
int marksobt[10], maxmarks[10];
float perc[10];
```

In order to calculate the percentage of marks obtained by each student, write the following statements after reading data of marksobt[10] and maxmarks[10] arrays:

```
for (i = 0; i < 10; i++)
    perc[i] = marksobt[i] * 100/maxmarks[i];
```

The above statements will multiply values of marksobt[i] data element with 100 and divide the results obtained by corresponding values of maxmarks[i] data elements.

In this way you can perform any type of arithmetic calculation an array elements.

Having understood declaration, initialisation and manipulation of 1- D arrays, we are now in a position to write complete programs using one-dimensional arrays:

18.3.4 Programs on 1-D Arrays

Let us write programs for solving two simple problems. The first problem is to store prices of 5 items along with their item codes in computer memory. After storing the data, we also want to display the data. This problem can be solved by declaring two 1-D arrays - icode[5] and price[5]. The complete program is as follows:

Program 18.1

```
/*Program to store and display codes and prices of 5 items*/
#include <stdio.h>
main( )
{
  int i; /*declaration of counter i for loop*/
  int icode[5]; /*declaration of icode[ ] array with 5 data elements*/
  float price[5]; /*declaration of price[ ] array with 5 data elements*/
  for (i = 0; i < 5; i++)
  {
        /*Accepting data for icode[ ] array*/
        printf ("\n Enter Item Code of Item %d", i + 1);
        /*The above statement will display Item no.*/
        /*i + 1 with the displayed string */
        scanf ("%d", icode[i]);
        /*Accepting data for price[ ] array */
        printf ("Enter Price of Item %d", i + 1);
        scanf ("%f", &price[i]);
  }
  /*Displaying data of 1-D arrays*/
  printf ("\n Details of Items/n");
  printf ("\n Item code\t Price");
  for (i = 0; i < 5; i++)
```

```
    printf ("\n %5d\t\t%7.2f", icode[i], price[i]);
    /*In the above statement %5d indicates that*/
    /*5 digits of integer will be displayed and*/
    /*%7.2f indicates that 7 digits including*/
    /*2 decimal places will be displayed*/
    /*This is required to align the data displayed on screen*/
    getche( );
}
```

Sample Inputs/Ouputs

When the above program is executed, you will get the following prompts to enter data: (We have entered sample data to show you the output).

Enter Item Code of Item 1 : 101
Enter Price of Item 1 : 59.50
Enter Item Code of Item 2 : 102
Enter Price of Item 2 : 139.00
Enter Item Code of Item 3 : 103
Enter Price of Item 3 : 3905.50
Enter Item Code of Item 4 : 104
Enter Price of Item 4 : 48.00
Enter Item Code of Item 5 : 105
Enter Price of Item 5 : 302.50

After entering this data, you will get the following output:

Details of Items

Item Code	*Price*
101	*59.50*
102	*139.00*
103	*3905.50*
104	*48.00*
105	*302.50*

As the program is properly documented with remark statements, the execution of program should be very much clear to you.

Now, consider another problem of storing and displaying marks of students using 1-D arrays. We want to store the roll numbers of 10 students along with their marks obtained and maximum marks in computer memory. After entering the data, we want to calculate the percentage of marks obtained by each student and store them in memory. Later on, we will display all the data. We are assuming that the maximum marks of each student is 100.

In order to solve this problem, we will write a program that will store data in four 1-D arrays- rollno[10], marksobt[10], maxmarks[10] and perc[10]

Although, as maximum marks of each student are same, we can declare a simple int data type variable for it and initialise it with 200. We can declare it as a subscripted variable (array) to illustrate you the concept of initialisation of an array. The complete program is written below:

Program 18.2

```
/*Program to store and display marks of 10 students*/
#include <stdio.h>
main( )
{
  int sno;/*sno is the serial number or counter for making a loop*/
  /*declaration of 4 1-D arrays*/
  int rollno[10], marksobt[10], maxmarks[10];
  float price[10];
  for (sno = 0; sno < 10; sno ++)
  {
        /*Accepting data of each student*/
        printf ("\n Enter Roll No. of Student %d:", sno+1);
        /*The above statement will also display student no. */
        scanf ("%d", &rollno[sno]);
        printf ("Enter Marks Obtained of Student %d:", sno+1);
        scanf ("%d", &marksobt[sno]);
  }
  /*Initialisation of data elements of array marksobt[10] */
  for (sno = 0; sno < 10; sno ++)
        maxmarks[sno] = 200
  /*Calculations of percentage of each student*/
  for(sno = 0; sno < 10; sno ++)
  perc[sno] = (float)marksobt[sno]*100/maxmarks[sno];
  /*Displaying the data of arrays*/
  printf ("\n\t\t Marks of Students");
  printf ("\n Roll No.\t Marks Obtained\t Max. Marks \t Percentage");
  for (sno = 0; sno < 10; sno ++)
     printf ("\n%5d\t\t %5d\t\t %6.2f", rollno[sno] marksobt[sno] max; marks[sno] perc[sno]);
  getche( );
  }
```

Sample Inputs/Outputs

When this program is executed, the following prompts are displayed (We have entered sample data):

Enter Roll No. of Student 1 : 2501
Enter Marks Obtained of Student 1 : 170
Enter Roll No. of Student 2 : 2502
Enter Marks Obtained of Student 2 : 123
Enter Roll No. of Student 3 : 2511
Enter Marks Obtained of Student 3 : 97
Enter Roll No. of Student 4 : 2512
Enter Marks Obtained of Student 4 : 200

Enter Roll No. of Student 5 : 2513
Enter Marks Obtained of Student 5 : 189
Enter Roll No. of Student 6 : 2515
Enter Marks Obtained of Student 6 : 101
Enter Roll No. of Student 7 : 2519
Enter Marks Obtained of Student 7 : 55
Enter Roll No. of Student 8 : 2520
Enter Marks Obtained of Student 8 : 200
Enter Roll No. of Student 9 : 2521
Enter Marks Obtained of Student 9 : 173
Enter Roll No. of Student 10 : 2522
Enter Marks Obtained of Student 10 : 120

After entering the data, the following output is displayed:

Marks of Students

Roll No.	*Marks Obtained*	*Max. Marks*	*Percentage*
2501	*170*	*200*	*85.00*
2502	*123*	*200*	*61.50*
2511	*97*	*200*	*48.50*
2512	*200*	*200*	*100.00*
2513	*189*	*200*	*94.50*
2515	*101*	*200*	*50.50*
2519	*55*	*200*	*27.50*
2520	*200*	*200*	*100.00*
2521	*173*	*200*	*86.50*
2522	*120*	*200*	*60.00*

This program does not need any explanation, as it is properly documented with remark statements.

Till this time, you must be familiar with the concept and usage of one-dimensional arrays. Now, it is the time to re-start our discussion on two-dimensional arrays.

18.4 TWO-DIMENSIONAL ARRAYS

In the earlier part of the chapter, we have defined the two-dimensional array along with an example. You can recall that a two-dimensional array has two subscripts and is logically similar to a table. Let us learn the methods to declare, initialise and manipulate two-dimensional arrays.

18.4.1 Declaration of 2-D Arrays

A two-dimensional array is declared in the following format:

```
<data-type> <array-name> [No. of rows] [No. of columns];
```

For example, an array to store sales made by 5 sales executives in 3 regions is declared as follows:

```
int sales[3][5];
```

where 3 is the number of rows *i.e.*, number of regions and 5 is the number of columns *i.e.*, number of sales executives (Refer Table 18.1).

As discussed in 1-D arrays, the data type of 2-D array can be declared as int, float, double, char or other derived type. So, you can also declare a 2-D array for storing a set of strings such as names of 5 students as illustrated below:

```
char name[5][21];
```

where 21 indicates the number of characters in the string *i.e.*, each name, including "\0 " (NULL) character.

18.4.2 Initialisation of 2-D Arrays

Similar to 1-D arrays, you can initialise array elements of 2-D arrays with values by the following two methods:

(*a*) Initialisation using a single instruction.

(*b*) Initialisation using a set of instructions.

Let us discuss these.

18.4.2.1 Initialisation Using a Single Instruction

You can initialise a two-dimensional array using a single instruction outside the function as illustrated in following examples:

(*i*)
```
char  name[5][21] = {"SHALU",
                     "HRITIK",
                     "RAJESH  PATHAK",
                     "NEERU  PATHAK",
                     "SURENDRA"};
```

(*ii*)
```
int  sales[3][5]  = {{3500,  950,  270,  1900,  459}
                     {450,  910,  7321,  521,  7102}
                     {370,  498,  876,  7120  131}} ;
```

or

```
int sales[3][5]  = {3500, 950, 270, 1900, 459, 450, 910, 7321, 521, 7102,
                    370, 498, 876, 7120, 131};
```

or

(*iii*)
```
float n[][2]  =  {5592.50,  359.18,  472.82,  132.91};
```

In the first example, a 2-D array contains names of 5 employees, where each name can be of maximum 21 characters including the string terminated character. In the second example, an integer 2-D array is initialised in two ways. You can use either of these two ways, but the number of elements must be r * c where r is number of rows and c is number of columns. In the given example, there are 3 rows and 5 columns, so total number of elements are 15. In the third example, the number of rows are not specified and there are 2 columns. So, it is optional to specify the number of columns but it is mandatory to specify the number of rows. So, the following declarations of 2-D arrays are incorrect:

```
float n [2] [ ] = {5592.50, 359.18, 472.82, 132.91};
float n [ ] [ ] = {5592.50, 359.18, 472.82, 132.91};
```

The above declarations are incorrect because the computer can not reserve memory space for data elements unless it is informed about the value of second subscript. However, just by specifying value of second subscript, the compiler can calculate the value of first subscript by counting elements.

18.4.2.2 Initialisation Using a Set of Instructions

Again similar to 1-D arrays, 2-D arrays can be initialised using a set of instructions written inside the function in the form of a loop. However, in 2-D arrays, nested loops are used, with 2 counters which refer 2 subscripts. The following example will make this procedure clear to you:

```
int r,c sales[3][5];
    for (r = 0; r < 3; r++)
    for (c = 0; c < 5; c++)
           sales[r][c]  = 0;
```

If the number of data elements are limited, the following initialisations are also correct:

```
float n[2][3];
n[0][0]  = 9132.50;
n[0][1]  = 139.00;
n[0][2]  = 297.50;
n[1][0]  = 45.00;
n[1][1]  = 0;
n[1][2]  = 2000.00;
```

Having understood the methods for declaration and initialisation of 2-D arrays, let us discuss the ways to manipulate 2-D arrays.

18.4.3 Manipulation of 2-D Arrays

Manipulation of two-dimensional arrays is again almost similar to that of one-dimensional arrays, except that nested loops with 2 counters are used in 2-D arrays instead of single loop with one counter. First of all, we will discuss the way to enter data into a 2-D array.

18.4.3.1 Entering Data into 2-D Array

The standard Input/Output functions, printf( ) and scanf( ) are used along with a nested loop construct to accept data from the user during execution of the program. Consider the problem of storing sales made by 5 executives in 3 regions in a 2-D array discussed in section 18.2.2.2 (Multi-dimensional Arrays). The following statements are written within the function to store the sales in 2-D array, sales[3][5]:

```
int r, c sales[3][5];
for (r = 0; r < 3; r++)
{
  printf ("\n Enter sales of region %d", r+1);
  for (c = 0; c < 5; c++)
  {
```

```
        printf ("\n\t Sales executive %d", c+1);
        scanf ("%d", &sales[r][c]);
    }
}
```

The first statement declares two counters r and c along with the array, sales[3][5]. The outer loop first initialises *r* with 0 while the inner loop first initialises c with c. Therefore, the first printf( ) function displays first time the following message:

Enter sales of region: 1

Similarly, the second printf( ) function first time displays the following message:

Sales Executive 1

The next scanf( ) function accepts the sales made by sales executive 1 in region 1 and stores it into the data element, sales[0][0]. Now, the counter c is incremented but *r* remains the same. So, the sales made by sales executive 2 in region 1 is accepted and is stored into the data element sales[0][1]. In this way, the sales made by all the 5 sales executives in region 1 are stored in sales[0][0], sales[0][1], sales[0][2], sales[0][3] and sales[0][4] data elements. Now c becomes 5 and the control comes out of inner loop as inner loop executes till c < 5. Then *r* is incremented and same steps are repeated to accept data for region 2. Similarly, the data for region 3 is accepted. Now *r* becomes 3 , hence the control comes out of outer loop as outer loop executes till *r* < 3. In this way, the data for 2-D array, sales[3][5] is accepted from the user and stored in all the data elements of the array. Now, we will discuss the procedure to read this data and display it on monitor.

18.4.3.2 Reading Data from 2-D Arrays

The data of 2-D arrays can be read by nested loops and printf( ) functions as illustrated below:

```
printf("\n Region No.\t Sales Executives No.\t Sales in Rs.");
for(r = 0; r < 3; r ++)
    for(c = 0; c < 5; c++)
printf ("\n %d\t\t\t%d\t\t%d", r + 1, c + 1, sales[r][c]);
```

The above statements will display the output in following form:

Region No.	*Sales Executives No.*	*Sales in Rs.*
1	*1*	*3500*
1	*2*	*950*
:	:	:
:	:	:
3	*5*	*131*

Now, let us discuss the way to perform calculations on the values of 2-D arrays.

18.4.3.3 Calculations on 2-D Arrays

Suppose, you want to calculate the region-wise total sales for the problem discussed above. In order to calculate region-wise total sales, we will declare an int type of variable, regtot. First, we will initialise it with zero before the beginning of inner loop and then we will add the values of array elements into it one by one as illustrated below:

```
int regtot;
int r, c, sales[3][5];
/*Accept the data*/
:
:
/*Perform calculations*/
for (r = 0; r < 3; r++)
{
        regtot = 0
        for (c = 0; c < 3; c++)
        {
                regtot = regtot + sales[r][c];
        }
        printf("\n The total sales of region %d is %d", r+1, regtot);
}
```

With the above statements, the total sales of each region will be displayed one by one on the screen.

In this way, you can perform any type of calculation on 2-D arrays.

Now, it is the time to write a complete program on 2-D arrays after having understood the methods of declaring, initialising and manipulating 2-D arrays.

18.4.4 Program on 2-D Arrays

Now, we will write the complete program to solve the problem discussed in section 18.2.2.2 (Multi-dimensional arrays). We will first store the sales made by 5 executives of 3 regions in a 2-D array and then display the data after performing necessary calculations so that total sales of each region and grand total sales can also be displayed with the output.

The complete program is as follows:

Program 18.3

```
/*Program to display sales analysis report using a 2-D array*/
#include <stdio.h>
main( )
{
  int r, c;/*r and c are counters indicating row and column*/
  int sales[3][5]; /*Declaration of 2-D array*/
  int regtot, gtot; /*The variables, regtot stores region-wise total sales*/
                  /*and gtot stores grand total sales*/
                  /*Accepting Data*/
  for (r = 0; r < 3; r++) /*Beginning of outer loop*/
  {
        printf ("\n Enter Sales of Region %d", r+1);
        for (c=0; c<5; c++)/ *Beginning of inner loop*)
        {
        printf ("\n\t Sales Executive %d", c + 1);
        scanf ("%d", &sales[r][c]);
        }
```

```
        /*End of Inner loop*/
}       /*End of Outer loop*/
  gtot = 0; /*Initialise grand total variable with 0*/
  /*Displaying data and performing calculations*/
  printf ("\n\t\t Region-Wise Sales Report");
  printf ("\n Region No.\t Sales Executive No.\t Sales in Rs.");
  /*loops for calculations and display of outputs*/
  for (r = 0; r < 3; r++)
  {
        regtot = 0; /*Initialise region total variable with 0*/
        for (c = 0; c < 5; c++)
        {
        /*Displaying data*/
        printf("\n%d\t\t\t%d\t\t%5d", r+1, c+1, sales[r][c];
        /*performing calculations*/
        regtot = regtot + sales[r][c];
        gtot = gtot + sales[r][c];
        }
  printf ("\n Total Sales of Region %d is \t\t%5d", r+1, regtot);
}
```

Sample Inputs/Outputs

On execution of above program, the following prompts will be displayed (sample data is entered here):

Enter Sales of Region 1

Sales Executive 1 2000

Sales Executive 2 492

Sales Executive 3 3120

Sales Executive 4 251

Sales Executive 5 8972

Enter Sales of Region 2

Sales Executive 1 1500

Sales Executive 2 5152

Sales Executive 3 530

Sales Executive 4 1730

Sales Executive 5 1498

Enter Sales of Region 3

Sales Executive 1 1375

Sales Executive 2 109

Sales Executive 3 4320

Sales Executive 4 450

Sales Executive 5 540

After entering this data, the following output will be displayed:

Region-Wise Sales Report

Region No.	Sales Executive No.	Sales in Rs.
1	*1*	*2000*
1	*2*	*492*
1	*3*	*3120*
1	*4*	*251*
1	*5*	*8972*
Total Sales of Region 1 is		*14835*
2	*1*	*1500*
2	*2*	*5152*
2	*3*	*530*
2	*4*	*1730*
2	*5*	*1498*
Total Sales of Region 2 is		*10410*
3	*1*	*1375*
3	*2*	*109*
3	*3*	*4320*
3	*4*	*450*
3	*5*	*540*
Total Sales of Region 3 is		*6794*
Grand Total Sales		*32039*

As the program is properly documented with remark statements and we have already discussed the concepts in detail, we are not explaining you the step wise step execution of the program. You are advised to enter this program on computer to understand its execution.

18.5 THREE-DIMENSIONAL ARRAYS

We have already discussed that in a three-dimensional array 3 subscripts are used (Refer section 18.2.2.2—Multi-dimensional Arrays). The first subscript denotes the parts of a table, the second denotes the rows and the third denotes the columns. So, a 3-D array is an array of 2-D arrays, where 2-D array is an array of 1-D arrays. Therefore, the declaration, initialisation and manipulation of 3-D arrays are almost similar to that of 2-D arrays except that a 3-D arary uses 3 subscripts, 3 counters and 3 loops (Nested) for manipulation of data. As a 3-D array is rarely required for any application, we will neither discuss its manipulation nor we will write any program using a 3-D array. However, we are discussing the ways of declaring and initialising 3-D arrays in brief.

18.5.1 Declaration of 3-D Arrays

A three-dimensional array is declared in the following format:

```
<data-type> <array-name> [No. of Parts of a table][No. of rows][No. of columns]
```

For example, in order to solve problem discussed in section 18.2.2.2 (Multi-dimensional arays), a 3-D array can be declared to store the sales of 2 types of products made by 5 sales executives in 3 regions, which is as follows:

```
int  sales[2][3][5];
```

where 2 is the number of parts of table *i.e.*, types of products, 3 is the number of rows *i.e.*, number of regions and 5 is the number of columns *i.e.*, number of sales executives (Refer Table 18.2).

As in the case of 1-D and 2-D arrays, the data type of 3-D arrays can be of int, char, float, double or any derived type.

18.5.2 Initialisation of 3-D arrays

Similar to 1-D and 2-D arrays, you can initialise array elements of 3-D arrays with values by the following two methods:

(*a*) Initialisation using a single instruction.

(*b*) Initialisation using a set of instruction.

Let us discuss these:

18.5.2.1 Initialisation Using a Single Instruction

You can initialise a three-dimensional array using a single instruction outside the function as illustrated in the following example (Refer Table 18.2):

```
int  sales[2][3][5]   = {
          { {1500,  292,  1620,  150,  5813},
            {1250,  1835,  20,  1500,  1100},
            {375,  100,  4100,  350,  270}},
            {500,  200,  1500,  101,  3159},
            {250,  3317,  510,  230,  398}
            {1000,  9,  220,  200,  270}}
                          }
```

18.5.2.2 Initialisation Using a Set of Instructions

Like 2-D arrays, you can also initialise a three-dimensional array using a set of instructions written inside the function in the form of a loop. However, you will use 3 counters, 3 subscripts and 3 loops (nested) as illustrated below (Refer Figure 18.3):

```
int  p,  r,  s  sales[2][3][5];
for  (p  =  0;  p  <  2;  p++)
     for  (r  =  0;  r  <  3;  r++)
          for  (s  =  0;  s  <  5;  s++)
               sales[p][r][s]  =  0;
```

Where p denotes product type, r denotes region and s denotes sales executive number.

Manipulation of data in 3-D arrays also follows this procedure.

If you can write program for 2-D arrays, you can definitely write program for 3-D arrays.

18.6 PASSING ARRAY TO A FUNCTION

There are basically two ways to pass arrays to a function-one by passing the values of an array to a function, and another, passing the location or memory address of an array. The first method is used when you call the function using 'Call by Value' method and the second one is used when you call the function using 'Call by Reference' method. As we have not yet discussed the concept of 'Pointers', we will discuss the second method in the next chapter on 'Pointers'. Here, we are discussing only 'Call by Value' method. Using this method, you can pass the individual array elements to a function. Let us discuss this method.

18.6.1 Passing Array Elements to a Function

In order to understand the procedure of passing array elements to a function, consider a 1-D array, num[ ] with 5 data elements having int data type and follow the steps discussed below for writing the program:

(*a*) Initialise each data element of the array, num[5] with same values, say 100.

(*b*) Calculate and display the total of these values before calling the function.

(*c*) Construct a loop and call the function numbers ( ) within loop by passing value of each array element.

(*d*) Define the formal parameter of function as unsubscripted int variable (not subscripted or array variable). Do you know, why? This is because you will pass value of only one element (not complete array) at one time.

(*e*) Now, change this value in called function (say, to 200).

(*f*) Return the new value to the calling function (which will return within loop).

(*g*) Add the new value to a variable, sum (which you would initialise to zero before loop) for calculating the new total.

(*h*) Display this new total (after calling the function) and compare it with earlier one (before calling the function). Will it be different?

(*i*) Construct a new loop to see total of array elements after calling the function and compare it with earlier one (before calling the function). Will it be different?

Now, the main question of discussion is whether such procedure of passing individual array elements to a function can change the values of array? Let us write the program, execute it and analyse the output.

Program 18.4

```
/*Program demonstrating the concept of passing array elements to a function */
#include <stdio.h>
main( )
{
  int i, num[5], sum = 0, newnum;
  /*Initialising array elements and calculating total*/
  for (i = 0; i < 5; i++);
  {
        num[i]  = 100;
        sum = sum + num[i];
  }
```

```
        printf ("\n The sum of array elements before calling the function is %d", sum);
        sum=0;
        for (i = 0; i < 5; i++)
           /*calling the function by passing value of each array element*/
              newnum = numbers(num[i]);
              sum = sum + newnum;
  }
  printf ("\n The sum of new numbers after calling the function is %d", sum);
  sum = 0;
  for (i = 0; i < 5; i++)
        sum = sum + num[i];
  printf ("\n The sum of array elements after calling the function is %d", sum);
  getche( );
}
int numbers (int n)
{
  n = 200;
  return(n);
}
```

Sample Inputs/Outputs

When the program is executed, the following output is generated:

The sum of array elements before calling the function is 500

The sum of new numbers after calling the function is 1000

The sum of array elements after calling the function is 500

Are you surprised with the output? Let us analyse the various steps of the program.

The output of first printf( ) function is not surprising. As each array element is initialised with 100, therefore sum of the values of all (*i.e.,* 5) array elements is 500. Now, the statement, newnum = numbers(num [i]), call the function, numbers( ) by passing the value of first data element, num[0] as the value of i is 0 in the beginning of loop. So, the value, 100 is passed to the function. In the called function, this value is stored in variable *n*. Here, the variable *n* is re-initialised with value 200. The statement, return (n) returns the value 200 to the calling function, where it is stored in another variable, newnum. The value of the variable, newnum is added to variable, sum for calculating the total. Now, i is incremented and again the function is called by passing value of data element, num[1]. In this way, the loop executes for 5 times and the function is also called 5 times. As after each call, newnum is 200, the new total becomes 1000. Therefore, the sum of new numbers after calling the function is displayed as 1000. The result which may be surprising to you is that the sum of the values of array elements after calling the function remains the same as it was before the calling of function.

So calling the function by passing individual values of array elements does not allow the function to access and modify the array. This is because the formal parameter of 'Call by value' method function calls does not store data in the corresponding array elements, but it stores data in the unsubscripted variable (which is *n* in the discussed example). If you will change the value of this unsubscripted variable, it will not be reflected in the array. Infact, you cannot access array elements from the called function, if values of the elements are passed to the function. So, how will you access array elements in the called function? This can be done by passing the entire array to function, which is actually a 'Call by Reference' method where address of array is passed. As stated earlier, we will discuss this method in the next chapter on "Pointers".

This finishes our discussion on arrays specially numeric arrays. However, we will discuss application of arrays by writing some programs at the end of this chapter. Now, we will discuss the character arrays or strings in detail.

18.7 CHARACTER ARRAYS (STRINGS)

Character Arrays store a string of characters such as name of a person or a set of strings such as names of persons. They are commonly called strings. We have already introduced character arrays in the earlier part of the chapter while discussing Declaration and Initialisation of Arrays (Refer sections 18.3.1, 18.3.2, 18.4.1 and 18.4.2). Let us summarise these concepts. Like numeric arrays, character arrays can be one-dimensional or two-dimensional. A one-dimensional character array is declared as illustrated below:

```
char  name[21];
```

A one-dimensional character array is a string of characters terminated by a null character '\0'. In the above example 21 indicates the number of characters including the null character.

A two-dimensional array is declared as illustrated below:

```
char  name[5][21];
```

A two-dimensional character array is a set of strings. In the above example, 5 indicates the number of strings and 21 indicates number of characters (including null) in each string.

A 1-D character array is initialised as illustrated below:

```
char name[ ]  =  {"SHIVANI"};
char name[ ]  =  {'M',  'A',  'R',  'C',  'H'  '\0'};
```

A 2-D character array is initialised as illustrated below:

char name[5][21] = {"SHALU", "HRITIK", "RAJESH PATHAK", "NEERU PATHAK", "SURENDRA"};

Now let us discuss the ways to manipulate strings or character arrays.

18.7.1 Manipulating Strings

The standard Input/Output functions, scanf( ) and printf( ) can be used to input and output the strings, respectively. However, scanf( ) function cannot accept the multi-word strings. (*e.g.*, RAJESH PATHAK). For accepting such strings, a string-based input function, gets( ) is used. Similarly, to display a string, a string-based output function, puts( ) is used. The main difference between puts( ) and printf( ) is that puts( ) function can display only one string at a time while printf( ) function can display many strings at one time. The other difference is that the line feed ('\n') character is not required with puts( ) function as puts( ) always displays the string on the next line. However, in printf( ), the line-feed character is required if you want to display output on next line.

Although we have already discussed these concepts in Chapter 15, we are writing a program to revise these concepts:

Program 18.5

```
/*Program demonstrating the used string-based Standard Input/Output Function*/
#include  <stdio.h>
main(  )
{
  char  name[21],  address[31];
  int  i;
  printf("\n  Enter  your  name:");
  scanf("%s",name);
  fflush(stdin);
  printf("\n  Enter  your  address:")
  gets(address);
  printf("\n  Hello");
  i  =  0;
  while(name[i] !='\0')
  {
        printf("%c",name[i]);
        i++;
  }
  puts("\n  Your  address  is  given  below:");
  puts(address);
  getche(  );
}
```

Sample Input/Output

When the above program is executed, you get the following prompts on screen (sample data is entered):

Enter your name: Kapil Dev

Enter your address: Tilak Nagar, New Delhi.

After entering the above data, the following output is generated:

Hello Kapil

Your address is given below:

Tilak Nagar, New Delhi.

In the above output, although you entered the name "Kapil Dev", you get the output as "Hello Kapil". Why is the first name displayed and not the last name? The reason is that scanf( ) function cannot be used to accept strings with many words. Note that %s is used instead of %c in scanf( ) function as the name variable is of string type. Also note that no ampersand (&) is put before the array variable, name. This is because an array name without brackets represent the address of that array. This concept will be discussed in detail in next chapter on pointers.

The string-based input function, gets( ) is used instead of scanf( ) to accept multiple word strings as illustrated in the gets(address) statement of the discussed program. You can see that as the address with multiple words is accepted using gets( ) function, the output generates the complete address. In the above program, while loop is executed to display each element of name[ ] array or string until null character is encountered. The puts( )

function has also been illustrated in the above program. When you use puts( ) function to display a string, there is no need to write '\n' after the end of that string or before the next output function as line-feed is automatically given after the display of string.

Now, let us discuss various string functions.

18.7.2 String Functions

For manipulating strings, C provides certain standard library string functions. The commonly used string functions are as follows:

(*a*) strupr( ) – It converts a string to upper case letters.
(*b*) strulwr( ) – It converts a string to lower case letters.
(*c*) strrev( ) – It reserves a string.
(*d*) strlen( ) – It calculates the length of a string.
(*e*) strcmp( ) – It compares two strings (without regard to case).
(*f*) strcat( ) – It concatenates two strings.
(*h*) strcpy( ) – It copies a string to another.

Depending upon the C compiler you use, you may need to include the header file, string.h while using these functions in your programs. Let us now discuss these functions with some examples.

18.7.2.1 The strupr( ) and strlwr( ) Functions

The strupr( ) function converts a string entered by you (whether it is in upper case or both lower and upper) to upper case letters as illustrated in the following program:

Program 18.6

```
/*Program to convert a string to uppercase */
#include <stdio.h>
#include <string.h>
main( )
{
   char str1[50];
   printf ("/n Enter a string in lower case:");
   gets (str1);
   printf ("/n The string in upper case is: %s", strupr(str1));
   getche( );
}
```

Sample Input/Output

When the above program is executed, the following prompt appears on the screen (sample data is entered):

Enter a string in lower case: I Love India

After entering the string, the following output is generated:

The string in upper case is: I LOVE INDIA.

The function strlwr( ) is just opposite to the function, strupr( ). It converts a string entered by you to lower case letters as illustrated in following program:

Program 18.7

```
/*Program to convert a string to lower case*/
#include <stdio.h>
#include <string.h>
main( )
{
  char str1[50];
  printf ("\n Enter a string in upper case:");
  gets (str1);
  printf ("\n The string in lower case is: %s", strlwr(str1));
  getche( );
}
```

Sample Input/Output

On execution, the following prompt is displayed (sample data is entered):

Enter a string in upper case: NEW DELHI IS THE CAPITAL OF INDIA.

The string in lower case is: new delhi is the capital of india.

18.7.2.2 The strrev( ) Function

The strrev( ) function reverses a string *i.e.,* stores the last character entered at first position, then second last character and so on. The following program illustrates the use of strrev( ) function and displays the string in reverse order.

Program 18.8

```
/*Program to reverse a string*/
#include <stdio.h>
#include <string.h>
main( )
{
  char str1[50];
  printf("\n enter a string:");
  gets(str1);
  printf("\n The string in reverse order is %s", strrev(str1));
  getche( );
}
```

Sample Input/Output

When the above program is executed, the computer prompts you.

Enter a string.

Suppose, you enter the string, NEW DELHI, the following output is generated:

IHLED WEN

18.7.2.3 The strlen( ) Function

Sometimes, you need to find the length of a string. C provides a simple way to do that. The strlen( ) function can be used to calculate the length of a string as illustrated in the following program:

Program 18.9

```
/*Program to calculate the length of a string*/
#include <stdio.h>
#include <string.h>
main( )
{
   char str1[50];
   int n;
   printf("\n Enter a string:");
   gets(str1);
   n = strlen(str1)
   printf("\n The length of string is %d", n);
   getche( );
}
```

Sample Input/Output

When the above program is executed, you are asked to enter a string as shown below (sample data is entered):

Enter a string: Hello Tulsi!

On entering this string, you get the following output:

The length of string is 12.

Note that the length of string is stored in int type of variable as shown in above program.

18.7.2.4 The strcmp( ) and strcmpi( ) Functions

You can also compare two strings to find whether they are identical or not. There are two main string functions to compare two strings— strcmp( ) and strcmpi( ). The strcmp( ) function compares the strings by ignoring whether they are in upper case or in lower case, while the strcmpi( ) considers the case of letters. If two strings are same but one is in capital and another is in small letters, the strcmpi( ) function will consider them as two different strings. Both these functions return the value zero if the strings are identical. They return a positive value if the first string is longer than the second string and return a negative value if the first string is shorter than the second string. The use of both these functions are illustrated in the following program:

Program 18.10

```
/*Program to compare two strings*/
#include <stdio.h>
#include <string.h>
main( )
{
  chr str1[50], str2[50];
  prinf ("\n Enter first string");
  gets(str1);
  printf ("\n Enter second string");
  gets(str2);
```

```
/*comparing strings with regard to case*/
if (strcmp(str1,str2)==0)
printf ("\n Both strings are identical (with regard to case)");
else
printf ("\n Both strings are not identical (with regard to case)");
/*comparing strings without regard to case*/
if (strcmpi(str1,str2)==0)
   printf ("\n Both strings are identical (without regard to case)");
else
   printf ("\n Both strings are not identical (without regard to case)");
getche( );
}
```

Sample Input/Outputs

When the above program is executed, the following input/output screen is displayed (sample strings are entered in 2 examples).

1. *Enter first string this is to certify that*
   Enter second string THIS IS TO CERTIFY THAT
   Both strings are not identical (with regard to case)
   Both strings are identical (without regard to case)
2. *Enter first string I am learning C*
   Enter second string I am learning C++
   Both strings are not identical (with regard to case)
   Both strings are not identical (without regard to case)

18.7.2.5 The strcat( ) Function

The strcat( ) function concatenates two strings. The second string is appended at the end of the first string as illustrated in the following program:

Program 18.11

```
/*Concatenating two strings*/
#include <stdio.h>
#include <string.h>
main( )
{
  char str1[50], str2[50];
  printf ("\n Enter first string");
  gets(str1)
  printf("\n Enter second string");
  strcat(str1, str2);
  puts("\n The first string is");
  puts(str1);
  puts("\n The second string is");
  puts(str 2);
  getche( );
}
```

Sample Input/Output

When the above program is executed, the computer asks you to enter two strings as shown below (Sample data is entered):

Enter first string Hello !

Enter second string How are you?

On entering the above data, the following output is generated:

The first string is

Hello ! How are you?

The second string is

How are you?

18.7.2.6 The strcpy( ) Function

The strcpy( ) function copies the contents of source string to the target string as illustrated in the following program:

Program 18.12

```
/*Program to copy a string*/
#include <stdio.h>
#include <string.h>
main( )
{
    char str1[50], str2[50];
    printf ("\n Enter a string");
    gets (str1)
    strcpy(str2, str1);
    puts ("\n The source string is");
    puts(str1);
    puts ("\n The target string is");
    puts (str2);
    getche( );
}
```

Sample Input/Output

On execution of the above program, the computer asks you to enter a string as shown below (sample data is entered).

Enter a string Good Morning

On entering the data, the following output is generated:

The source string is

Good Morning

The target string is

Good Morning

18.8 TYPICAL APPLICATIONS OF ARRAYS

Throughout the chapter, we have discussed the use of arrays in solving various problems. Let us write programs on the following typical applications of arrays:

(*a*) Conversion of a string to upper case/lower case
(*b*) Finding the pallindromes (words that are spelled the same forward or backward)
(*c*) Sorting of numbers
(*d*) Sorting of strings
(*e*) Transpose of a Matrix
(*f*) Addition of two matrices

18.8.1 Conversion of String to Upper/Lower Case

Although you can convert a string to upper case or lower case using the string functions, strupr( ) or strlwr (as discussed in previous section), there are two character-based functions which can do the same work. These functions are toupper( ) and tolower( ). The following program illustrates the use of these functions:

Problem 18.13

```
/*Program to convert a string to upper case/lower case*/
#include <stdio.h>
#define ARRSIZE 80
/*The #define is a preprocessor directive*/
/*that replaces every occurrence of ARRSIZE in the*/
/*program with 80*/
/*#define directive makes program easily understandable and manageable*/
main( )
{
  /*declaring array, sentence of size 80 characters*/
  char sentence[ARRSIZE];
  char char1, char2;
  int i = 0;
  printf("\n Enter a sentence:");
  gets (sentence);
  printf("\n The sentence in upper case is \n");
  while (sentence[i] != '\0')
  {
       /*Converting to upper case*/
       char1 = toupper(sentence[i]);
       putchar(char1);
       i++;
  }
  i = 0;
  printf ("\n The sentence in lower case is\n");
  while (sentence[i] != '\0')
  {
       /* converting to lower case*/
       char2 = tolower(sentence[i]);
       putchar(char2);
```

```
            i++;
        }
        getche( );
    }
```

Sample Input/Output

When the program is executed, the computer asks you to input data as shown below (sample data is entered):

Enter a sentence: For sure success, read LAXMI PUBLICATIONS Books.

After entering the data, the following output is generated:

The sentence in upper case is

FOR SURE SUCCESS, READ LAXMI PUBLICATIONS BOOKS

The sentence in lower case is

for sure success, read laxmi publications books

In the above program, there are two loops-one for converting a string to uppercase and another for converting a string to lower case. In both the loops, each character of the array, sentence[ ] is converted into upper or lower letter using the toupper( ) or tolower( ) function, respectively.

18.8.2 Finding the Palindromes

Palindromes are the words that are spelled same both forward and backward. For instance, radar, madam, etc. are palindromes. To write a program for finding whether the entered word is a palindrome, we follow the logic discussed below:

1. Declare two character arrays, word1[ ] and word2[ ].
2. Declare and initialise a variable, compare with *'y'*.
3. Declare and initialise two counters *i* and *j* with zeros.
4. Accept the word from user in array, word1[ ].
5. Find the length of word and store in *i* in order to make a loop.
6. Store the characters of array, word1[ ] in reverse order in array, word2[ ].
7. Now compare the two arrays character by character.
8. If there is any mismatch, store *'N'* to compare.
9. If compare = *'Y'*, display that word is a palindrome.
10. If compare = *'N'* display that word is not a palindrome.

In short, to find palindrome accept the word in one array, store reverse of it in another array and compare these two arrays. If they are matching, the word is a palindrome otherswise it is not. Now, let us write the program.

Program 18.14

```
/*Program to find palindromes*/
#include <stdio.h>
#include <string.h>
main( )
{
    /*Declaration of arrays*/
```

```
char word1[30], word2[30];
/*Declaration and initialisation of counters and flags*/
char compare ='y';
int i = 0, j = 0;
/*Accepting the word*/
printf("\n Enter a word:");
scanf("%s", word1);
/*Finding length of word*/
while (word1[i] != '\0')
i++;
i-- /*Decrement i as i was pointing to null character*/
/*Storing the reverse of word in second array*/
while (i > 0)
{
      word2[j] = word1[i]
      i--; /*Because storing the word backward*/
      j++; /*Because creating another array*/
}
/*Comparing two strings*/
i = 0; /*Because comparison begins from 0th element*/
while (word1[i]!= '\0') /*Do comparison while there is null character*/
{
      if (word[i]!= word[i]) /*comparing characters*/
      {
            compare = 'N';
            break;
      }
      i++
}
/* Displaying the output*/
if (compare=='y')
      printf ("\n The word is a palindrome");
else
      printf ("\n The word is not a palindrome");
getche( )
}
```

Sample Inputs/Outputs

Test the program with following sample data and see the output:

1. *Enter a word: radar*
   The word is a palindrome
2. *Enter a word: madam*
   The word is a palindrome
3. *Enter a word: Laxmi*
   The word is not a palindrome

4. *Enter a word: Arora*
   The word is not a palindrome
   ***(Note:** The program does not ignore case while comparison)*
5. *Enter a word: arora*
   The word is a palindrome

Execution of the above program must be clear to you as we have already explained the logic of program. You are advised to modify the program so that it ignores the case of letters while comparing.

18.8.3 Sorting of Numbers and Strings

The most useful application of arrays is to sort the elements of array in asscending or descending order. You can sort both numeric arrays (1-D arrays) and character arrays or strings (2-D arrays). Let us first develop the logic to sort the numbers in ascending order.

1. Declare an array, num[50].
2. Declare and initialise the numeric variables *i*, *j*, *c* and *t*. *i* and *j* are counters for making loops, *c* is the number of data elements you want to enter and *t* is a temporary location to store number.
3. Accept the number of data elements in *c*.
4. Accept the numbers and store in 1-D array, num[ ].
5. To sort the numbers, make a nested loop.

Perform outer loop beginning the value of *i* from 0 and incrementing by 1 till $i < c-1$. The logic is to compare the 1st number with 2nd and if 1st is bigger, interchange the numbers. Similarly, compare 2nd with 3rd, 3rd with 4th and so on. In the last, second last ($c-1$) will be compared with last (c) number. Therefore, loop ends before *i* becomes equal to $c-1$.

6. Perform inner loop beginning with the value of *j* from $i + 1$ (second number) by 1 till $j < c$. The loop ends before *j* becomes equal to *c*.
7. Within the loop, check if the numbers at *i*th location is bigger than number at *j*th location. If yes, interchange the numbers by storing num[*j*] to *t*, num[*i*] to num[*j*] and *t* to num[*i*].
8. Finally, display the data elements of array num[ ], which will be sorted out in ascending order. The above discussed logic is called *Bubble Sort*.

Let us write the program to sort the numbers using this logic.

Program 18.15

```
/*Program to sort numbers in ascending order*/
#include <stdio.h>
#define ASIZE 50 /*Directive that replaces*/
/*every occurrence of ASIZE with 50 in the program.*/
/*You can also write ASIZE in small case but then*/
/*you have to use the same case everytime.*/
main( )
{
  /*Declaration of counters and accumulators*/
```

```
    int i, j, c, t;
    int num[ASIZE] /*Declare array of size 50*/
    printf("\n How many numbers you want to sort?");
    scanf("%d", &c);
    printf("\n Enter %d numbers: \n", c);
    /*Accepting the numbers and storing in array*/
    for (i = 0; i < c; i++)
    {
        printf("Number %d", i + 1);
        scanf("%d", &num[i]);
    }
    /*Sorting the numbers*/
        for (i = 0; i < c - 1; i++) /*outer loop begins*/
        {
            for (j = i + 1; j < c; j++) /*Inner loop begins*/
            {
                /*Comparing two numbers*/
                if num[i] > num[j]
                {
                    t = num[j];
                    num[j] = num[i];
                    num[i] = t;
                }
            }
        }
    /*Displaying stored numbers*/
        printf("\n The sorted numbers are:");
    for (i = 0; i < c; i++)
        printf ("%d", num[i]);
    getche( );
}
```

Sample Inputs/Outputs

When the above program is executed, after entering the data, the following outputs are generated:

1. *How many numbers you want to sort? 5*
   Enter 5 numbers:
   Number 1 4
   Number 2 0
   Number 3 6
   Number 4 43
   Number 5 20
   The sorted numbers are: 0 4 6 20 43
2. *How many numbers you want to sort? 8.*
   Number 1 – 3

Number *2* *3*
Number *3* *0*
Number *4* *– 9*
Number *5* *34*
Number *6* *87*
Number *7* *0*
Number *8* *– 3*

The sorted numbers are: – 9 – 3 – 3 0 0 3 34 87

The execution of the above program must be clear to you. How will you sort the numbers in descending order? Just change the > sign to < sign in the statement, if (num[i] > num[1]) and execute the program.

Now, we will write the program to sort strings (say name of students). The logic of this program would be exactly same as followed in the program just discussed. The changes would be in coding of program, where you will have to declare character arrays and manipulate them accordingly. Let us first write the program and then discuss its execution.

Program 18.16

```
/*Program to sort strings in ascending order*/
#include <stdio.h>
#include <string.h>
#define numname 50 /*As we want to store max. 50 names */
main( )
{
  /*Declaration and initialisation of counters and accumulators*/
  int i, j, c;
  char name[numname][20];
  /*The above statement declares a 2-D array*/
  /*The length of string is 20 and there are */
  /*numname i.e., 50 strings max.*/
  char t[20]; /*declare a string to store temporary data*/
  printf("\n How many names you want to sort?");
  scanf("%d", &c);
  printf("\n Enter %d names: \n", c);
  /*Accepting the names*/
  for (i = 0; i < c; i++)
  {
        printf("Name %d", i + 1);
        scanf("%s", name[i]);
        /*Note that no & is written with array name*/
        /*in scanf( ) function and only one subscript is*/
        /*written. The reason will be explained while*/
        /*discussing 'Arrays and Pointers' in next chapter.*/
  }
  /*sorting the array*/
  for (i = 0; i < c - 1; i++)
```

```
    {
        for (j = i + 1; j < c; j++)
        {
            /*Comparing strings*/
            if (strcmpi(name[i], name[j]) > 0)
            {
                strcpy(t, name[j]);
                strcpy(name[j], name[i]);
                strcpy(name[i], t);
            }
        }
    }
    /*Displaying sorted names*/
    printf("\n The sorted names are:", c);
    for (i = 0; i < c; i++)
        printf("\n%s", name[i]);
    getche( );
}
```

Sample Input/Output

When the above program is executed, the following prompt comes on the screen:

How many names you want to sort?

Type 5 and press <Enter> key, Now computer asks you to enter 5 names as shown below (Sample Data is entered):

Enter 5 names
Name 1 Sonali
Name 2 Asha
Name 3 Mohit
Name 4 Shivani
Name 5 Komal

After entering the above data, the following output is generated:

Asha
Komal
Mohit
Shivani
Sonali

So, the names are sorted out in ascending order. You can sort these names in descending order too by the procedure explained in previous program. You may have noted that most of the statements written in this program are same with that of the previous program. The differences are in the following statements:

1. `char name[numname][20];`

   Here, we have declared a 2-D character array and not 1-D numeric array because a set of strings are stored in a 2-D array.

2. `scanf ("%s", name[i]);`

   This statement accepts the name of ith student *i.e.,* 0th, 1st, 2nd, 3rd, etc.

3. `if (strcmpi(name[i], name[j]) > 0)`

The above conditional statement uses the string function, strcmpi( ) to compare the strings name[i] and name[j] without regard to case (capital or small).

If the first string, name[i] is bigger than the second string, name[j], the strcmpi( ) function returns the value greater than 0. In that case, the next block of statement is executed.

4. `strcpy(t, name[j]);`

The above function copies the string, name[j] to t.

5. `strcpy(name[j], name[i]);`

The above function copies the string name[i] to name[j].

6. `strcpy(name[i], t);`

The above function copies the string to name[i].

Thus, the above 3 statements interchange the strings and hence the array is sorted.

18.8.4 Manipulating Matrices

The 2-D numeric arrays are mainly used to manipulate matrices. A *matrix* is a table of values organised in rows and columns. Let us first write a program to transpose a matrix. Transpose interchanges the data of rows and columns as explained below:

Consider a 3 × 3 matrix (3 rows and 3 columns), with following data:

$$\begin{bmatrix} 34 & 12 & 30 \\ 41 & 52 & 30 \\ 71 & 38 & 91 \end{bmatrix}$$

After transpose, the matrix will have data in following form:

$$\begin{bmatrix} 34 & 41 & 71 \\ 12 & 52 & 38 \\ 30 & 30 & 91 \end{bmatrix}$$

So, rows will become columns and columns will become rows during transpose.

The logic to develop this program is quite simple. Initialise the data of 2-D array, mat[3][3] and make a nested loop to display each element one by one by interchanging the positions of subscripts. For instance, if the data element mat[r][c] denotes the element for rth row and cth column, then mat[c][r] will denote the element for cth row and rth column. Let us write the program and see the output.

Program 18.17

```
/*Program to transpose a matix*/
#include <stdio.h>
main( )
{
  /*Declaring and initialising the matrix*/
```

```
int mat[3][3] =        {
                           {34, 22, 30},
                           {41, 52, 30},
                           {71, 38, 91}
                       };
  /*Declaring the transposed matrix*/
  int tranmat[3][3];
  int r, c; /*Variables for row and column*/
  /*Displaying the matrix*/
  printf("\n The first matrix is\n");
  for (r = 0; r < 3; r++)
  {
       for (c = 0; c < 3; c++)
       {
            printf("%d\t", mat[r][c]);
       }
       printf("\n");
  }
  /*creating and displaying transpose matix*/
  printf("\n The transposed matrix is /n");
  for (r = 0; r < 3; r++)
  {
       for (c = 0; c < 3; c++)
       {
            tranmat[r][c] = mat[c][r];
            printf("%d\t", tranmat[r][c]);
       }
       printf("\n");
  }
  getche( );
}
```

Sample Input/Output

On executing the above program, the following output is generated:

The first matrix is

34 12 30

[41 52 30]

71 38 91

The transposed matrix is

34 41 71

[12 52 38]

30 30 91

So, you see how simple it is!

Let us now write a program to add two matrices and store the total in 3rd matrix. Adding two matrices means adding their corresponding data elements and storing result in corresponding element of new matrix as illustrated in following example:

$$\begin{bmatrix}10 & 20 & 30\\40 & 50 & 60\\70 & 80 & 90\end{bmatrix} + \begin{bmatrix}1 & 2 & 3\\4 & 5 & 6\\7 & 8 & 9\end{bmatrix} = \begin{bmatrix}11 & 22 & 33\\44 & 55 & 66\\77 & 88 & 99\end{bmatrix}$$

Matrix 1 Matrix 2 Sum of Matrices 1 & 2

The logic to develop this program is also quite simple. First declare and initialise two matrices, mat1[3][3] and mat2[3][3] with some values within the program. Calculate the sum of these two matrices by making a nested loop for adding each element of matrix 1 to corresponding element of matrix 2 giving new element of matix 3 as shown below in the statement:

mat3[r][c] = mat1[r][c] + mat2[r][c]

where r and c are row and column numbers of matrices respectively.

Let us write the program and see the output on its execution:

Program 18.18

```
/*Program to add two matrices*/
#include <stdio.h>
main( )
{
  /*Declaring & initialising first matrix*/
 int mat1[3][3] = {
                              {10, 20, 30},
                              {40, 50, 60},
                              {70, 80; 90}
                  };
  /*Declaring & initialising second matrix*/
  int mat2[3][3] = {
                              {1, 2, 3},
                              {4, 5, 6},
                              {7, 8, 9}
                  };
  /*Declaring third matrix*/
  int r, c;/*declaring variables for rows and columns*/
  /*Displaying first matrix*/
  printf("\n The first matrix is \n");
  for (r = 0; r < 3; r++)
  {
        for (c = 0; c < 3; c++)
        {
        printf("%d\t", mat1[r][c]);
        }
        printf("\n");
}
  /*Displaying the second matrix*/
```

```
    printf("\n The second matrix is \n");
    for (r = 0; r < 3; r++)
    {
         for (c = 0; c < 3; c++)
         {
              printf("%d\t", mat2[r][c])
         }
         printf("\n");
    }
    /*Creating and displaying sum of matrices*/
    printf("\n The sum of two matrices are \n");
    for (r = 0; r < 3; r++)
    {
         for (c = 0; c < 3; c++)
         {
              mat3[r][c] = mat1[r][c] + mat2[r][c];
              printf("%d\t", mat3[r][c]);
         }
         printf("\n");
    }
    getche( );
}
```

Sample Input/Output

On execution of the above program, the following output is generated:

The first matix is

10 20 30
40 50 60
70 80 90

The second matrix is

1 2 3
4 5 6
7 8 9

The sum of two matrices are

11 22 33
44 55 66
77 88 99

So, you must have understood the application of arrays in solving mathematical and commerical problems. You are advised to think about such applications and write programs using arrays.

THEORY QUESTIONS

1. What is an Array? Explain with an example.
2. What are subscripts? Based on the number of subscripts, what are different types of arrays? Explain with examples.
3. How will you declare and initialise a
   (*a*) 1-D array
   (*b*) 2-D array
   Explain various methods along with suitable examples.
4. Explain with examples the procedure to enter data in a
   (*a*) 1-D array
   (*b*) 2-D array
5. How can you perform calculations on the data elements of
   (*a*) 1-D array
   (*b*) 2-D array
   Explain with examples.
6. Explain the procedure to declare and initialise a 3-D array with examples.
7. How will you pass array elements to a function using 'Call by Value' method? Explain with examples.
8. What are strings? How will you manipulate the strings? Explain the statements with examples.
9. Explain the following string functions with suitable programs:
   (*a*) strcat( )
   (*b*) strlen( )
   (*c*) strcpy( )
   (*d*) strrev( )
10. Explain the differences between the following string functions:
    (*a*) strcmp( ) and strcmpi( )
    (*b*) strlwr( ) and strupr( )
11. Write a program to accept a string from the user and convert it into upper case letters.
12. Write a program to sort the following numbers:
    37, 41, 22, 0, 9, 8, 1, 38, 172, 7
13. Write a program to sort the following names of cities: Delhi, Mumbai, Jaipur, Agra, Ambala, Chennai, Kolkata, Jodhpur, Lucknow, Aligarh.
14. Write a program to accept the item no., quantity and rate of 10 items Calculate the amount of each item and their sum and display the output in following format:

Komal Books

S. No.	Item No.	Quantity	Rate	Amount
1				
2				
:				
:				
10				
		Total =		

15. Write a program to multiply a matrix A (r × c) with a matrix B (c × n).
16. Write a program to find whether the words entered by user are palindromes (A palindrome is a word that is spelled same forward and backward *e.g.*, radar, level, etc.).
17. Write a program to store the marks obtained by 20 students in two subjects, Maths and English along with their roll numbers in 1-D arrays. Display the result in the following format:

National School Result

Roll No.	Marks in Maths	Marks in English	Total Marks

Highest total marks = obtained by roll no. =
Highest marks in Maths = obtained by roll no. =
Highest marks in English = obtained by roll no. =

18. Write a program to accept annual salary of 10 employees in 3 companies. Calculate and display the average salary of each company.
19. Write a program to calculate average of 10 numbers by passing arrays to a function using 'Call by Value' method.
20. Write a program to obtain the largest number from the 5 × 5 matrix.

WORKSHOP

1. Enter the Program no. 18.2 discussed in the chapter on your computer. Run it with the sample data given and analyse the output.
2. Enter the Program no. 18.3 discussed in the chapter on your computer. Run it with the sample data given and analyse the output. Modify this program and calculate the commission obtained by each sales executive. The commission is calculated as 7% of the sales.
3. Enter the Program 18.13 discussed in the chapter on your computer. Run it with sample data and analyse the output.
4. Enter the Program given in theory Question no. 17 (given above). Enter roll no. of 20 students of your class along with their marks in any two subjects. Run the program and analyse the results.
5. Enter the Program given in theory Question no. 12 (given above). Run it with the data given. Modify the program to accept data from the user and sort the numbers in descending order. Run the program with sample data and analyse the output.
6. Enter the following program and analyse the output:

```
#include <stdio.h>
main( )
{
      int x, y = 0;
      static int z[5] = {10, 22, 11, 70, 32};
      for (x = 0; x < 5; x++)
      if (x%2)==0)
```

```
        y += z[x];
    printf("%d", y);
}
```

7. Enter the following program and analyse the output:

```
#include <stdio.h>
int n[3][4] = {7, 2, 9, 8, 3, 5, 10, 11, 19, 0, 8, 2};
main()
{
   int x, y, z;
   for (x = 0; x < 3; x++)
   {
         z = 1000;
         for (y = 0; y < 4; y++)
         if (n[x][y] < z)
              z = n[x][y];
         printf ("%d", c);
   }
}
```

19
POINTERS

19.1 INTRODUCTION

Till now, we have written many programs in C. All the programs which we have discussed use variables (unsubscripted or subscripted) to store `data. You have learnt to manipulate data by accessing the value of variables. You know that data is stored in computer memory. In other words, the value of each variable is stored at particular location in computer memory, which is called its address. In C, you can access the data by referring its address. How will you refer that address? By the use of 'pointers', you can access any data in memory. 'Pointers' is the most fascinating and useful concept of C programming. You cannot call yourself a 'C programmer' unless you know pointers. Let us start learning the pointers in C and their applications in developing useful programs.

19.2 UNDERSTANDING POINTERS

The data items, which are stored in computer memory, occupy one or more contiguous memory cells. The adjacent memory cells are numbered consecutively (generally in hexa decimals) from the beginning to end of the memory area. The memory cells are actually registers in hardware terminology. Each memory cell is generally called 'address' in software terminology. So, whatever data item you store on computer has its own address. Even before storing, at the time of declaration of a variable, the space in memory is reserved for that variable. Consider the following declaration:

```
int num;
```

The above statement instructs the C compiler to reserve space in memory to hold the integer value. As an integer generally requires two contiguous bytes, 2 memory cells are reserved to store data. The above statement also associates the name num with that memory location. If you also initialise the variable num with certain value (say 25), that value is stored at the location as shown in the following statement and illustrated in Figure 19.1.

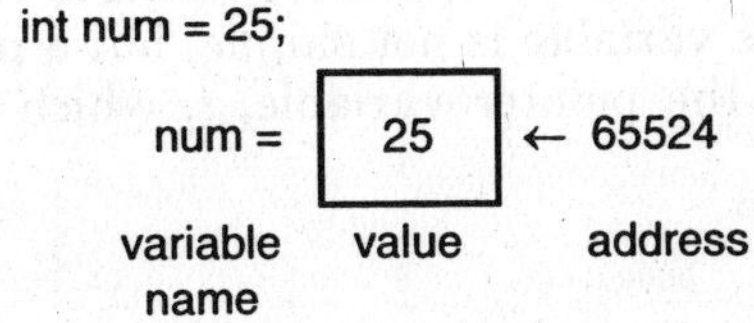

Figure. 19.1 *An example of value stored at memory location*

The address shown in Figure 19.1 (65524) is called the pointer as it is pointing to a memory location. You can display this address by the following statement:

```
printf("\n Address of variable num is %d", &num)
```

The expression, &num in the above statement is called the *address operator* as this operator evaluates the address of operand, num. You can assign this operator to another variable (say pnum) as shown below:

```
pnum = &num;
```

The variable, pnum in the above statement is a pointer, and hence is called a *pointer variable.* So, a pointer variable stores the address of another variable which can be a simple variable or a pointer variable. A simple variable, on the other hand, stores only the value and not the address.

The other difference between a simple variable and a pointer variable is that a simple variable can store value of any data type such as int, char, float, double, etc. while a pointer variable stores only integer value.

In the beginning of this section, we have discussed that the data items are stored in continguous memory cells and the compiler reserves space in these memory cells based on the data type. We also know that the typical memory requirements of different data types vary. For instance, an int type of variable reserves 2 bytes while a float reserves 4 bytes of space in memory. However, a pointer variable points to a single memory location. So, how are all the bytes accessed using a pointer? A pointer variable always points to (or store the address of) first byte of the variable and as the data items are stored in continuous memory cells, the subsequent bytes are accessed based on the data type.

With this discussion, the basic concept of pointers must be clear to you. We will learn to implement this concept in subsequent part of this chapter.

19.3 USING POINTERS

Let us learn to use pointers in our programs. Although, beginners generally find some difficulty in using pointers in their program. We believe if you follow the step wise step procedures discussed below, you will find the use of pointers simple and interesting. You are also advised to try all the examples on your computer for better understanding of the concepts.

19.3.1. Declaration of Pointers

The pointer variables must be declared in the program just like simple variables. However, the declaration of a pointer variable is somehow different as shown in the following general form:

```
<data-type> *<Name of Pointer variable>;
```

For example, the following declaration declares the pointer variable, pnum, which stores the address of a int variable:

```
int *pnum;
```

In the above declaration, * is unary operator, which is called the *indirection operator.* This operator indicates that the variable is not simple, but a pointer variable. Similarly, the following declaration declares the pointer variable, *i*, which stores the address of a float variable.

```
float *i;
```

The pointer variable can also store the address of another pointer (which is obviously an int variable) as illustrated in the following declaration:

```
int **j;
```

The two asterik symbols (**) indicate that the pointer variable is a pointer to pointer (and not pointer to simple variable). This concept would be clear to you when we will learn to initialise a pointer. Let us continue our discussion with the concept of initialisation of pointers.

19.3.2 Initialisation of Pointers

The initialisation of pointer variables is somehow different from the initialisation of simple variables. When you initialise a simple variable, you assign certain value to the variable. However, you cannot assign a value to the pointer variable. You can only assign the address (which you do not know because computer generates the address) to a pointer variable. This can be done in the following general form:

```
<Name of pointer variable> = &<Name of simple/pointer variable>;
```

For example,

```
pnum = &num;
```

In the above example, the address of variable, num is assigned to the pointer variable, pnum. You can also assign the address of the pointer variable, pnum to another pointer variable, j as shown below:

```
j = &pnum;
```

In the above initialisation, as the pointer variable, j stores the address of another pointer variable, pnum, the variable j is declared by putting two asteriks (**) before its name as discussed in previous sub-section (19.3.1). This type of pointer is called *pointer-to-pointer*. Similarly, you can create a pointer to pointer-to-pointer variable. In that case, you will put three asteriks (***) before the name of pointer variable during declaration. Theoretically there is no limit of creating pointers in this way, however you rarely require such extending pointer variables. Normally, you require either a pointer to simple variable or a pointer-to-pointer variable.

After declaring and initialising the pointers, you can manipulate them. Let us discuss the ways of manipulating pointers.

19.3.3. Manipulation of Pointers

Manipulation of pointers refers to access the value of variable to which the pointer points. For example, consider the following declaration and initialisation statements:

```
int num, *pnum; /*Declaration of variables */
num = 21; /* store 21 to simple variable, num */
pnum = &num; /* Initialisation of pointer variable, pnum */
```

The first statement declares two variables, one simple variable, and another pointer variable pnum. The second statement initialises the value, 21 to simple variable, num. The third statement assigns the address of simple variable, num to pointer variable, *pnum. Now, using the pointer variable, you can find the value of simple variable, num. How? Consider the following printf() statement:

```
printf("\n value of num is %d", *pnum);
```

What will be output of the above statement? The above statement will display the following output:

Value of num is 21

So, the expression, *pnum refers to the value at the address, pointed by the pointer variable, pnum. As pnum stores the address of variable, num and the value of num is 21. Therefore *pnum refers to 21. What will pnum refer to? Let us consider the following printf( ) statement:

```
printf ("\n Address of num is %d", pnum);
```

What will be the output of the above statement? 21 or something else? The above statement would display the following output:

Address of num is -12

So, the expression, pnum refers to the address of simple variable, num. This address may be - 12 or something else depending upon the location of memory cells where this data is stored in your computer. If you want that the address of a variable should be displayed in positive integers, use %u (unsigned integer) instead of %d as the format specifier in printf( ) statement as shown below:

```
printf ("\n Address of num is %u", pnum);
```

Now, the output of the above statement would be as follows:

Address of num is 65524

The general form to access the value of variable to which the pointer variable points is as follows:

```
*<Name of pointer variable>
```

Similarly, the general form to access the value of simple variable pointed by a variable to which another pointer variable points is as follows:

```
**<Name of pointer variable>
```

For example, if j is a pointer-to-pointer variable and stores the address of another pointer, pnum pointing to simple variable, num, j would be declared and initialised as follows.

```
int **j;
j = &pnum;
```

The value of a simple variable, num, pointed by the pointer variable, pnum to which another pointer variable, j points can be displayed by the following statement:

```
printf ("\n Value of num is %d", **j);
```

So, we manipulate the pointers in the procedure discussed above. Just by reading the above discussed procedures, you may not be able to understand this concept, unless you write a small program using the above concepts. Let us write a program that declare, initialise and manipulate pointers for displaying the addresses and values of various variables.

Program 19.1

```
/* Program to display value and address of a variable */
# include <stdio.h>
main()
{
      int num, *pnum, **j; /*Declaration of variables*/
      num = 21; /*storing the value 21 to num */
      pnum = &num; /*storing the address of num to pnum */
      j = &pnum; /*storing the address of pnum to j*/
      /* First way to display value and address*/
      printf("\n Value of the variable num is %d", num);
      printf(" Address of the variable num is %u", &num);
      /* Second way to display value and address */
      printf("\n Value of the variable num is %d", *pnum);
      printf("\n Address of the variable num is %u", pnum);
      /* Third way to display value and address */
      printf("\n Value of the variable num is %d", **j);
      printf("\n Address of the variable num is %u", *j);
      getche();
}
```

Sample Output

When you will run this program, you will get the following output:

Value of the variable num is 21
Address of the variable num is 65524
Value of the variable num is 21
Address of the variable num is 65524
Value of the variable num is 21
Address of the variable num is 65524

Explanation

You get the same output with all the three ways in the above program. It means, you can display the value of num by any of the following expressions:

```
num
*pnum
*jj
```

Similarly, you can display the address of num by any of the following expressions:

```
&num
pnum
*j
```

There is no doubt that the expressions, num and &num display the value and address of num respectively. As pnum stores the address of num, the expressions pnum and *pnum display the address and value (value at address) of num respectively. The third way is to use the expressions **j and *j. As j stores the address of pnum (as j = &pnum) and pnum stores the address of num (as pnum = &num), **j refers to value of num. This can also be explained as follows:

****j means value at *j**

***j means value at j**

But, j stores address of pnum

So, *j means value at (address of pnum)

But pnum stores address of num

So, *j means address of num

Therefore **j means value at (address of num), which is the value of num. So, **j refers to value of num. As already explained *j refers value at the address of pnum, which is the address of num, therefore *j refers to the address of num.

Now, let us consider the following statements of program and analyse the output:

(*i*) `int num, *pnum, **j;`
(*ii*) `num = 21;`
(*iii*) `pnum = #`
(*iv*) `j = &pnum;`
(*v*) `printf("\n %d", num);`
(*vi*) `printf("\n %d", pnum);`
(*vii*) `printf("\n %d", j);`
(*viii*) `printf("\n %d", *num);`
(*ix*) `printf("\n %d", *pnum);`
(*x*) `printf("\n %d", *j);`
(*xi*) `printf("\n %d", **num);`
(*xii*) `printf("\n %d", **pnum);`
(*xiii*) `printf("\n %d", **j);`

What will the output of the expressions written above? Are all the expressions written correctly? No. On compilation, there will be errors "Invalid indirection" in statement numbers, (*viii*), (*xi*) and (*xii*). Why? The reason is that the expressions *num, **num and **pnum are incorrect.

The expression *num indicates that num is a pointer variable, however num is a simple variable. Similarly, the expression **num is also invalid. The expression **pnum indicates that pnum is a pointer-to-pointer variable, however it is a pointer variable. Therefore, **pnum is also invalid. Now, what will be the output of statement numbers, (*v*), (*vi*), (*vii*), (*ix*), (*x*) and (*xiii*). Let us write the correct complete program, run it and see the output.

Program 19.2

```
/*Program to display the value of simple and pointer variables */
#include <stdio.h>
main()
{
   int num, *pnum, **j;
   num = 21;
   pnum = &num;
   j = &pnum;
   printf("\n num = %d", num);
```

```
    printf("\n pnum = %d", pnum);
    printf("\n j = %d",j);
    printf("\n *pnum=%d", *pnum);
    printf("\n *j = %d", *j);
    printf("\n **j = %d", **j);
    getche();
}
```

Sample Output

On execution, you may get the output similar to the one shown below:

num = 21

pnum = –12

j = –14

**pnum = 21*

**j = – 12*

***j = 21*

Explanation

(*a*) num = 21: As num is a simple variable and stores the value 21, so the output is num = 21.

(*b*) pnum = –12: pnum is a pointer variable that contains address of num (pnum =&num), therefore the output displays the address of variable, num which is here –12. (It may be different in your computer on different execution times.)

(*c*) j = –14: j is a pointer-to-pointer variable that contains address of another pointer, pnum (j = &pnum), therefore the output displays the address of pnum which is here –14.

(*d*) *pnum = 21: * pnum means * (&num) because pnum = &num.
As &num is – 12 (as stated in (*b*) above), so value at this address is 21 *i.e.,* value of num.

(*e*) *j = –12: * j means * (&pnum) because j = &pnum. As &pnum is – 14 (as stated in (*c*) above), so value at this address –12 (see (*b*) above).

(*f*) **j = 21: It has been already explained in previous program (see program 19.1).

So, you must have now understood the ways of declaring, initialising and manipulating arrays. We will now discuss various arithmetic operations that can be performed on pointers.

19.4 ARITHMETIC OPERATIONS ON POINTERS

The following arithmetic operations can be performed on pointers:

(*a*) Incrementation of pointers

(*b*) Decrementation of pointers

(*c*) Subtraction of two pointers

(*d*) Comparison of two pointers

Let us discuss these operations.

19.4.1 Incrementation of Pointers

You can add an integer value to a pointer as shown in the following example:

```
int n = 8, *pn;
pn = &n;
pn++
```

The expression, pn++ increments the pointer variable, pn by 1. This is called *incrementation of pointers*. Now, the pointer variable, pn points to the next memory location of same variable type. As the variable type of n is int and an int is always 2 bytes long, adding 1 to pointer variable, pn increments the memory address with 2. For instance, if the original memory location of n is 2000, the pn after increment will point to memory location 2002.

Similarly, incrementing pointers to char and float variables by 1 adds 1 and 4 to their memory addresses respectively (because char and float variables occupy 1 and 4 bytes respectively). You can increment pointers by any value as shown in following examples:

```
pn = pn + 5;
pn = pn + 10;
```

Addition of an integer value to a pointer is useful to manipulate arrays. As the data elements of an array are stored in continguous memory locations, you can know their values by incrementing their pointers. We will explain this concept in the next section on 'Pointers and Arrays'.

19.4.2 Decrementation of Pointers

You can also subtract an integer value from a pointer as illustrated below:

```
int n = 8, *pn;
pn = &n;
pn--;
```

The expression, pn-- decrements the pointer variable by 1. This is called *decrementation of pointers*. Now, the pointer variable, pn points to the previous memory location of same variable type. Decrementation of pointers work in same way as incrementation of pointers except that it subtracts the values based on data type. Like addition, subtraction of an integer value to a pointer value is useful to manipulate arrays. We will also explain this concept in the next section on 'Pointers and Arrays'.

19.4.3 Subtraction of Two Pointers

You can subtract one pointer from another if both point to the data elements of same array. As this concept is related to arrays, we will discuss it in next section on 'pointers and arrays'.

19.4.4 Comparison of Two Pointers

You can compare two pointers to know whether they point to same location or different. This is again useful in arrays, therefore we will discuss this concept in next section on 'Pointers and Arrays'.

So, you have seen the arithmetic operations, which can be performed on pointers. However, the following arithmetic operations on pointers are not allowed as they have no importance:

- Addition of two pointers.
- Multiplication of a pointer with a number.
- Division of a pointer with a number.

Let us now discuss the role of pointers in arrays, which is one of the major area of application of pointers.

19.5 POINTERS AND ARRAYS

We have discussed arrays in the last chapter. You know that an array is a collection of related or similar data elements stored in a contiguous area in the memory. We have also discussed in previous section that a pointer after incrementation always points to the next memory location of same variable.

Therefore, we can manipulate arrays using pointers. An array name is actually a pointer to the first element in that array. How? This can be explained by displaying the address of array elements by two methods— one using subscripted variables (arrays) and another using pointers. Let us first analyse one-dimensional arrays using both methods.

19.5.1 Manipulating 1-D Arrays

You can manipulate a one-dimensional array using both subscripted variables and pointers. To understand, how a 1-D array is stored in memory, consider an array of 6 numbers with the following declaration:

```
int n[6];
```

Let us initialise the data elements of this array and display their addresses by writing a small program.

Program 19.3

```
/*  Program to manipulate 1-D array without using pointers */
#include <stdio.h>
main()
{
   int n[ ] = {37,12,19,807,931,173};
   int c = 0;
   while (c < 6)
   {
      printf("\n Address of element %d is %u", c, &n[c]);
      printf("\n Value of element %d is %d", c, n[c]);
      c++;
   }
   getche();
}
```

Sample Output

When the above program is executed, the following output is obtained:

Address of element 0 is 65514
Value of element 0 is 37
Address of element 1 is 65516
Value of element 1 is 12
Address of element 2 is 65518
Value of element 2 is 19
Address of element 3 is 65520
Value of element 3 is 807
Address of element 4 is 65522
Value of element 4 is 931
Address of element 5 is 65524
Value of element 5 is 173

The above program displays the address and value of each data element. As the variable, n is of int type and occupies 2 bytes, the memory locations of various elements of the array differ by 2 as shown in the output and illustrated in Figure 19.2.

	Value	Address	
n[0]	37	65514	— I byte
		65515	— II byte
n[1]	12	65516	— I byte
		65517	— II byte
n[2]	19	65518	— I byte
		65519	— II byte
n[3]	807	65520	— I byte
		65521	— II byte
n[4]	931	65522	— I byte
		65523	— II byte
n[5]	173	65524	— I byte
		65525	— II byte

Note: Address of an element denotes the address of its first byte.

Figure. 19.2 *An example of Memory Map of an Array*

The value and address of each data element of an array can also be displayed using pointers. In the output of the above program, the address of 0th element is 65514. You can store this address to a pointer variable, say pn. By incrementing this pointer, you can display the value and address of each data element. Let us modify the above program by declaring the pointer variable, pn and manipulating the array using pointers.

Program 19.4

```
/*Program to manipulate 1-D array using pointers */
#include <stdio.h>
main()
{
   int n[ ] = {37, 12 19, 807, 931, 173};
```

```
    int c = 0;
    int *pn; /*Declaring the pointer variable.*/
    pn = &n[0] /*Initialising pointer with address of 0th element*/
    while (c < 6)
    {
            printf("\n Address of element %d is %u", c, pn);
            printf("\n Value of element % d is % d", c, *pn);
            pn++; /*Incrementing pointer*/
            c++;
    }
    getche();
}
```

Sample Output

On executing the above program, you will get the same output as shown in previous program (Program 19.3).

Let us analyse various statements of this program. The statement int *pn; declares a pointer variable for storing the address of 0th element of the array. Using the statement, pn = &n[0], the address of 0th element gets stored in the pointer variable, pn. The first printf( ) statement within while loop uses the expression, pn to display the address of each data element. As initially, pn points to 0th element, this printf( ) statement displays the address of 0th element. The second printf( ) statement uses the expression, *pn to display the value at memory location, pn, which is the value of first element. The next statement within the loop is pn++, which increments the pointer variable, pn by 1. So, when the loop is executed second time the pointer variable, pn points to the second element (1th) and hence its address and value is displayed. As the loop is executed 6 times based on the value of counter, c, the address and value of all the data elements are displayed one by one. In this way, you can access the value and address of any data element of an array.

The expressions, pn and *pn can also be written in some other ways. As pn, initially points to address of 0th element, it can be written as follows:

```
pn+0
```

Similarly, to refer to the 1th or second element. You can write the following expression:

```
pn+1
```

It means, the expression pn + c where c varies from 0 to 5, refers to the address of cth element. Similarly, it can be shown that the expression *(pn + c) refers to the value of cth element.

So, in the above discussed program you can display the output by the following statements:

```
printf("\n Address of element %d is %u", c, pn + c);
printf("\n Value of element %d is %d", c, *(pn + c);
```

The important point which you should keep in mind that you do not need to increment the pointer, pn as c is incremented. The expressions, pn + c and *(pn + c) can also be written as c + pn and *(c + pn) respectively according to the arithmetic rules. There is one more way to write these expressions. We know that the expressions, &n[c] and pn gives the address of cth element (compare Programs 19.3 and 19.4). We just discussed that the expressions pn, pn + c and (c + pn) are also same. If you can write the expression, pn + c also as &n[c], you can write the expression, c + pn as &c[n]. Similarly, the expressions *(c + pn) and c[n] are also same.

Let us summarise, what we have discussed. Referring to the Programs 19.3 and 19.4, if n[ ] is a 1-D array, pn is the pointer to the array and c is the counter incremented in the loop, the following expressions display the address of cth element:

```
pn + c
c + pn
&n[c]
&c[n]
```

So, all the above expressions are same. Similarly, the following expressions display the value of cth element:

```
*(pn + c)
*(c + pn)
n[c]
c[n]
```

All the above expressions are also same. Let us verify these concepts by re-writing the Program 19.4 to display the address and value of data elements of array, n[ ].

Program 19.5

```
/*Program to display address and values of data elements */
/* of an array using various similar expressions */
#include <stdio.h>
main()
{
 int n[ ] = (37, 12, 19, 807, 931 173);
 int *pn;
 int c;
 pn = &n[0];
 printf("\n Address of Elements :\n");
 for (c = 0; c < 6, c++)
 {
       printf("Element No. %d\t", c);
       printf("% u\t", pn + c);
       printf("%u\t", c + pn);
       printf("%u\t", &n[c]);
       printf("%u\t", &c[n]);
       printf("\n",);
 }
 printf("\n Value of Elements : \n");
 for (c = 0; c < 6; c++)
 {
       printf("Element No %d\t",c);
       printf("%d\t", *(pn + c));
       printf("%d\t", *(c + pn));
```

```
        printf("%d\t"; n[c]);
        printf("%d\t", c[n]);
        printf("\n");
    }
  getche();
}
```

Sample Output

When the above program is executed, you get the following output:

Address of Elements:

Element No. 0	*65514*	*65514*	*65514*	*65514*
Element No. 1	*65516*	*65516*	*65516*	*65516*
Element No. 2	*65518*	*65518*	*65518*	*65518*
Element No. 3	*65520*	*65520*	*65520*	*65520*
Element No. 4	*65522*	*65522*	*65522*	*65522*
Element No. 5	*65524*	*65524*	*65524*	*65524*

Value of Elements:

Element No. 0	*37*	*37*	*37*	*37*
Element No. 1	*12*	*12*	*12*	*12*
Element No. 2	*19*	*19*	*19*	*19*
Element No. 3	*807*	*807*	*807*	*807*
Element No. 4	*931*	*931*	*931*	*931*
Element No. 5	*173*	*173*	*173*	*173*

So, you see that the address and value elements can be displayed by any of similar expressions discussed above. Note that we are not incrementing the pointer variable, pn in the program. Why? This is because that we are incrementing c, which is being added to the pointer variable. If we will also increment pn, the pointer will point to next to next memory location. Do you want to verify this? Include the statement, pn++ within the loop and see the output. You will get incorrect results.

Having understood the role of pointers in 1-D arrays, let us analyse the differences between an array and a pointer.

19.5.1.1 Difference between Arrays and Pointers

Now let us come to one important point stated earlier in this section regarding definition of an array. We said that an array name is actually a pointer to the first element in that array. Do you want to see, how? Consider the previous program (Program 19.5) and analyse various expressions. In that program we stored the address of 0th element (first element) in a pointer variable, pn with the following expression:

```
pn = &n[0];
```

This expression can also be written as follows:

```
pn = n;
```

You can verify this by writing this expression in place of expression, pn = &n[0] and running the program again. You will see the same output. In the expression, pn = n, pn is

the pointer variable and n is the array name. So our statement 'An array name is actually a pointer to the first element in that array' is verified. If an array name is also a pointer, then what is the difference between an array and a pointer. The difference is itself stated in the above discussed statement. An array is a pointer with constant address (address of first element) which cannot be changed but a pointer is a variable to which an address can be stored, which can be assigned and changed in the program as discussed earlier in the chapter. The other difference is that an array is a collection of similar data elements stored in continguous memory locations while a pointer points a single address.

You can assign values to the data elements of an array but you cannot assign value to a pointer variable. A pointer variable can store only address or a NULL value. Another conceptual difference between an array and a pointer is that you cannot increment or decrement an array while you can increment or decrement a pointer. The practical differences (use in programs) between arrays and pointers have already been highlighted in the programs discussed above.

Now, we will discuss to manipulate a two dimensional array both by using subscripted variables and pointers.

19.5.2 Manipulating 2-D Arrays

As we have discussed in previous sub-section about the manipulation of 1-D arrays, a 2-D array can be manipulated both by using subscripted variables and pointers. To understand the use of pointers in 2-D arrays, we would first see, how data elements of a 2-D array are stored in memory. Consider a 2-D array with following declaration:

```
int mat[2][3];
```

The above declaration creates a 2-D array, mat with 2 rows and 3 columns. Let us initialise this array with values and analyse its memory map by writing a small program.

Program 19.6

```
/*Program to manipulate 2-D array without using pointers*/
#include <stdio.h>
main( )
{
   int mat[2][3] =    {{95, 172, 312},
                       {132, 81, 96}};
   int r, c;
   for (r = 0; r < 2; r++)
   {
         for (c = 0; c < 3; c++)
         {
                     printf("\n Element in row %d column %d", r,c);
                     printf("\t Address % u", &mat[r][c]);
                     printf("\t Value %d", mat[r][c]);
         }
   }
   getche( );
}
```

Sample Output

When the above program is executed, the following output is obtained:

Element in row 0 column 0 Address 65514 value 95

Element in row 0 column 1 Address 65516 value 172

Element in row 0 column 2 Address 65518 value 312

Element in row 1 column 0 Address 65520 value 132

Element in row 1 column 1 Address 65522 value 81

Element in row 1 column 2 Address 65524 value 96

On analysing the output, we observe that the address of each data element in 2-D array differs by 2 bytes just like elements of 1-D array. In the previous chapter on Arrays, we have discussed that a 2-D array is an array of 1-D arrays (see Section 18.2.2.2), where each row of a 2-D array is considered a 1-D array. So, the data of 2-D array is organised in memory, just like that of a 1-D array.

Hence, using pointers, you can display address and value of each data element just like the method discussed in case of 1-D array. Let us declare a pointer variable, pm and initialise with address of first element (*i.e.,* mat[0][0]) As there are 2 1-D arrays (2 rows) and each 1-D array (1 row) has 3 elements, we can increment the pointer variable 6 times (2 × 3) by making a loop to display address and value of each data element. The expression, pm will display the address while the expression, *pm will display the value of each data element. Let us write the program discussed above using pointers.

Program 19.7

```
/* Program to manipulate a 2-D array in linear order using pointers */
#include <stdio.h>
main( )
{
   int mat[2][3] = {{95, 172, 312},
                    {132, 81, 96}};
   int i;
   int *pm; /*Declaration of pointer variable */
   pm = &mat[0][0]; /*storing address of 1st element in pointer variable*/
   for (i = 0; i < 6; i++)
   {
         printf("\n Element  no % d", i);
         printf("\t Address %u", pm);
         printf("\t Value %d", *pm);
         pm++;
   }
   getche( );
}
```

Sample Output

When the above program is executed, the following output is obtained:

Element no. 0 Address 65514 Value 95

Element no. 1 Address 65516 Value 172

Element no. 2 Address 65518 Value 312

Element no. 3 Address 65520 Value 132
Element no. 4 Address 65522 Value 81
Element no. 5 Address 65524 Value 96

In the above program the loop is executed 6 times and in each loop the pointer variable increments by 1. In this way, you can easily display address and value of all the elements in a linear order. Now, suppose you want to access the data element based on their position in a particular row and column. Then, the above program will not solve your problem.

The program no. 19.6 (discussed earlier) can be used to access the data elements of a 2-D array based on their positions in particular row and column. However, that program does not use pointers. Now, we can modify this program by creating a pointer variable. This pointer variable will store the address of 0th element of each 1-D array of 2-D array. Let us first write the program, execute it and analyse its statements.

Program 19.8

```
/*Program to manipulate 2-D array in row-wise order using pointers*/
#include <stdio.h>
main( )
{
   int mat[2][3] = {{95, 172, 312};
                     {132, 81, 96}};
   int r, c;
   int *pm;
   for (r = 0; r < 2; r++)
   {
         pm = &mat[r][0];
         for (c = 0; c < 3; c++)
         {
               printf("\n Element in row %d column %d", r,c);
               printf("\t Address %u", pm);
               printf("\t value %u", *pm);
               pm++;
         }
   }
   getche( );
}
```

Sample Outupt

On execution of above program, you will get the following output:

Element in row 0 column 0 Address 65512 value 95
Element in row 0 column 1 Address 65514 value 172
Element in row 0 column 2 Address 65516 value 312
Element in row 1 column 0 Address 65518 value 132
Element in row 1 column 1 Address 65520 value 81
Element in row 1 column 2 Address 65522 value 96

The above program is somehow similar to previous 2 programs. We have created a nested loop in the program to refer data element of each row and column. The pointer variable, pm stores the address of 0th element of each row. Note that this initialisation statement of pointer is written after the first for loop. The reason is that we know that a 2-D array is an array of 1-D arrays and hence the address of 0th element of each row must be stored to the pointer variable each time, the row counter, r is incremented. The data elements of each row are accessed by incrementing the column variable, c and the pointer variable, pm within the inner for loop. In this way, all the elements of a 2-D array can be accessed row and column wise.

In the earilier part of this section (see Section 19.5.1), we have discussed the various ways of writing expressions, pn and *pn in a 1-D array. Similarly, in a 2-D array, the expressions, pm and *pm can be replaced by expressions pm + c or c + pm and * (pm + c) or *(c + pm) without incrementing the pointer variables. The reason is same as discussed in case of 1-D array. The reader is advised to go through the section 19.5.1 again to understand this concept.

19.6 POINTERS AND STRINGS

As discussed in the previous chapter (see Section 18.7), strings are the character arrays. Like numeric arrays, charater arrays are of two types— one-dimensional and two-dimensional character arrays. We can manipulate these character arrays using pointers. Let us first learn to manipulate one dimensional character arrays using pointers.

19.6.1 Manipulating 1-D Character Arrays

We have already discussed in the previous chapter that a one-dimensional character is declared as illustrated below:

```
char name[21];
```

Using pointers, you can declare the above array, name [21] as follows:

```
char *name;
```

In the above declaration, the pointer variable, name will store the address of 0th character of 1-D array, name[ ]. While declaring a 1-D character array using pointers, there is no need to specify the maximum number of data elements or characters.

You can initialise the name[ ] character array declared as pointer *name with value as illustrated below:

```
char *name = "Sapna";
```

or

```
char name = "Sapna";
```

The above initialisation statement will store the address of first element or character, 'S' in the pointer variable. You can manipulate this string by following statements in a loop:

```
printf("%c", *name);
name++;
```

Let us write a program to demonstrate the manipulation of 1-D character array using pointers.

Program 19.9

```
/* Program to demonstrate the use of pointers in a string*/
#include <stdio.h>
main( )
{
  char *name; /*Declaration of a string */
  int i = 0, j;
  printf("\n Enter your name:");
  gets(name);
  j = strlen(name); /*calculate length of string */
  printf("\n Your name is ");
  while (i <= j)
  {
        printf("%c", *name);
        name++;
        i++;
  }
  getche();
}
```

Sample Input/Output

When the above program is executed, the following prompt is displayed:

Enter your name:

Suppose you enter the name, Pawan Gupta, the computer displays the following output:

Your name is Pawan Gupta

The above program stores the 0th element of string or characters array in the pointer variable, name. The length of the entered string is calculated using strlen( ) function and gets stored in variable j. The variable, i is initialised with zero and the while loop is executed till i <= j. The printf ( ) statement initially displays the first character of string and then the pointer variable, name is incremented. We also increment the variable, i to count the number of loops executed. When loop is executed second time, the pointer variable, name points to the second character and hence second character is displayed. In this way the whole string is displayed.

Now, we will discuss the method to manipulate a 2-D character array using pointers.

19.6.2 Manipulating 2-D Character Arrays

As we have discussed in the previous chapter (see Section 18.7), a 2-D character array is declared as illustrated below:

```
char name[5][21];
```

The above declared 2-D character array, name[5][21] is a set of 5 strings where each string has maximum 21 characters including the null character.

You can declare such a 2-D character array by creating an array of pointers as illustrated below:

```
char *name[5];
```

As a 2-D array is an array of 1-D arrays, the above declaration will store the address of 0th element of each 1-D array (*i.e.*, a string) into the pointer variable, name. So, there will be an array of 5 pointers. Such an array of pointers to strings can be initialised as follows:

```
char *name[ ] = {"SHALU"
                 "RUCHI"
                 "RAJESH  PATHAK"
                 "NEERU  PATHAK"
                 "SURENDRA"};
```

As you can seen in the above initialisation statement that you do not need to mention the number of pointers (of subscripts) while initialising an array of pointers to strings. You can manipulate such an array both using subscripted variables, and pointer variables as illustrated in the following program.

Program 19.10

```
/*Program demonstrating the manipulation of an array*/
/* of pointers to strings*/
#include <stdio.h>
#include <stdlib.h>
main()
{
  char *name[5]; /*Declare an array of pointers*/
  int i;
  for (i = 0; i < 5; i++)
  {
      name[i] = malloc[20*sizeof(char)];
      printf("\n Enter name of person % d", i + 1);
      gets(name[i]);
  }
  printf ("\n The names you have entered are :");
  for (i = 0; i < 5; i++)
  {
      printf("\n Pointed by location no. %u", name + i);
      printf("\t value %s", *(name + i);
  }
  getche();
}
```

Sample Input/Output

When the above program is executed, you will be asked to enter name of persons as shown below (sample data is entered):

Enter name of person 1 Amitabh

Enter name of person 2 Aishwarya

Enter name of person 3 Anupam

Enter name of person 4 Ravinder

Enter name of person 5 Baldev Raj

After entering this data, you will get the following output:

The names you have entered are:

Pointed by location no. 65516 value Amitabh

Pointed by location no. 65518 value Aishwarya

Pointed by location no. 65520 value Anupam

Pointed by location no. 65522 value Ravinder

Pointed by location no. 65524 value Baldev Raj

Let us discuss various statements of this program. In the main() function, the first statement, char *name[5]; declares array of pointers to strings to store name of 5 persons. During declaration (without initialisation), it is necessary to mention the maximum number of pointers (or strings). However, it is optional to mention the number of characters in a string *i.e.,* the second subscript of 2-D array. After declaration, we declare an int variable i and perform a loop until i < 5 using for loop statement. The first statement within this loop is as follows:

```
name[i] = malloc[20*sizeof(char)];
```

The above statement uses a function, malloc( ). This function reserves a block of memory for the array variable, name[i]. The above function, malloc[20*sizeof(char)] allocates memory of 20 × 1 = 20 bytes for each string as maximum size of a string is assumed to be 20. The malloc( ) function always return a pointer to a character. It is necessary to include this function for assigning sufficient memory for the array, otherwise the program may give error during run time due to insufficient memory space. If you use malloc( ) function, you need to include the reader file, stdlib.h in the program.

The statement which we use to accept the string is gets(name[i]). Note that you do not need to put ampersand (&) before the array name as the array name itself is a pointer. The loop is executed 5 times to acceept 5 strings. Now, to display these strings, we create another for loop, which is again executed 5 times with value of *i* varying from 1 to 5. The following expression displays the address of each string:

```
name + i
```

As initially i would be 0, name + 0 will give the address of 0th element *i.e.,* first pointer to the string, which is 65516 in the output of above program. As this address points to the first string, the string can be displayed by following expression, *(name + 0). In general, each of the strings can be displayed by the following expression:

```
*(name + i)
```

Therefore, we have used the above expression for displaying each string. As initially i is 0, the expression, * (name + 0) displays the string, Amitabh. After this the variable i is incremented and the loop is executed second time. Now, the expression, name + 1 points to the second string. Note that its address in the output of above program is displayed as 65518 which is 2 bytes more than previous address. Why the difference is only 2 bytes and not 20 bytes?

The reason is that the expression, name + i is a pointer to the string and the pointer always contains whole numbers (integers), which occupy two bytes. As, we have declared an array of pointers to strings, their addresses differ by 2 bytes. Similarly, during 2nd execution of loop the expression *(name + 1) will display the second string, Aishwarya. In this way, the addresses of pointers to strings and the strings are displayed one by one.

Having understood the role of pointers to arrays and strings, let us understand how pointers are useful in functions.

19.7 POINTERS AND FUNCTIONS

In chapter-17, we have discussed that the values of the variables can be passed to the functions, such function calls are called *Call by Value* (see Section 17.2.2.1). However, using this type of call, you can return a single value to the calling function. Using pointers, you can return more than one value to the calling function. How? Using pointers, you can pass the addresses of variables (where calculations to be stored) to the functions and as addresses are passed and not values, the values are processed at their original locations, so infact you do not need to return values. Such calls are called *Calls by Reference.* Let us discuss these in detail.

19.7.1 Call By Reference

Using 'Call by Reference' method, you can pass the addresses of actual parameters of the calling function to the called function. In this method, the formal parameters become pointers to the actual parameters. Using these poniters, you can access the value of actual parameters from their original stored locations and manipulate them. Let us understand this method with an example. In the chapter 17, we wrote a program to calculate the area of a circle (Refer Program 17.6) by passing the value of radius, r (actual parameter) to the function, areafunc( ). In this called function, we calculated the area, a and returned its value to the calling function. Suppose, we want to calculate both area and perimeter of a circle using functions. You can pass the radius, *r* to two functions, areafunc( ) and perifunc( ) and return the values of area, a and perimeter, p from the respective functions to the called function. We have to call two functions, because each function can return only a single value. Before discussing the method of calling functions by reference, let us first write a program to solve the above problem by calling two functions using 'Call by Value' method.

Program 19.11

```
/* Program to demonstrate returning of two values from */
/* two functions without using pointers */
#include <stdio.h>
float areafunc(float); /*Function prototype*/
float perifunc(float); /*Function prototype*/
main()
{
   float r, area, peri;
   printf("\n Enter radius of the circle :");
   scanf("%f", &r);
   area = areafunc(r); /* calling first function*/
   peri = perifunc(r); /* calling second function*/
   printf("\n The area of the circle is %f", area);
   printf("\n The perimeter of the circle is %f", peri);
   getche();
}
```

```
float areafunc(float r)
{
  /* Area = πr^2 */
  return(3.14 * r * r); /* Calculating & returning area*/
}
float perifunc(float r)
{
  /* perimeter = 2πr^2*/
  return(2 * 3.14 * r); /*Calculating & returning perimeter*/
}
```

Sample Input/Output

When the above program is executed, you get the following message (sample data is entered):

```
Enter radius of the circle: 5
```

On entering the data, you get the following output:

```
The area of circle is 78.500000
The perimeter of circle is 31.400000
```

In the above program, we used two functions to return two values. However, using pointers you can solve the same problem by calling a single function. Let us first write the program and then understand the importance of various statements.

Program 19.12

```
/* Program to demonstrate the use of pointers in functions */
/* This program calls a function by reference and value*/
#include <stdio.h>
void apfunc(float, float*,float*); /* function prototype*/
main()
{
  float r, area, peri;
  printf("\n Enter radius of the circle :");
  scanf("%f", &r);
  apfunc(r, &area, &peri); /* call by reference & value */
  printf("\n The area of circle is %f", area);
  printf("\n The perimeter of circle is %f", peri);
  getche();
}
void apfunc(float x, float *y, float *z)
{
  *y = 3.14 * x * x;  /* Calculate area */
  *z = 2 * 3.14 * x;  /* Calculate perimeter*/
}
```

Sample Input/Output

When the above program is executed, you get the same input message and output as shown in previous program.

Let us understand the meanings of various statements. The function prototype is declared as follows:

```
void apfunc(float,  float*,  float*);
```

As the function apfunc does not return any value, its return value is stated as void in the above statement. The first parameter of function is radius r which is of float type. The second and third parameters pass the address of variables, area and peri which are of float type and hence are pointers. Therefore, the parameter types are specified as float, float * and float * for variables, r, area and peri respectively in the function prototype. This program accepts the radius of circle in the main( ) program and calls the function, apfunc( ) as follows :

```
apfunc(r, &area, &peri);
```

The above function call has 3 parameters –r, &area and &peri. This is actually a mixed call as you are passing the value of r but addresses of area and peri variables to the function, apfunc( ). Now, let us analyse the function definition statements. The first statement, void apfunc (float x, float * y, float * z) specifies that —

(*a*) The function is not returning any value, *i.e.,* its return type is void.

(*b*) The function has 3 formal parameters *x*, **y* and **z* for actual parameters, r, &area and &peri respectively.

(*i*) *x* is a simple float type variable which stores a value.

(*ii*) **y* is a pointer which stores address of variable, area.

(*iii*) **z* is a pointer which stores address of variable, peri.

Within the function definition, the first statement, $* y = 3.14 * x * x$ calculates the area while the second statement, $* z = 2 * 3.14 * x$ calculates the perimeter of the circle. Note that we have not written the return statement. Why?

Because the calculations are stored in the original locations due to passing of their addresses, so there is no point in returning any value. This is the unique and useful feature of pointers by which a calling function can pass more than one value to the called function.

In this way, the printf ( ) statements written in the main( ) program displays the area and perimeter of circle.

Passing the addresses to a function is one of the useful applications of pointers, which provides benefits to the programmers to develop complex software in C. Let us now conclude this chapter with the use of pointers in passing an entire array to a function.

19.8 POINTERS, ARRAYS AND FUNCTIONS

As discussed in previous chapter on functions, there are two ways to pass arrays to a function, first using 'Call by Value' method and second using 'Call by Reference'. Using 'Call by Reference' method, the entire array can be passed to the function by passing the base address of an array. Let us discuss this method.

19.8.1 Passing Entire Array to Function

To understand the method of passing entire array to a function, recall the program (Program 18.4) discussed in the previous chapter in Section 18.6.1 (Passing Array Elements to a Function). In that program, a 1-D array, num[5] was created and each data element of the array was initialised with same values, 100. The total of these values were calculated (which was 500) and displayed before calling the function. After this, a function was called by passing values of each array element one by one. The values stored in a new variable were changed to 200 one by one and returned to the main( ) function. When the total of array elements were again calculated, it remained at 500. The reason was that the data of array was not changed in the function and hence remained uneffected. You can change the data of array within the called function by passing the base address of the array to the called function. Let us modify that program, so that we can change the values of data elements within the calling function. The complete program, which passes an entire array to a function is discussed below:

Program 19.13

```
/* Program demonstrating the passing of entire array to a function */
#include <stdio.h>
void numbers(int*, int); /*prototype declaration*/
main()
{
   int i, num [5], sum = 0;
   /* Initialising array elements and calculating total */
   for (i = 0; i < 5; i++)
   {
         num[i] = 100;
         sum = sum + num[i];
   }
   printf("\n the sum of numbers before calling function is %d;", sum);
   /* Calling the function by passing entire array */
   numbers(&num[0], 5);
   /* Note that function is not returning any value */
   sum = 0;
   /* Calculating total after calling the function */
   for (i = 0; i < 5; i++)
         sum = sum + num[i];
   printf ("\n The sum of numbers after calling the function is %d", sum);
   getche();
}
/* function definition */
void numbers(int *n, int j)
{
   for (j = 0; j < 5; j++)
   {
         *n = 200; /*Store 200 to array element */
         n++; /*Increment pointer */
   }
}
```

Sample Input/Output

On execution, the following output is generated:

The sum of numbers before calling function is 500

The sum of numbers after calling function is 1000

Let us analyse the statements and the output. In the beginning of the program, the function prototype is declared as follows:

```
void numbers(int*, int);
```

The above statement specifies that the funtion is passing two parameters— one address of int variable, and another int value. It also specifies that the function will not return any value. In the main( ) function an array, num [5] is declared along with a counter, i and accumulator, sum which is initialised to 0. The first for loop calculates the sum of data elements and the first printf ( ) statement displays the sum of numbers before calling function, which comes to be 500. The next statement in the program is as follows:

```
numbers(&num[0],[5]);
```

This statement calls the function numbers( ) by passing the base address (of 0th element) of array and number of elements (which is 5) to it. The function calling statement can also be written as follows:

```
numbers(num, 5);
```

Note when you write in the above way, the array name without brackets or subscripts is writen as actual arguments.

We are also not returning any value to the calling function. So, whatever changes are done, they are done directly in the array elements. After encountering the function calling statement, the control goes to the called function definition. The function is defined as follows:

```
void numbers(int *n, int j);
```

In the above statement, the formal parameters *n and j stores the base address of array and number of elements respectively. The void word is written to specify that the function does not return any value. The above statement can also be written as follows:

```
void numbers (int num[], int j)
```

Note that when you write in the above way, specify the formal parameter for array by writing the array name with empty brackets with subscript. In this function, the loop is executed again and the value of all elements of array are changed one by one by following statements:

```
*n = 100;
n++;
```

The above two statements can be replaced by the following single statement.

```
num[j] = 200;
```

Now, the control goes back to the main program. The variable, sum is again initialised to 0 and the loop is executed to calculate the total of the values of all array elements. As the new value of each data element is 200 and there are 5 elements in the array, the total becomes 1000. Hence, you get the following output for the second printf ( ) statement.

The sum of numbers after calling function is 1000

In this way, you can manipulate an array within the called function by use of pointers.

So, now we have completed our discussion on pointers in this chapter. Let us write few programs for typical applications on pointers.

19.9 TYPICAL APPLICATIONS OF POINTERS

We have discussed the role of pointers in both arrays and functions. Let us write few programs on the following typical applications using pointers, arrays and functions.

(*a*) Swapping the value of two variables
(*b*) Counting number of different characters in a sentence.
(*c*) Finding largest value in a 1-D array
(*d*) Sorting numbers
(*e*) Sorting strings

As we have already discussed all the concepts related to arrays, functions and pointers, we are not explaining you the execution of these programs. Moreover, we have written these programs fully documented, so you will not face any problem in understanding them.

19.9.1 Swapping the Values

Using 'Calls by Reference' method of functions, you can easily swap the value of two variables as illustrated in the following program:

Program 19.14

```
/* Program to swap the values of two variables */
#include <stdio.h>
void swapnum(int*, int*) /* prototype declaration */
main()
{
  int num1, num2;
  printf("\n Enter first number ");
  scanf("%d", &num1);
  printf("\n Enter second number ");
  scanf("%d", &num2);
  swapnum(&num1, &num2); /*call by reference */
  printf("\n The first number is %d ", num1);
  printf("\n The second number is %d ", num2);
  getche();
}
/*Function definition*/
void swapnum(int *n1, int *n2)
{
  int t; /* Declaring a temp variable */
  /*Exchanging values */
  t  = *n1; /*storing value of n1 to t */
  *n1 = *n2; /*storing value of n2 to n1 */
  *n2 = t; /*storing value of t to n2 */
}
```

Sample Input/Output

When the above program is executed, the following messages are displayed (sample data is extended):

Enter first number 13

Enter second number 87

After entering the data, the following output is displayed:

The first number is 87

The second number is 13

So, the data of variables are exchanged with each other.

19.9.2 Counting the Characters

You know, a character in English can be a vowel, consonant, digit, space or any other character. We can write a program to count these different types of characters in a sentence. The following program calls a function by passing addresses of variables (Call by Reference) for counting various characters after accepting a sentence from the user:

Program 19.15

```
/*Program to count vowels, consonants, digits, spaces and other characters */
#include <stdio.h>
void countchar(char[], int*, int*, int*, int*, int*, int*);
/* The above statement is a function prototype having*/
/* 7 parameter types for array, no. of vowels, no. of consonants */
/* no of digits, no. of spaces, no. of other characters and total characters */
main()
{
  char sent[80]; /*Declare a variable for sentence */
  int v = 0; /* Declaration and initialisation of variable for vowel */
  int c = 0; /* Declaration and initialisation of variable for consonant */
  int d = 0; /* Declaration and initialisation of variable for digit */
  int s = 0; /* Declaration and initialisation of variable for spaces */
  int o = 0; /* Declaration and initialisation of variable for other char */
  int t = 0; /* Declaration and initialisation of variable for total char */
  printf("\n Enter a sentence:");
  gets(sent);
  countchar(sent, &v, &c, &d, &s, &o, &t)
  /* Calling function by reference */
  printf("\n The no. of vowels are % d ", v);
  printf("\n The no. of consonants are %d ", c);
  printf("\n The no. of digits are %d ", d);
  printf("\n The no. of spaces are %d ", s);
  printf("\n The no. of other characters %d ", o);
  printf("\n The total no. of characters are %d ", t);
  getche();
}
```

```
/* Function Definition */
void countchar(char sent1[],int*v1, int*c1, int*d1, int*s1, int*o1, int*t)
{
  int i = 0; /Initialise loop counter with 0 */
  char ch;
  /* Read the string until null character is encountered */
  while (sent[i] != '\0')
  {
        ch = toupper(sent1[i]) /*convert character to upper case */
        /* conditions for checking and counting characters */
        if (ch == 'A' || ch == 'E' || ch == 'I' || ch == 'o' || ch == 'U')
              *v1 = *v1 + 1; /*increment vowel counter*/
        else if (ch > = 'A' && ch < = 'Z')
              *c1 = *c1 + 1; /* Increment consonant counter */
        else if (ch > = '0' || ch < '9')
              *d1 = *d1 + 1 /*Increment digit counter */
        else if (ch == ' ' || ch == '\t')
              *s1 = *s1 + 1; /*Increment space counter */
        else
              /* otherwise increment other character counter */
              *o1 = *o1 + 1;
        i++; /*increment loop counter*/
  }
  *t = i-- ;/* Decrement loop counter and store in total counter */
}
```

Sample Input/Output

When the program is executed, the following message comes on the screen (sample data is entered):

Enter a sentence: Read books of Ashok Arora and Shefali Bansal for getting 100% marks

After entering the sentence, you will get the following output:

The no. of vowels are 19

The no. of consonants are 30

The no. of digits are 3

The no. of spaces are 11

The no. of other characters are 2

The total no. of characters are 65

19.9.3 Finding the Largest Number

You can find the largest number among the data elements of 1-D array by sending the entire array to a function and returning the largest value to the calling function as illustrated in the following program:

Program 19.16

```
/* Finding the largest value of 1-D array */
/* This program pass the entire array to a function */
#include <stdio.h>
int findlarge (int*, int); /*Function Prototype */
main()
{
  int n[10]; /*Declaration of 1-D array */
  int c, max; /*Declaration of variables */
  /* Accepting the values of array */
  for (c = 0; c < 10; c++)
  {
       printf("\n Enter the number %d ", c + 1);
       scanf("% d", &n[c]);
  }
  /* Calling the function by passing address of 0th element*/
  /* of array and the no. of elements */
  max = findlarge(&n[0], 10);
  printf("\n The largest number is %d", max);
  getche();
}
/*Defining the function*/
int findlarge (int *x, int j)
{
  int large = 0; /*Initialise largest to 0 */
  int i;
  for (i = 0; i < j; i++)
  {
       if (*x > large)/ *Compare value of data element with large */
            large = *x;
       x++; /*Increment the pointer */
  }
  return(large); /*Return the largest no. to calling function */
}
```

Sample Input/Output

When the program is executed, you are asked to enter the 10 numbers as shown below (sample data is entered):

Enter the number 1 65
Enter the number 2 45
Enter the number 3 73
Enter the number 4 87
Enter the number 5 236
Enter the number 6 432
Enter the number 7 388

Enter the number 8 82
Enter the number 9 83
Enter the number 10 33
After entering the data, you get the following output:
The largest number is 432.

19.9.4 Sorting the Numbers

In the previous chapter, we have already written the program for sorting the numbers stored in 1-D array (see Program 18.15). Now we will modify that program to apply the application to functions and pointers in solving such problems. The complete program is shown below:

Program 19.17

```
/* Sorting the numbers by use of arrays, functions and pointers */
#include <stdio.h>
#define ASIZE 50 /*Directive that replaces*/
/*every occurrence of ASIZE with 50 in the program */
main()
{
  int i, c;
  int num[ASIZE];/* Declare array of size 50*/
  printf("\n How many numbers you want to sort?");
  scanf("%d",&c);
  printf("\n Enter %d numbers: \n", c);
  /*Accepting the numbers and storing them in array */
  for (i = 0; i < c; i++)
  {
        printf("Number %d", i + 1);
        scanf("%d", &num[i]);
  }
  /*Calling the function by passing entire array*/
  sortnum(&num[0], c);
  printf("\n The sorted numbers are :",c); /*Displaying sorted nos. */
  for (i  = 0; i < c; i++)
        printf("%d", num[i]);
  getche();
}
/* Defining the function */
void sortnum (int *n, int d)
{
  int i, j, t; /*i and j are counters while t is temp variable */
  /*Sorting the numbers*/
  for (i = 0; i < d - 1; i++) /*Begin of outer loop */
```

```
    {
            for (j = i + 1; j < d; j++) /*Begin of Inner loop*/
            {
                    /*Comparing two numbers*/
                    if (num[i] > num[j])
                    {
                            t = n [j];
                            n[j] = n[i];
                            n[i] = t;
                    }
            }
    }
}
```

Sample Input/Output

When the above program is executed, you are asked to enter the data as shown below (Sample data is entered):

How many numbers you want to sort? 7
Enter 7 numbers:
Number 1 65
Number 2 45
Number 3 8
Number 4 0
Number 5 77
Number 6 34
Number 7 89
The sorted numbers are 0 8 34 45 65 77 89

19.9.5 Sorting the Strings

We have also written the program for sorting the strings in the previous chapter (see Program 18.16). Now we will modify the program to includes pointers and functions. The complete program in which an array of pointers to strings is declared and a function is called by passing an entire array is shown below:

Program 19.18

```
/* Program to sort strings in ascending order */
/* The program declares an array of pointers to strings*/
/* and call a function by passing the entire array */
#include <stdio.h>
#include <stdlib.h> /* Included for malloc() function */
#include <string.h>
#define numname 50 /*Directive to store 50 names */
main()
{
   int i, c;
```

```
    char *name[numname];
    /*The above statement declares an*/
    /*array of pointers to 50 strings*/
    printf("\n How many names you want to sort?");
    scanf("% d", &c);
    printf("\n Enter %d names \n", c);
    /*Accepting the names */
    for (i = 0; i < c; i++)
    {
        name[i] = malloc(20*sizeof(char));
        /* The above statement allocates memory */
        /* to store a string of 20 characters */
        printf("Name %d", i + 1);
        scanf("%s", name[i]);
        /* Note that no & is written with array name */
        /* in scanf() function and only one subscript is */
        /* written. The reason is that an array is */
        /* a pointer to strings */
    }
    /* calling the function by passing the entire array*/
    /* and no. of strings */
    sortstr(&name[0], c);
    /*Displaying the sorted names */
    printf ("\n The sorted names are :", c);
    for (i = 0; i < c; i++)
        printf("\n %s", name[i]);
    getche();
 }
 /* Defining the function */
 int sortstr (char *n[], int d)
 {
    int i, j;
    char t[20]; /*declare a string to store temporary data */
    /*Sorting the array*/
    for (i = 0; i < d - 1; i++) /*Outer loop */
    {
        for (j = i + 1; j < d; j++) /* Inner loop */
        {
            /* comparing strings */
            if (strcmpi(n[i], n[j] > 0)
            {
                strcpy(t, n[j]);
                strcpy(n[j], n[i]);
                strcpy(n[i], t);
```

```
            }
        }
    }
    return; /* As the function should return some value */
}
```

Sample Input/Output

When the above program is executed, the computer ask you to enter data (sample data is entered) as shown below:

How many names you want to sort? 7

Enter 7 names:

Name 1 Gaurav

Name 2 Kamal

Name 3 Ritwig

Name 4 Mohit

Name 5 Sarika

Name 6 Preeti

Name 7 Sidhartha

After entering the data, the following output is generated:

Gaurav

Kamal

Mohit

Preeti

Rituig

Sarika

Sidharth

This discussion finishes the chapter on pointers. We believe that you will find the concept of pointers easier and interesting if you will apply the concept to solve the problems practically.

THEORY QUESTIONS

1. What are pointers in C? Explain with an example.
2. Discuss the procedure for—
   (*a*) Declaration of pointers
   (*b*) Initialisation of pointers
   (*c*) Manipulation of pointers
   Explain with examples.
3. Write a program to display the value and address of a numeric variable using pointers.
4. Explain the arithmetic operations that can be performed on pointers with examples.
5. Write a program to display the address and value of each data element of 1-D numeric array, *x*[10] using pointers.

6. Write a program to display the address and value of each data element of 2-D numeric array, *x*[3][3] using pointers.
7. How can you manipulate 1-D character arrays using poniters? Explain with a program.
8. How can you manipulate 2-D character arrays using pointers? Explain with a program.
9. Explain the difference between 'Calls by Value' and 'Calls by Reference' functions with suitable examples.
10. How can you pass an entire array to a function? Explain with a program.
11. Correct errors (if any) in the following programs and write down their outputs:

(*a*)
```
main()
{
        int x = -3, y = -1;
        func1(x, &y)
        printf("x = %d, y = %d", x, y);
}
func1(x, y)
{
        int x, y;
        x = x * x;
        y = *y ** y;
}
```

(*b*)
```
main()
{
        int a = 5, b = 2;
        void func1(int a, int b);
        void func2(int *x, int *y);
        printf ("a = %d, b = %d", a, b);
        func1(a, b);
        printf("a = %d", b = %d", a, b);
        func2(*a, *b);
        printf("a = %d, b = %d", a, b);
}
func1(int a , int b)
{
        a = a + b;
        b = a - b;
}
func2(int *x, int *y)
{
      *x = *x + y;
      *y = *x - y;
}
```

WORKSHOP

1. Write and run the program using various statements given in Section 19.3.3 in the chapter, and analyse the output of the program.
2. Enter the Program no. 19.5 (given in chapter) on your computer. Run it and analyse the output of various statements.
3. Write and run a program to calculate the area and perimeter of a rectangle by calling a function by reference.
4. Enter and run the Program no. 19.14 (given in chapter). Analyse its output with different data.
5. Enter and run the Program no. 19.15 (given in chapter). Analyse its output with different data.
6. Write and run a program to find the smallest number of an array of 10 elements.
7. Enter the Program no. 19.17 in your computer and execute it with different set of numbers.
8. Write and run a program to sort the names of countries using array of pointers to strings.

❑❑❑

20

STRUCTURES

20.1 INTRODUCTION

C allows you to define different types of variables, such as int, float, char, etc. in your programs. In chapter 18, we have discussed the arrays, the collections of similar variables. C also allows you to define the collections of dissimilar variables, called structures. Using structures, you can define variables which can be collections of different data types such as int, float, char, double, various derived types and arrays. Why do you need structures? How do you declare, initialise and manipulate structure variables? What are the applications where structures can be used? We will discuss everything about structures in this chapter.

20.2 NEED OF STRUCTURES

In order to understand the need of structures, consider the following problem:

A computer company wants to store the prices of two models of PCs into the computer memory along with their model numbers and names. You can write the program to solve this problem by defining the following 6 variables:

1. modelno1 with int type.
2. modelname1 with char type.
3. price1 with float type.
4. model no2 with int type.
5. modelname2 with char type.
6. price2 with float type.

Let us write the program using these variables to solve the problem.

Program 20.1

```
/*Program to manipulate data using simple unsubscripted variables*/
#include <stdio.h>
main()
{
   int modelno1, modelno2;
   char modelname1[20], modelname2[20];
   float price1, price2;
   /*Accepting data of product 1 */
   printf("\n Enter model no. of product 1");
   scanf("%d", &modelno1);
   printf("\n Enter model name of product 1");
```

```
    fflush(stdin);
    gets(modelname1);
    printf("\n Enter price of product 1 ");
    scanf("%f", &price1);
    /*Accepting data of product 2*/
    printf("\n Enter model no. of product 2 ");
    scanf("%d", &modelno2);
    printf("\n Enter model name of product 2 ");
    fflush(stdin);
    gets(modelname2);
    printf("\n Enter price of product 2");
    scanf("%f", &price2);
    /*Displaying data of product 1*/
    printf("\n%d\t%s\t%8.2f", modelno1, modelname1, price1);
    /*Displaying data of product 2*/
    printf("\n%d\t%\s\t%8.2f", modelno2, modelname2, price2);
    getche();
}
```

Sample Input/Output

When the above program is executed, the computer asks you to enter the following data (sample data is entered):

Enter model no. of product 101

Enter model name of product 1 Pentium III

Enter price of product 1 20000

Enter model no. of product 2 102

Enter model name of product 2 Pentium 4

Enter price of product 2 25000

On entering this data, the following output is generated:

101	*Pentium III*	*20000.00*
102	*Pentium 4*	*25000.00*

The execution of this program would be very much clear to you as the program uses only simple variables. Although this program solves your problem, this is not the recommended way of writing the program. Why? The reason is that—

- The program does not use a single variable for a group of similar variables. This problem can be solved by use of array variables instead of simple ones.
- The program does not use a single variable for a group of dissimilar variables. Suppose you have to store a lot of information about a product, such as model configurations, quantity in stock, etc. besides model no., name and price, you would need to create many independent variables. This will make your program too unstructured to be maintained. So, there should be a way to group dissimilar variables into a single group. The solution is creating a structure variable. Let us learn to declare, initialise and manipulate these structure variables, simply called structures.

20.3 OVERVIEW OF STRUCTURES

A structure is a data type consisting of one or more variables having similar or dissimilar data types. Although generally dissimilar data types such as int, float char, etc. are grouped together in a structure, you can combine similar data types such as only int, only char etc. or even create a single variable in a structure. The structure variables can be initialised and manipulated in many ways. Let us first learn to declare a structure variable.

20.3.1 Declaring Structures

A structure is declared in the following format:

```
struct <structure-name>
{
   member 1;
   member 2;

   member n;
};
```

where struct is the key word,

<structure-name> is the name of structure,

member 1, member 2....member *n* are names of the variables along with their data types.

For example, you can declare a structure for the problem discussed in the beginning of the chapter as follows:

```
struct product
{
   int modelno;
   char modelname[20];
   float price;
}
```

After declaring the composition of the structure, you can declare the individual structure-type variables in the following format:

```
<storage class> struct <structure-name> var1, var2,.......,varn;
```

where <storage-class> is optional and specifies the type of storage *i.e.*, auto, static, etc.

<structure-name> is the name of structure.

var1, var2,....etc. are names of variables of type structure.

For example, as in the discussed problem, you want to store data of two products, you can declare two structure-type variables as shown below:

```
struct product p1, p2;
```

So, the complete structure declaration or definition for the discussed problem is as follows :

```
struct product
{
   int modelno;
   char modelname[20];
   float price;
}
struct product p1, p2;
```

This structure scan also be written in the following two ways:

```
1. struct product
   {
         int modelno;
         char modelname[20];
         float price;
   }p1, p2;
2. struct
   {
         int modelno;
         char modelname[20];
         float price;
   }p1, p2;
```

Note that in the second declaration, we have not written the structure name. If variable declarations are combined with the structure declaration, actually there is no need to write the structure name because structure is referred with the structure-type variable names and not with the structure name within the program.

As you can initialise simple and subscripted variables. Similarly you can initialise the structure variables. Let us discuss, how?

20.3.2 Initialisation of Structures

The structure, product declared above can be initialised in any of the following three ways:

```
1. struct product
   {
         int modelno;
         char modelname[20];
         float price;
   };
   struct product p1 = {101, "Pentium III", 20000};
   struct product p2 = {102, "Pentium 4", 25000};
2. struct product
   {
         int modelno;
         char modelname[20];
         float price;
```

```
    }p1 = {101, "Pentium III", 20000}, p2 = {102, "Pentium 4", 25,000};
3. struct
    {
          int modelno;
          char modelname[20];
          float price;
    }p1 = {101, "Pentium-III", 20,000},
     p2 = {102, "Pentium 4", 25,000};
```

In the above declaration and initialisation statements, the first data (101) written within brackets { } is stored in the first member (modelno) the second data ("Pentium III") is stored in the second member (modelname) and the third data(20000) in the third member of structure variable, p1. If you will not initialise any member of the variable, that will remain zero or blank depending on the type of variable.

Besides initialisation, you can also store the data in structure-type variables by accepting it from the user thorough standard input functions and display the data through standard output functions. Let us discuss the ways to manipulate structures.

20.3.3 Manipulation of Structures

Let us write a program to solve the problem discussed in the beginning of the chapter by use of structures in order to understand the way of manipulating structures. Before writing the program, it is important to discuss a new operator used to access structure variables. This new operator is called the *dot (.) operator*. Using this dot operator, the member modelno of structure variable, p1 can be accessed as follows:

```
p1.modelno
```

You can use this expression in scanf( ) and printf( ) functions as illustrated below:

```
scanf("%d", &p1 modelno);
printf("%d", p1.modelno);
```

The dot operator can also be used with string input/output functions as illustrated below:

```
gets(p1.modelname)
puts(p1.modelname);
```

Now, you can easily modify the program (Program 20.1) discussed in the beginning of the chapter by replacing structure variables in place of simple unsubscripted variables. The complete modified program is shown below:

Program 20.2

```
/*Program to manipulate data using structures*/
#include <stdio.h>
main()
{
    /*Declaration of structure*/
    struct product
    {
```

```
        int modelno.
        char modelname[20];
        float price;
    };
    struct product p1, p2; /*Two structure variables declared*/
    /*Accepting data of product 1*/
    printf("\n Enter model no. of product 1:");
    scanf("%d",&p1.modelno);
    printf("\n Enter mode name of product 1:");
    fflush(stdin); /*Erases memory buffer of standard input*/
    /*The above statement is necessary before*/
    /*gets() function, otherwise*/
    /*the problem may occur during run-time*/
    gets(p1.modelname);
    printf("\n Enter price of product 1:");
    scanf("%f", &p1.price);
    /*Accepting data of product 2 */
    printf("\n Enter model no. of product 2:");
    scanf("%d", &p2.modelno);
    printf("\n Enter modelname of product 2:");
    fflush(stdin);
    gets(p2.modelname);
    printf ("\n Enter price of product 2:");
    scanf("%f", &p2.price);
    /*Displaying data of product 1*/
    printf("\n%d\t%s\t%8.2f", p1.modelno., p1.modelname, p1.price);
    /*Displaying data of product 2*/
    printf("\n %d\t%s\t%8.2f", p2.modelno. p2.modelname p2.price);
    getche( );
}
```

Sample Input/Output

When the above program will be executed, you will get the same Input/Output messages as discussed in the previous program (Program 20.1).

So, in this way you can store data of many variables in a single structure type variable. However, this program can store data of only 2 products as you have declared only two structure type variables. If you need to store data of many products (say 10), you could not solve the problem easily using this type of structure declaration. For that, you need an array of structures. What is an array of structures? Let us discuss.

20.4 ARRAY OF STRUCTURES

Consider the same problem as discussed in previous two programs. Suppose the company wants to store data of its 10 products. Without using a structure, you can solve this problem by use of arrays. How? Let us first write the program and then analyse it.

Program 20.3

```
/*Program to manipulate data of 10 proudcts using arrays*/
#include <stdio.h>
main()
{
  /*Declaration of 3 1-D arrays*/
  int modelno[10];/*An array for storing model numbers*/
  char modelname[10][20]; /*An array for storing model names*/
  float price[10]; /*An array for storing prices*/
  int i;
  /*Accepting data of 10 products*/
  for (i = 0; i < 10; i++)
  {
         printf("\n Enter model no. of product %d: ", i + 1);
         scanf("%d", &modelno[i]);
         printf("\n Enter model name of product %d: ", i + 1);
         fflush(stdin);
         gets(modelname[i]);
         printf("\n Enter price of product %d: ", i + 1);
         scanf("%f", &price[i]);
  }
  /*Displaying data of 10 products */
  printf("\n Model No. Model Name\t Price");
  for (i = 0; i < 10; i++)
  printf("\n%d\t%s\t%8.2f",modelno[i], modelname[i], price[i]);
  getche();
}
```

Sample Input/Output

When the above program is executed, computer asks you to enter data of 10 products as shown below (sample data is entered):

Enter model no. of product 1 : 101
Enter model name of product 1 : Pentium III
Enter price of product 1 : 20000
Enter model no. of product 2 : 102
Enter model name of product 2 : Pentium 4
Enter price of product 2 : 25000
Enter model no. of product 3 : 103
Enter model name of product 3 : Laser Printer
Enter price of product 3 : 15000
Enter model no. of product 4 : 104
Enter model name of product 4 : Deskjet Printer
Enter price of product 4 : 5000
Enter model no. of product 5 : 105

Enter model name of product 5 : Hard disk
Enter price of product 5 : 3500
Enter model no. of procut 6 : 106
Enter model name of product 6 : Keyboard
Enter price of product 6 : 428.50
Enter model no. of product 7 : 107
Enter model name of product 7 : Mouse
Enter price of product 7 : 235.50
Enter model no. of product 8 : 108
Enter model name of product 8 : Floppy Drive
Enter price of product 8 : 245.50
Enter model no. of product 9 : 109
Enter model name of product 9 : Speakers
Enter price of product 9 : 350
Enter model no. of product 10 : 110
Enter model name of product 10 : CD Drive
Enter price of product 10 : 2350.50

After entering the data, the output will be displayed as follows:

Model No.	Model Name	Price
101	*Pentium III*	*20000.00*
102	*Pentium 4*	*25000.00*
103	*Laser printer*	*15000.00*
104	*Deskjet Printer*	*5000.00*
105	*Hard disk*	*3500.00*
106	*Keyboard*	*428.50*
107	*Mouse*	*235.50*
108	*Floppy Drive*	*245.50*
109	*Speaker*	*350.00*
110	*CD Drive*	*2350.00*

So, you get the desired output. As we have already discussed arrays in chapter 18, the statements of this program would be very much clear to you. Although the program solves your problem, it is not the right way to utilise the features of C. The problem with this program is that you have declared three arrays modelno[10], modelname[10] and price [10], which store data of 10 products. The better way is that you can declare an array of structures instead of 3 arrays of simple variables. If you will create an array of structures, you will not be needed to declare 10 different structure type variables. How do we declare an array of structures? It is very simple, let us understand it by solving the above discussed problem with an array of structures.

Program 20.4

```
/*Program to manipulate data of 10 products using array of structures*/
#include <stdio.h>
```

```
#include <stdlib.h>
main()
{
  /*Declaration of array of structures*/
  struct product
  {
        int modelno;
        char modelname[20];
        float price;
  };
  struct product p[10];/*Declare 10 subscripted variables of strucure type*/
  int i;
  for (i = 0; i < 2; i++)
  {
        printf("\n Enter model no. of product %d:", i + 1);
        scanf("%d", &p[i], modelno);
        printf("\n Enter model name of product %d:", i + 1);
        fflush(stdin);
        gets(p[i] modelname);
        prinf("\n Enter price of product %d:", i + 1);
        scanf("%f", &p[i].price);
  }
  /*Displaying data of 10 products*/
  printf("\n Model No. Model.Name\tPrice");
  for (i = 0; i < 2; i++)
  printf("\n%d\t%s\t%8.2f", p[i].modelno, p[i].modelname, p[i].price);
  getche();
}
```

Sample Input/Output

When the program will be executed, you will get the same input/output messages as shown in previous program (Program 20.3).

This is the better way to write program of such problems. You may have noticed that a subscripted structure type variable in an array of structures is declared similar to unscripted structure type variable in a structure. Let us compare both. A structure type variable, p1 for storing data of product 1 is declared as follows:

```
struct product p1;
```

On the other hand, a subscripted structure type variable, p[i] for storing data of 10 products (where *i* varies from 0 to 9) is declared as follows:

```
struct product p[i];
```

Similarly, the expressions to access data from unsubscripted and subscripted structure type variables are also similar as illustrated below:

`p1.modelno` for a simple structure type variable

`p[i].modelno` for a subscripted structure type variable

Having understood an array of structures, let us discuss some more features of structures which are used in development of real-life software.

20.5 NESTED STRUCTURES

As loops can be nested, structures can also be nested. It means that you can declare a structure within another structure. Nested stuctures are needed when data is organised in two groups. For example, a company can maintain data regarding products in one group (file) and data regarding invoices in another group. Consider the following two groups of data:

Group I data
- Product data
  - Model no.
  - Model name
  - Price

Group II data
- Invoice data
  - Invoice no.
  - Product details
  - Quantity
  - Amount

The amout is calculated by multiplying price (from product data) with quantity (from invoice data).

You can store these two groups of data in nested structures, which are declared as follows:

```
struct product
{
  int modelno;
  char modelname[20];
  float price;
};
struct invoice
{
  int invno;
  struct product p1;
  int qty;
  float amt;
};
struct invoice i1;
```

In the above declaration, the structure, invoice also describes the data of structure, product whose one structure type variable p1 is declared within the declaration of structure, invoice.

The members of struture, product are accessed by putting two dot operators with structure type variable names as illustrated below:

The expression, `i1.p1.modelno` accesses the model no.

The expression `i1.p1.modelname` accesses the model name

The expression `i1.p1.price` accesses the price.

However, the members of structure, invoice are accessed by putting single dot operator with structure type variable names as illustrated below:

The expression, `i1.inv.no` accesses the invoice no.

The expression, `i1.qty` accesses the qty.

The expression, `i1.amt` accesses the amt.

The amount can be calculated by the following statement:

```
i1.amt  =  i1.p1.price  *  i1.qty;
```

The standard input output functions such as scanf(), gets(), printf(), and puts() are used as usual with members of nested structures.

Now, let us write the complete program to manipulate data of nested structures.

Program 20.5

```
/*Program to manipulate data of nested structures*/
# include <stdio.h>
main()
{
   /*Declaration of inner structure*/
   /*Noticed that inner structure is declared first */
   struct product
   {
         int modelno
         char modelname[20];
         float price;
   };
   /*Declaration of outer structure*/
   struct invoice
   {
         int invno;
         struct product p1;
         int qty;
         float amt;
   };
   Struct invoice i1;
   /*Accepting the data of one invoice*/
   printf("\n Enter Invoice no.");
   scanf("%d", &i1.invno);
   printf("\n Enter model no. of product 1:");
   scanf("%d", &i1.p1.modelno);
   printf("\n Enter model name of product 1:");
   fflush(stdin);
   gets(i1.p1.modelname);
```

```
    printf("\n Enter price of product 1.:");
    scanf("%f", &i1.p1.price);
    printf("\n Enter quantity of product 1:");
    scanf("%d", &i1.qty);
    /*calculation of amount */
    i1.amt = i1.p1.price * i1.qty;
    /*Displaying the data of Invoice 1 */
    printf("\n Inv No.\t Modelno.\t Name\t Price\t Quantity\t Amount");
    printf("\n %d\t %d\t %s\t\ %8.2f\t%d\t %8.2f");
    i1.invno,i1.p1.modelno,i1.p1.modelname,i1.p1.price,i1.qty,i1.amount);
    getche():
}
```

Sample Input/Output

When the above program is executed, the following input prompts are displayed (sample data is entered):

Enter Invoice no. 1

Enter model no. of product 1 : 101

Enter model name of product 1 : Pentium III

Enter price of product 1 : 20000

Enter quantity of product 1 : 5

After entering the data, the output is displayed as shown below:

Inv. No.	*Model No.*	*Name*	*Price*	*Quantity*	*Amount*
1	*101*	*Pentium III*	*20000.00*	*5*	*100000.00*

As we have already discussed various statements used in the above program, you would not have any problem in understanding the execution of this program.

20.6 COPYING OF STRUCTURE VARIABLES

Using the assignment operator, you can copy the contents of one structure variable to another. There are two ways to copy the contents of structure variables—one, copying all the members with single statement, and two, copying each members separately. Let us discuss these two ways.

20.6.1 Copying All Members

Suppose you want to initialise a structure variable *a2* with data of another structure variable, *a1* of the same structure. This can be done, simply by the following statement.

a2 = *a1*;

where *a1* and *a2* are structure type variables of the same structure.

Let us write a program to verify this statement.

Program 20.6

```
/*Copying all members of a structure with single statement*/
#include <stdio.h>
main()
{
   /*Declaring a structure*/
   struct address
   {
         char colony[30];
         char city[20];
         char country[20];
   };
   struct address a1 = {"Tilak Nagar," "New Delhi", "India"};
   struct address a2;
   /*copying all the members of variable a2 to a1*/
   a2 = a1;
   /*Displaying contents of variable, a1*/
   printf("\n The first address is:");
   printf("\n %s, %s, %s", a1.colony, a1.city, a1.country);
   /*Displaying contents of variable, 92*/
   printf("\n The second address is:");
   printf("\n %s, %s, %s", a2.colony, a2.city, a2.country);
   getche()
}
```

Sample Input/Output

After running the program, the following output is generated:

The first address is:

Tilak Nagar, New Delhi, India

The second address is:

Tilak Nagar, New Delhi, India

Copying of all the members of structure variables at one go is possible as the data of structure variables is arranged in contingous memory locations just like arrays.

20.6.2 Copying Selective Members

Sometimes, you need to copy only the selective members of one structure variable to another. For instance, suppose the name and maximum marks of two student variables declared in a structure are same but their marks obtained are different. In that case, you do not need to copy all the members, so you have to copy them individually. To solve this problem, consider the following structure declaration:

```
struct
{
      char name[30];
      int mo;
```

```
        int mm;
}       s1 = {"Amit", 300, 400}, s2;
```

The name of student, stored in variable s1 can be copied to s2 as follows:

```
strcpy(s2.name,  s1.name)
```

where strcpy( ) is a function for string copy which we have discussed in chapter - 18 (see Section 18.7.2.7).

Similarly, the maximum marks of student, s1 can be copied to s2 by the following statement:

```
s2.mm  =  s1.mm
```

Let us now write the complete program to verify these statements.

Program 20.7

```
/*Program to copy selective members of a structure variable*/
#include <stdio.h>
#include <string.h>
main()
{
  /*Declaration & initialisation of structure*/
  struct
  {
        char name[30];
        int mo;
        int mm;
  }     s1 = {"Amit", 300, 400}, s2;
  /* Copying selective members of structure*/
  strcpy(s2.name, s1.name);
  s2.mo = 350;
  s2.mm = s1.mm;
  /*Displaying contents of variable, s1*/
  printf("\n The result of first student is:");
  printf("\n Name %s marks obtd %d out of %d", s1.name, s1.mo, s1.mm);
  printf("\n The result of second student is:");
  printf("\n Name: %s marks obtd %d out of %d", s2.name, s2.mo, s2.mm);
  getche();
}
```

Sample Input/Output

When the above program is executed, the following output is generated.

The result of first student is:

Name: Amit Marks obtd. 300 out of 400

The result of second student is:

Name: Amit Marks obtd. 350 out of 400

In this way, the contents of selective members of a structure variable are copied to another structure variables. Let us now conclude this chapter on the discussion on passing structures to functions.

20.7 PASSING STRUCTURES TO FUNCTIONS

You can pass a structure to a function in the following 3 ways:

(*a*) Passing selective structure members to a function

(*b*) Passing all structure members to a function *i.e.*, the whole stucture to a function.

(*c*) Passing address of structure variable to a function.

Let us first discuss the first two ways of passing structures to functions both of which pass the values and not addresses.

20.7.1 Passing Values of a Structure to a Function

The values of a structure variable can be passed to a function. Consider the following structure declaration:

```
struct
{
   int modelno;
   char modelname[20];
   float price;
} p1, p2;
```

The values of structure variables, p1 and p2 can be passed to two functions, dispdata1() and dispdata2 (), respectively in the following two different ways:

(*a*) By passing the individual members as illustrated below:

dispdata1(p1.model no, p1.modelname, p1.price);

(*b*) By passing the entire variable as illustrated below:

dispdata2(p2);

Let us modify the program discussed ealier in the chapter (see Program 20.2) by displaying data using functions to illustrate the above discussed ways of passing a structure to a function. The complete program is written below.

Program 20.8

```
/*Program to demonstrate the passing of structure values to a function*/
#include <stdio.h>
/*Declaration of function Prototypes */
void dispdata1(int, char*, float);
void dispdata2(struct product p);
struct product
{
   int modelno;
   char modelname[20];
   float price;
};
/*Note that 'Structure is declared outside*/
/*main() function, so that it becomes available*/
/*to all function.  The scope of structure variable should be global*/
main()
{
```

```
    /*Declaring structure variables*/
    struct product p1, p2;
    /*Accepting data of product 1*/
    printf("\n Enter model no. of product 1 :");
    scanf("%d", &p1.modelno);
    printf("\n Enter model name of product 1:");
    fflush(stdin);
    gets(p1.modelname);
    printf("\nEnter price of product 1:");
    scanf("%f", &p1.price);
    /*Accepting data of product 2*/
    printf("\n Enter model no. of product 2:");
    scanf("%d", &p2.modelno);
    printf("\n Enter model name of product 2:");
    fflush(stdin);
    gets(p2.modelname);
    printf("\n Enter price of product 2:");
    scanf("%f", &p2.price);
    /*calling function by passing individual members*/
    dispdata1(p1.modelno, p1.modelname, p1.price);
    /*calling function by passing entire structure variable*/
    dispdata2(p2);
    getche();
}
/*Definition of first function*/
void dispdata1(int mno, char *mname, float pr).
{
    printf("\n Model no. Model name\t Price");
    printf ("\n %d\t%s\t%8.2 f", mno, mname, pr);
}
/* Definition of second function*/
void dispdata2(struct product p)
{
    printf ("\n %d\t%s\t%8.2f", p.modelno, p.modelname, p.price);
}
```

Sample Input/Output

When the above program will be executed, you will get the same input/output messages as shown in first two programs of this chapter (see Input/Output of Programs 20.1 & 20.2)

As all the concepts regarding the statements written have already been discussed in this chapter and chapter 17 on functions, we are not explaining you the meaning of various statements written in this program. The reader is advised to revise the chapter 17 on functions to understand this program in a better way.

20.7.2 Passing Address of a Structure to a Function

Inspite of passing the values of a structure variable, you can pass its address to a function, which is called 'Call by Reference' as discussed during passing of addresses of actual parameters of the calling function to the called function in the previous chapter (see Section 19.7.1). To understand this method, let us declare a structure, employee, initialise it and pass its address to a function, dispdata() as illustrated in the following program:

Program 20.9

```
/*Program to demonstrate the passing of address*/
/*of a structure variable to a function*/
#include <stdio.h>
void dispdata(struct employee *e) /* Prototype declaration*
/*Declaration of structure */
struct employee
{
    int empno;
    char empname[20];
    int salary;
};
main()
{
   /*Declaration & initialisation of a structure variable*/
   struct employee e1 = {1201, "Dr. Surendra", 20000};
   dispdata(&e1); /*calling the function by passing address of variable*/
   getche();
}
/*Definition of function*/
void dispdata(struct employee *e)
{
   printf ("\n Employee no. %d", e -> empno);
   printf ("\n Employee name %s", e -> empname);
   printf ("\n Employee salary %d", e -> salary);
}
```

Sample Input/Output

When the above program is executed, the following output is generated:

Employee no. 1201
Employee name Dr. Surendra
Employee Salary 20000

As clear from the above program, you can pass the address of a structure variable, e1 to a function, dispdata( ) by the following statement:

```
dispdata(&e1);
```

In the definition of function, the formal parameter is written as type structure to pointer as shown below:

```
void dispdata (struct employee *e)
```

The expressions to access the members of structure within this function use -> operator instead of dot (.) operator as illustrated below:

e -> empno;
e -> empname;
e -> salary;

With this concept our discussion on Structures is over. You will find C very interesting if you will use combinations of arrays, functions, pointers and structures in solving real life problems.

20.8 TYPICAL APPLICATIONS OF STRUCTURES

Now, we are giving below few programs on typical applications of structures. As we have discussed each and every concept in detail, we will not explain you the statements of these programs.

20.8.1 Calculating Salary of an Employee

You can create structure variables for storing the salary detail of employees in an organisation. Infact, you will need to create an array of structures to store and process the data of many employees. Consider the details of an employee include employee no., employee name, basic salary, H.R.A. (House Rent Allowance), D.A. (Dearness allowance) and PF (Provident Fund). The net salary is calculated as follows:

Net salary = Basic + HRA + DA – PF

Let us write the program.

Program 20.10

```
/*Program to calculate net salary of 5 employees*/
/*Using an array of structures*/
#include <stdio.h>
main()
{
   /*Declaration of array of structures*/
   struct employee
   {
     int empno;
     char empname[20];
     int basic;
     int hra;
     int da;
     int pf;
     int net;
   };
   struct employee e[5];
   /*Accepting the data*/
   int i;
   for (i = 0; i < 5; i++)
```

```
    {
        printf("\n Enter data of employee %d:"; i + 1);
        printf("\n Emp. no. :");
        scanf("%d", &e[i]; empno);
        printf("\n Emp name:");
        fflush(stdin);
        gets(e[i]empname);
        printf("\n Basic :");
        scanf("%d", &e[i].basic);
        printf("\n HRA :");
        scanf("%d", &e[i].hra);
        printf("\n DA:");
        scanf("%d", &e[i].da);
        printf("\n PF :");
        scanf("%d", &e[i].pf);
        /*calculating net salary*/
        e[i].net = e[i].basic + e[i].hra + e[i].da - e[i].pf;
    }
    /*Displaying the data */
    printf("\n Emp. No.\t Name\t Basic\t HRA\t DA\tLess PF\t Net Salary");
    for (i = 0; i < 5; i++)
    {
        printf("\n%d", e[i].empno);
        printf("\t%s", e[i].empname);
        printf("\t%d", e[i].basic);
        printf("\t%d", e [i].hra);
        printf("\t%d", e[i].da);
        printf("\t%d", e[i].pf);
        printf("\t%d", e[i].net);
    }
    getche( );
}
```

Sample Input/Output

When the above program is executed, you are asked to enter data of 5 employees as shown below (sample data is entered):

Enter data of employee 1:
Emp no. : 2001
Emp name : Dr. Surendra
Basic : 20000
HRA : 500
DA : 1000
PF : 600
Enter data of employee 2 :

Emp no. : 2002
Emp name : Dr. Khetarpal
Basic : 50000
HRA : 5000
DA : 600
PF : 1000
Enter data of Employee 3 :
Emp. no. : 2003
Emp. name : Dr. Sonali
Basic : 25000
HRA : 5000
DA : 3000
PF : 4000
Enter data of Employee 4
Emp. No. 2004
Emp. name : Dr. Mehta
Basic : 35000
HRA : 5000
DA : 1000
PF : 500
Enter data of employee 5
Emp. No. : 2005
Emp Name : Dr. S. Kaur
Basic : 20,000
HRA : 2000
DA : 500
PF : 1000

After entering this data, you get the following output:

Emp. No.	Name	Basic	HRA	DA	Less Pf	Net Salary
2001	*Dr. Surendra*	*20000*	*500*	*1000*	*600*	*20900*
2002	*Dr. Khetarpal*	*30000*	*2000*	*1000*	*1000*	*32000*
2003	*Dr. Sonali*	*25000*	*5000*	*3000*	*4000*	*29000*
2004	*Dr. Mehta*	*28000*	*2000*	*1000*	*1000*	*30000*
2005	*Dr. S. Kaur*	*20000*	*2000*	*500*	*1000*	*21500*

20.8.2 Sorting Marks with Names of Students

In chapter 18 on Arrays, we have written a program to sort numbers in ascending order (see Problem 18.15). Suppose you want to organise marks of 5 students in descending order along with their names. How will you do? You can declare an array of structures to store names of students along with their marks. This data can be sorted easily as per the logic discussed in chapter 18 in Program 18.15. Let us write the program to accept the names and marks obtained of 5 students and sort the marks based on the same logic. The complete program is given below:

Program 20.11

```
/*Program to sort marks using array of structures*/
#include <stdio.h>
main ( )
{
   int i, j, t;
   char n[20]; /*temp variable to store name */
   /*Declaration of array of structures*/
   struct result
   {
         int marks;
         char name[20];
   };
   struct result r[5];
   /*Accepting data of students*/
   printf ("\n Enter names and marks of 5 students");
   for (i = 0; i < 5; i++)
   {
         printf("Student No. %d:", i + 1);
         printf("\n Name :");
         fflush(stdin);
         gets(r[i].name);
         printf("\n Marks:");
         scanf("%d", &r[i].marks);
   }
   /*Sorting marks in descending order*/
   for (i = 0, i < 4; i++)
   {
         for (j = i + 1; j < 5; j++)
         {
               /*comparing marks*/
               if (r[i].marks < r[j].marks)
               {
               /*Interchanging marks in array*/
               t = r[j].marks;
               r[j].marks = r[i].marks;
               r[i].marks = t;
               /*Interchanging names in array*/
               strcpy(n, r[j].name);
               strcpy(r[j].name, r[i].name);
               strcpy(r[i].name, n);
               }
         }
   }
```

```
/*Displaying sorted marks with names*/
printf("\n The marks in descending order are:");
printf("\n Marks/t Name");
for (i = 0; i < 5; i++)
  printf ("\n %d\t%s", r[i].marks, r[i].name);
getche();
}
```

Sample Input/Output

When the above program is executed, the following messages come on the screen (sample data is entered):

Enter marks of 5 students
Student No. 1
Name : Gaurav
Marks : 300
Student No. 2
Name : Komal
Marks : 400
Student No. 3
Name : Shalu
Marks : 350
Student No. 4
Name : Ravinder
Marks : 320
Student No. 5
Name : Anupam
Marks : 290

On entering this data, you will get the following output:

Marks	*Name*
400	*Komal*
350	*Shalu*
320	*Ravinder*
300	*Gaurav*
290	*Anupam*

Hence, the marks are sorted and the corresponding names are also arranged accordingly.

THEORY QUESTIONS

1. What are structures? Why are they needed? Explain with example.
2. Discuss the procedures to declare, initialise and manipulate a structure with suitable examples.
3. What is an array of structures? Write a progam to declare and manipulate an array of structures.
4. What are nested structures? Why are they needed? Explain with an example.

5. How can you copy the values of members of a structure variable to another? Explain different ways by writing a program.
6. How can you pass a structure to a function. Explain various ways with programs.
7. Write a program to enter to employee records with following details:

```
Employee Code char[4]
Employee Name char[20]
Salary       int
```

After entering the data, display it in following format:

Employee Details

S. No.	Code of Employee	Name of Employee	Salary
1			
2			
3			

8. Write a program to enter item nos. and prices of 10 items. Arrange the items in ascending order of their prices using array of structures.

WORKSHOP

1. Enter the Program no. 20.2 (discussed in chapter) on your computer. Execute it and analyse the output.
2. Enter the Program no. 20.3 (discussed in chapter) on your computer. Execute it and analyse the output.
3. Enter and execute the Program no. 20.9 on your computer. Analyse its output.
4. Write and enter a program to store and display the roll no., name and age of students of your class using an array of structures. Execute the program and analyse its output.

GLOSSARY

Abacus. A rudimentary first computing device which was developed in 3000 BC. It consists of a row of wires held in a wooden frame having beads stung on them. It is used for calculations by sliding the heads along the wires.

Absolute Address. An explicit identification of a memory location.

Abstract Class. A class created as a master structure. It is also known as an abstract superclass in object terminology.

Abstraction. In object oriented programming, the act of representing essential features of the objects without giveing details.

Access. (i) To retrieve data from an external storage device (such as hard disk or floppy disk). (ii) To log to a computer system or network.

Access Rights. The privileges that are granted to a user to read, write and delete files on the computer system.

Accumulator. A register that acts as a temporary store in the Arithmetic and Logic Unit (ALU) for storing the result of an arithmetic or logic operation.

ActiveX. A collection of technologies used to enable different software components to interact. This allows the functionality of web pages to be increased by including animations in them. It was developed by Microsoft.

ActiveX Documents. The extensions to Microsoft's OLE (Object Linking and Embedding) document architecture that allows a container application to use the full capabilities of server applications.

Ada. A high level programming language designed for process control, embedded and logistics applications.

Adder. A logic circuit that adds two numbers. It can also subtract two numbers using 2's complement arithmetic.

Address. (*i*) An exact location in memory or external storage device where a unit of data (byte) is stored. (*ii*) To refer or manage a storage location.

Address Bus. A bus that is used to carry the signals specifying memory locations for data. It consists of 20 to 64 separate hardware lines.

Advanced RISC. Acronym for Advanced Reduced Instruction Set Computing. A specification designed by MIPS Computer Systems for a RISC microchip architecture and system environment to provide binary compatibility among software applications.

Aldus. The software company that pioneered desktop publishing with its PageMaker software. Aldus was acquired by Adobe.

ALGOL. Acronym for ALGOrithmic Language. The first structured procedural programming language that was developed as an international language for the expression of algorithms between people and machines.

Algorithm. A set of instructions or mathematical formula given to computer to perform a specific task.

Alias. A short name for a person or group using E-mail. It is simpler and easier to remember than the full name.

Alternate Key. Any candidate key in a database which is not designated as the primary key.

alt. Newsgroups. Internet newsgroups that are part of the alternative hierarchy.

America Online. An online informative service, based in Vienna that provides Internet access, E-mail, News, Educational and Entertainment services .

AmiPro. A full-fledged, multi-featured Windows-based word processor with DTP features, developed by Lotus Development Corporation.

Analog. Any device that represents changing values by a continuously variable physical quantity (such as current, voltage or frequency).

Analog Computer. A special purpose computer that represent and store data in continuously varying physical quantities such as current, voltage or frequency.

Analytical Engine. A digital computer, built by Charles Babbage, an English mathematician in the year 1834.

AND Gate. A logic gate whose output is 'true' only when all inputs are 'true', otherwise the output is 'false'.

Animation. The creation of moving pictures on a PC using multimedia software.

Anonymous. The standard login name used to obtain access to a public FTP file archive on the internet.

ANSI. Acronym for American National Standards Institute. A nonprofit organization of business and industry groups, founded in 1918, devoted to the development of voluntary standards (such as recommendations for the programming languages) in the United States.

ANSI C. A version of the C programming language standardized by the ANSI C Programming Language Committee. Also called as Standard C.

Anti-virus Program. An application program that detects and removes a virus.

API. Acronym for Application Program Interface. Language and message format used by an application program to perform tasks such as managing files and displaying information on the computer screen.

APL. Acronym for A Programming Language. A high-level, interactive, scientific programming language famous for its brevity and matrix-manipulation capabilities.

Apple (Apple Computer, Inc.). One of the first and the largest independent manufacturer of non-IBM-compatible PCs.

Apple Macintosh. A popular series of personal computers, introduced by the Apple Computer Corporation in January 1984, which incorporate a graphical user interface.

Applet. A small program generally written in Java, which can be downloaded onto a user's computer through Internet.

Application. A computer program designed to perform a specific task, such as accounting, payroll, inventory, scientific analysis, word processing, or desktop publishing.

Application Generator. A software development tool for generating source or machine code according to the specifications given the developer.

Application Package. A application software that is created for a specific purpose or a particular industry.

Application Programmer. A computer professional who develops application programs in a user organisation.

ARCHIE. A collection of servers that maintain a database of information on various information resources on the Internet for search purpose.

Archive. A backup storage device consisting of magnetic tape or disk containing files copied from another storage device.

Archive Site. A site on the Internet that stores files which are usually downloaded through anonymous FTP, retrieved through Gopher or viewed on the World Wide Web.

ARCnet. Acronym for Attached Resource Computer Network. A form of token bus network architecture for PC-based LANs. It was developed by Datapoint Corporation.

Arithmetic and Logic Unit (ALU). A part of the central processing unit of a computer in which arithmetic and logic operations are performed.

Arithmetic Operator. An operator that performs the arithmetic operations such as addition, subtraction, multiplication and division. An arithmetic operator usually takes one or two arguments.

ARPANET. The first Internet, developed by ARPA (Advance Research Projects Agency) of the Department of Defense, United States in 1969. ARPANET effectively linked together scientific and academic researchers in the USA.

Array. A collection of similar data items that are arranged in a particular order in computer memory.

Array Processor. A group of interconnected, identical processors operating simultaneously, generally under the control of a central processor.

ASCII. Acronym for American Standard Code for Information Interchange. A standard 7-bit code adapted by microcomputer manufacturers for representations of 128 characters to facilitate the transfer of data between different computer components. An extended version of ASCII is an 8-bit code that represents 256 characters.

Assembler. A program that translates an assembly language code into machine language code.

Assembly Language. A low level programming language that has instructions written using abbreviations and codes called Mnemonics.

Asynchronous Data Transmission. In asynchronous mode of data transmission only one character (byte) is transmitted at a time. There is no perceptible method for the receiving device to sample the incoming signal precisely to recover the transmitted data.

Asynchronous Protocol. A communication protocol that controls an asynchronous transmission.

AT. Acronym for Advanced Technology. IBM's first 286-based PC, introduced in 1984.

ATM. (*i*) Acronym for Asynchronous Transfer Mode. A network technology capable of transmitting data, audio and video in real time. (*ii*) Acronym for Automatic Teller Machine. A banking terminal that accepts deposits and gives cash to the PIN holder.

Attributes. (*i*) The columns of a relational database table. (*ii*) The characteristic of an entity.

ATX. A specification, introduced by Intel in 1995 for PC motherboard architecture with built-in audio and video capabilities.

Audio CD. A music Compact Disc (CD) format that has replaced the phonograph record.

AutoCAD. Full-featured computer aided design program from AutoDesk Inc. that runs on IBM/Mac PCs, VAXs and UNIX workstations.

Authoring Program. A program that is used to develop multimedia presentations.

Authorware. A popular multimedia authoring program used for creating interactive learning programs on Windows and Macintosh.

AUTOEXEC. BAT. A batch file (set of commands) that is automatically executed by the DOS operating system when the computer is started.

Auxiliary storage. The device used to keep programs and data in computer's internal memory.

Backbone. A network of computer networks that may be linked to other network of computer networks.

Back End. In client/server database applications, the database that runs on the server.

Backup. A file, device or system used as a substitute in the event of a loss of data.

Bandwidth. Amount of data that can be fit through a network connection. In broadcasting, bandwidth is the measure of the spectrum between the highest frequency and the lowest. Unit of bandwidth is hertz (Hz.). For analog circuits the bandwidth is generally expressed in Hertz (Hz.) and is calculated by subtracting the lowest possible frequency from the highest possible frequency. For digital circuits, bandwidth is generally expressed in bits per seconds (bps). In simple terms, bandwidth describes the capacity of the physical network to carry data traffic.

Baseband. The sum of frequencies representing the total information to be transmitted.

BASIC. Short for Beginner's All-purpose Symbolic Instruction Code. A high-level programming language developed by John Kemeny and Thomas Kurtz at Dartmouth College in the mid-1960s.

Batch Processing. A method of data processing in which data is processed in batches.

Batch Program. A program that executes without interacting with the user.

BAT file (BATch file). A file of DOS commands, in which the commands are executed one after the other automatically without intervention of the user.

Baud Rate. The speed at which a modem can transmit data.

BBS. Acronym for Bulletin Board System. A computer system equipped with one or more modems through a network access that serves as an information centre for remote users.

BCD. Acronym for Binary Coded Decimal. A coding scheme for data representations that converts each digit of a decimal number into its 6 bits binary equivalent.

Benchmark Test. A standard test or point of reference used to measure a computer's performance against its competitors.

Binary Logic. A computer logic that deals with binary variables and logical operations.

BIOS. Acronym for Basic Input-Output System. A set of low level instructions stored in Read Only Memory (ROM), which provides basic control over the peripheral devices of the computer.

BIT. Acronym for BInary digiT. The basic unit of information in the binary numbering system, representing either 0 (for off) or 1 (for on).

Bitmap. A format for storing simple graphic files in computer.

biz. Newsgroups. Usenet newsgroups that are part of the biz. hierarchy, devoted to discussions related to business.

BMP file. Acronym forBit MaP file. A Windows and OS/2 bitmapped graphics file format.

Bomb. A program residing on a computer unknown to the user, which can destroy the system.

Book Keeping. Maintaining account books in a prescribed manner.

Boolean Algebra. An algbebra, developed in 1847 by the English mathematician George Boole which deals with binary numbers.

Boolean Expression. An expression that yields a Boolean value (true or false).

Boolean Operator. An operator designed to work with Boolean values. The most commonly used Boolean operators are AND (logical conjunction), OR (logical inclusion), XOR (exclusive or) and NOT (logical negation).

Boot. The process of starting or resetting a computer. At the time of booting, the operating system is loaded into the computer's memory.

Boot Disk. A floppy disk containing all the necessary files for an operating system to start on a computer.

Bootstrap. A bootstrap is a short program whose function is to load another longer program into a computer.

Boot Virus. A virus written into the boot sectors of a floppy disk.

BPS. Acronym for Bits Per Second. The transmission speed on networks and communication is measured in BPS.

Bridge. A device that connects two networks into one large logical network so that information can flow between them.

Bridge Router. A device that supports the functions of both a bridge and router.

Broadband. Term associated with the microwave or cable systems which have a very high bandwidth and carry a large number of voice channels generally above 300.

Brouter. Internetworking device which functions as a bridge as well as a router.

Browser. A software which helps in getting information from text, graphics, sound and even video through Internet. For example, World Wide Web is a popular browser.

Bug. An error in coding or logic that causes a program to produce incorrect results.

Bulk Storage. A storage medium which stores large amounts of data. It has relatively slow access time.

Bus. An electronic pathway either between hardware devices in a computer or workstations in a network along which data signals are sent.

Bus Bridge. A device that connects two similar or dissimilar buses together.

Bus Network. A topology for LAN (Local Area Network) in which all nodes are connected to a main communication line.

BYTE. Short for BinarY digiT Eight. A group of 8 bits that holds the equivalent of a single character such as a number, letter or other symbol.

C. A general purpose high level programming language, developed by Dennis Ritchie at AT&T's Bell Labs in the early 1970s.

C++. An object-oriented version of C language, developed by Bjarne Stroustrup of Bell Labs.

Cache. Pronounced as "cash". A relatively small section of the very fast memory (often static RAM) on the disk controller board used for storing the contents of frequently accessed memory locations and their addresses.

Cache Card. An expansion card that increases a system's cache memory.

CAD. Short for Computer Aided Design. The use of a computer for design work in fields such as engineering or architecture, with the computer's graphics capabilities substituting for work that traditionally would have been done with pencil and paper.

CAE. Acronym for Computer Aided Engineering. An application that enables the user to analyse engineering test and designs created with a computer.

CAI. Acronym for Computer Aided (or Computer Assisted) Instruction. A computer-based educational program designed to serve as a teaching tool.

Call. A statement that transfers program execution to some section code to perform a specific task in a program.

Card. A printed circuit board or adapter that can be plugged into a computer to provide added functionality.

Cartridge. A removable device containing a magnetic tape, magnetic disk, printer ink ribbon, etc.

Cascading Windows. A sequence of successive, overlapping windows in a graphical user interface.

CBT. Acronym for Computer Based Training. A computer based teaching methodology.

CC. Acronym for Courtesy Copy. A directive to an e-mail program to send a complete copy of a given piece of mail to another computer user.

CD. Short for Compact Disc. A non-magnetic, polished, optical disk used to store large amounts of digital information.

CD ROM. Short for Compact Disc Read Only Memory. A high-capacity, optical storage device that uses compact disc technology to store large amounts of information (more than 600 MB) on a single 4.72 inch disc.

Celeron. Intel's family of budget-priced microprocessors.

Cellular Phone. A sophisticated electronic instrument which is a piece of digital engineering and uses cellular technology to enable its users to communicate while on move.

Censorware. Software that imposes restrictions on what Internet sites, newsgroups or files may be accessed by the user.

Central Processing Unit (CPU). The main part of a computer that carries all the instructions given by a program.

CGA. Acronym for Color/Graphics Adapter. One of the early graphics adapters capable of several character and graphic modes.

Chain Printer. A type of printer that uses type slugs linked together in a chain as its printing mechanism.

Character Printer. A type of printer that produces a single character at a time, printing them in the order in which they appear in a line.

Chat. Real-time conversation via Internet. When a participant types a line of text and then presses the Enter key, participant's words appear on the screens of the other participants, who can then respond in kind. Most online services support chat on the Internet.

Chip. A set of microminiaturized electronic circuits used in computers.

CHKDSK. A DOS utility program that checks the disk space, number of files, lost clusters, etc. on the disk.

CIO. Acronym for Chief Information Officer. The executive officer in charge of all information processing in an organization.

Client. (*i*) A device or an application program that makes use of the services provided by a server. (*ii*) An object that uses the resources of another in object-oriented programming.

Client Application. An application that runs in a workstation or personal computer on a network.

Client/Server. A computing architecture in which the client is the requesting computer (PC or workstation) and the server is the supplying computer (LAN file server, mini/mainframe computer) on the network.

Client/Server Networking. In Client/Server networking, the server is centralised and has the large database, large internal memory, user interface and application software.

Clip art. Simple artwork in digital form designed for use in publications or Web pages.

Clipper. Originally a dBASE compiler from Nantucket Corp., but later became a complete stand-alone development environment for DOS-based applications.

Clock. An electronic device that provides a series of pulses at extremely regular intervals of time.

Clock Speed. The internal speed of a computer or processor normally expressed in Megahertz.

Cluster. An area on a disk that stores data on a hard disk or a floppy disk.

CMOS. Acronym for Complementary Metal Oxide Semiconductor. The battery-backed memory used to store parameter values needed to boot PCs.

CMOS Setup. A system configuration utility loaded at boot time, for setting up certain system options such as date, time, etc.

COBOL. Acronym for Common Business Oriented Language. A high level compiler based programming language which became very popular for development of commercial applications on PCs and mini/mainframe computers.

Code Division Multiple Access (CDMA). A communication access where a large number of communicating persons overlap the same frequency band in the same frequency and time.

COM file (COMmand file). An executable DOS program that takes up less than 64K and fits within one segment.

Command. An instruction given to a computer program that, when issued by the user, causes an action to be carried out.

COMMAND.COM. The command interpreter for MS-DOS.

Communication Program. A software program that exchanges information between two computers on a network.

Communication Protocol. A set of standards designed to enable computers to communicate and exchange data with one another.

Communication System. A system that is used for sending messages, documents and data within and outside the organisation.

Comp. Newsgroups. Usenet newsgroups that are part of the comp. hierachy, devoted to discussions of computer hardware, software, etc.

Compiler. A program that translates a high-level programming language code into a machine language program code.

Compressed file. A file whose contents have been compressed by a special utility program so that it occupies less space on a disk or other storage device as compared to an uncompressed or normal file.

Computer. An electronic machine that processes data according to a set of instructions that are stored internally.

Computer System. A complete computer installation including the CPU, the peripherals and the operating system which are designed to work and interact with each-other and with the user.

Conceptual DDL. A type of data description language using which the database administrator defines the overall logical schema.

Conceptual Schema. The overall logical model of the database.

CONFIG.SYS. A special text file that contains various system parameters loaded during booting of a computer.

Conventional Memory. The amount of RAM required by computer to operate in real mode.

CORBA. Acronym for Common Object Request Broker Architecture. A specification with the help of which pieces of program (objects) communicate with other objects in other program even if the two programs are written in different programming language and are running on different platforms.

Cordless Phone. Low power, long range phones that enable communication while the user can move around in a fixed area.

Cost Accounting System. The system that provides reports to managers for cost planning and cost control of operations.

CPS. Acronym for Characters Per Second. The measurement of the speed of a dot-matrix printer.

CPU Cycle. The smallest unit of time recognized by the CPU (central processing unit) typically a few hundred millionths of a second.

Cray-1. An early supercomputer developed in 1976 by Seymour Cray.

Crop. To cut off part of an image in computer graphics such as unneeded sections of a graphic or extra white space around the borders.

Cursor. (*i*) A blinking character on the display screen to indicate the position of the next character to be typed. (*ii*) A pen or puck like device used with a graphics tablet.

Cybercafe. A shop that offers access to PCs or other terminals that are connected to the Internet, usually for per-hour basis.

Cyberspace. The universe of environments, such as the Internet, in which persons interact by means of connected computers.

Cyberworld. The world of computers and communications.

Cylinder. The group of all tracks that reside in the same location on every disk surface.

Data. (*i*) Raw facts and figures which are processed by the computer to produce information. (*ii*) Any form of information either on a paper or an electronic medium.

Database. A collection of interrelated data, which can be used by one or more applications so that it can be integrated and stored in a shared and organised way. It has controlled redundancy, consistency and integrity with a provision of data independence.

Database Administrator (DBA). The person who is responsible for the overall control of the database management system.

Database Management System (DBMS). Application software that organises and manages the data in a database.

Data Bus. An internal pathway across which data is transferred to and from the processor or to and from the memory.

Data Communication. The transfer of digital information from one computer to another over a communication link.

Data Compression. Any method of encoding data so that it takes less storage space than its original form.

Data Definition. The way of defining and storing data.

Data Description Language (DDL). Languages that describe the database objects as perceived by the user or programmer. Also called Data Definition Languages.

Data File. A file consisting of data in the form of text, numbers or graphics.

Datagram Service. In this approach all packets carry full address of its destination and sequence identity. Each packet takes routes independently without a pre-established route and re-assemble and resequence at the receiving device.

Data Independence. A feature of database that makes the programming independent of data storage.

Data Integrity. The accuracy of data and its conformity to its expected value, especially after being transmitted or processed.

Data Manipulation Language (DML). A type of language responsible for manipulating or processing of data objects defined by a DDL.

Data Processing (DP). A term used to describe work done by mini and mainframe computers (not PCs) in a data center or business environment. Also called as Electronic Data Processing (EDP).

Data Structure. Data representation at the external level.

Data Type. The set of values that the variable is allowed to take and the operations that can be performed on it eg. integers, real numbers, strings,etc.

Data Warehouse. A database that is very large in size and can access all the company's information.

DB2. Acronym for DATABASE 2. A relation DBMS from IBM that was originally developed for its mainframes.

dBASE. A very popular industry-standard database management system developed by Ashton-Tate Corporation.

Debug. To find and remove errors in a computer program.

Decision Tree. A binary tree in which every non termianl node represents a decision.

Demodulation. In communications, the means by which a modem converts data from analog signals to digital signals.

Desktop. (*i*) On-screen representation of a desktop in a graphical user interface (such as Macintosh and Windows). (*ii*) A term attached to any application performed on a PC.

DeskTop Publishing (DTP). The use of a personal computer to produce high-quality documents for commercial printing and publication.

Device. Any computer peripheral or hardware component that can send or receive data.

Developer/2000. A client/server application development system for Windows and Macintosh from Oracle.

Diagnostics. Software routines that test hardware components (memory, keyboard, disks, etc.) for finding their faults. In personal computers, they are often stored in ROM and activated on startup.

Dial-up access. Connection to a data communication network through a switched telecommunication network.

Dial-up networking. Connection to a remote network through use of a modem.

Difference Engine. A mechanical computing device designed by Charles Babbage in 1823 to produce mathematical tables.

Digitizer. An input device that converts graphical information into digital data by tracing the image with a puck. Also known as a digitizing tablet.

Digital Audio Tape (DAT). A magnetic audio-tape storage medium for recording digitally coded audio information.

Digital Camera. A type of camera that stores photographed images electronically.

Digital Computer. A computer that represent and store data in discrete quantities or numbers.

Digitalisation. Process of transformation of analogue signals into digital signals.

Digital Signal. A signal that is made up of on and off pulses of electricity. The digit 1 stands for the ON state whereas the digit 0 is used to represent the OFF state.

Digital Subscriber line. A digital technology which permits high bandwidth transmission over twisted pair copper wiring.

Direct Access. The ability of a computer to find and go straight to a particular storage location in memory or on disk to retrieve or store an item of information.

Direct Access Storage Device (DASD). A storage device such as a hard disk, whose data can be accessed directly, without having to read all the preceding data.

Director. A popular multimedia authoring program for Windows and Macintosh from Macromedia.

Directory. A catalog for filenames and other directories stored on a disk.

Disk Cache. A part of Random Access Memory (RAM) set aside for temporarily holding information read from the disk.

Disk Controller Card. A peripheral circuit card that manages and controls the operation of disk drives in a computer.

Disk Drive. A peripheral storage device that reads and writes on the magnetic or optical disks.

Diskpack. A form of disk storage used in a specially designed disk drive from which it can be removed and replaced by another pack of the same type.

Distributed Database. The database where the data is not stored at a single physical location but is distributed on many geographically dispersed computers, connected with a network or communication link.

Documentation. Narrative and graphical description of a system in form of instruction manuals, tutorials and reference guides.

Document Management System. A system that includes computerised tools for generation, storage, processing and distribution of documents.

Domain. In relational database, the pool of values from which the actual values appearing in a given column are drawn.

Domain Name System (DNS). Mechanism of documenting and distributing information about the name and address of the computer attached to the Internet.

DOS. Acronym for Disk Operating System. A very popular disk operating system for PCs, originally developed by Microsoft. Also called as MS DOS.

Dot Matrix Printer (DMP). A type of printer that produces characters made up of dots using a wire-pin print head.

Download. In communications (such as Internet), the transfer of a file or files from one computer to another over a network (using a modem).

Drag. To move an image or a window from one place on the screen to another by "grabbing" it and pulling it to its new location using the mouse.

DRAM. Acronym for Dynamic RAM. A common type of computer memory, having high storage capacity which has to be refreshed after every few milliseconds.

Drum Plotter. A plotter in which paper is wrapped around a large revolving drum, with a pen that moves back and forth at the uppermost point on the drum.

DSS Database Management System. Enables decision maker to create, maintain and query Decision Support System (DSS) database by the processes of retrieval, data reconfiguration (sorting, exchanging columns and joining data, graphical presentations) selection and projection tasks.

DSS Generator. The software used to develop Decision Support Systems (DSS) and coordinate its processing tasks.

DSS Model Management System. Enables the creation, maintenance and application of quantitative and statistical prototypes or models to manipulate the Decision Support System (DSS) data as per the needs of the decision maker.

Dumb Terminal. A terminal with combination of keyboard and screen that has no processing capability. It is used to input information to a large, remote computer such as mini/mainframe computer.

Dump. A copy of some or all of the contents of a storage device at a particular instance in order to safeguard against loss of data, to check for errors in a program or for some other purpose.

DVD. Acronym for Digital Video Disk. A family of optical discs that have the same overall dimensions of a CD but have significantly higher capacities.

Dynamic Storage. Information storage systems whose contents are lost when the power goes off.

EBCDIC. Acronym for Extended Binary Coded Decimal Interchange Code. An 8-bit code used to represent 256 different characters.

E-Bomb. Short for E-mail bomb. A technique used by some hackers in which a target is put on a large number of mailing lists so that the network traffic and storage are tied up.

E-Commerce. Acronym for Electronic Commerce. Selling products and services online on the Internet.

Economic Order Quantity (EOQ). The optimum quantity of ordering materials that minimizes the procurement cost, inventory carrying cost and stock-out cost.

EDI. Acronym for electronic data interchange. A set of standards for controlling the transfer of business documents, such as purchase order and invoices, between computers.

Editor. A program that creates files or makes changes to existing files.

EDRAM. Acronym for Enhanced DRAM. A high-speed DRAM chip.

EEPROM. Acronym for Electrically Erasable Programmable Read Only Memory. Pronounced as "e-e-prom". A memory chip whose contents can be erased by using a high voltage and can be re-programmed either within the computer or from an external source.

EGA. Acronym for Enhanced Graphics Adapter. A video adapter standard that provides medium-resolution text and graphics.

EISA. Acronym for Extended Industry Standard Architecture. Pronounced as "ee-sah". A PC bus standard that extends the AT-bus (ISA bus) to 32 bits and allows more than one processor to share the bus.

Electronic Mail. The service which allows the user to use his computer for sending message to another computer without requiring the receiving person to be logged onto the destination computer at the time of it being sent. Popularly called as 'E-mail'.

Embedded SQL. SQL statements written into a high-level programming language such as C or Pascal.

Encrypt. To encode information in such a way that it is unreadable to only those individuals who possess the key to the code.

Encryption. The process of encoding data to prevent unauthorized access, especially during transmission.

End user. The person for whom a hardware or software product is designed as opposed to the developer.

ENIAC. Acronym for Electronic Numerical Integrator and Calculator. It was the first electronic computer using vacuum tubes.

Entity. An object, person or an event about which data is stored.

Environment. (*i*) The complete set of hardware and software resources including the CPU, operating system, system utilities, programming languages and the user interface available to the user of a system (*ii*) The operating system needed to execute a program.

EPABX. Acronym for Electronic Private Automatic Branch Exchange. An electronic system of telephone network, where individual subscriber's telephones are connected.

EPROM. Acronym for Erasable Programmable Read Only Memory. Pronounced as "e-prom." A memory chip whose contents can be erased by ultra-violet light and can be re-programmed.

Ethernet. A type of local area network (LAN) using a bus or star topology.

Executable Program. A program that can be run on the computer without the need of source and object programs.

Expert System. In artificial intelligence, a problem-solving and decision-making system that uses knowledge base of human expertise.

External DDL. A type of data description language using which the application programmers describe their sub-schemas.

External Modem. A self-contained modem that is connected via cable to the serial port of a computer.

External Schema. The user-oriented way of viewing the data. Also called User View.

Extranet. A private network that uses Internet protocols and the public telephone system to share business information and operations with customers, suppliers and so on.

Facsimile telegraphy. The most widely used office automation system for transmitting images of documents and photographs/ graphics from one location to another through a telephone line. Popularly known as Fax.

FAT. Acronym for (File Allocation Table. The part of the DOS, Windows and OS/2 file system that keeps track of where data is stored on disk.

Fax (Facsimile). The electronic transmission of copies of documents through telephone lines for reproduction at a remote location. Conventional fax machines scan an original document, transmit an image of the document as a bit map and reproduce the received image on a printer.

Fax Modem. An adapter that fits into a PC expansion slot and provides many of the capabilities of a fax machine.

FDISK. A DOS and Windows utility that is used to partition a hard disk, which is necessary before high-level formatting.

Feasibility Study. A study carried out before development of a computer system in order to establish that the proposed system is possible and can serve a useful purpose.

Field. A physical unit of data that collectively makes up a record in a data file. It is the lowest level of the database.

File. (*i*) A named collection of data stored on disk, appearing to the user as a single unit. (*ii*) A group of related records in a database. Synonym to 'Table' in a relational database.

File Allocation Table (FAT). A table maintained by the operating system to manage disk space used for file storage.

File Manager. A module of an operating system that controls the physical placement and access to a group of program files.

File Server. A high-speed computer in a network that stores data and program files which are accessed by client computers on the network.

File Transfer Protocol (FTP). A utility to transfer files to and from the remote servers and the user's machine.

Financial Accounting. Preparation of financial statements based on the account books.

Fingerprint Recognition. A technology used to control access to a computer, network or other device or to a secure area through a user's fingerprints.

Firewall. A method for keeping a network secure.

Fixed Disk. A non-removable hard disk found in personal computers.

Flatbed Scanner. A type of scanner in which the page to be scanned is stationary behind a glass window while the head moves past the page, similar to a photocopier.

Flip-flop. An electronic circuit that has two stable states, either of which can be maintained until the circuit is made to switch or 'flip' to the other state.

Floppy Disk. A round, removable external storage device, enclosed in a square protective jacket.

FLOPS. Acronym for Floating-point Operations Per Second. The number of arithmetic operations that can be performed on floating-point numbers in a period of one second, expressed in megaflops.

Folder. A location on the storage media that contains files and can also contain nested folders. Folders are equivalent to directories and subdirectories in DOS.

Font. A set of characters of the same typeface and style.

Formatting. The process of initializing a disk so that it can be used to store information.

FORTRAN. Acronym for FORmula TRANslator. The first compiler-based high-level programming language, mainly used for development of scientific applications.

Fourth Generation Computer. Computers currently in use and designed in the period from about 1970.

Fourth Generation Language (4GL). A user friendly programming language, more advanced than high level languages.

FoxPRO. A dBase IV-compatible DBMS from Microsoft, widely used for development of DOS/Windows based applications.

Freeware. A software distributed to others free of cost, but the author retains copyright of the software.

Frequency. Number of cycles that an electromagnetic wave makes in a second.

Frequency Division Multiple Access (FDMA). In FDMA , the frequency spectrum is divided into number of frequency slices. Each frequency slice is used as a communication channel.

Front End. In a client/server application, the part of the program that runs on the client.

Front End Processor. A specialized processor that manipulates data received from the communications channel before passing it on to the main processor.

Full Duplex Data Transmission. In a full duplex system of data transmission, data flows in both directions simultaneously.

Fuzzy Logic. A type of logic that deals with ideas of possibility and probability. Fuzzy logic could have a range of values such 'true', 'very true', not very true', etc.

Gateway. A device used to interconnect two dissimilar LANs. The Gateway operates on network layer and above.

General Purpose Language. A programming language, designed for a variety of applications and uses. For example, Ada, Basic, C or Pascal are general purpose languages.

General Purpose Register. A register within a microprocessor that is available for any use rather than being reserved for a specific use by the processor design or operating system.

GIF. Acronym for Graphics Interchange Format. A graphics file format used for transmitting faster image files on the Internet.

GigaByte (GB). A higher unit of memory, equivalent to approximately one billion bytes and exactly 2^{30} or 1,073,741,824 bytes.

GigaHertz (GHz). One billion cycles per second.

GOPHER. A menu driven system which enables the user to navigate within the Internet information resources.

Gopherspace. The total set of information on the Internet that is accessible as menus and documents through Gopher.

Grabber Hand. A screen tool that is shaped like a hand and is used to move objects within a window.

Graphical User Interface (GUI). A popular, graphics-based user interface that allows users to select files, programs, menu options or commands by pointing to pictorial representations (icons) on the screen.

Groupware. Network software designed for use by a group of people all working either on the same project or the related projects sharing same data.

Hacker. A person who fidles with systems software, usually without authorization.

Half Duplex Data Transmission. In a half duplex system of data transmission data flows in the forward and backward directions to the receiving and the sending devices but not simultaneously.

Hard Disk. The primary computer storage medium, made of one or more aluminum or glass platters, coated with a ferromagnetic material.

Hardware. Any physical component of a computer system.

Hashing. A procedure to determine the address of a record by transforming the record key value into an arithmetic formula.

Hertz (Hz). A unit of frequency.

Hexadecimal (Hex.). The base-16 numbering system that uses the digits 0 to 9, followed by the letters A to F as equivalents to the decimal numbers from 0 through 15.

Hierarchical Database. A database in which records are grouped in such a way that their relationships form a branching, treelike structure.

Hierarchical Structure. A type of data structure where the records are organised into different levels of hierarchy.

High Level Language (HLL). A machine-independent programming language that uses English-like syntax in which each statement is translated into several lines of machine language instructions.

Home Page. The Web page that appears each time the user start a Web browser.

HTML. Acronym for Hypertext Markup Language. The markup language used for documents on the World Wide Web.

Hub. A centralised distribution point for all traffic on a network just like a warehouse distribution centre.

Hybrid Computers. Computers that incorporate the technology of both analog and digital computers.

Hypermedia. The combination of text, video, graphic images, sound, hyperlinks and other elements in the form of Web documents.

Hypertext. Text linked together in a complex web of associations in which the user can browse through related topics.

IBM-compatible Computer. Any personal computer compatible with the original IBM PC.

Image Processing System. A system used to electronically capture, store, process and retrieve images of documents.

Impact Printer. A printer that drives an inked ribbon mechanically against the paper to form marks such as dot-matrix, daisy wheel, etc.

Indexed Sequential File Organisation. A file organisation where the records are stored sequentially along with an index.

Information. Data which has some meaning or value.

Information System. A business application of the computer made up of the database, application programs, manual and machine procedures among which the computer systems perform the processing.

Ink Jet Printer. A type of printer in which fine drops of quick-drying ink are projected on to the paper to form the character.

Input Device. Any device that transfers data, programs or signals into a computer system.

Input/Output (I/O). The transfer of data between the computer and its peripheral devices such as disk drives, keyboard, monitor and printer.

Institute of Electrical and Electronic Engineers (IEEE). A membership organization, founded in 1963, including engineers, students and scientists.

Instruction. A statement given to computer to perform a task.

Integrated Circuit. The formal name for the chip. More than one transistor are fabricated on a single piece of semiconductor material.

Integrated Software. An application software that combines the functions of several different application programs such as a spreadsheet, database, word processor, etc. into a single package.

Intelligent Network. A terminal with its own memory, processor and firmware that can perform certain function independent of its host computer.

Intelligent Terminal. A terminal connected to a large computer with built-in processing capability which can perform certain operations independently from the remote computer, but does not usually have any external storage device.

Interface. An interaction between two hardware devices, a user and a program or operating system, or between two application programs.

Internal DDL. A type of data description language using which the database administrator defines the internal schema, which represents the physical storage of data.

Internal Modem. An internal modem is an expansion card inserted into an expansion slot on a computer's motherboard.

Internal Schema. The actual storage design of database.

Internet. The world's largest computer network, consisting of millions of computers, connected through telephone lines and supporting billions of users all over the world.

internet (abbreviation for internetwork). A set of computer networks, made up of a large number of smaller networks, using different networking protocols.

Internet Account. A generic term for a registered username at an Internet Service Provide (ISP).

Internet Explorer. A web browsing software from Microsoft.

Internet Protocol (IP). Connection-less protocol for Internet communication.

Internet Relay Chat (IRC). A service on the Internet which allows the users to communicate real-time.

Internet Service Provider. An organization that provides access to the Internet.

Internetware. A network operating system and intranet server from Novell.

Internet working. The process of connecting individual LANs to create WANs and connecting WANs to form even larger WANs.

Interpreter. A programming-language translator that converts high-level program source code into machine language object code one line at a time.

Interrupt. A signal sent to a processor to suspend its current task.

Intranet. A network of computers within the closed perimeters of the office.

Inventory. Concerned with the stock of raw materials and finished goods available in the firm.

IO.SYS. One of two hidden system files installed on an MS-DOS startup disk.

ISDN. Acronym for Integrated Services Digital Network. A worldwide digital communications network for transmitting audio, video and data over a digital communications line.

ISO/OSI reference model. Short for International Standards Organization/Open Systems Interconnection reference model. A layered architecture (plan) that standardizes levels of service and types of interaction for computers exchanging information through a communication network.

J. A high-level mathematical programming language which can run on a variety of platforms such as DOS, Windows, OS/2, etc.

Java. A programming language for Internet and intranet applications from Sun.

JCL. Acronym for Job Control Language. A special kind of programming language by means of which a user can communicate with the operating system of a computer.

Job. A specified amount of processing performed as a unit by a computer.

Joystick. A popular multi-directional pointing input device, used exclusively for playing computer games and using CAD applications.

Kernel. The central module of an operating system that is loaded first and remains in memory. It is responsible for memory, process and task management.

Keyboard. A manually operated input device for converting letters, digits and other characters into coded form. It is the most commonly used means to communicate with a computer.

Kilobyte (KB). A basic unit of memory, equivalent to 1024 bytes.

KiloHertz (KHz). One thousand cycles per second

Knowledge Base. Stores information about the particular domain in an expert system.

LAN Server. A network operating system from IBM that runs as a server application under OS/2 and supports DOS, Windows and OS/2 clients.

LAN Station. A workstation in a local area network.

Laptop Computer. A small portable PC with a flat screen and keyboard that can be folded together.

LaserDisc. An optical disk used for full-motion video.

LaserJet. A family of desktop laser printers from HP.

Laser Printer. A high-resolution non-impact printer that uses a laser beam to write the images on a paper.

Leased Line. A private communications channel leased from a common carrier.

LED Display. A device used in some calculators, digital clocks, etc. to display numbers and letters.

Library Function. A subroutine that is part of a function library.

Light Pen. A light-sensitive input device shaped like a pen, used to draw and make menu selections on the screen.

Linux. A version of the UNIX System V Release 3.0 kernel developed for PCs with 80386 and higher-level microprocessors.

LISP (LISt Processing). A high level programming language used for the development of artificial intelligence applications.

Liveware. People who use computers.

Load. To place information from storage into memory for processing.

Loader. A utility program that loads a program into main store ready for execution.

Local Area Network (LAN). A communication network made up of servers, workstations, network operating system and communication channels within a confined geographical area with capability of sharing files and other resources between several users.

Local News Groups. Newsgroups that are devoted to a geographically limited area such as a city or educational institution.

Logic Gate. A n electronic device used to control the flow of signals in a computer.

Logical Operator. An operator that manipulates binary values at the bit level.

Logo. A programming language used for teaching young children.

Low Level Format. The sector identification on a disk that the drive uses to locate sectors for reading and writing.

Low Level Language. A machine-dependent programming language.

Lycos. A search tool that is used to discover information related to any subject on the World Wide Web and the rest of the Internet.

Machine Code. The code used to represent the instructions in the instruction set of a particular computer.

Machine Instruction. An instruction in machine code that can be directly executed by a processor or microprocessor.

Machine Language. The native binary language consisting of zeros and ones, used internally by the computer.

Macintosh (Mac.). A popular range of personal computers introduced in 1984 by Apple Computer Inc. featuring a very popular graphical user interface.

Macromedia. A software company specializing in multimedia authoring tools.

Macro Virus. Virus that works by using the macro language of an application to hide virus code. When a document is opened with an infected macro, the virus is loaded into memory.

Magnetic Disk. A computer disk enclosed in a protective case (hard disk) or jacket (floppy disk) and coated with a magnetic material that enables data to be stored in the form of changes in magnetic polarity (with one polarity representing a binary 1 and the other a 0) on many small sections (magnetic domains) of the disk surface.

Magnetic Tape. A sequential storage medium used for data collection, backup and historical purposes.

Mailbox. A network user's area for storing incoming E-mail messages.

Mail Client. An E-mail program that resides in the user's computer and has access to mail servers on the network.

Mailing List. A system that allows users to send E-mail to one address and all of the other subscribers to the list.

Mainframe Computer. A very large and fast multi-user computer system, used in a centralised location where many terminals are connected to one CPU.

Management Accounting System. The system that provides reports to managers for strategic and tactical decisions.

Management Information System. A computer-based system for providing information to various levels of management needed for management activities and decision making.

Math Coprocessor. A type of processor that performs high-speed floating point operations.

Megabyte (MB). A higher unit of memory, equivalent to approximately one million bytes and exactly 2^{20} or 1,048,576 bytes.

MegaHertz (MHz). A unit of processor's clock speed, refers to one million cycles per second.

Memory. RAM (Random Access Memory) chips installed in the computer.

Memory Address Register (MAR). A register used for holding the address of the next location in main store to be executed.

Memory Allocation. Reserving memory for specific purposes during execution of a program.

Memory-resident. The programs that permanently reside in memory.

Metropolitan Area Network (MAN). A public high-speed computer network, that serves customers in the same city or region with capability of voice and data transmission over a distance of up to 50 miles.

Microcomputer. Any computer based on a single-chip micro-processor. Popularly called as Personal Computer.

Microprocessor. A CPU on one single chip. Also called Processor.

Microsoft (Microsoft Corporation, USA). The leading personal computer software company, founded in 1975 by Bill Gates and Paul Allen.

MIPS (Million of Instructions Per Second). A unit of the processing speed of a computer's CPU.

Mnemonic. Pronounced as "nem-onic". A name or code used to represent complex instructions of low level languages (such as assembly language).

MODEM (MOdulator/DEModulator). A device that allows a computer to transmit information over a telephone line.

Monitor. A high-resolution video output device capable of displaying text and graphics.

Motherboard. The main printed circuit board in a computer that contains the central processing unit, co-processor, memory chips, I/O interface, expansion slots and other logic circuits.

Mouse. A small pointing input device with one or more buttons, mainly used to move cursor, draw sketches/diagrams, etc. It is also used for selecting a text/object/menu-option etc. in a graphical user interface such as Windows.

Multimedia. A latest computer technology that displays information using a combination of full-motion video, animation, sound, graphics and text with a high degree of user interaction.

Multiprocessing. The ability of an operating system to use more than one CPU in a single computer.

Multitasking. The simultaneous execution of two or more programs in one computer.

Multi-user. A computer system or operating environment that supports more than one simultaneous users.

Nanosecond (ns). The unit of the speed of computer memory and logic chips, equivalent to one-billionth of second.

Natural language. A language spoken or written by humans.

Natural Language processing. The study of computer system that can react to and understand both spoken and written natural language.

Navigate. To move from one page to another on the Web.

Netiquette. Short for network etiquette. Proper manners when conferencing between two or more users on an online service or the Internet.

Netizen. A person who participates in online communication through the Internet and other networks.

Netscape Communicator. A site of Web browsing and groupware tools from Netscape.

Netscape Navigator. A Web Browser produced by Netscape Communication Corporation.

NetWare. A popular multi-user, multitasking network operating system from Novell, Inc., that runs on all PC/ATs.

Network. A group of computers and associated peripherals, connected by a communication channel and capable of sharing files/resources between several users.

Network Operating System. An operating system that includes the capability for connecting computers and devices to a local area network (LAN).

Network Security. The authorization of access to files and directories in a network.

Network Structure. A type of data structure where a given entity can have any number of superiors and subordinates.

Newsgroup. A discussion group on the Internet devoted on one topic.

Node. A point in a computer network where communication lines are interconnected.

Normalisation. A process of decomposition of more complex data structures into relations.

Norton Utilities. Widely-used utility programs for DOS, Windows and Macintosh from Symantec which are used to search, edit and undelete files, restore damaged files, etc.

Notebook Computer. A small portable PC, about the size of a book, with a flat screen and a keyboard that can be folded together.

Notepad. A special area of memory used when moving data or graphics from one place or file to another.

Object. (i) Any distinct, separate entity such as block of text/graphics etc. that can appear on the desktop. (ii) A self-contained module of data and functions in an object-oriented program.

Object Oriented Programming (OOP). A latest approach of programming that views a problem as a collection of objects that model the real world things.

Object Oriented Databases. Databases that store objects as a whole and not as separate entities.

Office Automation. The use of computers, networks and telecommunication technologies to integerate the traditional office information functions including word processing, filing, electronic mail, voice mail, fax, and desktop publishing.

OLAP. Acronym for OnLine Analytical Processing. Decision support software that allows the user to quickly analyze information that has been summarized into multidimensional views and hierarchies.

OLE. Acronym for Object Linking and Embedding. Pronounced as "oh-lay." A Windows compound document protocol for application-to-application communications.

OLTP. Acronym for Online Transaction Processing. A system for processing transactions and updating master files on line in a database management system.

Operating System (OS). The most essential system software, responsible for allocating system resources, including memory, processor time, disk space and peripheral devices.

Optical Disk. A thin, circular disk which can store/retrieve information using laser light.

Optical Scanner. An input device that uses light-sensing equipment to scan paper and translating the pattern into a digital signal that can be manipulated by either optical character recognition software or graphics software.

Oracle. The most popular RDBMS (Relational Database Management System) for microcomputers.

OR Gate. One of the three basic logic gates from which all digital systems can be built. The output of an OR circuit is 'true' if any input is 'true'.

OS/2. Short for Operating System/2. IBM's multitasking graphical user interface operating system designed to work with 32-bit microprocessors

OSI Model. Acronym Open System Interconnection Seven Layers Model. Network communication model as specified by International Standards Organisation (ISO).

Output Device. A device that displays/prints documents, data, instructions and information on a computer.

Overlay. A section of a program designed to reside on a storage device and loaded into memory when needed.

P5. Intel's internal working name for the Pentium microprocessor.

P6. The Intel code name for the Pentium Pro, which is optimized for 32-bit applicaions.

Packaged Software. An general purpose application software that meets the requirements of a wide variety of users.

Packet. A block of data transmitted.

Page Printer. A printer (such as Laser printer) that prints one page at a time.

Paging. A one way wireless communication system that allows the users to receive messages on the move.

Palmtop. A hand-sized computer having no keyboard but the screen serves both as an input and output device.

Parallel Port. An input/output port that manages information of 8 bits at a time, mainly used to connect a parallel printer.

Parallel Processing. An architecture that can perform multiple operations on systems containing two or more processors.

Parallel Transmission. A type of transmission where eight separate wires are used to send each bit simultaneously.

Parity Bit. An extra or redundant bit attached to the byte, character or word, often used to detect transmission errors.

Partition. A logical division of hard disk created at the time of formatting.

Partition Boot Sector. The first sector in the partition of a computer's bootable hard disk, used to store information required for booting.

Pascaline. A calculating machine developed in 1642 by a French mathematician, Blaise Pascal.

Password. The string of characters entered by a user to verify his or her identity on a system.

PC/XT. An upgraded model of the original IBM Personal Computer, introduced in 1983 . It was the first PC that had a hard disk.

Peer to Peer Networking. Low cost LANs where each workstation may act as a server to any other workstation.

Pen Computer. A class of computers whose primary input device is a pen (stylus) instead of a keyboard.

Pentium. The latest 64-bit microprocessor introduced by Intel in 1993.

Pentium 4. The latest Intel Pentium processor, designed to deliver end-user appreciable performance gains for Visual Internet including Internet audio/ video streaming, 3D graphics, digital photography, speech recognition, etc.

Pentium II. The successor to the Pentium Pro from Intel.

Pentium MMX. A Pentium CPU that contains additional instructions for improved multimedia performance.

Pentium Pro. The sixth generation of the Intel x86 family of CPU chips.

Perl. Acronym for Practical Extraction and Report Language. A script programming language which has a syntax similar to C.

Personal Computer. A type of digital computer, most popular among all users. Also called a microcomputer.

Pixel. The smallest element on a video display screen.

Physical Address. An address that corresponds to a hardware memory location.

Physical Data Independence. If the data is designed in such a way that the physical storage techniques of the data can be changed without changing the application programs then this level of data independence is called as physical data independence.

PKUNZIP. A shareware utility program that uncompresses files compressed by the PKZIP shareware utility program.

PKZIP. One of the most widely used shareware compression programs available in both MS DOS and Windows forms.

Platform. The underlying hardware or software system on which application programs run.

Plotter. An output device used to draw high-resolution charts, graphs, layouts and other diagrams especially of CAD applications.

Plug and Play. The ability of an operating system such as Windows 98 to recognize new hardware that has been attached to a computer and to configure the system automatically to use the hardware.

Portal. A Web site having collection of links, content and services, designed to guide users to view information they are likely to find interesting on the Internet.

PostScript. A page description language, introduced by Adobe in 1985 having a series of instructions for drawing graphics and placing text on a page.

PostScript Font. A font defined in terms of the PostScript page-description language rules.

Primary Key. The key field in a database file that serves as the unique identifier of a specific record.

Primary Storage. The main storage area of computer to which the microprocessor has direct access.

Printer. The most common output device that provides printed output on a paper or a film.

Procedural Language. A programming language that is split into named basic sections or procedures.

Procedure. In a program, a named sequence of statements that generally perform a single task.

Processing. The manipulation of data by a computer for generating the information.

Programming Language. A language used to write a set of instructions (program) in a computer.

PROM. Acronym for Programmable Read Only Memory. A type of ROM chip that is programmed after its manufacturing.

Protocols. Rules of data communication.

Prototyping. A working model of a new computer system or a software for testing and refinement.

Puck. An input device used to enter information about a drawing to the computer.

QBASIC. A BASIC interpreter from Microsoft that comes with DOS starting with DOS 5.

QIC. Acronym for Quarter Inch Cartridge. A type of magnetic tape used for backup purposes.

Query Language. A subset of the data manipulation language, that is used for the retrieval and display of data from a database.

Query By Example (QBE). IBM's old relational database which is specially designed for use in a visual terminal.

QWERTY Keyboard. A common type of keyboard is a keyboard that has keys arranged in a certain order similiar to a manual typewriter.

RAD. Acronym for Rapid Application Development. In object-oriented programming, a method of software development in which a programmer uses a library of prebuilt objects for developing the programs.

RAID. Acronym for Redundant Array of Independent Disks. A disk subsystem that provides increased performance and fault tolerance.

RAM. Acronym for Random Access Memory. A volatile memory of computer that can be read from and written to by the user.

RAM Disk. Short for Random Access Memory Disk. A storage technique in which a portion of main store is set aside to be used in place of a disk to provide faster processing.

Random File Organisation. A file organisation where the records are stored at the storage location numbers called addresses.

RDBMS. Acronym for Relational Database Management System. An application software that organises and manages data in a relational database by supporting SQL (Structured Query Language) features.

Read/write Head. A component of disk drive used to read and write data.

Realtime System. Any computer based system such as air-traffic control, Process Control or defense systems in which the time at which the output is produced is of importance.

Reboot. Reloading of the operating system into computer's memory.

Record. A group of fields in a file.

Recursion. The ability of a routine in a program to call itself again.

Register. A set of bits of high-speed memory within a microprocessor or other electronic device used to store data.

Relation. In mathematical language, given a collection of sets S1, S2, ... Sn, R is a relation on these n sets, if it is a set of ordered n tuples <s1,s2,...sn> such that s1 belongs to S1, s2 belongs to S2,... sn belongs to Sn and items Sn are domains of R.

Relational Database. A database model in which the data always appears to the user as a set of two-dimensional tables with rows and columns, where each table is constructed using a special case of construct, called a relation.

Relational Operator. An operator that allows the programmer to compare two (or more) values or expressions. Typical relational operators are greater than (>), equal to (=), less than (<), not equal to (<>), greater than or equal to (>=), and less than or equal to (<=).

Relational Structure. A type of data structure where data is viewed as organised in tables.

Relationship. An association between entities.

Relative Address. An address expressed as a difference with respect to some numerical value used as a reference, known as a base address. Addition of a base address to a relative address gives an Absolute Address.

Remote Login. The action of logging into a computer at a distant location by means of a data communication connection with the computer.

Removable Disk. A disk module that is inserted into the drive for reading and writing and can be removed when not required.

Reorder Level. The level of inventory of an item at which an order for purchase is placed so that it is not run out of stock.

Repeater. Equipment used for expansion of LAN by boosting the signals to accommodate long distances.

Report Generator. A software development tool , commonly part of a database management program that uses a report form created by the user to view and print the contents of a database.

Resident Program. A program that always remains in computer's memory.

Resolution. The degree of sharpness of a printed or displayed image. It is generally expressed in dots per inch (dpi).

Restore. To copy files from a backup storage device to their normal location, especially to replace files that were accidentally lost or deleted.

Ring Network. A LAN (local area network) topology in which devices (nodes) are connected in a closed loop or ring.

Robot. A computer controlled mechanical device that has been engineered to perform many simple repetitive tasks.

Robotics. A field of artificial intelligence that is concerned with design, manufacturing and implementation of computer controlled mechanical devices (Robots).

ROM . Acronym for Read Only Memory. A semiconductor-based memory chip that stores information permanently and does not erase its contents when power is switched off.

ROM BIOS. Acronym for Read Only Memory Basic Input/Output System. A PC's BIOS stored in a ROM chip.

Router. A bridge like device that interconnects several types of LANs. The main function of router is to provide the best route for the packets of information through the interconnection of LANs.

RS-232-C Standard. An accepted industry standard for serial communication connections.

Save. To store data, information or instructions in external memory (stoarge device) of a computer.

Scandisk. A utility in Windows 95/98 and DOS that detects and repairs errors on disk.

Scanner. An input device that enters information from a paper into a computer by scanning it.

Schema. The view of the data as a whole represented as a graph, table, chart and mathematical formulas. Also called Model.

Screen Saver. A utility program of Windows that displays a moving image on the screen after a set time interval if no keyboard or mouse actions have been performed.

SCSI. Acronym for Small Computer System Interface. A standard high-speed parallel interface used to attach peripheral devices to a PC.

Search Engine. A tool used for finding information on the Internet.

Secondary Storage. Any data storage medium other than a computer's internal memory.

Second Generation Computers. Computers designed in the mid and late 1950s and early 1960s, characterised by the use of transistors their electronic circuitry.

Sector. The triangular storage region on a disk, generally with a capacity of 512 bytes.

Security. Prevention or protection of data against unauthorised access in a computer system or a network.

Sequential Access. A method of storing or retrieving information that requires the program to start reading data from the beginning and continues until the desired data is found.

Sequential File Organisation. A file organisation where the records are arranged sequentially in a predetermined order.

Serial Bus. A type of bus such as Ethernet that transmits data serially.

Serial Transmission. In serial transmission, each byte of information takes eight time slots for transmission.

Server. A high-speed computer in a network that makes access to files, printing, communications or other services available to users.

Shareware. A form of software distribution through information services that makes copyright programs freely available on a trial basis but users are expected to register their copy and pay a small fee to the program developer.

Signal. Form of electromagnetic waves that need a range of frequency depending upon the distance of the transmission to carry transmission data.

SIM Card. Acronym for Subscriber Identity Module Card. A smart card designed for use with a GSM (Global System for Mobile Communications) mobile phones for storing a subscriber's personal identifier, billing information and other data.

Simple Mail Transfer Protocol (SMTP). Used for communication of various proprietary E-mail System.

Simplex Transmission. One way transmission of data between two endpoints in a network.

Sleep Mode. A power management mode that shuts down all unnecessary computer operations to save energy after it has received no input or other activity for a specified period of time.

SLIP. Acronym for Serial Line Internet Protocol. A data link protocol that allows transmission of TCP/IP data packets over dial-up telephone connections. It enables a computer or a LAN to be connected to the Internet.

Software. Programs required to operate a computer.

Software Piracy. The illegal copying and distribution of the copyright software.

Sort. To organize a set of records in a database file in a particular order.

Sound Card. A type of expansion board on a PC that allows the playback and recording of sound.

Source Code. Program statements written by a programmer or developer in a programming language other than machine language.

Speaker. An output device of a multimedia PC for producing sound and music.

Speech Recognition. The process of changing spoken words into code which a computer can use.

Spreadsheet Program. An application program used to create tables, reports, graphs and databases by using formulas and performing arithmetic calculations.

Stand-alone System. A system designed to meet specific individual needs without relying on any other application software to perform the assigned task.

Star Network. A LAN (Local Area Network) topology in which each device (node) is connected to a central computer in a star-shaped configuration.

Static RAM. A type of Random Access Memory (RAM) in which information remains stable as long as power supply is provided.

Storage Allocation. The allocation of specified areas of storage to the various processing tasks running in a computer.

Structured Query Language (SQL). A query language originally developed by IBM for use in mainframe applications but now adapted on all types of computers to query and process data in a relational database.

Supercomputer. The biggest and fastest computer, having many CPUs (Central Processing Units) that operate in parallel.

SuperVGA (SVGA). An enhancement to the VGA (Video Graphics Array) display adapter by providing better resolutions to the monitor.

Surfing. Searching or scanning online material on Internet.

Switch. A high speed bridge that segments a LAN traffic such that it switches packets from one segment of LAN to another in a matter of milliseconds.

Sybase SQL Server. A distributed RDBMS which runs on most servers except mainframe.

Synchronous Data Transmission. In synchronous mode of data transmission, a block of characters is transmitted one at a time.

Syntax Error. A programming error in which the grammatical rules of the programming language are not followed.

System. A set of componentsthat work together to achieve a goal.

System Administrator. The person responsible for administering the use of a multi-user computer system.

Systems Analysis. The analysis of a system during development of software.

Systems Analyst. A person who analyses and designs the software.

Table. A highly structured database file in a relational database.

Tape Drive. A storage device that moves magnetic tape during reading and writing of data.

TCP/IP. Acronym forTransmission Control Protocol/Internet Protocol. A communication protocol that includes media access, session communications, file transfer and e-mail, developed by Defense Advanced Research Projects Agency (DARPA).

Technical Writer. The person responsible for writing the hardware and software documentation such as tutorials, user manuals, etc.

Telecommunication. The transmission of all forms of information including digital data, voice, fax, sound and video from one computer to another by a telephone line.

Teleconferencing System. An electronic means of communication for conducting seminars and training programmes in an organisation.

Teleprinter. A typewriter terminal with a keyboard and built-up printer.

Teletext. A computer related technology for transmitting text through a telephone line.

TELNET. A service on the Internet which allows users to use resources of the remote servers.

Terabyte (TB). Highest unit of memory, equivalent to 2^{40} or 1,099,511,627,778 bytes.

Terminal. A visual display unit with a keyboard.

Text Editor. A software utility program used for input and editing of information in textual form.

Thermal Printer. A non impact printer that uses heat to generate an image on a specially treated paper.

Third Generation Computer. The computers produced from the mid-1960s to the 1970s that used integrated circuits in place of transistors.

Third Generation Language. A high-level programming language such as FORTRAN, COBOL, BASIC, Pascal and C which uses common English words for writing a program.

Throughput. A measure of the overall performance of a computer system i.e. the amount of work performed in a given period.

Time-sharing. The use of a computer system by more than one individual at the same time.

Token Ring Network. A type of network connected in a loop or ring in which a message is passed from one computer to the next unit it reaches its destination.

Toner. Powdered pigment device that is commonly used in a Laser printer.

Toner Cartridge. A disposable container that holds toner for a laser printer.

Topology. Layout of the cabling in connecting devices in a network.

Touch Pad. Small, flat, rectangular pointing input device of computer which is sensitive to pressure and motion.

Track. The concentric circular storage region on the disk.

Trackball. An input device used to move the cursor by rotated it by the user's fingers.

Translator. A program that converts a program written in one language into the equivalent program in another language.

Troubleshoot. A process of finding problems in the hardware of a computer system.

TSR. Acronym for Terminate and State Resident. MS DOS programs that always stay in memory.

Tuple. The row of a relational database table.

Turbo C. A C compiler from Borland used to create a wide variety of commercial products.

Turnaround Time. The time that elapses between the submission of a job to a computer and the return of the results.

Uniform Resource Locator (URL). Address of a web page or web resource in World Wide Web.

Uninstall. To completely remove software from a computer.

UNIX. A 32 bit multi-user, multitasking, portable operating system originally developed by AT&T that runs on all types of computers.

UPS. Acronym for Uninterruptible Power Supply. A battery-powered device connected between a computer and automatically provides backup power in the event of power failure..

Unsubscribe. To remove oneself as a recipient on a mailing list on Internet.

USENET. A worldwide network of Unix systems with thousands of subject-based newsgroups on Internet.

User Interface. The way a user interacts with the computer.

Username. The name by which a user is identified on a computer or network.

Utility Program. A program that supports the operating system by providing additional services such as file compression, virus scanning, disk management, etc.

Vaccine. Anti-virus programs that detect and remove computer viruses.

VERONICA. A search tool for scanning particular files in a gopher space.

Very Small Aperture Terminal (VSAT). A sophisticated personal satellite earth station that provides links for various communication of data, video and voice over long distances.

VGA. Acronym for Video Graphics Array. A video adapter for monitors, introduced by IBM along with the IBM PS/2 line of computers in 1987.

Video Adapter. The electronic components that generate the video signal sent through a cable to a video display.

Video CD. A compact disc format used to hold full-motion video.

Videotape. A magnetic tape used for recording full-animation video images.

Videotext. The modern means of computer-based telecommunication where the data is superimposed upon TV signals and the message is displayed on television sets.

Virtual Reality. A way of creating a three-dimensional image of an object or scene.

Virus. A program that copies itself to other programs, spreads from one system to another in order to damage the software and data without the knowledge or permission of the user.

Virus Scanner. An application program that detects, removes and prevents a virus attack.

Visual Basic. A programming language and environment developed by Microsoft.

Visual C++. A Microsoft application development system for the programming language C++ that runs both under DOS and Windows.

Visual Display Unit (VDU). An output device used to display information on a screen.

Voice Mail. A computer system that can store telephone messages in memory for later retrieval by a user.

Voice Modem. A modulation/demodulation device that supports a switch to change between telephony and data transmission modes.

Volatile Memory. A type of memory whose contents are lost as soon as the power supply to the memory is switched off.

VRML. Acronym for Virtual Reality Modeling Language. A language for creating interactive three-dimensional image sequences and possible user interaction with them.

Web. A set of interlined documents in a hypertext system.

Web Authoring Software. A Web site development system that allows creating of Web pages like a desktop publishing program.

Web Browser. A program that allows Internet users to view and to explore information on the World Wide Web.

Web Designer. A person who creates a Web site.

Web Page. An electronic document on the Web.

Website. A collection of web pages containing important information about the company's business.

Wide Area Network (WAN). A communications network that connects users across a wide area crossing the geographical boundaries of cities or states.

Win32. The application programming interface in Windows 95 and Windows NT that enables applications to use the 32 bit instructions available on 80386 and higher processors.

Windows 1.0. The first version of Microsoft Windows, introduced in 1985.

Windows 2.0. An upgrade to Windows 1.0, introduced in 1988.

Window 2000. A line of desktop operating systems and network servers announced by Microsoft in 2000.

Windows 3.0. A complete overhaul of Microsoft windows, introduced in 1990.

Windows 3.1. The first major upgrade to Windows 3.0 introduced in 1992.

Windows 3.1.1. The final release of Windows 3.1.

Windows 95. An operating system with a graphical user interface for 80836 and higher processors released by Microsoft Corporation in 1995.

Windows 98. An operating system with a graphical user interface for 486 and higher processors released by Microsoft Corporation in 1998.

WordStar. The most popular full-featured word processing program for DOS and Windows.

World Wide Web (WWW). A vast collection of online documents distributed over the Internet.

Worm. A type of virus that is introduced into a host and replicates itself across computer.

XBase. A generic term denoting any of the programming environments derived from the original dBase programming languages created by Ashton-Tate, Inc.

Yahoo. A popular search engine for Internet resources.

Zoom. To make an image or text larger on the visual display unit.

101-keys Keyboard. A computer keyboard modeled after the enhanced keyboard introduced by IBM for the IBM PC/AT.

1.2 M. Acronym for 1.2 Megabyte. Refers to the storage capacity for high-density 5.25 inch floppy disks.

1.44 M. Acronym for 1.44 Megabyte. Refers to the storage capacity for high-density 3.5 inch floppy disks.

286. The second generation of the Intel x86 family of CPU chips.

386. The third generation of the Intel x86 family of CPU chips.

3D Animation. Animating objects that appear in a three-dimensional space.

3D Audio. Audio reproduction that simulates sounds coming from all directions.

486. The fourth generation of the Intel x86 family of CPU chips.

56-kbps Modem. A standard for a modem that communicates data at 56 Kbps downstream and 33.6 Kbps upstream.

APPENDICES

Appendix A

MODEL QUESTION PAPER

Computer and Languages

CS-101/201

FIRST/ SECOND SEMESTER EXAMINATION

Time: 2 hours *Total Marks: 50*

Note: Attempt ALL questions.

1. Attempt any *Four* parts: 3 × 4 = 12

(*a*) Draw the block diagram of a Digital Computer. Explain the role of each functional unit in brief.

(*b*) What is an Operating System? Explain its major functions in brief. Explain the salient features of Multiprogramming and Multitasking operating systems.

(*c*) Explain the difference between –

(i) Main Memory and Auxiliary Memory

(*ii*) ROM and RAM

(*iii*) Sequential File and Indexed File

(d) Write the following MS DOS commands along with complete syntax:

(*i*) FORMAT

(*ii*) DEL

(*iii*) XCOPY

(*e*) Write short notes on the following –

(*i*) Character Printers

(*ii*) HDD

(*iii*) DVD

(*f*) Why do people prefer to use Windows 98 instead of DOS? Write the steps to do the following in Windows 98:

(*i*) To make a folder 'Exam' in C:drive

(*ii*) To copy a file 'Test.doc' from floppy to 'Exam' folder in C:drive

2. Attempt any *Four* parts: 3 × 4 = 12

(a) Explain the following UNIX commands with the complete syntax:

(*i*) grep

(*ii*) sort

(*iii*) cut

(b) Perform the following operations in vi editor:

(*i*) Search the string 'Examination System' and then change 'Examination' to 'Admission'

(*ii*) Revert to the last saved version of a file.

(*iii*) To save and exit from vi

(*c*) Differentiate among the following terms:

(*i*) FTP and Telnet

(*ii*) Download and Upload

(*iii*) Alt and Biz Newsgroups

(*d*) Write short notes on the following terms (with examples):

(*i*) Domain Name System

(*ii*) Search Engine

(*iii*) Hyperlinks

(e)

(*i*) What is E-mail? How will you compose and send a message using E-mail to your friend using Outlook Express? Explain.

(*ii*) Give the full form of following abbreviated terms:

(a) HTML

(*b*) SGML

(*c*) DNS

(f)

(*i*) How will you read and reply a message in PINE or Elm.

(*ii*) How will you create an address book in PINE?

OR

How will you create an alias in Elm?

3. Attempt any *Three* parts: 4 × 3 = 12

(*a*) Explain the use of following operators in C:

(*i*) Ternary Operator

(*ii*) Increment Operator

(*iii*) Assignment Operator

(*b*) Write a program in C to find the sum of the following series:

(*c*) Write a program in C to print the Pascal triangle as shown below:

```
1   1
1   2   1
1   3   3   1
1   4   6   4   1
```

(*d*) Write a program in C to determine whether the year entered by user is a leap year or not.

4. Attempt any *Two* parts: 7 × 2 = 14

(a) What are Functions? Explain the scope of global and local variables with examples. Write a function to calculate factorial of a number entered by user.

(*b*)

(*i*) What are Pointers? How are the pointers initialised? Explain with examples.

(*ii*) How can an array element be accessed by pointer? Write a program in C to find the smallest number in an array using pointers.

(*b*) What are Structures? Define a structure which stores the roll no., name and marks of 10 students. Write a program in C to display the name and roll no. of a student who gets the maximum marks.

Appendix B

ASCII CHART

ASCII Value	Character	ASCII Value	Character
000	NUL	039	'
001	SOH	040	(
002	STX	041	)
003	ETX	042	*
004	EOT	043	+
005	ENQ	044	,
006	ACK	045	–
007	BEL	046	.
008	BS	047	/
009	HT	048	0
010	LF	049	1
011	VT	050	2
012	FF	051	3
013	CR	052	4
014	SO	053	5
015	SI	054	6
016	DLE	055	7
017	DC1	056	8
018	DC2	057	9
019	DC3	058	:
020	DC4	059	;
021	NAK	060	<
022	SYN	061	=
023	ETB	062	>
024	CAN	063	?
025	EM	064	@
026	SUB	065	A
027	ESC	066	B
028	FS	067	C
029	GS	068	D
030	RS	069	E
031	US	070	F
032	blank	071	G
033	!	072	H
034	”	073	I
035	#	074	J
036	$	075	K
037	%	076	L
038	&	077	M

ASCII Value	Character	ASCII Value	Character
078	N	103	g
079	O	104	h
080	P	105	i
081	Q	106	j
082	R	107	k
083	S	108	l
084	T	109	m
085	U	110	n
086	V	111	o
087	W	112	p
088	X	113	q
089	Y	114	r
090	Z	115	s
091	[	116	t
092	\	117	u
093	]	118	v
094	↑	119	w
095	—	120	x
096		121	y
097	a	122	z
098	b	123	{
099	c	124	|
100	d	125	}
101	e	126	~
102	f	127	DEL

Appendix C

C LIBRARY FUNCTIONS

Function	Type	Purpose	Include File
abs(i)	int	Returns the absolute value of i.	stdlib.h
atof(s)	double	Converts string s to a double-precision quantity.	stdlib.h
atoi(s)	int	Converts string s into an integer.	stdlib.h
atol(s)	long	Converts string s to a long integer.	stdlib.h
exit(u)	void	Closes all files and buffers and terminates the program.	stdlib.h
fclose(f)	int	Closes file f. Returns 0 if the file is successfully closed.	stdio.h
fgetc(f)	int	Enters a single character from file f.	stdio.h
fgets(s,i,f)	char	Enter string s, containing i characters, from file f.	stdio.h
fopen(s1,s2)	FILE*	Opens a file named s1 of s2 type. Returns a pointer to a file.	stdio.h
fprintf(f,...)	int	Sends data items to file f.	stdio.h
fputc(c,f)	int	Sends a single character to file f.	stdio.h
fputs(s,f)	int	Sends string s to file f.	stdio.h
fread(s,i1,i2,f)	int	Inputs i2 data items each of size i1 bytes, from file f to string s.	stdio.h
free(p)	void	Frees a block of allocated memory whose starting address is indicated by p.	malloc.h or stdlib.h
fscanf(f,...)	int	Inputs data items from file f.	stdio.h
fseek(f,l,i)	int	Moves the pointer for file f at distance 1 bytes from location i (i may represent pointer position or end-of-file).	stdio.h
ftell(f)	longint	Returns the current pointer position within file f.	stdio.h
fwrite(s,i1,i2,f)	int	Sends i2 data items, each of size i1 bytes from string s to file f.	stdio.h
getc(f)	int	Inputs a single character from file f.	stdio.h
getchar()	int	Inputs a single character from the standard input device.	stdio.h
isalnum(c)	int	Determines if argument is alphanumeric.	ctype.h
isalpha(c)	int	Determines if the argument is alphabetic. Returns non-zero value if true; 0 otherwise.	ctype.h
isascii(c)	int	Determines if the argument is an ASCII character. Returns non-zero value if true, 0 otherwise.	ctype.h

Function	Type	Purpose	Include File
isdigit(c)	int	Determines if argument is a decimal digit. Returns non-zero value if true; 0 otherwise.	ctype.h
islower(c)	int	Determines if argument is in lower-case character. Returns non-zero if true, 0 otherwise.	ctype.h
isspace(c)	int	Determines if argument is a whitespace character. Returns non-zero value if true; 0 otherwise.	ctype.h
isupper(c)	int	Determines if argument is in upper case. Returns non-zero value if true; 0 otherwise.	ctype.h
malloc(u)	void	Allocates u bytes of memory. Returns a pointer to the beginning of the allocated space.	malloc.h or stdlib.h
pow(d1,d2)	double	Returns d1 raised to the power d2.	math.h
printf(...)	int	Sends data items to the standard output device.	stdio.h
putchar(c)	int	Sends a single character to the output device.	stdio.h
puts(s)	int	Sends the string s to the standard output device.	stdio.h
scanf(....)	int	Allows input of data items from the standard ouput device.	stdio.h
strcmp(s1,s2)	int	Compares two strings. Returns a –ve value if s1 < s2, 0 if s1 = s2, +ve if s1 > s2.	string.h
strcpy(s1,s2)	char*	Copies string s2 to string s1.	string.h
strlen(s)	int	Returns the number of characters in string s.	string.h
toascii(c)	int	Converts value of argument to ASCII.	ctype.h
tolower(c)	int	Converts value of argument to lower-case.	ctype.h or stdlib.h
toupper(c)	int	Converts letter to upper-case.	ctype.h or stdlib.h
rewind(f)	void	Moves the pointer to the beginning of file f.	stdio.h

Appendix D

COMMONLY USED TURBO C MENU COMMANDS

Hot Key	Menu Function
<F1>	Displays Help Screen (Help)
<F2>	Saves active editor file (File/Save)
<F3>	Opens a file (File/Open)
<F4>	Executes to cursor location (Run/Go to Cursor)
<F5>	Zooms the active window (Window/Zoom)
<F6>	Cycles through open windows (Window/Next)
<F7>	Traces into subroutines (Run/Trace into)
<F8>	Steps over subroutine calls (Run/Step Over)
<F10>	Activates the menu bar
<Alt+F1>	Displays previous Help Screen (Help/Previous topic)
<Alt+F3>	Closes active window (Window/Close)
<Alt+F5>	Displays user screen (Window/User Screen)
<Alt+F9>	Compiles active program (Compile/Compile)
<Alt+Spacebar>	Goes to System menu
<Alt+C>	Goes to Compile menu
<Alt+D>	Goes to Debug menu
<Alt+E>	Goes to Edit menu
<Alt+F>	Goes to File menu
<Alt+H>	Goes to Help menu
<Alt+O>	Goes to Options menu
<Alt+R>	Goes to Run menu
<Alt+S>	Goes to Search menu
<Alt+W>	Goes to Window menu
<Alt+X>	Exits Turbo C to DOS (File/Exit)
<Ctrl+F9>	Executes active program (Run/Run)

Appendix E

COMMONLY USED TURBO C OPERATION COMMANDS

Function	Keystroked
Character left	<Left arrow> or <Ctrl+S>
Character right	<Right arrow> or <Ctrl+D>
Word left	<Ctrl+left arrow> or <Ctrl+A>
Word right	<Ctrl+right arrow> or <Ctrl+F>
Line up	<Up arrow> or <Ctrl+E>
Line down	<Down arrow> or <Ctrl+X>
Page Up	<PgU> or <Ctrl+R>
Page down	<PgDn> or <Ctrl+C>
Beginning of line	<Home> or <Ctrl+Q/S>
End of line	<End> or <Ctrl+Q/D>
Insert line	<Ctrl+N>
Delete line	<Ctrl+Y>
Delete block	<Ctrl+K/Y>
Delete till end of line	<Ctrl+Q/Y>
Delete a character to the left of cursor	<Backspace> or <Ctrl+H>
Delete character at current cursor position	<Delete> or <Ctrl+G>
Copy block of lines to edit a file	<Ctrl+K/C>
Copy block of lines to clipboard	<Ctrl+Ins> or <Edit/Copy>
Delete block	<Ctrl+Del> or <Edit/Clear>
Mark block begin	<Ctrl+K/B>
Mark block end	<Ctrl+K/K>
Move block from clipboard	<Shift+Ins> or <Edit/Paste>
Invoke main menu	<F10>
Language help	<Ctrl+F1>
Open file	<File/open> or <F3>
Save file	File/save> or <F2>

EXAMINATION PAPERS

B. TECH

SECOND SEMESTER EXAMINATION, 2000–2001

COMPUTER AND LANGUAGES

Time : Two Hours *Total Marks : 50*

Note : *(i) Attempt ALL questions.*

UNIT 1

1. Explain the various steps in booting of a computer system.

Or

Discuss the effect of booting the computer system with following CONFIG.SYS file

```
[menu]
menuitem = one
menuitem = two
[common]
dos = high
buffers = 20
[one]
files = 40
device = c:\dos\himen.sys
device = c:\dos\mouse.sys
[two]
files = 30
device = c:\dos\mouse.sys
```

2

2. Explain the role of file manager with respect to WINDOWS 98. **2**

3. Write the following MS-DOS commands along with complete syntax.

(*i*) COPY

(*ii*) RENAME

(*iii*) FORMAT

Or

Discuss the salient features of multiprogramming and multi-tasking. **3**

4. State the sequence of operations needed for (CMOS) setup to introduce a slave Hard Disk. **3**

UNIT 2

5. What do you understand by environment variables ? What environment will it create after the execution of the following sequence of commands ?

HOME = /home/rama

LOGNAME = rama

MAIL = /ver/spool/mail/rama

PATH = /bin :/ursr/bin :

PS1 = '$'

PS2 = '>'

SHELL = /bin/ksh

TERM = ansi 3

6. Discuss the different tools and services available on Internet.

Or

Discuss the utility of Netscape Navigator Browser of Internet in brief. 2

7. Write commands to open, close, save files in Edit. What commands are used to :

(*i*) cut and paste a paragraph

(*ii*) delete a line

(*iii*) insert a line

Or

Explain the access control mechanism of file and directory attributes in UNIX. 3

8. Differentiate between Gopher and www.

Or

Explain the purpose of Usenet in Internet. 2

UNIT 3

9. Write a program in C to print the Pascal triangle.

```
1   1
1   2   1
1   3   3   1
1   4   6   4   1
```

4

10. Write a C-program to determine that a given year is a leap year or not.

Or

Write a C-program that accepts 6-digit positive integer. If the number is even, then add up its digits or else multiply the individual digits and print the result. 4

11. (*a*) Rewrite the following for statement into an equivalent while statement

```
for  (i=j;  i<k;  i++)
  if  (in[i]  ==  '?')
    Q++;
```

(*b*) Put parenthesis in the following expression :

a = b + c * d < < 2 & B

(c) Rewrite the following if statement into an equivalent simple statement [i can be either ∅ or 1]

```
if  (i  =  ∅)
        i  =  1;
else
        i  =  ∅;
```
3

12. Write a recursive program in C which finds greatest common divisor (GCD) of two positive integers. 4

UNIT 4

13. Write appropriate declarations and assign the given initial values for each variable.

(a) floating point variable : a = – 8.2

(b) long integer variable : big = 1 2 3 4 5 6 7 8 9

(c) integer variables : u = 711 (octal), v = ffff (hexadecimal)

Or

A C-program contains the following declarations and initial assignments :

```
int  i=8,  j=5;
float  x=0.005,  y=-0.01;
char  C='c';
```

Determine the value of each of the following expressions :

(a) (i – 3 * j) % (C + 2 * d) / (x – y)

(b) 2 * ((i/5) + (4 * (j – 3)) % (i + j – 2) 3

14. State in at most two sentences what the following function does

```
void  function-unknown  (int  *x,  int  *y)
{
  *x  =  *x  +  *y;
  *y  =  *x  -  *y;
  *x  =  *x  -  *y;
}
```
4

15. Consider the following function for searching for integer x in an array with n elements. The array is assumed to contain integers in non-decreasing order. The function returns TRUE if x appears in the array and FALSE otherwise. The function is not correct. Give an example to show the reason why the function is not correct.

```
int  binary-search  (int  a[],  int  n,  int  x)
{
  int  i=0,  j=n-1,  k;
  while  (i<=j)  {
  k  =  (i+j)/2;
  if  (a[k]  ==  x)
                return  TRUE;
  else  if  (a[k]  <  x)
                  i  =  k;
  else
                  j  =  k;
}
```

```
return  FALSE;
}
```

4

16. What is the output of the following program :

```
#include  <stdio.h>
main  ()
{
    int  j,k,x  =  Ø;
    for  (j=Ø;  j<5;  ++j)
    for  (k=Ø;  k<j;  ++k)
    {
        x  +=  (j+k-1);
        printf("%d",  x);
        break;
    }
   printf("\nx  =  %d",  x);
}
```

4

□□□

B. TECH

FIRST SEMESTER EXAMINATION, 2001–2002

COMPUTER AND LANGUAGES

Time : Two Hours | *Total Marks : 50*

Note : *(i) Attempt ALL questions.*

1. Attempt any Four parts of the following : **3 × 4 = 12**

(*a*) Explain the following in context of Computer :

(*i*) Secondary Memory

(*ii*) Cache Memory

(*iii*) Main Memory

(*b*) What are the advantages of WINDOWS 95/98 over DOS ? Explain the following terms related with WINDOWS :

(*i*) MyDocument

(*ii*) Recycle Bin

(*c*) What do you mean by Multitasking System ? How is it different from Multiprocessing System ?

(*d*) Write DOS Commands to do the following :

(*i*) Create directory "ABC" at root.

(*ii*) Copy file "Readme.Txt" from root to "ABC" directory.

(*iii*) Delete directory "ABC" with all of its subdirectories and files.

(*e*) Write steps to do the following in WINDOWS 95/98 :

(*i*) Create a folder in MyDocument.

(*ii*) Copy a file from one folder "X" to another folder "Y".

(*iii*) Send a file from folder "X" to Recycle Bin.

(*f*) What are output devices used in Digital computer ? Discuss any two of them.

2. Attempt any Four parts of the following : **3 × 4 = 12**

(*a*) List any two major features of UNIX operating system. What is the difference between absolute and relative path names of a UNIX file ?

(*b*) What is Web Browser ? Explain in brief.

(*c*) What are Search Engines ? List any two popular Search Engines.

(*d*) What are E-mails ? How are they sent ? Explain how an attachment is made to the mail.

(*e*) Explain the following with respect to DOS Editor, EDIT :

(*i*) List the different menu options and explain any one.

(*ii*) How do you set colours ?

(*f*) Explain the salient features of PINE or ELM.

3. Attempt any Four parts of the following : **3½ × 4 = 14**

(*a*) State the fundamental data types and their size used in 'C' Language. Explain the difference between Postfix and Prefix increment operators. Show how it affects the result of an Expression.

(*b*) Write a 'C' program to sort an array of integers in ascending order.

(*c*) Write a 'C' program to find the sum of the series—

$1 + X + X^2 + X^3 + \ldots\ldots\ldots\ldots\ldots X^n$

(*d*) What are pointers in 'C' ? How is a pointer initialized ? Explain with a suitable example.

(*e*) Write a program in 'C' to calculate sine and cosine values of the angles 0, 10°, 20°, ... 180° and print the result in tabular form.

(*f*) What are functions ? Explain the difference between iterative and recursive function calls.

4. Attempt any Two parts of the following : **6 × 2 = 12**

(*a*) (*i*) Differentiate between Structure and Union.

(*ii*) Write a program to accept the element of the structure; EMP–NO, BASIC–PAY, NAME. Display the same structure along with DA, CCA and GROSS–SALARY. DA and CCA are to be calculated as follows :

DA = 51% of basic pay

CCA = Rs. 100=00 consolidated.

(*b*) Using pointer, write a function that receives a character string and a character as argument and deletes all occurrences of this character in this string. Function should return the corrected string without space.

(*c*) (*i*) What are arrays ? How are they declared in 'C' ?

(*ii*) Write a program in 'C' to transpose a matrix of size N × N.

❑❑❑

B. TECH

SECOND SEMESTER EXAMINATION, 2001–2002

COMPUTER AND LANGUAGES

Time : Two Hours *Total Marks : 50*

Note : *(i) Attempt ALL the questions.*

1. Attempt any FOUR of the following : **3 × 4 = 12**

(*a*) What is a general purpose machine ? Explain von Neumann machine's features.

(*b*) What are differences in

(*i*) Static versus Dynamic memories,

(*ii*) Volatile versus Non-Volatile memory,

(*iii*) RAM and ROM ?

(*c*) Find out the average access time for a fixed head disk rotating at 3000 rpm and contains 10 sectors in a track.

(*d*) What is a device controller ?

(*e*) State whether the following are True or False :

(*i*) Cache memory increases load on main memory.

(*ii*) The principle of locality says that all the references to data have to be to the same memory location.

(*iii*) Memory hierarchy is built in computer system as the main memory cannot store very large data.

(*iv*) An interrupt may be generated by a clock. This is known as a timer interrupt.

(*v*) In case multiple interrupts occur at the same time, then only one of the interrupts will be acknowledged and rest will be lost.

(*f*) What is a file manager in Windows ? Explain the purpose for what the following commands are used :

(*i*) File Menu → Copy Command.

(*ii*) View Menu → Split Command.

(*iii*) View Menu → Select Drive Command.

2. Answer any FOUR of the following : **3 × 4 = 12**

(*a*) Write the UNIX equivalent of the following DOS commands :

DIR DEL COPY TYPE CD MD RD REN

(*b*) What will be the effect of following UNIX commands ?

umask

chmod 777 abc.c

chmod ug+rw a=x ff.out

chmod u+t mydir

(*c*) In vi editor, what is the purpose of .exe file ? What is the difference between yank and delete ?

(*d*) How do PINE and ELM compare with other mail programs under UNIX and WINDOWS ?

(*e*) Write short notes on any *three* of the following :

(*i*) SMTP

(*ii*) POP

(*iii*) MIME

(*iv*) UUCP

(*f*) Explain the following terms :

(*i*) Search Engines

(*ii*) URL

(*iii*) Browsing

3. Attempt any TWO of the following : **6.5 × 2 = 13**

(*a*) Explain the following in 'C' Language :

(*i*) What are 4 relational and two logical operators ?

(*ii*) What are the 6 bitwise operators ?

(*iii*) What is ternary operator ?

(*iv*) Give the precedence and associativity of the operators : && → * & + =

(*b*) (*i*) What will be the output of the following program ?

```
main()
{
    int  i=4,  j=-1,  k=0,w,x,y,z;
    w=i||j||k;
    x  =  i&&j&&k;
    y  =  i||j&&k;
    z  =  (i>3?k:i*4);
    printf(w,x,y,z);
}
```

(*ii*) Discuss modular programming, structured programming and object oriented programming techniques.

(*c*) (*i*) What are the differences between a compiler and an interpreter ?

(*ii*) Distinguish between the following :

(1) Actual and formal arguments

(2) Global and local variables

(3) Automatic, static and extern variables

(*iii*) State the fundamental (basic) data types and their sizes used in 'C' language.

4. Attempt any TWO of the following questions : **6.5 × 2 = 13**

(*a*) (*i*) State whether True or False :

(1) All structure elements are stored in contiguous memory locations.

(2) Address of a floating point variable is always a whole number.

(3) The array int num[26] has twenty-six elements.

(4) The expression num[1] designates the first element in the array.

(*ii*) Create a structure to specify data on students given below :

Roll number, Name, Department, Course, Year of joining

Assume that there are not more than 450 students.

Write a function to print names of all students who joined in a particular year.

(*b*) (*i*) What will be the output of the following program ?

```
main()
{
    int  a[5]={5,1,15,20,25};
    int  i,j,k  =  1,m;
    i  =  ++a[1];
    j  =  a[1]++;
    m  =  a[i++];
    printf(i,j,m);
}
```

(*ii*) What is the relationship between the data item represented by a variable *v* and the corresponding pointer variable *pv* ?

(*c*) (*i*) What do you understand by pointer arithmetic ? Explain.

(*ii*) Write a function that swap (exchanges the value of) two integers. Write the main function and make the call to swap ( ) function on the arguments taken through command line arguments.

❑❑❑

B. TECH

FIRST SEMESTER EXAMINATION, 2002–2003

COMPUTER AND LANGUAGES

Time : Two Hours *Total Marks : 50*

Note : (*i*) *This question paper contains FOUR questions.*

(*ii*) *Attempt ALL the questions.*

1. Attempt any FOUR of the following : **3 × 4 = 12**

(*a*) What are the different sections of CPU ? Explain the functions of each of them.

(*b*) What is multiprogramming OS ? What are the main advantages of multi-programming ?

(*c*) What purpose does the operating system serve to the computer ? Name various popularly used operating systems.

(*d*) What do you mean by DOS ? Write the DOS commands for the following operations :

(*i*) to display all the files having the (. ext) extension but different file names.

(*ii*) to combine FILE1 and FILE2 into a new file name, FILE3.

(*iii*) to move file from one directory to another.

(*e*) Explain the role of the following objects in Windows 95/98 :

(*i*) Control Panel

(*ii*) Desk Top

(*iii*) Recycle Bin

(*f*) What do you mean by files and directories ? Explain their functions in brief.

2. Attempt any FOUR of the following : **3 × 4 = 12**

(*a*) Explain Environment Variables used in Unix. Which command is used for finding the values of environment variables ?

(*b*) Give syntax and use of the following Unix commands :

(*i*) grep

(*ii*) chmod

(*iii*) stty

(*c*) Write commands to perform the following operations in EDIT editor :

(*i*) to cut a block

(*ii*) to paste the block

(*iii*) to find a text

(*d*) Differentiate between :

(*i*) FTP and Telnet

(*ii*) HTTP and HTML

(*e*) Write commands to perform the following operations in vi editor :

(*i*) to insert a text before the current position of a cursor.

(*ii*) to insert the text after the current position of a cursor.

(*iii*) to insert the text after the line in which the cursor is placed.

(*f*) What is Elm ? Write the steps to perform the following operations in Elm :

(*i*) message composition

(*ii*) replying or forwarding a mail

(*iii*) print a message on a printer

3. Attempt any FOUR of the following : **3 × 4 = 12**

(*a*) Explain the following terms :

(*i*) Compiler

(*ii*) Interpreter

(*iii*) Linker

(*b*) Draw flow-chart for summing N natural numbers.

(*c*) List the advantages of higher level language over low level language.

(*d*) What do you mean by an identifier ? How is a user-defined identifier different from a keyword ?

(*e*) Write a C-program to calculate compound interest for the given principal amount, rate of interest and the number of years.

(*f*) Determine the value of each of the following expressions if $i = 8, j = 5, x = 0.005, y = -0.01$

(*i*) $2 * x + (y == 0)$

(*ii*) $(i > 0) \| (j < 5)$

(*iii*) $(x > y) \&\& (i > 0) \&\& (j < 5)$

4. Attempt any TWO of the following : **7 × 2 = 14**

(*a*) Determine the output that will be generated by each of the following C-programs :

(*i*)
```
#include <stdio.n>
int funct (int count);
main()
{
int a, count;
for (count=1; count<=5; ++count)
{
a = funct1(count);
printf ("%d", a);
}
}
int funct1(int x)
{
int y;
```

```
y = x*x;
return(y);
}
```

(*ii*)
```
#include <stdio.n>
main()
{
int i, j, k, x=0;
for (i=0; i<5; ++i)
for (j=0; j<i; ++j)
{
switch(i+j-1)
{
case -1:
case 0:
  x+ = 1;
  break;
case 1:
case 2:
case 3:
  x+ = 2;
default :
  x+ = 3;
}
printf ("%d", x);
}
printf ("\nx=%d",x);
}
```

(*b*) **Write a C-program to sort an array of numbers. The maximum and minimum numbers alongwith their difference should be given as output.**

(*c*) (*i*) **Write a C-program to display the address and the content of a pointer variable.**

(*ii*) **What is a structure ? How does a structure differ from an array ?**

❑❑❑

B. TECH

SECOND SEMESTER EXAMINATION, 2002–2003

COMPUTER AND LANGUAGES

Time : Two Hours *Total Marks : 50*

Note : *(i) Attempt ALL the questions.*

1. Attempt any FOUR of the following : **3 × 4 = 12**

(*a*) What is the purpose of command interpreter ? Why is it usually separate from the Kernel ?

(*b*) Differentiate between :

(*i*) Primary and Secondary memories

(*ii*) Data and Information

(*iii*) Single user and Multiuser Operating systems

(*c*) What is virtual memory technique ?

(*d*) Describe how multiplatter disks are organized into tracks and sectors. How is information on the disk referenced ?

(*e*) State the purpose and syntax of the following DOS commands :

(*i*) XCOPY

(*ii*) ATTRIB

(*iii*) PATH

(*iv*) DISKCOPY

(*v*) PROMPT

(*f*) Write command(s) to perform the following operations in Windows environment :

(*i*) To create a shortcut of an application

(*ii*) To move a folder from one directory to another directory

(*iii*) To rearrange icons namewise on the desktop

(*iv*) To change the attributes of a file

(*v*) To search a file having name "UPTU.DOC"

(*vi*) To change the screen saver.

2. Answer any THREE of the following : **4 × 3 = 12**

(*a*) In context to UNIX, state whether the following are True or False :

(*i*) A file having protection 466 cannot be read by anybody.

(*ii*) The 1s-1 < f-name> command shows whether f-name is a file or directory.

(*iii*) Only the owner of a file and the super-user can change the access permission of a file.

(*iv*) The rm-r command deletes the files and not the directories.

(*b*) Give any two commands which can change the vi editors mode from escape to insert. How can you perform cut-paste and copy-paste operations in vi ?

(*c*) Write short notes on any Two :

(*i*) DNS

(*ii*) Web Browser

(*iii*) ELM

(*d*) What is URL ? Give the syntax of an URL by a suitable example.

(*e*) What is PINE ? How can you compose and send a message using PINE ?

3. Attempt any TWO of the following : 6.5 × 2 = 13

(*a*) Answer the following in context to C :

(*i*) What is the purpose of escape sequences ?

(*ii*) How does switch statement differ from nested if ?

(*iii*) Why have all variables to be declared before they are used in a 'C' program ?

(*b*) (*i*) Determine the values of the following expressions if a = 5, b = 3, c = – 8 :

(1) a > b || a > c

(2) c ! = (a + b)

(3) a & b

(4) a | b

(*ii*) Why do successful compilation/execution of a 'C' program generate two additional files with extension . obj and . exe ? Explain.

(*c*) (*i*) Distinguish between the following :

(1) Call by value and Call by reference.

(2) Struct and Union.

(*ii*) Differentiate between :

(1) int abc[5][10] and int * b[5];

(2) int *fn (int); and int (*fn) (int);

4. Attempt any TWO of the following : 6.5 × 2 = 13

(*a*) (*i*) Discuss different modes in which a file can be opened by giving suitable examples.

(*ii*) Write a 'C' program to rearrange a list of names in ascending order.

(*b*) (*i*) What will be the output of the following program ?

```
int f(int)
main ()
{
  int i;
  for (i=1; i<5; i++)
     printf("%d\n",f(i));
}
int f(int n)
{
  static int x=1;
```

```
    int  y=3;
    x=n;
    return  x+n+y;
  }
```

(*ii*) Write a C program to convert all lowercase letters of an input string into uppercase and vice-versa.

(*c*) (*i*) int a[4] = {10, 20, 30, 40}, * p;

p=a;

What is meant by :

(1) p++

(2) *p

(3) *++p

(*ii*) Write a C program which accepts count and message on command line and prints message for count number of times on the screen.

□□□

ANSWERS

B. TECH

SECOND SEMESTER EXAMINATION, 2000–2001

COMPUTER AND LANGUAGES

UNIT 1

1. Steps in Booting. Refer Section 4.2.6, Page 77.

Or

Effect of Booting with Config.sys File. Config.sys is a text file created in the root directory of the DOS boot disk. It contains the parameters to configure DOS when DOS is first loaded in memory. With the given CONFIG.SYS file, the booting will be effected as follows :

The DOS will be configured based on the choice of menu. If the choice will be 1, the following parameters will be executed :

files = 40
device = C:\dos\himem.sys
device = C:\dos\mouse.sys

If the choice will be two, the following parameters will be executed :

files = 30
device = C:\dos\mouse.sys

However, in any of these cases, the following parameters will be executed :

dos = high
buffers = 20

All these parameters are discussed below :

(1) buffers = 20

This command allocates memory for 20 disk buffers when the system is started.

(2) device = C:\dos\himem.sys

This command loads the device driver, 'himem.sys' from the 'dos' sub-directory into computer's memory.

(3) dos = high

This command specifies that MS-DOS should load a part of itself into the high memory area.

(4) files = 40

This command specifies that maximum 40 files can be opened.

(5) device = C:\dos\mouse.sys

This command loads the device driver, 'mouse.sys' from the 'dos' sub-directory into computer's memory.

2. Refer Section 5.9, Page 118.

3. (*i*) Refer Section 4.5.1, Page 85.

(*ii*) Refer Section 4.5.3, Page 87.

(*iii*) Refer Section 4.8.1, Page 92.

Or

Refer Section 3.3.1, Page 54.

Refer Section 3.3.3, Page 54.

4. The sequence of operations needed for CMOS setup to introduce a slave hard disk are as follows :

1. Switch on the computer and press <Del> key before booting.
2. You will see the AMIBIOS HIFLEX SETUP UTILITY menu on the screen.
3. Select the 'Standard CMOS Setup' option from the menu.
4. Press <Tab> keys to jump to 'Sec Slave' option and select the type of secondary slave hard disk.
5. Press <ESC> key.
6. Select 'Save Settings and Exit' option from the Utility menu.

UNIT 2

5. Refer Page 178, Section 7.11.1.

When these sequence of commands are executed, the following environment is created :

1. The login directory is /home/rama.
2. This variable shows your username as rama.
3. The mail variable determines where all the incoming mail addressed to the user is to be stored *i.e.,* /ver/spool/mail/rama.
4. The first search is made in /bin directory. If the specified file is not found here, then the search is made in /usr/bin directory.
5. The shell has two prompts *i.e.,* PS1 and PS2. The user can change the values of PS1 and PS2.
6. The 'SHELL' determines the type of shell that the user gets when he logs on.
7. 'TERM' indicates the terminal type. Here the terminal type is ANSI.

6. Refer Section 8.4, Page 194.

Or

Refer Section 9.3.3, Page 207.

7. To open a file, press Alt + F + O keys.

To close a file, press Alt + F + C keys.

To save a file, press Alt + F + S keys.

(*i*) To cut and paste a paragraph, follow the steps given below :

STEP1. Select a block of text.

STEP2. From the 'Edit' menu, select the 'cut' option.

STEP3. Take the cursor at the desired location.

STEP4. From the 'Edit' menu, select the 'Paste' option.

(*ii*) To delete a line, press the Ctrl + Y keys together.

(*iii*) To insert a line, press the ENTER key.

Or

Refer Section 6.7.1, Page 139.

Refer Section 6.7.10, Page 143.

8. Refer Section 9.3.1, Page 205.

Refer Section 9.3.2, Page 206.

Or

Refer Section 8.4.6, Page 197.

UNIT 3

9.
```
/*  Program  to  print  the  Pascal  triangle  */
#include <stdio.h>
void  main()
{
     int  n=11,r;
     for(r=1;  r<=  4;  r++)
     {
         printf("\n%d",  n);
         n  =  n*11;
     }
     getche();
}
```

10.
```
/*  Program  to  determine  whether  a  given  year  */
/*  is  leap  year  or  not  */
#include  <stdio.h>
void  main()
{
     int  year;
     printf("\n  Enter  an  year  :");
     scanf("%d",  &year);
     if((year%4  ==  0  &&  year%100  !=  0  ||  year%400  ==0)
             printf  ("\n  This  is  a  leap  year");
     else
             printf  ("\n  This  is  not  a  leap  year");
     getche();
}
```

Or

```
/*  Program  to  find  sum  and  multiplication  of  */
/*  digits  of  a  six-digit  positive  integer  */
#include  <stdio.h>
void  main()
{
     long  int  num,  storenum;
     int  sum=0,  mult=1,  digit;
     printf("\n  Enter  a  number  :");
```

```
scanf("%ld", &num);
storenum = num;
do
{
   digit = num % 10;
   sum = sum + digit;
   mult = mult * digit;
   num = num/10;
}while (num!=0);
if (storenum %2 == 0)
   printf("\n The sum of digits of number % ld is %d",
                                          storenum,sum);

else
   printf ("\n The multiplication of digits of number %ld is
                                          %d", storenum,sum);

getche();
}
```

11. (*a*)
```
for (i=j; i<k; i++)
      if (in[i]=='?')
            Q++;
```

The equivalent while statement of the above for statement is as follows :

```
i=j;
while (i<k)
{
      if (in[i] == '?')
            Q++;
      i++;
}
```

(*b*) a = b + c * d << 2 & B

After putting parenthesis in the above expression, the expression is written as follows :

a = ((b + (c * d)) << 2) & B

(*c*)
```
if   (i=0)
      i=1;
else
      i=0;
```

There is an error in above if statement, the correct statement will be :

```
if   (i==0)
      i=1;
else
      i=0;
```

The above if statement can be written into an equivalent simple statement using conditional operator as shown below :

i = (i==0) ? 1 : 0;

12.
```
/* Program to find GCD of 2 positive integers */
#include <stdio.h>
void main()
{
    int a,b,g;
    printf("\n Enter the value of a");
    scanf("%d",&a);
    printf("\n Enter the value of b");
    scanf("%d", &b);
    g = gcd(a, b);
    printf("\n GCD of %d and %d is %d", a,b,g);
}
int gcd(int x, int y)
{
    int z;
    if (y%x != 0)
    {
        z = y % x;
        z = gcd(z, x);
    }
    return(z);
}
```

UNIT 4

13. (*a*) float a = – 8.2;

(*b*) long int big [a] = {1, 2, 3, 4, 5, 6, 7, 8, 9};

(*c*) int u = 0711, v = 0Xfff;

Or

Given, int i = 8, f = 5;
float x = 0.005, y = – 0.01;
char C = 'c';

(*a*) Value of

(i – 3 * j) % (C + 2 * d) / (x – y)

= (8 – 3 × 5) % ('c' + 2 × d) / (0.005 – (– 0.01))

As d is undefined, the value of above expression cannot be calculated.

(*b*) Value of

2 * ((i/5) + (4 * (j – 3)) % (i + j – z)

= 2 × ((8/5) + (4 × (5 – 3)) % (8 + 5 – 2)

= 2 × (1 + (4 × 2)) % (11)

= 2 × 9 % 11

= 18 % 11 = 7

14. This function swaps the value of two variables x and y. If $x = 2$ and $y = 4$, then after execution of this function, x will be, 4 and y will be z. This is a 'Call by Reference' method of functions call.

15. The given function is not correct due to the reason explained below :

Consider an array,

a [ ] = {0, 1, 2, 5, 8, 10, 12, 15, 18, 20}

Suppose we want to search item, 12, then the function will run perfectly because the item, 12 exists in the array, and the function will return value 1 or TRUE. However, if we want to search item, 13, the function will not run perfectly as there would be an end less loop. During each loop, the value of various variable would be as follows :

i	j	k	a[k]
0	9	4	8
4	9	6	12
6	9	7	15
6	7	6	12
6	7	6	12

This is because i would be always less than 7. Actually, the statements i = k; and j=k are incorrect. They should be as follows :

i = k + 1; and j = k – 1;

16. The output will be as follows :

0 1 3 6

$x = 6$.

❑❑❑

B. TECH

FIRST SEMESTER EXAMINATION, 2001–2002

COMPUTER AND LANGUAGES

1. (*a*) (*i*) Refer Section 1.11, Page 32.

(*ii*) **Cache Memory.** Cache memory is a fast-speed memory which is readily available during processing. A computer system stores data in a cache memory temporarily. The main purpose for a cache memory is to provide data for different parts of the hardware. So, it is possible to level out slower and faster computer peripherals.

(*iii*) Refer Section 1.8, Page 19.

(*b*) Refer Page 106, Section 5.3, 5.3.1.

(*i*) **MyDocument.** The 'MyDocument' icon is present on the desktop of your computer. It is used to view the name of document that you have recently opened. When you double-click on the 'My Computer' icon, a window opens up to show its contents. It shows you the icons of the latest fifteen documents that you have used.

(*ii*) **Recycle Bin.** Refer (First Semester Exam 2002–2003) Q. 1.(*e*) (*iii*).

(*c*) Refer Section 3.3.3, 3.3.2 Page 54.

(*d*) (*i*) C:\> MD \ABC ↵

(*ii*) C:\> COPY Readme.Txt C:\ABC ↵

(*iii*) C:\> DEL \ABC*.* ↵

C:\> RD \ABC ↵

(*e*) (*i*) **Step 1** : Double-click the 'My Documents' icon present on the desktop.

Step 2 : Right-click the mouse button.

Step 3 : Select the 'New' option.

Step 4 : Select the 'Folder' option.

Step 5 : Give the desired name to the folder.

(*ii*) **Step 1** : Go to Windows Explorer.

Step 2 : Double-click on the 'X' folder and select the file to be copied.

Step 3 : Right-click the mouse-button and select the 'Copy' option.

Step 4 : Open the 'Y' folder.

Step 5 : Right-click the mouse button and select the 'Paste' option.

(*iii*) **Step 1** : Go to Windows Explorer.

Step 2 : Open the 'X' folder.

Step 3 : Select the file and right-click the mouse button.

Step 4 : Select the 'Delete' option.

Step 5 : Click OK button.

(*f*) Refer Section 1.10, Page 27.

2. (*a*) Refer Section 6.2.4, Page 128.
Refer Section 6.5.7, Page 138.
(*b*) Refer Section 8.4.1, Page 194.
(*c*) Refer Section 8.4.2, Page 195.
(*d*) Refer Section 10.2, Page 227.
Refer Section 10.3, Page 234.
(*e*) (*i*) The different menu options present in a DOS Editor are :
- File
- Edit
- Search
- Options
- Help

Let us explain the 'Edit' menu option. Under the 'Edit' menu, the following commands are available :
* Cut : It is used to cut a line or a block of text.
* Copy : It is used to copy a line or a block of text.
* Paste : It is used to paste a line or a block of text.
* Clear : It is sed to delete a block of text.

(*ii*) We set colours in EDIT by the following way :
Step 1 : Load EDIT by giving the following command :
C:\>EDIT <Enter>
Step 2 : Select 'Colors.....' option from the 'Options' menu.
Step 3 : Select the Foreground and Background colours for different types of text items such as Normal Text, Selected Text, Window Border, etc.
Step 4 : Finally click on <OK> button.

(*f*) Refer Section 11.2.2, Page 253.
Refer Section 11.6.2, Page 266.

3. (*a*) Refer Section 14.4.5.1, Page 324 and Section 15.2.4, Page 337.
(*b*) Refer Program 18.15, Page 450.
(*c*) Refer Program 17.21, Page 417.
(*d*) Refer Section 19.2, Page 461 and Section 19.3.2, Page 463.
(*e*)
```
/* Program to calculate sine and cosine values */
/* of the angles 0,10,20,........,180 degree */
#include <stdio.h>
#include <math.h>
void main()
{
   float xdeg, xrad, sinx, cosx;
   printf("\n x in degree \t sinx\t\t cosx");
   for (xdeg=0; xdeg <=180; xdeg=xdeg+10)
   {
```

```
        xrad  =  3.14  *  xdeg/180;
        sinx  =  sin  (xrad);
        cosx  =  cos  (xrad);
        printf("\n%3.0f\t\t  %f\t  %f", xdeg,  sinx,  cosx);
    }
    getche();
}
```

(*f*) Refer Section 17.2, Page 390 and Section 17.5.3, Page 403.

4. (*a*) (*i*)

<table>
<tr><th>Structure</th><th>Union</th></tr>
<tr><td>1. Each member within a structure is assigned its own unique storage area within the computer's memory.
2. Structures do not conserve memory.
3. Example :
<pre>struct cloth
{
   char brand[20];
   float price;
   char description[20];
} c1, c2;</pre></td><td>1. Each member within a union shares the same storage area in memory.
2. Unions conserve memory.
3. Example :
<pre>union desc
{
   char colour[20];
   int size;
};
struct cloth
{
   char brand[20];
   float price;
   union desc description;
   c1, c2;</pre></td></tr>
</table>

(*ii*)
```
/*  Program  to  accept  and  display  structure  elements  */
#include  <stdio.h>
main()
{
    struct  employee
    {
        int  empno;
        char  name[20];
        float  basic;
        float  da;
        float  cca;
        float  gs;
    };
    struct  employee  e1;
    printf("\n  Enter  Employee  No.  :");
    scanf("%d",  &e1.empno);
    printf("\n  Enter  Employee  Name  :");
    fflush(stdin);
    gets(e1.name);
```

```
        printf("\n  Enter  Basic  Pay  :");
        scanf("%f",  &e1.basic);
        /*  calculations  */
          e1.da  =  51  *  e1.basic/100;
          e1.cca  =  100.00;
          e1.gs  =  e1.basic  +  e1.da  +  e1.cca;
        /*  Displaying  data  */
        printf("\n  Employee  No.:  %d",  e1.empno);
        printf("\n  Employee  Name:  %s",  e1.name);
        printf("\n  Basic  pay:  %f",  e1.basic);
        printf("\n  DA  :  %f",  e1.da);
        printf("\n  CCA  :  %f",  e1.cca);
        printf("\n  Gross  Salary  :  %f",  e1.gs);
        getche();
    }
```

(*b*)
```
/*  Program  to  correct  a  string  */
#include  <stdio.h>
char*  strfunc(char*,  char);
void  main()
{
  char  *str1,  ch,  *str2;
  puts("Enter  a  string  :");
  gets(str1);
  puts("Enter  a  character  :  ");
  ch  =  getchar();
  str2  =  strfunc(str1,  ch);
  puts("The  corrected  string  is");
  puts(str2);
  getche();
}
char*  strfunc(char  *str1a,  char  ch1)
{
  int  i=0,  j=0;
  char*  str2a;
  while(str1a[j]  !=  '\0')
  {
    if(str1a[i]  !=  ch1  &&  str1a[i]  !='  ')
    {
      str2a[j]  =  str1a[i];
      j++;
    }
    i++;
  }
  return(str2a);
}
```

(*c*) (*i*) **Arrays.** An array is a collection of related or similar data elements stored in a contiguous area in the memory, which is referred by a common name.

Arrays are classified into two categories—One-dimensional and Multi-dimensional arrays.

An array containing a single subscript is called a **One-dimensional array.** For example, rollno[i] is a one-dimensional array.

An array containing multiple or more than one subscripts is called a **Multi-dimensional array.** A multi-dimensional array is generally either a two-dimensional or a three-dimensional array. For example, sales[i][j] is a two-dimensional array and sales[i][j][k] is a three-dimensional array.

Declaration of Arrays

Refer Section 18.3.1, Page 424,
Section 18.4.1, Page 430 and
Section 18.5.1, Page 436.

(*ii*) Refer Program 18.17, Page 454.

❑❑❑

B. TECH

SECOND SEMESTER EXAMINATION, 2001–2002

COMPUTER AND LANGUAGES

1. (*a*) **General Purpose Machine.** A machine that follows instructions for general requirements such as sales analysis, financial accounting, invoicing, etc. is called a General Purpose Machine. For example, Personal Computer is a general purpose machine.

Features of von Neumann Machine. von Neumann Machine represented the data and program in digital form. It is the basis for nearly all digital computers. It had five basic parts—the memory, the arithmetic logic unit, the program control unit, the input and output unit (See Figure 1.4 on Page 11).

The memory consisted of 4096 words. A word consisted of 40 bits. Each word could hold either 20-bit instructions or a 39-bit signed integer.

There was a special 40-bit register inside arithmetic logic unit. This register was called the accumulator. The main drawback of von Neumann machine was that it did not have floating-point arithmetic.

(*b*) (*i*) **Static Versus Dynamic Memories :**

Static Memories. The static memories are made of semi-conductors. They need to be refreshed less often. Static memory is faster and more expensive than Dynamic memory.

Dynamic Memories. The Dynamic memories are made up of capacitors. They needs to be refreshed thousands of times per second. Dynamic memory is generally slower than static memory. It is less expensive.

(*ii*) **Volatile Versus Non-volatile Memories :**

Volatile Memories. The contents of the volatile memory are erased off as and when the power is switched off. It is temporary in nature.

Non-volatile Memories. The contents of the non-volatile memory are not erased off as and when the power is switched off. It is permanent in nature.

(*iii*) **RAM and ROM :**

RAM. Refer Section 1.8.1, Page 19.

ROM. Refer Section 1.8.2, Page 20.

(*c*) Given, Speed of disk = 3000 rpm

No. of Sectors per track = 10

To find,

Average Access Time = ?

Average Access Time = Average Latency Time + Average Seek Time

$$(T_a) \qquad (T_l) \qquad (T_S)$$

$$T_l = \frac{1}{2} \times \text{Max. time taken in 1 revolution}$$

3000 revolutions take = 60 sec

$$1 \text{ revolution takes} = \frac{60}{3000} = \frac{1}{50} \text{ sec}$$

So, $$T_l = \frac{1}{2} \times \frac{1}{50} = \frac{1}{100} \text{ sec.}$$

As, the head disk is fixed (not movable), its seek time is always zero.

So, $$T_s = 0$$

Hence, $$T_a = T_l + T_s = \frac{1}{100} + 0 = \frac{1}{100} \text{ sec.}$$

$$= \frac{1}{100} \times 1000 = 10 \text{ millisecond}$$ **Ans.**

(*d*) **Device Controller.** Device Controller is a part of I/O device. It is generally contained on a board plugged into the card cage. It connects to its device by a cable attached to a connector on the back of the card cage. The function of a device controller is to control its I/O device and handle bus access. Examples of device controllers are Keyboard and Video Controller.

(*e*) (*i*) False (*ii*) False
(*iii*) True (*iv*) True
(*v*) False.

(*f*) The file manager controls the reading and writing of files. It handles communication between applications and files on block devices such as disk drives of various kinds.

(*i*) **File Menu → Copy Command :**

The copy command is used to duplicate the contents of one file or folder to another file or folder.

(*ii*) **View Menu → Split Command :**

The split command is used to split the window screen into two parts.

(*iii*) **View Menu → Select Drive Command :**

The 'Select Drive' command is used to select the specified drive from the available drives (A, B, C, D, F, etc.).

2. (*a*) DIR — ls
DEL — rm
COPY — cp
TYPE — cat
CD — cd
MD — mkdir
RD — rmdir
REN — mv

(*b*) Unmask : It sets the default permissions to all (0, 2, 2)
Chmod 777 abc.c : It grants all the (r, w, x) permissions to all the users (owner group and others) for the file named abc.c.

Chmod ug+rw a=x ff.out : It grants the read and write permission to owner and group for the file named ff.out. For the same file, it also grants the execute permission to all others.

Chmod U+t mydir : It sets the sticky bit of mydir.

(*c*) The editor used by UNIX is vi. The set command is used to set the environment variables manually. Alternatively, they may also be set automatically by placing the commands (but withuot colons) in a file named .exe. This file must be located in the home directory.

Difference between yank and delete

The Yank command is used to copy whereas the delete command is used to delete a line or a block of lines.

(*d*) PINE and ELM run on only UNIX systems over Internet. However other mail programs under windows such as Rediffmail, Yahoomail, etc. do not require UNIX operating system. They are more user-friendly than PINE and ELM as they provide graphical user interface (GUI). Also Refer Section 11.2.1, Page 252 and Section 11.6.2, Page 266.

(*e*) (*i*) **SMTP.** It stands for Simple Mail Transfer Protocol. It is used for sending E-mail messages between servers. Most E-mail systems that send mail over the Internet use SMTP to send messages from one server to another, the messages can then be retrieved with an E-mail client using either POP or IMAP.

(*ii*) **POP.** It stands for Post Office Protocol. It is used to retrieve E-mail from a mail server. Most E-mail applications (sometimes called an E-mail client) use the POP protocol although some can use the newer IMAP (Internet Message Access Protocol).

(*iii*) **MIME.** It stands for Multi-purpose Internet Mail Extension. It is a way to attach any kind of file to an E-mail message.

(*iv*) **UUCP.** It stands for UNIX-to-UNIX Copy Protocol. It is used for copying files between consenting UNIX systems and for handling E-mail. It is mostly superseded, but still used in low budget situations.

(*f*) (*i*) **Search Engines.** Refer Section 8.4.2, Page 195.

(*ii*) **URL.** Refer Section 9.2, Page 203.

(*iii*) **Browsing.** Refer Section 8.4.1, Page 194.

3. (*a*) (*i*) Refer Section 15.2.2, Page 335 and Section 15.2.3, Page 336.

(*ii*) **Bitwise Operators.** Bitwise Operators manipulate individual bits within a word of memory. The six bitwise operators are :

1. **One's Complement Operator (~).** This operator inverts the bits of its operand *i.e.,* 1s become 0s and 0s become 1s.

   For example, if x = 11011010 01110010

   then $\sim x$ = 00100101 10001101

2. **Bitwise and (&).** An expression having bitwise and operator returns 1 if both bits are 1, otherwise it returns 0.

   For example, if x = 11011010 01110010

   and y = 01101101 11010111

   then $x \,\&\, y$ = 01001000 01010010

3. **Bitwise or (¦).** An expression having bitwise or operator returns 1 if one or both bits are 1, otherwise it returns 0.

   For example, if x = 11011010 01110010
   and y = 01101101 11010111
   then $x \mid y$ = 11111111 11110111

4. **Bitwise Exclusive or (^).** An expression having bitwise exclusive or operator returns 1 if one bit is 1 and other is 0, otherwise it returns 0.

   For example, if x = 11011010 01110010
   and y = 01101101 11010111
   then x ^ y = 10110111 10100101

5. **Bitwise Shift Left (<<).** This operator causes all the bits in the first operand to be shifted to the left by a number of positions. The number of positions are indicated by a second operand. The overflow left most bits in the original operand are lost. The vacant right most bits are filled with 0_s.

   For example, if x = 11011010 01110010
   then x << 3 = 11010011 10010000

6. **Bitwise Shift Right (>>).** This operator causes all the bits in the first operand to be shifted to the right by a number of positions. The number of positions are indicated by a second operand. The underflow right most bits in the original operand are lost. The vacant left most bits are filled with 0s.

   For example, if x = 11011010 01110010
   then x >> 3 = 00011011 01001110

(*iii*) **Ternary Operator.** Ternary operator is also called conditional operator. Refer Section 15.2.6, Page 339 for explanation on conditional operator.

(*iv*) **Precedence and Associativity of Operators**

Operator Category	*Operators*	*Associativity*
Arithmetic	*	L → R
Arithmetic	+	L → R
Logical and	&&	L → R
Assignment	=	R → L
Bitwise	& >>	R → L

(*b*) (*i*) No output will come because printf( ) statement is written incorrectly. If the printf( ) statement will be written as follows :

printf("%d %d %d %d", w, x, y, z);

Then, the following output will come :

1 0 1 0

(*ii*) **Modular Programming.** Modular programming is also called Procedure oriented programming.

For discussion on procedure oriented programming, Refer Section 12.2.1, Page 278.

Structured Programming. Refer Section 13.4, Page 299.

Object-oriented Programming. Refer Section 12.2.2, Page 279.

(*c*) (*i*) Refer Sections 2.3.2 and 2.3.3, Page 40.

(*ii*) (1) **Actual and Formal Arguments**

<table>
<tr><th>Actual Arguments</th><th>Formal Arguments</th></tr>
<tr><td>1. They are defined in the calling function statement. For example, in the following part of program :<pre>main()
{
    :
    area = areafunc(l,b);
    :
}</pre>l and b are actual arguments.</td><td>1. They are defined in the definition of function. For example, in the following part of program :<pre>main()
{
    :
    area = areafunc(a,b);
    :
    areafunc(a,b)
    int a,b;
    {
      :
    }</pre>a and b are formal arguments.</td></tr>
<tr><td>2. Their scope is global.</td><td>2. Their scope is local.</td></tr>
<tr><td>3. They are also called actual parameters or simply arguments.</td><td>3. They are also called formal parameters or simply parameters.</td></tr>
</table>

(2) Global and Local Variables

Refer Section 17.6.1, Page 404.

(3) Automatic, static and enter n variables

Refer Table 17.1, Page 409.

(*iii*) Refer Section 14.4.5.1, Page 324.

4. (*a*) (*i*) (1) True

(2) True

(3) True

(4) False.

(*ii*) **Declaring a Structure**

```
struct  student
{
   int  rollno;
   char  name[20];
   char  dept[20];
   char  course[25];
   int  year;
};
struct  student  S[450];
```

Function to print names

The complete program with function is written below :

```
#include <stdio.h>
typedef struct
{
        int rollno;
        char name[20];
        char dept[20];
        char course[25];
        int year;
}student;
void main()
{
        int i;
        void func1(student *pt);
        student s[450]
        for (i=0; i<450; i++)
        {
          puts("Enter Roll No.");
          scanf("%d", &s[i].rollno);
          fflush(stdin);
          puts("Enter Name");
          gets(s[i].name);
          puts("Enter Dept");
          gets(s[i].dept);
          puts("Enter Course");
          gets(s[i].course);
          puts("Enter year");
          scanf("%d" & s[i].year);
          fflush (stdin);
        }
        func1(s);
        getche();
}
void func1(student *s1)
{
        int i,y;
        printf("\n Enter the year for displaying name");
        scanf("%d", &y);
        for (i=0; i<3; i++)
        {
          if (s1[i].year==y)
          printf("\n Name %s", s1[i].name);
        }
}
```

(*b*) (*i*) No output will come because printf( ) statement is incorrectly written. If the printf( ) statement will be written as follows :

printf ("%d %d %d," i, j, m);

Then, the output will be :

3 2 15

(*ii*) The data item represented by a variable v contains the value of variable while the corresponding pointer variable, pv contains the address of variable.

Example :

```
int v, * pv; /* Declaration of variables */
v = 21; /* Store 21 to variable, v */
pv = &v; /* Initialisation of pointer variable */
```

(*c*) (*i*) Refer Section 19.4, Page 467.

(*ii*) Refer Program 19.14, Page 486.

❑❑❑

B. TECH

FIRST SEMESTER EXAMINATION, 2002–2003

COMPUTER AND LANGUAGES

1. (*a*) Refer Section 1.7, Page 17.

(*b*) Refer Section 3.3.1, Page 54.

Refer Section 3.5.2.2, Page 60.

(*c*) Refer Section 3.2, Page 53.

The various popularly used operating systems are :

- MS-DOS
- OS/2
- Windows NT
- UNIX
- Netware
- MVS
- OS/400
- UMS.

(*d*) Refer Section 4.2, Page 73.

(*i*) To display all the files having the (. ext) extension but different file names, give the following command :

C:\> DIR *.ext <Enter>

(*ii*) To combine FILE1 and FILE2 into a new file name, FILE3, give the following commands :

A > TYPE FILE1 > FILE3 <Enter>

A > TYPE FILE2 >> FILE3 <Enter>

(*iii*) To move file from one directory to another, give the following command :

C:\>move\dirname\file1 \dir\file1 ↵

(*e*) (*i*) **Control Panel.** The control panel is available in Windows 95/98. It is the most important utility that allows you to change your system settings. The control panel contains a number of other small utilities such as Desktop, Mouse, Printer, Keyboard, etc. You can easily change the settings of your hardware through Control Panel.

(*ii*) **Desktop.** Desktop is the first screen that appears when Windows 95/98 gets loaded. This is the total visible area of your screen that keeps your important software, folders, shortcuts, etc. Any program that is used frequently can be placed on the desktop.

(*iii*) **Recycle Bin.** In Windows 95/98, whenever a file or a folder is deleted, it is sent to the Recycle Bin. This avoids the possibility of accidental deletion of your important files and folders. A file or a folder can always be restored back to its original location.

(*f*) Refer Section 4.3, Page 78.

2. (*a*) Refer Section 7.11.1, Page 178.

The SET command is used to find the value of environment variables.

(*b*) (*i*) $ grep "pattern" filename ↵

The grep command is used to find the matching pattern from a file. If the specified pattern is found then it shows that line of the file.

(*ii*) $ chmod [for whom] operation permission file name.

The chmod command is used to change the access permission to a file.

(*iii*) $ stty echo erase char

The stty command is used to change the erase character from # to something else.

(*c*) (*i*) To cut a block of text, simply select the text and press the <Ctrl + X> keys together.

(*ii*) To paste a block of text, press the <Ctrl + U> keys together.

(*iii*) To find a text, press the <Ctrl + F> keys together.

(*d*) (*i*) FTP : Refer Section 8.4.5, Page 195.

Telnet : Refer Section 8.4.7, Page 199.

Also refer Section 8.4.7.2, Page 200.

(*ii*) **HTTP.** HTTP stands for Hyper Text Transport Protocol. This protocol is used for interaction between the computers on the Internet. Any computer on the Internet that uses the HTTP protocol is called a Web Server and any computer that can access that server is called a Web Client. The HTTP allows different types of computers on the Internet to interact with each other.

HTML. Refer Section 9.3.1.2, Page 206.

(*e*) (*i*) Press 'i' to insert a text before the current position of a cursor.

(*ii*) Press 'a' to append character after the current character.

(*iii*) Press 'o' to insert a line immediately after the line in which the cursor is placed.

(*f*) Refer Section 11.6.1, Page 266.

(*i*) **Message Composition.** Refer Section 11.7.1, Page 269.

(*ii*) **Replying or forwarding a mail.** Refer Section 11.7.2, Page 270.

(*iii*) **Print a message on a printer.** Refer Section 11.7.3, Page 271.

3. (*a*) (*i*) Refer Section 2.3.3, Page 40 and Section 14.5.2, Page 330.

(*ii*) Refer Section 2.3.2, Page 40.

(*iii*) Refer Section 14.5.3, Page 331.

(*b*)

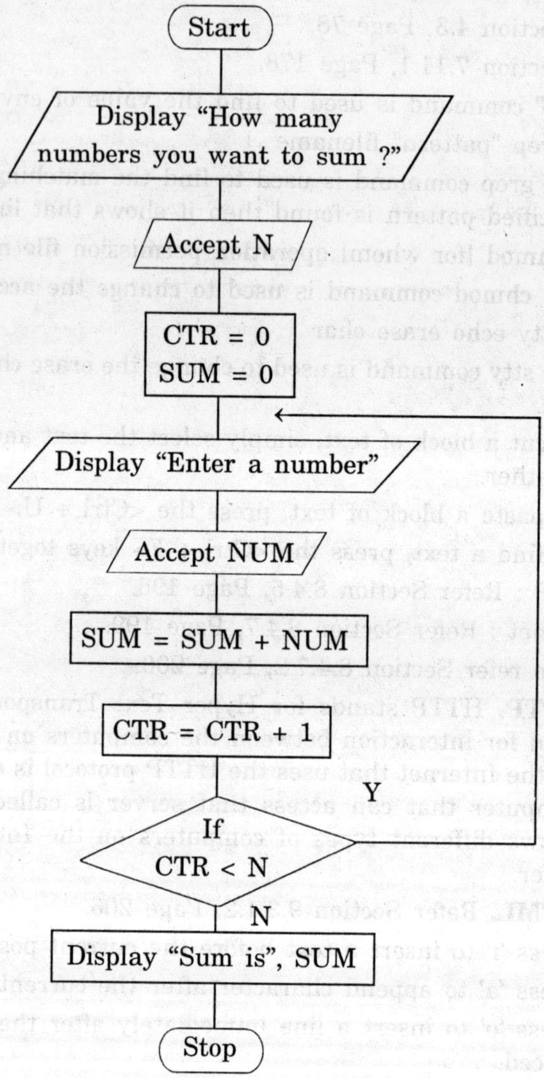

(*c*) **Advantages of High Level Languages over Low Level Languages**

(*i*) High level languages do not require a deep understanding of the hardware.

(*ii*) They use common English words.

(*iii*) They are machine independent.

(*iv*) They are more suitable for developing commercial applications.

(*v*) Some high level languages such as FORTRAN and PASCAL are more suitable for developing scientific applications.

(*vi*) High level languages are easier to learn.

(*d*) Refer Section 14.4.3, Page 323 and Section 14.4.4, Page 324.

(e)
```
/* Program to calculate compound interest */
/* Compound interest is calculated by the formula */
/* F = P (1 + i)^n */
/* Where F represents Future accumulation */
/* P represents Principal amount */
/* i represents decimal form of interest rate */
/* i = r/100, where r is interest rate */
/* n represents number of years */
#include <stdio.h>
#include <math.h>
main()
{
    float f, i, n, p, r;
    printf("\n Enter the principal amount :");
    scanf("%f", &p);
    printf("\n Enter the interest rate :");
    scanf("%r", &r);
    printf("\n Enter the number of years :");
    scanf("%n", &n);
    i = r/100;
    f = p * pow((1 + i), n);
    /* pow is the library function for exponentiation */
    printf("\n The Future accumulation is %f", f);
}
```

(f) (i) Given, $x = 0.005$

$y = -0.01$

So, the value of expression,

$2 * x + (y = = 0)$ is

$= 2 \times 0.005 + (-0.01 = = 0)$

$= 0.010 + 0$

$= 0.010$ **Ans.**

(ii) Given, $i = 8$

$j = 5$

So, the value of expression,

$(i > 0) \| (j < 5)$ is

$= 8 > 0 \| 5 < 5$

$= 1 \| 0$

$= 1$ **Ans.**

(ii) Given, $x = 0.005$

$y = -0.01$

$i = 8$

$j = 5$

So, the value of expression,

$(x > y)$ && $(i > 0)$ && $(j < 5)$ is

= (0.005> – 0.01) && (8 > 0) && (5 < 5)
= 1 && 1 && 0
= 0 **Ans.**

4. (*a*) (*i*) 1 4 9 16 25

(*ii*) 1 6 11 16 21 24 29 32 35 38

$x = 38.$

(*b*)
```
/* Program to sort numbers in ascending order */
#include <stdio.h>
main()
{
  int i,j,c,f;
  int num[50];
  printf("\n How many numbers you want to sort?");
  scanf("%d",&c);
  printf("\n Enter %d numbers : \n", C);
  for (i=0; i<c; i++)
  {
     printf("Number %d", i+1);
     scanf("%d", &num[i]);
  }
  for (i\0; i<c-1; i++)
  {
  for (j=i+1, j<c; j++)
  {
     if (num[i] > num[j])
     {
       t = num[j];
       num[j] = num[i];
       num[i] = t;
     }
  }
}
printf("\n The maximum number is %d", num[c-1]);
printf("\n The minimum number is %d", num[0]);
printf("\n The difference of maximum and minimum number is");
printf("%d", num[c-1]-num[0]);
getche();
}
```

(*c*) (*i*) Refer Program 19.1, Page 465.

(*ii*) **Structure.** A structure is a data type consisting of one or more variables having similar or dissimilar data types. Although generally dissimilar data types such as int, float, char, etc. are grouped together in a structure, you can combine similar data types such as only int, only char etc. or even create a single variable in a structure.

For example, a structure is declared as follows :

```
struct product
{
   int modelno;
   char modename[20];
   float price;
}
struct product p1, p2;
```

Difference between Structure and Array

Structure	*Array*

1. It consists of one or more variables having similar or dissimilar data types.
2. Example :
`struct employee`
`{`
`int empno;`
`char empname[20];`
`int salary;`
`} e1;`
To above example declares one structure variable `e1` with dissimilar datatypes.
	1. It consists of related or similar data elements.
	2. Example :
	`float price[10]`
	The above example declares one-dimensional subscripted variable, `price` with data type float having 10 data items.

❑❑❑

B. TECH

SECOND SEMESTER EXAMINATION, 2002–2003

COMPUTER AND LANGUAGES

1. (*a*) Refer Section 6.3, Page 129.

(*b*) (*i*) Refer Section 1.11, Page 32.

Refer Section 1.8, Page 19.

(*ii*) Refer Section 2.7.2.1, Page 46.

(*iii*) Refer Section 3.5.1.1, Page 57.

Refer Section 3.5.1.2, Page 57.

(*c*) **Virtual Memory Technique.** Virtual memory technique is an implementation of the non-contiguous storage allocation. In this technique, the effective address generated by a machine instruction in the program is considered to have two parts. The first part refers to the program components being referenced and the second part refers to the word number in that program component. Program components are allocated contiguous storage. So, their address translation consists of the start address of their allocated storage area. However, when word number is added to this address, the absolute address of the physical location to be accessed is given. The range of main storage addresses are called the physical address space while the range of program addresses is called the virtual address space.

(*d*) Winchester disk consists of one or more disk platters. In a multiplator disk, the upper surface of the top plate and the lower surface of the bottom plate are not used. A set of corresponding tracks on all other used surfaces is called a cylinder. So, if the disk pack has 10 disk plates, it will have 18 recording surfaces or in other words 18 tracks per cylinder. The number of sectors per track varies and is generally 8 or above per track. The information on the disk is referenced by the drive number, cylinder number, surface number (o .. n) and sector number.

(*e*) (*i*) Refer Section 4.8.5, page 95.

(*ii*) Refer Section 4.10.2, page 98.

(*iii*) Refer Section 4.6.8, page 90.

(*iv*) Refer Section 4.8.4, page 94.

(*v*) Refer Section 4.6.7, page 89.

(*f*) (*i*) **To create a shortcut of an application.** Shortcuts are made for the files and folders that are frequently used. Follow the steps given below :

STEP 1. Open Window's Explorer and select the file or the folder on which a shortcut has to be created.

STEP 2. From the 'File' menu, select 'Create Shortcut' option.

STEP 3. Drag the shortcut icon onto the desktop.

(*ii*) **To move a folder from one directory to another**

STEP 1. Open Window's Explorer and select the folder to be moved.

STEP 2. From the 'Edit' menu, select the 'Cut' option.

STEP 3. Select the location or the folder where you want to place the folder.

STEP 4. From the 'Edit' menu select the 'Paste' option.

(*iii*) **To re-arrange icons name-wise on the desktop**

STEP 1. Right-click the mouse button and select the 'Arrange Icons' option.

STEP 2. From the cascading menu, select the 'by Name' option.

(*iv*) **To change the attributes of a file**

STEP 1. Select the file icon whose attributes are to be changed.

STEP 2. Right-click your mouse button and select the 'Properties' option.

STEP 3. The 'Properties' window comes up. Change the file attributes such as read only, hidden, archive, etc. and click on the OK button.

(*v*) **To search a file having name "UPTU.DOC"**

STEP 1. Click at START button.

STEP 2. Select Search → For files or folders.

STEP 3. Type the name of the file as UPTU.DOC in the search box.

STEP 4. Click at the 'Search Now' button.

(*vi*) **To change the screen saver**

STEP 1. Right click on the desktop and select the 'Properties' option.

STEP 2. Choose the 'Screen Saver' tab.

STEP 3. Select the desired screen saver.

STEP 4. Click at the OK button.

2. (*a*) (*i*) False

(*ii*) True

(*iii*) True

(*iv*) False.

(*b*) The commands that change the mode of the vi editor from command mode to input mode are :

Press A or a

Or

Press i or I

Cut-Paste operations in vi

Suppose, we want to cut 3 lines and place them at a new location. So, press 3dd, then move the cursor to the desired location and press the 'P' key.

Copy-Paste operations in vi

Suppose we want to copy 3 lines and place them at a new location. So, press 3yy, move the cursor to the desired location and press the 'p' key.

(*c*) (*i*) **DNS**

Refer Section 9.2.1, Page 203.

(*ii*) **Web Browser**

Refer Section 9.3, Page 205.

(*iii*) **ELM**

Refer Section 11.6.1, Page 266.

(*d*) Refer Section 9.2, Page 203.

Refer Section 9.2.1, Page 203.

Refer Section 9.2.2, Page 204.

(*e*) Refer Section 11.2.1, Page 252.

Refer Section 11.3.1, Page 255.

3. (*a*) (*i*) Escape sequences are used to express certain non-printing characters such line feed, null, etc. as well as the double quote ("), the apostrophe ('), the question mark (?) and the backslash. They always represent single characters, though they are written in terms of two or more characters as illustrated below :

Escape Sequence	Character expressed
\n	line feed
\o	null
\"	Quotation mark
\'	Apostrophe
\?	Question Mark
\\	Backslash

(*ii*) Refer Section 16.5, Page 361.

(*iii*) Refer Section 14.4.8, Page 326.

(*b*) (*i*) Given $a = 5$, $b = 3$, $c = -8$

(1) $a > b \parallel a > c$

$= 5 > 3 \parallel 5 > -8$

$= 1 \parallel 1$

$= 1$ **Ans.**

(2) c! = $(a + b)$

$= -8$!= $(5 + 3)$

$= -8$!= 8

$= 1$ **Ans.**

(3) a & b

$= 5$ & 3

& is a bitwise and operator let us first find bit values of numbers 0 to 8 :

Decimal	Binary
0	0000
1	0001
2	0010
3	0011
4	0100

5	0101
6	0110
7	0111
8	1000

So, $a = 5$ *i.e.,* 0101

$b = 3$ *i.e.,* 0011

$a \& b = 1$ *i.e.,* 0001 **Ans. 1**

(4) $a \mid b$

¦ is a bitwise or operator.

$a = 5$ *i.e.,* 0101

$b = 3$ *i.e.,* 0011

$a \mid b = 7$ *i.e.,* 0111 **Ans. 7**

(*ii*) Refer Section 14.5.2, Page 330 and Section 14.5.3, Page 331.

(*c*) (*i*) (1) Refer Section 17.2.2.1, Page 395 and Section 19.7.1, Page 481.

(2) Refer answer of Q. 4(*a*) (*i*) of First Semester Exam., 2001–2002.

(*ii*) (1) int abc[5][10] and int *b [5]

int abc[5][10]	*int *b [5]*
1. This statement declares a 2–D array with name abc and integer data-type to store data in 5 rows and 10 columns. 2. It does not use pointers.	1. This statement declares a 2–D array, which is represented as an array of pointers to 1–D arrays. 2. In this statement, *b* is a 5–element array of pointers to integer quantities.

(2) int *fn (int); and int (*fn) (int);

*int *fn (int);*	*int (*fn) (int);*
This declaration indicates a function that accepts an integer argument and returns a pointer to an integer.	This declaration indicates a pointer to a function that accepts an integer argument and returns an integer.

4. (*a*) (*i*) **File Opening Modes :**

1. "r" — This mode opens an existing file for reading only. So, "r" is a read mode.
2. "w" — This mode opens a new file for writing only. If the file exists, its contents are overwritten. So, "w" is a write mode.
3. "a" — This mode opens an existing file for adding new data at the end of the file. If the file does not exist, a new file is created. So "a" is a append mode.
4. "r+" — This mode opens an existing file for both reading and writing.

5. "w+" — This mode opens a new file for both reading and writing. If the file exists, its contents are overwritten.
6. "a+" — This mode opens an existing file for both reading and appending. If the file does not exist, a new file is created.

Examples :

1. f1 = fopen("student.dat", "r");
2. f2 = fopen("sale.dat", "w");
3. f3 = fopen("pr1.c", "a");
4. f4 = fopen("p2.c", "r+");
5. f5 = fopen("bill", "w+");
6. f6 = fopen("invoice", "a+");

(*ii*) See Page 491, Program 19.18.

(*b*) (*i*) **Output**

5
7
9
11

(*ii*) Refer Program 18.6, Page 442 and Program 18.7, Page 443.

(*c*) (*i*) Given,

int a[4] = {10, 20, 30, 40}, *p;

p = a;

(1) p++ refers to the address of next data element in array, a

(2) *[refers to the value of current data element in array, a

(3) *++p refers to the value of next data element in array, a

(*ii*)
```
/* Program to display a message for a given no. of times */
#include <stdio.h>
main()
{
  int n, count;
  char message[79];
  printf("\n Enter your message");
  scanf("%S", message);
  fflush(stdin);
  printf("\n How many times, you want to display");
  scanf("%d", &count);
  for(n=1; n<=count; n++)
       printf("\n%s", message);
  getche ();
}
```

❑❑❑

SELECTED REFERENCES

Arora, Ashok and Shefali Bansal: *Information Technology for 'O' Level Module 1.1*, New Delhi: Cybertech Publications, 2002.

Arora, Ashok and Shefali Bansal: *Computer Fundamentals*, New Delhi: Excel Books, 1999.

Arora, Ashok and Shefali Bansal: *PC Tools for sManagers*, New Delhi: Amexcel Publications, 1999.

Arora, Ashok and Akshaya Bhatia: *Information Systems for Managers*, New Delhi: Excel Books, 1999.

Arora, Ashok and Akshaya Bhatia: *Computer and Information Management*, New Delhi: Amexcel Publications, 1999.

Athey, Thomas H.: *Systematic Systems Approach*, Englewood Cliffs, New Jersey: Prentice-Hall, 1982.

Awad, Elias M.: *Systems Analysis and Design*, 2nd Edition, New Delhi: Galgotia Publications, 1979.

Barcomb: *Office Automation*, Bedford, Mass.: Digital Press, 1989

Bartee: Thomas C.: *Digital Computer Fundamentals*, 6th Edition, New Delhi: Tata McGraw-Hill, 1991.

Basandra, S.K.: *Computers for Managers*, New Delhi: Global Business Press, 1994.

Basandra, S.K.: *Computers Today*, New Delhi: Galgotia Publications, 1995

Black, U.: *Computer Networks*: Protocols, Standards and Interfaces, 2nd Edition, New Delhi: Prentice-Hall of India, 1996.

Cady, G.H. and Pat McGregor: *Mastering the Internet*, New Delhi: BPB Publications, 1995.

Cascio, Wayne F., and Elias M. Awad: *Human Resources Management*: An Information Systems Approach, Reston, Va.: Reston, 1981.

Chadwick, M. and J.A. Hannah: *Expert Systems for Personal Computers—An Introduction to AI*, New Delhi: Galgotia Publications, 1990.

Charniak, E. and D. McDermott: *Introduction to AI*, Reading, Mass.: Addison-Wesley, 1985.

Chorafas. D. and H. Steinmann: *Object Oriented Databases*, Englewood Cliffs, New Jersey: Prentice-Hall, 1993.

Codd, E.: *Relational Model for Database Management*, Reading, Mass.: Addison-Wesley, 1990.

Comer, D.: *Internetworking with TCP/IP (Vols. I-III)*, New Delhi: Prentice-Hall of India, 1995.

Date, C.J.: *An Introduction to Database Systems*, Vol. I, 3rd Edition, Reading, Mass.: Addison-Wesley, 1990.

Date, C. J.: *Database—A primer, Reading*, Mass.: Addison-Wesley, 1984.

Davis, Gordon B. and Margrethe H. Olson: *Management Information Systems*, Conceptual Foundations, Structure and Development, 2nd Edition, New York: McGraw-Hill, 1985.

Davis, Rosco K., and Patrick G. McKeown: *Quantitative Models for Management*, Boston: Kent, 1981.

De Macro, T.: *Structured Systems Analysis and Design*, New York: Yourdon Press, 1978.

Desai, B.C.: *An Introduction to Database Systems*, Galgotia Publications, 1997.

Drucker, Peter F: *Management, Tasks, Responsibilities, Practices*, New York: Harper & Row, 1979.

Galbraith, Jay R.: *Organisation Design, Reading, Mass.*: Addison-Wesley, 1977.

Gottfried, Byron S.: *Schaum's Outline of Theory and Problems of Programming with C*, New Delhi: Tata McGraw-Hill, 1990.

Gupta Sanjeev and Shameena Gupta: *Internet for Business Managers*, New Delhi: Excel Books, 2001.

Hawryszkiewyez, I.T.: *Introduction to System Analysis and Design*, 2nd Edition, New Delhi: Prentice-Hall of India, 1991.

Jalote, Pankaj: *An Integrated Approach to Software Engineering*, New Delhi: Narosa, 1991.

Kanetkat Yaashwant: *Let us C*, 3rd Edition, New Delhi: BPB Publications, 1999.

Lacy, M.: *Understanding Computer Systems Architecture*, New Delhi: BPB Publications, 1993.

Laudon, Kenneth C. and Jane P.Laudon: *Management Information Systems: Organization and Technology*, 4th Edition, New Delhi: Prentice-Hall of India, 1998.

Lcvy, J.R.: *Welcome to Networking*, New Delhi: BPB Publications, 1994.

Loomis, M.: *Data Management and File Structures*, 2nd Edition, New Delhi: Prentice-Hall of India, 1983.

Lowe, Doug : *Client/Server Computing for Dummies*, 2nd Edition, Comdex Computer Publishing, 1996.

Lotia, Manohar and Pradeep Nair: *Modern All About Motherboard*, New Delhi: BPB Publications, 1996.

Lucas, Henry C.: *The Analysis, Design and Implementation of Information Systems*, New York: McGraw-Hill, 1981.

Majumdar, A.K. and P. Bhattacharyya: *Database Management Systems*, Tata McGraw-Hill, 1996.

Mano, M. Morris: *Digital Design, 2nd Edition*, New Delhi: Prentice-Hall of India, 1991.

Martin, E. W., W.D. Daniel, A.H. Jeffrey, and C.P. Willian: *Managing Information Technology: What Manages Need to Know*, New York: Machmillan, 1991.

Martin, James: *Computer Data-base Organisation*, 2nd Edition, New Delhi: Prentice-Hall of India, 1977.

Martin, James: *Principles of Data-base Management*, New Delhi: Prentice-Hall of India, 1976.

Martin, James: *Telecommunications and the Computer*, 3rd Edition, New Delhi: Prentice-Hall of India, 1992.

Martin, James, and Joe Leben: *Strategic Information Planning Methodologies*, Englewood Cliffs, New Jersey: Prentice-Hall, 1989.

McGovern, T.: *Data Communications—Concepts and Applications, Englewood Cliffs, New Jersey*: Prentice-Hall, 1988.

Mintzberg, Henry: *The Structuring of Organisations, Englewood Cliffs*, New Jersey: Prentice-Hall, 1979.

Moscove, Stephen A. and Mark G. Simkin : *Accounting Information Systems*, New York: John Wiley & Sons, 1981.

Murdick, R.G., J.E. Ross and J.R. Clagget: *Information Systems for Modern Management*, 3rd Edition, New Delhi: Prentice-Hall of India, 1984.

Murdick, Robert G.: *MIS: Concepts and Design, Englewood Cliffs*, New Jersey: Prentice-Hall, 1980.

Norton, P.: *Peter Norton's Introduction to Computers*, New York: McGraw-Hill, 1995.

Obrien, J.A., Jr.: Management Information Systems, Chicago: Irwin, 1990.

Parker, Charles and Thomas Case: *Management Information Systems*, 2nd Edition, New York: McGraw-Hill, 1993.

Perry, T.J. and J.G. Lateer: *Understanding Oracle*, New Delhi: BPB Publications, 1991.

Prakash, Naveen: *Introduction to Database Management*, New Delhi: Tata McGraw-Hill, 1991.

Rajaraman, V.: *Fundamentals of Computer*, New Delhi: Prentice-Hall of India, 1996.

Rajaraman, V.: *Analysis and Design of Information Systems*, New Delhi: Prentice-Hall of India, 1991.

Rathbone, Andy: *Upgrading and Fixing PCs for Dummies*, New Delhi: Comdex Computer Publishing, 1995.

Sanders, D.H.: *Computers Today*, 3rd Edition, New York: McGraw-Hill, 1988.

Scott Morton, M.S.: *Management Decision Support System*, Cambridge, Mass.: Harvard University Press, 1972.

Shepherd, Robert D.: *Introduction to Computers and Technology*, New Delhi: Pentagon Press, 2001.

Simon, H.: *The New Science of Management Decisions, Englewood Cliffs*, New Jersey: Prentice-Hall, 1977.

Simpson, Alan: *Understanding dBase IV*, New Delhi: BPB Publications , 1989.

Senn, James A.: *Analysis and Design of Information Systems*, New York: McGraw-Hill, 1984.

Singh, Bhagat and Thomas L. Naps: *Introduction to Data Structures*, New Delhi: Galgotia Publications, 1996.

Sinha, P.K.: *Computer Fundamentals*, New Delhi: BPB Publications, 1992.

Sox, Charlene W.: *Introduction to Office Automation*, Englewood Cliffs, New Jersey: Prentice-Hall, 1990.

Sprague, R.H. and E.D. Carlson: *Building Effective Decision Support Systems*, Englewood Cliffs, New Jersey: Prentice-Hall, 1982.

Tanenbaum, Andrew S.: *Structure Computer Organisation*, 3rd Edition, New Delhi: Prentice-Hall of India, 1993.

Tanenbaum, Andrew S.: *Computer Networks*, 2nd Edition, New Delhi: Prentice-Hall of India, 1988.

Titman, Lionel G.: *The Effective Office*, New Delhi: Excel Books, 1995.

Turban, E.: *Decision Support and Expert Systems*, New York: Macmillan, 1988.

Ullman, J.D.: *Principles of Database Systems*, New Delhi: Galgotia Publications, 1995.

Ward, John, Pat Griffiths, and Paul Whitmore: Strategic *Planning for Information Systems*, New York: John Wiley & Sons, 1986.

Wilkinson, Joseph W.: *Accounting and Information Systems*, 2nd Edition, New York: John Wiley & Sons, 1986.